파고다교육그룹 언어교육연구소, 안병남(Bobby Ahn) | 저

PAGODA TOEFL

80+

Reading
Listening
Speaking
Writing

PAGODA Books

PAGODA TOEFL 80+ R/L/S/W

초 판 1쇄 인쇄 2024년 2월 18일
초 판 1쇄 발행 2024년 2월 21일

지 은 이 | 파고다교육그룹 언어교육연구소, 안병남(Bobby Ahn)
펴 낸 이 | 박경실
펴 낸 곳 | **PAGODA Books** 파고다북스
출판등록 | 2005년 5월 27일 제 300-2005-90호
주 소 | 06614 서울특별시 서초구 강남대로 419, 19층(서초동, 파고다타워)
전 화 | (02) 6940-4070
팩 스 | (02) 536-0660
홈페이지 | www.pagodabook.com

ISBN 978-89-6281-915-1 (13740)

파고다북스 www.pagodabook.com
파고다 어학원 www.pagoda21.com
파고다 인강 www.pagodastar.com
테스트 클리닉 www.testclinic.com

낙장 및 파본은 구매처에서 교환해 드립니다.

2023년 7월
New iBT TOEFL®의 시작!

TOEFL 주관사인 미국 ETS(Educational Testing Service)는 iBT TOEFL® 시험에서 채점되지 않는 더미 문제가 삭제되면서 시간이 개정 전 3시간에서 개정 후 2시간 이하로 단축됐으며, 새로운 라이팅 유형이 추가되었다고 발표했다. 새로 바뀐 iBT TOEFL® 시험은 2023년 7월 26일 정기 시험부터 시행된다.

- 총 시험 시간 기존 약 3시간 ⋯› 약 2시간으로 단축
- 시험 점수는 각 영역당 30점씩 총 120점 만점으로 기존과 변함없음

영역	2023년 7월 26일 이전	2023년 7월 26일 이후
Reading	지문 3~4개 각 지문 당 10문제 시험 시간 54~72분	지문 2개 각 지문 당 10개 시험 시간 36분
Listening	대화 2~3개, 각 5문제 강의 3~5개, 각 6문제 시험 시간 41~57분	28문제 대화 2개, 각 5문제 강의 3개, 각 6문제 시험 시간 36분
Speaking	*변함없음 4문제 독립형 과제 1개 통합형 과제 3개 시험 시간 17분	
Writing	2문제 통합형 과제 1개 독립형 과제 1개 시험 시간 50분	2문제 통합형 과제 1개 수업 토론형 과제 1개 시험 시간 30분

목차

Reading

iBT TOEFL® Reading 개요 18

>> I. Identifying Details 22
Lesson 01 Sentence Simplification 22
Lesson 02 Fact & Negative Fact 28
Lesson 03 Vocabulary 34
Lesson 04 Reference 40

>> II. Making Inference 46
Lesson 01 Rhetorical Purpose 46
Lesson 02 Inference 50

>> III. Recognizing Organization 54
Lesson 01 Insertion 54
Lesson 02 Summary 60
Lesson 03 Category Chart 72

>> IV. Actual Tests 80
Actual Test 1 80
Actual Test 2 89

* MP3파일은 www.pagodabook.com에서 무료로 다운로드 가능합니다.

Listening

iBT TOEFL® Listening 개요 100

>> I. Conversations 102

Lesson 01 Main Idea 104
Lesson 02 Details 110
Lesson 03 Function & Attitude 116
Lesson 04 Connecting Contents 122
Lesson 05 Inference 130

>> II. Lectures 138

Lesson 01 Main Idea 140
Lesson 02 Details 146
Lesson 03 Function & Attitude 152
Lesson 04 Connecting Contents 158
Lesson 05 Inference 164

>> III. Actual Tests 170

Actual Test 1 170
Actual Test 2 184

Speaking

iBT TOEFL® Speaking 개요 200

>> I. Independent Task 202

Q1 선택 말하기 202
Lesson 01 표현 익히기 204
Lesson 02 이유 제시하기 216
Lesson 03 문장으로 말하기 219

>> II. Integrated Task 224

Q2 읽고 듣고 말하기: 대학 생활 224
Lesson 01 표현 익히기 226
Lesson 02 읽기 정리 230
Lesson 03 듣기 정리 234
Lesson 04 정리해서 말하기 238

>> III. Integrated Task 246

Q3 읽고 듣고 말하기: 대학 강의 246
Lesson 01 표현 익히기 248
Lesson 02 읽기 정리 252
Lesson 03 듣기 정리 256
Lesson 04 정리해서 말하기 260

>> IV. Integrated Task 268

Q4 듣고 말하기: 대학 강의 268
Lesson 01 표현 익히기 270
Lesson 02 듣기 정리 274
Lesson 03 정리해서 말하기 278

>> V. Actual Tests 286

Actual Test 1 286
Actual Test 2 292

Writing

iBT TOEFL® Writing 개요 300

>> I. Integrated Task 302
Lesson 01 노트테이킹 304
Lesson 02 요약하기 314
Lesson 03 정리하기 324
Lesson 04 노트 & 답변 연결하기 334

>> II. Academic Discussion Task 342
Lesson 01 스트레스 관련 주제 350
Lesson 02 분위기 관련 주제 354
Lesson 03 사람들과의 관계 관련 주제 358
Lesson 04 관점의 확장 관련 주제 362
Lesson 05 조언 관련 주제 366
Lesson 06 편리함 관련 주제 370
Lesson 07 시간 활용 관련 주제 374

>> III. Actual Tests 378
Actual Test 1 378
Actual Test 2 382

이 책의 구성과 특징

>> New TOEFL 변경 사항 및 최신 출제 유형 완벽 반영!

2023년 7월부터 변경된 새로운 토플 시험을 반영, iBT TOEFL® 80점 이상을 목표로 하는 학습자를 위해 최근 iBT TOEFL의 출제 경향을 완벽하게 반영한 문제와 주제를 골고루 다루고 있습니다.

Reading

>> 문제 유형별 Lesson 구성으로 원하는 유형 선택 학습 가능!

문제 유형별로 Lesson을 구성해, 자주 나오는 유형이나 학습자가 특히 취약한 유형을 골라 iBT TOEFL® 전문 연구원이 제시하는 문제 풀이 전략을 학습할 수 있도록 하였습니다.

Listening

>> 배경지식을 통한 Lecture 내용 파악!

각 Lecture 단원의 Lesson에 등장하는 지문 주제들의 주요 배경지식과 어휘 등을 정리하여 Lecture의 이해도를 높일 수 있도록 구성하였습니다.

>> 전체 미국인 버전과 미국인+영국인 버전 두 가지 음원 온라인 다운로드로 제공!

iBT TOEFL® Listening 영역 듣기에서는 주로 미국인 성우들이 등장하지만, 때에 따라서는 영국인 성우가 일부 등장하는 경우가 있습니다. 이에 따라 학습자들의 학습 편의와 효과적인 시험 대비를 위해 본 교재에서는 2가지 유형의 듣기 음원을 제공하고 있습니다.

- 전체 미국인 성우 버전 음원: 보다 익숙한 발음으로 듣기 연습을 하고 싶은 학습자분들을 위해 모든 내용을 미국인 성우가 녹음한 버전입니다.
- 미국인 + 영국인 버전: 실제 Listening 시험에서의 미국인과 영국인 음성 비중을 반영하여, 미국인 성우와 함께 영국인 성우가 일부 포함된 버전입니다.

Speaking

>> 문제 유형별 표현 정리 제공!

각 문제 유형별로 자주 쓰이는 유용한 표현을 예문과 함께 수록해, MP3 파일을 들으면서 반복적으로 암기할 수 있도록 구성하였습니다.

>> 단계별로 점진적인 학습 가능!

혼자 공부하는 사람도 충분히 따라올 수 있도록, 효율적인 노트 정리부터 답변 말하기까지 차근차근 단계별로 학습을 구성하였습니다. 함께 제공되는 예시 노트 및 답변을 통해 학습자가 자신의 답변을 직접 비교해 보고 보완할 수 있습니다.

Writing

>> 유형별 표현 정리 제공!

유형별로 자주 쓰이는 유용한 표현들을 예문과 함께 수록해, 실제 시험에 그대로 적용해서 사용할 수 있도록 있도록 구성하였습니다.

>> 단계별로 점진적인 학습 가능!

혼자 공부하는 사람도 충분히 따라올 수 있도록, 효율적인 노트 정리부터 답변 작성하기까지 차근차근 단계별로 학습을 구성하였습니다. 함께 제공되는 예시 노트 및 답변을 통해 학습자가 자신의 답변을 직접 비교해 보고 보완할 수 있습니다.

iBT TOEFL® 개요

1. iBT TOEFL® 이란?

TOEFL은 영어 사용 국가로 유학을 가고자 하는 외국인들의 영어 능력을 평가하기 위해 개발된 시험이다. TOEFL 시험 출제 기관인 ETS는 이러한 TOEFL 본연의 목적에 맞게 문제의 변별력을 더욱 높이고자 PBT(Paper-Based Test), CBT(Computer-Based Test)에 이어 차세대 시험인 인터넷 기반의 iBT(Internet-Based Test)를 2005년 9월부터 시행하고 있다. ETS에서 연간 30~40회 정도로 지정한 날짜에 등록함으로써 치르게 되는 이 시험은 Reading, Listening, Speaking, Writing 총 4개 영역으로 구성되며 총 시험 시간은 약 2시간이다. 각 영역별 점수는 30점으로 총점 120점을 만점으로 하며 성적은 시험 시행 약 4~8일 후에 온라인에서 확인할 수 있다.

2. iBT TOEFL®의 특징

1) 영어 사용 국가로 유학 시 필요한 언어 능력을 평가한다.

각 시험 영역은 실제 학업이나 캠퍼스 생활에 반드시 필요한 언어 능력을 측정한다. 평가되는 언어 능력에는 자신의 의견 및 선호도 전달하기, 강의 요약하기, 에세이 작성하기, 학술적인 주제의 글을 읽고 내용 이해하기 등이 포함되며, 각 영역에 걸쳐 고르게 평가된다.

2) Reading, Listening, Speaking, Writing 전 영역의 통합적인 영어 능력(Integrated Skill)을 평가한다.

시험이 4개 영역으로 분류되어 있기는 하지만 Speaking과 Writing 영역에서는 [Listening + Speaking], [Reading + Listening + Speaking], [Reading + Listening + Writing]과 같은 형태로 학습자가 둘 또는 세 개의 언어 영역을 통합해서 사용할 수 있는지를 평가한다.

3) Reading 지문 및 Listening 스크립트가 길다.

Reading 지문은 700단어 내외로 A4용지 약 1.5장 분량이며, Listening은 3~4분 가량의 대화와 6~8분 가량의 강의로 구성된다.

4) 전 영역에서 노트 필기(Note-taking)를 할 수 있다.

긴 지문을 읽거나 강의를 들으면서 핵심 사항을 간략하게 적어두었다가 문제를 풀 때 참고할 수 있다. 노트 필기한 종이는 시험 후 수거 및 폐기된다.

5) 선형적(Linear) 방식으로 평가된다.

응시자가 시험을 보는 과정에서 실력에 따라 문제의 난이도가 조정되어 출제되는 CAT(Computer Adaptive Test) 방식이 아니라, 정해진 문제가 모든 응시자에게 동일하게 제시되는 선형적인 방식으로 평가된다.

6) 시험 응시일이 제한된다.

시험은 주로 토요일과 일요일에만 시행되며, 시험에 재응시할 경우, 시험 응시일 3일 후부터 재응시 가능하다.

7) Performance Feedback이 주어진다.

온라인 및 우편으로 발송된 성적표에는 수치화된 점수뿐 아니라 각 영역별로 수험자의 과제 수행 정도를 나타내는 표도 제공된다.

3. iBT TOEFL®의 구성

시험 영역	Reading, Listening, Speaking, Writing
시험 시간	약 2시간
시험 횟수	연 30~40회(날짜는 ETS에서 지정)
총점	0~120점
영역별 점수	각 영역별 30점
성적 확인	응시일로부터 4~8일 후 온라인에서 성적 확인 가능

시험 영역	문제 구성	시간
Reading	● 독해 지문 2개, 총 20문제가 출제된다. ● 각 지문 길이 700단어 내외, 지문당 10개 문제	36분
Listening	● 대화(Conversation) 2개(각 5문제씩)와 강의(Lecture) 3개(각 6문제씩)가 출제된다.	36분
Break		10분
Speaking	● 독립형 과제(Independent Task) 1개, 통합형 과제(Integrated Task) 3개 총 4개 문제가 출제된다.	17분
Writing	● 통합형 과제(Integrated Task) 1개(20분) ● 수업 토론형 과제 (Writing for Academic Discussion) 1개(9분)	30분

4. iBT TOEFL®의 점수

1) 영역별 점수

Reading	0~30	Listening	0~30
Speaking	0~30	Writing	0~30

2) iBT, CBT, PBT 간 점수 비교

기존에 있던 CBT, PBT 시험은 폐지되었으며, 마지막으로 시행된 CBT, PBT 시험 이후 2년 이상이 경과되어 과거 응시자의 시험 성적 또한 유효하지 않다.

5. 시험 등록 및 응시 절차

1) 시험 등록

온라인과 전화로 시험 응시일과 각 지역의 시험장을 확인하여 신청할 수 있으며, 일반 접수는 시험 희망 응시일 7일 전까지 가능하다.

❶ 온라인 등록

ETS 토플 등록 사이트(https://www.ets.org/mytoefl)에 들어가 화면 지시에 따라 등록한다. 비용은 신용카드로 지불하게 되므로 American Express, Master Card, VISA 등 국제적으로 통용되는 신용카드를 미리 준비해 둔다. 시험을 등록하기 위해서는 회원 가입이 선행되어야 한다.

❷ 전화 등록

한국 프로메트릭 콜센터(00-7981-4203-0248)에 09:00~17:00 사이에 전화를 걸어 등록한다.

2) 추가 등록

시험 희망 응시일 3일(공휴일을 제외한 업무일 기준) 전까지 US $60의 추가 비용으로 등록 가능하다.

3) 등록 비용

2023년 US $220(가격 변동이 있을 수 있음)

4) 시험 취소와 변경

ETS 토플 등록 사이트나 한국 프로메트릭(00-7981-4203-0248)으로 전화해서 시험을 취소하거나 응시 날짜를 변경할 수 있다. 등록 취소와 날짜 변경은 시험 날짜 4일 전까지 해야 한다. 날짜를 변경하려면 등록 번호와 등록 시 사용했던 성명이 필요하며 비용은 US $60이다.

5) 시험 당일 소지품

❶ 사진이 포함된 신분증(주민등록증, 운전면허증, 여권 중 하나)
❷ 시험 등록 번호(Registration Number)

6) 시험 절차

❶ 사무실에서 신분증과 등록 번호를 통해 등록을 확인한다.
❷ 기밀 서약서(Confidentiality Statement)를 작성한 후 서명한다.
❸ 소지품 검사, 사진 촬영, 음성 녹음 및 최종 신분 확인을 하고 연필과 연습장(Scratch Paper)을 제공받는다.
❹ 감독관의 지시에 따라 시험실에 입실하여 지정된 개인 부스로 이동하여 시험을 시작한다.
❺ Reading과 Listening 영역이 끝난 후 10분간의 휴식이 주어진다.
❻ 시험 진행에 문제가 있을 경우 손을 들어 감독관의 지시에 따르도록 한다.
❼ Writing 영역 답안 작성까지 모두 마치면 화면 종료 메시지를 확인한 후에 신분증을 챙겨 퇴실한다.

7) 성적 확인

응시일로부터 약 4~8일 후부터 온라인으로 점수 확인이 가능하며, 시험 전에 종이 사본 수령을 신청했을 경우 약 11-15일 후 우편으로 성적표를 받을 수 있다.

6. 실제 시험 화면 구성

TOEFL

CONTINUE

General Test Information

This test measures you ability to use English in an academic context. There are 4 sections.

In the Reading section, you will answer questions to 2 reading passages.

In the Listening section, you will answer questions about 2 conversations and 3 lectures.

In the Speaking section, you will answer 4 questions. One of the questions asks you to speak about familiar topics. Other questions ask you to speak about lectures, conversations, and reading passages.

In the Writing section, you will answer 2 questions. The first question asks you to write about the relationship between a lecture you will hear and a passage you will read. The second questions asks you to write a response to an academic discussion topic.

There will be directions for each section which explain how to answer the question in that section.

Click Continue to go on.

전체 Direction

시험 전체에 대한 구성 설명

TOEFL Reading

REVIEW HELP BACK NEXT

Question 1 of 30

00:53:28

Tundra

Tundras are areas that have long, cold winters and very short summers. The average annual temperatures of these regions are usually below zero. Because of the long cold season, the soil has a layer of permafrost, permanently frozen earth that often extends to a depth of 200 feet.
There are two types of tundra: Arctic and Alpine. Arctic tundra, found around the North Pole, is the most well known. Alpine tundra can be found at the tops of tall cold mountains, like the highest peaks in the Swiss Alps.
The plants in all tundra regions have shallow roots to allow them to grow in the shallow layer of surface soil that does thaw in summer. Animals that live in the tundra regions are also adapted to breed and raise their young quickly during the short summers.
There are two main risks to people living in tundra areas; hypothermia, the lowering of the body's core temperature, and frostbite, the constriction of blood vessels in parts of the body.

The word annual in the passage is closest in meaning to

- ordinary
- diurnal
- conventional
- yearly

Reading 영역 화면

지문은 왼쪽에, 문제는
오른쪽에 제시

Listening 영역 화면

수험자가 대화나 강의를 듣는
동안 사진이 제시됨

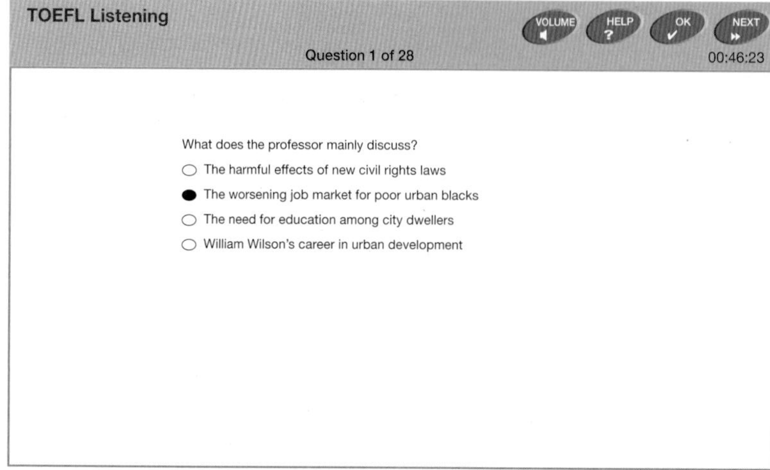

Listening 영역 화면

듣기가 끝난 후 문제 화면이 등장

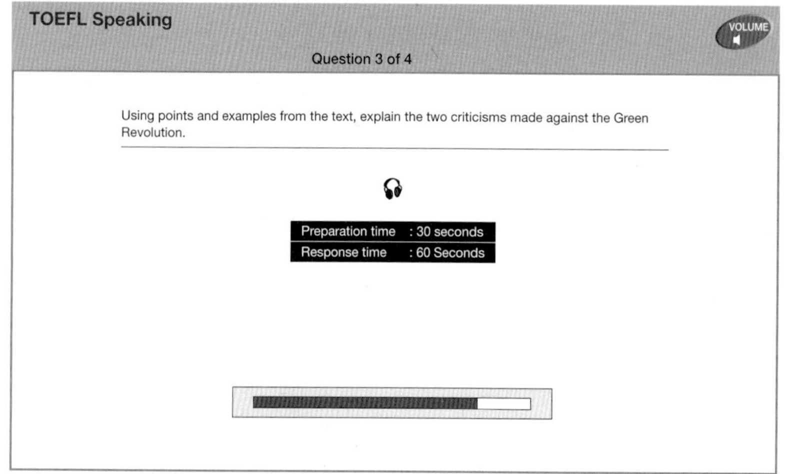

Speaking 영역 화면

문제가 주어진 후, 답변을 준비하는 시간과 말하는 시간을 알려줌

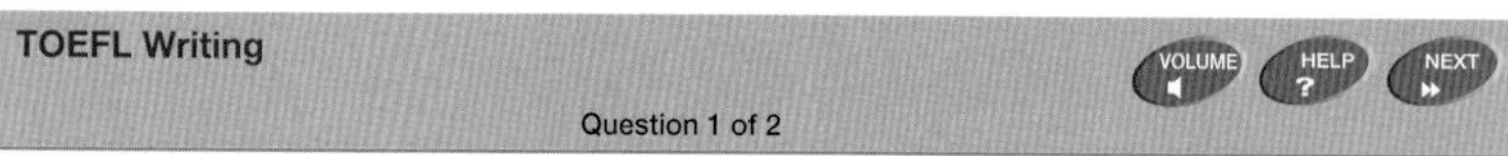

In the late 14th century, an unknown poet from the Midlands composed four poems titled *Pearl*, *Sir Gawain and the Green Knight*, *Patience*, and *Cleanness*. This collection of poems is referred to as Cotton Nero A.x and the author is often referred to as the Pearl Poet. Up to this day, there have been many theories regarding the identity of this poet, and these are three of the most popular ones.

The first theory is that the author's name was Hugh, and it is based on the *Chronicle of Andrew of Wyntoun*. In the chronicle, an author called Hucheon (little Hugh) is credited with writing three poems, one of which is about the adventures of Gawain. Not only that, but all three poems are written in alliterative verse, as are all four of the poems in *Cotton Nero A.x*. Since they are written in the same style and one poem from each set concerns Gawain, some people contend that all of the *Cotton Nero A.x* poems were written by Hugh.

The second theory is that John Massey was the poet, and it is supported by another poem called *St. Erkenwald* and penmanship. Although the actual authorship of *St. Erkenwald* is unknown, John Massey was a poet who lived in the correct area and time for scholars to attribute it to him. This manuscript was written in very similar handwriting to that of the Pearl Poet, which indicates that one person is likely the author of all five of the poems.

The third theory is that the poems were actually written by different authors from the same region of England. This comes from the fact that there is little linking the poems to each other. Two are concerned with the Arthur legends, but the only link connecting the other two is that they describe the same area of the countryside. They also seem to be written in the same dialect. Taken together, these facts indicate that they were written in the same region, but they probably were not written by the same person.

Writing 영역 화면

왼쪽에 문제가 주어지고 오른쪽에 답을 직접 타이핑할 수 있는 공간이 주어짐

복사(Copy), 자르기(Cut), 붙여넣기(Paste) 버튼이 위쪽에 위치함

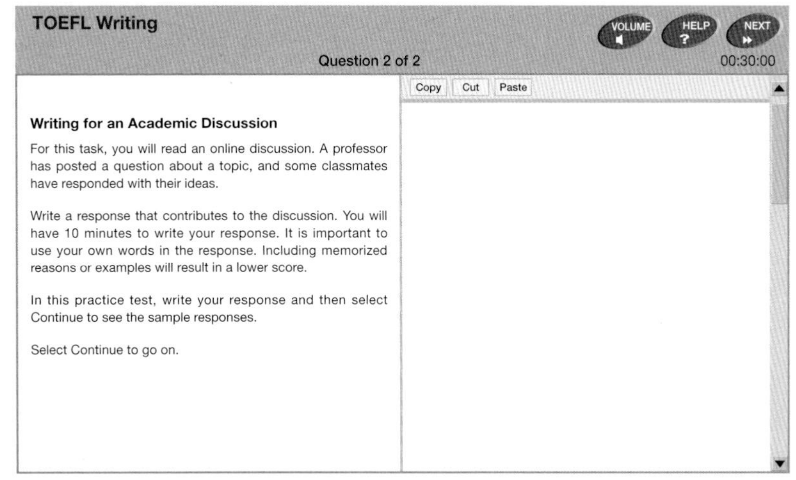

Writing 영역 화면

왼쪽에 문제가 주어지고 오른쪽에 답을 직접 타이핑할 수 있는 공간이 주어짐

복사(Copy), 자르기(Cut), 붙여넣기(Paste) 버튼이 위쪽에 위치함

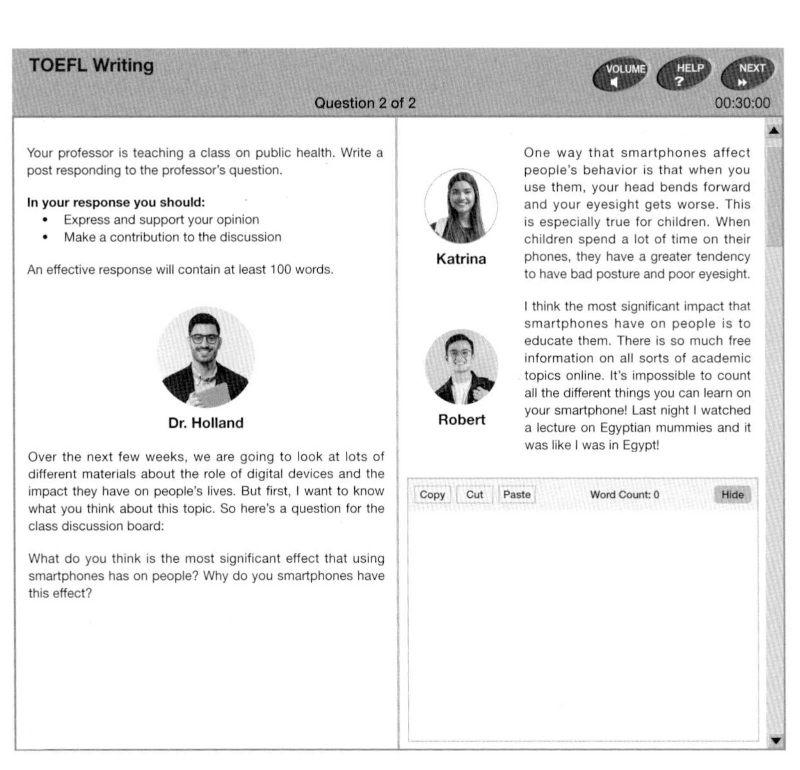

Writing 영역 화면

왼쪽에 문제가 주어지고 오른쪽에 답을 직접 타이핑할 수 있는 공간이 주어짐

복사(Copy), 자르기(Cut), 붙여넣기(Paste) 버튼이 타이핑하는 곳 위쪽에 위치함

Reading

I. Identifying Details

- Lesson 01 Sentence Simplification
- Lesson 02 Fact & Negative Fact
- Lesson 03 Vocabulary
- Lesson 04 Reference

II. Making Inference

- Lesson 01 Rhetorical Purpose
- Lesson 02 Inference

III. Recognizing Organization

- Lesson 01 Insertion
- Lesson 02 Summary
- Lesson 03 Category Chart

IV. Actual Tests

Actual Test 1

Actual Test 2

iBT TOEFL® Reading 개요

1. Reading 영역의 특징

1. 지문의 특징

Reading 영역에서는 영어권 대학의 학습 환경에서 접할 수 있는 전공별 강좌의 입문 내지 개론 수준의 지문이 다뤄지며 다양한 분야의 주제가 등장한다.

① 자연 과학: 화학, 수학, 물리학, 생물학, 의학, 공학, 천문학, 지질학 등

② 인문: 역사, 문화, 정부 정책, 문학, 그림, 조각, 건축, 연극, 춤, 특정 인물의 일대기 또는 업적 등

③ 사회 과학: 사회학, 심리학, 인류학, 경제학 등

Reading 영역에서 출제되는 글의 종류는 크게 설명(Exposition), 논증(Argumentation), 역사적인 인물 혹은 역사적인 사건의 서술(Historical/Biographical Event Narratives)로 나눌 수 있으며, 수필이나 문학 작품은 포함되지 않는다. 각 지문은 논지가 매우 분명하며 객관적인 논조로 전개되는 잘 짜인 글이다. 각 지문에는 제목이 주어지며 때로는 지문과 관련된 그림이나 사진, 도표, 그래프, 지도 등이 포함되기도 한다. 또한 용어 설명(Glossary) 기능이 있어 지문에서 밑줄 표시가 된 어휘에 마우스를 갖다 대면 그 영어 뜻이 화면 하단에 제공된다. 이러한 어휘는 일반적으로 난이도가 매우 높거나 특수한 용어다.

2. 문제의 특징

각 지문당 10개의 문제가 주어지며 크게 3가지 유형으로 나뉜다.

① 사지선다형

② 지문에 문장 삽입하기

③ 지문 전반에 걸쳐 언급된 주요 사항을 분류하여 요약표(Summary)나 범주표(Category Chart)에 넣기

※ 하나의 지문에는 Summary와 Category Chart 중 한 가지 유형의 문제만 출제되며, 이 두 문제 유형에는 부분 점수(총점 2~3점)가 있다.

2. Reading 영역의 구성

Reading 영역에서는 총 10개의 문제 유형을 통해 지문에 대한 이해도를 다각도로 평가한다. 지문 길이가 700단어 내외로 상당히 긴 편이기 때문에 자칫 어렵다고 생각할 수 있지만, 문제 풀이에 필요한 정보는 모두 지문에서 찾을 수 있다. 따라서 다양한 주제의 지문을 접하면서 실제 시험 문제 유형에 익숙해지고 나면 TOEFL의 그 어느 영역보다도 고득점에 유리한 영역이다.

TOEFL 시험의 첫 번째 영역인 Reading 지문은 기존 3~4개에서 2개로 바뀌면서 시험 시간도 36분으로 줄었다.

Part 구성	지문 수	문제 수	시험 시간
Part 1	2개	20 문제	36분

3. Reading 영역의 문제 유형

Reading 영역을 통해 평가하고자 하는 기본 능력은 다음과 같다.

- Basic Comprehension: 지문에 대한 기초적인 이해도
- Reading to Learn: 문장/문단 전후 관계 파악 및 전체 지문과의 연관성에 대한 이해도
- Inferencing: 지문 전체의 흐름에 대한 이해에 기반한 저자 의도 파악 능력

<Reading 영역의 10가지 문제 유형>

문제 유형	문제 설명	문제 개수
Basic Comprehension		
어휘 (Vocabulary)	문맥 안에서 특정 어휘가 어떤 뜻으로 사용되었는지 선택지 가운데 가장 비슷한 유의어를 고르는 문제	1~2
지시어 (Reference)	문맥에서 대명사나 관계대명사 등이 지칭하는 명사를 고르는 문제	0~1
문장 요약 (Sentence Simplification)	지문에서 음영 표시된 문장을 가장 잘 간결하게 바꾸어 쓴 것을 선택지 중에서 고르는 문제	0~1
사실 정보 찾기 (Factual Information)	지문을 바탕으로 문제를 통해 특정 정보의 사실 여부를 파악하거나 육하원칙에 따라 묻는 정보를 찾는 문제	2~3
틀린 정보 찾기 (Negative Fact)	지문에서 언급되지 않았거나 지문의 정보에 비춰볼 때 잘못된 것을 가려내는 문제	1

Reading to Learn		
요약 완성 (Summary)	제시된 지문에 대한 요약의 글을 완성시키는 문제로서 선택지의 6개 문장 가운데 요약에 포함되어야 할 문장 3개를 고르는 문제	0~1
분류 (Category Chart)	지문에서 언급된 요점 혹은 그 외 중요한 정보를 분류표의 카테고리에 맞게 분류하는 문제	0~1
Inferencing		
추론 (Inference)	지문에서 명백하게 언급된 사실은 아니지만 지문의 내용을 통해 추론하는 문제	0~2
의도 파악 (Rhetorical Purpose)	글을 쓰는 방식에 대한 저자의 의도를 파악하는 문제	1~2
문장 삽입 (Insertion)	주어진 한 문장을 지문의 정해진 부분에 표시된 네 곳 중 가장 알맞은 위치에 끼워 넣는 문제	1
총 문항 수		10

4. 기존 시험과 개정 시험 간 Reading 영역 비교

	기존 iBT (~2023년 7월 전)	개정 후 iBT (2023년 7월 이후)
지문 개수	3~4개	2개
지문당 문제 수	10문제	10문제
지문당 평균 시간	18분	18분
전체 시험 시간	54~72분	36분

- 지문 길이, 난이도, 문제 난이도에는 변화가 없다.

PAGODA TOEFL 80+ R/L/S/W

I. Identifying Details

Lesson

01 Sentence Simplification

Lesson Outline

- 문장 요약(Sentence Simplification) 문제는 지문에 표시된 특정 문장을 가장 정확하고 간결하게 요약한 보기를 찾아내는 문제다. 문장의 세부적인 내용보다는 핵심 내용에 집중해야 하며, 일종의 패러프레이징(paraphrasing) 문제라고도 할 수 있으므로 문장의 주요 정보를 파악하는 것이 가장 중요하다.
- 이 유형의 문제는 한 지문당 0~1개가 출제된다.

Typical Questions 

- Which of the sentences below best expresses the essential information in the highlighted sentence in the passage? Incorrect choices change the meaning in important ways or leave out essential information.

다음 중 지문에 음영 표시된 문장의 핵심 정보를 가장 잘 표현한 문장은 무엇인가? 오답은 의미를 크게 왜곡하거나 핵심 정보를 누락하고 있다.

Learning Strategies

Step 1 지문에 음영으로 표시된 문장을 보고 핵심 내용을 간추린다.

⋯› 너무 세부적이거나 지문의 흐름에 중요한 내용이 아니면 핵심 내용에 포함되지 않는다.

⋯› 만약 음영 표시된 문장에 대명사 등의 지시어가 있다면 앞 문장을 보고 그것이 무엇을 가리키는지 정확히 파악하고 넘어가도록 하자. 핵심 내용 이해에 도움이 된다.

Step 2 주어진 보기들 중 핵심 정보를 가장 정확히 담고 있는 보기를 고른다. 물론 보기는 지문에 쓰인 것과 다른 단어를 사용하여 패러프레이징된다는 점을 기억해야 한다. 즉, 지문과 동일한 단어가 쓰인 보기가 있더라도 핵심 내용을 담고 있지 않거나 핵심 내용과 다른 정보를 담은 오답일 수 있다.

Step 3 정답을 고른 뒤 다른 보기들의 오답 여부를 확인하고 넘어가자. 문제에서 말하듯 오답은 문장의 의미를 왜곡하고 바꾸거나 핵심 정보가 빠져 있다. 오답을 검토하는 것도 Sentence Simplification 유형을 이해하는 데 큰 도움이 된다.

Example

(...) Features of the Gothic style including elaborate facades which frequently bore sculptures depicting Biblical scenes and a preference for vertical movement, evident in its tall towers and pointed arches, were aimed at conveying a sense of majesty about the Church. (...)

Q. Which of the sentences below best expresses the essential information in the highlighted sentence in the passage? Incorrect choices change the meaning in important ways or leave out essential information.

1 지문에 음영으로 표시된 문장을 보고 핵심 내용을 간추린다.

Features of the Gothic style [including elaborate facades which frequently bore sculptures depicting Biblical scenes and a preference for vertical movement, evident in its tall towers and pointed arches,] were aimed at conveying a sense of majesty about the Church.

문장의 길이가 길면 혼란이 올 수도 있고 압도될 수도 있지만 찬찬히 읽으며 잔가지, 즉 세부 사항들을 쳐내고 핵심 내용만 남겨보자. 위에 주어진 예시의 경우 [ ] 안에 들어간 내용이 Gothic style의 특징들, 즉 세부 사항들이다. 이 문장의 핵심은 '[이러한 특징의] 고딕 양식은 **교회의 위엄을 전달하려고 의도되었다**'는 것이다.

2 주어진 보기들 중 핵심 정보를 가장 정확히 담고 있는 것을 고른다. 보기를 살펴보자.

Ⓐ The purpose of elaborate sculptures on the exterior illustrating Biblical scenes and the extreme height found in Gothic buildings was to evoke reverence about the Church.

··· 고딕 건물들에서 볼 수 있는 ~의 목적은 교회에 대한 존경심을 불러일으키기 위한 것이었다

Ⓑ From the decorative Biblical sculptures in the outer walls, towers, and arches of the church, it is evident that Gothic style means to instill awe in viewers.

··· 고딕 양식은 보는 사람들에게 경외심을 불어넣으려는 것이 명백하다

Ⓒ Sculptures, which are one of the features of Gothic architecture meant to express grandeur, often showed a preference for Biblical scenes and vertical movement.

··· 조각품들은 성경에 나오는 장면들과 수직적 움직임에 대한 선호를 흔히 보였다

Ⓓ Gothic style centers primarily on intricate Biblical sculptures and an inclination for height to communicate a sense of reverence about the Church.

··· 고딕 양식은 복잡한 성경적 조각들과 높이에 주로 중점을 둔다

핵심 내용만 봐도 무엇이 정답인지 매우 명백하다. 정답은 Ⓐ로, '~ were aimed at'이 'The purpose of ~'로 패러프레이징되었다.

3 정답을 고른 뒤 다른 보기들의 오답 여부를 확인하고 넘어가자. 핵심 내용을 잘 파악했는지 다시 살펴본다. Ⓑ는 단순한 경외심이 아니라 '교회에 대한' 존경심을 불러일으키기 위한 것이었으므로, Ⓒ는 특정 조각품을 선호했다는 것이 핵심 내용이 아니므로, Ⓓ는 특정 세부 사항에 주로 중점을 두었다는 것이 핵심 내용이 아니므로 오답이다.

Practice

01

Inca Sacrifices

Five centuries after Inca priests sacrificed three young children on a snow-covered peak in Argentina, archaeologists discovered them frozen in nearly perfect condition. Approximately two feet above the body of the sacrificed boy, three miniature llama figurines were found. It is presumed that the Incas may have offered the llama figurines along with the sacrifices to help ensure the fertility of the llama herds. In front of the three llama figurines were placed two male figurines, one made of gold and the other of spondylus shell, as if to suggest that they were leading the animals. These two male figurines may have been meant to represent one of two things: they could have been meant to represent the deities believed to be the natural owners of the llamas, most likely the mountain gods, or the Inca nobles who were responsible for overseeing the royal herds of animals dedicated to the gods.

Which of the sentences below best expresses the essential information in the highlighted sentence in the passage? Incorrect choices change the meaning in important ways or leave out essential information.

Ⓐ The two statuettes might be either the mountain gods, the owners of the llamas in nature, or the Inca's ruling class in charge of the royal animals which were meant to be offerings to the gods.

Ⓑ The two figures probably show the gods who took care of the mountains, or the Inca nobles who watched the llama herds that belonged to the gods.

Ⓒ One of the figures is thought to have been the owner of the llamas in nature, and the other the Inca authority who supervises the king's llama herds, which would become offerings to the gods.

Ⓓ Small male figures usually symbolize the gods who were thought to be the llamas' owners in nature, the mountain gods, or the Inca royal family who chose the offerings to the gods.

02

Type of Volcanoes

People have a stereotypical idea of what volcanoes look like, but geologists generally group volcanoes into four main types: cinder cones, composite volcanoes, shield volcanoes, and lava domes. Some of our most impressive mountains are composite volcanoes, which are also sometimes called stratovolcanoes. These volcanoes typically feature steep slopes and huge symmetrical cones built by periodic flows of lava, volcanic ash, and cinders. They can rise as high as 8,000 feet above their bases. Some famous examples of this kind of volcanic mountain include Mount Cotopaxi in Ecuador, Mount Shasta in California, Mount St. Helens in Washington, Mount Fuji in Japan, and Mount Hood in Oregon. Most composite volcanoes have craters at their summits, which can contain one central vent or a cluster of vents. As lava flows from breaks in the crater wall or cracks in the sides of the cone, they form dikes and ridges that act as gigantic ribs that help strengthen the cone. The essential feature for a volcano to be considered a composite volcano is the alternating layers of material that form a conduit system that allows magma to rise from deep within the earth's crust and spill out through cracks and fissures.

Which of the sentences below best expresses the essential information in the highlighted sentence in the passage? Incorrect choices change the meaning in important ways or leave out essential information.

Ⓐ The uniformity of the layers in a composite volcano allows it to form a conduit system for magma to rise from great depths.

Ⓑ The conduit system that allows magma to rise from great depths earns this volcano type its name.

Ⓒ This type of volcano is characterized by the different strata of material that channel magma from deep within the Earth.

Ⓓ Composite volcanoes are essentially a conduit system for the transportation of viscous magma.

03

Global Warming

Global warming is the increase in the average temperature of the Earth's near-surface air and oceans over recent decades and its projected continuation. Global average air temperatures near the Earth's surface have risen 0.74 ± 0.18 °C over the past century. [1] The Intergovernmental Panel on Climate Change (IPCC) has concluded that "most of the observed increase in globally averaged temperatures since the mid-20th century is very likely due to the observed increase in anthropogenic greenhouse gas concentrations." Natural phenomena such as solar variation combined with volcanoes probably had a small warming effect from pre-industrial times until 1950, but have had a small cooling effect since 1950. These basic conclusions have been endorsed by at least 30 scientific societies and academies of science. [2] Interestingly, despite the ample evidence collected to support global warming trends, as well as the support of these findings by the world's top scientists, there are still those who dismiss the idea of the phenomenon. However, these naysayers tend to be members of special interest groups who stand to lose money if measures are taken to curtail global warming.

1. Which of the sentences below best expresses the essential information in the highlighted sentence in the passage? Incorrect choices change the meaning in important ways or leave out essential information.

Ⓐ An organization on climate change believes that the increase in global temperature was caused by greenhouse gas emissions from industries in the late 20th century.

Ⓑ Global temperature has increased since the mid-20th century because of increased greenhouse gas emissions from human activities, according to one organization.

Ⓒ A study by an organization suggests that global warming started when the industrial revolution produced a lot of factories and machines that replaced human beings.

Ⓓ An organization has provided solid evidence that the increase in average global temperature didn't happen until the mid-20th century due to the population explosion.

2. Which of the sentences below best expresses the essential information in the highlighted sentence in the passage? Incorrect choices change the meaning in important ways or leave out essential information.

Ⓐ There are people who suspect global warming because of the evidence provided by the world's eminent scientists.

Ⓑ World-class scientists have already collected enough evidence to prove that the phenomenon called global warming exists.

Ⓒ People don't trust even world-famous scientists because they didn't provide much evidence of their theories.

Ⓓ Some people still have doubts about global warming even with a lot of supporting evidence and opinions.

04

Head Injuries

People often complain about helmet laws for those who ride motorcycles and rules that specify helmets as necessary gear for cycling, inline skating and a host of other recreational activities. [1] Though helmets may be uncomfortable, there are strong reasons for why their use is encouraged because no one knows when an accident will occur, and many injuries that occur while riding motorcycles and bicycles, or while doing other recreational activities, are injuries to the head. A severe head injury may damage cerebral blood vessels and cause bleeding into the cranial cavity. If blood is forced between the dura mater (a protective membrane) and the cranium (skull), the condition is known as an *epidural hemorrhage*. If the flow of blood goes between the lower layer of the dura mater and the brain, it is called a *subdural hemorrhage*. [2] The symptoms of these conditions vary depending on whether the damaged vessel is an artery or a vein because arterial blood pressure is higher than the blood pressure of veins, which means that artery damage can cause more rapid and severe distortion of neural tissue than vein damage. Since the nature of a head injury cannot always be immediately determined, it is important to receive medical attention quickly.

1. Which of the sentences below best expresses the essential information in the highlighted sentence in the passage? Incorrect choices change the meaning in important ways or leave out essential information.

Ⓐ Wearing helmets should be mandatory for all bike riders since many bikers injure their heads while bike-riding.

Ⓑ Well-made helmets are essential because when bikers fall, they usually get the biggest injury to their head.

Ⓒ It is urgent to produce comfortable helmets so that bikers may feel safe and have a pleasant time while riding a bike.

Ⓓ People ought to wear helmets when enjoying active recreational activities like riding a bike because accidents in such cases are likely to result in head injuries.

2. Which of the sentences below best expresses the essential information in the highlighted sentence in the passage? Incorrect choices change the meaning in important ways or leave out essential information.

Ⓐ Damage to an artery causes various conditions depending on whether the affected area is close to the heart.

Ⓑ If the damaged vessel is an artery, there may be a more serious condition because the blood pressure in arteries is higher than that in veins.

Ⓒ Artery damage usually leads to a fatal condition because it directly affects the neural tissues of the brain.

Ⓓ An artery is more important than a vein in terms of neural conditions, because the blood pressure in arteries is higher than that in veins.

Lesson

02 Fact & Negative Fact

Lesson Outline

- 사실 및 틀린 정보 찾기(Fact & Negative Fact) 문제는 지문에 제시된 세부 정보에 관해 묻는 문제이다. Fact 문제는 지문에 제시된 내용과 일치하는 보기를, Negative Fact 문제는 지문에 제시되지 않았거나 지문의 내용과 다른 보기를 고르는 문제다. 수험자가 이미 알고 있는 배경 지식과는 상관 없이 지문에 언급된 내용만으로 문제를 풀어야 한다.
- 이 유형의 문제는 한 지문당 3~4개가 출제된다.
- 질문이 출제된 단락의 번호가 문제와 함께 제시되며 해당 단락은 [➡]로 표시된다.

Typical Questions 

Fact

- Which of the following does paragraph X mention?
  다음 중 X단락에서 언급된 것은 무엇인가?
- According to paragraph X, why/how/what ~?
  X단락에 따르면, 왜/어떻게/무엇이 ~인가?
- According to paragraph X, which of the following is true of ~?
  X단락에 따르면, 다음 중 ~에 대해 사실인 것은 무엇인가?

참고 가끔 정답을 두 개 고르라는 문제도 출제된다.

Negative Fact

- According to the passage, which of the following is NOT true of ~?
  지문에 따르면, 다음 중 ~에 대해 사실이 아닌 것은 무엇인가?
- All of the following are mentioned in paragraph X EXCEPT
  다음 중 X단락에서 언급되지 않은 것은

Learning Strategies

Step 1 문제를 읽은 뒤 해당 내용이 지문의 어느 부분에서 나왔는지 확인한다. 문제에서 '단락 X'라고 직접 말해줄 때도 있다.

···› Reading 영역에서는 문제 순서가 거의 지문의 흐름대로 나오는 경우가 많으므로 참고하자.

Step 2 패러프레이징된 보기가 있다는 점을 염두에 두고, 보기를 전부 읽어보며 오답인지 정답인지 하나씩 확인해 나가자.

Example

Q. According to paragraph 6, why did the International Style become popular?

❶ 문제를 읽은 뒤 해당 내용이 지문의 어느 부분에서 나왔는지 확인한다. 문제에서 '단락 X'라고 직접 말해줄 때도 있다.

···› 6단락에서 'International Style'이라는 단어를 찾는다.

6 ➡ Nonetheless, this idea, which came to be known as **International Style, served as a prototype for all modern cities which deal with the problem of accommodating high-density urban populations.** Modern design leaned towards ridding buildings of decorative elements and placing priority on function over form. By utilizing mass-produced, inexpensive building materials such as glass and reinforced concrete, large-scale urban development was made possible. Today, the construction of high-rise buildings with minimalist, repetitive structures is creating a sense of uniformity in cities throughout the world.

이 '국제 양식'은 '고밀도 도시 인구를 수용하는 문제에 대처하는 모든 현대 도시의 원형이 되었다'라고 나와 있다. 뒤에 국제 양식에 관한 설명이 더 이어진다.

❷ 보기를 하나씩 읽어보며 확인하도록 하자.

(A) It created similar-looking cities throughout the world.

···› 지문에 언급된 내용이긴 하지만 이것 때문에 국제 양식이 인기를 끈 것은 아니다.

(B) The materials it used kept the costs of large-scale urban development low.

···› '국제 양식이 사용한 자재가 대규모 도시 개발의 비용을 줄였다'고 한다.

(C) It attempted to address the problem of urban sprawl in modern times.

···› '국제 양식이 현대의 도시 확산 문제를 다루려고 시도했다'고 한다. 이는 지문에 나오지 않은 내용이다. 지문에 언급된 문제는 '고밀도 도시 인구를 수용하는 것'이다.

(D) It did not have any of the decorative elements from the previous era.

···› 국제 양식에 관해 부분적으로 옳지만 '전혀(any of)'라는 단어가 맞지 않는다. 장식적인 요소를 없애는 쪽으로 기울었다는 언급은 있지만 장식적 요소가 전혀 없었다고 말하고 있지는 않다.

답은 (B)이다. '고밀도 도시 인구 수용을 위해 대량 생산된 값싼 건축 자재를 이용해 대규모 도시 개발이 가능해졌다(By utilizing mass-produced, inexpensive building materials such as glass and reinforced concrete, large-scale urban development was made possible.)'는 내용이 지문에 나와 있다. 보기가 항상 패러프레이징된다는 점을 기억해야 한다.

Practice

01

Sand Dune

The field of physical geography defines dunes as hills that are formed by a process known as deposition, occurring when wind blows sand eroded from mountains to areas with high volumes of sand. The shape that is created when sand reaches its destination is determined not only by a dune's mass but also by the wind system in its area, both of which affect the number and positioning of slip faces, basically the steep sides of a dune. Furthermore, dunes are classified in terms of the positioning and number of slip faces they exhibit. Of all the dune types, the crescentic dune is the most prevalent dune shape on Earth, even though it comprises only a small percentage of the Earth's dune area. This fact results from the dune's relatively small mass, as the world's largest crescentic dunes are up to thirty meters in height and four kilometers in length and width. The crescentic dune displays its individual slip face on its concave side. Additionally, it is formed by a wind blowing in a single direction, and it can move, another important consideration in the study of dunes, faster and farther than any other type of dune. These are, once more, inherent traits for a small dune like the crescentic.

According to the passage, which of the following is NOT true of crescentic dunes?

Ⓐ Their movement and shape are stable for being so small.

Ⓑ They are the most frequently occurring dunes.

Ⓒ They can move more swiftly than other types.

Ⓓ They are generally smaller in scale than other dune types.

02

The Galapagos Islands

The Galapagos Islands are an archipelago of volcanic islands located 900 km west of South America. These islands are perfect for organisms' evolution because they are neither too far from nor too close to the mainland, allowing animals to travel only sporadically. Natural phenomena such as wind or ocean currents sometimes carry a few individuals of a mainland species to an island in the archipelago. If the individuals successfully reproduce on the island, their descendants may establish a population. The vast expanse of ocean that isolates the island from the mainland geographically impedes their interaction with other members of their species. Thus, over generations the island population diverges from the mainland species. Individuals of the diverging population may in turn colonize other islands in the archipelago, repeating the evolutionary process. Habitats and selection pressures that differ between the islands can foster even more divergence from the ancestral species. For example, finches living in the Galapagos Islands, also known as Darwin's finches, were most likely blown in by a storm. Over a long period of time, and hundreds of generations, these finches have evolved into 15 different species, all with varying beak size and shape. These various finches all come from the same ancestors, but they have diverged into separate species with noticeable behavioral differences from island to island.

According to the passage, the island species differ from the mainland population because

Ⓐ of the absence of enemies

Ⓑ they establish a strong social network among themselves

Ⓒ the immense ocean functions as an obstruction

Ⓓ they evolve on the island over generations

03

The Rise of Civilization

Data from diverse sources indicate that the first obvious examples of agricultural evidence date back to somewhere around 5,000 BCE in Mesopotamia, North Africa, India, or China. Clearly, in the beginning, farming was not their major way of obtaining food and served only as a supplement to their main method: hunting and gathering. The first people who tried to harvest crops had no reliable techniques or the know-how to sustain themselves purely from growing crops. However, the sudden advance in agriculture was started by people that lived near rivers and planted seeds in floodplains. This allowed people to get a stable source of water from the river instead of relying on unpredictable or seasonal rainfall. This changed the way people lived as nomadic groups of people were able to settle in one place and grow into a community. The increase in food accessibility triggered the expansion of the population, which in turn led to irrigation to bring water to the city to support the demands of the people. Because of the surplus of agricultural products, settled agriculture brought about the development of property rights and legal mechanisms to bring laws into effect. This in turn gave rise to a concept of more complex and hierarchical government organization.

According to the passage, what caused the development of an organized government?

Ⓐ Reliable hunting techniques which led to the waning dependency on farming

Ⓑ The increasing food availability that led to the need to protect their harvest from invaders

Ⓒ The source of water that was directed into the community for fishing

Ⓓ The need to enforce property laws

04

Thermoregulation

All living organisms are influenced by the external temperatures of their environment. Changes in the ambient temperature of its surroundings can cause an animal's body temperature to fluctuate. Therefore, an animal's ability to regulate its body temperature is vital to its survival in extreme environments. As such, animals indigenous to extremely cold climates have evolved various mechanisms for thermoregulation. Most land mammals and birds react to the cold by raising their fur or plumage, which reduces the flow of heat and lowers the energy cost of keeping warm. For example, an arctic fox dressed in its winter fur can sit comfortably in -50 degrees Celsius weather without any need to change its metabolic rate to warm up. Another mechanism employed by animals is shutting down circulation to peripheral systems in order to prevent further heat loss by regulating the blood flow. An Alaskan husky dog may have a core temperature of 38 degrees Celsius, but the temperature in its forelimbs may be 14 degrees and the pads of its feet 0 degrees. As a result, heat loss is reduced by lowering the temperature in the limbs to several degrees below that of the body core, where most of its vital organs are located. The polar bear has dense fur, a layer of blubber up to 11 centimeters thick and black skin for absorbing the heat from light, making it an excellent insulation machine. Some animals also possess behavioral adaptations, such as rolling up into a ball to preserve body heat.

According to the passage, all of the following are polar bears' adaptations to living in a cold area EXCEPT

(A) a thick layer of fatty tissue

(B) a thick coat of hair

(C) the ability to mitigate the cold by varying its blood flow

(D) hide pigmentation that soaks up sunlight

Lesson
03 Vocabulary

Lesson Outline

- 어휘(Vocabulary) 문제는 지문에 음영 표시된 단어 또는 구와 의미가 같거나 맥락상 비슷한 단어를 찾는 문제다.
- 이 유형의 문제는 한 지문당 1~2개가 출제된다.

Typical Questions 

- The word "▒▒▒" in paragraph X is closest in meaning to
  X단락의 단어 '▒▒▒'와 의미상 가장 가까운 것은
- The phrase "▒▒▒" in paragraph X is closest in meaning to
  X단락의 구 '▒▒▒'와 의미상 가장 가까운 것은

Learning Strategies

Step 1 문제에 음영 표시된 단어·구를 찾아 정확한 의미를 파악한다.
→ 한 단어가 여러 가지 다른 의미를 가질 수 있다는 점을 기억해야 한다.
→ 음영 처리된 단어·구의 뜻을 모르는 경우, 앞뒤 문장과 문단의 흐름을 통해 대략적인 의미를 유추해 보도록 한다.

Step 2 주어진 보기 네 개 중 음영 표시된 단어·구와 의미상 가장 비슷한 보기를 찾는다.

Step 3 정답을 고른 뒤 다른 보기들의 오답 여부를 확인하고 넘어가자. 네 개 보기의 뜻이 각각 무엇인지, 음영 표시된 단어·구를 선택한 보기로 대체해도 의미 파악에 문제가 없는지 문맥을 다시 한 번 확인한다.

Example

Q. The word "elevated" in paragraph 5 is closest in meaning to

Ⓐ raised
Ⓑ installed
Ⓒ assembled
Ⓓ advanced

1 문제에 음영 표시된 단어·구를 찾아 어떤 의미로 쓰였는지 봐야 한다. 5단락에서 elevated라는 단어를 찾는다.

(...) These buildings were framed by large parks, and the residential areas around them were elevated on pillars. Le Corbusier's plan was shocking, and it was rejected by the Paris government. (...)

elevate라는 단어는 '올리다, 높이다'라는 뜻을 가지고 있다. 수동의 형태로 쓰였으므로 '올려진, 높여진'이라는 의미가 된다.

2 주어진 보기 네 개 중 음영 표시된 단어·구와 의미상 가장 비슷한 보기를 찾는다.

Ⓐ raised 올려진
Ⓑ installed 설치된
Ⓒ assembled 조립된
Ⓓ advanced 진보된

elevated와 가장 의미가 가까운 Ⓐ raised가 정답이다. 보기는 보통 제시된 단어보다 약간 더 쉽거나 더 흔히 쓰는 단어들로 출제되므로, 제시된 단어를 모른다 해도 해당 위치에 각각의 보기를 대신 넣어 보며 제시어를 추론하는 것이 가능할 때도 있다.

3 정답을 고른 뒤 다른 보기들의 오답 여부를 확인하고 넘어가자. Ⓓ advanced는 were ~ on pillars 사이 빈칸에 들어가기에는 의미상 어색하므로 가장 쉽게 오답임을 알 수 있다. Ⓑ installed와 Ⓒ assembled는 얼핏 보면 were ~ on pillars 사이 빈칸에 들어가기에 적절해 보이지만, 문장의 주어가 residential areas이므로 문맥상 맞지 않는다는 것을 알 수 있다.

Practice

01

Tundra

Of all the biomes in the world, tundra is the coldest, and it is known for its harsh conditions. It has long, frigid winters and very short summers. There are a low variety of organisms and little human settlement because it is almost devoid of precipitation, the soil is barren and the growing season is short. In addition, tundra has an underground layer of permanently frozen soil called permafrost that extends to a depth of about 20 feet. To endure these surroundings, tundra flora and fauna have special adaptations. Tundra-dwelling plants are able to survive by growing shallow roots in the topsoil that does thaw, and animals have adapted to breeding and raising their young quickly during the short summer. There are two distinct types of tundra: Arctic tundra, which is found around the North Pole, and Alpine Tundra, which is located at the tops of tall, cold mountains such as the Himalayas or the highest peaks in the Alps.

1. The word "frigid" in the passage is closest in meaning to

Ⓐ chilly

Ⓑ dormant

Ⓒ existing

Ⓓ persistent

2. The word "dwelling" in the passage is closest in meaning to

Ⓐ supporting

Ⓑ decimating

Ⓒ inhabiting

Ⓓ verging

02

Animal Cycles

Certain critical cycles typically regulate animal behavior. One of the most obvious manifestations of these cycles is called the circadian rhythm, which refers to their behavioral pattern based on a 24-hour cycle. The circadian clock affects the basic drives of an animal, such as hunger, sleep and excretion. On top of daily cycles, animals are also affected by circannian rhythms, which operate on an annual basis. Determined primarily by seasonal changes, an animal's circannian rhythm is what drives activities like hibernation, reproduction, and migration. For instance, with the onset of winter, ground squirrels choose hibernation as the best way to cope with the frigid temperatures during the season. Before they go into dormancy, they consume more food than usual because doubling their body weight is a prerequisite for the long cold winter.

1. The word "onset" in the passage is closest in meaning to

   (A) integration

   (B) start

   (C) feat

   (D) abundance

2. The phrase "cope with" in the passage is closest in meaning to

   (A) consider

   (B) handle

   (C) advocate

   (D) retard

03

The Relationships between Organisms

Even in the absence of blossoms, many plants make and secrete nectar through extrafloral nectaries: structures that produce nectar on leaves and stems. These plants are usually found in areas where ants are abundant, such as the tropics and temperate areas. Although some types contain amino acids, nectar is mainly composed of water and dissolved sugar. These plants have developed ways to attract ants and coexist with them. Ants are persistent defenders, and they protect these plants from invaders such as flower-eating insects and other herbivores. These species of plants and the ants cannot live without each other. The highly active worker ants need much energy to support their busy lifestyle. Therefore, these plants exploit them by providing extrafloral nectar, giving the ant a profuse source of energy. In exchange for this favor, ants guard the plant from other insects which may compete with ants for the valuable resource, and they also ward off herbivores that feed on the leaves of this plant.

1. The word "persistent" in the passage is closest in meaning to

Ⓐ lasting

Ⓑ ensuing

Ⓒ firm

Ⓓ exclusive

2. The word "Therefore" in the passage is closest in meaning to

Ⓐ Hence

Ⓑ Notwithstanding

Ⓒ Furthermore

Ⓓ Meanwhile

04

Direct Carving

Traditionally, sculptures began with preliminary models made by the artist out of clay. These were then passed on to studio assistants who finalized the production in stone, plaster, or bronze. In fact, it was quite unusual for neoclassical sculptors to actually pick up mallet and chisel since the assistants were usually far more adept at carving than the original artists. In the 20th century, however, direct carving appeared as a novel way of creating sculptures without the use of intermediate clay models. Either working from memory or the subject itself, the sole artist worked on carving alone. Direct carving, as an approach to form composition, is considered a breakthrough in modern art and a revival of techniques derived from primitive art. A critical aspect of direct carving is the artist's decision to present the nature of the medium, working to reveal its appealing aesthetic and textural qualities. The subject matter and final form of direct carving often evolves from the shape, texture, or grain of the medium employed.

1. The word "adept" in the passage is closest in meaning to

(A) fast

(B) abrupt

(C) sturdy

(D) competent

2. The word "employed" in the passage is closest in meaning to

(A) congregated

(B) utilized

(C) considered

(D) hired

Lesson

04 Reference

Lesson Outline

- 지시어(Reference) 문제는 지문에 음영 표시된 단어 또는 구가 무엇을 가리키는지 찾는 문제다. 여기서 해당 단어나 구는 대명사인 경우가 많다. 영어는 앞에 나온 단어를 다시 반복하지 않기 위해 대명사를 쓰기 때문에 해당 대명사가 의미하는 원래 단어가 무엇인지 묻는 것이다. It, They, Its, Their, That 등의 대명사가 자주 등장한다.
- 이 유형의 문제는 한 지문당 1개 정도 출제되며, 아예 출제되지 않을 때도 있다.

Typical Questions

- The word "   " in the passage / in paragraph X refers to

  지문/X단락의 단어 '   '가 가리키는 것은

- The phrase "   " in paragraph X refers to

  X단락의 구 '   '가 가리키는 것은

Learning Strategies

Step 1 문제에 음영 표시된 단어·구를 지문에서 찾는다. 보통 문제에서 '단락 X'에 있다고 말해준다.

Step 2 음영 표시된 단어·구를 찾은 뒤 이 단어나 구가 해당 문장 안에서 무엇을 가리키는지 파악한다. 단어·구가 들어 있는 문장을 읽어보면 보통 답이 눈에 들어오지만, 난이도가 높을 경우에는 그 앞의 문장까지 살펴봐야 할 수도 있으므로 찬찬히 읽어보고 의미를 파악하자.

보통 음영 표시된 단어·구가 가리키는 대상은 앞에서 먼저 제시되지만, 간혹 뒤에 나오는 경우도 있으므로 주의한다.

Step 3 정답을 고른 뒤 다른 보기들의 오답 여부를 확인하고 넘어가자. 일단 정답을 음영 표시된 부분에 넣어보고 의미가 여전히 맞는지 읽어본 뒤, 오답들을 훑어보며 비슷한 것은 없는지 확인한다.

Example

The boundary between the Cretaceous and Paleogene periods is clearly defined throughout the world. In areas where the boundary is exposed, the rocks above and below the border have often quite distinct colors. Moreover, there is always a thin band of clay separating the two. When Luis Alvarez and his son were studying geologic formations in Italy in the 1970s, his son pointed out the clay layer to his father. Although scientists knew at the time that it marked the end of the age of reptiles, no one really knew why it had formed and what its true significance was.

Q. The word "it" in paragraph 5 refers to

Ⓐ world
Ⓑ layer
Ⓒ Italy
Ⓓ age

1 문제에 음영 표시된 단어·구를 지문에서 찾는다.

Although scientists knew at the time that it marked the end of the age of reptiles, no one really knew why it had formed and what its true significance was.

2 음영 표시된 단어·구를 찾은 뒤 이 단어나 구가 해당 문장에서 어떤 것을 가리키는지 파악한다. '그것'이 파충류 시대의 종말을 표시한다고 했으므로 앞에 있는 문장을 살펴보자.

When Luis Alvarez and his son were studying geologic formations in Italy in the 1970s, his son pointed out the clay layer to his father.

알바레즈와 아들이 지형을 연구하고 있을 때 아들이 점토층을 가리켰다는 내용이다. 이 문장 바로 뒤에 it이 있는 문장이 따라나오면서 '그것은 파충류 시대의 종말을 나타냈다'고 했으므로 점토층이 답이라는 것을 알 수 있다. 따라서 Ⓑ가 정답이다.

3 정답을 고른 뒤 다른 보기들의 오답 여부를 확인하고 넘어가자. 의미상 it으로 대체될 수 있으면서 marked의 주어가 되기에 맥락상 자연스러운 단어는 layer 밖에 없다는 것을 확인할 수 있다.

Practice

01

Quilting

Quilting is the process of sewing together two or more layers of cloth, often with a layer of padding between them. It was initially used to make clothing to shield the wearer from frigid weather, and for a while it was put to use as armor padding. However, as firearms appeared, it could no longer function as a cushion against impact. Therefore, it has been used mainly as an insulating cover against cold air since then. In the 18th and 19th centuries, quilting was often a communal activity, involving women and girls within a family, or in a larger community. 'Quilting bees' in which teams spent time working together on one quilt were essential social events in many communities, and were typically held in the agricultural off-season, between periods of high demand for farm labor. Quilts were frequently made to commemorate major life events, mostly wedding ceremonies. During this period, women employed quilts to articulate their concerns about social issues and to fortify the bonds among them.

1. The word "it" in the passage refers to

Ⓐ quilt

Ⓑ clothing

Ⓒ wearer

Ⓓ weather

2. The word "their" in the passage refers to

Ⓐ events

Ⓑ communities

Ⓒ ceremonies

Ⓓ women

02 Echolocation

1 ➠ Most animals rely on their sense of sight to find their way around and perform important daily tasks. However, some animals live in dimly lit or dark environments which render their vision almost useless, while others have such poor vision that they have to rely on other senses to avoid obstacles and find food. Many of these animals, like whales, dolphins, bats, and shrews, rely on a technique called echolocation.

2 ➠ Animals that use this technique emit short, extremely high-pitched sounds and then listen for the echoes to bounce back to them. They then carefully interpret the echoes to determine an object's size, direction of movement, and distance from them. The time interval between the emission of the sound and the return of the echo indicates the distance to the object. The longer the interval is, the further away it is. The volume of the echo tells the animal the size and texture of the object. In fact, echolocation is so effective that researchers have observed bats using it to locate and avoid thin wires while flying at great speeds.

1. The word "others" in paragraph 1 refers to

Ⓐ tasks

Ⓑ animals

Ⓒ environments

Ⓓ senses

2. The word "it" in paragraph 2 refers to

Ⓐ technique

Ⓑ direction

Ⓒ distance

Ⓓ object

03

Volcanoes

1 ➡ Because volcanoes channel magma—super-heated molten rock—out from beneath the Earth's crust onto the surface, some regard them as the Earth's plumbing system. Volcanic eruptions generally take place near the boundaries of the continental or tectonic plates, although some known as hot spot volcanoes are located over extremely active points beneath the surface of continental plates. On land, volcanoes, which generally do not last long, either form broad, flat cones as a result of the build-up of the material from previous eruptions, or cinder cones, which are much like a chimney. Underwater volcanoes sometimes form steep pillars which eventually break the surface of the ocean, forming new islands.

2 ➡ Active volcanoes are those that are currently releasing steam, different types of lava, and gases like carbon dioxide at present. These often also produce pyroclastic flows, which are fast moving rivers of fluidized hot gas, ash, and rock. They may also become lahars, mixtures of rock, mud, and water with the consistency of concrete that flow from the volcano down through river valleys at high speeds. Areas with active volcanoes are often popular tourist spots because they have nature's miracles like hot springs, geysers, and mud pots. But by bad fortune, they also often have earthquakes.

3 ➡ It can be hard to say whether volcanoes are in an active state. Some volcanoes that have shown no activity for a certain amount of time are classified as dormant, but they have the potential to erupt again without warning. Others that are deemed to have permanently ceased are classified as extinct. People are so confident that extinct volcanoes will never erupt again that resorts have been built in the craters of some of these volcanoes.

1. The word "which" in paragraph 1 refers to

Ⓐ cinder cones

Ⓑ volcanoes

Ⓒ pillars

Ⓓ islands

2. The word "they" in paragraph 2 refers to

Ⓐ river valleys

Ⓑ areas with active volcanoes

Ⓒ tourist spots

Ⓓ earthquakes

04

Mantle

1 ➡ The first stage of terrestrial planetary evolution is *differentiation*, which is the separation of material based on its density. In this stage, heavier materials steadily sink to the center of the bodies to form a solid, metallic core, which in turn is surrounded by a relatively thin surface crust. At present, the Earth is composed of three main layers; the hard yet thin layer where we currently dwell, generally known as the crust; a central ball of molten iron, which is the core; and the mantle, the area between the two, which actually represents two thirds of the Earth's matter. Unlike the hard crust, the nature of the mantle is quite flexible and it resembles a thick liquid.

2 ➡ The mantle is not uniform but has three distinct structural areas. At the point where the crust and the mantle meet, both of them are a random mixture of different types of rock. Deeper into the mantle, the rock gradually becomes malleable, thus creating a soft zone. It is this zone that enables the tectonic plates of the crust to move about. Below the soft zone is the transition zone, where softer minerals become crystals, and it is the place through which slabs of surface rocks descend and slag from the core rises into the mantle. This area is in constant motion, so there are formations of thick and thin spots where heat energy can rise from the core, sometimes reaching the surface.

3 ➡ Not much is known about the rest of the mantle because it cannot be studied directly. Rather it is studied through seismic measurements of earthquakes that occur as far below the Earth's surface as the transition zone, but no deeper.

1. The phrase "the two" in paragraph 1 refers to

Ⓐ planetary evolution and differentiation

Ⓑ material and density

Ⓒ the crust and the core

Ⓓ the core and the mantle

2. The phrase "this zone" in paragraph 2 refers to

Ⓐ the crust

Ⓑ the mantle

Ⓒ the soft zone

Ⓓ the transition zone

II. Making Inference

Lesson

01 Rhetorical Purpose

Lesson Outline

- 의도 파악(Rhetorical Purpose) 문제는 지문에 음영 표시된 단어·구·절의 역할을 묻거나 지문에서 해당 단어·구·절, 크게는 문단이 왜, 어떤 목적을 위해 언급되었는지 찾는 문제다. 'Rhetorical'은 '수사적인'이라는 의미로, 이 수사적 표현에는 직유, 은유와 반복 등 다양한 방법이 있다. 음영 표시된 내용을 통해 지문이 말하고자 하는 것이 무엇인지 그 의미를 정확히 파악해야 한다.
- 이 유형의 문제는 한 지문당 1~2개가 출제된다.

Typical Questions 

- The author mentions ▒▒▒ in order to 글쓴이가 ▒▒▒를 언급하는 이유는
- Why does the author mention ▒▒▒ in paragraph X/in the passage?
  X단락에서/지문에서 글쓴이가 ▒▒▒를 언급하는 이유는 무엇인가?
- In paragraph X, the author mentions ▒▒▒ to
  X단락에서 글쓴이가 ▒▒▒를 언급하는 이유는
- What is the purpose of paragraph X as it relates to paragraph Y?
  Y단락과 관련하여 X단락의 목적은 무엇인가?

Learning Strategies

Step 1 문제에 음영 표시된 단어·구·절을 지문에서 찾자.

⋯› Vocabulary 문제나 Reference 문제와 달리 더 깊은 의미를 파악해야 하는 문제이므로 해당 문장뿐 아니라 앞과 뒤의 문장까지 함께 고려해야 한다는 점에 유의하자.

⋯› 음영 표시된 내용은 앞뒤 문장의 내용에 반박하거나, 비교·대조하거나, 예시를 들기 위한 장치인 경우가 많다.

Step 2 보기들을 하나씩 읽으며 정답을 찾는다. 해당 단어·구·절이 어떤 식으로 앞뒤 문장과 관계를 맺고 있는지, 논리적 관계와 논리 전개 방식에 초점을 맞춘다.

Step 3 앞서 배운 대로 다른 보기들의 오답 여부를 확인하는 것을 잊지 말자. 저자의 의도 및 설명 방식 면에서는 맞는 것처럼 보이지만, 지문의 세부 정보와 다른 내용이 담긴 오답도 있을 수 있다.

Example

Griffith was working with two different strains of the pneumonia bacteria. A strain of bacteria is a population of bacterial cells that all descend from one parent cell, with one or more inherited characteristics that make it different from other strains. One of the strains Griffith used had a protective covering that made its surface smooth, while the other's surface was rough. Therefore, they were designated as type S and type R. The covering made it difficult for an organism's immune system to detect the bacteria, so it was virulent. That means it was capable of surviving and reproducing long enough to cause disease symptoms and be transmitted to other organisms. The R strain lacked this covering.

Q. In paragraph 2, the author mentions that The R strain lacked this covering to

Ⓐ emphasize that it was rarely transmitted to other organisms

Ⓑ explain the role of the protective covering that bacterial strains have

Ⓒ indicate that it was non-virulent

Ⓓ show how Griffith distinguished it from type S

1 문제에 나온 단어·구·절을 지문에서 찾자. 해당 내용은 제시된 문단의 맨 마지막 문장으로 등장하고 있다.

2 보기들을 하나씩 읽으며 정답을 찾는다.

Ⓐ emphasize that it was rarely transmitted to other organisms
→ R형 균주가 다른 생물에 옮겨지는 경우가 거의 없다는 점을 강조하기 위해서

Ⓑ explain the role of the protective covering that bacterial strains have
→ 박테리아성 균주가 가진 보호막의 역할을 설명하기 위해서

Ⓒ indicate that it was non-virulent
→ R형 균주가 치명적이지 않다는 점을 가리키기 위해서

Ⓓ show how Griffith distinguished it from type S
→ 그리피스가 R형 균주를 S형 균주와 구분한 방법을 보여주기 위해서

R형 균주에 보호막이 없다는 점이 명시되기 전에 나온 내용을 살펴보자. 보호막 때문에 면역 체계가 박테리아를 잘 감지하지 못해서 박테리아가 치명적이었다고 나와 있다. 그리고 R형 균주에는 이 보호막이 없었다는 내용이 나오므로 박테리아가 가진 보호막의 역할, 즉 면역 체계에 잘 감지되지 않게 해주는 역할을 설명하고 있음을 알 수 있다. 따라서 Ⓑ가 정답이다.

3 다른 보기들의 오답 여부를 확인하는 것을 잊지 말자. S형 균주가 다른 생물체에 전파 가능하며 치명적이라는 언급은 있으나, R형 균주가 그렇지 않다는 말은 지문에 없으므로 Ⓐ와 Ⓒ는 오답이다. 또한 지문에는 그리피스가 서로 다른 두 개의 균주로 작업했다는 언급은 있지만 둘을 어떻게 구분했는지 그 방법에 대해서는 언급된 바가 없으므로 Ⓓ도 오답이다.

Practice

01

The Manufacturing Belt

The Manufacturing Belt is an area in the northeastern and north-central United States where the economy was formerly based on heavy industries and manufacturing. Unfortunately, the expansion of international free trade agreements in the 1960s made it much cheaper to produce heavy industrial goods like steel in third world countries and import them into the United States than to produce them there. This led to factory closures all over the Manufacturing Belt, decimating the area's economy. During each successive recession, starting with one in 1969, manufacturing jobs disappeared and were replaced by lower-paying service industry jobs. The area's new name, the Rust Belt, is a reference to the rusting machinery left over from the industrial days and a figurative reference to the general decline of the region.

Why does the author mention third world countries in the discussion of the Manufacturing Belt?

Ⓐ To indicate that the economy of the area was fragile

Ⓑ To show that the area would recover from the effects

Ⓒ To explain how the region's economy was set back

Ⓓ To indicate the severity of the impact on the economy

02

Archaeopteryx

Archaeopteryx is the oldest-known animal fossil that is generally accepted as a bird because its feathers were very similar in structure and design to modern-day bird plumage. In fact, the first-known fossils of Archaeopteryx discovered clearly show traces of the feathers that the animal had. Other scientists, however, believe Archaeopteryx was closer to a dinosaur because it had many dinosaur characteristics that birds lack. Unlike modern birds, Archaeopteryx had small teeth as well as a long bony tail. Its three fingers bore claws and moved independently, unlike the fused fingers of living birds. Also, skeletal structures related to flight seem to be incompletely developed, which suggests that Archaeopteryx may not have been able to sustain flight for great distances. These structures, therefore, cannot be said to have evolved for the purpose of flight, because they were already present in dinosaurs before either birds or flight evolved.

Why does the author mention small teeth as well as a long bony tail in the passage?

Ⓐ To explain why Archaeopteryx are intriguing to scientists

Ⓑ To give examples of features that are more like dinosaurs

Ⓒ To confirm the fact that Archaeopteryx was a bird

Ⓓ To show the way in which Archaeopteryx hunted its prey

03 Fuel in Europe

Britain faced serious energy shortage problems during the 18th century. Prior to that time, wood was the primary source of fuel and an essential building material. However, due to the population increase in large cities consumption of wood rose, resulting in rapid deforestation throughout the European continent as well as Britain. The supply was limited as the result of deforestation, while demand was continuously rising to the point where there was not enough lumber for essential housing and industries. Moreover, other alternative fuels, such as coal, were not available at the time due to certain limits in infrastructure and known methods of production. Therefore, Britain's iron industry, which called for lumber to burn to melt iron ore in blast furnaces to produce raw iron, languished due to the limited supply of wood in the 1790s. At that time, the vast forests of Austria made it possible for it to become the world's largest iron producer for a few decades until it too reached the same barrier Britain had already experienced.

The author mentions Austria in the passage in order to

(A) show how a pattern repeated itself in Europe

(B) show that wood is not the best material to be used for energy

(C) show how much more advanced Britain was at the time

(D) show why the iron industry was so vital in that time period

04 Fossils

Fossils are marks or remains left by a myriad of flora and fauna that inhabited the Earth thousands to millions of years ago. Some fossils are the hard parts of organisms such as seashells or bones that were preserved after a plant or animal died, while others are the tracks or trails of animals moving about. The majority of fossils are found in sedimentary rocks. Such fossils are formed from plant or animal remains that were quickly buried under mud or sand that collected on the bottoms of rivers, lakes, swamps, and oceans. After thousands of years, pressure turned the sediment into rock. At the same time, minerals seeped into the remains and replaced the organic material. This eventually created a stone replica of the organism. Other fossils are entire plants or animals that have been preserved in ice, tar, or solidified sap. For example, small bugs or invertebrates got trapped in tree sap, and as the sap turned into amber over time, they became fossilized. Places where there are few scavengers such as bacteria or fungi, which would decompose the organism, are ideal for fossilization.

In the passage, the author mention seashells or bones in order to

(A) emphasize the importance of the presence of decomposers

(B) contrast fossils of organisms' hard parts to those of tracks or trails

(C) illustrate which parts of organisms are likely to become fossils

(D) give an example of fossils which are found in solidified sap

Lesson
02 Inference

Lesson Outline

- 추론(Inference) 문제는 지문에서 명시되지는 않았지만 지문의 내용을 바탕으로 추론·유추할 수 있는 것을 찾는 문제다. 지문 내용에 관한 전문적인 지식을 요구하는 것이 아니므로, 지문 내용만 이해하면 수월하게 추론할 수 있다.
- 이 유형의 문제는 한 지문당 1~2개 정도 출제되지만, 아예 출제되지 않는 경우도 가끔 있다.

Typical Questions 

- In paragraph X, what does the author imply about ~?
  X단락에서 글쓴이가 ~에 대해 암시하는 것은 무엇인가?
- According to paragraph X, what can be inferred about ~?
  X단락에 따르면, ~에 대해 추론 가능한 것은 무엇인가?
- It can be inferred from paragraph X that X단락에서 추론할 수 있는 것은
- Which of the following can be inferred from paragraph X?
  다음 중 X단락에서 추론 가능한 것은 무엇인가?

참고 문제에 infer, imply라는 단어가 들어가면 Inference 유형이다.

Learning Strategies

Step 1 문제에서는 항상 특정 단어·절을 제시하며 그것에 관해 무엇을 추론할 수 있는지 묻는다. 따라서 그 단어·절이 지문의 어느 부분에 위치했는지 먼저 확인해야 한다.

→ 추론 문제이기 때문에 해당 문장뿐만 아니라 앞뒤의 문장도 파악해야 한다.

Step 2 이제 보기를 확인하며 지문에서 언급된 내용을 바탕으로 추론 가능한 것들인지 확인하자. 언제나 그렇듯 패러프레이징의 중요성을 잊지 말자. 지문에서 쓰인 단어가 그대로 들어갔다고 해서 항상 정답이 되지는 않는다. 어떤 Inference 문제는 해당 단어·절이 들어간 문장 전체의 패러프레이징이라고 해도 될 정도로 표현만 다르게 쓰인 비슷한 내용이 정답인 경우가 있다.

→ 보통 한두 문장을 연결해서 추론하는 문제가 많으며, 때로는 한 단락의 내용을 바탕으로 추론하는 문제가 출제되기도 한다.

Step 3 정답을 고른 뒤 다른 보기들의 오답 여부를 확인하고 넘어가자. 지문에서 아예 언급하지 않은 내용을 이야기하지는 않는지, 아니면 지문에 나온 내용을 어떤 식으로 틀리게 유추했는지 살펴본다.

Example

Q. Which of the following can be inferred about 19th century Europe from paragraph 4?

1 문제에서 제시된 단어나 절이 지문의 어디에 위치했는지 파악하자. 4단락에서 19th century Europe을 찾는다.

During the following Age of Enlightenment, many rulers undertook ambitious plans to redesign their capitals as symbols of their regime's status and wealth. One city that typifies this process is Paris, France. **By the 19th century**, Paris was massively overcrowded, and poverty, pollution, and disease wracked much of the city. When Emperor Napoleon III came to power in 1852, he commissioned Georges-Eugene Haussmann to oversee a comprehensive public works project, which he did from 1853 until his dismissal in 1870. As Napoleon III had been inspired by Hyde Park in London, Haussmann built new large parks and replanted some of the older existing ones in the city to provide the citizens with more green space.

2 이제 보기를 확인하며 지문의 내용에서 추론 가능한 내용인지 확인하자.

Ⓐ London went through a wide-scale renovation similar to that of Paris.

→ 런던이 지문에서 언급되기는 했지만, 런던의 대규모 개선 작업에 관한 내용은 유추할 수 없다.

Ⓑ There was much social turbulence in 19th century Paris.

→ 역시 지문에서 언급되지 않았으므로 유추할 수 없다.

Ⓒ Haussmann was one of the most influential architects of the day.

→ 오스만이 지문에서 언급된 것은 사실이지만, 이 사람이 당시 가장 영향력 있는 건축가 중 한 사람이었다는 내용 역시 지문에서 유추하기 어렵다.

Ⓓ Napoleon III was not the only ruler who sought to renovate his capital.

→ '나폴레옹 3세가 수도를 개선하려고 한 유일한 통치자가 아니었다'고 한다. 단락 맨 앞에 '많은 통치자들이 수도를 다시 설계하려고 했다'는 내용이 있으므로 19세기 유럽에서 수도를 개선하려고 한 통치자는 나폴레옹 3세 한 사람만이 아니었다는 것을 유추할 수 있다.

위와 같은 이유로 정답은 Ⓓ가 된다.

Practice

01

Women in the Olympics

According to Greek mythology, the Olympic Games always included a women's festival called the Heraia. It took place every four years just before the men's and may well have been open to girls from all the Greek states. There were three footraces, one for each of the three age divisions. These divisions are not cited exactly in the ancient sources, but scholars guess that they ranged from ages six to eighteen. The winners of the Heraia, just like the victors in the men's games, received an olive wreath crown and a share of the single ox slaughtered for the patron deity on behalf of all the game's participants. The Heraia victors attached painted portraits of themselves to Hera's temple in the Olympic sanctuary. Though the paintings are long gone, the niches on the temple columns into which they were set are still evident.

Which of the following can be inferred from the passage about the winners of the Heraia?

Ⓐ Some of them later married the winners of the Olympics.

Ⓑ Some of them later became members of religious orders.

Ⓒ They became mythical goddesses to future generations of girls.

Ⓓ They were held in high esteem for their accomplishments.

02

Gorillas

Primatologists continue to study the relationships between various gorilla populations in order to determine just how many species there are. Until recently, it was mostly agreed that there are three gorilla species: the Mountain Gorilla, the Western Lowland Gorilla, and the Eastern Lowland Gorilla. However, the present agreement is that there are only two species of gorilla, and that each of these has two subspecies. The first of these two species is the Western Gorilla, with its two subspecies, the Western Lowland Gorilla and the Cross River Gorilla. The second of these two species is the Eastern Gorilla, with its two subspecies, the Mountain Gorilla and the Eastern Lowland Gorilla. Another subspecies, sometimes called the Bwindi Gorilla, has been proposed as an additional third subspecies for the Eastern Gorilla, though this proposal has not been entirely accepted among primatologists.

According to the passage, which of the following can be inferred about animal species?

Ⓐ There are always two subspecies under one species.

Ⓑ The scientific classification of gorilla species has never changed.

Ⓒ The standards scientists use to classify animal species can change over time.

Ⓓ Primatologists have recently finalized the classification of gorilla species.

03

The First Civilization

No one has been able to accurately determine when or where small groups of nomadic hunter-gatherers first embarked on creating civilization. Despite the absence of solid evidence, there is a general belief that civilization began approximately 10,000 years ago, when people may have inadvertently planted seeds in the ground as a way of preserving them. It would have surprised the initial farmers to see a sapling break through the surface of the soil where they had previously buried seeds. This was the initial momentum for the development of farming methods, and it eventually made it possible to produce enough food to support a large scale population in a small area. This fact can easily be seen in historical records, which clearly show that farming and the first large scale civilizations developed more or less contemporaneously.

What can be inferred about the first farmers according to the passage?

Ⓐ They had knowledge about the way to choose proper soil for planting seeds.

Ⓑ They were able to preserve all of their seeds in the ground.

Ⓒ It is most likely that the first people discovered farming practices by chance.

Ⓓ It is definitively known when the first farmers started to preserve seeds.

04

Moths

Moths vary greatly in size, ranging in wingspan from about 4 millimeters to nearly 300 millimeters. Highly diversified, they live in all but polar habitats. They are insects closely related to butterflies. Like butterflies, the wings, bodies, and legs of moths are covered with dust-like scales that come off if the insect is handled. There are, however, several differences between butterflies and moths. Although some moth species are active during the day, moths generally tend to be nocturnal. Compared to butterflies, they have stouter bodies and proportionately smaller wings. Whereas butterflies are known for their bright-colored wings, moths are usually dull colors like black, gray, brown and white with zigzag patterns that help them stay hidden. Another difference is their antennae. Unlike butterflies which have thin antennae in the shape of a golf club, moths have distinctive feathery antennae. Additionally, when at rest, they fold their wings, wrap them around their body, or hold them extended at their sides.

It can be inferred from the passage that moths

Ⓐ usually have an extraordinarily huge wingspan

Ⓑ have more delicate bodies than other insects

Ⓒ can exist in a wide array of habitats

Ⓓ are usually diurnal like butterflies

III. Recognizing Organization

Lesson

01 Insertion

Lesson Outline

◎ 문장 삽입(Insertion) 문제는 삽입이라는 단어가 의미하는 것처럼 문제에서 제시하는 하나의 문장을 지문에 표시된 네 개의 [■] 중 어느 위치에 넣을지 찾는 문제다. 해당 문장을 어디에 넣었을 때 앞뒤 문장의 의미가 가장 자연스럽게 연결되는지 알아보는 게 중요하다.

◎ 이 유형의 문제는 한 지문당 1개가 출제되며, 보통 9번 문제로 나온다.

Typical Questions 

- Look at the four squares [■] that indicate where the following sentence could be added to the passage.
  지문에 다음 문장이 들어갈 수 있는 위치를 나타내는 네 개의 사각형[■]을 확인하시오.

  〈삽입 문장〉

  Where would the sentence best fit? 이 문장이 들어가기에 가장 적합한 곳은?

Learning Strategies

Step 1 문제에서 제시되는 문장을 읽어보고 의미를 이해한다.

⋯› 제시된 삽입 문장은 두 문장을 이어주는 역할을 하기 때문에 어떤 뜻인지 정확히 파악하고 있어야 한다.

Step 2 이제 네 개의 사각형[■]이 어디에 위치했는지 확인해 본다. 보통 해당 단락에서 한 문장씩 건너 표시되어 있다. [■] 앞뒤의 문장을 읽어보며 삽입 문장이 어떤 문장들과 가장 잘 어울리고, 가장 잘 연결되는지 찾아본다.

⋯› 해당 단락 전체를 읽어보고 의미를 파악하면 내용 흐름이 더 명확히 눈에 들어오기 때문에 답 찾기가 더 수월해진다.

Example

Q. Look at the four squares [■] that indicate where the following sentence could be added to the passage.

Roman construction methods developed from the Greek model.

Where would the sentence best fit?

1. 지문에서 제시하는 문장을 읽어보고 의미를 이해한다.

= 로마의 건축 방식은 그리스 모델에서 발달했다.

2. 이제 네 개의 사각형[■]이 어디에 위치했는지 확인해 본다. 보통 해당 단락에서 한 문장씩 건너 표시되어 있다. [■] 앞뒤의 문장을 읽어보며 삽입 문장이 어떤 문장들과 가장 잘 어울리고, 가장 잘 연결되는지 찾아 본다.

One of the hallmarks of organized development throughout the history of Europe has been grid pattern streets that run in cardinal directions. [■A] [1] Many treatises cite the cities of the Greeks and Romans as the inspiration for European construction. [■B] [2] Towns in Ancient Greece were laid out on a grid system with a public square or marketplace in the center. [■C] [3] The Romans, in tandem with their far-reaching conquests, built hundreds of cities across their empire according to a plan that provided both security and easy movement. [■D]

[■A] 뒤에 오는 문장[1]은 '많은 논문이 그리스와 로마 도시들을 유럽 건축에 영감을 준 것으로 꼽는다'고 설명한다.
[■B] 뒤에 오는 문장[2]은 '고대 그리스의 마을들은 중앙에 광장이나 시장을 둔 격자형 체계로 설계됐다'고 설명한다.
[■C] 뒤에 오는 문장[3]은 '로마인들은 그들의 광범위한 정복과 동시에 안보와 쉬운 이동을 제공하려는 계획에 따라 제국 각지에 수백 개의 도시를 지었다'고 설명한다.
[■D] 뒤에는 아무 내용이 없으므로 제시된 문장이 맨 뒤에 들어가는 것이 가장 적합한지 본다.

'로마의 건축 방식은 그리스 모델에서 발달했다'는 내용을 생각했을 때, 문장 2에서 고대 그리스의 건축 시스템이 나온 뒤 문장 3에서 로마인들의 건축 계획이 언급되었으므로 제시된 문장이 이 두 문장 사이에 들어갈 때 연결이 가장 매끄럽다. 따라서 [■C]가 정답이다.

Practice

01

Steam Engines

Floods in the coal mines were the most devastating hazard confronted by English miners in the 18th century. It was James Watt's steam engine that eventually addressed this predicament. Watt's early steam engines allowed water to be effectively pumped out of deep mines. [■A] His first steam engine was installed in 1776, and it caused a paradigm shift in the production lines of factories worldwide. [■B] First of all, the advent of factory steam engines facilitated better outcome and shorter time for production. [■C] Moreover, there was no longer a need for water power as a factory power source, so places for factory construction became less restricted, allowing them to be built anywhere. [■D] Finally, because factories with steam engine power called for manual laborers in large numbers, there was mass population movement from the countryside to the ever-expanding urban centers. The influence of mass movement transformed England from a cottage industry and agrarian society into a factory-based, urban-dwelling industrial powerhouse within fifty years.

Look at the four squares [■] that indicate where the following sentence could be added to the passage.

Watt, however, was interested in developing steam engines for use in factories.

Where would the sentence best fit?

02

The Orion Nebula

When we look at the Orion Nebula with all of its young stars and collection of dust and gases, what we are seeing amidst the chaos is a star factory and what our own solar system may have looked like in its infancy. [■A] The ages of the stars that make up the nebula are between roughly 300,000 and 2 million years old, which is very young for stars. In comparison, our own Sun is 4.5 billion years old. [■B] The smallest of these young stars are usually reddish in color and low in mass. In addition to these smaller stars, there are four gigantic hot stars that form the Trapezium. The Trapezium can be considered the heart of the nebular star factory. The largest of these four stars, Theta 1 Orionis C, is around 20 times as large as our Sun and about 100,000 times as bright. In fact, it is so bright that it can light up the entire nebula on its own. [■C] The immediate area around the Trapezium is crowded with hundreds of lesser stars because of the abundance of basic nebular materials. [■D] All of this raw material for forming stars makes this area one of the most densely congested clusters of stars anywhere in the known regions of our galaxy.

Look at the four squares [■] that indicate where the following sentence could be added to the passage.

The stars of the Trapezium emit ultraviolet radiation that causes the dust and gases of the nebula near them to shine brightly.

Where would the sentence best fit?

03

The Purpose and Study of Chemistry

1 ➡ Life has changed more in the past two centuries than in all of the previously recorded history of mankind. The population of the earth has increased greater than fivefold since 1800, and human life expectancy has nearly doubled due to our ability to control the spread of diseases, synthesize medicines, and increase the yields of food crops. Our modes of transportation have changed from horseback to automobiles and airplanes because of our ability to harness the energy available in petroleum. Many goods that we now manufacture are made of ceramics and polymers, rather than wood and metal, because of our ability to create materials with properties unlike any found in the natural world.

2 ➡ In one way or another, directly or indirectly, each of these life-changing developments involves chemistry, or the study of the composition, properties, and transformations of matter. [■A] Likewise, chemistry is in a great many ways responsible for the profound social changes that have taken place over the past two hundred years. [■B] Furthermore, chemistry is at the core of the current revolution in molecular biology that is exploring the ins and outs of how life is genetically controlled. [■C] In fact, no educated person today can truly understand the world around us without at least a basic knowledge of chemistry. [■D]

Look at the four squares [■] that indicate where the following sentence could be added to the passage.

Chemistry is responsible for the changes that take place in the natural world.

Where would the sentence best fit?

04

American Revolutionists and Their System of Government

1 ➡ As with any influential document, the underlying purposes of the Constitution of the United States can only be revealed through the study of the conditions and events which led to its composition and subsequent adoption by the people. Firstly, it must be remembered that there were two great factions at the time of the adoption of the U.S. Constitution. One party emphasized strength and efficiency in government and the other its popular aspects.

2 ➡ Naturally, the men who led in stirring up the revolt against the dominating presence of Great Britain and in keeping the fighting temper of the Revolutionists at a high level were the boldest and most radical of thinkers—men like Thomas Jefferson, Samuel Adams, Thomas Paine, and Patrick Henry. [■A] Generally, these men neither held large property nor possessed much practical business experience. But, in an era of disorder, they consistently put more stress upon personal liberty than on social control. [■B] These men pushed to the extreme the doctrine of human rights which had evolved in England during the trials and tribulations of the small land holders and commercial classes against the power of the aristocracy. [■C] These conditions corresponded to the prevailing economic conditions in America at the close of the 18th century. [■D] A number of these radicals viewed all government, especially of a highly centralized nature, as a spawn of evil. Government was tolerated only because it is necessary to maintain some kind of order, but at the same time, it must be kept to a minimum through constant vigilance.

Look at the four squares [■] that indicate where the following sentence could be added to the passage.

As they associated strong government with monarchy, they came to believe that the best government was one which governed least.

Where would the sentence best fit?

Lesson

02 Summary

Lesson Outline

- 요약(Summary) 문제는 말 그대로 지문을 네 문장으로 요약하는 문제다. 다만 맨 처음에 올 문장, 즉 '도입 문장(Introductory Sentence)'은 문제에서 제시되며 수험자는 뒤에 올 3개 문장을 보기에서 골라야 한다.
- 이 유형의 문제는 한 지문당 1개가 출제되며, 아예 출제되지 않을 때도 있다. 다만 출제되지 않을 경우 Category Chart 유형의 문제가 대신 나온다. 지문을 '요약하는' 문제이므로 맨 마지막 문제로 출제된다.

Typical Questions 

Directions: An introductory sentence for a brief summary of the passage is provided below. Complete the summary by selecting the THREE answer choices that express the most important ideas in the passage. Some sentences do not belong in the summary because they express ideas that are not presented in the passage or are minor ideas in the passage. ***This question is worth 2 points.***

지시문: 지문을 간략하게 요약한 글의 첫 문장이 아래 제시되어 있다. 지문의 가장 중요한 내용을 표현하는 세 개의 선택지를 골라 요약문을 완성하시오. 일부 문장들은 지문에 제시되지 않았거나 지문의 지엽적인 내용을 나타내기 때문에 요약문에 포함되지 않는다. *이 문제의 배점은 2점이다.*

〈도입 문장〉

-
-
-

Answer Choices

참고 보기는 보통 6개가 주어진다.

Ⓐ --------------------- Ⓓ ---------------------

Ⓑ --------------------- Ⓔ ---------------------

Ⓒ --------------------- Ⓕ ---------------------

Drag your answer choices to the spaces where they belong.
To remove an answer choice, click on it. To review the passage, click on **View Text**.
선택한 답안을 맞는 곳에 끌어다 넣으시오.
선택한 답안을 삭제하려면, 답안에 대고 클릭하시오. 지문을 다시 보려면 지문 보기를 클릭하시오.

Learning Strategies

Step 1 도입 문장(Introductory Sentence)은 해당 지문을 관통하는 중심 문장이다. 이 문장을 중심으로 뒤에 오게 될 나머지 세 문장이 결정되므로 잘 읽어보자.

⋯› 문제에서 말하듯 '가장 중요한' 개념을 찾아야 한다. 문제에서는 '어떤 문장은 지문에 나오지 않았거나 중요한 내용이 아니기 때문에 답이 될 수 없다'고 명확히 밝히고 있다.

Step 2 각 단락을 한 문장으로 요약한다면 어떻게 요약할지 생각해 보자. 보통 각 단락을 요약한 문장이나 그 단락에서 가장 중요한 내용을 담은 문장이 답이다. 다시 한 번 기억해야 할 점은 지나치게 세부적인 내용은 답이 될 수 없다는 것이다.

Step 3 정답을 고른 뒤 오답 보기를 확인해 보자. 사소한 점을 언급했는지, 지문에 나오지 않은 내용이나 틀린 내용을 제시하고 있는지 짚고 넘어간다.

Example

1 ➡ The cities of Europe are known for their unique blend of classical and modern architecture, which reflects a long and complex history involving a series of transformations. One of the hallmarks of organized development throughout the history of Europe has been grid pattern streets that run in cardinal directions.

2 ➡ Many treatises cite the cities of the Greeks and Romans as the inspiration for European construction. Towns in Ancient Greece were laid out on a grid system with a public square or marketplace in the center. Roman construction methods developed from the Greek model. The Romans, in tandem with their far-reaching conquests, built hundreds of cities across their empire according to a plan that provided both security and easy movement. Strict geometrical order was imposed, with the city center holding a square for conducting business and city services surrounded by a compact grid of wide, linear roads inside a rectangular defensive wall.

3 ➡ Even though different architectural styles came into vogue, it did not create discord in the cityscape because these styles synthesized with features from previous ones. Therefore, even though parts of the cities were rebuilt throughout different eras, they blended in harmoniously.

4 ➡ Nonetheless, this idea, which came to be known as International Style, served as a prototype for all modern cities which deal with the problem of accommodating high-density urban populations. Modern design leaned towards ridding buildings of decorative elements and placing priority on function over form.

Directions: An introductory sentence for a brief summary of the passage is provided below. Complete the summary by selecting the THREE answer choices that express the most important ideas in the passage. Some sentences do not belong in the summary because they express ideas that are not presented in the passage or are minor ideas in the passage. ***This question is worth 2 points.***

The cities of Europe underwent centuries of change in architectural style to reach their current appearance.

-
-
-

Answer Choices

(A) With the advent of modernism, urban design concepts steered away from ornate elements and stayed true to functional aesthetics.

(B) The emphasis on a grid system to provide efficient transportation and security began with the Ancient Greeks and Romans and persisted in European cities.

(C) Many European leaders wanted to display the majesty of their nations by reintroducing Greek and Roman architectural styles.

(D) The decorative elements in modern buildings were round and symmetrical while those from classical buildings were pointed.

(E) The renovation of cities cleared up overcrowding and laid down the foundations for public health facilities.

(F) While many styles influenced European cities over the centuries, they were essentially based on previous styles that blended to create the current cityscape.

Drag your answer choices to the spaces where they belong.

To remove an answer choice, click on it. To review the passage, click on **View Text**.

1 도입 문장을 중심으로 뒤에 오게 될 나머지 세 문장이 결정되므로 잘 읽어보자.

→ '유럽의 도시들은 현재의 모습에 이르기까지 건축 양식에 있어 수백 년간의 변화를 거쳤다'가 중심 내용이라는 점을 기억한다.

2 각 단락을 한 문장으로 요약한다면 어떻게 요약할지 생각해 보자.

단락 1: 제시된 도입부 문장으로 요약 가능하다.
단락 2: 격자형 체계를 강조하며 고대 그리스 및 로마인들의 영향을 받았다고 한다. → Ⓑ
단락 3: 다양한 건축 양식이 유행했지만 과거 양식들의 특징과 합쳐졌다고 한다. → Ⓕ
단락 4: 오늘날의 디자인은 장식적인 요소보다 기능에 더 우선 순위를 둔다고 한다. → Ⓐ

3 정답을 고른 뒤 오답 보기를 확인해 보자. 오답은 지문에 나온 내용이 아니거나, 지문에 나왔지만 지나치게 세부적이라 중요 핵심 문장이라고 하기 어려운 것들이다.

Lesson 02 Recognizing Organization

Practice

01

Animal Communication

1 ➡ Due to the fact that animals either possess only basic auditory communication skills or lack them altogether, many animals rely on visual communication methods. Insects and birds, especially, possess very sophisticated visual systems of communication. These visual systems primarily belong to two different categories—passive signals and active signals—and may be used separately or in a combination of the two.

2 ➡ Passive signals require no energy expenditure on the part of the animal. This is due to the fact that passive signals are part of their physical appearance. For instance, butterflies come in a variety of colors and in a multitude of designs. With brightly colored eyespots, stripes and solid colors, butterflies are able to communicate their gender, age and species. These passive signals also inform creatures of other species that they are inedible or poisonous. Likewise, many species of birds display different patterns of colors for much the same reason as butterflies, especially to differentiate gender and to initiate reproduction.

3 ➡ The use of active signals is much more physical and requires energy from the creatures using them. Courtship and mating rituals are one area in which active signals are displayed with vigor. Some insects will perform intricate airborne dances to attract mates. At night, fireflies produce certain flashes that communicate that they are ready to reproduce or that they have already done so. Certain bird species also perform mating dances. A male prairie chicken may spend hours strutting and hopping in circles around a female trying to convince her to mate with him. Birds also make use of active signals to warn their flock of danger such as the approach of a predator by beating their wings or rapidly taking flight. These visual warnings quickly spread throughout the flock and are copied in turn by other members.

Directions: An introductory sentence for a brief summary of the passage is provided below. Complete the summary by selecting the THREE answer choices that express the most important ideas in the passage. Some sentences do not belong in the summary because they express ideas that are not presented in the passage or are minor ideas in the passage. *This question is worth 2 points.*

Birds and insects have implemented visual measures to communicate.

-
-
-

Answer Choices

Ⓐ Visual forms of communication are extremely obvious.

Ⓑ Active signals can show willingness and ability to mate as well as warn others of danger.

Ⓒ Birds use elaborate decoration to send out passive signals about their species.

Ⓓ Fireflies use flashes of light in a sequence that represents language.

Ⓔ Passive signals are sent by the communicator's physical features.

Ⓕ There are two types of visual systems in animal communication.

02

Animal Cognition

1 ➡ In the first part of the 20th century, animal psychology was full of experiments that sought to uncover basic thought processes that could then be used to explain the advanced intellect of humans. Derived from the psychology movement known as behaviorism, these experiments were intended to classify specific behaviors through identifying a relationship between a stimulus and a response. The data from these experiments would then be used to explain the behavior scientifically, disregarding the influences of mental or emotional states, which, it was presupposed, animals didn't experience.

2 ➡ Then, in the late 1950s, developments in cognitive psychology made it the predominant form for explaining the behavior of both humans and animals. It addressed behavior from the opposite direction of behaviorism as it was concerned with internal states and their effects on outcomes rather than stimulus and response. In addition, animal behavior was analyzed by comparing it to what was known of human mental processes. Previously, the common animals used in behaviorist experiments were birds, dogs, and rats. However, cognitive psychologists chose to direct their research towards primates like monkeys and apes since they share a developed limbic system with and are genetically similar to humans. This shared neurological trait, which is involved in emotion, motivation, and the connection of emotions to memory, could hypothetically give researchers more reasonable grounds for applying their theories to human behavior.

3 ➡ Since cognitive psychology became the standard for analyzing animal cognition, it has found many parallels between human and animal behavior. Research on animal cognition has been centered in the areas of language, memory, and problem-solving. It has been found that monkeys possess a similar short-term memory phenomenon to humans, but the most progress has been made in researching spatial memory. Animals are particularly talented at remembering where objects are spatially. A prime example of this occurs in squirrels, which store their food supplies in hiding places covering broad areas. Despite radical changes in the environment, they can proficiently remember their storage locations by using spatial memory.

Directions: An introductory sentence for a brief summary of the passage is provided below. Complete the summary by selecting the THREE answer choices that express the most important ideas in the passage. Some sentences do not belong in the summary because they express ideas that are not presented in the passage or are minor ideas in the passage. *This question is worth 2 points.*

Discoveries in animals' thought processes have given scientific insight into human beings' cognitive operations.

-
-
-

Answer Choices

(A) Early attempts at understanding human thought processes were carried out by analyzing the way animals behave.

(B) With all of the advances in behavioral sciences and research techniques, it is still impossible to fully explain all behaviors.

(C) Cognitive psychology reversed the way psychologists observed and explained behavior, causing them to even change the animals used in experiments.

(D) Monkeys and apes share most of the same genetic material and behavioral patterns as human beings.

(E) Cognitive psychology is the preferred method for analyzing animals' behavior, with attention placed on memory, problem-solving, and language.

(F) Profound changes in a landscape might confuse and disorient animals that don't have a refined spatial memory.

03

The Columbian Exchange

1 ➡ Following the arrival of Christopher Columbus's expedition in the Caribbean, waves of conquerors and colonists came to the Americas. When these Europeans interacted with the Native Americans, they exchanged many things either intentionally or by chance. Much of this exchange took place in the form of actual trade. Whether positive or negative, these exchanges had dramatic effects on both the New World and the Old World.

2 ➡ Columbus brought back many souvenirs to his Spanish sponsors from the Caribbean. His original mission had been to open a new trade route to the spices and other riches of Asia. Having essentially failed that mission, the king and queen of Spain took interest in what he did find. These included new crops like maize, tomatoes, potatoes, pumpkins and chocolate, some of which later became staples in the European diet. What interested the Spanish the most about the Americas, though, was gold because of its monetary value and rarity. The Spanish conquerors sent small armies of soldiers to explore the land they had claimed and bring back all of the gold. On the other hand, the Europeans introduced many crops to the Americas as well, the most important being sugar cane and coffee. They also brought many animals including chickens, pigs and cows, but the animal that became the most important to the Native Americans was the horse.

3 ➡ However, this exchange also had its downside. The Europeans brought warfare and oppression, but unknown to them at the time, they also brought something far worse than swords and guns: new diseases. Europe had suffered for centuries through many plagues that sometimes destroyed whole villages. Over time, the survivors of these plagues built up immunities to the epidemics. Diseases like smallpox, influenza, cholera, typhus, and the Pest were still serious in Europe, but they spread to the new land, and devastated the Native Americans. It is impossible to accurately estimate the mortality rate, but it is estimated that within 130 years, foreign diseases had killed 80 to 90 percent of Native Americans from Canada to Argentina. These diseases were spread through conquest, colonization and even brief trade meetings. When the English came later to colonize North America, only a small fraction of the local inhabitants remained.

Directions: An introductory sentence for a brief summary of the passage is provided below. Complete the summary by selecting the THREE answer choices that express the most important ideas in the passage. Some sentences do not belong in the summary because they express ideas that are not presented in the passage or are minor ideas in the passage. *This question is worth 2 points.*

When Christopher Columbus discovered the New World, he opened the way for trade between Europe and the Americas.

-
-
-

Answer Choices

Ⓐ The main goal of the expedition was a military takeover of valuable trading ports in Asia, but they failed to reach that continent.

Ⓑ The most significant exchanges at the time involved gold from the Americas and livestock from Europe.

Ⓒ The Spanish sent armies throughout Central and South America to find gold and they conquered many tribes.

Ⓓ These exchanges had lasting effects for both continents in both positive and negative ways.

Ⓔ Despite their intent, the Europeans brought diseases that nearly wiped out most of the native population.

Ⓕ Foreign crops, livestock, technology and riches all changed hands with the Native Americans.

04

Inca Roads

1 ➡ The Inca people first established their civilization in the highlands of Peru in the 13th century. The Inca Empire was the largest empire in South America before the Spanish conquered the region. In order to connect and more easily rule this vast empire, the Inca created a network of roads which made up the most extensive transportation system in the Americas at the time. From their capital in Cusco, the Inca incorporated many neighboring cultures; some joined peacefully, while others were convinced by military force. The Inca imposed their own culture throughout their empire much like Alexander the Great did in his own. They required the people to speak their language, Quechan, and they had to worship the Incan sun god, Inti, above all others. Likewise, they believed the systematic network of roads helped to maintain and spread their unique culture.

2 ➡ The Inca road system consisted of two main north-south running roads that were linked to each other and outlying areas by many smaller connecting roads. The western road ran mostly along the coastal plain, but it curved in closer to the foothills of the Andes near desert areas. The eastern one, which was paved with stone usually one to three meters wide, ran through the high mountain valleys and grasslands of the Andes Mountains. Along the roads there were rest stops called tambos which were spaced about one day's walk apart, with larger ones every five to six days apart. Travelers could rest in the stone buildings and replenish their supplies from food stocked up there.

3 ➡ The Incas never developed wheels, and horses were introduced later by the Spanish, so the traffic on these roads consisted of people and llamas. As a result, when the roads crossed steep slopes, they would often have long flights of stairs to make walking easier. In sandy areas they built low walls to keep the sand from blowing onto the road. Furthermore, where the roads went through steep areas, they would build taller walls to keep people from falling. At their height, the roads stretched for a total of 40,000 kilometers. However, after the Spanish invaded in 1533, the roads were no longer maintained. The Spanish tore up some sections, and others deteriorated under the metal shoes of their horses. Most of the system was eventually reclaimed by nature, but there are efforts today to restore as much of it as possible.

Directions: An introductory sentence for a brief summary of the passage is provided below. Complete the summary by selecting the THREE answer choices that express the most important ideas in the passage. Some sentences do not belong in the summary because they express ideas that are not presented in the passage or are minor ideas in the passage. *This question is worth 2 points.*

The Incas built an extensive network of roads to connect the largest empire in the Americas.

-
-
-

Answer Choices

(A) The road system included two main roads that stretched across the empire from north to south.

(B) The Inca modeled their conquest of neighboring tribes on Alexander the Great's campaign.

(C) With the extensive road system, the Inca wanted to integrate the empire by spreading their language and religion.

(D) The roads had special rest stops where travelers could restock their foodstuffs and sleep at night.

(E) Although the Inca took the great care in making their roads, they were not maintained later.

(F) There continues to be conservation efforts underway today to restore the roads to their former state.

Lesson

03 Category Chart

Lesson Outline

- 분류(Category Chart) 문제는 지문에서 제시된 정보를 각각 알맞은 범주(category)에 분류해서 넣는 문제다. 문제에서 제시된 5~7개의 보기 중 주어진 범주에 맞는 보기를 클릭해서 순서에 상관 없이 표의 [•] 옆에 끌어다 놓으면 된다.

- 이 유형의 문제는 한 지문당 1개가 출제되거나, 아예 출제되지 않을 때도 있다. 요약(Summary) 문제와 함께 출제되는 경우는 거의 없다.

Typical Questions 

Directions: Complete the table by matching the sentences below. Select the appropriate sentences from the answer choices and match them to the category to which they relate. TWO of the answer choices will NOT be used. ***This question is worth 3 points.***

지시문: 아래 문장들을 알맞게 넣어 다음 표를 완성하시오. 선택지 중 적절한 문장들을 골라 관계된 개념과 연결하시오. 선택지 두 개는 정답이 될 수 없다. ***이 문제의 배점은 3점이다.***

Answer Choices	Category A
Ⓐ ---------------------	•
Ⓑ ---------------------	•
Ⓒ ---------------------	•
Ⓓ ---------------------	**Category B**
Ⓔ ---------------------	
Ⓕ ---------------------	•
Ⓖ ---------------------	•

참고 질문 내용은 지문에 따라 조금씩 다르지만, 거의 항상 'Select the appropriate choices/sentences ~ (적절한 보기/문장들을 선택하시오)'와 같이 제시된다.

각 범주에 표시된 [•]를 통해 해당 범주에 몇 개의 정답이 들어갈지 알 수 있다. 선택지는 보통 5~7개가 주어지며 이 중에서 2~3개 선택지는 정답이 될 수 없다는 점에 주의하자.

Learning Strategies

Step 1 먼저 문제에서 어떤 범주에 대해 묻는지 본다. 비교·대조 문제가 가장 일반적이고 자주 등장한다.

···› 보통 두 가지 범주에 대해 물으므로 각 범주가 지문의 어디에서 언급되었는지 찾아본다.

···› 범주가 언급된 부분을 찾으면, 그 부분을 자세히 읽어보며 비교·대조되는 부분을 찾는다.

Step 2 주어진 선택지는 많지만 이중에서 몇 개는 정답이 될 수 없다는 점에 유의하면서, 이제 각 선택지를 하나씩 읽어보고 어떤 선택지가 지문에서 언급되었는지 파악한다. 그리고 이 선택지가 들어갈 범주를 다시 확인한다.

Step 3 오답 확인의 중요성은 아무리 강조해도 지나치지 않다. 걸러낸 오답을 보며 이 오답이 지문에서 언급되지 않은 내용인지, 아니면 지문과 아예 다른 내용인지 확인해 보도록 한다.

Example

Nocturnal vs. Diurnal

1 ➡ There are two basic sleep cycles in the animal kingdom—diurnal and nocturnal. Animals that are active during the day and sleep at night are diurnal. Those who are active at night and sleep during the day are nocturnal.

2 ➡ Nocturnal animals usually have highly developed senses of hearing and smell to compensate for the absence of light. Some have specially adapted eyesight. This usually involves the animals having enlarged pupils, the black part of the eye, or sometimes even larger-than-usual eyes. It is the pupils that allow light to enter the eyes, so by having larger pupils, nocturnal animals' eyes allow more light to enter the eye, enabling the animals to see more clearly at night. Some other nocturnal animals have special adaptations to help them find their way around in the dark. Many bats use a type of natural sonar. They emit a high-pitched sound and listen to the echoes of that sound to find nearby objects or prey.

3 ➡ Diurnal animals, on the other hand, are active during the daylight hours. Their senses are equally balanced. Their eyes generally have small pupils to prevent too much light from entering the eye. On the other hand, many have a large number of cone cells, allowing them to see in color. Once the sun sets, diurnal animals have difficulty moving around as they cannot see well in low light. Animals are not the only diurnal organisms; some flowering plants, like Namaqualand daisies, only open their flowers in daylight, closing them again when it is cloudy or dark. However, with the advent of electric lighting, many diurnal animals, including pets and city-dwelling birds, are remaining active long into the night.

Directions: Complete the table by matching the sentences below. Select the appropriate sentences from the answer choices and match them to the category to which they relate. TWO of the answer choices will NOT be used. ***This question is worth 3 points.***

Answer Choices	Nocturnal	Diurnal
Ⓐ These animals are often blind. Ⓑ These flowering plants only open their flowers in daylight. Ⓒ These animals have stronger senses of smell and hearing. Ⓓ These animals have small pupils to allow as much light as possible to enter their eyes. Ⓔ Some of these animals have large eyes to facilitate better sight. Ⓕ Electric light has lengthened the active period of these animals. Ⓖ These animals sleep during the day.	• • •	• •

❶ 먼저 문제에서 어떤 범주에 대해 묻는지 본다. 문제를 보면 Nocturnal/Diurnal로 범주가 나뉘어져 있으므로 이 두 생물을 분류하는 특징에 관해 묻는다는 것을 알 수 있다. 이제 Nocturnal/Diurnal 동물들의 특징이 지문의 어디에서 언급되었는지 찾아본다. 해당 부분을 읽어보며 각 범주의 특징을 파악한다.

❷ 주어진 선택지는 많지만 이중에서 몇 개는 정답이 될 수 없다는 점에 유의하며 각 선택지를 하나씩 읽어본다.

Ⓐ These animals are often blind.

⋯› 지문에서 언급되지 않은 내용이다. 따라서 범주에 넣지 않는다.

Ⓑ These flowering plants only open their flowers in daylight.

⋯› 주행성(diurnal)이 동물뿐 아니라 식물에도 있다고 하며 예로 든 Namaqualand daisies의 특징이다. 따라서 Diurnal 범주에 들어간다.

Ⓒ These animals have stronger senses of smell and hearing.

⋯› 야행성(nocturnal) 동물의 특징 중 맨 첫 번째로 언급되는 내용이다. 따라서 Nocturnal 범주에 들어간다.

Ⓓ These animals have small pupils to allow as much light as possible to enter their eyes.

⋯› 작은 동공은 주행성 동물의 특징이며 이는 햇빛을 적게 받아들이기 위한 것이므로 틀린 설명이다. 따라서 범주에 넣지 않는다.

Ⓔ Some of these animals have large eyes to facilitate better sight.

⋯› 어둠 속에서 더 잘 보기 위해 더 큰 눈을 가지는 경우가 있다고 지문에서 언급되었다. 따라서 Nocturnal 범주에 들어간다.

Ⓕ Electric light has lengthened the active period of these animals.

⋯› 전기 불빛 때문에 이 동물들의 활동 시간이 길어졌다고 주행성 동물의 특징에 나와 있다. 따라서 Diurnal 범주에 들어간다.

Ⓖ These animals sleep during the day.

⋯› 낮 시간에 잠을 잔다는 내용이므로 Nocturnal 범주에 들어간다.

따라서 정답은 Nocturnal: Ⓒ, Ⓔ, Ⓖ / Diurnal: Ⓑ, Ⓕ가 된다.

3 오답 확인의 중요성은 아무리 강조해도 지나치지 않다. 범주에 넣지 않은 Ⓐ와 Ⓓ를 다시 읽어보고 확인한다.

Lesson 03 Recognizing Organization

Practice

01

Fungi vs. Plants

1 ➡ Living things are organized for study into large, basic groups called kingdoms. Fungi were listed in the Plant Kingdom for many years. Then scientists learned that fungi show a closer relation to animals, but are unique and separate life forms. Now, fungi are placed in their own kingdom. The principal reason for this is that none of them possess chlorophyll, so, unlike plants, they cannot synthesize their own carbohydrates. They obtain their supplies either from the breakdown of dead organic matter or from other living organisms.

2 ➡ Furthermore, the walls of fungal cells are not made of cellulose, as those of plants are, but of another complex sugar-like polymer called chitin, the material from which the hard outer skeletons of shrimps, spiders, and insects are made. The difference between the chemical composition of the cell walls of fungi and those of plants is of enormous importance because it enables the tips of the growing hyphae, the threadlike cells of the fungus, to secrete enzymes that break down the walls of plant cells without having any effect on those of the fungus itself.

Directions: Complete the table by matching the sentences below. Select the appropriate phrases from the answer choices and match them to the category to which they relate. TWO of the answer choices will NOT be used. *This question is worth 3 points.*

Answer Choices	Fungi	Plants
Ⓐ They have no chlorophyll.	• Ⓐ	• Ⓑ
Ⓑ They synthesize their own carbohydrates.	•	•
Ⓒ They acquire carbohydrates exclusively from dead organic matter.	•	
Ⓓ Their cell walls contain the same kind of material as shrimp and insect shells.		
Ⓔ They cannot synthesize carbohydrates.		
Ⓕ They use chlorophyll to produce their own food.		
Ⓖ They possess hyphae which secrete enzymes that have no effect on plant cells.		

02

Left and Right Brain Hemispheres

1 ➡ The human brain, while being one organ, is divided into two halves, or hemispheres. Each hemisphere has different functions and processes information in different ways. Depending on the task being performed, one hemisphere or the other is more dominant.

2 ➡ The left hemisphere focuses on details. It is better at logical and analytical thought. When performing structured tasks that involve following various steps or when concentration on a particular part of our environment is required, the left side of the brain is used. The left side of the brain, one specialty of which is symbolic thought, enables people to decode language to find the literal or superficial meaning. However, the detail-oriented left hemisphere is not good at spatial perception, that is, the ability to discern the relationship between objects in view. That requires less attention to detail.

3 ➡ In contrast, the right hemisphere processes information on a more general level. It is the part of the brain that provides an overall view of places, things, and situations. Since the right hemisphere is the center of human imagination, people rely on this hemisphere when performing open-ended tasks requiring a creative approach. When processing language, it is the right hemisphere that enables people to understand humor, emotion, and metaphors, thereby providing connotative or contextual meanings. Furthermore, the right hemisphere is the source of our spatial awareness, enabling us to analyze our environment three dimensionally and judge distances.

Directions: Complete the table by matching the phrases below. Select the appropriate phrases from the answer choices and match them to the category to which they relate. TWO of the answer choices will NOT be used. *This question is worth 3 points.*

Answer Choices	Left	Right
Ⓐ enables us to notice details in our environment	•	•
Ⓑ enables us to judge distances	• Ⓖ	•
Ⓒ enables us to dream		• Ⓔ
Ⓓ enables us to solve problems creatively		
Ⓔ enables us to put things in context		
Ⓕ enables us to structure problems that need to be solved		
Ⓖ enables us to understand language literally		

03

Education and Schooling

1 ➡ In the United States, the common belief is that schools are where people must go for an education. However, some people believe that going to school interrupts a child's education. The difference between schooling and education suggested by this statement is important.

2 ➡ Education is much more broad and all-inclusive than schooling. There are no limits in education. Education includes both formal schooling and a whole world of informal learning. The agents of education can be a respected grandparent, people debating on a radio talk show, another child, or a famous scholar. While schooling is predictable in some ways, education is often spontaneous. For instance, a casual conversation with a stranger may introduce a person to a new subject they previously knew little about. People begin their educations in infancy and never stop. It is a lifelong process that starts long before a person starts school, and should continue to be an integral part of a person's entire life.

3 ➡ Schooling, on the other hand, is a more formalized and specific process. The general pattern of schooling varies little from one setting to another. Children usually arrive at school at the same time, sit in assigned seats, are taught by adults, do homework, take exams, etc. The segments of reality that are being taught, whether they are the alphabet or simple calculating, usually have been limited by the boundaries of the subject being taught. For instance, high school students are aware that they are not likely to learn the truth concerning political problems in their communities or what new techniques filmmakers are exploring. Definite boundaries exist in the course of formalized schooling.

Directions: Complete the table by matching the sentences below. Select the appropriate sentences from the answer choices and match them to the category to which they relate. TWO of the answer choices will NOT be used. ***This question is worth 3 points.***

Answer Choices	Education	Schooling
Ⓐ People are involved in it from birth to death.	•	•
Ⓑ Its context is usually the same everywhere.	•	•
Ⓒ What it may produce is largely predictable.	•	
Ⓓ There are no limits to it.		
Ⓔ It interferes with the continuity of study.		
Ⓕ It is often unexpected and unplanned.		
Ⓖ It should be totally disregarded as being useful in human development.		

04

Hardwoods vs. Softwoods

1 ➡ In woodworking and construction, the types of wood that are used are usually divided into two groups: hardwood and softwood. The reasoning behind these groupings would seem to be fairly obvious. As a rule, hardwoods tend to be harder than softwoods. However, this is not always the case. Hardwoods are indeed denser than softwoods, but not all of them are harder. For example, balsa wood is one of the softest types of wood on the planet, but it is actually designated as a hardwood. Therefore, the genuine distinction between these two types of wood is more elaborate.

2 ➡ The true discrepancy between hardwoods and softwoods has to do with the type of tree that they come from. Hardwoods are deciduous trees, which are broad-leafed trees that lose their leaves every autumn and typically produce hard shelled seeds. These include trees like maple, oak, cherry, and mahogany. Softwoods are usually evergreens, which means that they do not drop their leaves seasonally, and their foliage is thin and needle-like. Their seeds are usually contained in a cone (which is why they are often called conifers) and they do not have a hard, protective shell. This group includes pine, fir, spruce, and cedar, among others.

3 ➡ These differences between the two groups are all observable from the outside, but the most important difference lies within. At a microscopic level, the structure of the trees is dissimilar. Softwoods have long, vertically growing cells that provide strength and carry water and nutrients up through the tree. They transfer materials through their cells' walls, which means that they can retain water within them. This is how they can stay green all year. Hardwoods have a system of vessels that transport those materials much like blood vessels in animals. The vessels look like pores in the wood, and their walls are made of strong cells called vessel elements. Their walls afford added strength to the tree, and the other cells that surround them are packed tightly together, making the wood denser. However, they do not function as well in the winter, which is why these trees lose their leaves every year.

Directions: Complete the table by matching the phrases below. Select the appropriate phrases from the answer choices and match them to the category to which they relate. TWO of the answer choices will NOT be used. ***This question is worth 3 points.***

Answer Choices	Hardwoods	Softwoods
(A) contain tube-like structures to carry water and nutrients	•	•
(B) usually grow at higher altitudes in dense forests	•	•
(C) are non-deciduous trees which have evergreen leaves	•	
(D) typically have harder cells of higher density		
(E) shed their foliage on an annual basis		
(F) produce seeds with hard shells contained in a cone		
(G) are able to store moisture in their cellular structure		

Actual Test 1

TOEFL Reading

Reading Section Directions

The Reading section measures your ability to understand academic passages in English. A clock at the top of the screen will show you how much time is remaining.

Most questions are worth 1 point, but the last question for each passage is worth more than 1 point. The directions for the last question indicate how many points you may receive.

Some passages include a word or phrase that is underlined in blue. To see a definition or an explanation, click on the word or phrase.

You may skip a question and return to it later, provided there is time remaining. To move on to the next question, click **NEXT**. To return to a question, click **BACK**.

Click **REVIEW** to access the review screen. The screen will show which questions have been answered and which have not been answered. You may go directly to any previous question from the review screen.

Click **CONTINUE** to proceed.

TOEFL Reading

Two Types of Planets

1 ➡ All of the planets in our solar system including the Earth are arranged on nearly the same flat plane with roughly oval orbits around the Sun. Considering that there are only eight planets in the solar system, it is striking how much diversity exists among them. Yet over the past two centuries as more and more has been discovered about our neighbors, it has gradually become clear that the planets can be grouped into two broad categories. The terrestrial planets are small worlds that contain high-density, rocky material, and the Jovian planets are low-density giants composed mostly of gases like hydrogen and helium. Beyond being a convenient classification of the planets, these categories have proven very revealing in helping us understand how our solar system came to be.

2 ➡ Mercury, Venus, Earth, and Mars are terrestrial planets. The term terrestrial comes from the Latin word *terra* which means earth. Thus, the term is meant to indicate that all of these planets are similar to Earth in important ways, and indeed they do have several features in common. First of all, they are all similar in size and, more importantly, are significantly smaller than the Jovian planets. The smallest of the Jovian planets, Neptune, is over fifty times larger than the largest of the terrestrial planets, Earth. Also, the terrestrial planets all orbit close to the Sun relative to the other planets. The distances between the orbits of the planets increase the further out from the Sun they are. Consequently, the orbits of the four terrestrial planets are grouped close to the Sun, while the outer four planets have immense distances between their orbits. Being closer to the Sun, the terrestrial planets are warmed by its heat energy. In addition, the terrestrial planets all have an atmosphere, which helps to retain the

1. Based on the information in paragraph 1, what can be inferred about planet classification?

Ⓐ No more research needs to be done to further categorize the planets in our solar system.

Ⓑ The density and matter of a planet plays an important role in its classification.

Ⓒ Our solar system can be split into more than 8 groups.

Ⓓ Planet classification enabled us to explain how other celestial objects began.

2. The word "retain" in paragraph 2 is closest in meaning to

Ⓐ produce

Ⓑ reflect

Ⓒ keep

Ⓓ increase

3. Why does the author mention Neptune in paragraph 2?

Ⓐ To demonstrate a difference in composition between terrestrial and Jovian planets

Ⓑ To provide evidence that Jovian planets are better located than terrestrial planets

Ⓒ To illustrate how small terrestrial planets are compared to Jovian planets

Ⓓ To explain why terrestrial planets are closer to the Sun than Jovian planets

TOEFL Reading

Sun's heat and accounts for the much higher average temperatures of the terrestrial planets as compared to their more distant cousins. However, the most significant distinguishing feature of the terrestrial planets is their dense composition. Their surfaces are composed primarily of silicate rocks and they have recorded their violent histories, accounting for the dramatic landscapes of these planets, which are marked by comet impact craters, canyons, mountains, and volcanoes.

3 ➡ Jupiter, Saturn, Uranus, and Neptune are called Jovian planets. The term is derived from the name of the Roman god Jove, also called Jupiter, and hence designates their similarity to the planet Jupiter. The four Jovian planets are the true giants in our solar system, dwarfing the terrestrial planets. Also, with orbits that take them so far away from the Sun's warmth, they are the most frigid of all the planets, with the outermost planets reaching below -200 degrees Celsius. Another conspicuous feature of the Jovian planets is their surfaces. Despite their seemingly solid appearance, these planets are composed primarily of gases; therefore, unlike the rocky terrestrial planets, they do not have a well-defined surface. [■A] Instead, their atmospheres, which are mostly hydrogen and helium, become more and more dense closer to the core, blending into a liquid interior under very intense pressures. [■B] Also prominent are the spectacular systems of rings and moons that encircle all four of these gaseous giants. [■C] In marked contrast to the terrestrial planets, which have at most two moons, Jupiter has 63 moons. [■D] When one considers the dramatic differences between them, it is clear that terrestrial planets have radically different characteristics from Jovian planets.

4 ➡ The phenomenal differences between the Jovian and terrestrial planets are explained by the different ways they formed at the birth of our solar system. The current theory holds that the solar system was originally a huge rotating

4. Which of the sentences below best expresses the essential information in the highlighted sentence in the passage? Incorrect answer choices change the meaning or leave out essential information.

Ⓐ Craters, canyons, mountains and volcanoes account for the dramatic landscape of the terrestrial planets with rocky surfaces.

Ⓑ Because they have had violent histories, these planets have craters.

Ⓒ Therefore, their surfaces, covered with craters, canyons, mountains and volcanoes are mostly silicate rock.

Ⓓ Terrestrial planets, due to their rocky, silicate surfaces, show signs of historic trauma evidenced by various geographical features.

5. The word they in paragraph 3 refers to

Ⓐ Jovian planets

Ⓑ terrestrial planets

Ⓒ orbits

Ⓓ surfaces

6. According to paragraph 3, what is distinctive about Jovian planets in comparison to terrestrial planets?

Ⓐ They were formed before the development of terrestrial planets.

Ⓑ They consist primarily of gases.

Ⓒ Their atmospheres are made primarily of hydrogen.

Ⓓ Their cores are relatively solid.

cloud known as a solar nebula. This cloud was made up primarily of gases like helium and hydrogen, along with much smaller amounts of denser material. As this cloud spun, it gradually flattened to become a disk with a denser area at the center. Our solar system was formed out of this cloud as the gases condensed and coalesced. Gases condense in conditions of low temperature and high pressure. However, the conditions near the center of the nebula were too intense for this to happen. So the planets that formed there were composed mostly of compounds with high melting points such as silicates and metals, and thus were smaller since these compounds were less plentiful. These became the terrestrial planets. Farther out in the nebula, where conditions were more favorable, the gases could condense and be drawn together by gravity to form the Jovian planets. This explains the differences in composition, size, and density between the two kinds of planets in our solar system.

7. According to paragraph 4, which of the following is true about our solar system?

Ⓐ It was created by compacting gases.
Ⓑ Gases compact then condense before they coalesce.
Ⓒ Gases contract when temperatures fall and pressure increases.
Ⓓ Gravity played a role only in the formation of the Jovian planets.

8. The word "coalesced" in paragraph 4 is closest in meaning to

Ⓐ combined
Ⓑ arranged
Ⓒ disseminated
Ⓓ expanded

TOEFL Reading

9. Look at the four squares [■] that indicate where the following sentence could be added to the passage.

Thus, there is no precise distinction between the exterior atmosphere and the interior surface.

Where would the sentence best fit?

Click on a square [■] to add the sentence to the passage.

10. **Directions:** Complete the table by matching the sentences below. Select the appropriate sentences from the answer choices and match them to the category to which they relate. TWO of the answer choices will NOT be used. ***This question is worth 3 points.***

Answer Choices	Terrestrial Planets	Jovian Planets
Ⓐ In terms of size, they dwarf the other category of planets. Ⓑ They are compact compared to the other category of planets. Ⓒ They warm up by shuffling closer to the Sun's heat energy. Ⓓ Planets in this group are comparable in size to one another. Ⓔ They have a rocky exterior. Ⓕ They are characterized as having many moons. Ⓖ There is an inadequate supply of gas on these planets.	• • •	• •

Drag your answer choices to the spaces where they belong.
To remove an answer choice, click on it. To review the passage, click on **View Text**.

TOEFL Reading

Gutenberg and Metal Type Printing

1 ➡ [■A] Movable type is a system of printing and typography that uses movable cast-metal pieces to represent individual symbols and characters. [■B] The development of movable type began with woodblock printing in ancient Egypt. [■C] Later building on these developments, 15th century German printer and goldsmith, Johannes Gutenberg, gained fame by implementing a novel printing system using movable metal type as one of its components. [■D] Before printing technology arrived in Europe, books had to be meticulously copied by hand by monks. Woodblock printing was quickly adopted when it reached Europe because it was easier and more dependable than copying by hand, but it wasn't much faster.

2 ➡ Before metal type, printing was accomplished through a relatively slow method—woodblock printing. This arduous process necessitated the carving out of text and illustrations from the surface of wooden blocks, using one block for each printed page. Then in late 13th century China, it was replaced by movable wooden type. This allowed printers to use individual pieces that could be fitted together to form words and eliminated the need to carve out a completely new image any time a new page was to be printed. Production times profoundly decreased, but there were still limitations to using wood as a printing instrument. Wood is a durable material; however, when faced with the stresses of repeated printing, it wears down, needing fairly regular replacement. Furthermore, because of wood's natural grain and veining, characters had to be carefully chiseled out, affecting the clarity of the letters and requiring more time to produce.

3 ➡ To overcome these limitations, attempts at using metal to form type were made. For this, carved wooden pieces were pressed into sand to form a negative of each character or

11. What is the function of paragraph 1 as it relates to the rest of the passage?

Ⓐ It introduces some historical background about the subject and a person who influenced its development.

Ⓑ It provides the background of a person who revolutionized the field of paper printing.

Ⓒ It illustrates a major technological change in printing and the methods used to create movable type.

Ⓓ It identifies the subject and the consequences of an invention that revolutionized the way paper was printed.

12. According to paragraph 2, which of the following is NOT a limitation of wood used for printing?

Ⓐ It deteriorates relatively quickly.

Ⓑ It takes a long time to carve.

Ⓒ It has a texture that affects the readability of the letters.

Ⓓ It is not readily available in some locations.

13. According to paragraph 3, which of the following is NOT true of Gutenberg's printing?

Ⓐ Prints from his press were clearer and more uniform than those of other printing techniques.

Ⓑ Gutenberg developed an ink used exclusively for printing.

Ⓒ Gutenberg used his machines for olive oil and wine production.

Ⓓ It was a dependable process for creating printed pages.

TOEFL Reading

symbol. Molten metals such as bronze, copper, iron, and tin were then poured into matrices, or molds, to cast type. Metal movable type like this had been evolving for several centuries in Asia before Johannes Gutenberg was able to create a practical and efficient printing system. Unlike the inventors who placed their attention on the individual mechanical parts used in printing, Gutenberg addressed the process by considering all of the parts involved in printing as a whole. He was able to create a process for producing metal movable type, which differed from earlier attempts as he used copper matrices to produce sharper images than had previously been made. Furthermore, Gutenberg developed new oil-based inks designed especially for printing. These inks were made using turpentine, soot, and walnut oil, and they had an oily consistency that made them excellent for application using a printing press. Lastly, he created a technique for printing that used a wooden printing press structurally similar to the screw-type machines used for olive oil and wine production, which allowed uniform pressure to be applied to all parts of the printed page. The effect was a consistent print that had ink evenly distributed throughout the image.

4 ➡ Gutenberg's most famous book printing is the *Gutenberg Bible*, of which he produced 180 copies. While this book was not the first one printed with his movable type process, it is the one that serves not only as an icon of Gutenberg, but also as the beginning of the age of the printed book. With his invention, Gutenberg ushered in a printing era lasting several centuries, and the processes for creating movable metal type remained unchanged for almost as long, resulting in profound effects on most societies around the world. This was mainly due to metal type's high durability. It allowed printing to become an economical choice for recording information, facilitating a proliferation of printed materials. In fact, metal type's effectiveness would influence societies by making printed materials available to not

14. The word "it" in paragraph 4 refers to

Ⓐ printing
Ⓑ *Gutenberg Bible*
Ⓒ movable type process
Ⓓ icon

15. Which of the following sentences below best expresses the essential information in the highlighted sentence in the passage? Incorrect answer choices change the meaning in important ways or leave out essential information.

Ⓐ It is known that movable metal type influenced many societies around the world.
Ⓑ Gutenberg's printing methods endured for hundreds of years, influencing cultures worldwide.
Ⓒ Gutenberg redesigned his invention numerous times, allowing the durable equipment to be used for several centuries.
Ⓓ Societies around the world provided input for Gutenberg when he was developing movable metal type.

16. According to paragraph 4, which of the following sentences about the *Gutenberg Bible* is true?

Ⓐ It was Gutenberg's first printing using his newly created printing process.
Ⓑ It was the first book ever created using a printing machine.
Ⓒ It was printed with movable metal type and oil-based inks.
Ⓓ It was the result of profound changes in most European societies.

only the educated elite but also to the masses. Indeed, in metal type's early years, this was seen as a threat to the upper classes, and in some societies, state governments would make laws limiting metal type printing to only their use.

5 ➡ It is believed that Gutenberg helped establish the Renaissance by producing a reliable and efficient way to reproduce writings and images in mass quantities. Metal-type printing enabled the mass production of books for the first time, with news and information spreading across Europe faster than ever before. It also made books much cheaper, which caused a rapid increase in literacy. People were exposed to new ideas and subjects that they would not have been able to study in the past. Indeed, the exchange of ideas rapidly accelerated, sparking the beginning of the scientific revolution.

17. According to paragraph 4, early metal type was seen as a threat to the upper classes because

Ⓐ printing was more efficient than it had been in the past
Ⓑ books could now be accessed by the lower classes of society
Ⓒ they would now have to create laws limiting who could produce books
Ⓓ the masses were now printing books using movable metal type

18. The word "reliable" in paragraph 5 is closest in meaning to

Ⓐ reputable
Ⓑ decent
Ⓒ complex
Ⓓ dependable

TOEFL Reading

19. Look at the four squares [■] that indicate where the following sentence could be added to the passage.

By the 8th century A.D., the Chinese were using this technique to print whole books filled with text and illustrations.

Where would the sentence best fit?

Click on a square [■] to add the sentence to the passage.

20. **Directions:** An introductory sentence for a brief summary of the passage is provided below. Complete the summary by selecting the THREE answer choices that express the most important ideas in the passage. Some sentences do not belong in the summary because they express ideas that are not presented in the passage or are minor ideas in the passage.
This question is worth 2 points.

Movable type is a printing process of great historical importance.

-
-
-

Answer Choices

Ⓐ Paper prints have existed since the 1400s, the period in which Gutenberg began developing his well-known printing system.

Ⓑ Wooden type required great care on the part of craftsmen as it had to be chiseled out and took a long time.

Ⓒ Printing was originally accomplished by using an entire block of carved wood, but this was later replaced with movable wood type.

Ⓓ Because metal is a very durable material, it is quite useful for forming the types used in the printing process.

Ⓔ Gutenberg revolutionized printing by creating a printing system that used movable metal type as one of its components.

Ⓕ Gutenberg's accomplishments increased the rate at which information was exchanged, sparking new influential movements.

Drag your answer choices to the spaces where they belong.
To remove an answer choice, click on it. To review the passage, click on **View Text**.

Actual Test 2

TOEFL Reading

Reading Section Directions

The Reading section measures your ability to understand academic passages in English. A clock at the top of the screen will show you how much time is remaining.

Most questions are worth 1 point, but the last question for each passage is worth more than 1 point. The directions for the last question indicate how many points you may receive.

Some passages include a word or phrase that is underlined in blue. To see a definition or an explanation, click on the word or phrase.

You may skip a question and return to it later, provided there is time remaining. To move on to the next question, click **NEXT**. To return to a question, click **BACK**.

Click **REVIEW** to access the review screen. The screen will show which questions have been answered and which have not been answered. You may go directly to any previous question from the review screen.

Click **CONTINUE** to proceed.

TOEFL Reading

Earthquake Prediction

1 ➡ Earthquakes are among the most devastating natural disasters that affect the planet, and their unpredictable nature makes them even more serious. The accurate prediction of seismic events has long been a goal of scientists that could help to prevent the massive loss of lives that often accompanies such widespread destruction. Unfortunately, no reliable way of predicting earthquakes has been identified, but scientists continue to research many promising methods of earthquake prediction that fall into two broad categories: long-term prediction and short-term prediction.

2 ➡ The long-term prediction of earthquakes is done by studying the historical record of seismic activity along a particular segment of a fault zone. By plotting out a timeline of when past earthquakes occurred and the magnitude of each quake, scientists can create a pattern of activity that allows them to determine the average interval between events of a particular size. By studying these gaps in seismic activity, they can determine the average length of time that passes between events of a significant magnitude. Based upon when the last quake of a particular size occurred, they can make an educated guess as to when the next one may strike. Since this method deals with average amounts, it can only be used to predict when an earthquake has the potential to occur. This means that they cannot be more accurate than a specified time interval of a few years to a few decades.

3 ➡ Short-term prediction is focused on being able to determine when the next earthquake will occur accurately enough to evacuate people from the surrounding area before it hits. In order to do so, scientists devote their time to studying events that occurred shortly before previous earthquakes called precursors. Throughout history, a variety of physical and

1. **Which of the following best expresses the essential information in the highlighted sentence? Incorrect answer choices change the meaning in important ways or leave out essential information.**

   (A) Thankfully, scientists have developed reliable methods to predict when earthquakes will occur, and these fall into two basic categories.

   (B) Unfortunately, scientists may never discover any way to accurately predict earthquakes in the long term, but short term methods show promise.

   (C) Scientists have not discovered any fool-proof way to predict earthquakes, but they are researching many potential methods that fit into long and short-term prediction.

   (D) Scientists have developed many ways to predict earthquakes, however they are only useful for broad, long-term predictions.

2. **According to paragraph 2, how is long-term prediction of earthquakes done?**

   (A) By comparing quakes of similar size on a fault segment with those of nearby faults

   (B) By analyzing seismic gaps identified in earthquake activity patterns

   (C) By comparing historical timelines of quakes on various segments of a fault

   (D) By calculating the average time interval between every earthquake

3. **The word "specified" in paragraph 2 is closest in meaning to**

   (A) stated

   (B) observed

   (C) typical

   (D) definite

chemical phenomena have been observed both by survivors and by scientists who were in the area prior to the events. Easily observed phenomena include deformation of land features and changes in water chemistry and the water level in wells and lakes. Others that require sophisticated devices to detect are more directly related to altered seismic activity. Fault zones are never completely stable, so there are frequent small tremors and seismic waves, but as an earthquake becomes imminent, the speed of seismic waves, the frequency of stronger tremors, which are called foreshocks, and the electrical resistance of rocks can all be altered.

4 ➡ One theory that explains many of these precursors is referred to as the dilatancy model. As the rocks that are under pressure along a fault line approach their breaking point, they can increase in volume significantly. [■A] This swelling, or dilation as it is called, is the result of microcracks forming between the crystalline layers of the rock. [■B] This alters the density of the rock, which changes how it transmits seismic energy, and the water also alters its electrical conductivity. [■C] When dilation occurs throughout large rock formations, it can dramatically alter the shape of the land as the inevitable quake rupture approaches. [■D] One such area of uplift that has scientists concerned has developed near Los Angeles along the San Andreas Fault. Since long-term prediction shows that a high magnitude quake in this area is likely to happen soon, scientists are monitoring this feature, which is called the Palmdale Bulge, very closely for further precursors. Dilatancy can also affect groundwater movement and water quality in wells or lakes. As water fills the rock fissures, the volume of water in wells and lakes may drop. The chemistry of the water can also be altered as gases and minerals are released from the rocks as they split apart. In particular, levels of radon gas have been shown to increase in water as tension increases along fault zones. The frequency and intensity of tremors also tend to increase, and then abruptly decline immediately before a major quake begins. This

4. According to paragraph 3, all of the following are precursors of earthquakes EXCEPT

Ⓐ changes in geological features
Ⓑ resistivity of rocks
Ⓒ instability of fault zones
Ⓓ increased seismic activity

5. The word "imminent" in paragraph 3 is closest in meaning to

Ⓐ of much significance
Ⓑ great in intensity
Ⓒ occurring in short intervals
Ⓓ about to happen

6. Why does the author mention the San Andreas Fault in paragraph 4?

Ⓐ To provide an example of a precursor event that changes land formation
Ⓑ To explain why this area is called the Palmdale Bulge
Ⓒ To introduce a region which is a counter-example of the dilatancy model
Ⓓ To highlight the effectiveness of long-term prediction in identifying a high-risk area

7. According to paragraph 4, which of the following is true about precursor events involving water?

Ⓐ The concentration of radon in water filling the rock fissures decreases.
Ⓑ Changes in groundwater levels increase the frequency of foreshocks.
Ⓒ Minerals released from rocks cause a change in water chemistry.
Ⓓ Bodies of water experience a volume increase.

calm before the storm is believed to be caused by a momentary increase in rock strength before the water impregnates them.

5 ➡ The phenomena in the dilatancy model can be organized into a typical sequence of events. In Stage I, stress builds up in an area of the fault zone. In Stages II and III, the effects of dilatancy are felt as the rocks expand and water fills in the micro-fissures. Stage IV is the large magnitude quake, and Stage V is the aftermath of the event, which often includes further strong tremors called aftershocks. Unfortunately, these stages are not uniform in length in every earthquake, nor do the precursors guarantee that a large quake will even occur. Every seismic event is unique, which makes it extremely difficult to use precursor events to accurately predict when a quake will happen. For example, when the Loma Prieta earthquake struck in 1989, two magnitude 5 foreshocks preceded the earthquake by 15 and 2 months, and in each case scientists predicted that a stronger earthquake would strike within a few days. However, no quake occurred, and people were unprepared when the magnitude 6.9 earthquake finally came. With further research and analysis, many scientists believe refinement of the dilatancy model is possible, or that a new, better method may be developed.

8. How is paragraph 5 organized?

Ⓐ It outlines the dilatancy model and then provides reasons why a new method of quake prediction needs to be developed.

Ⓑ It explains how the dilatancy model is divided into five stages and its limitations in real-life application.

Ⓒ It shows the progression of a major earthquake and the reason why prediction of earthquakes is difficult.

Ⓓ It groups precursor events into five distinct categories and provides real-life examples of how they manifest.

TOEFL Reading

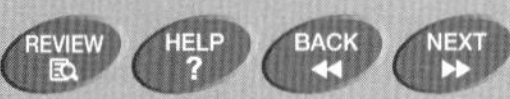

9. Look at the four squares [■] that indicate where the following sentence could be added to the passage.

The weaker grains in the rock separate and groundwater flows into the openings, forcing them to stay apart.

Where would the sentence best fit?

Click on a square [■] to add the sentence to the passage.

10. **Directions:** An introductory sentence for a brief summary of the passage is provided below. Complete the summary by selecting the THREE answer choices that express the most important ideas in the passage. Some sentences do not belong in the summary because they express ideas that are not presented in the passage or are minor ideas in the passage. ***This question is worth 2 points.***

While accurate prediction of earthquakes has been a scientific goal for many years, no completely reliable method has been found yet.

-
-
-

Answer Choices

(A) While a sequence of stages of major quakes is known, the duration of each stage is not identical, making prediction hard.

(B) An example of land deformation is the Palmdale Bulge along the San Andreas Fault where a high-magnitude quake is likely to take place soon.

(C) Stages I through III of the dilatancy model are precursor events that precede the major quake and aftershocks that are labeled Stages IV and V respectively.

(D) Events like land swelling, increasing foreshocks, and changes in water levels are indicators of an impending earthquake.

(E) By creating a timeline of seismic activity, scientists identify a pattern that helps them predict when the next quake of a similar size may occur.

(F) Prediction of the Loma Prieta quake failed because scientists failed to accurately predict how long after the preceding foreshocks the quake would take place.

Drag your answer choices to the spaces where they belong.
To remove an answer choice, click on it. To review the passage, click on **View Text**.

TOEFL Reading

The Development of Motion Pictures

1 ➡ The development of motion pictures began in the mid-19th century with the invention of the zoetrope. Artists would create a series of drawings that showed various stages of movement, for example of a couple dancing. These drawings were placed within a cylinder that had an opening for a person to look through. When the cylinder was rotated at an appropriate speed, it would appear to the viewer that the dancers were actually moving instead of the cylinder. This optical illusion is called the phi phenomenon, and it occurs because as humans view a series of images in rapid succession, our eyes perceive continuous movement. The images of the dancers do not change, but our mind processes the information in such a way that it appears to be one image that moves. By the 1870s, camera technology had advanced far enough that artist Eadweard Muybridge was able to use a series of cameras to replicate this phenomenon.

2 ➡ Eadweard Muybridge was a professional photographer who was famous for his images of natural landscapes and studies of the western United States. In 1872 he was approached by Leland Stanford to help him settle a question about the movement of horses. Many people believed that when a horse moves at a trot or a gallop, it keeps at least one foot on the ground for balance. [■A] The shutter speeds of cameras had become fast enough that Muybridge was able to line up 24 in a row to capture the movement of the horse. [■B] As a jockey rode the horse past the cameras at 36 miles per hour, it triggered trip wires that activated the cameras. [■C] Some of the resulting photographs showed that the horse did indeed have all of its feet in the air at times. [■D] Muybridge converted the images into silhouettes and placed them together into a device of his own design to project them onto a screen for an audience

11. Why does the author mention phi phenomenon in paragraph 1?

(A) To introduce the concept which makes motion pictures viable

(B) To emphasize the versatility of our visual abilities

(C) To explain why zoetropes came in a cylindrical form

(D) To suggest that artists who produced zoetropes were clearly scientists

12. The word "converted" in paragraph 2 is closest in meaning to

(A) reproduced

(B) transferred

(C) changed

(D) applied

13. What can be inferred about Muybridge's work in paragraph 2?

(A) He specifically requested the jockey to ride the horse at a certain speed.

(B) Cameras were not advanced enough to take multiple shots with a single lens.

(C) It was the first time he ever worked with a moving animal.

(D) He inadvertently provided a breakthrough in the field of zoology.

14. The word "flexible" in paragraph 3 is closest in meaning to

(A) fragile

(B) bendable

(C) adaptable

(D) stiff

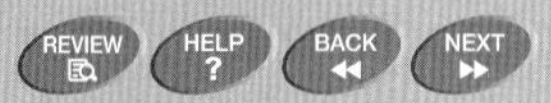

to view, thus creating the first motion picture exhibition.

3 ➡ The next great innovation in motion pictures came in the late 1880s with the creation of celluloid photographic film and cameras that could take photographs in sequence through a single lens. The flexible celluloid allowed strips of film to be rolled onto reels that fed the camera, which allowed a few minutes instead of a few seconds of action to be filmed. After meeting Muybridge, Thomas Edison decided to develop his own motion picture camera and an exhibition apparatus. The final result was the Kinetoscope, which passed the film strip between a lamp and a viewing lens. Unfortunately, only one person at a time could use a Kinetoscope, so when the first commercial motion picture house opened in New York City in 1894, the owner had to purchase ten machines. Despite the considerable investment this required, Kinetoscope parlors were launched in major cities across the country, and Edison's company reaped great profits.

4 ➡ Due to the amount of revenue that Kinetoscopes were generating, Edison did not feel compelled to develop a projection system. However, his counterparts in other companies recognized that films shown to larger audiences would be far more profitable because of the machine to viewer ratio. Much of the innovation took place at other companies, but Edison was eventually approached to mass produce the end result, the Vitascope. This machine used a high-intensity light bulb to project the film onto a wall or sheet, and the technology remained essentially the same for decades. The earliest films that were produced seem simple by today's standards, but they had a profound effect on the viewing public. They were filmed from one perspective and depicted an action or event with no alteration. They showed dancing, athletic events, scenes from nature, and famously, a train arriving at a station. The angle the train movie was shot from made it appear as though the train was coming at the viewers, and

15. Which of the following is NOT mentioned in paragraph 3 about the Kinetoscope?

Ⓐ It made use of celluloid film.

Ⓑ It projected film strips a few minutes long through a viewing lens.

Ⓒ It allowed only one viewer at a time.

Ⓓ It required significant financial investment for its use.

16. According to paragraph 4, why was Edison late in joining the move toward a projection system?

Ⓐ His Kinetoscope business would suffer with an increased machine to viewer ratio.

Ⓑ He believed there could be no further innovation beyond his Kinetoscope.

Ⓒ He did not have the foresight to realize that larger audiences would be more profitable.

Ⓓ His company was the last to be approached about mass producing a projection system.

17. Which of the following best expresses the essential information in the highlighted sentence? Incorrect answer choices change the meaning in important ways or leave out essential information.

Ⓐ The film of a train was shot in such a way that it made the audience think that the train would crash into them, so they ran away.

Ⓑ The film of a train showed it approaching the station at a bad angle and hitting people, which terrified the audience.

Ⓒ The train in one film was shown approaching the camera at great speed, which made some of the audience afraid.

Ⓓ The film of a train was very popular because the angle of the camera made it look like the train was going to strike the viewers.

TOEFL Reading

some people close to the screen fled their seats in panic.

5 ➡ The second phase of films began to tell stories, and they also incorporated different scenes and shots from multiple distances and angles. These films were only 5 to 10 minutes long, because film reels could only hold that much film. Sound did not become available until the late 1920s when the technology became commercially viable. So, any dialogue between characters or explanation of the story had to be achieved via using a blank screen with writing called a title card. For this reason, movies from this era of cinema are referred to as "silent films," but theater owners would often employ a pianist or organist to play music to accompany the scenes. The films were often distributed with prepared sheet music to ensure that the music played was appropriate, and some films had complete scores for large theaters employing orchestras. When sound technology became adequate to include a soundtrack with speech, music, and sound effects, film studios transitioned to making "talking pictures" seemingly overnight.

18. All of the following are mentioned in paragraph 5 EXCEPT

Ⓐ how films emerged as a medium for storytelling

Ⓑ the progress of relatively sophisticated filmmaking techniques in early films

Ⓒ the time period in which the transition to "talking pictures" took place

Ⓓ the reason why theater owners prepared sheet music for orchestras

TOEFL Reading

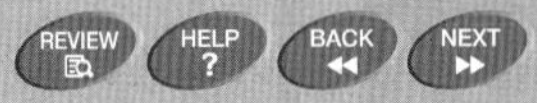

19. Look at the four squares [■] that indicate where the following sentence could be added to the passage.

Others maintained that the horse had all four feet off of the ground at certain points.

Where would the sentence best fit?

Click on a square [■] to add the sentence to the passage.

20. **Directions:** An introductory sentence for a brief summary of the passage is provided below. Complete the summary by selecting the THREE answer choices that express the most important ideas in the passage. Some sentences do not belong in the summary because they express ideas that are not presented in the passage or are minor ideas in the passage. ***This question is worth 2 points.***

Motion pictures rapidly developed from a scientific novelty to a form of mainstream entertainment in the late 19th and early 20th century.

-
-
-

Answer Choices

(A) Muybridge's clever set up of cameras allowed him to provide the verdict that horses did indeed have all four feet off the ground when galloping.

(B) Edison's Kinetoscope was an innovation on its own, but it also was the first to allow the public to consume short films as a form of entertainment.

(C) Sensing great profitability with larger audiences, many jumped into developing a projection system, resulting in the Vitascope.

(D) Early "silent films" made up for the lack of sound by including title cards and live music accompaniment until the transition to "talking pictures" took place.

(E) Even though early Kinetoscope parlors had to make a heavy investment upfront, the high demand for them offset that cost.

(F) The phi phenomenon, which allows us to perceive a sequence of still images as moving, is the scientific breakthrough that drove the film industry.

Drag your answer choices to the spaces where they belong.
To remove an answer choice, click on it. To review the passage, click on **View Text.**

Listening

I. Conversations

Lesson 01 Main Idea
Lesson 02 Details
Lesson 03 Function & Attitude
Lesson 04 Connecting Contents
Lesson 05 Inference

II. Lectures

Lesson 01 Main Idea
Lesson 02 Details
Lesson 03 Function & Attitude
Lesson 04 Connecting Contents
Lesson 05 Inference

III. Actual Tests

Actual Test 1
Actual Test 2

iBT TOEFL® Listening 개요

1. Listening 영역의 구성

Listening 영역은 약 2개의 파트로 구분되며, 각 파트에는 대화(Conversation), 강의(Lecture) 및 토론(Discussion)의 청취 지문이 등장한다. 대화 지문은 2개가 출제되며, 강의 지문은 3개가 출제된다.

* Conversation 지문 2개, 지문당 각 5문제 출제

* Lecture 지문 3개, 지문당 각 6문제 출제

2. Listening 영역의 특징 및 학습 방법

1) 반드시 노트 필기를 한다.

iBT TOEFL®에서는 청취 지문을 듣는 동안 주어진 필기 용지(Scratch Paper)에 들은 내용을 필기할 수 있다. 따라서 강의나 토론과 같은 긴 지문을 들을 때, 기억력에 의존하기보다는 강의의 중요한 내용과 예측 가능한 문제의 답을 미리 노트 필기하면 문제의 정답을 좀 더 쉽게 찾을 수 있다.

2) 다양한 대화와 주제에 익숙해지자.

iBT TOEFL®은 실제 영어 사용 국가에서 학업을 할 수 있는 능력을 평가하는 TOEFL 본래의 목적에 충실하도록 변화한 만큼, 시험의 내용 또한 실제와 흡사하게 변화했다고 볼 수 있다. 대화의 내용이 좀 더 캠퍼스 상황으로 한정되었고, 대화와 강의의 길이가 길어졌으며, 주저하며 말하거나 대화 중간에 끼어든다거나 하는 자연스러운 청취 지문이 제시되고 있다. 발음에 있어서는 미국식 발음 외에 영국이나 호주식 발음도 가끔 청취 지문에 등장하여 다양한 언어가 사용되는 학업 상황을 좀 더 현실적으로 보여주고 있다.

3) 전체 내용을 이해한다.

iBT TOEFL®에서는 지문 전반의 내용을 이해하여 전체 주제를 찾거나(Main Idea Question) 또는 특정 정보의 상호 관계를 파악하는 문제(Connecting Content Question)가 많이 등장한다.

4) 억양이나 톤에 주의한다.

iBT TOEFL®에서 특히 눈에 띄는 문제 유형은 지문의 일부분을 다시 듣고 화자의 억양, 목소리 톤, 문맥상 전후 관계를 통해 정보에 대한 화자의 태도나 목적을 파악하는 문제 유형이다. 태도 파악 문제(Attitude Question)와 의도 파악 문제(Function Question)라고 불리는 이 문제 유형들은 지문의 의미 그 자체만으로 정답을 찾기보다는 특정 부분의 문맥상 의미를 파악하여 선택지에서 올바른 답을 골라야 한다.

3. Listening 영역의 문제 유형

iBT Listening 영역에서는 크게 5개의 문제 유형이 출제된다. 아래의 표는 Listening 영역의 문제를 유형별로 나누어 각 유형별 특징과 출제 문항 수를 표시해 놓은 것이다.

< iBT Listening 영역의 5가지 문제 유형>

주제 찾기 문제 Main Idea Question	강의나 대화의 목적 또는 전반적인 흐름을 묻는 문제 예) What is the conversation mainly about? 대화는 주로 무엇에 관한 것인가?
세부 사항 찾기 문제 Details Question	강의나 대화의 주요한 정보들에 관해 묻는 문제 예) What are the characteristics of ~? ~의 특징은 무엇인가?
의도 및 태도 파악 문제 Function & Attitude Question	화자가 특정 문장을 언급한 의도나 문장에 담긴 화자의 태도나 관점을 묻는 문제 예) Listen again to part of the conversation. Then answer the question. Why does the student say this: 대화의 일부를 다시 듣고 질문에 답하시오. 학생은 왜 이렇게 말하는가:
관계 파악 문제 Connecting Contents Question	강의나 대화에 주어진 정보들 간의 유기적 관계를 묻는 문제 (e.g. 인과, 비교, 추론하기, 결과 예측하기, 일반화하기) 예) Why does the professor say ~? 교수는 왜 ~라고 말하는가? In the conversation, the speakers discuss ~. Indicate in the table below ~. 대화에서 화자들은 ~에 대해 논의한다. ~인지 아래 표에 표시하시오.
추론 문제 Inference Question	강의나 대화를 통해 유추할 수 있는 것을 묻는 문제 예) What is the student most likely to do next? 학생이 다음에 무엇을 할 것 같은가?

4. 기존 시험과 개정 시험 간 Listening 영역 비교

	기존 iBT (2023년 7월 전)	개정 후 iBT (2023년 7월 이후)
지문 개수	대화 2~3개 강의 3~5개	대화 2개 강의 3개
지문당 문제 수	대화 각 5문제 강의 각 6문제	대화 각 5문제 강의 각 6문제
전체 시험 시간	41~57분	36분

• 지문 및 질문 유형은 기존과 동일하다.

I. Conversations

Introduction

iBT TOEFL Listening Conversations

TOEFL Listening에서 대화(Conversation) 유형은 총 2개 출제된다. 보통 교수와 학생, 또는 대학교 직원과 학생의 대화를 다룬다. 보통 1 지문당 450~550단어의 길이로 이루어져 있으며(약 3분), 대화를 듣고 1~5번 문제를 풀게 된다. 필기용 종이가 제공되기 때문에 대화를 들으면서 노트 필기와 요약이 가능하다.

Conversation Question Types

대화 하나당 다섯 문제를 풀게 되며 문제 유형은 아래와 같이 총 다섯 가지이다.

1. **주제 찾기(Main Idea):** 대화의 주제·목적 찾기
2. **세부 사항 찾기(Details):** 대화를 들으며 알 수 있는 세부 내용 찾기
3. **의도 및 태도 파악(Function & Attitude):** 듣기 지문의 일부를 다시 듣고 화자가 어떠한 말을 한 이유 또는 무언가에 대한 화자의 태도 파악하기
4. **관계 파악(Connecting Contents):** 대화가 연결된 방식 또는 무언가가 언급된 이유 파악하기
5. **추론(Inference):** 대화를 통해 유추할 수 있는 내용 찾기

Conversation Topic Types

대화 주제는 크게 두 가지로 분류할 수 있다.

1. **집무 시간(Office Hours):** 교수·지도교수의 집무 시간에 교수 연구실에서 이루어지는 대화로, 주로 학생이 교수에게 성적과 과제, 전공·진로 상담, 인턴십, 취업 등에 관해 다양하게 묻는 내용이다. 때로는 교수가 학생을 불러 학업이나 과제와 관련해 묻는 대화도 있다.

2. **교내 서비스 관련(Service-Related):** 캠퍼스 내 모든 곳에서 이루어지는 대화로, 학생과 대학교 직원 간의 대화로 구성된다. 주로 도서관, 구내 식당, 기숙사 관련 내용이 많으며 교내 주차 문제부터 책 대출, 등록금 납부까지 다양한 문의 사항이 나온다.

Tips

이 대화의 주제·중심 내용이 무엇인가?

대화의 주제가 무엇인지 파악하지 못한다면 결코 그 대화를 잘 이해했다고 볼 수 없다. 대화의 주제와 중심 내용은 보통 대화가 시작되고 나서 거의 바로 확인할 수 있다. 학생이나 교수, 직원의 말을 통해 왜 이 대화가 이루어지고 있는지, 학생이 왜 찾아왔는지에 집중하자. 주제·중심 내용을 묻는 문제는 반드시 한 문제씩 출제되며 가장 기본적인 사항이므로 절대 놓치지 말자.

세부 정보를 파악하라!

주제·중심 내용을 알면 그에 맞춰 세부 정보를 파악할 수 있다. 세부 정보 문제 역시 대화 하나당 1~2개의 문제가 반드시 출제되므로 대화의 처음부터 끝까지 긴장을 놓지 말고 듣자. 세부 정보 문제로 많이 나오는 내용은 흔히 다음과 같다.

❶ 화자(주로 학생)의 문제

❷ 그 문제·상황이 발생한 원인과 이유

❸ 그 문제·상황을 해결하기 위한 방법·수단(주로 교수나 직원이 제안)

❹ 대화에서 등장한 예시·설명

❺ 그 외의 세부 정보

화자의 말투와 대화 분위기는 어떤가?

의도 및 태도 파악 문제(Function & Attitude Question)에서는 특히 화자의 말투와 대화의 분위기 등을 파악하는 내용이 많이 나온다. 대화를 듣고 있으면 문제점이나 고민 사항, 불만 내용 등을 알 수 있으며 그에 따라 화자의 어투와 분위기 역시 달라진다. 화자가 불만을 갖고 비꼬아서 말할 수도 있고, 화를 내거나 아쉬워하는 등 다양한 상황이 등장하므로 오가는 대화 속의 명확한 의미를 파악할 수 있도록 하자.

정답은 정직하게 출제되지 않는다!

대화에서 나온 단어가 문제 보기에 그대로 출제되는 경우는 거의 없다. 같은 내용이지만 다른 말로 약간 변화를 주며, 이 때문에 혼란이 올 수 있지만 단어 자체를 보지 말고 내용과 뜻에 집중하자. 이렇게 같은 의미를 다른 말로 바꿔 표현하는 것을 패러프레이징(paraphrasing)이라고 하며 Listening뿐만 아니라 Reading과 Writing, Speaking 영역에서도 흔히 나타난다. 수험자가 방심하도록 일부러 대화에서 등장한 단어와 똑같은 단어를 문제 보기에 출제할 때도 있다는 점을 명심하자.

Lesson

01 Main Idea

Lesson Outline

주제 찾기 문제(Main Idea Question)는 대화의 목적 또는 주된 내용을 묻는 문제로, 모든 듣기 지문에 한 문제씩 반드시 출제된다. 대부분의 듣기 지문에는 전체 주제나 목적이 분명하게 진술되어 있으나 일부 지문에는 주제가 간접적으로 암시되어 있기 때문에 충분한 연습이 없으면 의외로 많은 시간을 소비하기 쉬운 문제 유형이기도 하다.

이 Lesson에서는 주제 찾기 문제를 풀 때 알아 두어야 할 지문 구조와, 답이 다른 말로 바뀌어 쓰였을 때 주제를 찾는 연습을 해보도록 하자.

Lesson Point

Point 1 도입부 + 표시어(signal) = 주제!

Point 2 너무 일반적이거나 너무 구체적인 보기는 오답이다.

Point 3 보기에서 키워드가 패러프레이즈되어 있을 확률이 높다.

Point 4 대화에서는 문제점이 주제!

Point 5 끝까지 듣고 주제를 고르면 모든 보기가 답으로 보인다. 도입부에 집중하자.

Typical Questions

- What is the conversation mainly about? 대화는 주로 무엇에 관한 것인가?
- What are the speakers mainly discussing? 화자들은 주로 무엇에 관해 이야기하고 있는가?
- What is the main topic of the conversation? 대화의 주제는 무엇인가?
- Why does the student go to see his professor? 학생은 왜 교수를 찾아가는가?
- Why does the student go to the registrar's office? 학생은 왜 학적부 사무실을 찾아가는가?

Learning Strategies

1 '주제 찾기' 표시어(signal)를 공략한다!

도입부에서 주제가 나올 것을 미리 알려 주는 표시어를 파악하고, 그 뒤에 나오는 내용, 즉 주제를 집중해서 듣는다.

• I was wondering (I wonder) if you can ~.	~해 주실 수 있는지 궁금해서요.
• Actually, I am here to talk about ~.	사실, 제가 온 이유는 ~에 대해 이야기하기 위해서예요.
• I want to talk to you about ~.	~에 대해 말씀 드리고 싶어요.
• I have some problems regarding ~.	~에 문제가 좀 있어요.
• I have some questions about ~.	~에 관해 여쭤볼 게 좀 있어요.
• The reason why I'm here is ~.	제가 여기 온 이유는 ~예요.
• Yeah, I'm looking for ~.	네, 저는 ~를 찾고 있어요.
• I'm interested in ~.	저는 ~에 관심이 있어요.
• I was thinking about ~.	~하려고/~에 대해 생각하고 있었어요.
• I was supposed to ~.	저는 ~해야 해요.

2 패러프레이징(paraphrasing)에 주의한다!

대화에 나온 단어가 문제 보기에 그대로 쓰이는 경우는 거의 없다. 따라서 전반적인 내용을 잘 파악한 뒤 보기와 일치하는 내용을 고르는 것이 중요하다.

Ex The use of electricity has increased → the increase in the use of electricity [절 → 명사구]

Ex Many people often encounter difficulties when they first use the tool. → A lot of people frequently face challenges when they use the device for the first time. [동사/형용사/명사 등을 다른 단어로 대체]

Example

Woman: Professor | Man: Student

 C01_EX

Listen to a conversation between a student and a professor.

W Hello, Joel, I'm glad you could find time to meet me.

M Of course, Professor. Is something wrong?

W Well, I sincerely hope not. You are aware that you were supposed to arrange a meeting with me to discuss your term paper, aren't you?

M Yes, but I don't remember when the deadline for scheduling the meeting was...

W It is tomorrow. So you can see why I was concerned. Have you made any progress on your paper?

M Oh! I'm so sorry! I thought I still had a week or so. But, yes, I have chosen my topic, and I have gotten started on my research.

W That is very good to hear. What have you selected as a topic to write about?

M Well, you said that we should write about the history of our neighborhoods. I grew up near a hat factory in Concord—maybe you are familiar with it?

W I think so, after all Concord is not far from here. Are you referring to Massachusetts Millinery?

M Yes, I am.

W That is a very good choice. That company has been around for a long time.

M Yes. It was founded nearly 150 years ago, in 1867.

W That is going to be a lot of history for you to cover. Have you decided on what type of focus to take to narrow down your perspective?

M Yes. Growing up in the shadow of the landmark has always made it feel like a part of my home. I want to focus more on the history of the owners' families than the business side of the factory, so I have been approaching it from a genealogical angle.

Q. Why did the professor want to see the student?

Ⓐ The student forgot the due date of his term paper and turned it in late.

Ⓑ She was worried that the student was still confused about the topic.

Ⓒ The student had not contacted her to discuss the progress of his paper.

Ⓓ She wanted to explain why she is not going to give the student extra time for the paper.

학생과 교수의 대화를 들으시오.

여 안녕, 조엘. 나와 만날 시간이 있다니 다행이네요.

남 그럼요, 교수님. 무슨 문제가 있나요?

여 음, 진심으로 없기를 바라요. 학생의 학기말 리포트를 논의하기 위해 나와 회의할 시간을 잡았어야 한다는 걸 알고 있죠, 그렇죠?

남 네, 하지만 회의 날짜를 정하기로 한 기한이 언제였는지 기억이 안 나네요...

여 내일이에요. 내가 왜 걱정했는지 알겠죠. 리포트에 어떤 진척이라도 있나요?

남 아! 정말 죄송해요! 아직 한 주 정도 더 시간이 있다고 생각했어요. 하지만, 네, 주제를 정했고 리서치를 시작했어요.

여 다행이네요. 무엇을 주제로 정해서 쓰기로 했나요?

남 음, 우리 근처 이웃의 역사에 대해 써야 한다고 말씀하셨죠. 저는 콩코드의 모자 공장 근처에서 자랐어요. 아마 교수님도 아실지 모르겠네요.

여 그런 것 같아요. 어쨌든 콩코드는 여기에서 멀지 않으니까요. 매사추세츠 여성용 모자 제작 공장에 대해 말하고 있는 건가요?

남 네, 맞아요.

여 매우 좋은 선택이네요. 그 회사는 꽤 오래된 곳이니까요.

남 네, 거의 150년 전인 1867년에 세워졌어요.

여 학생이 다루기에는 역사의 범위가 너무 넓을 텐데요. 관점을 좀 더 좁히기 위해 어디에 집중할지 결정했나요?

남 네, 이 역사적인 건물 근처에서 자랐다는 것이 이곳을 제가 저희 집의 일부처럼 느끼도록 만들었어요. 공장쪽 사업보다 공장 주인 가족들의 역사에 집중하고 싶고, 그래서 계보의 각도에서 접근했어요.

Q. 교수는 왜 학생을 보고자 했는가?

(A) 학생이 학기말 리포트의 마감 기한을 잊어 제출을 늦게 했다.

(B) 학생이 여전히 주제에 대해 헷갈려 했기에 걱정했다.

(C) 학생이 리포트의 진척에 대해 논의하기 위한 연락을 하지 않았다.

(D) 왜 학생에게 리포트 기한 연장을 해줄 수 없는지를 설명하고자 했다.

해설 학생이 교수에게 무슨 문제가 있냐고 묻자 교수가 리포트를 논의할 회의 시간을 잡았어야 하는데 학생이 연락을 하지 않았다고 대화 도입부에 밝히고 있다. 따라서 정답은 (C)이다. 한편, (A)가 교묘하게 패러프레이즈되었다는 점을 발견할 수 있다. 학생이 리포트 자체를 제출하는 것이 아니라 리포트 논의를 위한 회의 시간을 잡는 것이 대화의 목적인데, '리포트 마감 기한'으로 내용이 살짝 바뀌어 출제되었다. 문제 보기들은 패러프레이징을 통해 본문에 쓰인 단어에서 살짝 바뀌어서 출제된다는 점을 항상 기억하고 보기를 주의 깊게 읽도록 하자.

Lesson 01 Conversations

어휘 sincerely adv 진심으로 | arrange v 마련하다, 주선하다 | discuss v 논의하다 | term paper 학기말 리포트 | deadline n 마감일 | concerned adj 염려하는 | progress n 진전, 진척 | millinery n 여성 모자 제작업/판매업 | narrow down 좁히다, 줄이다 | genealogical adj 족보의, 계보의

Practice

Passage 1 Listen to part of a conversation between a student and a professor. C01_P01

Note-taking

Q. Why did the student come to see the professor?

Ⓐ To provide the reason why the student missed a class

Ⓑ To ask for a handout that the student did not receive

Ⓒ To discuss ideas for the student's next writing assignment

Ⓓ To talk about an assignment that the student failed to complete

Passage 2 Listen to part of a conversation between a student and a professor. C01_P02

Note-taking

Q. Why did the student want to speak to the professor?

Ⓐ She needs a new sports reporter for the school newspaper.

Ⓑ She has a problem with the school newspaper's sports reporter.

Ⓒ She wants to become a sports reporter for the school newspaper.

Ⓓ She wants to create a sports section in the school newspaper.

Passage 3 Listen to part of a conversation between a student and a housing officer. C01_P03

Q. What are the speakers discussing?

Ⓐ Hiring workmen to repaint the school dormitories

Ⓑ Problems with a painting in a dormitory room

Ⓒ Applying to have a dormitory room repainted

Ⓓ Organizing access to a student's room in order to paint it

Passage 4 Listen to part of a conversation between a student and a registrar. 

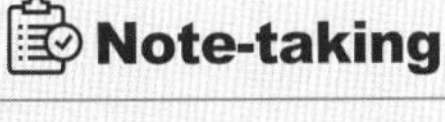

Q. What is the conversation mainly about?

Ⓐ Plans to open a new swimming pool on the campus

Ⓑ Registration for swimming classes at the new campus pool

Ⓒ The opening ceremony for an on-campus swimming pool

Ⓓ Hiring swimming instructors for the new campus swimming pool

Lesson

02 Details

Lesson Outline

세부 사항 찾기 문제(Details Question)는 TOEFL Listening 문제에서 가장 빈도수가 높은 문제 유형으로, 지문의 세부 사항에 대해 질문한다. 세부 사항 찾기 문제는 주로 대화에서 다루는 문제점과 연관된 자세한 사항, 화자가 강조하거나 반복해서 말하고 있는 사항, 주제를 뒷받침하는 예나 특징으로 사용된 것 등을 묻고, 2개의 답을 선택해야 하는 경우도 있기 때문에 정확도가 중요하다.

이 문제 해결의 관건은 전반적인 내용 파악을 바탕으로 한 정확한 노트 필기(note-taking)이다. 전체 내용의 흐름을 이해한다고 해도 자칫 세부적인 질문에 대해서는 답이 기억 나지 않을 수 있기 때문에 노트 필기를 활용하여 정확도를 높여야 한다. 자신만의 노트 필기 방법을 연습하고 그 안에서 답을 찾는 연습을 해 보자.

Lesson Point

Point 1 세부 사항 찾기 = 최고 빈출 문제 유형!

Point 2 문제점과 해결책에 주목한다.

Point 3 노트 필기(note-taking) 실력 없이는 고득점으로 갈 수 없다.

Point 4 표시어(signal)를 바탕으로 한 정확하고 간결한 노트 필기를 연습한다.

Typical Questions 

- What does the professor offer to do? 교수는 무엇을 해주겠다고 제시하는가?
- What are two key features of ~? ~의 두 가지 주요 특징은 무엇인가?
- What are the characteristics of ~? ~의 특징들은 무엇인가?
- What is the reason that ~? ~하는 이유는 무엇인가?
- According to the student, what is ~? 학생에 의하면, ~은 무엇인가?
- What does the [student/professor] say about ~? [학생은/교수는] ~에 관해 무엇이라고 말하는가?

Learning Strategies

1 '세부 사항 찾기' 표시어(signal)를 공략한다!

세부 사항 표시어를 바탕으로 한 정확한 노트 필기를 통해 강조 또는 반복되는 내용을 정리한다. 표시어를 들으면 다음에 어떤 내용이 나올지 짐작이 가능하다. 특히 아래와 같은 표시어가 나오면 화자가 무언가에 관해 예를 들 거라는 점을 미리 예측할 수 있고, 이러한 예시는 세부 사항 문제로 출제될 가능성이 높다.

• such as ~	예를 들면, ~와 같은
• things like ~	~와 같은 것들
• for instance,	예를 들어,
• in this case,	이 경우에 있어서,
• referred to as ~	보통 ~로 불리는/~라 하는

위의 표시어를 바탕으로 노트 필기(note-taking)를 한다. 언급된 내용이 너무 길면 자신이 알아볼 수 있는 줄임말과 축약형을 사용해 간단하고 빠르게 적도록 하자.

2 패러프레이징(paraphrasing) 역시 잊지 말자!

세부 사항 문제에서도 화자가 했던 말을 그대로 문제에 쓰기보다는 내용은 같지만 쓰이는 단어는 다른 것으로 바꾸는 패러프레이징이 보기에 등장한다. 그 점에 유의하며 보기를 하나씩 잘 살펴보고, 같은 단어를 포함한 보기가 아니라 지문의 내용에 부합하는 보기를 고르도록 하자.

Ex Read it **carefully** → careful reading is **required** [부사 → 형용사]

Ex A person should never **make** an important decision alone. → An important decision should not be **made** alone. [능동태 → 수동태]

Example

Man: Professor | Woman: Student

C02_EX

Listen to part of a conversation between a student and a professor.

W Excuse me, professor. Maria told me you wanted to speak with me?

M Paola, yes, I do. Please have a seat. I'm not interfering with your schedule today, am I?

W What? Oh, no. No, I'm not busy today. My next class doesn't start for two more hours.

M Good. Is that true of your schedule in general? What I mean to say is do you usually have much free time? Do you have a job this semester?

W Uh, I'm not sure where you are going with this.... No, I do not have a job this semester. I am ahead of schedule with my major courses, so I am taking some electives to fill up my schedule. Only three of my remaining mandatory courses were available this semester, so this semester my schedule is pretty light. [1] May I ask why you are so interested in my schedule?

M [1] Of course, are you familiar with our night math program?

W Kind of. I know that it exists. [2] I also took part in one when I was in high school.

M Oh really? What did you think of it?

W Well, it was at a community college. My parents enrolled me in it. Not because I was bad at math or anything.

M Of course, you wouldn't be pursuing a doctorate in physics if you were.

W Exactly. But, to answer your question, I wasn't very impressed by it. They thought it would be like an advanced class, but I found it was far too easy for me. I dropped out after just a few sessions.

M That doesn't surprise me. [2] That program was probably very similar to ours, which is a remedial math program. It is aimed at adults who find their math skills to be lacking, and not intended for advanced students.

1. Why did the professor want to see the student?

Ⓐ To discuss her class schedule for the upcoming semester

Ⓑ To tell her to work harder to become a math teacher

Ⓒ To persuade her to become a volunteer at a math teaching center

Ⓓ To encourage her to take more elective courses next year

2. According to the conversation, what is true about the school's night math program?

Ⓐ It usually takes place at national universities.

Ⓑ It teaches math to high school students and adults.

Ⓒ It accepts students who usually excel at math.

Ⓓ It is an introductory math course for freshmen.

W Yeah, most of the students were much older than me. But the class level was beneath me, so I quit.

M And rightly so. [1] But tell me, would you be interested in teaching such a program?

학생과 교수의 대화를 들으시오.

여 실례합니다 교수님, 마리아가 교수님께서 절 보길 원하셨다고 했는데요?

남 파올라, 맞아요. 자리에 앉아요. 오늘 학생의 일정을 내가 방해하고 있는 건 아니죠, 그렇죠?

여 네? 아, 아니에요. 오늘은 바쁘지 않거든요. 다음 수업이 시작하기까지는 2시간이 남았어요.

남 좋아요. 학생의 시간표 전반적으로 그런 식인가요? 내 말은, 남는 시간이 많나요? 이번 학기에 하는 일이라도 있어요?

여 음, 무슨 말씀을 하려고 하시는지 잘 모르겠어요.... 아니요. 이번 학기에는 일을 하지 않아요. 제 전공 과목 수업들은 앞서 있어서 스케줄을 채우기 위해 선택 과목을 몇 개 듣고 있어요. 남아 있는 필수 과목들 중에서 이번 학기에 세 개밖에 열리지 않아서 시간표가 꽤 한가한 편이에요. [1] 왜 제 스케줄에 대해 궁금해하시는지 여쭤봐도 되나요?

남 [1] 물론이죠. 우리 학교의 야간 수학 프로그램에 대해 알고 있나요?

여 약간은요. 있다는 건 알아요. [2] 제가 고등학교 때 들었던 적이 있거든요.

남 정말인가요? 그 프로그램을 어떻게 생각했죠?

여 음, 전문 대학에서 들은 거였어요. 부모님이 저를 등록시키셨죠. 제가 수학을 못해서라거나 그런 건 아니었어요.

남 그럼요. 만약 그랬다면 물리학 박사 학위를 목표로 하고 있지 않겠죠.

여 맞아요. 하지만 교수님의 질문에 답하자면, 그다지 깊은 인상을 받지 못했어요. 부모님은 이 프로그램이 고급반 수업 같을 거라고 생각하셨지만, 저에겐 너무 쉬웠어요. 몇 번 듣고 그만두었죠.

남 놀랍지는 않네요. [2] 그 프로그램은 아마 우리가 가진 프로그램과 매우 비슷한 거였을 거예요. 수학 보충 프로그램 같은 거죠. 고급반 학생들을 위한 것이 아니라, 수학 능력이 부족하다고 느끼는 성인들을 위해 만들어진 프로그램이니까요.

여 네, 대부분의 학생들이 저보다 나이가 훨씬 많았지만, 수업의 레벨이 제 실력보다 낮았기에 그만뒀어요.

남 그만두기를 잘한 거죠. [1] 하지만 말해줄 수 있어요? 혹시 그런 프로그램을 가르치는 데 관심이 있나요?

1. 교수는 왜 학생을 보고자 했는가?

Ⓐ 학생의 다음 학기 스케줄을 논의하기 위해
Ⓑ 수학 교사가 되기 위해 더 열심히 공부하라고 말하기 위해
Ⓒ 수학 교육 센터에서 자원 봉사자로 일하라고 설득하기 위해
Ⓓ 내년에 더 많은 선택 과목을 들으라고 학생을 장려하기 위해

해설 학생이 교수가 왜 자신의 스케줄에 관해 궁금해 하는지를 묻자 교수가 '물론이죠'라고 대답하며 야간 수학 프로그램 이야기를 꺼낸다. 그리고 대화 마지막 부분에도 학생에게 직접 가르치는 일에 관심이 있는지 물었으므로 정답은 (C)이다. 한편, 'volunteer'라는 단어를 사용하여 수학 프로그램을 가르치는 일을 패러프레이즈했다는 점을 눈여겨보자.

2. 대화에 의하면, 학교의 야간 수학 프로그램에 대해 옳은 것은 무엇인가?

Ⓐ 보통 국립 대학에서 진행된다.
Ⓑ 고등학생들과 성인들에게 수학을 가르친다.
Ⓒ 수학을 매우 잘 하는 학생들을 받아들인다.
Ⓓ 1학년생들을 위한 수학 입문 수업이다.

해설 학생이 먼저 '고등학교 때 들었다'고 밝혔고, 뒤에 교수가 '수학 능력이 부족하다고 느끼는 성인들을 위해 만들어진 프로그램'이라고 설명했으므로, 정답은 (B)이다. 교수가 야간 수학 프로그램에 관해 설명하기 시작할 때부터 이 프로그램의 특징을 노트 필기해 두는 것이 큰 도움이 된다.

어휘 interfere **v** 방해하다, 간섭하다 | ahead of ~앞에, ~보다 빨리 | elective **n** 선택 과목, 교양 과목 | mandatory **adj** 필수의 | familiar **adj** 익숙한, 친숙한 | take part in ~에 참가하다 | enroll **v** 등록하다, 명부에 올리다 | pursue **v** 추구하다 | doctorate **n** 박사 학위 | physics **n** 물리학 | impress **v** 깊은 인상을 주다 | advanced **adj** 고급의, 상급의 | drop out 중도 하차하다 | remedial **adj** 보충하는, 개선하는 | aim **v** ~을 목표로 하다 | intend **v** 의도하다, 생각하다 | rightly **adv** 당연히, 마땅히

Practice

Passage 1 Listen to part of a conversation between a student and a professor. C02_P01

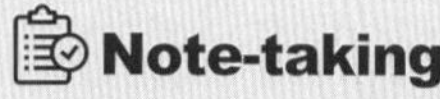

Q. What will the woman do a presentation on?

Ⓐ Reasons that the war was fought

Ⓑ The beginning of the American Civil War

Ⓒ Why poor Southerners opposed the war

Ⓓ The experiences of African American soldiers

Passage 2 Listen to part of a conversation between a student and a professor. C02_P02

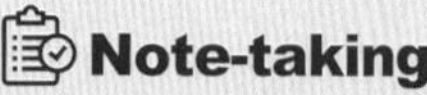

Q. What document does the man need to get?

Ⓐ A copy of his transcript

Ⓑ A letter of recommendation

Ⓒ A certificate of his language ability

Ⓓ An essay written in French

정답 및 해석 | P. 31

Passage 3 Listen to part of a conversation between a student and a university employee. C02_P03

Q. What does the woman want to do?

Ⓐ Get a refund for a course

Ⓑ Drop a class she cannot handle

Ⓒ Add a class to her schedule

Ⓓ Look up her grade point average

Passage 4 Listen to part of a conversation between a student and a professor.

Q. What does the man need to do first?

Ⓐ Visit an art exhibition

Ⓑ Write a report

Ⓒ Locate a partner to work with

Ⓓ Select a destination

Lesson

03 Function & Attitude

Lesson Outline

의도 및 태도 파악 문제(Function & Attitude Question)는 화자의 말이나 표현에 집중해야 한다. 의도 파악(Function) 문제의 경우 화자가 어떤 말을 한 목적과 그 말 속에 내재된 숨은 의도를 파악해야 하며, 주로 짧은 구간을 다시 들려주고 문제를 푸는 방식으로 출제된다. 태도 파악(Attitude) 문제는 화자의 태도와 감정, 또는 확신하는 정도를 파악하는 문제가 출제된다.

Lesson Point

Point 1 직역보다는 지문의 문맥이나 화자의 말투 또는 억양을 통해 파악한다.

Point 2 다시 들려줄 때도 있지만 기억력에 의존해 풀어야 하는 경우가 많으니 주의하자!

Point 3 다시 들었던 표현이 선택지에 그대로 나오는 경우 오답일 확률이 높다.

Point 4 생소한 표현은 반드시 정리 및 숙지한다.

Point 5 노트 필기보다는 글의 흐름과 이야기하는 사람들의 분위기, 그리고 속뜻을 파악하는 것이 중요하다.

Typical Questions

의도 파악(Function)

- Listen again to part of the conversation. Then answer the question. Why does the student say this: — 대화의 일부를 다시 듣고 질문에 답하시오. 학생은 왜 이렇게 말하는가:
- Listen again to part of the conversation. Then answer the question. What does the student mean when he/she says this: — 대화의 일부를 다시 듣고 질문에 답하시오. 학생은 다음과 같이 말하며 무엇을 의미하는가:

태도 파악(Attitude)

- What is the man's attitude toward ~? — ~에 관한 남자의 태도는 어떠한가?
- What is the student's opinion about ~? — ~에 관한 학생의 의견은 무엇인가?

Learning Strategies

의도 및 태도 파악 빈출 표현

의도·태도 파악 문제와 관련하여 대화에 자주 등장하는 표현들을 알아두자.

'동의함' 관련 표현

- You can say that again! — 정말 그래요! (=전적으로 동의해요)
- You can't be more right about that. — 정말 맞는 말이에요. (=이보다 더 맞는 말을 할 수는 없을 거예요.)
- You are on the right track. — 잘하고 있어요. (=옳은 방향으로 나아가고 있어요.)
- You hit the nail on the head. — 정곡을 찔렀네요.
- Let me elaborate on that a little. — 거기에 대해서 내가 좀 더 자세히 설명할게요.

'동의하지 않음' 관련 표현

- You've got to be kidding me. — 농담하시는 거죠?
- I doubt that ~. — ~할/~일 것 같지 않아요.
- That may be true, but ~. — 그게 사실일 수도 있는데요. 그런데 ~

'혼란스러움' 관련 표현

- I'm not sure I understand the problem. — 제가 그 문제에 대해 제대로 이해한 건지 모르겠네요.
- I didn't know such a thing even existed! — 그런 게 있는지도 몰랐어요!
- It just doesn't make sense. — 이건 그냥 말이 안 돼요.

'불확실함' 관련 표현

- I'm not so sure about that. — 거기에 대해서는 잘 모르겠어요. (=확신할 수 없어요.)
- You can't be serious. — 그럴 리가요. (=정말 진심은 아니겠지.)
- Are you sure? — 확실해요?

Example

Man: Professor | Woman: Student

C03_EX

Listen to part of a conversation between a student and a professor.

W Hello, Professor Buelle.

M Good morning, Lucy. Have a seat. I just wanted to know how you are doing with preparations for your performance coming along?

W Pretty well, I guess. I didn't realize how hard it can be to choreograph a ten-minute performance alone.

M [1] Yes, it can be a lot of work. It takes commitment—a lot of commitment in terms of time and effort. Which dancer are you basing your performance on, if you don't mind my asking?

W [1] I don't mind. Um, I am creating a performance in the style of Isadora Duncan.

M Oh really? Then I think I can see why you are having a difficult time with it. Duncan was a pioneer of dance. Some even call her the creator of modern dance.

W Yes, she has a unique style that is definitely true. With ballet, the movements are so rigid and precise, but her dancing flowed. The movements were so much more natural.

M Indeed, that was an important part of her philosophy of dance. She took much of her inspiration from ancient Greece and combined it with her sense of freedom. Some critics referred to it as her "American love of freedom," but her work was not very well received in America. Most of her fame came in Europe, which is also where she established her schools.

W Right, and her love of Greece made the costume at least easy. She usually wore a tunic reminiscent of ancient Greek clothing. It is fairly easy to make, and it allows for so much more range of movement than a corseted ballet outfit.

M Yes, her style of dress had many benefits. [2] Have you done any research about Isadora's life? It is important to understand an artist's experiences and motivation if you want to accurately emulate their style.

1. Listen again to part of the conversation. Then answer the question.

Why does the student say this:

Ⓐ She does not know what to say about the professor's previous comment.

Ⓑ She is okay with the professor checking the progress of her project.

Ⓒ She is annoyed by the fact that the professor is pressuring her.

Ⓓ She still has not decided what to do with her performance theme.

2. What is the professor's opinion about understanding an artist?

Ⓐ He sees that it will allow the student to achieve better grades on her performance.

Ⓑ He feels that it can explain how the artist came up with such choreography.

Ⓒ He thinks it helps one to imitate the artist's style and performance better.

Ⓓ He believes that it inspires one to create more radical and innovative styles.

학생과 교수의 대화를 들으시오.

여 안녕하세요, 뷰엘 교수님.

남 안녕하세요, 루시. 자리에 앉아요. 공연 준비는 어떻게 되고 있는지 알고 싶어서요.

여 잘 되고 있는 것 같아요. 10분짜리 공연의 안무를 혼자 짠다는 것이 얼마나 어려운 건지 깨닫지 못했어요.

남 [1] 그래요, 매우 할 일이 많죠. 헌신이 필요해요. 시간과 정성 면에서 말이죠. 물어봐도 괜찮다면, 어떤 무용수에 기반을 두고 공연을 작업하고 있나요?

여 [1] 물어보셔도 괜찮습니다. 음, 이사도라 던컨의 스타일로 공연을 만들고 있어요.

남 오, 그래요? 그러면 왜 학생이 어려워하고 있는지 알 것 같네요. 던컨은 춤의 선구자였어요. 어떤 이들은 심지어 그녀를 현대 무용의 선구자라고 부르기도 하죠.

여 맞아요. 그녀는 분명히 진정하고 참신한 스타일을 갖고 있어요. 발레의 경우 움직임이 뻣뻣하고 정확하지만 그녀의 춤은 흐르는 듯했어요. 움직임이 훨씬 더 자연스러웠죠.

남 정말 그래요. 그녀가 가진 춤에 대한 철학의 중요한 부분이었죠. 던컨은 고대 그리스에서 많은 영감을 받았고 그것을 자유에 대한 그녀의 감각과 결합시켰어요. 어떤 비평가들은 그것을 그녀의 "자유에 대한 미국식 사랑"이라고 불렀지만 그녀의 작품은 미국에서 큰 호응을 얻지 못했어요. 명성의 대부분은 유럽에서 얻었는데, 이곳에 그녀는 학교들도 세웠죠.

여 네, 그리고 그리스에 대한 그녀의 사랑은 의상을 적어도 편하게 만들었어요. 그녀는 보통 고대 그리스의 옷을 연상시키는 튜닉을 입었죠. 꽤 만들기 쉬울 뿐 아니라 코르셋을 입어야 하는 발레 의상보다 훨씬 더 넓은 범위의 움직임을 가능하게 했어요.

남 네, 그녀의 드레스 스타일은 많은 이점이 있었죠. [2] 이사도라의 삶에 대해서도 조사해 봤나요? 예술가들의 스타일을 정확히 모방하고 싶다면 그들의 경험과 동기 부여를 이해하는 것이 중요해요.

1. 대화의 일부를 다시 듣고 질문에 답하시오.

> 남 그래요, 매우 할 일이 많죠. 헌신이 필요해요. 시간과 정성 면에서 말이죠. 물어봐도 괜찮다면, 어떤 무용수에 기반을 두고 공연을 작업하고 있나요?
>
> 여 물어보셔도 괜찮습니다.

학생은 왜 이렇게 말하는가:

> 여 물어보셔도 괜찮습니다.

Ⓐ 교수가 방금 말한 것에 대해 어떻게 대답해야 할지 모른다.

Ⓑ 교수가 그녀의 프로젝트가 어떻게 진행되고 있는지 확인하는 것이 괜찮다.

Ⓒ 교수가 그녀를 재촉한다는 사실에 짜증이 났다.

Ⓓ 공연의 주제를 어떻게 해야 할지 여전히 결정하지 못했다.

해설 학생이 왜 이 말을 했는지에 대한 이유를 묻는 의도 파악 문제이므로 대화의 맥락을 파악해야 한다. 교수가 학생에게 공연 준비에 대해 물으며 어떤 무용수에 기반을 두고 작업하고 있는지 '물어봐도 괜찮으냐(if you don't mind ~?)'고 했고, 학생은 '신경 쓰지 않습니다(=괜찮습니다)', 즉 물어봐도 괜찮다고 대답한 것이므로 학생은 교수가 자신의 프로젝트 진행 상황을 확인해도 신경 쓰지 않음을 알 수 있다. 정답은 (B)이다.

2. 예술가를 이해하는 것에 대한 교수의 의견은 어떠한가?

Ⓐ 학생이 그녀의 공연에서 더 좋은 성적을 내도록 도와줄 것이라고 본다.

Ⓑ 어떻게 예술가가 이러한 안무를 창조해냈는지 설명해줄 수 있다고 느낀다.

Ⓒ 예술가의 스타일과 공연을 더 잘 모방하도록 도와준다고 생각한다.

Ⓓ 더 극단적이고 혁신적인 스타일을 창조하도록 영감을 준다고 믿는다.

해설 상황이나 문제에 대한 화자의 의견·태도를 파악하는 태도 파악 문제이므로 화자가 대상에 관해 어떤 태도와 관점을 가졌는지 알아야 한다. 대화의 맨 마지막 부분을 보면 교수가 학생에게 '예술가의 스타일을 정확히 모방하고 싶다면 그의 경험과 동기 부여를 이해하는 것이 중요합니다'라고 했으므로 예술가를 이해하는 것이 스타일을 모방하는 데 도움을 준다고 생각하고 있음을 알 수 있다. 즉 교수는 예술가를 이해하면 스타일과 공연을 더 잘 따라 할 수 있다고 보고 있으므로 정답은 (C)이다.

어휘 choreograph v 안무를 하다 | definitely adv 분명히, 틀림없이 | rigid adj 뻣뻣한 | philosophy n 철학 | inspiration n 영감 | fame n 명성 | tunic n 튜닉(고대 그리스나 로마인들이 입던 헐렁한 웃옷) | reminiscent adj 연상시키는 | corseted adj 코르셋을 입은 | emulate v 모방하다, 따라 하다

Practice

Passage 1 Listen to part of a conversation between a student and a librarian. C03_P01

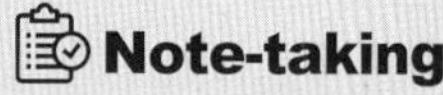

Q. What does the woman mean when she says this:

Ⓐ The librarian should not bother the student.

Ⓑ The student still has much information to find.

Ⓒ Certain materials cannot be removed from the library.

Ⓓ The copier may damage the books if she uses it.

Passage 2 Listen to part of a conversation between a student and a professor. C03_P02

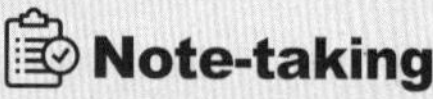

Q. Why does the professor say this:

Ⓐ To indicate that the student should change her topic

Ⓑ To emphasize the importance of regular attendance

Ⓒ To suggest that the student wrote her paper incorrectly

Ⓓ To express concern about the student's performance

Passage 3 Listen to part of a conversation between a student DJ and a radio director.

C03_P03

Q. What is the woman's attitude about her responsibilities?

Ⓐ She thinks that some tasks are tedious.

Ⓑ She wants the rules to be made clearer.

Ⓒ She is ignoring the man's suggestions.

Ⓓ She feels the changes are unnecessary.

Passage 4 Listen to part of a conversation between a student and a manager.

C03_P04

Q. What is the woman's opinion of the man's request?

Ⓐ She thinks that it is completely unreasonable.

Ⓑ She wants to help him, but the rules do not allow it.

Ⓒ She believes that she may be able to accommodate him.

Ⓓ She feels that he should be more considerate of other students.

Lesson

04 Connecting Contents

Lesson Outline

관계 파악 문제(Connecting Contents Question)는 지문의 정보가 서로 어떻게 관련되었는지 묻는 문제이다. 대화에서 아예 나오지 않을 때도 있으나 보통 1개가 출제된다. 주로 어떤 내용이 왜 언급되었는지 묻는 문제가 많이 나오지만, 짝이나 순서 맞추기 문제가 출제되기도 한다.

Lesson Point

Point 1 전체 흐름을 통해 전반적인 구조를 파악하는 문제 유형

Ex How is the conversation organized?

···› 초반부와 중반부의 구조를 파악한다!

Point 2 특정 정보를 강조한 후, 그 정보의 역할을 묻는 문제 유형

Ex Why does the professor mention ~?

···› 해당 특정 정보의 구조적 성격을 파악한다!

Typical Questions

언급 이유

- Why does the professor say ~? 교수는 왜 ~라고 말하는가?
- Why does the student mention ~? 학생은 왜 ~를 언급하는가?

짝 맞추기

- In the conversation, the speakers discuss ~. Indicate in the table below ~.
  대화에서 화자들은 ~에 대해 논의한다. ~인지 아래 표에 표시하시오.

	Category A	Category B
Characteristic 1		
Characteristic 2		
Characteristic 3		

순서 맞추기

- Put the following steps in order. 다음 단계들을 순서에 맞게 배열하시오.

Step 1	
Step 2	
Step 3	

Learning Strategies

1 내용의 흐름을 파악한다.

대화에서 지문의 요점은 다음과 같은 방식으로 전개된다.

▶ **유형 1** ① 문제 제기 ···› ② 문제 세부 설명 ···› ③ 해결책 제시

▶ **유형 2** ① 불만 제기 ···› ② 불만 세부 설명 ···› ③ 관련 인물의 사과 또는 해결책 제시

▶ **유형 3** ① 건의 사항 제시 ···› ② 세부 설명 ···› ③ 관련 인물의 동의 또는 거절

▶ **유형 4** ① 학생이 교수에게 질문 제시 ···› ② 수업 관련 내용 언급 ···› ③ 교수의 답변

▶ **유형 5** ① 교수가 학생을 부름 ···› ② 수업 관련 내용 언급 ···› ③ 함께 과제나 그 외의 해결책 논의

2 특정 정보를 사용한 의도를 파악한다.

특정 문장이나 내용의 역할을 파악할 때 주로 등장하는 표시어를 알아두면 도움이 된다.

주제 소개

- I came here to discuss ~. ~에 대해 논의하러 왔어요.
- I have a question about ~. ~에 대해 질문이 있어요.
- I'm having a problem with ~. ~에 문제가 있어요.
- The reason why I came here is because ~. 제가 여기 온 이유는 ~이에요.

예시

- Let's imagine ~. ~라고 상상해 봐요.
- Let's look at it this way: 이렇게 생각해 보세요.
- Let's suppose ~. ~라고 가정해 봐요.
- I can give you an example about ~. ~에 대한 예시를 드릴 수 있어요.

여담

- Incidentally, 그건 그렇고,
- As far as I remember, 제가 기억하기로는,
- That reminds me of ~. 그건 ~를 떠올리게 하네요.
- By the way, I have experienced ~. 그나저나, 저는 ~를 경험했어요.

결론

- Thank you, I will go there right now. 고맙습니다. 지금 바로 거기로 갈게요.
- Let me [get/print] this material for you. 제가 이 자료를 [갖다 드릴게요/출력해 드릴게요].
- Can I get his/her contact information? 그 사람의 연락처를 알 수 있을까요?
- I really appreciate your help. 도와주셔서 정말 고마워요.

Example

Man: Professor | **Woman:** Student

C04_EX

Listen to part of a conversation between a student and a professor.

W Hello, Professor Carter. I came to see you because of the article you assigned for us to read about Francis Bacon. A few questions came into my mind while I was reading it. You referred to him as the "father of the scientific method," didn't you?

M Actually, I was quoting Voltaire. Bacon is widely regarded as the creator of the modern approach to science, though. He did not formulate the scientific method as we know it today, but he placed great importance on inductive reasoning. He argued that knowledge must be based upon our observations of the natural world.

W Scientists didn't observe things before him?

M Of course they did, but the fundamental basis for their knowledge and reasoning was flawed. They believed that the senses and the human mind were imperfect, which made them unreliable. He agreed with them on that basic point, but he also realized that our flawed senses were our only tools with which to make any sense of the world. So, he said that we must doubt everything until we can prove it is true. [1] We should never assume that something is true.

W [1] That sounds logical. How did people arrive at conclusions before that?

M [1] Largely by deductive reasoning—what is referred to as syllogism. They also relied upon classical texts, like those of Aristotle and the other ancient Greek philosophers.

W [1] Wait, what is syllogism? That sounds familiar....

1. Why does the professor mention syllogisms?

(A) To give an example of the modern decision-making method

(B) To criticize the student for missing too many class sessions recently

(C) To explain the method people used in the past to arrive at conclusions

(D) To suggest the student use it as well when she conducts her own experiment

M [1] I should hope so. It was mentioned in class before, after all. A syllogism is a logical argument that is based upon two or more statements that are generally agreed to be correct. As in Aristotle's classic example: "All men are mortal. Socrates is a man. Therefore, Socrates is mortal."

W Yes, I remember that. But, that isn't necessarily true, right? I mean, that statement is, but other such arguments may not be.

M Correct. So, [2] Bacon did not like this type of deductive reasoning. Logical proof was not enough, and observation was key. So, he said that you must observe, and then experiment. He insisted that scientists must manipulate nature in order to test their hypothesis, but not to prove themselves right. Their goal should be to prove their ideas wrong. They must always doubt what they think they know.

W Can you give me an example?

M People had no idea where diseases really came from. So, Bacon advised scientists to expose healthy people to all of the outside influences that they thought might cause disease: cold, dampness, smells, etc. If one of these got someone sick, then they should repeat the experiment again and again, until it was established that this was a likely cause. When enough scientists reached the same conclusion independently, then it could be considered a truth.

W That sounds like a lot to understand. Anyways, thank you for your help, professor. I'll go and read the article more thoroughly.

2. In the conversation, the speakers discuss Francis Bacon and his theories. Indicate in the table below whether each of the following is one of his theories.

Click in the correct box for each sentence.

	Yes	No
(A) Experiment is more important than observation.		
(B) Proving a hypothesis is deeply related to nature.		
(C) Observation is required for deductive reasoning.		
(D) A person needs to doubt even proved hypothesis.		

학생과 교수의 대화를 들으시오.

여 안녕하세요, 카터 교수님. 프랜시스 베이컨에 대해 읽으라고 정리해주신 자료 때문에 왔습니다. 읽다가 몇 가지 질문이 생겼거든요. 교수님께서는 베이컨을 '과학적 방법의 아버지'라고 하셨어요, 그렇죠?

남 사실, 나는 볼테르가 한 말을 인용한 겁니다. 베이컨은 과학에 대한 현대적 접근법의 창시자로 널리 인정받고 있어요. 오늘날 우리가 아는 과학적 방법을 만든 것은 아니지만, 그는 귀납적 추리에 큰 중요성을 두었어요. 그는 지식이 우리의 자연 세계 관찰에 기반을 두어야 한다고 주장했죠.

여 베이컨 이전의 과학자들은 사물을 관찰하지 않았나요?

남 물론 했지만, 그들의 지식과 추리의 근본적 기반에 결함이 있었어요. 그들은 감각과 인간의 생각이 불완전하다고 믿었기 때문에 그것을 신뢰할 수 없었어요. 베이컨은 그들의 그러한 기본적 요점에는 동의했지만 세계를 어떻게든 이해하기 위해서는 우리의 불완전한 감각이 우리가 사용할 수 있는 유일한 도구라는 것을 깨달았습니다. 그래서 그는 어떠한 것을 사실이라고 증명할 수 있을 때까지 모든 것을 의심해야 한다고 주장했죠. [1] 무언가가 진실이라고 가정해서는 절대 안 된다는 겁니다.

여 [1] 논리적으로 들리네요. 그 전에는 사람들이 어떻게 결론을 내렸나요?

남 [1] 대개 연역적 추리로요. 삼단 논법이라고 불리죠. 그리고 아리스토텔레스나 다른 고대 그리스 철학자들의 고문서에 의지하기도 했어요.

여 [1] 잠깐만요, 삼단 논법이 무엇인가요? 들어본 것 같은데요....

남 [1] 그랬기를 바라요. 전에 수업에서 언급한 것이니까요. 삼단 논법은 일반적으로 옳다고 동의한 두 개 이상의 주장에 기반한 하나의 논리적인 주장입니다. 아리스토텔레스의 고전적 예시를 들면, "모든 인간은 죽는다. 소크라테스는 인간이다. 그러므로 소크라테스 역시 죽는다."

여 네, 기억해요. 하지만 그게 진짜로 맞지는 않잖아요, 그렇죠? 제 말은, 방금 이야기하신 건 맞지만, 다른 주장들은 맞지 않을 수도 있어요.

남 그렇습니다. 그래서 [2] 베이컨은 이러한 연역적 추리를 좋아하지 않았어요. 논리적 증명은 충분하지 않았으며 관찰이 열쇠였습니다. 그래서 그는 우리가 관찰을 하고 난 뒤에 실험해야 한다고 말했죠. 과학자들은 자신이 옳다는 것을 증명하기 위해서가 아니라, 가설을 시험하기 위해 자연을 조종해야 한다고 주장했습니다. 과학자들의 목표는 그들의 생각이 틀렸다는 것을 증명하는 것이어야 한다는 거죠. 그들이 안다고 생각하는 것을 항상 의심해야 했습니다.

여 예시를 들어주실 수 있나요?

남 사람들은 질병이 어디에서 오는 것인지 전혀 알지 못했습니다. 그래서 베이컨은 과학자들에게 그들이 생각하는 '병을 초래할 수 있는 외적 영향'에 건강한 사람들을 노출시키도록 조언했죠. 추위, 습기, 냄새 등등 말이에요. 만약 이들 중 하나가 누군가를 아프게 만들었다면 그 실험을 몇 번이고 다시 반복했습니다. 이것이 가능한 원인일 수도 있다는 것이 정립될 때까지요. 충분한 수의 과학자들이 독립적으로 같은 결론에 이르렀을 때 이것은 사실로 여겨질 수 있는 겁니다.

여 이해할 것이 참 많은 것 같네요. 어쨌든 도와주셔서 감사합니다, 교수님. 가서 그 자료를 더 철저히 읽어볼게요.

1. 교수는 왜 삼단 논법을 언급하는가?

Ⓐ 현대의 의사 결정 방법의 한 예시를 들기 위해

Ⓑ 최근 학생이 수업에 너무 많이 빠진 것을 지적하기 위해

Ⓒ 결론에 도달하기 위해 과거의 사람들이 사용했던 방법을 설명하기 위해

Ⓓ 학생이 실험을 할 때에도 삼단 논법을 써 보도록 제안하기 위해

해설 교수가 무언가를 언급한 이유를 묻는 문제이므로 앞뒤 맥락을 살펴보자. 학생이 "그 전에는 사람들이 어떻게 결론을 내렸나요?"라고 묻자 교수가 "대개 연역적 추리로요. 삼단 논법이라고 불리죠."라고 대답한다. 과거의 사람들이 이용한 방법을 물은 것이기 때문에 (C)가 정답이다.

2. 대화에서 화자들은 프랜시스 베이컨과 그의 이론들을 논의한다. 다음 각 사항이 그의 이론인지 아닌지를 아래 표에 표시하시오.

각 문장에 대해 맞는 칸에 표시하시오.

	Yes	No
Ⓐ 실험이 관찰보다 더 중요하다.		✓
Ⓑ 가설을 증명하는 것은 자연과 깊이 관련되어 있다.	✓	
Ⓒ 관찰은 연역적 추리에 반드시 필요하다.		✓
Ⓓ 사람은 심지어 증명된 가설도 의심해봐야 한다.		✓

해설 교수가 프랜시스 베이컨에 관해 설명하고, 그 설명이 옳은 내용인지를 가려내는 문제이다. 두 번째 주장을 보면 베이컨이 "가설을 시험하기 위해 자연을 조종해야 한다고 주장했다"는 교수의 설명과 부합하므로 Yes이다. 나머지 주장은 교수의 설명과 일치하지 않으므로 모두 No다.

어휘 assign v 맡기다, 배정하다 | scientific adj 과학의, 과학적인 | method n 방법 | approach n 접근법, 접근 | formulate v 만들어내다; 표현하다 | inductive reasoning 귀납적 추리 | argue v 주장하다 | observation n 관찰 | fundamental adj 근본적인 | flawed adj 결함이 있는 | imperfect adj 불완전한 | unreliable adj 신뢰할 수 없는 | prove v 증명하다, 입증하다 | logical adj 논리적인 | conclusion n 결론, 판단 | deductive reasoning 연역적 추리 | syllogism n 삼단 논법 | classical text 고문서 | philosopher n 철학자 | familiar adj 익숙한 | argument n 주장 | statement n 진술, 의견(주장) | generally adv 일반적으로 | mortal adj 유한한 생명의, 언젠가는 반드시 죽는 | proof n 증거 | experiment v 실험하다 | insist v 주장하다, 고집하다 | manipulate v 조종하다, 조작하다 | hypothesis n 가설, 추정 | doubt v 의심하다 | disease n 질병 | expose v 노출시키다 | influence n 영향 | dampness n 습기, 눅눅함 | establish v 정립하다, 수립하다 | independently adv 독립적으로 | thoroughly adv 철저히

Practice

Passage 1 Listen to part of a conversation between a student and a professor. C04_P01

1. In the conversation, the speakers discuss the requirements of a research paper. Indicate in the table below which of the requirements apply to the student's assignment.

Click in the correct box for each phrase.

	Yes	No
Ⓐ Conduct research at the library on Childhood Behavioral Development		
Ⓑ Make predictions about behavioral patterns that may arise		
Ⓒ Locate children to participate in the behavioral study		
Ⓓ Observe the test subjects to see if their behavior corresponds with research		

2. Why does the professor mention the assistant in the psychology department?

Ⓐ To express how annoyed he is by the student's attitude
Ⓑ To direct the student to someone else who can provide help
Ⓒ To show the student the first step for starting her assignment
Ⓓ To tell the student that he needs to help someone else right now

Passage 2 Listen to part of a conversation between a student and a university employee.

C04_P02

1. In the conversation, the speakers discuss the process by which documents may be obtained. Indicate in the table below whether each of the following is indicated about that process. Click in the correct box for each sentence.

	Yes	No
(A) The person must come to the university in person.		
(B) There is a limit to the number of documents that can be obtained.		
(C) The person must present a valid identification card.		
(D) The transcripts take a week to process.		
(E) The person may access the documents on the university website.		

2. Why does the man mention a fellow alumnus?

(A) To tell the woman that she misunderstood him
(B) To show the woman has wrong information
(C) To ask the woman to make an exception
(D) To persuade the woman that she could be wrong

Lesson

05 Inference

Lesson Outline

추론 문제(Inference Question)는 하나의 정보를 토대로 답을 찾는 것이 아니라, 지문에서 주어진 여러 정보 간의 관계에 대해 답하거나 그 정보를 기반으로 추론하는 문제이다. 대화에서 따로 언급되지는 않았지만 대화의 내용과 맥락을 통해 유추·추론할 수 있는 사실을 묻는다.

Lesson Point

Point 1 5개 문제 유형 중 최고난도의 문제 유형!

Point 2 문제에 imply, infer, next, result, cause, conclude 등의 단어가 있으면 추론 문제!

Point 3 들은 것 또는 노트 필기한 것을 바탕으로 제시된 정보의 특징을 추론 또는 유추한다.

Point 4 보기에서 키워드가 패러프레이징 된 것을 찾으면 정답!

Typical Questions

- What is the student most likely to do next? 학생이 다음에 무엇을 할 것 같은가?
- What does the student imply about ~? 학생은 ~에 관해 무엇을 암시하는가?
- What can be inferred about the woman? 여자에 대해 무엇을 추론할 수 있는가?
- What can be inferred from the student's situation? 학생의 상황으로부터 무엇을 추론할 수 있는가?
- What can be concluded about ~? ~에 관해 어떤 결론을 내릴 수 있는가?

Learning Strategies

대화 주제의 특징을 나타내는 표시어(signal)를 공략한다!

주제의 주요 특징 및 예시에 관해 유추·추론하는 문제가 나오므로, 주제의 특징과 관련된 원인, 문제, 해결책 등을 나타내는 표시어를 중심으로 노트 필기하며 듣는다.

원인

- It all started with ~. 모든 일은 ~로부터 시작되었어요.
- It happened because ~. ~때문에/~해서 생긴 일이에요.
- I did X and Y happened ~. 제가 X했는데 Y가 되었어요(발생했어요).
- I had to do X because ~. ~때문에/~해서 제가 X해야만 했어요.

문제

- I have a problem with X, so I came to ~. X로 인한 문제가 있어서, ~하러 왔어요.
- I could not do X, so ~. X할 수가 없어서 ~해요.
- I am concerned because ~. ~때문에/~해서 걱정이 돼요.
- The thing is, I ~. 사실, 저는 ~.
- I have to tell you that ~. ~라는 것을 말씀드려야겠네요.
- It seems that ~ is a problem. ~가 문제인 것 같아요.

해결책

- What about ~? ~는/~하는 건 어떨까요?
- Why don't you ~? ~하는 게 어때요?
- If I were you, I would ~. 제가 당신이라면, ~하겠어요.
- I had the same problem, I did ~. 저도 똑같은 문제를 겪었는데, 저는 ~했어요.
- I want to suggest doing ~. ~해 보시라고 말씀 드리고 싶어요.

Example

Man: Student | Woman: Professor

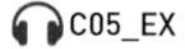

Listen to part of a conversation between a student and a professor.

M Excuse me, Professor Zhang. Can I bother you for a minute?

W Come in, Joel. Of course you can. What can I help you with? I'm sure it's no bother.

M [1] Well, the council has decided that they want to invite a band to play at our fall festival.

W [1] That sounds like a good idea to me. In fact, don't they usually have some musical entertainment?

M [1] Yes, they do. But, it's usually local bands—student bands actually—that play at the festival. But, the vice president's cousin is in a band whose career is just starting to take off, so we decided to invite them to play.

W Again, that sounds like a good idea. Is there a problem?

M Unfortunately, there is. They are eager to play here, and they are going to be on a break during their tour at the time. But, they would need us to pay their expenses. The treasurer said that we would have to have a fundraiser to earn the money.

W Do you have any ideas as to what kind of fundraiser you want to organize?

M So far, the best solution we have been able to come up with is a carwash. People always have cars that need to be washed.

W That is true, but it isn't going to raise much money. You cannot charge much, and there are only so many cars that you can wash in one day. How about you hold an auction? You can publicize your event and make money at the same time.

M An auction? What could we auction off?

1. What can be inferred about the university's fall festival?

Ⓐ It features some kind of music performance every year.

Ⓑ It has many different types of entertainment including auctions.

Ⓒ It helped a few local bands to gain popularity.

Ⓓ It holds an annual auction to raise money for the musicians.

2. What will the student most likely do next?

Ⓐ Call local stores and museums to ask for their help

Ⓑ Fill out an application form to participate in the auction event

Ⓒ Meet Professor Singh to persuade her to become his advisor

Ⓓ Contact Professor Zhang's friend to ask detailed questions

W Well, anything really. You can go around to local businesses and ask them for products to auction. You can also go to libraries and museums. As long as you endorse them during the auction—you know, say which company donated the item and praise them—most businesses will happily donate something. It's a very inexpensive form of advertising for them. Since people will be trying to outbid each other, you should be able to make money fairly quickly.

M That sounds like a great idea, but where would we host such an event?

W You just need an empty lecture hall. Those rooms can hold quite a few people, and they already have AV systems installed.

M You seem to know a lot about this. Have you ever organized an auction before?

W No, [2] not personally, but a colleague of mine organized one at Crichton College last year. They were able to raise enough money to fund two events.

M [2] OK, I will propose this at the next council meeting, which is tonight. Could you put me in touch with your colleague?

W [2] Certainly. Her name is Professor Rhona Singh. She is a tenured professor at Crichton. I have one of her business cards right here.

M Thank you for all of your help, Professor Zhang.

학생과 교수의 대화를 들으시오.

남 실례합니다, 장 교수님, 잠시 시간을 내주실 수 있으세요?

여 들어와요, 조엘. 물론 가능하죠. 어떻게 도와줄까요? 귀찮은 일이 아닐 거라고 확신해요.

남 [1] 음, 위원회에서는 우리 학교의 가을 축제에 공연해줄 밴드를 초청하기로 결정했어요.

여 [1] 좋은 생각 같네요. 사실 항상 음악 공연이 있지 않나요?

남 [1] 네, 맞아요. 하지만 축제에서 공연했던 건 보통 지역 밴드, 사실 학생 밴드였어요. 그렇지만 부회장의 사촌이 이제 막 잘 나가기 시작한 밴드의 멤버여서 그 밴드를 초대하기로 결정했어요.

여 다시 말하지만 좋은 생각이에요. 문제가 있나요?

남 불행히도 있습니다. 그 밴드 역시 우리 학교 축제에서 공연하고 싶어 하고, 그 시기에 공연 투어를 잠시 쉬거든요. 그렇지만 비용을 우리가 내주길 원해요. 회계 담당자분이 그 돈을 벌기 위해 저희가 모금 행사를 해야 할 거라고 말하더군요.

여 어떤 종류의 모금 행사를 조직할지 생각한 게 있나요?

남 저희가 지금까지 생각해낸 것들 중 가장 좋은 해결책은 세차였어요. 사람들은 항상 세차를 필요로 하니까요.

여 맞아요. 하지만 많은 돈을 벌진 못할 거예요. 세차에 많은 비용을 청구할 수도 없고, 그리고 하루에 세차를 할 수 있는 차 역시 한정되어 있으니까요. 경매를 개최하는 건 어때요? 학교 축제를 알리고 동시에 돈도 벌 수 있잖아요.

남 경매요? 저희가 경매에 무엇을 내놓을 수 있을까요?

여 음, 사실 아무 거나요. 지역의 사업체들을 돌아다니면서 경매에 내놓을 물건을 요청할 수 있어요. 도서관이나 박물관에 갈 수도 있죠. 학생이 경매 중간에 이 사업체들을 홍보해주기만 한다면, 즉 어떤 회사에서 이 물건을 내놓았는지 말하고 그 회사를 칭찬한다면, 대부분의 사업체들에서 기쁘게 무언가를 기부할 거예요. 그들에게 있어 매우 값싼 방식의 광고니까요. 사람들이 서로를 이기려고 금액을 부를 테니, 돈을 꽤 빨리 벌 수 있죠.

남 정말 좋은 생각이네요. 하지만 이런 행사를 어디서 열 수 있나요?

여 그저 빈 강당만 하나 있으면 돼요. 그런 강당은 꽤 많은 수의 사람을 수용할 수 있고, 이미 시청각 시스템이 설치되어 있으니까요.

남 경매에 대해 아시는 게 많은 것 같네요. 전에도 경매를 주관해 본 적이 있으세요?

여 아니에요. [2] 개인적으로 해 본 적은 없지만 동료 교수가 작년에 크라이튼 대학에서 경매를 주관했어요. 두 개의 행사에 자금을 댈 수 있을 정도로 충분한 돈을 모았죠.

남 [2] 알겠습니다. 오늘 밤에 있는 위원회 회의에서 경매를 제안해 볼게요. 동료분의 연락처를 가르쳐주실 수 있으신가요?

1. 대학의 가을 축제에 관해 무엇을 추론할 수 있는가?

Ⓐ 매년 어떠한 종류의 음악 공연이 있는 것이 특징이다.

Ⓑ 경매를 포함해 많은 다양한 여흥 거리가 있다.

Ⓒ 몇몇 지역 밴드들이 인기를 얻는 것을 도왔다.

Ⓓ 음악가들을 위한 기금을 모으려고 매년 경매를 연다.

해설 학생이 가을 축제에 밴드를 초대하겠다고 하자 교수가 늘 음악 공연이 있지 않느냐고 물었고, 학생이 그렇다고 대답했으므로 가을 축제에 항상 어떠한 종류의 음악 공연이 있었다는 점을 유추할 수 있다. 정답은 (A)이다.

2. 학생이 무엇을 할 것 같은가?

Ⓐ 지역의 가게와 박물관들에 전화를 걸어 도움을 요청한다

Ⓑ 경매 행사에 참석하기 위해 지원서를 작성한다

Ⓒ 싱 교수를 만나 지도 교수가 되어 달라고 설득한다

Ⓓ 장 교수의 친구에게 연락하여 더 자세한 질문들을 물어본다

해설 학생이 경매 행사를 조직하는 데 관심을 보이자 교수가 자신의 동료가 경험이 있다고 했고, 학생이 그 동료와 연락할 수 있게 해달라고 부탁한다. 교수가 승낙하며 동료의 명함을 주었으므로 학생이 조만간 교수의 동료에게 연락해 조언을 구할 것이라는 점을 알 수 있다. 정답은 (D)이다.

여 [2] 물론이죠. 로나 싱 교수예요. 크라이튼 대학의 종신 재직 교수죠. 여기 명함 한 장이 있어요.

남 도와주셔서 감사합니다, 장 교수님.

어휘 bother n 성가신 일 | council n 위원회, 의회 | entertainment n 오락, 여흥 | vice president 부회장 | take off 도약하다 | unfortunately adv 불행히도 | eager adj 간절히 바라는, 열렬한 | expense n 비용 | treasurer n 회계 담당자 | fundraiser n 모금 행사 | earn v 벌다 | organize v 조직하다, 준비하다 | solution n 해결책 | carwash n 세차 | auction n 경매 | publicize v 알리다, 홍보하다 | product n 제품 | endorse v 홍보하다, 지지하다 | donate v 기부하다 | praise v 칭찬하다 | inexpensive adj 비싸지 않은 | advertising n 광고 | outbid v 더 비싼 값을 부르다 | host v 주최하다 | empty adj 비어 있는 | install v 설치하다 | personally adv 개인적으로 | colleague n 동료 | fund v 자금을 대다 | tenured professor 종신 재직 교수

Practice

Passage 1 Listen to part of a conversation between a student and a professor. C05_P01

Q. What can be inferred about the professor?

Ⓐ He works on the campus literary magazine.

Ⓑ He often submits stories to the magazine.

Ⓒ He does not think the woman is qualified.

Ⓓ He is a well-known and popular author.

Passage 2 Listen to part of a conversation between a student and a registrar. C05_P02

Q. What can be inferred about the student's situation?

Ⓐ His academic advisor didn't tell him he should take the course.

Ⓑ The class always fills up very quickly every semester.

Ⓒ He was not sure if the class was required to graduate.

Ⓓ He already had a full schedule in his freshman year.

Passage 3 Listen to part of a conversation between a student and a housing officer. C05_P03

Q. What is implied about the school housing policy?

(A) The school housing policy allows some exceptions.

(B) All the freshmen must live in the dormitories.

(C) The school housing policy does not allow any exceptions.

(D) Seniors must leave the dorm immediately after school finishes.

Passage 4 Listen to part of a conversation between a student and an administrator. 

Q. What does the administrator imply about the Asian Studies class?

(A) It is not likely that the student will get into the class.

(B) The class is not very useful to students with his major.

(C) There are not many people interested in taking it.

(D) The class is usually held in the evening.

II. Lectures

Introduction

iBT TOEFL Listening Lectures

TOEFL Listening에서 강의(Lecture) 유형은 총 3개 출제된다. 교수 혼자 강의하는 유형과 교수가 강의하는 도중 학생이 한두 마디 질문을 하는 유형이 있다. 보통 1 지문당 550~850단어의 길이로 이루어져 있으며(약 4~5분), 강의를 듣고 1~6번 문제를 풀게 된다. 대화와 마찬가지로 필기용 종이가 제공되기 때문에 강의를 들으면서 노트 필기와 요약이 가능하다.

Lecture Question Types

강의 하나당 여섯 문제를 풀게 되며 문제 유형은 아래와 같이 총 다섯 가지이다.

1. **주제 찾기(Main Idea):** 강의의 주제·목적 찾기
2. **세부 사항 찾기(Details):** 강의를 들으며 알 수 있는 주제 관련 세부 내용 찾기
3. **의도 및 태도 파악(Function & Attitude):** 교수나 학생이 어떠한 말을 한 이유 또는 무언가에 대한 화자의 태도 파악하기
4. **관계 파악(Connecting Contents):** 강의가 연결된 방식 또는 무언가가 언급된 이유 파악하기
5. **추론(Inference):** 강의를 통해 유추할 수 있는 내용 찾기

Lecture Topic Types

강의 주제는 크게 두 가지로 분류할 수 있으며, 각각의 대분류 아래에 다음과 같은 주제들이 주로 등장한다.

1. **과학(Science)**

   건축(Architecture), 천문학(Astronomy), 생물학(Biology), 화학(Chemistry), 공학(Engineering), 환경 과학(Environmental Science), 지질학(Geology), 기상학(Meteorology), 고생물학(Paleontology), 물리학(Physics), 생리학(Physiology)

2. **인문학(Humanities)**

   인류학(Anthropology), 고고학(Archaeology), 미술(Art), 경영학(Business Management), 경제학(Economics), 영화 연구(Film Studies), 역사(History), 언어학(Linguistics), 문학(Literature), 음악(Music), 사진술(Photography), 심리학(Psychology)

Tips

이 강의의 주제·중심 내용이 무엇인가?

대화와 마찬가지로 강의의 주제와 중심 내용은 일반적으로 강의가 시작되고 나서 거의 바로 파악할 수 있다. 교수의 도입부 설명을 통해 이 강의가 무엇에 관한 강의인지 알 수 있다. 강의의 주제·중심 내용을 묻는 문제는 반드시 한 문제씩 출제되며 강의 전체의 맥락을 잡는 데 있어서 가장 기본적인 사항이므로 주의해서 듣도록 하자.

세부 정보를 파악하라!

강의의 주제와 중심 내용을 알면 그에 맞춰 세부 정보를 파악할 수 있다. 세부 정보 역시 강의 하나당 1~2개의 문제가 반드시 출제되므로 처음부터 끝까지 긴장을 놓지 말고 듣자.

화자의 말투와 대화 분위기는 어떤가?

의도 및 태도 파악 문제(Function & Attitude Question)는 강의에서도 찾아볼 수 있다. 대화와 마찬가지로 강의 맥락 속에서 화자의 의견과 태도를 파악해야 하는 문제가 나온다. 교수가 특정 주제를 비꼬아서 말할 수도 있고, 주제에 관해 찬성하거나 반대하는 등 다양한 형식이 등장하므로 상황 속의 명확한 의미를 파악할 수 있도록 하자.

강의에서도 노트 필기를 놓치지 말자!

강의는 대화에 비해 더 길며, 어렵거나 익숙하지 않은 주제가 나오면 듣는 도중에 집중력이 흐트러지기 쉽다. 노트 필기를 하며 강의 주제의 요점과 특징을 알아보기 쉽도록 간단히 정리하는 법을 익혀보자.

정답은 정직하게 출제되지 않는다!

대화와 마찬가지로 강의 또한 교수나 학생이 말한 단어가 문제 보기에 그대로 출제되는 경우는 거의 없다. 특정 단어에만 너무 초점을 맞추지 말고 전반적인 내용과 뜻에 집중하도록 하자. 내용을 먼저 이해한 후 같은 단어가 아니라 다른 단어를 사용했더라도 같은 의미를 나타내는 패러프레이징된 표현을 골라낼 수 있어야 한다.

주제에 대한 친밀감을 높이자!

강의 지문의 경우 대학교 전공 수업 수준의 내용이 등장하다 보니, 조금 생소한 주제와 단어가 나오면 내용 자체를 따라잡는 데 어려움을 겪고 당황하는 경우가 많다. 다양한 강의 주제에 익숙해질 수 있도록 자주 등장하는 주제에 대한 배경지식과 핵심 어휘를 꼭 익혀두자.

Lesson

01 Main Idea

Lesson Outline

주제 찾기 문제(Main Idea Question)는 강의나 토론을 듣고 주제를 찾는 문제로, 지문마다 한 문제씩 반드시 출제된다. 대부분의 경우 교수가 강의 주제를 직접 말하므로 크게 어렵지 않지만, 가끔 너무 세부적인 내용에 집중하게 되면 강의 내용 전체를 포함하지 않는 선택지를 고르게 되므로 주의해서 전체를 보아야 한다.

Lesson Point

Point 1 도입부 + 교수가 말하는 표시어(signal) = 강의의 주제!

Point 2 너무 세부적인 내용을 다루는 보기는 오답이다.

Point 3 보기에서 키워드가 패러프레이징 되어 있을 확률이 높다.

Point 4 강의에서는 주제가 곧 Main Idea!

Point 5 끝까지 듣고 주제를 고르면 모든 보기가 답으로 보인다. 도입부에서 교수가 하는 말에 집중하자.

Typical Questions 

- What is the [lecture/discussion/talk] mainly about? [강의/토론/담화]는 주로 무엇에 관한 것인가?
- What is the professor mainly discussing? 교수는 주로 무엇을 논의하고 있는가?
- What is the main idea of the lecture? 강의의 요지는 무엇인가?
- What is the main purpose of the lecture? 강의의 주요 목적은 무엇인가?
- What is the speaker talking about? 화자는 무엇에 관해 이야기하고 있는가?

Learning Strategies

'주제 찾기' 표시어(signal)를 공략한다!

대화와 마찬가지로 강의/토론의 도입부에서 교수가 하는 말 중 주제가 나올 것을 미리 알리는 표시어를 파악하고, 그 뒤에 나오는 주제를 집중해서 듣는다.

- Today, we're going to talk about ~. — 오늘 우리는 ~에 대해서 이야기할 겁니다.
- Okay, let's start with ~. — 좋아요, ~부터 시작합시다.
- I'd like to focus on ~ today. — 오늘은 ~에 초점을 맞춰 보고자 합니다.
- What I'd like to talk about today is ~. — 제가 오늘 하려는 이야기는 ~입니다.
- Today, I want to take a look at ~. — 오늘은 ~에 대해 살펴보고자 합니다.
- Our discussion for today is going to be ~. — 오늘 우리가 토론할 것은 ~입니다.
- Today, I would like to turn our attention to ~. — 오늘은 ~로 관심을 돌려 볼 겁니다.
- The topic we're going to focus on today is ~. — 오늘 우리가 초점을 두고자 하는 주제는 ~입니다.
- Last time, we talked about ~, and we're going to continue ~. — 지난 시간에는 ~에 대해 이야기했었는데요, 계속해서 ~해 보겠습니다.

Example

Man: Professor

Listen to part of a lecture in an art history class.

M Pablo Picasso is an artist who tried his hand at just about every medium imaginable and was successful at pretty much everything he attempted. He was a painter, printmaker, sculptor, ceramicist, poet, playwright, and stage designer who is known as a co-founder of the Cubist movement, collage, and the invention of constructed sculpture, and for developing and exploring a diverse array of other artistic styles. Along with Marcel Duchamp and Henri Matisse, Picasso is viewed as one of the chief artists who embodied the revolutionary artistic movements in visual arts at the beginning of the 20th century. Picasso was extraordinarily prolific throughout his life, and he achieved worldwide fame and amassed great personal wealth for his artistic accomplishments. From a very early age, Picasso displayed immense artistic talent, and although he began painting in a very realistic manner, his style shifted as he experimented with other techniques and theories of art. For this reason, critics and historians typically categorize his works into different periods defined by their stylistic, technical, and thematic content.

After World War I, he and many other artists returned to a more neoclassical style of art, and he painted some realistic portraits, like those of his wife Olga Khokhlova. He entered into an exclusive contract with art dealer Paul Rosenberg, and he began to become wealthy. He half-heartedly entered the Surrealist movement for a time, but after the Spanish Civil War, he seems to have fully embraced Cubism as his predominant style. After the German bombing of Guernica, Spain, he produced his most famous cubist painting, *Guernica*, which depicted the horrors of war and its effects on humanity.

Q. What is the lecture mainly about?

Ⓐ Characteristics of cubism and its influence

Ⓑ A pioneer who worked with the natural environment

Ⓒ An artist's struggles to become famous

Ⓓ A famous artist's life and artistic styles

미술사 강의의 일부를 들으시오.

남 파블로 피카소는 상상할 수 있는 모든 표현 수단을 시도했었고, 그가 시도했던 거의 모든 것들에 성공을 거두었던 예술가입니다. 그는 화가, 판화 제작자, 조각가, 도예가, 시인, 극작가, 그리고 무대 디자이너였으며 입체파 운동의 공동 창설자, 콜라주, 건축 조형물 발명으로 알려져 있고, 다른 여러 다양한 예술 양식을 발전시키고 탐구한 것으로도 잘 알려져 있습니다. 마르셀 뒤샹과 앙리 마티스와 함께 파카소는 20세기 초에 혁명적 예술 운동을 시각 예술에 구현했던 가장 주요한 예술가 중의 한 명으로 여겨집니다. 그는 전 생애에 걸쳐 엄청나게 다작을 했으며 세계적인 명성을 얻었고 그의 예술적 성취로 굉장한 개인적 부를 축적했습니다. 파카소는 어렸을 때부터 월등한 예술적 재능을 보였으며 처음 그림을 시작했을 때는 매우 현실적인 방식으로 작품 활동을 했으나 예술의 다른 기법과 이론들을 가지고 실험하면서 화풍이 바뀌었습니다. 이러한 이유로 비평가들과 역사학자들은 일반적으로 그의 작품들을 화풍, 기법, 그리고 주제에 기반해 서로 다른 시대들로 분류합니다.

1차 세계 대전 뒤, 그와 다른 많은 예술가들은 좀 더 신고전주의적인 화풍으로 돌아왔는데, 파카소는 그의 아내 올가 코클로바의 것과 같은 몇 점의 현실적인 초상화들을 그렸습니다. 그는 폴 로젠버그라는 미술상과 독점 계약을 맺었고 부유해지기 시작했죠. 그는 건성으로 초현실주의 운동에 잠시 동참하기도 했지만, 스페인 내전 후 그는 입체주의를 자신의 가장 두드러진 화풍으로 받아들인 것처럼 보입니다. 스페인의 게르니카가 독일에게 폭격을 당한 뒤 그는 그의 가장 유명한 입체파 작품인 〈게르니카〉를 그렸는데, 이 작품은 전쟁의 공포와 전쟁이 인류에 미치는 영향을 묘사했습니다.

Q. 강의는 주로 무엇에 관한 것인가?

Ⓐ 입체주의의 특징과 그 영향
Ⓑ 자연 환경으로 작품 활동을 한 선구자
Ⓒ 유명해지기 위한 한 예술가의 분투
Ⓓ 유명한 예술가의 삶과 화풍

교수가 강의 초반부터 파블로 피카소라는 주제를 언급하며 그의 삶과 화풍에 관해 계속 설명하고 있으므로 정답은 (D)이다. 강의의 전반적인 내용을 포괄할 수 있는 선택지를 골라야 한다는 점을 잊지 말자. 강의에서 언급된 내용이더라도 주제가 아닌 세부 내용일 경우는 주제 찾기 문제에서는 오답이므로 주의해야 한다.

Lesson 01 Lectures

어휘 medium n 수단 | imaginable adj 상상할 수 있는 | successful adj 성공한 | attempt v 시도하다 | printmaker n 판화 제작자 | sculptor n 조각가 | ceramicist n 도예가 | playwright n 극작가 | co-founder n 공동 창시자/창업자 | collage n 콜라주 | invention n 발명 | construct v 건설하다, 구성하다 | sculpture n 조형물, 조각품, 조각 | explore v 탐구하다 | diverse adj 다양한 | array n 모음, 무리 | embody v 구현하다, 상징하다 | revolutionary adj 혁명적인 | visual art 시각 예술 | extraordinarily adv 엄청나게 | prolific adj 다작하는 | worldwide adj 전 세계적인 | amass v 축적하다, 모으다 | accomplishment n 성취 | immense v 엄청난, 어마어마한 | realistic adj 현실적인 | shift v 이동하다 | typically adv 일반적으로 | categorize v 분류하다 | thematic adj 주제의 | neoclassical adj 신고전주의의 | portrait n 초상화 | exclusive contract 독점 계약 | half-heartedly adv 건성으로 | surrealist n 초현실주의자 | embrace v 받아들이다, 안다 | predominant adj 두드러진, 우세한, 뚜렷한 | humanity n 인류

Practice

Passage 1 Listen to part of a lecture in a science class. L01_P01

Q. What is the lecture mainly about?

Ⓐ The importance of alternative fuels

Ⓑ The difficulty of finding an energy source to replace oil

Ⓒ The different types of alternative fuels

Ⓓ Environmental safety

Passage 2 Listen to part of a lecture in a history class. L01_P02

Q. What is the main idea of the lecture?

Ⓐ How aggression forced the Pueblo to move to a new type of housing

Ⓑ The interest of modern scholars in the Utah cliff dwellings

Ⓒ What cliff dwellings are and why they were helpful to the Pueblo people

Ⓓ Rain and its impact on the Pueblo people's cliff dwellings

정답 및 해석 | P. 44

Passage 3 Listen to part of a lecture in a biology class.

L01_P03

Q. What is the main idea of the lecture?

Ⓐ Tetrastigma and how it sustains the Rafflesia

Ⓑ Photosynthesis and how plants rely on it to survive

Ⓒ Rafflesia and how it differs from most plants

Ⓓ Rafflesia's strong odor and unusual size

Passage 4 Listen to part of a discussion in a geology class.

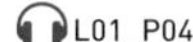

Q. What aspect of plate tectonics does the professor mainly discuss?

Ⓐ The formation of tectonic plates

Ⓑ How tectonic plates move

Ⓒ The different types of tectonic plates

Ⓓ How plates are destroyed

Lesson

02 Details

Lesson Outline

세부 사항 찾기 문제(Details Question)는 TOEFL Listening 문제에서 가장 빈도수가 높은 문제 유형이며, 강의에서는 한 개에서 세 개까지 출제된다. 대화와 마찬가지로 지문의 세부 사항에 대해 묻는데, 강의 주제에 관한 자세한 내용, 교수가 강조하거나 반복해서 말하는 사항, 또는 주제를 뒷받침하는 예나 특징으로 사용된 것을 묻는다.

하나 이상의 답을 선택해야 하는 경우도 있기 때문에 문제를 풀 때 정확도가 중요하며, 정확한 노트 필기가 생명이다. 특히 강의 지문 특성상 기억해야 할 세부 내용이 많고 어려운 용어도 많아서 전체 강의의 흐름을 이해했다 하더라도 세부적인 내용은 잘 기억이 나지 않을 수 있기 때문에 노트 필기를 최대한 활용해야 한다. 모르는 단어를 포함해서 빠르게 노트 필기하는 방법을 꾸준히 연습하고 그 필기한 내용을 재구성해 답을 찾는 연습을 해 보자.

Lesson Point

Point 1 강의 지문 최고 빈출 문제 유형!

Point 2 특징(characteristic)과 예시(example)에 주목한다.

Point 3 빠른 노트 필기 연습이 고득점으로 가는 관건이다.

Point 4 표시어(signal)를 바탕으로 한 정확하고 재구성하기 쉬운 노트 필기를 연습한다.

Typical Questions

- What [is/are] the characteristic(s) of ~? ~의 특징(들)은 무엇인가?
- What does the professor talk about ~? 교수는 ~에 관해 뭐라고 말하는가?
- What does ~ [show/demonstrate]? ~는 무엇을 [나타내는가/보여주는가]?
- According to the professor, [why/what] is ~? 교수에 의하면, [왜/무엇]인가?
- What [is/are] the reason(s) for ~? ~의 이유(들)는 무엇인가?
- What point does the professor make by ~? 교수가 ~함으로써 주장하고자 하는 것은 무엇인가?

Learning Strategies

'세부 사항 찾기' 표시어(signal)를 공략한다!

세부 사항 표시어를 바탕으로 한 정확한 노트 필기를 통해 강조·반복되는 내용을 정리한다.

정의

- X means ~. X는 ~를 의미합니다.
- X is called ~. X는 ~라고 불립니다.
- X is referred to as ~. X는 ~를 나타냅니다.

서술 및 나열

- Some X, but others Y. 일부는 X하지만 나머지는 Y합니다.
- Not only X, but also Y. X뿐만 아니라, Y이기도 합니다.
- In other words 다시 말해서
- The reason why ~ ~의 이유는

강조

- You should remember that ~. ~를 기억해야 합니다.
- We need to make sure ~. ~를 확실히 해 둘 필요가 있습니다.
- It's interesting to note that ~. ~는 매우 흥미로운 사실입니다.
- It is quite a surprise ~. ~라니 참으로 놀라운 일입니다.
- This could actually mean ~. 이것은 사실 ~임을 의미합니다.
- In fact 사실은, 실은

예시

- For example 예를 들어
- Let's take ~ for example. ~를 예로 들어 봅시다.
- To illustrate this 이것을 설명하기 위해서

비유

- Similarly 비슷하게, 유사하게
- Likewise 똑같이, 비슷하게
- In the same manner 마찬가지로

반전

- But/Yet/However 그렇지만, 그러나
- While/Whereas ~인 데 반해, 반면
- Contrary to ~ ~와는 반대로
- In contrast to ~ ~와 대조적으로
- On the other hand 다른 한편으로는
- On the contrary 그와는 반대로
- Although X, Y. 비록 X이긴 하지만, Y입니다.
- The problem is ~. 문제는 ~입니다.

Example

Woman: Professor

Listen to part of a lecture in a marine biology class.

W In our last class, we discussed Darwin's journey on the Beagle and the concept of evolution that he developed after observing the finches of the Galapagos Islands. Beginning as one species, those birds adapted to the unique environment of their particular islands and their morphology changed. These adaptations led to the development of new species. As you know, this phenomenon is not limited to those islands or to birds. Indeed all animals have undergone this process to some degree, including fish. Some types of fish have remained fairly static for millions of years, like sharks, while others have continued to change. The fish in the suborder Notothenioidei, which live in the Southern Ocean, fit into this category. Because they make their home in the frigid waters surrounding Antarctica, they have adapted in many ways to survive.

Many millions of years ago, the globe looked very different. There was a single supercontinent called Pangaea, and the rest of the planet's surface was ocean. The seas around this supercontinent were fairly warm, and they supported a wide variety of species of fish—much like the Caribbean today. [1] Due to plate tectonics, the supercontinent split apart, and the pieces drifted on their plates to form the current continents. As the landmass that would become Antarctica moved south, many of the fish species abandoned the area because the water around it was getting colder. However, the Notothenioidei stayed.

The South Pole does not receive much sunlight, and it is even darker in the water, especially at over 1,000 meters down! [2] So, some of these species have developed large eyes to allow them to see in very low light conditions. Unfortunately, large eyes contain a lot of fluid, which would freeze in such cold water. So, the fish have developed a

1. According to the professor, what happened to the fish species after the split of the supercontinent?

Ⓐ Many species moved to regions with milder climates.

Ⓑ Most of them migrated from the south to the north.

Ⓒ They quickly adapted to survive without the interconnected land.

Ⓓ Many species ended up going extinct afterward.

2. Which characteristic allowed the Notothenioidei to survive in the Antarctic?

Ⓐ Protective eyelids

Ⓑ Thick proteins

Ⓒ More bone mass

Ⓓ Being cold-blooded

special transparent eyelid that allows them to see without allowing the eye to freeze. They also have an extremely low amount of red blood cells. The extremely cold and stable temperature allows there to be a higher concentration of oxygen in the water than there would be in warmer regions. So, the fish don't need many red blood cells to transport oxygen throughout their bodies. As a result, their blood is only 1 percent hemoglobin, compared to the 45 percent found in other fish.

해양 생물학 강의의 일부를 들으시오.

W 지난 시간에 우리는 비글에서의 다윈의 여행과 갈라파고스 제도의 되새들을 관찰한 뒤 그가 발전시킨 진화의 개념에 대해 이야기했습니다. 하나의 종으로 시작된 이 새들은 특별한 제도의 독특한 환경에 적응했고, 이들의 형태는 변화되었습니다. 이러한 적응은 새로운 종의 발생으로 이어졌습니다. 여러분도 알다시피 이 현상은 그 제도에만 국한된 것이 아니며, 새들에게만 국한된 것도 아닙니다. 실제로 모든 동물들이 어느 정도 이 과정을 거쳤는데, 물고기도 포함됩니다. 상어와 같은 몇몇 종류의 물고기는 수백만 년 동안 꽤나 변화 없이 남아 있었던 반면, 다른 종들은 계속해서 변화했죠. 남쪽 바다에 서식하는 남극암치아목이라는 아목에 속하는 물고기가 이 분류에 속합니다. 이들은 남극 대륙을 둘러싼 매우 차가운 물에서 서식하기 때문에 생존하기 위해 많은 방법으로 적응했습니다.

수백만 년 전, 지구는 매우 다른 모습을 갖고 있었습니다. 판게아라고 불리는 하나의 초대륙이 있었고 지구 표면의 나머지 부분은 바다였습니다. 이 초대륙을 둘러싼 바다는 꽤 따뜻했으며 매우 다양한 물고기 종들이 살고 있었습니다. 오늘날의 카리브해와 매우 비슷했죠. [1] 판구조론에 의해 이 초대륙은 분열되었고 조각난 땅들은 흘러가서 현재의 대륙이 되었습니다. 후에 남극 대륙이 될 땅덩어리가 남쪽으로 이동할 때 많은 종의 물고기들이 그 지역을 떠났는데, 이는 주변의 물이 점점 차가워졌기 때문이었죠. 그러나 남극암치아목 물고기들은 남았습니다.

남극은 햇빛을 그다지 많이 받지 않고, 물 속은 한층 더 어두운데, 특히 1,000미터가 넘는 수심에서는 훨씬 그렇겠죠! [2] 그래서 이들 중 몇몇 종은 매우 어두운 환경에서도 볼 수 있도록 커다란 눈으로 발달되었습니다. 불행하게도 커다란 눈에는 액체가 많이 포함되어 있는데 이렇게 차가운 물에서는 얼어붙고 말죠. 그래서 이 물고기들은 눈이 얼어붙지 않으면서 볼 수 있도록 특별한 투명 눈꺼풀을 발생시켰습니다. 그리고 이들은 극도로 적은 양의 적혈구를 가지고 있습니다. 그 매우 차갑고 안정적인 수온은 따뜻한 지역에 비해 물 속 산소 농도를 더 높게 만듭니다. 그래서 이 물고기들은 몸을 통해 산소를 운반해줄 적혈구들이 그다지 많이 필요하지 않습니다. 그 결과, 다른 물고기들의 피는 45%가 헤모글로빈인 반면 이들의 피에는 헤모글로빈이 단 1%입니다.

1. 교수에 의하면, 초대륙의 분열 뒤 물고기 종들에게 무슨 일이 일어났는가?

Ⓐ 많은 종들이 더 온화한 기후의 지역으로 옮겨갔다.
Ⓑ 대부분의 종들이 남쪽에서 북쪽으로 이주했다.
Ⓒ 서로 연결된 대륙 없이도 빠르게 생존에 적응했다.
Ⓓ 많은 종들이 그 뒤 멸종에 이르렀다.

해설 강의에서 초대륙이 분열된 뒤 남극 대륙이 될 땅덩어리가 남쪽으로 이동할 때 많은 종류의 물고기가 그 지역을 떠났는데, 물이 점점 차가워졌기 때문이었다는 내용이 나오므로 정답은 (A)이다. 한편, 물이 점점 차가워져서 옮겼다는 말이 '더 온화한 기후로 이동했다'라는 의미로 살짝 바꿔 패러프레이즈되었다는 점을 눈여겨보자.

2. 어떠한 특징이 남극암치아목 물고기들이 남극에서 살아남을 수 있도록 했는가?

Ⓐ 보호용 눈꺼풀
Ⓑ 두꺼운 단백질
Ⓒ 더 높은 골밀도
Ⓓ 냉혈성

해설 교수가 이 물고기 중 몇몇 종은 환경에 적응하기 위해 커다란 눈으로 발달되었고, 나아가 눈이 얼어붙지 않게 하려고 투명 눈꺼풀까지 발생시켰다고 설명했으므로 정답은 (A)이다. 투명 눈꺼풀(transparent eyelid)이 보호용 눈꺼풀(protective eyelid)로 패러프레이즈되었다.

어휘 concept n 개념 | evolution n 진화 | finch n 되새 | adapt v 적응하다 | particular adj 특정한, 특별한 | morphology n 형태, 형태학 | adaptation n 적응, 순응 | phenomenon n 현상 | undergo v 겪다, 받다 | static adj 변화가 없는, 정지 상태의 | suborder n 아목 | Notothenioidei n 남극암치아목 | frigid adj 몹시 추운 | Antarctica n 남극 대륙 | globe n 지구, 세계 | supercontinent n 초대륙(수억 년 전 존재했던 거대 대륙) | surface n 표면 | plate tectonics 판구조론 | continent n 대륙 | landmass n 땅덩어리, 대륙 | abandon v 떠나다, 버리다 | South Pole n 남극 | transparent adj 투명한 | eyelid n 눈꺼풀 | red blood cell 적혈구 | stable adj 안정적인 | concentration n 농도 | transport v 운반하다, 수송하다 | hemoglobin n 헤모글로빈, 혈색소

Practice

Passage 1 Listen to part of a lecture in an architecture class.

L02_P01

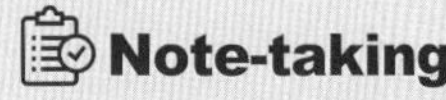

Q. According to the professor, what advantage did adobe bricks have over adobe balls in the rain?

Ⓐ They could let rain sit on top of the bricks.

Ⓑ They were flat, which kept the water from soaking in.

Ⓒ They were slanted, which allowed the rain to run off.

Ⓓ They wouldn't roll as much as the adobe balls did.

Passage 2 Listen to part of a discussion in a psychology class.

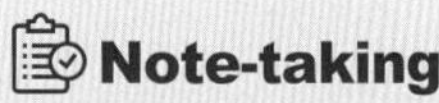

Q. How does the professor reward her daughter for reading?

Ⓐ By giving her extra free time

Ⓑ By buying her more books

Ⓒ By giving her drawing supplies

Ⓓ By buying her music

Passage 3 Listen to part of a lecture in a biology class.

L02_P03

Q. According to the professor, what provides most of the energy needed in the water cycle?

Ⓐ Wind

Ⓑ The Sun

Ⓒ Heat from the Earth's core

Ⓓ Energy released when water evaporates

Passage 4 Listen to part of a lecture in an astronomy class.

L02_P04

Q. When does a new lunar month start?

Ⓐ When the Moon reaches its fullest point

Ⓑ On the 15th of each month of the Gregorian solar calendar

Ⓒ When the Moon is in its new phase

Ⓓ Approximately half a day before the start of each solar month

Lesson

03 Function & Attitude

Lesson Outline

의도 및 태도 파악 문제(Function & Attitude Question)는 화자의 말이나 표현에 집중해야 한다. 의도 파악(Function) 문제의 경우 화자, 특히 교수가 강의 중 어떠한 말을 한 목적과 그 말 속에 내재된 의도를 파악해야 한다. 학생이 교수에게 질문한 내용에 관해 출제될 때도 있다. 주로 '짧은 구간을 다시 들려주고 풀기' 방식으로 출제되며, 태도 파악(Attitude) 문제는 강의 중의 특정 내용에 대한 화자의 태도와 감정, 또는 확신 정도를 파악하는 문제가 주로 출제된다.

Lesson Point

Point 1 앞뒤 문맥과 화자의 말투를 종합해서 들리는 그대로가 아닌 숨겨진 뜻을 파악한다.

Point 2 말을 번복 또는 수정하거나 여담처럼 말하는 부분에 주의해서 듣는다.

Point 3 개인적인 의견을 말하는 부분이 태도 파악(Attitude) 문제로 나오는 경우가 많으니 주의!

Point 4 다시 들었던 표현이 선택지에 그대로 나오는 경우 오답일 확률이 높다.

Point 5 노트 필기보다는 감각을 사용해서 화자의 말투를 파악한다.

Typical Questions

의도 파악(Function)

- Listen again to part of the lecture. Then answer the question. Why does the professor say this:
  강의의 일부를 다시 듣고 질문에 답하시오. 교수는 왜 이렇게 말하는가:
- What does the professor mean when he/she says this:
  교수는 다음과 같이 말하며 무엇을 의미하는가:

태도 파악(Attitude)

- What is the professor's attitude toward ~?
  ~에 대한 교수의 태도는 어떠한가?
- What does the professor feel by saying ~?
  ~라고 말할 때 교수는 어떤 감정을 느끼고 있는가?
- What is the professor's opinion about ~?
  ~에 대한 교수의 의견은 무엇인가?

Learning Strategies

의도 및 태도 파악 빈출 표현

의도·태도 파악 문제와 관련하여 강의에 자주 등장하는 표현들을 알아두자.

'확신' 관련 표현

- As you can see, — 보시다시피,
- I'm sure you all know that ~. — ~라는 건 다들 아실 겁니다.
- You all remember this, right? — 다들 이 내용 기억하시죠, 그렇죠?
- I guarantee that ~. — ~라는 걸 보장합니다.

'동의하지 않음' 관련 표현

- I have some other opinions for ~. — ~에 대해서 저는 좀 다른 의견을 갖고 있어요.
- I doubt that ~. — (제 생각에는) ~할 것 같지 않아요.
- That may be true, but ~. — 그게 사실일 수도 있겠지만, 그러나 ~.
- Contrary to that, the evidence suggests ~. — 그와 반대로, 그 증거는 ~임을 보여줍니다.
- This is different from what we know ~. — 이건 우리가 ~에 대해 알고 있는 것과는 다릅니다.
- However, now we know that ~. — 그러나, 이제 우리는 ~라는 걸 압니다.

'혼란스러움' 관련 표현

- I'm not sure if I understand your question. — 제가 질문을 제대로 이해했는지 모르겠군요.
- Can you elaborate on that again? — 그것에 대해 다시 자세히 설명해 주실 수 있을까요?
- I don't think that makes sense. — 이해가 안 돼요.
- I know that it is confusing, but ~. — 헷갈리는 내용이라는 건 알아요, 하지만 ~.

'불확실함' 관련 표현

- We can't be certain that ~. — ~라고 확신할 수는 없습니다.
- It is not safe to say ~. — ~라고 말하는 건 위험한 발언이죠.
- Are we sure about this? — 여기에 대해서 다들 확신하나요?
- Hmm... — 흠...

Example

Man: Professor

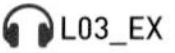 L03_EX

Listen to part of a lecture in an Earth science class.

M Today, we will be talking about the benefits and limitations of wind energy. As you know, the majority of energy that is utilized by human beings is generated by the combustion of fossil fuels, but their supply is finite, so alternatives must be found. Nuclear reactors generate vast amounts of electricity, but their fuel is also limited, and they produce toxic waste far more dangerous than the pollution created by burning coal, oil, and gas. Many areas rely upon hydroelectric plants to generate electricity, which is renewable, but dependent upon many factors including location and average rainfall. There are two other options that are gaining popularity, which are wind and solar power, but these also have their limitations. Now, as I said earlier, let's start with wind energy.

Harnessing wind energy is hardly a new concept, and it dates back well into prehistoric time. The first use for wind energy was most likely the sails on ships, and people have used windmills for over 2,000 years to pump water and grind grain. The first time a windmill was built with the express purpose of generating electricity was in Scotland in 1887, and it was quickly replicated in the United States. Since then, wind generators have been a common solution to providing power to buildings located in remote or isolated areas.

The ability to provide power in areas where conventional power plants are impractical is only one of the advantages of wind power. The most important is that it is an infinite resource. As long as the Earth possesses an atmosphere, there will be wind. In addition, it generates no pollution once the installation of the wind turbines for a wind farm has been completed. True, they incorporate synthetic materials that are made from oil, and the pieces must be transported to site, but they compensate for this via the energy they produce in the first

Q. Why does the professor mention synthetic materials?

Ⓐ To show some harmful effects of wind farms on the environment

Ⓑ To name the substances needed for constructing wind turbines

Ⓒ To explain how they influence the performance of wind plants

Ⓓ To describe the process of generating electricity from wind energy

few months. The farms also use only a fraction of the land that conventional plants require. A wind farm may cover a large area, but the foundations of the turbines and their attendant structures only use a small portion of the surface, leaving the rest open for agriculture or other purposes. To name some limitations of wind power, well, wind is not stable. It constantly fluctuates in strength, and some days may have no wind at all.

지구 과학 강의의 일부를 들으시오.

남 오늘 우리는 풍력의 이점과 한계에 대해 이야기할 겁니다. 여러분도 알고 있듯이, 인간이 사용하는 에너지의 대다수는 화석 연료의 연소로 만들어지지만, 화석 연료의 공급은 유한하기에 대체 연료를 반드시 찾아야만 하죠. 원자로가 막대한 양의 전기를 생산하지만 이들의 연료 역시 제한되어 있을 뿐만 아니라, 석탄, 석유, 가스를 태움으로써 만들어지는 오염 물질보다 훨씬 위험한 독성 폐기물을 만들어 냅니다. 많은 분야에서 수력 발전 시설이 만드는 전기에 의존하고 있는데, 이는 재생 가능하지만 장소와 평균 강우량에 따라 달라집니다. 인기를 얻고 있는 다른 두 가지 방법이 있는데, 이는 풍력과 태양열입니다. 그러나 이 둘에도 한계가 있어요. 이제 아까 말했던 대로 풍력에 대해 먼저 시작해 봅시다.

풍력 에너지를 이용하는 것은 새로운 개념이 아니며 선사 시대까지 거슬러 올라가 찾아볼 수 있습니다. 최초의 풍력 에너지 이용은 아마도 배에 달린 돛이었을 가능성이 가장 크고, 사람들은 2,000년이 넘게 물을 끌어 올리고 곡식을 빻는 데 풍차를 사용해 왔죠. 전기 발전을 위한 분명한 목적으로 풍차가 지어진 최초의 시기는 1887년의 스코틀랜드에서였습니다. 그리고 미국에서도 빠르게 풍차를 도입했죠. 그 뒤로 풍력 발전소는 외지거나 외딴곳에 있는 건물들에 전력을 공급하는 일반적인 해결책이 되어 왔습니다.

전통적인 발전소를 세울 수 없는 지역에 전력을 공급할 수 있는 능력은 풍력이 가진 이점들 중 겨우 하나일 뿐입니다. 가장 중요한 것은 무한한 자원이라는 것이죠. 지구에 대기가 존재하는 이상 바람은 존재할 테니까요. 그리고 일단 풍력 발전 단지에 터빈이 설치되고 나면 전혀 오염을 만들어내지 않습니다. 사실, 터빈에 석유로 만들어진 합성 물질들이 포함되어 있으며 터빈 부품들이 현장으로 운송되어야 하지만, 이는 풍력 발전소가 세워지고 처음 몇 달 동안 생산하는 에너지로 보상받을 수 있습니다. 풍력 발전 단지들은 또한 전통적인 발전소들이 필요로 했던 많은 토지의 극히 일부만 사용합니다. 풍력 발전 단지가 넓은 지역에 걸쳐 세워질 수도 있지만 터빈의 기초와 보조 구조물들은 표면의 작은 부문만을 사용하기에 남은 부분의 땅을 농업이나 다른 목적에 사용할 수 있게 됩니다. 풍력의 한계 몇 가지를 들자면, 음, 바람은 안정적인 것이 아닙니다. 그 센 정도가 계속해서 변하며 어떤 날에는 바람이 아예 안 불 수도 있죠.

Q. 교수는 왜 합성 물질을 언급하는가?

Ⓐ 풍력 발전 단지가 환경에 끼치는 몇몇 해로운 영향을 보여주려고

Ⓑ 풍력 터빈 건설에 필요한 물질을 말하려고

Ⓒ 합성 물질이 풍력 발전소의 성능에 어떻게 영향을 주는지 설명하려고

Ⓓ 풍력으로 전기를 발생시키는 과정을 묘사하려고

해설 터빈의 설치와 관련된 이야기를 하는 부분에서 이 터빈에 석유로 만들어진 합성 물질이 포함되어 있다고 했으므로 정답은 (B)이다. 합성 물질(synthetic materials)이 물질(substances)로 대체되었다는 점을 눈여겨보자.

Lesson 03 Lectures

어휘 limitation n 한계, 제한 | wind energy 풍력 | majority n 대다수 | generate v 만들어 내다 | combustion n 연소, 불에 탐 | fossil fuel 화석 연료 | finite adj 유한한 | alternative n 대안 | nuclear reactor 원자로 | vast adj 막대한 | toxic adj 독성의 | pollution n 오염 | coal n 석탄 | hydroelectric adj 수력 전기의 | renewable adj 재생 가능한 | dependent adj 의존하는 | rainfall n 강우량 | harness v 이용하다, 활용하다 | prehistoric adj 선사 시대의 | sail n 돛 | windmill n 풍차 | pump v (물을) 펌프로 퍼 올리다 | grind v 갈다 | express adj 분명한 | replicate v 복제하다 | remote adj 외진 | isolated adj 외떨어진 | conventional adj 전통적인, 관습적인 | impractical adj 비현실적인 | infinite adj 무한한 | turbine n 터빈 | incorporate v 포함하다 | synthetic material 합성 물질 | compensate v 보상하다 | fraction n 부분, 일부 | attendant adj 수반되는 | agriculture n 농업 | stable adj 안정적인 | constantly adv 끊임없이 | fluctuate v 변동하다

Practice

Passage 1 Listen to part of a lecture in a genetics class. L03_P01

Q. Listen again to part of the lecture. Then answer the question.
Why does the professor say this:

(A) To imply that people's ideas about the animals may be incorrect
(B) To show that people are mistaking a dog breed for a hybrid
(C) To indicate that coywolf is an inaccurate name for the species
(D) To state that she does not think that it is a new organism at all

Passage 2 Listen to part of a lecture in a biology class. L03_P02

Q. Listen again to part of the lecture. Then answer the question.
What does the professor imply by saying this:

(A) The expedition found the only organisms that existed.
(B) The surveyors were not well educated about marine biology.
(C) The techniques that the scientists were using were primitive.
(D) The scientists were using the best technology available to them.

Passage 3 Listen to part of a lecture in a marketing class.

L03_P03

Q. What is the professor's attitude toward product-driven companies?

(A) She feels that their focus is too limited.

(B) She thinks that they should do more internal research.

(C) She believes that they are more successful.

(D) She advises against working for them.

Passage 4 Listen to part of a lecture in a biology class.

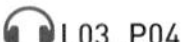

Q. What is the professor's opinion about Antonie van Leeuwenhoek?

(A) He feels that he brought the Age of Enlightenment in the Netherlands.

(B) He believes that he is given too much credit in the scientific community.

(C) He thinks that his innovations were integral to the discovery of cells.

(D) He regards him as the first scientist to ever view organic cells.

Lesson

04 Connecting Contents

Lesson Outline

관계 파악 문제(Connecting Contents Question)는 지문의 정보가 서로 어떻게 관련되었는지 묻는 문제로, 강의에서 나올 경우 보통 1개가 출제된다. 강의에서 어떤 내용이 언급되었는지 묻는 문제가 많이 나오며 짝이나 순서 맞추기 문제가 출제되기도 한다.

Lesson Point

Point 1 전체 흐름을 통해 전반적인 구조를 파악하는 문제 유형:

Ex How is the lecture organized?

⋯› 강의에서 언급되는 정보들 간의 전체적인 상관관계를 파악하며 듣는다!

⋯› 노트 필기 시 간단한 구조도를 그려가며 정리하는 것도 도움이 된다.

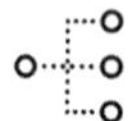

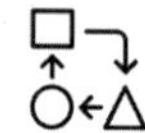

Point 2 특정 정보와 관련된 화자의 의도/정보의 역할을 묻는 문제 유형:

Ex Why does the professor mention ~?

⋯› 해당 정보의 구조적 성격을 파악한다!

⋯› 주제와 상관 없어 보이는 특정 정보가 갑자기 등장하는 경우, 주제 강조 목적의 예시나 비유로 쓰이는 경우가 많다.

Typical Questions

언급 이유

- Why does the professor say ~? 교수는 왜 ~라고 말하는가?
- Why does the student mention ~? 학생은 왜 ~를 언급하는가?
- How is the lecture organized? 강의는 어떻게 구성되어 있는가?

짝 맞추기

- In the lecture, the professor listed ~. Indicate which of the following features are mentioned in the lecture. 강의에서 교수는 ~를 열거한다. 다음 중 어느 특징이 강의에서 언급되었는지 표시하시오.

	Category A	Category B
Characteristic 1		
Characteristic 2		
Characteristic 3		

순서 맞추기

- Put the following steps in order. 다음 단계들을 순서에 맞게 배열하시오.

Step 1	
Step 2	
Step 3	

Learning Strategies

1 내용의 흐름을 파악한다.

강의에서 지문의 요점은 다음과 같은 방식으로 전개된다.

▶ **유형 1** ① 주제 ···› ② 정의/설명 ···› ③ 예시 ···› ④ 영향
▶ **유형 2** ① 주제 ···› ② 원인 ···› ③ 결과
▶ **유형 3** ① 주제 ···› ② 과정 1, 2, 3
▶ **유형 4** ① 주제 ···› ② 설명 ···› ③ 찬성 vs. 반대 ···› ④ 결론
▶ **유형 5** ① 주제 ···› ② 비교 ···› ③ 대조
▶ **유형 6** ① 주제 ···› ② 특징 1, 2, 3

2 특정 정보를 사용한 의도를 파악한다.

특정 문장이나 내용의 역할을 파악할 때 주로 등장하는 표시어를 알아두면 도움이 된다.

주제 소개

• Let's move on to ~.	~로 넘어가겠습니다.
• The next topic of discussion is ~.	다음으로 논의할 주제는 ~입니다.
• What we're going to cover in the remainder of the lecture is ~.	남은 강의 시간에 다룰 내용은 ~입니다.
• We've looked at X, and now I'd like to mention Y.	X를 들여다봤으니, 이제 Y에 대해 이야기하고 싶군요.

예시

• Let's imagine that X is Y.	X가 Y라고 상상해 봅시다.
• Let's look at an example of ~.	~의 예를 한 번 봅시다.
• Let's suppose ~.	~라고 가정해 봅시다.
• One example of X is ~.	X의 한 예는 ~입니다.

여담

• Incidentally,	그건 그렇고,
• I have a personal anecdote concerning ~.	~에 대한 개인적인 일화가 있습니다.
• That reminds me of ~.	그건 ~를 떠올리게 하는군요.
• One time, I had a chance of ~.	한번은, ~할 기회가 있었습니다.

결론

• I'd like to end with ~.	~로 끝내고 싶습니다.
• Let me just run over X again.	X를 다시 한번 간략하게 훑어봅시다.
• So far we've seen that ~.	지금까지 우리는 ~에 대해 알아보았습니다.
• So, just to quickly recap, ~.	그럼, 빠르게 요약해 보면, ~.

Example

Woman: Professor | Man: Student

L04_EX

Listen to part of a discussion in an engineering class.

W As we continue our discussion of electromagnetic radiation today, we will be focusing on light generation. Before humans harnessed electricity, we relied upon the light generated by the Sun and from combustion. This severely limited the tasks that we could perform at night or in rooms without windows. Many scientists attempted to develop artificial means of generating light, and the first successful electric lamp was created by Humphry Davy in 1802. Davy had created a powerful battery, and he passed the current from that battery through a thin strip of platinum, which he chose because it has an extremely high melting point. It did not generate a bright light, nor did it last long enough to be usable, but it did prove the principle of incandescence and provide the precedent for future experimenters.

M Professor, didn't Thomas Edison invent the first light bulb?

W No, actually, he did not. Some historians list as many as 22 inventors who developed incandescent lamps before Edison, including Joseph Swan, who actually created the first practical lamp. Edison and Swan did not work together, but the companies that produced their products eventually merged. (C) The reason that Edison receives so much credit is because his version of the bulb incorporated the best aspects of others. (B) It had an effective material for the filament based on Swan's work, (A) a better vacuum inside the bulb using Herman Sprengel's magnificent vacuum pump, and high resistance that allowed it to operate using his centralized power distribution system. He is remembered while other equally qualified scientists have been forgotten because he created not only components, but also an integrated system of lighting that included his generators and power distribution system.

Q. The professor explains the characteristics of Edison's light bulb, which incorporated elements of other inventors' work. Match each of the following to the inventor.

	Swan	Sprengel	Edison
Ⓐ An efficient vacuum pump to remove the air			
Ⓑ A filament made of a practical substance			
Ⓒ A comprehensive power distribution system			

공학 수업 중 토론의 일부를 들으시오.

여 오늘 전자기 방사선에 대한 이야기를 계속하면서 빛 생성에 집중해 보도록 하겠습니다. 인류가 전기를 활용하기 전 우리는 태양과 연소에서 생성되는 빛에 의존했어요. 이는 밤이나 창문이 없는 방에서 우리가 할 수 있는 업무를 심각하게 제한했습니다. 많은 과학자들이 빛을 생성시키는 인공적인 수단을 발전시키려고 시도했고, 1802년에 험프리 데이비가 첫 번째의 성공적인 전등을 만들어 냈습니다. 그는 강력한 건전지를 만들었고 얇은 백금 조각을 통해 이 건전지로부터 전류를 통하게 했습니다. 백금은 매우 높은 용해점을 가지고 있기에 이것을 선택한 것이었죠. 이 전등은 밝은 빛을 만들어내지 않았고 사용 가능할 만큼 길게 지속된 것도 아니었지만, 백열의 원리를 증명했으며 미래의 실험자들을 위한 선례가 되었습니다.

남 교수님, 토마스 에디슨이 최초의 전구를 발명하지 않았나요?

여 아니오, 사실 아닙니다. 어떤 역사가들은 에디슨 전에 백열전등을 만든 발명가를 많게는 22명까지 열거할 수 있는데, 이는 최초의 실용적인 전등을 만든 조셉 스완을 포함합니다. 에디슨과 스완은 함께 일한 것은 아니었지만 이들의 제품을 생산한 회사들은 결국 합병했죠. (C) 에디슨이 그렇게 많은 인정을 받는 이유는 그의 전구가 다른 이들의 가장 뛰어난 점을 포함했기 때문입니다. (B) 스완의 제품에 기반한 필라멘트를 위한 효율적인 재료와 (A) 헤르만 스프렝겔의 멋진 진공 펌프를 사용한 전구 안의 더 성능 좋은 진공, 그리고 그의 집중 전력 시스템을 이용하여 작동하게 한 높은 저항값이 그것이죠. 동일하게 자격을 갖춘 다른 과학자들이 잊혀진 반면 에디슨이 기억된 이유는 그가 부품들만 만든 것이 아니라 그의 발전기와 배전 시스템을 포함한 조명의 통합 시스템을 발명했기 때문입니다.

Q. 교수는 다른 발명가들의 작업 요소를 포함한 에디슨의 전구가 가진 특징들을 설명한다. 다음 각 사항을 발명가와 연결하시오.

	스완	스프렝겔	에디슨
Ⓐ 공기를 제거하기 위한 효율적인 진공 펌프		✓	
Ⓑ 실용적인 물질로 만들어진 필라멘트	✓		
Ⓒ 포괄적인 배전 시스템			✓

해설 강의에서 '스완의 제품에 기반한 필라멘트를 위한 효율적인 재료', '스프렝겔의 멋진 진공 펌프를 사용한 전구 안의 더 성능 좋은 진공', '그(에디슨)의 집중 전력 시스템을 이용하여 작동하게 한 높은 저항값'이라고 말한 데서 정답을 찾을 수 있다.

어떻게 보면 제품의 세부 정보를 묻는 '세부 사항 찾기 문제'와 비슷하다고 할 수 있다. 세부적인 내용, 특히 여러 인물과 특성이 나올 경우 반드시 노트 필기를 하도록 하자.

어휘 electromagnetic radiation 전자기 방사선 | light generation 빛 생성 | harness v 이용하다, 활용하다 | electricity n 전기, 전력 | rely v 의존하다, 기대다 | combustion n 연소 | severely adv 심하게, 엄격하게 | task n 일, 과업 | perform v 행하다, 실시하다 | artificial adj 인공의 | electric lamp 전등 | current n 전류 | strip n 가느다란 조각 | platinum n 백금 | melting point 용해점 | usable adj 사용할 수 있는, 쓸모 있는 | principle n 원리, 원칙 | incandescence n 백열 | precedent n 전례 | historian n 역사가 | inventor n 발명가 | incandescent adj 백열의 | practical adj 실용적인 | merge v 합병하다, 합치다 | incorporate v 포함하다 | aspect n 측면, 양상 | effective adj 효과적인 | filament n 필라멘트 | vacuum n 진공 | magnificent adj 멋진, 훌륭한 | resistance n 저항 | operate v 작동하다 | centralized adj 집중된 | power distribution 배전 | equally adv 동일하게 | qualified adj 자격이 있는 | component n 부품 | integrated adj 통합된 | generator n 발전기

Practice

Passage 1 Listen to part of a lecture in an art history class. L04_P01

Q. Why does the professor mention Dadaism in the lecture?

Ⓐ To contrast it with Surrealism as an art form

Ⓑ To illustrate why one movement was more popular

Ⓒ To explain what influenced the creation of surrealism

Ⓓ To compare the techniques that the artists used

Passage 2 Listen to part of a lecture in an ecology class. L04_P02

Q. Why does the professor talk about the different oil clean-up methods?

Ⓐ To classify them into traditional and non-traditional methods

Ⓑ To indicate the scale of the environmental catastrophe

Ⓒ To examine why some were more effective than others

Ⓓ To emphasize the difficulty of cleaning up the Exxon Valdez oil spill

Passage 3 Listen to part of a lecture in an American history class.

L04_P03

Q. The professor described some of the events that occurred during the life of Chief Tecumseh in the lecture. Put those events in the correct order. Drag each answer choice to the space where it belongs. One of the answer choices will not be used.

Ⓐ The Shawnee and other tribes sided with the British in the War of 1812.

Ⓑ Tecumseh tried to rally other Native American Tribes to form a confederacy.

Ⓒ The United States purchased the Louisiana Territory from France.

Ⓓ The Indian Removal Act was passed by the United States government.

Ⓔ Tecumseh became the chief of his tribe, the Shawnee.

1	
2	
3	
4	

Passage 4 Listen to part of a lecture in an astronomy class.

L04_P04

Q. In the lecture, the professor listed many features of the planet Uranus. Indicate which of the following features are mentioned in the lecture.
Click in the correct box for each sentence.

	Yes	No
Ⓐ The planet rotates on a horizontal axis.		
Ⓑ Its orbit lies between Jupiter and Saturn.		
Ⓒ Its temperature is the lowest in the solar system.		
Ⓓ The planet looks blue because of its atmosphere.		
Ⓔ Its atmosphere is composed mostly of methane.		

Lesson

05 Inference

Lesson Outline

추론 문제(Inference Question)는 지문에서 주어진 여러 정보 간의 관계에 대해 답하거나 그 정보를 기반으로 추론해서 답을 찾는 문제이다. 강의에서 따로 언급되지는 않았지만 강의 전체의 내용과 맥락을 통해 추론·유추할 수 있는 사실을 묻는다.

Lesson Point

Point 1 5개 문제 유형 중 최고난도의 문제 유형!

Point 2 문제에 imply, infer, next, result, cause, conclude 등의 단어가 있으면 추론 문제!

Point 3 들은 것(노트 필기한 것)을 바탕으로 제시된 정보의 특징을 유추, 추론한다.

Point 4 너무 깊게 생각하여 강의 내용을 벗어난 추론을 하지 않도록 주의!
추론의 근거는 어디까지나 화자가 한 말 안에 있어야 한다.

Typical Questions

- What will the professor most likely do next? 교수는 다음에 무엇을 할 것 같은가?
- What does the professor imply about ~? 교수는 ~에 관해 무엇을 암시하는가?
- What can be inferred about ~? ~에 대해 무엇을 추론할 수 있는가?
- What can be inferred from the professor's explanation about ~? 교수의 ~에 대한 설명으로부터 무엇을 추론할 수 있는가?
- What will the professor discuss next? 교수는 다음에 무엇에 대해 이야기하겠는가?
- What can be concluded about ~? ~에 관해 어떤 결론을 내릴 수 있는가?

Learning Strategies

주제의 특징을 나타내는 표시어(signal)를 공략한다!

주제의 주요 특징 및 예시에 관해 유추 · 추론하는 문제가 나오므로, 주제의 특징과 관련된 원인, 결과, 비교, 대조 등을 나타내는 표시어를 중심으로 노트 필기하며 듣는다.

원인

- The reason why it happened was ~. 그 일이 발생한 이유는 ~였습니다.
- This is due to ~. 이것은 ~때문입니다.
- This is caused by ~. 이것은 ~에 의해 야기되었습니다.
- What happened was ~. 무슨 일이 일어났는가 하면 ~.
- How did it happen? Well, ~. 어떻게 그 일이 일어났을까요? 자, ~.

결과

- As a result 그 결과로
- This results in ~. 이는 결과적으로 ~가/~하게 됩니다.
- X comes as a result of Y. Y의 결과로 X가 되게 됩니다.
- This led to ~. 이는 ~로 이어졌습니다.
- Consequently 그 결과, 따라서

비교

- Both X and Y X와 Y 모두
- Similarly 비슷하게, 유사하게
- Likewise 똑같이, 비슷하게
- In the same way 같은 방법으로
- In a similar fashion 유사한 방식으로

대조

- Whilst/While/Whereas X, Y. X인데 반해, Y입니다.
- On the contrary 그와는 반대로
- In contrast 그에 반해서
- On the other hand 다른 한편으로는
- However/But 그렇지만, 그러나

Example

Woman: Professor

L05_EX

Listen to part of a lecture in a biology class.

W Over the last fifty years, anthropogenic global warming has been causing the polar ice caps to steadily shrink, which is reducing the polar bears' natural habitat. As you know, the majority of a polar bear's diet consists of seals, which they use the ice to capture. Seals must surface to refill their lungs before diving again to hunt their own prey, so they often emerge from holes in the ice to breathe. Polar bears lurk by such holes, patiently waiting for a seal to breach the surface, at which point the bear will seize the defenseless creature in its jaws and wrest it from its aquatic home. The vitamin and nutrient dense meat and blubber of the seals satisfy all of the bears' dietary needs. They do most of their hunting in the spring and summer, when they pack on needed weight for the long polar winter. But, with increasingly less ice to stage their ambushes from, these giants are unable to gorge themselves. Like all organisms, the bears must prioritize their energy usage, so if they cannot feed enough, they are less likely to reproduce. Even if they do mate, there is less chance that their offspring will survive long enough to learn to hunt. In 2004, archaeologists discovered a polar bear jawbone that has been dated to 110,000 to 130,000 years old, which provided some interesting information through its DNA. By analyzing the mitochondrial DNA of ancient and modern polar bears and comparing it with that of other ancient and modern bear species, they have concretely proven that polar bears are actually a highly specialized form of brown bear. This relationship has been further proven by the confirmation of polar bear-grizzly bear hybrids. Dubbed "grolar bears," these animals may point to the future of the species. If they continue to interbreed, that could hasten the disappearance of polar bears, but their DNA would live on in their descendants. So, when the conditions once again become more favorable, the traits that define polar bears may emerge again, allowing the rebirth of the species.

Q. What can be inferred from the professor's explanation about "grolar bears"?

(A) Grolar bears can be a future solution for the survival of polar bears.

(B) The method to interbreed polar bears and grizzly bears has yet to be discovered.

(C) Grolar bears can survive extreme weather conditions that polar bears cannot.

(D) The advance of science will be able to lengthen the survival of grolar bears.

생물학 강의의 일부를 들으시오.

여 지난 50년간 인류로 인해 야기된 지구 온난화가 극지방의 만년설을 지속적으로 줄어들게 만들고 있는데, 이는 북극곰들의 자연 서식지를 감소시키고 있어요. 여러분도 알겠지만 북극곰의 대부분의 음식 섭취는 바다표범으로 이루어지는데, 이들을 잡기 위해 얼음을 이용합니다. 바다표범들은 먹이를 사냥하러 물에 다시 들어가기 전에 물 밖으로 나와 폐에 숨을 채워야만 하는데, 숨을 쉬기 위해 종종 얼음에 난 구멍을 통해 올라옵니다. 북극곰들은 이들 구멍 주변에 숨어서 참을성 있게 바다표범이 수면 위로 올라오길 기다리는데, 올라오는 순간 무방비 상태의 바다표범을 턱으로 물어 물 속의 집으로부터 끄집어내서 잡습니다. 바다표범 고기와 지방에 잔뜩 함유된 비타민과 영양분은 북극곰의 음식으로 필요한 영양소들을 모두 만족시켜주죠. 사냥의 대부분을 봄과 여름에 해서 긴 극지방의 겨울에 대비해 필요한 무게를 늘립니다. 그러나 몰래 숨어있다가 기습하는 데 필요한 얼음이 점점 녹고 있기에 이 거대한 곰들은 배를 불리지 못하고 있어요. 모든 생물들과 마찬가지로 이 곰들은 에너지 사용에 우선 순위를 매겨야만 하는데, 그래서 충분히 먹이를 섭취하지 못하면 번식을 할 가능성이 줄어듭니다. 그리고 짝짓기를 한다 해도 이들의 새끼가 사냥을 배울 때까지 생존할 가능성은 적습니다. 2004년에 고고학자들은 약 11만 년에서 13만 년 전으로 추정되는 북극곰의 턱뼈를 발견했는데, 이 뼈의 DNA를 통해 흥미로운 정보를 제공했습니다. 고대와 현대의 북극곰들의 미토콘드리아 DNA를 분석하고 고대와 현대의 곰 종들의 DNA를 비교했을 때 이는 북극곰들이 사실 매우 전문화된 불곰의 한 종류라는 것을 명확하게 증명했어요. 이 관계는 북극곰과 회색곰 잡종에 대한 확인을 통해 더 증명되었습니다. '그롤라곰'이라고 별명 붙여진 이 곰들은 종의 미래에 중요한 핵심이 될 수도 있습니다. 이들이 계속해서 이종 교배를 한다면 이는 북극곰이 더 빨리 사라지도록 만들 가능성이 있지만, 이들의 DNA는 후손들을 통해 전해질 겁니다. 그래서 환경이 좀 더 좋아진다면 북극곰을 정의하는 이 특징들이 다시 나타나서 북극곰 종의 부활로 이어질 수도 있죠.

Q. '그롤라곰'에 대한 교수의 설명에서 무엇을 유추할 수 있는가?

(A) 그롤라곰들은 북극곰의 생존에 있어 미래의 해결책이 될 수 있다.

(B) 북극곰과 회색곰을 이종 교배시키는 방법은 아직 발견되지 않았다.

(C) 그롤라곰들은 북극곰들이 생존할 수 없는 극단적인 기후에서도 생존할 수 있다.

(D) 과학의 발전은 그롤라곰의 생존을 더 연장할 수 있을 것이다.

해설 북극곰의 턱뼈를 통해 과학자들은 북극곰이 아주 전문화된 불곰의 한 종류라는 점을 밝혀냈으며 북극곰과 회색곰 잡종, 즉 '그롤라곰'을 통해 이것을 확인했다고 강의에서 나온다. 이 점을 이용해 두 종이 계속해서 이종 교배를 하게 하여 북극곰의 DNA를 계속 남길 수 있다고 했으므로 북극곰의 미래 생존 가능성을 염두에 두고 있다는 점을 알 수 있다.

어휘 anthropogenic adj 인류 발생의(인류로부터 만들어진) | global warming 지구 온난화 | steadily adv 꾸준히, 착실하게 | shrink v 줄어들다, 오그라들다 | reduce v 줄이다, 축소하다 | habitat n 서식지 | majority n 다수, 가장 많은 수 | consist v 이루어져 있다 | seal n 바다표범 | capture v 잡다, 포획하다 | surface v 수면으로 올라오다 | refill v 다시 채우다 | lung n 폐 | emerge v 나오다, 모습을 드러내다 | lurk v 숨어 있다, 도사리다 | patiently adv 참을성 있게 | breach v 구멍을 뚫다 | seize v 붙잡다, 움켜잡다 | defenseless adj 무방비의, 방어할 수 없는 | jaw n 턱 | wrest v 비틀다 | aquatic adj 물속에서 자라는 | blubber n 해양 동물의 지방 | satisfy v 만족시키다 | dietary adj 음식물의 | pack v 싸다, 꾸리다 | ambush n 매복 | gorge v 실컷 먹다 | prioritize v 우선 순위를 매기다 | reproduce v 복사하다, 복제하다 | mate v 짝짓기를 하다 | offspring n 새끼, 자식 | analyze v 분석하다 | mitochondrial adj 미토콘드리아의 | concretely adv 구체적으로, 명확하게 | specialized adj 전문화된 | confirmation n 확인, 확정 | hybrid n 잡종 | dub v 별명을 붙이다 | interbreed v 이종 교배하다 | hasten v 재촉하다 | descendant n 자손, 후손 | define v 정의하다, 규정하다 | rebirth n 부활

Practice

Passage 1 Listen to part of a lecture in an American history class. L05_P01

Q. What can be inferred about the whaling industry in the United States?

Ⓐ It exported oil products around the world.

Ⓑ It was the largest contributor to the nation's export.

Ⓒ It contributed greatly to the country's economy.

Ⓓ It supported the industrialization of the nation.

Passage 2 Listen to part of a lecture in a biology class. L05_P02

Q. What is implied about blood plasma?

Ⓐ It is the main component in blood.

Ⓑ It allows wounds to heal more quickly.

Ⓒ It defends the body against illnesses.

Ⓓ It is a watery yellow fluid produced by the body.

정답 및 해석 | P. 61

Passage 3 Listen to part of a lecture in an environmentology class.

L05_P03

Q. What can be deduced about El Niño from the lecture?

Ⓐ It results in increased rainfall throughout the world.

Ⓑ It contributes to a sharp increase in boating accidents.

Ⓒ It causes natural disasters around the world.

Ⓓ It brings about problems on the Atlantic side of South America.

Passage 4 Listen to part of a lecture in an ecology class.

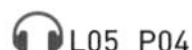

Q. What does the professor imply about current agricultural practices?

Ⓐ Raising large herds of animals compacts the soil.

Ⓑ Too much salt is building up in the soil.

Ⓒ Fertilizers accumulate in the ground water.

Ⓓ Farmers are using up the land that can be farmed.

Actual Test 1

TOEFL Listening

Now put on your headset.

Click on **Continue** to go on.

TOEFL Listening

Changing the Volume

To change the volume, click on the Volume icon at the top of the screen. The volume control will appear. Move the volume indicator to the left or to the right to change the volume.

To close the volume control, move the mouse pointer to another part of the screen.

You may now change the volume.
When you are finished, click on **Continue**.

TOEFL Listening

Listening Section Directions

This section measures your ability to understand conversations and lectures in English. You should listen to each conversation and lecture only once.

After each conversation or lecture, you will answer some questions about it. The questions typically ask about the main idea and supporting details. Some questions ask about the purpose of a speaker's statement or a speaker's attitude. Answer the questions based on what is stated or implied by the speakers.

You may take notes while you listen. You may use your notes to help you answer the questions. Your notes will not be scored.

In some questions, you will see this icon: 🎧 This means that you will hear, but not see, part of the question.

Most questions are worth 1 point. If a question is worth more than 1 point, it will have special directions that indicate how many points you can receive.

You must answer each question. Click **NEXT** after you have answered a question. Then click **OK** to confirm and proceed to the next question. You cannot return to an earlier question once you have clicked **OK**.

A clock will be displayed at the top of the screen to show how much time remains. It only counts down while you are answering a question - not while you are listening to a conversation or lecture.

Conversation 1

[1-5] Listen to part of a conversation between a student and a librarian.  L_AT1_01

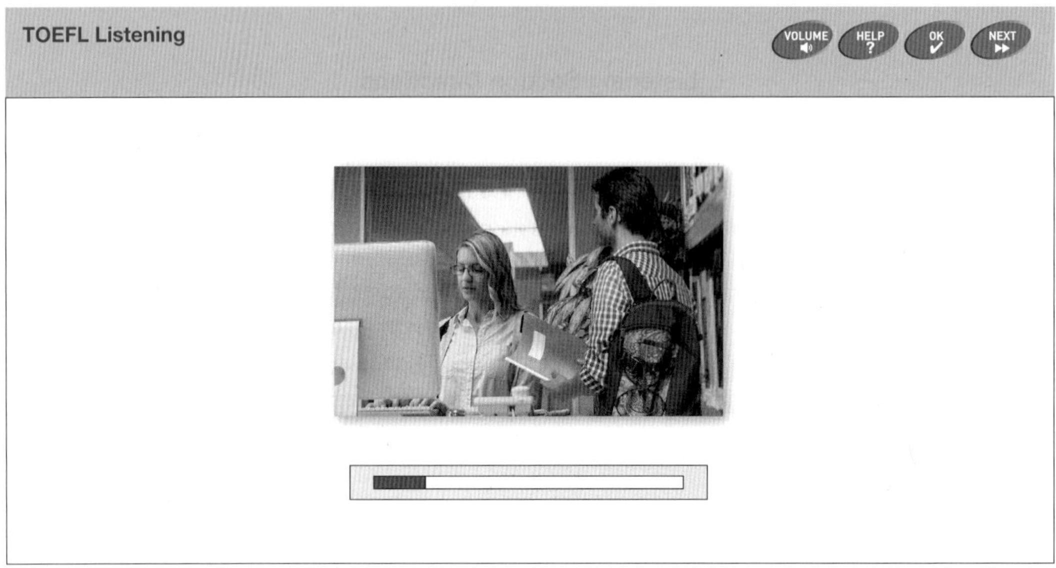

1. **Why does the student go to the library?**

Ⓐ To check out some materials for a paper he is writing

Ⓑ To find out why he is receiving notices from the library

Ⓒ To inquire about obtaining notes for a psychology lecture

Ⓓ To request a timeline for picking up reserve materials

2. **What is a key feature of the library's checkout policy?**

Ⓐ Seniors are permitted to keep books out without a time limit.

Ⓑ Seniors are permitted to keep books out longer with some restrictions.

Ⓒ All underclassmen must return books as soon as seniors request them.

Ⓓ Seniors and underclassmen have the same library privileges.

3. **Listen again to part of the conversation. Then answer the question.**

What does the student imply when he says this:

Ⓐ He does not comprehend the rules of the book return policy.

Ⓑ He is irritated about the ineffective book return policy.

Ⓒ He thinks the policy regarding a senior extension is unfair.

Ⓓ He believes that the library should lengthen the policy time.

4. **What is true about the return request?**

Ⓐ It is something that does not happen that often.

Ⓑ It guarantees a semester-long checkout for seniors.

Ⓒ It requires students to fill out a form.

Ⓓ It has to be fulfilled within a week.

5. **What is the likely outcome of the conversation?**

Ⓐ The student will be allowed to keep the book until the completion of his project.

Ⓑ The student will no longer be able to check books out from the library.

Ⓒ The student will return the book but receive it back sooner than thought.

Ⓓ The student will not utilize the services of the library any longer.

Lecture 1

[6-11] Listen to part of a lecture in an astronomy class. 

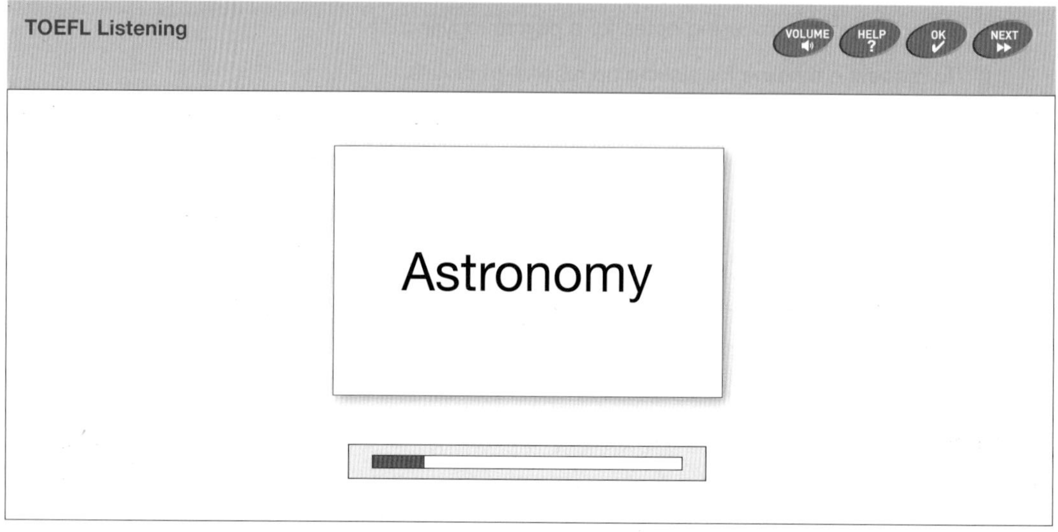

6. What is the topic of this lecture?

Ⓐ Pluto and its constantly-changing position in the solar system

Ⓑ Pluto and the space agencies that are fighting to reach it first

Ⓒ The characteristics of Pluto and the ongoing process of learning about it

Ⓓ Pluto and the type of spacecrafts that have explored there

7. **What does the professor imply about the discovery of Pluto?**

Ⓐ The mistake was not very important to the discovery of Pluto.

Ⓑ Pluto exists only as a mathematical possibility.

Ⓒ Pluto was only discovered because of a mistake.

Ⓓ We know about Pluto only because of its influence on Neptune's orbit.

8. **How does the professor account for the fact that so little is known about Pluto?**

Ⓐ Pluto cannot be seen clearly even with our best telescope.

Ⓑ Pluto is large and is located very far from Earth.

Ⓒ Pluto has only been observed from other planets.

Ⓓ Pluto has a circular orbit, which makes it invisible for long periods.

9. **What does the professor say are the characteristics of Pluto's atmosphere?**
Choose 2 answers.

Ⓐ It is not affected by Pluto's orbit.

Ⓑ It is composed of methane, carbon monoxide, and nitrogen.

Ⓒ It is very stable.

Ⓓ It stays frozen for hundreds of years at a time.

Ⓔ The snow and ice covering Pluto melt spontaneously.

10. **Listen again to part of the lecture. Then answer the question.**

Why does the professor say this:

Ⓐ He thinks that the students can understand based on what he has already said.

Ⓑ He thinks that the students couldn't possibly understand why it is important.

Ⓒ He thinks that the students already knew why the probe is important.

Ⓓ He thinks the students will find this boring because they already know a lot about it.

11. **What will the professor probably talk about next?**

Ⓐ He will go on to discuss the New Horizons mission in more detail.

Ⓑ He will move to a discussion about Mars and the Hubble telescope.

Ⓒ He will talk about the possibility of humans living on Pluto.

Ⓓ He will discuss the costs and benefits of space exploration.

PAGODA TOEFL 80+ R/L/S/W

TOEFL Listening

Listening Directions

You will now begin the next part of the Listening Section.

You must answer each question. After you answer, click on **NEXT**. Then click on **OK** to confirm your answer and go on to the next question. After you click on **OK**, you cannot return to previous questions.

Click on **CONTINUE** to go on.

Conversation 2

[1-5] Listen to part of a conversation between a student and a cafeteria manager.  L_AT1_03

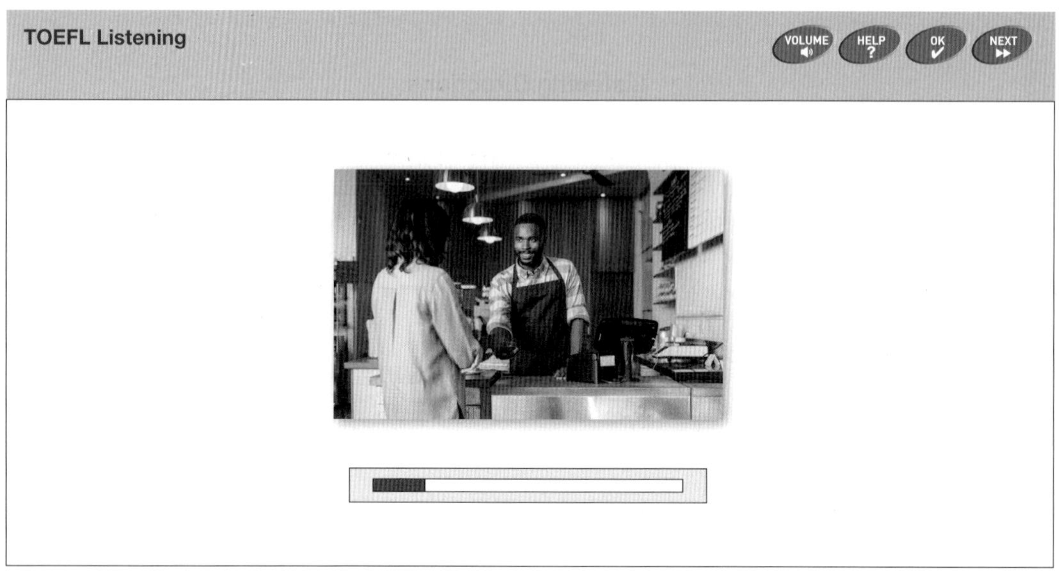

1. Why does the student go to see the cafeteria manager?

Ⓐ To make a complaint about the quality of the food

Ⓑ To apply for a vacant work position at the cafeteria

Ⓒ To ask about information involving a baking class

Ⓓ To substitute a working shift for a sick friend

2. What is the man's attitude at the beginning of the conversation?

Ⓐ He is trying to show that he is too busy to talk at the moment.

Ⓑ He is implying that the student is not qualified for the job.

Ⓒ He is stating that the cooking class has filled up.

Ⓓ He is wondering if the woman filled the lunch order.

3. What made the student want to register for the cooking class?

Ⓐ She wants to improve her cooking skills because she lives alone.

Ⓑ She wants to learn to bake a cake to cheer up her injured friend.

Ⓒ She is trying to impress her parents, who are coming to visit.

Ⓓ She is considering changing her major to the culinary arts.

4. Listen again to part of the conversation. Then answer the question.

Why does the student say this:

Ⓐ She is excited that she got a job working at the cafeteria.

Ⓑ She is angry because she thinks the manager overcharged her.

Ⓒ She is very happy because the class will be beneficial to her.

Ⓓ She is upset at the man because he gave away her spot in the class.

5. What are two items that the student needs to bring to the cooking class? Choose 2 answers.

Ⓐ Spatula

Ⓑ Apron

Ⓒ Beater

Ⓓ Old clothes

Lecture 2

[6-11] Listen to part of a discussion in a marine biology class. L_AT1_04

6. What is the discussion mainly about?

Ⓐ The life cycle of the fiddler crab

Ⓑ The role of the fiddler crab in its local ecosystem

Ⓒ The fiddler crab's features and patterns of behavior

Ⓓ The dating rituals of the fiddler crab

7. **What are the main characteristics of fiddler crabs mentioned by the professor? Choose 3 answers.**

Ⓐ They filter their food from mud.
Ⓑ They are most active during high tide.
Ⓒ They live in networks of small tunnels.
Ⓓ They breathe air.
Ⓔ Their main food is small birds and fish.

8. **According to the professor, how can male and female crabs be differentiated?**

Ⓐ Female fiddler crabs' claws are both the same size, whereas the males' aren't.
Ⓑ Female fiddler crabs remain in their burrows more than males do.
Ⓒ Female fiddler crabs look for food in the intertidal region, while males don't.
Ⓓ Both male and female fiddler crabs wave their claws during dating.

9. **What does the professor infer when she talks about goliath beetles and walruses?**

Ⓐ Male fiddler crabs have the same body parts as these creatures.
Ⓑ Male fiddler crabs have structures that look very similar to the structure of these organisms.
Ⓒ The behavior of male fiddler crabs is similar to these creatures.
Ⓓ The enlarged claw of male fiddler crabs has a function similar to body parts of these creatures.

10. **Put the following words in the same order as the professor used when talking about the characteristics of the crabs.**

Ⓐ Mating Behavior
Ⓑ Habitat
Ⓒ Body Structure
Ⓓ Feeding Behavior

1	
2	
3	
4	

11. **Listen again to part of the discussion. Then answer the question.**

Why does the professor say this:

Ⓐ To help students understand that crabs mate very often during their lifetime
Ⓑ To demonstrate ways that females behave and ways that males try to get their attention
Ⓒ To add humor and interest and give students a vivid image that they will more easily remember
Ⓓ To help students see that crabs behave strangely during breeding season

Lecture 3

[12-17] Listen to part of a lecture in a psychology class.

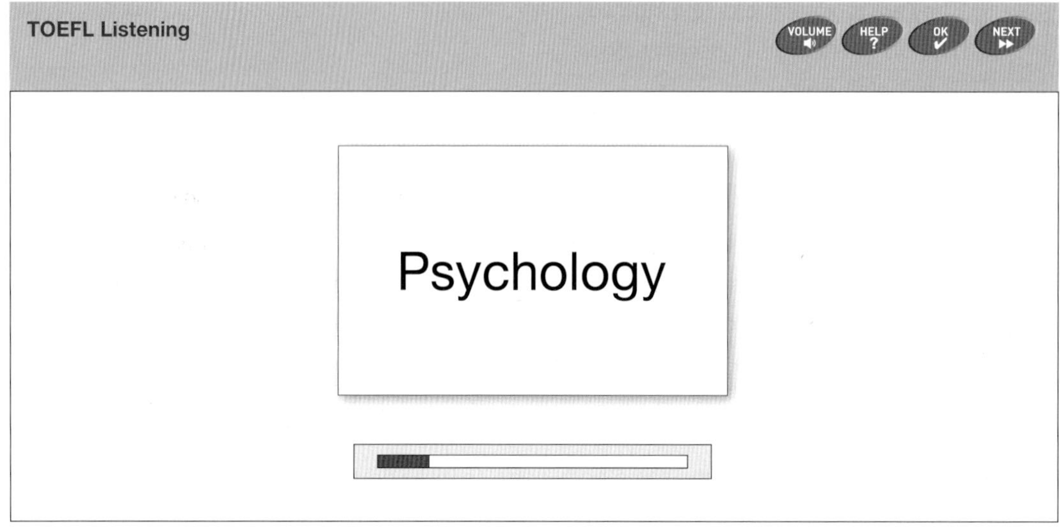

12. What is the lecture mainly about?

Ⓐ Using cooking to learn about other things

Ⓑ John Dewey's personal life

Ⓒ Reforms in rote-learning techniques

Ⓓ A revolutionary development in education

13. What does the professor say about memorization?

(A) It's a critical part of student-centered learning.

(B) It's not a useful indicator of practical intelligence.

(C) It can be used in any classroom situation.

(D) It cannot be influenced by repetition.

14. How is the lecture organized?

(A) The spokesperson gives a biographical account of a prominent figure in 20th-century education.

(B) The professor shows students feedback received from a class that used a learner-centered style.

(C) The teacher introduces an alternative form of education followed by its pros and cons.

(D) The instructor discusses a traditional teaching method before presenting John Dewey's alternative.

15. According to the professor, what does her son do to learn about geometry?

(A) He uses toys to construct different things.

(B) He breaks his toys into pieces.

(C) He attends a public school taught by Dewey.

(D) He practices making buildings outside in nature.

16. What is the professor's attitude toward her son's playing with wooden blocks?

(A) She is disappointed that he has to use toys to learn a subject taught in schools.

(B) She likes the structures he creates with the wooden toy blocks.

(C) She feels that his public school should use this type of learning in its classrooms.

(D) She is happy he is enjoying himself while naturally learning about geometry.

17. Listen again to part of the lecture. Then answer the question.

Why does the professor say this:

(A) Since the students are already cooperating with each other, the professor doesn't want to do any lecturing in the next class.

(B) Since she lectures during the class, the students will be listening to her rather than cooperatively working toward their goals together.

(C) Since each student is already in charge of achieving his or her goals, the professor feels it is unnecessary to do any lecturing.

(D) Since listening isn't necessary in a learner-centered class, the professor feels it doesn't need to be practiced in the next class.

Actual Test 2

TOEFL Listening

Now put on your headset.

Click on **Continue** to go on.

TOEFL Listening

Changing the Volume

To change the volume, click on the Volume icon at the top of the screen. The volume control will appear. Move the volume indicator to the left or to the right to change the volume.

To close the volume control, move the mouse pointer to another part of the screen.

You may now change the volume.
When you are finished, click on **Continue**.

TOEFL Listening

Listening Section Directions

This section measures your ability to understand conversations and lectures in English. You should listen to each conversation and lecture only once.

After each conversation or lecture, you will answer some questions about it. The questions typically ask about the main idea and supporting details. Some questions ask about the purpose of a speaker's statement or a speaker's attitude. Answer the questions based on what is stated or implied by the speakers.

You may take notes while you listen. You may use your notes to help you answer the questions. Your notes will not be scored.

In some questions, you will see this icon: 🎧 This means that you will hear, but not see, part of the question.

Most questions are worth 1 point. If a question is worth more than 1 point, it will have special directions that indicate how many points you can receive.

You must answer each question. Click **NEXT** after you have answered a question. Then click **OK** to confirm and proceed to the next question. You cannot return to an earlier question once you have clicked **OK**.

A clock will be displayed at the top of the screen to show how much time remains. It only counts down while you are answering a question - not while you are listening to a conversation or lecture.

Conversation 1

[1-5] Listen to part of a conversation between a student and a resident assistant. 

1. What is the conversation mainly about?

Ⓐ The speakers are discussing a problem with the dormitory lease.

Ⓑ The speakers are debating the benefits of living in the dorm.

Ⓒ The speakers are wondering where a late student is.

Ⓓ The speakers are trying to resolve a roommate issue.

2. What is implied about the school's policy toward student problems in the dorms?

Ⓐ The school has very strict regulations regarding students' behavior.

Ⓑ The school would prefer that students solve problems on their own.

Ⓒ The school never permits students to change rooms in mid-semester.

Ⓓ The school allows students to change rooms at any point in the year.

3. What does the housing officer tell the student to do?

Ⓐ She insists that the student solve the problem on his own with the roommate.

Ⓑ She directs the student to take up the problem with the Dean of Students.

Ⓒ She suggests that the student gather the signatures needed to change rooms.

Ⓓ She advises the student to coordinate schedules with the roommate.

4. What does the student say about the R.A.'s second suggestion?

Ⓐ He is concerned about his new roommate's current roommate.

Ⓑ He believes it will be effective since he already got their signatures.

Ⓒ He is worried since he needs to persuade a few people.

Ⓓ He thinks it can work out very well since he already knows what to do.

5. Listen again to part of the conversation. Then answer the question.

What does the student mean when he says this:

Ⓐ The student would like the R.A. to repeat the instructions.

Ⓑ The student is upset he has to do the appropriate paperwork.

Ⓒ The student understands the signatures are most important.

Ⓓ The student doubts that he will be able to get all the signatures.

Lecture 1

[6-11] Listen to part of a discussion in a history class.  L_AT2_02

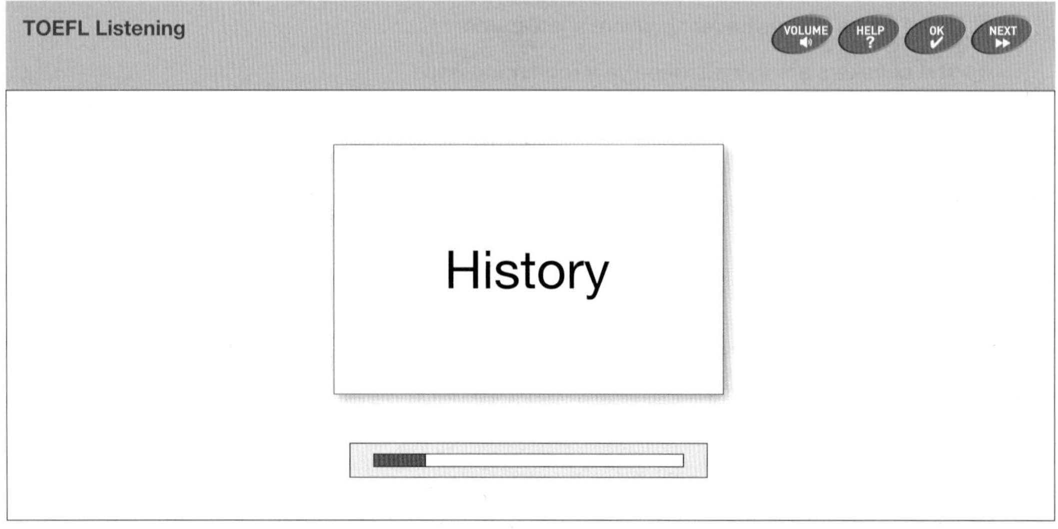

6. What is the discussion mainly about?

Ⓐ The time-consuming process of excavating the Nebra sky disk

Ⓑ The interesting discovery that was made in Germany

Ⓒ The lives of people who lived during the Neolithic period

Ⓓ The astrological observances made with an ancient calendar

7. What is true about the Nebra sky disk?

Ⓐ It was invented for ritual purposes.

Ⓑ Its age has yet to be discovered.

Ⓒ It was made of gold, bronze, and silver.

Ⓓ Its diameter is about one meter.

8. Why did scientists assume that the Nebra sky disk was some form of calendar? Choose 2 answers.

Ⓐ The area that it was found is deeply related with astrology.

Ⓑ The numbers carved on the disk showed similarities with today's calendar.

Ⓒ There are some celestial bodies portrayed on the surface of the disk.

Ⓓ People during the Neolithic period had already been using calendars.

9. What can be inferred about the Nebra sky disk and other artifacts?

Ⓐ Their original burial site cannot solely prove their authenticity.

Ⓑ There are various ways to prove that they were forged.

Ⓒ They were almost sold to another country by the hunters.

Ⓓ Their existence proved the widespread use of iron in the region.

10. Why does the professor mention a piece of birch bark?

Ⓐ To show the interesting use of trees during the Neolithic period

Ⓑ To emphasize the importance of small objects for a burial ritual

Ⓒ To introduce another important discovery from the Bronze Age

Ⓓ To explain how scientists discovered the burial date of the artifacts

11. Why does the professor say this: 🎧

Ⓐ He is telling the students that many things still need to be revealed.

Ⓑ He sees the difficulty of determining whether the disk is authentic or not.

Ⓒ He finds it interesting to see the earliest trade route of mankind.

Ⓓ He is excited that the authenticity of the disk was finally made certain.

PAGODA TOEFL 80+ R/L/S/W

TOEFL Listening

Listening Directions

You will now begin the next part of the Listening Section.

You must answer each question. After you answer, click on **NEXT**. Then click on **OK** to confirm your answer and go on to the next question. After you click on **OK**, you cannot return to previous questions.

Click on **CONTINUE** to go on.

Conversation 2

[1-5] Listen to part of a conversation between a student and a registrar. 

1. **Why does the student go to the registrar's office?**

Ⓐ She wants to check an error on her tuition bill.

Ⓑ She needs to pay a political seminar fee.

Ⓒ She wants to sign up for a required class.

Ⓓ She has signed up for the wrong class.

2. **What is the man's attitude toward the student at the beginning of the conversation?**

Ⓐ He is annoyed by the fact that the student could not register the class herself.

Ⓑ He is puzzled why the student took so long to register for the class.

Ⓒ He is irritated that the student is taking so long to complete the registration.

Ⓓ He is not sure if the class is really important for the student.

3. **What suggestions does the registrar give to the student? Choose 2 answers.**

Ⓐ He suggests that the student make up the course in the summer.

Ⓑ He suggests that the student get an override from the professor.

Ⓒ He suggests that the student try to audit the class and wait.

Ⓓ He suggests that the student take the class at a different university.

4. **Listen again to part of the conversation. Then answer the question.**

What does the student mean when she says this:

Ⓐ She thinks the idea doesn't sound necessary.

Ⓑ She does not understand why there are so many people on the list.

Ⓒ She thinks she will get into the course soon in the semester.

Ⓓ She thinks that she will not be admitted into the class this semester.

5. **What will the student most likely do?**

Ⓐ Find an open spot to audit the required course

Ⓑ Visit City Hall to sign up for the political seminar

Ⓒ Go and see Professor Peterson regarding her grade

Ⓓ Visit Professor Peterson's office to ask for help

Lecture 2

[6-11] Listen to part of a lecture in a biology class.

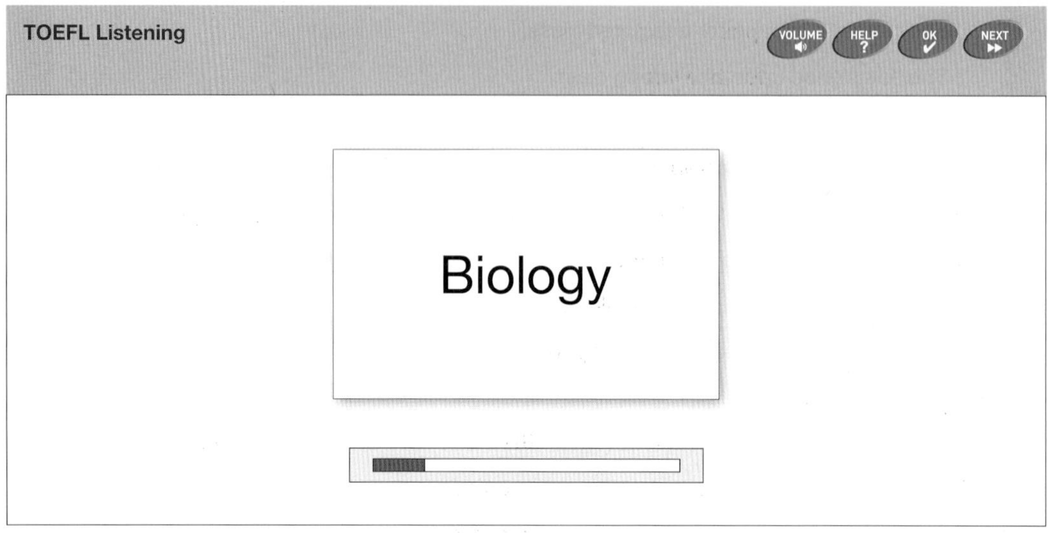

6. What is the topic of the lecture?

Ⓐ Self-pollination and how plants do it

Ⓑ The way farmers can make more money

Ⓒ The different ways plants create new plants

Ⓓ Cross-pollination and what makes it happen

7. What does the professor say about pollen?

Ⓐ It is commonly seen in the springtime.

Ⓑ It makes all flowers yellow in color.

Ⓒ It is helpful for protecting flowers.

Ⓓ It is the male portion of a plant.

8. What is the professor's attitude toward wind as a pollinator of large areas?

Ⓐ He feels the wind is the best for them.

Ⓑ He thinks the wind is better for flowers.

Ⓒ He wants more information.

Ⓓ He isn't sure the wind is strong enough to be effective.

9. How can honeybees be compared to the bees native to the area?

Ⓐ They are less expensive than native bees.

Ⓑ They are larger than native bees.

Ⓒ They aren't as efficient at pollinating as native bees.

Ⓓ They pollinate plants faster than native bees.

10. Listen again to part of the lecture. Then answer the question.

Why does the professor say this:

Ⓐ To develop ideas for discussion in the next class

Ⓑ To talk about how pollination fertilizes plants

Ⓒ To inform students what they will be reading about for homework

Ⓓ To describe the process that creates new plants

11. How does the professor conclude the lecture?

Ⓐ By assigning homework and reviewing the lecture

Ⓑ By answering questions about pollination

Ⓒ By telling students to read about vegetables

Ⓓ By giving a homework assignment and asking a question

Lecture 3

[12-17] Listen to part of a discussion in a business class. L_AT2_05

12. What aspects of advertising is the professor mainly discussing?

Ⓐ The costs and benefits of advertising

Ⓑ The types of messages that companies try to send through advertisements

Ⓒ The main elements companies must consider when planning advertisements

Ⓓ The four types of advertising media

13. Listen again to part of the discussion. Then answer the question.

Why does the professor say this:

Ⓐ She does not think the students need another definition.

Ⓑ She wants to give a definition that is a little easier to understand.

Ⓒ She feels like the students should be able to understand the first definition.

Ⓓ She's trying to say that the first definition is not confusing.

14. What is the market in the 4 M's of advertising?

Ⓐ The method used to show the advertisements

Ⓑ Who will buy the product and how much they need it

Ⓒ The number of people who will see the TV commercial

Ⓓ The style the company uses to make the ad

15. According to the professor, how is market related to media?

Ⓐ Market and target consumers are more important than the media form.

Ⓑ The media that is chosen is more important than the market.

Ⓒ The target customer must be established before determining which form of media to use.

Ⓓ The media message should be chosen first, then companies can decide whom to target.

16. Why is time important in terms of the third M, 'money'?

Ⓐ It gets the most viewership and maximizes the number of potential consumers.

Ⓑ It reminds existing consumers of a certain product again to purchase.

Ⓒ It can estimate the number of people who watch the Super Bowl.

Ⓓ It attracts different groups of people who can affect a company's sales.

17. How does the professor conclude the discussion?

Ⓐ By repeating the main topic of the lecture

Ⓑ By giving several examples of the main topic

Ⓒ By asking the students if they can remember something

Ⓓ By reminding the students the most important example of the lecture

Speaking

I. Independent Task Q1 선택 말하기

- Lesson 01 표현 익히기
- Lesson 02 이유 제시하기
- Lesson 03 문장으로 말하기

II. Integrated Task Q2 읽고 듣고 말하기: 대학 생활

- Lesson 01 표현 익히기
- Lesson 02 읽기 정리
- Lesson 03 듣기 정리
- Lesson 04 정리해서 말하기

III. Integrated Task Q3 읽고 듣고 말하기: 대학 강의

- Lesson 01 표현 익히기
- Lesson 02 읽기 정리
- Lesson 03 듣기 정리
- Lesson 04 정리해서 말하기

IV. Integrated Task Q4 듣고 말하기: 대학 강의

- Lesson 01 표현 익히기
- Lesson 02 듣기 정리
- Lesson 03 정리해서 말하기

V. Actual Tests

Actual Test 1

Actual Test 2

iBT TOEFL® Speaking 개요

1. Speaking 영역의 특징

Speaking 영역은 수험자가 영어권 국가에서 공부할 때 효율적으로 담화를 통해 자기 생각을 표현할 수 있는 능력, 즉 교실 안팎에서 읽고 들었던 정보에 대해서 이야기하고 자신의 가치관 및 의견을 말할 수 있는 능력을 측정하는 데 그 목적이 있다. 상황별 상세 목적은 다음과 같다.

❶ in class: 수업 시간에

다양한 주제의 학술 토론

교수나 다른 학생과 질문하고 질문에 답하기

자신의 의견 및 주장 말하기

❷ around campus: 캠퍼스 주변에서

다른 학생들과 친숙한 주제에 대한 일상의 대화(음악, 여행, 세계적 이슈, 정치 등)

서점, 기숙사, 도서관 같은 곳에서의 대화

2. Speaking 영역의 구성

진행 시간	문제 개수	문제 형태
총 17분	4개	1. Independent Task(문제 1번) 독립형 과제에서는 질문에 대한 개인적 의견을 말한다. 2. Integrated Task(문제 2번, 3번, 4번) 통합형 과제에서는 읽거나 들은 정보를 바탕으로 질문에 답한다.

3. Speaking 영역의 시험 유형 및 시간 배분

		문제 유형		시간 배분
독립형	Q1. 선택	두 가지 상반되는 선택 사항을 주고 선호하는 것을 선택하거나 찬/반 입장을 이유와 함께 설명	말하기	준비 시간 15초 답변 시간 45초
통합형	Q2. 상황 설명 <캠퍼스 관련>	• 읽기 캠퍼스와 관련된 상황에 관한 지문 • 듣기 읽기 지문에 관한 두 사람의 대화 • 말하기 읽기 지문에 관한 화자의 의견을 요약하는 문제	읽기 ↓ 듣기 ↓ 말하기	읽기 시간 45 / 50초 준비 시간 30초 답변 시간 60초
	Q3. 일반적 개념과 구체적 개념 <학술적 주제>	• 읽기 학술적 주제와 일반적 개념 지문 • 듣기 읽기 지문의 구체적 내용 강의 • 말하기 읽기와 듣기를 통해 얻은 정보를 요약하는 문제	읽기 ↓ 듣기 ↓ 말하기	읽기 시간 45 / 50초 준비 시간 30초 답변 시간 60초
	Q4. 요약 <학술적 주제>	• 듣기 학술적 주제에 관련된 강의 • 말하기 강의의 주제와 세부사항을 파악하여 요약하는 문제	듣기 ↓ 말하기	준비 시간 20초 답변 시간 60초

4. 기존 시험과 개정 시험 간 Speaking 영역 비교

	기존 iBT (~2023년 7월 전)	개정 후 iBT (2023년 7월 이후)
문제 개수	4개	
독립형 과제	1개	
통합형 과제	3개	
시험 시간	17분	

• 통합형 과제의 읽기와 듣기의 길이 및 난이도에는 변화가 없다.

I. Independent Task

Q1 선택 말하기

Introduction

1번 문제는 '선택 말하기' 문제로, 질문에서 제시한 두 가지 행동이나 상황, 의견 중 수험자가 마음에 드는 것을 선택하는 선호 문제 또는 어떤 주제에 관한 찬성이나 반대를 표하는 동의 문제가 나온다. 주로 학교 또는 일상 생활과 관련된 내용이 출제된다.

화면 구성

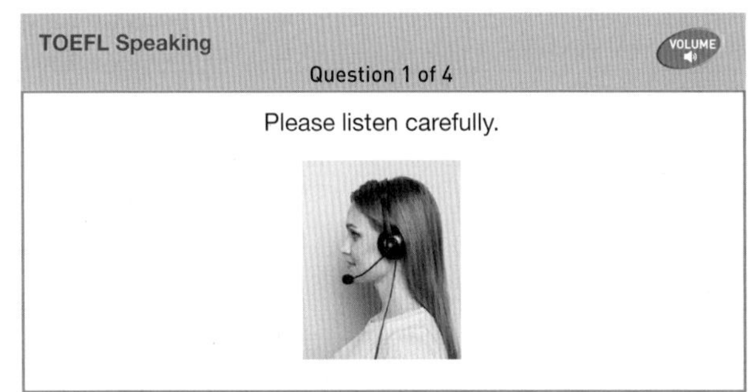

• 안내: 1번 문제에 관한 설명을 들려준다.

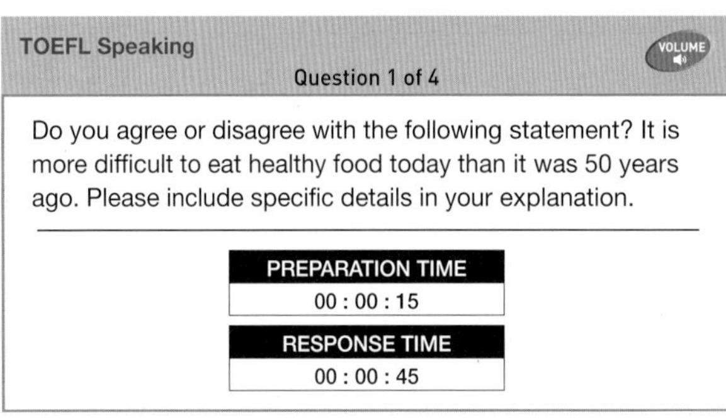

• 문제: 1번 문제가 화면에 글로 제시되는 동시에 음성으로 문제를 읽어준다.

• 답변: 준비 시간 15초, 대답 시간 45초가 주어진다.

Sample Questions

- Do you think the Internet has influenced human society in a negative way or a positive way? 인터넷이 인간 사회에 부정적인 방식 또는 긍정적인 방식 중 어떤 식으로 영향을 끼쳤다고 생각하는가?
- Some students like to study at home. Others prefer studying in the library. Which place do you prefer to study and why?
  어떤 학생들은 집에서 공부하는 것을 좋아한다. 다른 학생들은 도서관에서 공부하는 것을 선호한다. 당신이 공부하기를 선호하는 곳은 어디이며 그 이유는 무엇인가?
- Television has had a negative influence on society. Do you agree or disagree with this opinion and why?
  텔레비전은 사회에 부정적인 영향을 끼쳤다. 당신은 이 의견에 동의하는가 아니면 동의하지 않는가? 그 이유는 무엇인가?

Learning Strategies

Step 1 **문제를 파악하면서 답을 머릿속으로 정한다.**

– 시간이 많이 주어지지 않으므로 문제를 읽는 동시에 답을 결정하도록 한다.

Step 2 **머릿속으로 정한 답을 정리한다.**

– 종이와 연필이 주어지므로 답변과 구체적인 이유를 간단한 단어들로 표현해 본다.

Step 3 **정리한 답에 설명과 예를 덧붙여 문장으로 만들어 말한다.**

Example

Q. Do you agree or disagree with the following statement? It is more difficult to eat healthy food today than it was 50 years ago. Please include specific details in your explanation.

당신은 다음 진술에 동의하는가 아니면 동의하지 않는가? 오늘날 건강한 식품을 먹는 것은 50년 전보다 더 어렵다. 설명에 구체적인 세부 사항을 포함하시오.

❶ 나의 선택 생각하기

- disagree 동의하지 않음

❷ 답변과 구체적인 이유 정리하기

1. **more ppl care about their health** 더 많은 사람들이 건강에 신경을 씀
   - organic food production ↑ 유기농 제품 생산 ↑
   - easy to get 구하기 쉬움
2. **sci/med/tech development** 과학/의학/기술 발전
   - valuable info. 귀중한 정보
   - search what is good for us 우리에게 무엇이 좋은지 찾음

❸ 문장으로 말하기

I disagree with the idea that it is more difficult to eat healthy food today than it was 50 years ago.
나는 오늘날 건강한 식품을 먹는 것이 50년 전보다 더 어렵다는 생각에 동의하지 않는다.

I have two reasons to support my opinion. First, more and more people are looking for organic food and are careful about their health. To meet this demand, farmers produce more organic food ingredients, and those are easier to see in markets these days.
내 의견을 뒷받침할 두 가지 이유가 있다. 첫째, 점점 더 많은 사람들이 유기농 식품을 찾고 있고 건강에 신경을 쓴다. 이러한 수요에 부응하기 위해 농부들은 더 많은 유기농 식품 재료들을 생산하고, 오늘날 그러한 것들을 시장에서 더 쉽게 볼 수 있다.

Secondly, the rapid development of science, medicine, and technology has revealed many valuable facts regarding food. With this information, we can search for what is good for us and eat it. For these reasons, I disagree with the given statement.
둘째, 과학, 의학, 그리고 기술의 빠른 발전은 식품에 관해 많은 귀중한 사실을 밝혀냈다. 이 정보를 가지고 우리는 우리에게 좋은 것이 무엇인지 찾을 수 있고 섭취할 수 있다. 이러한 이유들로 인해 나는 주어진 진술에 동의하지 않는다.

Lesson

01 표현 익히기

1. 비교·대조 관련 표현

Q1_01

01. similarly 비슷하게, 마찬가지로

Similarly, I experienced the same thing when I was in college.
비슷하게 나는 대학에 다닐 때 같은 일을 경험했다.

02. likewise 마찬가지로, 게다가

Likewise, the new computer lab will be able to ensure more student participation.
마찬가지로 새로운 컴퓨터실은 더 많은 학생 참여를 보장할 수 있을 것이다.

03. unlike ~와 달리

Unlike an online course, traditional classes require students to be present in the classroom.
온라인 수업과 달리, 전통적인 수업들은 학생들에게 교실에 있을 것을 요구한다.

04. however 하지만, 그러나

However, the best solution can be drawn from paying more attention to details.
하지만 가장 좋은 해결책은 세부 사항에 더 주의를 기울임으로써 얻을 수 있다.

05. as well as ~에 더하여, ~뿐만 아니라, ~만큼

The benefit of creative writing influences children as well as adults.
창조적 글쓰기의 이점은 성인들뿐만 아니라 아이들에게도 영향을 미친다.

06. different from
~와 다른

They were different from the ones I enjoyed a few years ago.
그것들은 몇 년 전에 내가 즐겼던 것들과 달랐다.

07. whereas
~하지만, ~한 반면에

Many students struggled with chemistry, whereas others did quite well.
많은 학생들이 화학에 어려움을 겪었던 반면에 다른 학생들은 상당히 잘했다.

08. despite, in spite of
~에도 불구하고

Despite the fear, I was able to finish my presentation in front of the whole class.
두려움에도 불구하고, 나는 반 전체 앞에서 발표를 끝마칠 수 있었다.

09. though, even though, although
비록 ~일지라도, ~라 해도

Even though I was getting upset, I tried to calm my voice down.
기분이 나빠지고 있었음에도, 나는 목소리를 낮추려고 애썼다.

10. alternatively
그 대신, 그렇지 않으면

Alternatively, I can take the course online to save money and time.
그 대신 나는 돈과 시간을 절약하기 위해 온라인 강의를 들을 수 있다.

11. otherwise
그렇지 않으면, 그 외에는

I will try to register for the class today, otherwise I won't have time.
나는 오늘 수강 신청을 할 것이다, 그렇지 않으면 시간이 없을 것이다.

12. instead of

～ 대신에

Instead of joining the hockey team, I decided to go for the soccer team.
하키팀에 들어가는 대신 나는 축구팀으로 가기로 결정했다.

13. in short

간단히 말해서, 요컨대

In short, I must start preparing for my midterm exam.
간단히 말해서, 나는 중간고사 준비를 시작해야 한다.

14. to be sure

틀림없이, 분명히

There was, to be sure, an open position in the library.
분명히 도서관에는 빈 일자리가 하나 있었다.

15. after all

결국, 요컨대

After all, it was my turn to answer the questions of my classmates.
결국 내가 반 친구들의 질문에 답할 차례였다.

16. meanwhile

한편, 그동안

Meanwhile, I invited my friends to the book discussion club tonight.
한편 나는 오늘 밤에 있을 책 토론 클럽에 친구들을 초대했다.

17. at last

마침내, 드디어

At last I was able to concentrate on my book.
드디어 나는 책에 집중할 수 있었다.

18. finally
마침내, 마지막으로

I finally finished the reading assignment an hour before the class started.

나는 수업이 시작하기 한 시간 전에 마침내 독서 과제를 끝냈다.

19. subsequently
그 뒤에, 이어서

Subsequently, the professor distributed the class syllabus to everyone.

그 뒤에 교수님은 모두에게 수업 계획서를 나눠줬다.

20. eventually
결국, 마침내

He eventually quit working part-time at the cafeteria because his schedule was too tight.

그의 일정이 너무 빡빡했기 때문에 그는 결국 카페테리아 아르바이트를 그만두었다.

21. currently
현재, 지금

The professor asked me if I'm currently participating in any projects.

교수님은 내가 현재 어떠한 프로젝트에 참여하고 있는지 물었다.

22. in the meantime
그 사이에, 그동안

In the meantime, we decided to visit the museum in downtown.

그동안 우리는 시내에 있는 박물관에 가기로 결정했다.

23. in the past
과거에

The noise from the construction was much louder in the past.

건설 현장에서 들려오는 소음은 과거에 훨씬 더 요란했다.

Practice 1

Q1_02

>> 주어진 우리말 표현과 같은 뜻이 되도록 빈칸을 채워 보시오.

01. The old software ran very slowly ____________ the new one ______________ at lightning speed.

그 옛날 소프트웨어는 아주 느리게 작동하는 **반면에** 새것은 빛의 속도로 **작동하는 것처럼 보인다.**

02. ________________ the weather will be very ____________ today's weather.

나는 날씨가 오늘의 날씨와는 매우 **다를 것이라고 들었다.**

03. ____________, he decided to ____________________ while waiting for his friend to arrive.

한편 그는 친구가 도착하길 기다리는 동안 **커피숍에 들르기로** 했다.

04. I can still ____________________ even though I don't know him __________ Bryan does.

나는 브라이언**만큼** 그를 **잘** 알지는 않지만 여전히 **그를 당신에게 소개해줄** 수 있어요.

05. ____________, we decided to drop the project since __________________ ____________.

결국 물자가 부족했기 때문에 우리는 그 프로젝트를 그만두기로 결정했다.

06. ____________, they need funding from the government _________________.

간단히 말해서, 그들은 **연구를 계속하기 위해** 정부로부터 자금이 필요하다.

07. ____________________ he was sick since his face was ________ his usual one.

그의 얼굴이 평소**와 같지 않았기** 때문에 **나는** 그가 아프다는 것을 **알아차릴 수 있었다.**

08. ________ having a difficult time, she ________________ with her new project.

힘든 시간을 겪고 있었음**에도 불구하고** 그녀는 새 프로젝트에 **인내심을 갖으려고 노력했다.**

09. After I ____________________________, I thought the world is a small place ____________.

옛 고등학교 선생님과 마주친 뒤 나는 세상은 **결국** 작은 곳이라고 생각했다.

10. ________________, we started to ____________________ for the construction project.

그동안 우리는 그 건설 프로젝트를 위한 **새 계획을 발전시키기** 시작했다.

11. ____________ it looks small, ________________ the kitchen area is in fact quite spacious.

비록 작아 보**이지만** 실제로는 부엌 공간이 꽤나 넓다는 것을 **보실 수 있을 겁니다**.

12. At the bus station, I noticed that ______________________ were dressed ____________.

버스 정류장에서 나는 **버스를 기다리는 사람들**이 **비슷하게** 옷을 입었다는 것을 알아차렸다.

13. ________________ long pause, the match was able to begin ____________.

20분간의 긴 멈춤 **뒤에** 경기는 **마침내** 시작될 수 있었다.

14. The store clerk said that shops in the area ______________________ unless ____________ noted.

가게 직원은 그 지역의 가게들이 **따로** 명시되어 있지 않은 한 **신용카드를 받지 않는다**고 말했다.

15. __________, it was announced that schools in the district ________________ for a snow day.

그러나 그 지역 학교들이 폭설 휴일로 **수업을 취소할 것**이라고 공지되었다.

16. ________________________ for an extra 30 minutes until both parties ________ came to an agreement.

그 회의는 양측이 **마침내** 합의에 이를 때까지 30분 연장되어 **계속 진행되었다**.

17. Since the road is ____________________________, everybody needs to make a detour.

그 도로가 **현재 공사 중**이기 때문에 모두가 우회해서 가야 한다.

18. ____________________ on the positive side ____________ just complaining about them.

나는 그저 불평만 하는 **대신 사물을** 긍정적인 면에서 **보고 싶다**.

2. 선호·동의 관련 표현

Q1_03

01. I prefer

나는 ~를 선호한다

I prefer to drink tea in the morning rather than in the afternoon.

나는 오후보다 오전에 차를 마시는 것을 선호한다.

02. I like *A* better than *B*

나는 B보다 A를 더 좋아한다

I like jogging in the morning better than jogging at night.

나는 밤에 조깅하는 것보다 아침에 조깅하는 것을 더 좋아한다.

03. I would rather

나는 차라리 ~를 하겠다

I would rather go sightseeing tomorrow since the weather will be much better.

날씨가 훨씬 더 좋을 것이기 때문에 나는 차라리 내일 관광을 가겠다.

04. I'm more interested in

나는 ~에 더 관심이/흥미가 있다

I'm more interested in acting since I have been doing it for many years.

나는 수년간 연기를 해왔기 때문에 연기에 더 관심이 있다.

05. *A* appeals to me more than *B*

A가 B보다 더 끌린다

Having a cup of tea for breakfast appeals to me more than drinking coffee.

나는 아침으로 차 한 잔을 마시는 것이 커피를 마시는 것보다 더 끌린다.

06. I don't mind -ing

~하는 것을 신경 쓰지 않는다, ~해도 된다

I don't mind working overtime since the due date is tomorrow.

마감일이 내일이므로 초과 근무를 해도 상관없다.

07. I enjoy

나는 ~를 즐긴다

I enjoyed the play we watched two weeks ago at the new theater in downtown.

나는 2주 전 시내의 새 극장에서 우리가 봤던 연극을 즐겼다.

08. I agree with

나는 ~에 동의한다

I agree with the idea that the new software should be installed to improve the company's system.

나는 회사의 시스템을 향상시키기 위해 그 새로운 소프트웨어를 설치해야 한다는 생각에 동의한다.

09. I disagree with

나는 ~에 반대한다

It is true that I respect him a lot, but I still have to disagree with what he said at the meeting.

내가 그를 무척 존경하는 것은 사실이지만, 나는 여전히 그가 회의에서 한 말에 반대할 수밖에 없다.

10. exactly

정확히, 틀림없이

Even though I don't remember exactly when the event was held, it was still a lot of fun.

그 행사가 정확히 언제 열렸는지 기억나진 않지만, 그래도 무척 즐거웠다.

11. there is no doubt

~에는 의심의 여지가 없다

There was no doubt in my mind when I decided to change my major.

내가 전공을 바꾸기로 결심했을 때 내 마음에는 한치의 의심도 없었다.

12. I'm afraid

(유감스러운 내용을 말할 때) ~인 것 같다, ~이다

I'm afraid the repairman is still working on the air conditioner on the 5th floor.

수리 기사가 여전히 5층에서 에어컨 작업을 하고 있는 것 같다.

13. I have to side with 나는 ~의 편을 들어야 한다

I have to side with the latter one because it goes well with the color of my wall.
나는 후자가 내 벽의 색과 잘 맞기 때문에 후자의 편을 들어야겠다.

14. I suppose 나는 ~라고 추측한다, ~인 것 같다

I suppose that is how the artist expresses her perspective of the world.
내 생각엔 그것이 그 예술가가 자신의 세계관을 표현하는 방식인 것 같다.

15. I'm going to say 나는 ~라고 말하겠다

I'm going to say the situation is quite different compared to the past.
나는 과거에 비해 상황이 상당히 다르다고 말하겠다.

16. totally 완전히

I totally forgot my dentist's appointment because I was so busy today.
나는 오늘 너무 바빴기 때문에 치과 예약을 완전히 잊어버렸다.

17. not ~ necessarily 반드시 ~는 아니다

I don't think it is necessarily a bad thing since it increased the popularity of the product.
나는 그것이 제품의 인기를 높여줬기 때문에 반드시 나쁜 것이라고 생각하지는 않는다.

18. add something 무언가를 추가하다

She wanted to add something to the idea I suggested for the project.
그녀는 내가 그 프로젝트를 위해 제안한 아이디어에 무언가를 추가하고 싶어했다.

19. for sure 확실히, 틀림없이

I told him that I'll be at the meeting for sure by 2 o'clock.

나는 그에게 2시까지 회의에 틀림없이 참석할 거라고 말했다.

20. personally 개인적으로

Personally, I want to start working on the project timeline first.

개인적으로 나는 프로젝트 시간표를 작업하는 일을 먼저 시작하고 싶다.

21. what I mean is 내 말은 ~이다

What I mean is there is still an ongoing debate over this matter.

내 말은 이 문제에 대해 여전히 논쟁이 계속되고 있다는 것이다.

22. it is generally accepted that ~가 일반적으로 받아들여진다

It is generally accepted that people have to be motivated by something to achieve success.

사람들이 성공을 이루려면 무언가에 동기 부여가 되어야 한다는 것이 일반적으로 받아들여진다.

23. I'd go along with 나는 ~에 찬성한다

I'd go along with his idea because it will save us lots of time.

그의 아이디어가 우리에게 많은 시간을 절약해 줄 것이기 때문에 나는 그것에 찬성한다.

24. make a good point 좋은 지적을 하다

She made a good point during the lecture, and the professor was impressed by her question.

그녀는 강의 시간에 좋은 지적을 했고 교수는 그녀의 질문에 깊은 인상을 받았다.

Practice 2

Q1_04

>> 주어진 우리말 표현과 같은 뜻이 되도록 빈칸을 채워 보시오.

01. ____________________ anywhere for my vacation ______________ it is a quiet place.

나는 조용한 곳**이기만 하다면** 휴가로 어디를 **가든 신경 쓰지 않는다**.

02. ______________, I think the author's first book ______________________________ his most recent one.

개인적으로 나는 그 작가의 첫 번째 책이 가장 최근에 나온 책**보다 더 흥미로웠다고** 생각한다.

03. ______________ I can spare some time to mow the lawn ____________________.

부모님을 돕기 위해 잔디를 깎을 시간을 좀 낼 수 있을 **것 같다**.

04. ______________ working out at the gym ______________ because there is hardly anyone there.

그곳에는 사람이 거의 없기 때문에 **나는 밤 늦게** 헬스장에서 운동하는 것**을 즐긴다**.

05. ______________ choose a small bag than a big one since it is __________________.

나는 큰 가방보다 작은 가방이 **들고 다니기 쉬울** 것이므로 **차라리** 작은 가방을 택하**겠다**.

06. ____________________ astronomy since _________________________ when I was young.

나는 어렸을 때 **별을 보는 것을 좋아**했기 때문에 천문학에 **더 관심이 있다**.

07. _________________________, I was ______________ prepared for the public speech.

2주간의 연습 후, 나는 공개 연설을 위해 **완전히** 준비가 되었다.

08. ______________ the idea partially because ______________________________.

나는 제안할 더 좋은 것이 있기 때문에 그 생각에 부분적으로 동의한다.

09. __________ the second applicant because ________________________________.

나는 그가 더 경험이 많기 때문에 두 번째 지원자를 선호한다.

10. ______________ this house ______________ the first one because ____________

________________________.

나는 이 집의 뒷마당이 훨씬 더 크기 때문에 첫 번째 집보다 이 집을 더 좋아한다.

11. _________________ I agree with the first statement because ___________________

_______________.

나는 작은 도시에서 자랐기 때문에 첫 번째 말에 동의한다고 말하겠다.

12. That is not ______________ true because _________________________ the result.

충분한 증거가 결과를 보여주기 때문에 그것이 반드시 사실은 아니다.

13. ____.

그가 올 수 있는지 보려면 나는 공연이 정확히 언제 시작하는지 알아야 한다.

14. ____.

내 말은 회사가 연구와 개발에 더 많은 돈을 쓸 예정이라는 것이다.

Lesson
02 이유 제시하기

1. 생각 정리하는 법

1. 선택

생각해 보지 않은 주제라 어느 한쪽을 선택하는 것이 어렵다 하더라도, 질문이 요구하는 대로 한쪽을 선택해서 답변하도록 한다. 모호한 태도를 보일 경우 답변 또한 애매해질 수 있다. 또한 더 많은 아이디어가 떠오르는 쪽을 선택하는 것이 편하다.

2. 구체적인 이유

보통 두 가지 이유가 적당하다. 다만 세부적인 예시와 설명을 추가해야 하므로 너무 구체적인 이유는 피하는 것이 좋고, 일반적인 이유를 제시하도록 한다.

3. 예시·설명·근거

앞에서 두 가지 이유를 제시했다면 각 이유에 관한 구체적인 예시와 설명, 근거를 덧붙인다. 실제로 경험한 적이 없거나 지금까지 생각해 본 적이 없는 질문이 나오더라도 사실에 집착할 필요 없이 떠올릴 수 있는 가상의 아이디어를 제시하면 된다.

2. 생각한 내용 노트로 정리

노트 정리

선택 disagree 동의하지 않음

이유 1. more ppl care about their health 더 많은 사람들이 건강에 신경을 씀

예시·설명·근거

- organic food production ↑ 유기농 제품 생산 ↑
- easy to get 구하기 쉬움

2. sci/med/tech development 과학/의학/기술 발전

예시·설명·근거

- valuable info. 귀중한 정보
- search what is good for us 우리에게 무엇이 좋은지 찾음

Practice

정답 및 해석 | P. 98

>> 다음 질문을 읽고 아래 노트 정리를 완성해 보시오.

01 **Students at many high schools are required to take art classes like music or painting in addition to academic courses, while others are not. Which do you think is better and why? Give reasons and examples to support your opinion.**

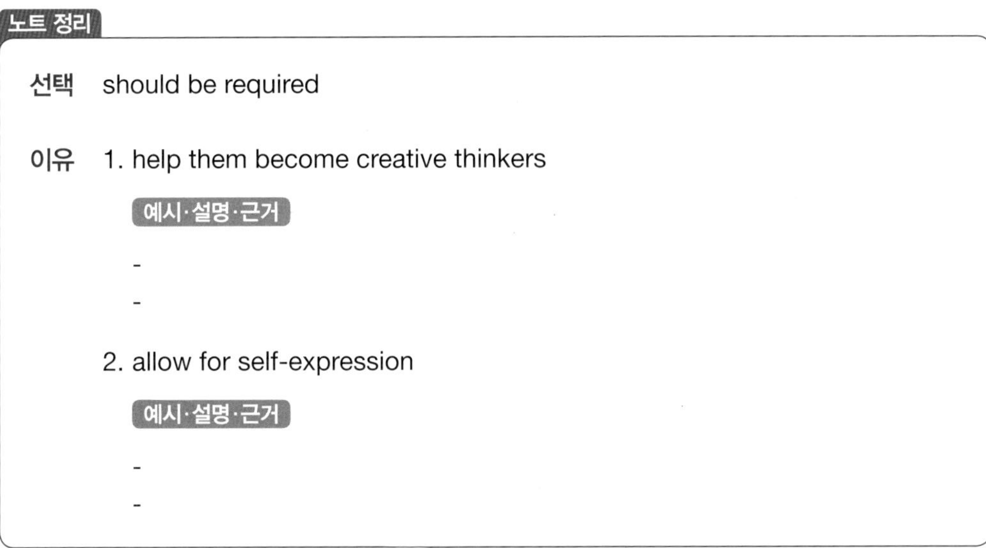
노트 정리

선택 should be required

이유 1. help them become creative thinkers

예시·설명·근거

-
-

2. allow for self-expression

예시·설명·근거

-
-

02 **Do you agree or disagree with the following statement? Video games can actually be beneficial to children. Please include specific examples in your explanation.**

노트 정리

선택 agree

이유 1. improve many skills

예시·설명·근거

- visual skill, problem solving, creativity
- accomplish many different objectives

2. ________________

예시·설명·근거

-
-

03 **While attending university, some students only take classes that focus on the specific career path they have chosen, whereas others prefer to take a wide variety of courses that provide them with broader knowledge. Which do you think is better and why?**

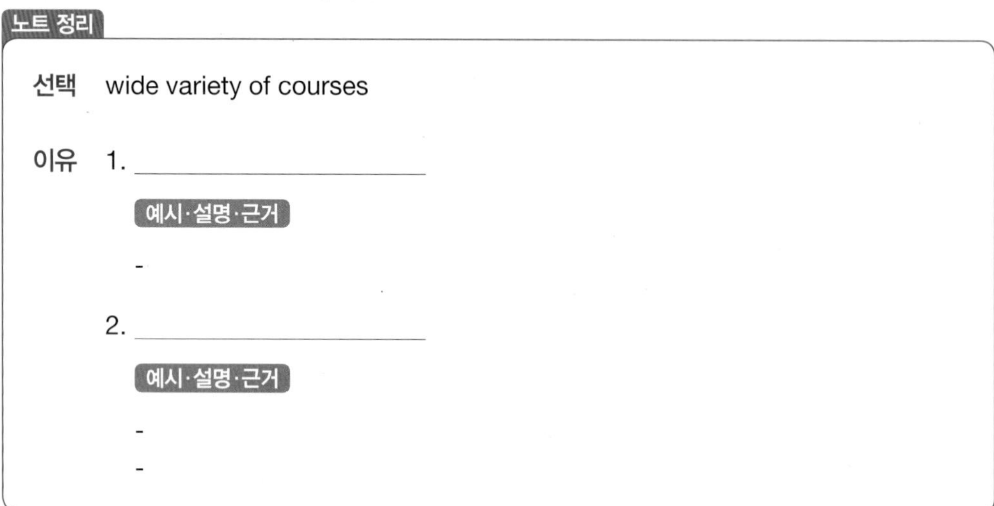

04 **Do you agree or disagree with the following statement? Students should gain some experience in a field before they can complete a degree in it.**

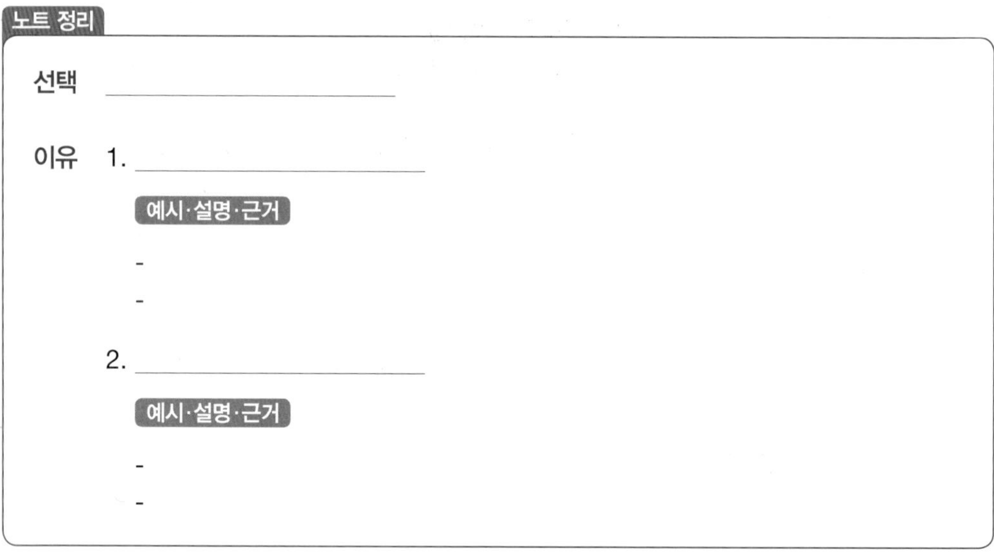

Lesson
03 문장으로 말하기

말하기 전략

간단한 노트 필기로 생각을 정리한 뒤에 45초 동안 그 내용에 기반한 답변을 말한다.
정리한 내용 순서와 같이 먼저 내가 선택한 것이 어떤 것인지 말한 후 이유를 제시하고 예시·설명·근거를 덧붙인다.

1. 선택

답변을 시작하며 바로 나의 선택 사항을 이야기하도록 한다. 질문을 패러프레이즈해도 좋고, 그대로 다시 인용하여 읽어도 상관없다.

2. 이유

앞에서 배운 표현들을 토대로 이유를 제시한다. 특별하게 선택 이유가 생각나지 않는다면, 내가 선택하지 않은 사항에 대해서 왜 그것을 선택하지 않았는지를 설명하는 것도 좋은 방법이다.

3. 예시·설명·근거

이유와 마찬가지로 앞에서 배운 다양한 표현들을 토대로 예시·설명·근거를 제시한다. 보통 한 문장에서 두 문장 정도로 설명하는 것이 시간 배분에 좋다. 시간이 남는 경우에는 자신의 선택을 다시 한 번 요약한다.

실전 적용 예시

- I disagree with the idea that it is more difficult to eat healthy food today than it was 50 years ago.
  나는 오늘날 건강한 식품을 먹는 것이 50년 전보다 더 어렵다는 생각에 동의하지 않는다.
- I have two reasons to support my opinion. First, more and more people are looking for organic food and are careful about their health.
  내 의견을 뒷받침할 두 가지 이유가 있다. 첫째, 점점 더 많은 사람들이 유기농 식품을 찾고 있고 건강에 신경을 쓴다.
- To meet this demand, farmers produce more organic food ingredients, and those are easier to see in markets these days.
  이러한 수요에 부응하기 위해 농부들은 더 많은 유기농 식품 재료들을 생산하고, 오늘날 그러한 것들을 시장에서 더 쉽게 볼 수 있다.
- Secondly, the rapid development of science, medicine, and technology has revealed many valuable facts regarding food.
  둘째, 과학, 의학, 그리고 기술의 빠른 발전은 식품에 관해 많은 귀중한 사실을 밝혀냈다.
- With this information, we can search for what is good for us and eat it. For these reasons, I disagree with the given statement.
  이 정보를 가지고 우리는 우리에게 좋은 것이 무엇인지 찾을 수 있고 섭취할 수 있다. 이러한 이유들로 인해 나는 주어진 진술에 동의하지 않는다.

Practice

>> '생각 정리'와 주어진 우리말 표현을 참고하여 질문에 대한 대답을 완성해 보시오.

01 **For academic success, some students like to take courses online. Others prefer to study in traditional courses on campus. Which do you prefer and why? Include details and examples to support your explanation.**

문제 듣기 Q1_05
예시 답변 Q1_06

생각 정리	문장으로 만들기
선택 online course 온라인 수업	I think I'd have to say that ______________. 나는 **온라인 수업을 듣는 것을 선호한다**고 말해야 할 것 같다.
이유 1 convenient - easy access - anywhere & anytime 편리함 – 쉬운 접근 – 어디서든 & 어느 때나	The first reason is because ______________. To be more specific, online courses ______________. If there's any computer device with an Internet connection, I can easily access my online lectures ______________. 첫 번째 이유는 **그것이 아주 편리하기** 때문이다. 좀 더 구체적으로 말하자면, 온라인 수업은 **쉽게 접근할 수 있다.** 인터넷 연결이 되는 컴퓨터 장치만 있으면 **어디서든, 어느 때나** 온라인 강의를 쉽게 이용할 수 있다.
이유 2 economical - work & study - tuition fee & time 경제적 – 일 & 학업 – 등록금 & 시간	Another reason is that ______________. For example, a few years ago, I had a chance to take some online courses. Back then, I had to ______________, so I thought taking online courses would be pretty convenient. I realized that it was not only convenient but also more ______________ since I didn't physically have to go to school. So, for these reasons, I prefer to take online courses. 또 다른 이유는 **그것이 경제적이기도 하다**는 것이다. 예를 들어, 몇 년 전에 나는 온라인 수업을 몇 개 들을 기회가 있었다. 당시 나는 **일과 학업을 동시에 해야 했기** 때문에 온라인 수업을 듣는 것이 상당히 편리할 것이라고 생각했다. 나는 온라인 수업이 편리할 뿐만 아니라 **더 싼 등록금과** 학교에 물리적으로 가지 않아도 되기 때문에 **시간 절약 면에서** 더 **경제적**이기도 하다는 것을 깨달았다. 그래서 이러한 이유들로 나는 온라인 수업을 듣는 것을 선호한다.

02 **Would you rather study in a large class or a small class? Explain your answer and include details and examples to support your explanation.**

문제 듣기 Q1_07
예시 답변 Q1_08

생각 정리	문장으로 만들기
선택 small class 작은 수업	I would rather study ____________________. 나는 **작은 규모의 수업에서** 공부하는 것을 택하겠다.
이유 1 more individual attention - professor knows me 더 많은 개인적 집중 – 교수님이 나를 알고 계심	That's because there is ____________________ ____________________ in a small class. I've taken large classes before, and the ____________________ ____________________. I think it makes a class a lot better when the teachers know a little bit about the students. 왜냐하면 작은 수업에서는 **교수님으로부터 훨씬 더 많은 개인적인 관심이 주어지기** 때문이다. 나는 전에 큰 수업을 들은 적이 있는데 **교수님은 내 이름조차 모르셨다.** 나는 교사가 학생들에 관해 약간이라도 알고 있을 때 수업이 훨씬 더 나아진다고 생각한다.
이유 2 more chances to participate - questions & discussions - add to learning experience 더 많은 참여 기회 – 질문 & 토의 – 학습 경험에 도움이 됨	Also, in a small class, students have ____________________ ____________________. For example, they can ____________________, which can definitely help students to develop strong communication skills. This will eventually ____________________ ____________________ at school. 또한 작은 수업에서는 학생들이 **수업에 참여할 기회를 더 많이** 갖게 된다. 예를 들어, **질문을 하거나 토의에 참여할 수 있는데,** 이는 학생들이 강력한 의사소통 능력을 개발하는 데 분명히 도움을 줄 것이다. 이는 결국 학교에서의 **학습 경험 전반에 도움이 될** 것이다.

03 **Some universities require first-year students to live on campus in dormitories. Other universities allow first-year students to live off-campus. Which policy do you think is better for first-year students and why? Include details and examples to support your explanation.**

문제 듣기 Q1_09
예시 답변 Q1_10

생각 정리	문장으로 만들기
선택 dorm 기숙사	I think that, for first-year students, it's ______________________ ______________________. 나는 1학년 학생들의 경우, **교내 기숙사에서 사는 것이 훨씬 낫다**고 생각한다.
이유 1 fit in at the univ. - make new friends - clubs & group activities 대학교에 적응함 – 새 친구들 사귐 – 동아리 & 그룹 활동	The main reason is that it can ______________________ ____________. Since they're on campus, it's ____________ ______________________. They can also ____________ ______________________. 주된 이유는 이것이 **그들이 대학교에 적응하는 데 도움을 줄** 수 있기 때문이다. 그들은 교내에 있으므로 **새 친구들을 사귀는 것이 더 쉽다**. 그들은 또한 **더 쉽게 동아리나 그룹 활동에 참여**할 수 있다.
이유 2 less stressful - no chore - less domestic responsibility 스트레스를 덜 받음 – 해야 하는 집안일 없음 – 돌봐야 할 가사 적음	Another good reason is that it is ______________________ ______________ because there are ______________ ______________. If it's their first time living alone, it could be really stressful as they would have to do the cooking and cleaning all by themselves. Living in a dorm, they ______________________ ______________________. 또 다른 좋은 이유는 **처리해야 하는 집안일이 없기** 때문에 **기숙사에서 사는 것이 스트레스가 덜하다**는 것이다. 만약 혼자 사는 게 처음이라면 요리와 청소를 전부 스스로 해야 하기 때문에 무척 스트레스를 받을 수도 있다. 기숙사에 살면 **그만큼 많은 가사를 돌보지 않아도 된다**.

04 **Would you rather organize a trip yourself or take a trip organized by a tour company and why? Include details and examples to support your explanation.**

문제 듣기 Q1_11
예시 답변 Q1_12

생각 정리	문장으로 만들기
선택 organize myself 스스로 계획	________________ than take a trip organized by a tour company. 나는 여행사에서 기획한 여행을 가는 것보다 **내 스스로 여행을 계획하겠다.**
이유 1 like to be spontaneous - change my plans 즉흥적으로 행동하는 것을 좋아함 – 계획을 바꿈	That is because ________________, and I like to be ________________ if I hear of something new or better than my original plan. For example, if I visited a new city, and found out that there was a festival I had not expected, ________________ ________ stick to my original plans. 왜냐하면 **나는 휴가를 갔을 때 즉흥적으로 행동하는 것을 좋아하며**, 만약 원래 계획보다 새롭거나 더 나은 것을 듣게 되면 **내 계획을 바꿀 수 있는 것**을 좋아하기 때문이다. 예를 들어, 만약 새로운 도시에 갔는데 내가 예상하지 못했던 축제가 있다는 것을 알게 되면, **나는** 원래 계획을 고수하기**보다는 거기에 갈 것이다.**
이유 2 tour company - follow their plans - restricted by time 여행사 – 자신들의 계획을 따름 – 시간 제약	But ________________, I would probably have to give up going to that festival and ________ ________. So, if I organize a trip myself, I ________ ________________, and I might enjoy my trip more. 그러나 **만약 내가 여행사와 같이 갔다면** 나는 아마 축제에 가는 것을 포기하고 **그들의 계획에 따라야** 했을 것이다. 그래서 만약 스스로 여행을 계획하면 나는 **시간에 제약을 받지 않아도 되고**, 여행을 더 즐길 수 있을지 모른다.

Q1. Lesson 03
Independent Task

Q2 읽고 듣고 말하기: 대학 생활

Introduction

2번 문제는 '읽고 듣고 말하기' 문제로, 화면에 제시되는 글을 읽고 들려주는 대화를 들은 뒤 질문에 답하는 문제다. 읽기와 듣기 내용에 따라 크게 대학 생활과 대학 강의로 나눌 수 있다. 전자는 대학 생활과 관련된 학교 측의 공지나 캠퍼스 신문 기사 등이 읽기 지문으로 나오며, 이어서 그 내용과 관련된 학생들의 대화를 들려준다. 질문은 읽기 지문의 내용에 대해 대화의 화자가 어떤 의견을 갖고 있는지, 그리고 화자가 그렇게 생각하는 이유는 무엇인지를 묻는다.

화면 구성

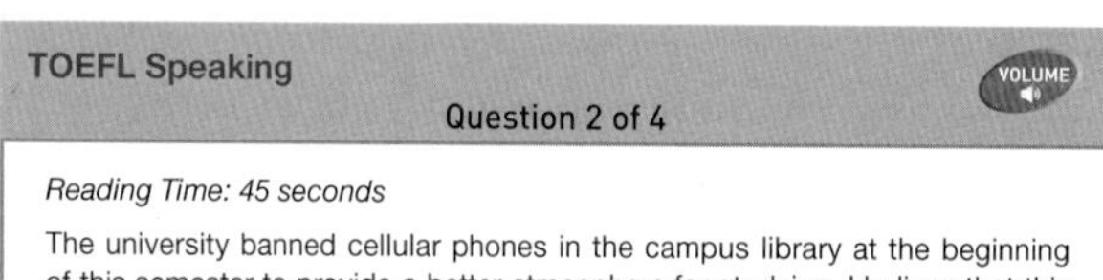

TOEFL Speaking
Question 2 of 4
VOLUME

Reading Time: 45 seconds

The university banned cellular phones in the campus library at the beginning of this semester to provide a better atmosphere for studying. I believe that this has had some unforeseen repercussions. Firstly, there is increased competition for the computers there. Students need those computers to locate books in the library, but most people are using them to access the Internet. If students could use their smartphones in the library, this would be less of a problem. In addition, many students miss important calls from their classmates, family members, and employers, which can cause serious problems.

- Michio Wada

• 안내: 2번 문제에 관한 설명을 들려준다.

• 읽기: 지문이 화면에 제시된다. (100자 이하)
읽기 시간 45/50초가 주어진다.

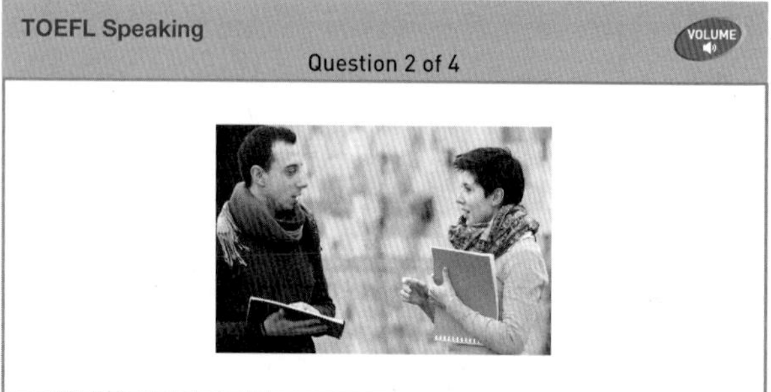

• 듣기: 사진과 함께 읽기 지문과 관련된 대화를 들려준다. (60~90초 길이)

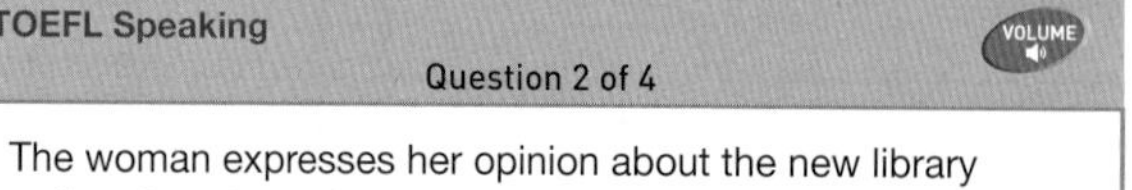

TOEFL Speaking
Question 2 of 4
VOLUME

The woman expresses her opinion about the new library policy. State her opinion and explain the reasons she gives for holding that opinion.

PREPARATION TIME
00 : 00 : 30

RESPONSE TIME
00 : 00 : 60

• 문제: 2번 문제가 화면에 글로 제시되는 동시에 음성으로 문제를 읽어준다.

• 답변: 준비 시간 30초, 대답 시간 60초가 주어진다.

Learning Strategies

Step 1 **읽기 지문의 핵심 내용을 찾는다.**

Step 2 **대화를 들으며 찬성 또는 반대의 의견을 고수하는 내용에 집중한다.**
– 대화의 화자가 읽기 지문의 내용에 찬성하는지 또는 반대하는지, 그리고 왜 그렇게 생각하는지 정리한다.

Step 3 **주어진 30초를 활용하여 정리한 내용을 바탕으로 연습해 본다.**
– '읽기 지문 정리 → 화자의 의견 → 화자가 그렇게 생각하는 이유' 순서로 답한다.

Example

Q. The woman expresses her opinion about the new library policy. State her opinion and explain the reasons she gives for holding that opinion.
여자는 새로운 도서관 정책에 대한 자신의 의견을 표현하고 있다. 그녀의 의견에 대해 서술하고 그렇게 생각하는 이유가 무엇인지 설명하시오.

❶ 읽기 지문 정리하기

The letter in the campus newspaper states that the university is banning cellular phones in the campus library to provide a better atmosphere for studying.
대학 신문에 실린 편지는 학교가 더 나은 면학 분위기를 제공하기 위해 교내 도서관에서 휴대전화를 금지한다고 말한다.

❷ 읽기 지문에 대한 대화 속 화자의 의견 밝히기

The woman agrees with this new policy. 여자는 이러한 새로운 정책에 동의한다.

❸ 화자가 그렇게 생각하는 이유 설명하기

First, she thinks that there are many places around campus where students can use computers to access the Internet instead of using their mobile phones. Secondly, if students are expecting an important call, they can call them back outside, where they will not be bothering other students. No matter how quietly people answer their calls, if the person on the other end of the line is in a noisy location, the conversation will eventually get louder.
첫째, 그녀는 학생들이 휴대전화를 사용하는 대신 인터넷에 접속하기 위해 컴퓨터를 사용할 수 있는 장소가 교내에 많이 있다고 생각한다. 둘째, 만약 학생들이 중요한 전화를 기다린다면, 다른 학생들을 방해하지 않는 바깥에서 전화를 다시 걸 수도 있다. 아무리 조용히 전화를 받는다고 해도, 통화하는 상대방이 시끄러운 장소에 있으면 결과적으로 대화 소리가 더 커질 것이다.

Lesson
01 표현 익히기

관련 표현

Q2_01

01. I think/believe/see/feel
나는 ~라고 생각한다

I believe that moving to another dormitory would be better.
나는 다른 기숙사로 옮기는 것이 더 나을 것이라고 생각한다.

02. he/she suggests that
그/그녀는 ~를 제안한다/시사한다

She suggests that the cafeteria should provide more vegetarian options.
그녀는 카페테리아에서 더 많은 채식주의 옵션을 제공해야 한다고 제안한다.

03. he/she states that
그/그녀는 ~라고 말한다

He states that the policy would not really help students register for classes.
그는 그 정책이 학생들이 수업 등록을 하는 데 그다지 도움이 안 될 거라고 말한다.

04. prefer *A* over *B*
B보다 A를 선호하다

The woman prefers having a café next to the library over having it on the first floor.
여자는 카페가 1층에 있는 것보다 도서관 옆에 있는 것을 선호한다.

05. according to
~에 따르면

According to the announcement, library hours will be extended during finals week.
공지에 따르면, 도서관 운영 시간이 기말고사 주간에 연장될 것이다.

06. he/she agrees
그/그녀는 ~에 동의한다

He agrees that renovating the music building will be beneficial to students.
그는 음악과 건물을 보수하는 것이 학생들에게 유익할 것이라는 데 동의한다.

07. he/she disagrees
그/그녀는 ~에 동의하지 않는다

She disagrees with the school policy because it will cost too much money.
여자는 너무 많은 돈이 들 것이기 때문에 그 학교 정책에 동의하지 않는다.

08. therefore
따라서, 그러므로

Therefore, it will be better to apply a quiet-hour policy to all dormitories.
그러므로 모든 기숙사에 조용한 시간 정책을 적용하는 것이 더 나을 것이다.

09. he/she thinks *A* is a good idea
그/그녀는 A가 좋은 생각이라고 생각한다

He thinks renting a car downtown is a good idea.
남자는 시내에서 차를 대여하는 것이 좋은 생각이라고 생각한다.

10. he/she mentions
그/그녀는 ~를 언급한다

She mentions cafeteria hours because she is interested in working there.
여자는 카페테리아에서 일하는 것에 관심이 있기 때문에 그곳의 운영 시간을 언급한다.

11. he/she is against
그/그녀는 ~에 반대한다

He is against the idea of turning the park into a parking lot.
그는 그 공원을 주차장으로 바꾸려는 생각에 반대한다.

12. one reason is that
한 가지 이유는 ~이다

One reason is that students simply do not have enough time to do it.
한 가지 이유는 학생들이 그저 그것을 하기에 충분한 시간이 없다는 것이다.

13. plan to
~할 계획이다

The university is planning to expand its art gallery by the end of the semester.
그 대학은 이번 학기 말까지 미술관을 확장할 계획이다.

14. be beneficial to
이익이다, 도움이 되다

It is beneficial to provide more options to students since they are busy.
학생들은 바쁘기 때문에 그들에게 더 많은 선택권을 제공하는 것이 도움이 될 것이다.

15. notice, announcement
알림, 공지

The school announcement was published in the campus newspaper as well.
학교의 공지 사항은 교내 신문에도 실렸다.

16. *A* should be
A는 ~여야 한다

The student says the orientation date should be postponed.
그 학생은 오리엔테이션 날짜가 미뤄져야 한다고 말한다.

17. in order to
~하기 위해

The university decided to change the schedule in order to increase overall participation.
대학은 전반적인 참여를 늘리기 위해 일정을 바꾸기로 결정했다.

18. it is necessary/unnecessary
~는 필요하다/불필요하다

It is necessary to install the new software system for extra security.
추가 보안을 위해 새 소프트웨어 시스템 설치가 필요하다.

19. the advantage/disadvantage is
장점은/단점은 ~이다

The advantage of this policy is that it will encourage students to exercise more.
이 정책의 장점은 학생들이 운동을 더 하도록 장려할 것이라는 점이다.

20. it is because
~ 때문이다

It is because the date always coincides with the midterm exams week.
그것은 날짜가 항상 중간고사 주간과 겹치기 때문이다.

Practice

Q2_02

정답 및 해석 | P. 101

>> 주어진 우리말 표현과 같은 뜻이 되도록 빈칸을 채워 보시오.

01. ______________________ the funding should be used to purchase new equipment.
한 가지 이유는 자금이 새로운 장비를 구매하는 데 사용되어야 한다는 **것이다.**

02. ______________________ student tutors ______________________ other students well.
나는 학생 개인 지도 교사들이 다른 학생들을 잘 **도와줄 수 있을 거라고 믿는다.**

03. ______________________ some additional research at the library ________________ finish my essay.
나는 내 리포트를 끝내**기 위해** 도서관에서 추가 조사**를 해야 한다.**

04. ________________ the announcement, the school festival will feature some local musicians.
공지**에 따르면,** 학교 축제에 지역 뮤지션 몇 명이 출연할 것이다.

05. ______________________ the freshmen students who ______________________ the university yet.
그것은 대학교**에** 아직 **익숙하지 않은** 1학년 학생들**에게 유익하다.**

06. ________________ that cutting the budget will be a bad move for the university.
그는 예산 삭감이 대학에 나쁜 조치가 될 거라고 **시사한다.**

07. ________________ with the idea that ______________________ at the gym.
그녀는 학생들이 체육관에서 **더 많은 장비를 필요로 한다**는 생각**에 동의하지 않는다.**

08. ________________, as of May 1st, renovations of parking lot A will begin.
그러므로 5월 1일자로 주차장 A의 보수 공사가 시작될 것이다.

09. ________________ the change ________________ because it will provide cleaner air.
그는 그 변화가 더 깨끗한 공기를 제공할 것이기에 **좋은 생각이라고 생각한다.**

10. ______________________ to require everyone to attend the seminar.
모두에게 그 세미나에 참석하도록 요구하는 것**은 불필요하다.**

Q2. Lesson 01
Integrated Task

Lesson

02 읽기 정리

읽기 정리 전략

읽기 지문에서는 주제와 중요한 세부 내용을 빠르게 찾는 것이 무엇보다 중요하다. 노트 정리를 통해 간단하게 주제와 세부 내용을 찾아 적는 연습을 해 보자.

Tip 1

일반적으로 제목이나 도입부에서 지문의 주제가 제시되므로 주제를 먼저 파악해 노트에 적은 후 그 뒤로 이어지는 내용 중에서 주제와 관련된 핵심 내용을 찾도록 한다.

Tip 2

읽기 지문 내용이 뒤에 들려주는 대화와 연결되므로 읽기 지문에서 다루는 내용을 잘 파악해 두면 듣기에 도움이 된다.

노트 정리 예시

읽기 지문

The university banned cellular phones in the campus library at the beginning of this semester to provide a better atmosphere for studying. I believe that this has had some unforeseen repercussions. Firstly, there is increased competition for the computers there. Students need those computers to locate books in the library, but most people are using them to access the Internet. If students could use their smartphones in the library, this would be less of a problem. In addition, many students miss important calls from their classmates, family members, and employers, which can cause serious problems.

- Michio Wada

노트 정리

cellphones banned in the library: negative 휴대전화가 도서관에서 금지됨: 부정적

- increased competition for the computers → noisier 컴퓨터 경쟁이 증가함 → 더 시끄러움
- miss important calls 중요한 전화를 놓침

Practice

정답 및 해석 | P. 102

>> 다음 지문을 읽고 먼저 아래에 노트 정리를 한 후, 주어진 질문에 답해 보시오.

01

문제 듣기 Q2_03
예시 답변 Q2_04

Dear Editor,

The center of our campus is currently taken up by a large parking lot, which detracts from the university as a whole. I propose that this parking lot be removed and replaced with a park. Since all of the administration buildings have their own small parking lots, and large parking lots have been built both north and south of campus for student use, I think that the central lot has become unnecessary. Replacing the asphalt with grass and trees would not only make the area more aesthetically pleasing, it would also make the air cleaner.

- Clara Bowes

노트 정리

▶ **Question: What does the student propose?**

02

문제 듣기 Q2_05

예시 답변 Q2_06

Dormitories and Classrooms Renovation

Due to the recent increase in complaints regarding cold dormitory rooms and classrooms, the university's board of directors has decided to renovate many buildings on campus. As heating costs have risen, we will be replacing the windows in some buildings and upgrading the climate control systems in others. To take full advantage of warm weather, this process will begin in April and continue through the summer. Classes in affected buildings will have to be relocated, and a list of affected courses can be found on the university website. The dormitory improvements will not begin until June, so student accommodations will be unaffected.

노트 정리

▸ **Question: What has the university's board of directors decided to do?**

03

문제 듣기
Q2_07
예시 답변
Q2_08

Car Rental Program on Campus

The president of the university announced today that the school has formed a partnership with the car rental agency near campus on 8th Street. Since the campus is located on the east side of town, it is a long way for students to go downtown for shopping or entertainment. It is also difficult to travel outside of the city for weekend trips. This new partnership will help students move around more easily. Students will still have to pass the customary requirements to rent a vehicle, but if they present their university ID, they will receive a 50% discount on any rental.

노트 정리

▸ **Question: What has the university announced?**

Lesson

03 듣기 정리

듣기 정리 전략

대화 듣기에서는 두 화자 사이에 오가는 대화를 들으며 읽기 지문 내용에 찬성/반대 의견을 표현하는 화자에게 집중한다. 화자가 찬성하는지 또는 반대하는지, 그리고 그렇게 생각하는 이유가 무엇인지 듣고 정리하는 연습을 해 보자.

Tip 1

일반적으로 대화 도입부에서 화자가 읽기 지문의 주제에 대한 자신의 찬성/반대 입장을 나타내고 시작하므로 처음부터 집중해서 들어야 한다.

Tip 2

화자가 찬성/반대하는 이유만 가지고는 말할 내용이 부족할 수 있으므로 각각의 이유에 대한 구체적인 근거도 반드시 같이 메모해 두자.

노트 정리 예시

듣기 지문

M: Did you see this letter in the campus newspaper about the library? What do you think?

W: I can see the logic behind what he said, but I don't agree. I don't think that relaxing the rule is the correct solution. Every dormitory and hall and the university center has computer labs in them where people can use computers to access the Internet.

M: That is true. I just came from the one in Michener Hall. Okay, but what about missing calls?

W: If they are expecting an important call, they can call them back outside. If it is really important, I am sure the person who is calling them will understand.

M: I guess, but couldn't people just talk quietly in the library? People have conversations when they do research or study together there.

W: Sure, they could. But, what if the person on the other end of the line is in a noisy location? Then they would have to talk loudly to be heard by them. It is just easier to ban them completely.

M: I think you're right.

노트 정리

주제 relaxing the rule X 규칙 완화 X

woman: not agree w/ the letter 여자: 편지에 동의하지 않음

- many computer labs → can access the Internet 많은 컴퓨터실 → 인터넷 접속 가능
- important call → call them back outside 중요한 전화 → 밖에서 다시 전화함
  in a noisy location: have to talk loudly 시끄러운 곳: 크게 말해야 함

Practice

정답 및 해석 | P. 104

>> 다음 대화를 듣고 먼저 아래에 노트 정리를 한 후, 주어진 질문에 답해 보시오.

01

문제 듣기
Q2_09
예시 답변
Q2_10

노트 정리

▶ **Question: What does the woman think? Why does she think that way?**

02

문제 듣기
Q2_11
예시 답변
Q2_12

노트 정리

▶ **Question: What does the woman think? Why does she think that way?**

03

문제 듣기
Q2_13
예시 답변
Q2_14

▶ **Question: What does the man think? Why does he think that way?**

04

문제 듣기
Q2_15
예시 답변
Q2_16

▶ **Question: What does the man think? Why does he think that way?**

05

문제 듣기
Q2_17
예시 답변
Q2_18

▸ Question: **What does the woman think? Why does she think that way?**

06

문제 듣기
Q2_19
예시 답변
Q2_20

▸ Question: **What does the woman think? Why does she think that way?**

Lesson

04 정리해서 말하기

말하기 전략

앞서 연습한 것을 토대로, 이제 읽기와 듣기의 내용을 연결하여 정리한 뒤 말하기 연습을 해 보자.

1. 읽기

앞서 연습한 것처럼 주제를 찾는다. 학교 측의 공지 또는 학생이나 교수의 건의 사항이 읽기 지문으로 나온다. 주제와 그 주제에 관련된 세부 내용을 요약할 수 있어야 한다.

2. 듣기

공지 또는 건의 사항을 읽은 학생들의 대화로 구성된다. 둘 중 한 학생이 특히 강력하게 자신의 의견을 표현하는데 이 학생의 말에 주목하도록 하자. 다른 학생의 말은 맞장구를 치는 것이거나 일반적인 질문이므로 굳이 노트에 적을 필요는 없다. 그 학생이 왜 읽기 지문의 내용에 찬성 또는 반대하는지, 그 이유는 무엇인지 간단히 정리한다.

3. 읽기&듣기 정리해서 말하기

정리한 읽기 지문의 주제를 먼저 말하고, 중요 세부 사항을 간략하게 덧붙인다. 그 뒤에 들려준 대화 속의 학생이 이 내용에 찬성하는지 또는 반대하는지를 말하고, 그 이유를 설명한다.

실전 적용 예시

- **읽기 지문의 주제**

  The letter in the campus newspaper states that the university is banning cellular phones in the campus library to provide a better atmosphere for studying.

  대학 신문에 실린 편지는 학교가 더 나은 면학 분위기를 제공하기 위해 교내 도서관에서 휴대전화를 금지한다고 말한다.

- **대화 속 학생의 의견**

  The woman agrees with this new policy.

  여자는 이러한 새로운 정책에 동의한다.

- **학생의 의견에 대한 이유**

  First, she thinks that there are many places around campus where students can use computers to access the Internet instead of using their mobile phones. Secondly, if students are expecting an important call, they can call them back outside, where they will not be bothering other students. No matter how quietly people answer their calls, if the person on the other end of the line is in a noisy location, the conversation will eventually get louder.

  첫째, 그녀는 학생들이 휴대전화를 사용하는 대신 인터넷에 접속하기 위해 컴퓨터를 사용할 수 있는 장소가 교내에 많이 있다고 생각한다. 둘째, 만약 학생들이 중요한 전화를 기다린다면, 다른 학생들을 방해하지 않는 바깥에서 전화를 다시 걸 수도 있다. 아무리 조용히 전화를 받는다고 해도, 통화하는 상대방이 시끄러운 장소에 있으면 결과적으로 대화 소리가 더 커질 것이다.

Practice 1

>> 다음 지문을 읽고 대화를 들으며 각각의 노트 정리를 완성해 보시오.

01

문제 듣기
Q2_21

Reading Time: 50 seconds

Recreation Center Renovations

We are sorry to announce that the Recreation Center will be closed for the summer session, from June 1st to September 15th, for renovations. It has been more than ten years since the facility was built, and since then, the student population has expanded. The current Recreation Center is no longer able to accommodate the increasing number of students on campus, so the plans will include the expansion of the pool, gym, and weight room as well as the purchase of new weight and cardio machines. We apologize for any inconvenience this may cause you, and we hope to see you all in September!

읽기 – 노트 정리

주제

- close Jun 1~Sep 15 for renovations
- expansion: pool, gym, etc.

▶ **Now listen to two students talking about the announcement.**

듣기 – 노트 정리

의견

이유 1.

- always go to the gym, hardly anyone there

2. no need for new equipment

- they are all quite new

02

문제 듣기
Q2_22

Reading Time: 50 seconds

Announcement on the Removal of TV in the Cafeteria

Please be advised that the large LCD TV in the main cafeteria at Raleigh House will be moved to the Recreation Center at the end of this month. The first reason brought up was that quite a few students have meetings and study in the cafeteria, and the noise from the television disturbs them. Also, the cafeteria is an important place to talk and get to know one another. Having the LCD TV in the cafeteria interferes with this. Therefore, to help build relationships among students, we have decided to move the TV to the Recreation Center on the third floor. For further information, please contact the Housing Committee.

읽기 – 노트 정리

주제

- TV noise = disturb students who meet & study
- students should talk & get to know

▶ Now listen to two students talking about the announcement from the Housing Committee.

듣기 – 노트 정리

의견

이유 1. ppl just want to relax

- meet & study ppl should go somewhere quiet

2.

-

Practice 2

>> 다음 지문을 읽고 대화를 들으며 각각 노트 정리를 한 후, 주어진 질문에 답해 보시오.

01

문제 듣기 Q2_23

예시 답변 Q2_24

TOEFL Speaking

Question 2 of 4

Reading Time: 50 seconds

Parking Lot Under Construction

All parking permit holders should be aware that Lot C, located next to the Registrar's Office, will be closed for construction. With the increase in enrollment over the past five years, the number of people parking in the lot has also increased dramatically. To increase capacity, the university is planning to build a four-story parking garage on the site of Parking Lot C from the beginning of August until the end of October. While the parking lot is under construction, Lot C permit holders can park in any of the other parking lots on campus.

TOEFL Speaking

Question 2 of 4

TOEFL Speaking

Question 2 of 4

The man expresses his opinion about the announcement by the Facilities Management Department. State his opinion and explain the reasons he gives for holding his opinion.

PREPARATION TIME
00 : 00 : 30

RESPONSE TIME
00 : 00 : 60

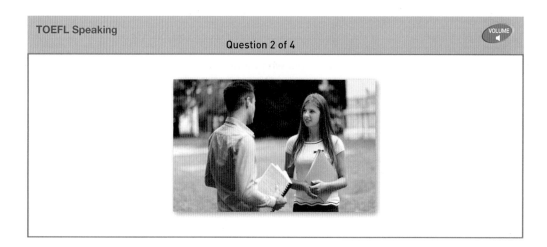

읽기 – 노트 정리

주제

듣기 – 노트 정리

의견

이유 1.

2.

읽기&듣기 정리해서 말하기

02

문제 듣기
Q2_25
예시 답변
Q2_26

TOEFL Speaking

Question 2 of 4

Reading Time: 45 seconds

School of Engineering Orientation

Welcome back from the summer break! Once again, the faculty of the School of Engineering will be hosting its annual orientation activities; but this year, due to students' complaints, there will be a few changes. In previous years, the faculty hosted a barbeque and a hiking trip on the first weekend in September. This year, however, the events are scheduled for Wednesday, September 20th, between noon and 4 o'clock. Additionally, students can choose which of the planned events they wish to attend. Students may sign up for the preferred activity on the webpage of the School of Engineering by noon on the 19th.

TOEFL Speaking

Question 2 of 4

TOEFL Speaking

Question 2 of 4

The woman gives her opinion about the announcement. State her opinion and explain the reasons she gives for holding that opinion.

PREPARATION TIME
00 : 00 : 30

RESPONSE TIME
00 : 00 : 60

읽기 – 노트 정리

주제

듣기 – 노트 정리

의견

이유 1.

2.

읽기&듣기 정리해서 말하기

Q3 읽고 듣고 말하기: 대학 강의

Introduction

3번 문제는 '읽고 듣고 말하기' 문제로, 대학 강의에 관련된 문제다. 2번 문제와 마찬가지로 읽기와 듣기를 연계하여 강의를 요약하는 것이 목표다. 먼저 강의 주제에 관한 짧은 읽기 지문이 제시된 후, 그 지문에 관한 교수의 설명을 듣게 된다.

화면 구성

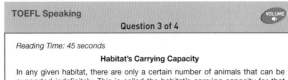

TOEFL Speaking VOLUME
Question 3 of 4

Reading Time: 45 seconds

Habitat's Carrying Capacity

In any given habitat, there are only a certain number of animals that can be supported indefinitely. This is called the habitat's carrying capacity for that organism. Normally, the population of an animal species fluctuates mildly without upsetting the balance, and it will not increase or decrease significantly over time. However, if the balance is disturbed, the population will fall drastically. This is usually due to outside factors, but some species simply reproduce too quickly. Due to such overpopulation, they consume too much of their available food source, which leads to a population crash. Sometimes this becomes a repeating cycle.

- 안내: 3번 문제에 관한 설명을 들려준다.
- 읽기: 지문이 화면에 제시된다. (100자 이하)
  읽기 시간 45/50초가 주어진다.

TOEFL Speaking VOLUME
Question 3 of 4

- 듣기: 사진과 함께 읽기 지문과 관련된 강의를 들려준다. (60~90초 길이)

TOEFL Speaking VOLUME
Question 3 of 4

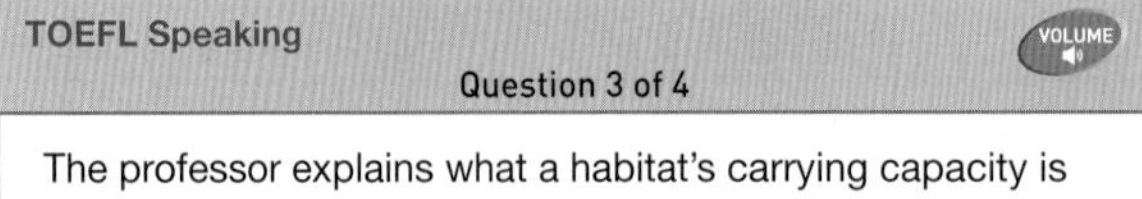

The professor explains what a habitat's carrying capacity is by giving an example of the cinnabar moth. Explain how this example demonstrates the topic.

PREPARATION TIME
00 : 00 : 30

RESPONSE TIME
00 : 00 : 60

- 문제: 3번 문제가 화면에 글로 제시되는 동시에 음성으로 문제를 읽어준다.
- 답변: 준비 시간 30초, 대답 시간 60초가 주어진다.

Learning Strategies

Step 1 **읽기 지문의 핵심 내용을 찾는다.**

– 주제는 보통 굵은 글씨체의 제목으로 나와 있다. 글을 읽으며 무엇에 관한 내용인지 파악한다.

Step 2 **교수의 강의를 들으며 강의가 주제를 어떻게 드러내는지 파악한다.**

– 교수는 보통 예시를 통해 강의 주제를 설명하는 경우가 많다. 이 예시와 관련된 내용을 노트 필기로 간략하게 정리해 둔다.

Step 3 **주어진 30초를 활용하여 정리한 내용을 바탕으로 연습해 본다.**

– '읽기 지문 정리 → 교수의 예시 → 예시 세부 설명' 순서로 답하는 것이 일반적이다.

Example

Q. The professor explains what a habitat's carrying capacity is by giving an example of the cinnabar moth. Explain how this example demonstrates the topic.

교수는 진홍나방의 예를 들어 서식지의 수용력이 무엇인지 설명하고 있다. 이 예가 주제를 어떻게 입증하는지 설명하시오.

❶ 읽기 지문 정리하기

The reading passage explains what a habitat's carrying capacity is. The carrying capacity of a habitat is the number of organisms that it can support.

읽기 지문은 서식지의 수용력이 무엇인지 설명한다. 서식지의 수용력은 서식지가 지탱할 수 있는 생물의 숫자이다.

❷ 읽기 지문과 관련해 교수가 강의에서 전달하는 내용 밝히기

To illustrate this concept more clearly, the professor gives the example of the cinnabar moth.

이 개념을 더 명확히 설명하기 위해 교수는 진홍나방을 예로 든다.

❸ 강의 세부 내용 설명하기

The moth feeds on a plant called ragwort, which makes the moth toxic. Since it is poisonous, the only factor that limits its population is carrying capacity. Sometimes there are fewer ragwort plants for the caterpillars to eat, which leads to a population crash of moth. Then, when the plant population returns to normal, the large supply of food allows many larvae to survive. Then the cycle repeats itself.

이 나방은 금방망이라는 식물을 먹으며 이는 나방이 독성을 갖게 한다. 독성을 가졌으므로 나방의 개체 수를 제한하는 것은 수용력뿐이다. 때로는 애벌레가 먹을 금방망이가 더 적어서 나방 개체군 파괴로 이어진다. 그 뒤 그 식물의 개체 수가 정상으로 돌아오면, 많은 먹이 공급이 많은 유충들이 생존하게 해준다. 그리고 이 주기는 되풀이된다.

Lesson

01 표현 익히기

관련 표현

Q3_01

01. the professor explains 교수는 ~를 설명한다

The professor explains the concept of animal adaptations in the lecture.
교수는 강의에서 동물 적응의 개념을 설명한다.

02. the professor gives an example of 교수는 ~의 예시를 든다

The professor gives an example of this from her own experience.
교수는 자신의 경험에서 이것의 예시를 든다.

03. the professor describes 교수는 ~를 서술한다

The professor describes how this example relates to credence goods.
교수는 이 예시가 어떻게 신뢰재와 관련되는지 서술한다.

04. the professor talks about 교수는 ~에 관해 이야기한다

The professor talks about two different forms of polygamy in the lecture.
교수는 강의에서 다혼의 두 가지 다른 형태에 관해 이야기한다.

05. one example of *A* is A의 한 예는 ~이다

One example of adaptive reuse is the Tate Gallery in London.
건물 전용(轉用)의 한 가지 예는 런던의 테이트 갤러리다.

06. a common example is　　한 가지 흔한 예는 ~이다

A common example is this bird species often found in tropical regions.
한 가지 흔한 예는 열대 지역에서 흔히 발견되는 이 새 종이다.

07. another type of *A* is　　A의 또 다른 종류는 ~이다

Another type of polygamy is called polyandry, and it is less common than polygyny.
다혼의 또 다른 종류는 일처다부제이며 이는 일부다처제보다 덜 흔하다.

08. the professor talks about his/her personal experience to

교수는 ~하기 위해 그/그녀의 개인적 경험에 관해 말한다

The professor talks about his personal experience to explain what group think is.
교수는 집단 사고가 무엇인지 설명하기 위해 자신의 개인적 경험에 관해 이야기한다.

09. the first/second example is　　첫 번째/두 번째 예는 ~이다

The first example is easily found in Arctic regions.
첫 번째 예는 북극 지역에서 쉽게 볼 수 있다.

10. we can observe　　우리는 ~를 관찰할 수 있다

We can observe this phenomenon mostly in suburban areas.
우리는 이 현상을 주로 교외 지역에서 관찰할 수 있다.

11. it is true that ~는 사실이다

It is true that the birds in the area have decreased in the past few years.

그 지역의 새들이 최근 몇 년간 감소한 것은 사실이다.

12. according to the reading 읽기 지문에 의하면

According to the reading, many animals avoid predators with the help of physical adaptations.

읽기 지문에 의하면, 많은 동물들이 신체적 적응의 도움으로 포식자를 피한다.

13. as you know 여러분도 알다시피

As you know, the amount of sunlight it absorbs has its limits.

여러분도 알다시피, 그것이 흡수하는 햇빛의 양에는 한계가 있습니다.

14. there's another example of ~의 또 다른 예가 있다

There's another example of revealing coloration, which is the peanut bug.

경고색의 또 다른 예가 있는데, 바로 악어머리뿔매미이다.

15. the lecture is mainly about 강의는 주로 ~에 관한 것이다

The lecture is mainly about the overestimation of one's own capability.

강의는 주로 자신의 능력을 과대 평가하는 것에 관한 것이다.

Practice

Q3_02

정답 및 해석 | P. 115

>> 주어진 우리말 표현과 같은 뜻이 되도록 빈칸을 채워 보시오.

01. ______________________ how two organisms ______________________.

두 생물이 **서로에게서 이익을 얻는 또 다른 예가 있다.**

02. ______________________ it is almost impossible to ______________________ ______________________.

교수는 그 곤충을 나뭇가지와 구분하는 것이 거의 불가능하다고 **설명한다.**

03. ______________ how this theory works in a laboratory setting.

우리는 이 이론이 실험실 환경에서 어떻게 기능하는지 **관찰할 수 있다.**

04. ___________________________ business forecasting in the lecture.

교수는 강의에서 경기 예측**의 한 예를 든다.**

05. ______________________ how this animal behaves ______________________.

한 가지 흔한 예는 이 동물이 **포식자에게 위협당할 때** 행동하는 방식**이다.**

06. ______________________, a placebo effect ______________________.

읽기 지문에 의하면, 플라시보 효과는 **누구에게나 일어날 수 있다.**

07. ______________________ psychological strategies called defense mechanisms.

강의는 주로 방어 기제라고 불리는 심리학적 전략**에 관한 것이다.**

08. ______________________ the Notothenioidei fish, which inhabits the Antarctic.

두 번째 예는 남극 지역에 서식하는 남극암치아목과 물고기**다.**

09. _________________________________ what we saw in the Philippines.

문화변동의 또 다른 종류는 우리가 필리핀에서 본 것**이다.**

10. ___________________________ her personal experience to show the process of learning new information.

교수는 새 정보를 배우는 과정을 보여주기 위해 자신의 개인적 경험**에 관해 이야기한다.**

Lesson

02 읽기 정리

읽기 정리 전략

읽기 지문에서는 강의 주제를 잘 기억하는 것이 무엇보다 중요하다. 노트 필기를 통해 간단하게 주제와 관련한 세부 내용을 정리하는 연습을 해 보자.

Tip 1

읽기 지문의 제목은 읽기 지문과 그 뒤에 이어질 강의의 내용 전체에 관한 주제가 된다. 따라서 노트 필기를 할 때 제일 먼저 읽기 지문 제목을 적어 두도록 한다.

Tip 2

읽기 지문은 이어서 듣게 될 강의 내용을 이해할 수 있도록 강의에서 다루는 내용의 기본 개념이나 배경 지식을 다룬다. 따라서 읽기 지문의 내용을 제대로 파악해 두어야 강의 듣기도 수월하다.

노트 정리 예시

읽기 지문

Habitat's Carrying Capacity

In any given habitat, there are only a certain number of animals that can be supported indefinitely. This is called the habitat's carrying capacity for that organism. Normally, the population of an animal species fluctuates mildly without upsetting the balance, and it will not increase or decrease significantly over time. However, if the balance is disturbed, the population will fall drastically. This is usually due to outside factors, but some species simply reproduce too quickly. Due to such overpopulation, they consume too much of their available food source, which leads to a population crash. Sometimes this becomes a repeating cycle.

노트 정리

Habitat's Carrying Capacity 서식지의 수용력

= # of animals that can be supported in a habitat 한 서식지에서 지원할 수 있는 동물의 수

- disturbed balance → population will fall drastically 깨진 균형 → 개체 수 크게 감소
- overpopulation → food source ↓ → population crash 과잉 개체 수 → 식량원 ↓ → 개체군 파괴

Practice

정답 및 해석 | P. 115

>> 다음 지문을 읽고 먼저 아래에 노트 정리를 한 후, 주어진 질문에 답해 보시오.

01

문제 듣기 Q3_03
예시 답변 Q3_04

The Principle of Allocation

For all organisms, their ultimate purpose is to reproduce. However, many are unable to obey this most primal of directives. Their time and resources are limited, so they must allocate their energy to the most important task at that time. This is called the principle of allocation. Organisms have other basic needs, like finding food, locating shelter, and migrating. When food is scarce, they have less energy to put towards reproduction, which can consume much time and energy. This does not apply to many insects that only mate once during their brief lifetimes. However, species that can potentially mate many times must favor their own survival over potential offspring.

▸ **Question: What is the principle of allocation?**

02

문제 듣기
Q3_05
예시 답변
Q3_06

Synomones

One means of communication utilized in nature is the use of scent compounds. These typically take two forms: pheromones, which are chemical signals used to communicate with other members of the same species, and allelochemicals, which are used for interspecies communication. One type of allelochemicals called synomones benefit both organisms, and they are an intense area of study. One example is when plants that are being eaten release scent compounds to attract predators like parasitic wasps that prey upon the insects attacking them.

▸ **Question: According to the passage, what are synomones?**

03

문제 듣기
Q3_07
예시 답변
Q3_08

Adaptive Reuse

Adaptive reuse is the practice of repurposing buildings to fulfill a new role, often preserving the exterior shell of the building while renovating the interior. In many cases, these buildings would have been demolished to make room for the construction of an entirely new structure. However, some buildings have great historical and societal value which leads the community to save them. If a building is still structurally sound, and the site is ecologically viable, then it may become a candidate for adaptive reuse. The buildings that are typically treated in this manner are industrial buildings like factories and power plants, political buildings like palaces and courthouses, and community buildings like churches and schools.

노트 정리

▶ Question: **What is adaptive reuse?**

Lesson

03 듣기 정리

듣기 정리 전략

듣기에서는 교수의 강의를 들으며 읽기 지문과 강의 내용이 어떻게 연관되는지에 집중한다. 대부분의 경우 교수는 주제와 관련한 예시를 들고 세부 설명을 한다. 강의 초반에 주제를 간단하게 다시 정리해 주기도 한다.

Tip

듣기가 끝난 후 주어지는 질문에서는 교수가 강의에서 언급한 예시 등 주요 사항에 대해 필수적으로 물어보므로, 핵심어 위주로 빠르게 노트 필기를 하는 연습을 해야 한다. 일반적으로 강의는 다음과 같은 구조로 진행된다.

읽기 지문에 관련된 주제 언급 → 주요 사항 → 구체적 설명 (→ 주요 사항 2 → 구체적 설명)

노트 정리 예시

듣기 지문

W: Yesterday, we were talking about the carrying capacity of habitats. Some species cause their own population crashes due to overpopulation and overconsumption. One species that typifies this pattern is the cinnabar moth. The cinnabar moth has very few natural predators in its native forest habitat because it is poisonous. You see these bright red markings on the moth's black wings? Those markings signify that the moth is dangerous to eat. You see, as caterpillars, these insects feed on a plant called ragwort. This plant produces toxins that the caterpillars take into their bodies, making them poisonous. So, the only thing that limits their population is their habitat's carrying capacity. One year, there was less rain than usual, so there were fewer ragwort plants for them to eat. With fewer plants to eat, many caterpillars died before they became adults. This meant that only a few moths could mate and lay eggs, which led to a population crash. Then, the rainfall returned to normal levels the following year, so the ragwort plant population quickly returned to its former size. Since there were many plants, the surviving cinnabar moth caterpillars had plenty of food. And within just a few years, their population had once again reached its former size. This process often repeats with cinnabar moths.

노트 정리

주제 **the carrying capacity of habitats** 서식지의 수용력

예시 the example of the cinnabar moth 진홍나방의 예

- caterpillars: feed on a ragwort plant → make them toxic 유충: 금방망이 식물 섭취 → 독성을 갖게 함
- fewer ragwort → population crash 더 적은 금방망이 → 개체군 파괴
- plant population returns → allows many larvae to survive 식물 개체 수 복구 → 많은 유충들이 생존하게 함

Practice

정답 및 해석 | P. 117

>> 다음 강의를 듣고 먼저 아래에 노트 정리를 한 후, 주어진 질문에 답해 보시오.

01

문제 듣기 Q3_09

예시 답변 Q3_10

노트 정리

▶ **Question: What does the principle of allocation say about certain animals?**

02

문제 듣기 Q3_11

예시 답변 Q3_12

노트 정리

▶ **Question: What is the example of synomones?**

03

문제 듣기
Q3_13
예시 답변
Q3_14

노트 정리

▸ Question: **What is the example of adaptive reuse?**

04

문제 듣기
Q3_15
예시 답변
Q3_16

노트 정리

▸ Question: **What is the example of appeasement behavior?**

05

문제 듣기
Q3_17
예시 답변
Q3_18

▸ Question: **What is the example of agonistic buffering?**

06

문제 듣기
Q3_19
예시 답변
Q3_20

▸ Question: **How does the professor explain the concept of information overload?**

Lesson

04 정리해서 말하기

말하기 전략

앞서 연습한 것을 토대로, 이제 읽기와 듣기의 내용을 연결하여 정리한 뒤 말하는 연습을 해 보자.

1. 읽기

일반적이고 이론적인 전문 용어나 개념, 특정 현상과 이에 대한 부연 설명이 주어지는데, 뒤에 이어질 강의 내용에 대한 사전 설명이라고 생각하고 읽는다.

2. 듣기

읽기 지문의 주제에 대한 구체적인 부연 설명, 예시, 반증, 또는 그 개념을 적용, 응용한 예가 주어지는데, 뒤에 나올 질문에서는 강의 내용을 중점적으로 물어보므로 집중해서 들으며 필기한다.

3. 읽기&듣기 정리해서 말하기

30초의 준비 시간 동안에는 노트 필기를 참고해서 '읽기 지문의 주제 → 강의에 언급된 예시와 세부 설명' 순으로 말할 내용의 구성을 정리한다. 마지막에 시간이 남는 경우 강의 주제를 다시 한 번 요약해주면 좀 더 논리 정연한 인상을 줄 수 있다.

실전 적용 예시

• **읽기 지문의 주제**

The reading passage explains what a habitat's carrying capacity is. The carrying capacity of a habitat is the number of organisms that it can support.

읽기 지문은 서식지의 수용력이 무엇인지 설명한다. 서식지의 수용력은 서식지가 지탱할 수 있는 생물의 숫자이다.

• **강의에 언급된 예시**

To illustrate this concept more clearly, the professor gives the example of the cinnabar moth.

이 개념을 더 명확히 설명하기 위해 교수는 진홍나방을 예로 든다.

• **예시 세부 설명**

The moth feeds on a plant called ragwort, which makes the moth toxic. Since it is poisonous, the only factor that limits its population is carrying capacity. Sometimes there are fewer ragwort plants for the caterpillars to eat, which leads to a population crash of moth. Then, when the plant population returns to normal, the large supply of food allows many larvae to survive. Then the cycle repeats itself.

이 나방은 금방망이라는 식물을 먹으며 이는 나방이 독성을 갖게 한다. 독성을 가졌으므로 나방의 개체 수를 제한하는 것은 수용력뿐이다. 때로는 애벌레가 먹을 금방망이가 더 적어서 나방 개체군 파괴로 이어진다. 그 뒤 그 식물의 개체 수가 정상으로 돌아오면, 많은 먹이 공급이 많은 유충들이 생존하게 해준다. 그리고 이 주기는 되풀이된다.

Practice 1

>> 다음 지문을 읽고 강의를 들으며 각각의 노트 정리를 완성해 보시오.

01

문제 듣기
Q3_21

Reading Time: 50 seconds

The Peak-End Rule

When people are asked to describe certain events that have happened in their lives, a psychological phenomenon termed as the peak-end rule often comes into play. The peak-end rule states that a person is most likely to focus on the highlights or the last parts of his or her experience and discard virtually all other information when describing the event as a whole. The main reason is that people have a tendency to recall their experiences with ease when strong, either negative or positive, emotions are attached to them. Minor emotions and information are often disregarded in the process of remembering and describing the overall experience of the event.

읽기 – 노트 정리

주제 The Peak-End Rule

-

-

▶ **Now listen to part of a lecture on this topic in a psychology class.**

듣기 – 노트 정리

예시 1. family trip

-

2. movie

-

02

문제 듣기
Q3_22

Reading Time: 50 seconds

Fixed Action Patterns

In the animal kingdom, there are some species that show fixed action patterns, which are complex instinctive behavior produced in response to specific stimuli. One important aspect is that the response is normally elicited by a set of perceptions, such as shapes, color combinations, or specific smells, rather than by specific objects in the environment. Another important feature is that, once started, a fixed action pattern does not stop until the entire action sequence is completed. Even if the stimulus is no longer present, the organism would still show the same behavioral pattern since it is a kind of reflex response.

읽기 – 노트 정리

주제 Fixed Action Patterns

- specific stimuli → show fixed action pattern
-
-

▸ **Now listen to part of a lecture on this topic in a biology class.**

듣기 – 노트 정리

예시 1. stickleback fish

-

2. graylag goose

-

Practice 2

>> 다음 지문을 읽고 강의를 들으며 각각 노트 정리를 한 후, 주어진 질문에 답해 보시오.

01

문제 듣기 Q3_23

예시 답변 Q3_24

TOEFL Speaking

Question 3 of 4

Reading Time: 45 seconds

Polygamy

In the animal kingdom, different types of mating patterns have evolved in order to maximize the chance of increasing the number of young. The most common type among animals is called polygamy, where one male or female mates with two or more other partners at the same time. Within this multiple-partner mating system, the fittest animals have more partners than those with relatively less power or dominance. In a general zoological sense, polygamy can be categorized as either polygyny or polyandry. In polygyny, a male mates with more than one female; whereas in polyandry, one female partners with several males.

TOEFL Speaking

Question 3 of 4

The professor talks about polygamy in the animal kingdom. Use the examples from the lecture to explain what the types of polygamy are and how they benefit organisms that practice them.

PREPARATION TIME
00 : 00 : 30

RESPONSE TIME
00 : 00 : 60

읽기 – 노트 정리

주제

듣기 – 노트 정리

예시 1.

2.

읽기&듣기 정리해서 말하기

02

문제 듣기 Q3_25

예시 답변 Q3_26

TOEFL Speaking

Question 3 of 4

Reading Time: 50 seconds

Film Techniques

In filmmaking, various camera shots are used to give viewers a better comprehension of the film's story. One of the shots often used is called an "establishing shot." Usually shown at the beginning of the movie, it gives viewers general ideas about the whole movie, so it provides the basic context or background information. There is another type called a "bridging shot," which makes a smooth transition between two different scenes. If there is a jump or a break in the flow of a story, perhaps in time or place, a bridging shot can be inserted to cover the gaps between those disconnected scenes, helping viewers to avoid any confusion.

TOEFL Speaking

Question 3 of 4

TOEFL Speaking

Question 3 of 4

The professor is discussing two different shots used in filmmaking. Using points and examples given in the lecture, describe these shots and how they are used.

PREPARATION TIME
00 : 00 : 30

RESPONSE TIME
00 : 00 : 60

읽기 – 노트 정리

주제

듣기 – 노트 정리

예시 1.

2.

읽기&듣기 정리해서 말하기

Q4 듣고 말하기: 대학 강의

Introduction

4번 문제는 대학 강의에 관련된 내용을 들은 뒤 질문에 답하는 문제다. 교수가 수업 내용의 일부를 설명하며, 보통 수업의 주제와 그 주제를 뒷받침하는 예시에 관해 자세히 말한다. 질문은 강의의 주제가 무엇이며 그 주제의 예시로는 무엇이 있는지, 또는 예시가 주제를 어떻게 뒷받침하는지 등을 묻는다.

화면 구성

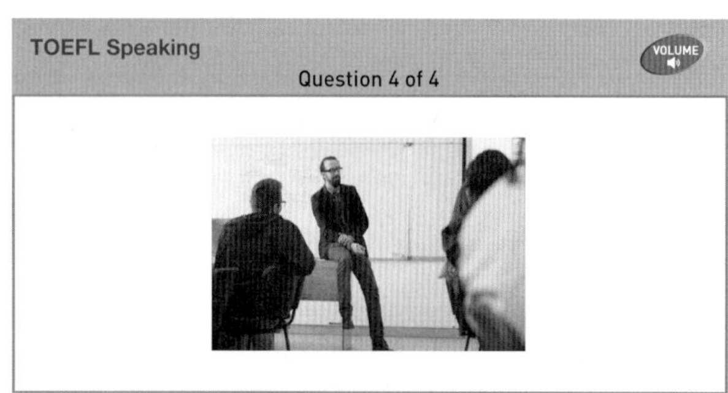

• 안내: 4번 문제에 관한 설명을 들려준다.
• 듣기: 사진과 함께 강의를 들려준다. (60~90초 길이)

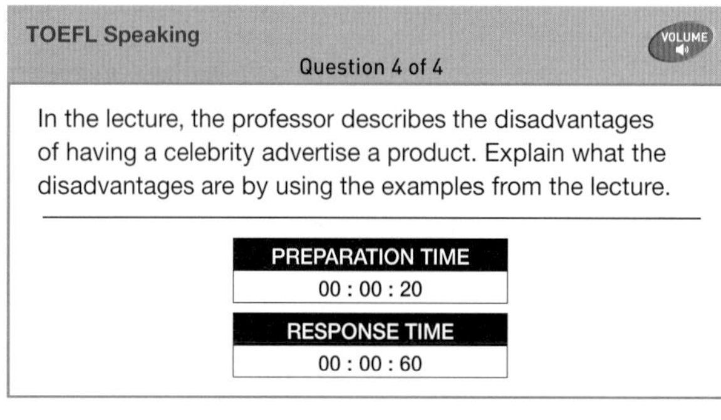

• 문제: 4번 문제가 화면에 글로 제시되는 동시에 음성으로 문제를 읽어준다.
• 답변: 준비 시간 20초, 대답 시간 60초가 주어진다.

Learning Strategies

Step 1 **교수의 강의를 들으며 교수가 논의하는 주제가 무엇인지 찾는다.**

- 그 주제를 간략히 설명할 방법을 찾는다.
- 그 주제에 관해 어떤 예시나 하위 분류가 등장하는지 파악한다.
- 예시나 하위 분류가 주제와 어떻게 연결되는지 정리한다.

Step 2 **주어진 20초를 활용하여 정리한 내용을 바탕으로 연습해 본다.**

- '강의 주제 요약 → 주제 관련 분류·예시' 순서로 답한다.

Example

Q. In the lecture, the professor describes the disadvantages of having a celebrity advertise a product. Explain what the disadvantages are by using the examples from the lecture.

강의에서 교수는 유명인이 제품을 광고하게 하는 것의 단점들을 묘사하고 있다. 강의의 예들을 사용하여 그러한 단점들이 무엇인지 설명하시오.

❶ 강의 주제 정리하기

In the lecture, the professor talks about a common advertising method: hiring a celebrity to endorse a company's product. However, having celebrities promote a company's product can sometimes backfire for the following two reasons.

강의에서 교수는 흔한 광고 방법에 대해 이야기하는데 그것은 기업의 제품을 홍보하기 위해 유명인을 고용하는 것이다. 그러나 유명인으로 하여금 기업의 제품을 홍보하게 하는 것은 때때로 다음의 두 가지 이유로 인해 역효과를 낳을 수 있다.

❷ 주제와 관련해 제시된 세부 내용 설명하기

The first one is overshadowing. An example of overshadowing is when a beverage company hires a singer to promote their drink. After some time, the company finds out that their sales did not increase much, but the singer's music sales did. This is called overshadowing. The second problem is compromising behavior by a celebrity. For instance, when an athlete does not wear the company's shoes that he has been promoting, people will lose confidence in the shoes. Also, a celebrity could do something that results in legal problems. This can seriously harm the company's image, so the company severs its ties with the celebrity after the incident.

첫 번째는 뒤덮기다. 뒤덮기의 한 예는 음료 생산 기업이 자사의 음료를 홍보하기 위해 가수를 고용하는 경우다. 얼마간의 시간이 지난 후, 기업은 매출이 그다지 증가하지 않았지만, 그 가수의 음반 매출은 증가했음을 알게 된다. 이것을 뒤덮기라고 부른다. 두 번째 문제는 유명인의 위태로운 행동이다. 예를 들면, 어떤 운동선수가 자신이 홍보하는 기업의 신발을 신지 않을 때, 사람들은 그 신발에 대한 신뢰를 잃을 것이다. 또한 유명인이 법적인 문제로 귀결될 수 있는 어떤 일을 할 수도 있다. 이것은 기업의 이미지를 심각하게 손상할 수 있기 때문에, 기업은 그 사건 이후 그 유명인과의 관계를 끊는다.

Lesson
01 표현 익히기

관련 표현

Q4_01

01. the lecture is about 강의는 ~에 관한 것이다

The lecture is about how the interaction between cultures influences people.
강의는 문화들 사이의 교류가 어떻게 사람들에게 영향을 주는지에 관한 것이다.

02. the lecture's main idea is 강의의 주제는 ~이다

The lecture's main idea is the experiments about recalling newly learned information.
강의의 주제는 새로 배운 정보 기억하기에 관한 실험들이다.

03. the professor explains 교수는 ~를 설명한다

The professor explains the factors that influence population size.
교수는 인구 크기에 영향을 주는 요인들을 설명한다.

04. the professor talks about 교수는 ~에 관해 말한다

The professor talks about the population of deer in a certain area.
교수는 특정 지역의 사슴 개체 수에 관해 말한다.

05. according to the lecture/professor 강의/교수에 따르면

According to the professor, the space is too limited to accommodate all the organisms.
교수에 따르면, 그 공간은 모든 생물을 수용하기엔 너무 좁다.

06. the professor gives an example of 교수는 ~의 예시를 든다

The professor gives an example of monkeys to explain this emotional attachment.
교수는 이 감정적 애착을 설명하기 위해 원숭이의 예시를 든다.

07. the first/second example is 첫 번째/두 번째 예시는 ~이다

The second example is the way frogs lay their eggs.
두 번째 예시는 개구리가 알을 낳는 방식이다.

08. for example, instance 예를 들어

For example, it can significantly reduce the air pollution level.
예를 들어, 그것은 공기 오염 수치를 크게 줄일 수 있다.

09. for these reasons 이러한 이유로

For these reasons, many researchers are observing the newly discovered trend.
이러한 이유로 많은 연구원들이 새로 발견된 트렌드를 관찰하고 있다.

10. there are two types of ~에 두 종류가 있다

There are two types of these birds, and they both occupy a small region.
이 새에는 두 종류가 있으며, 둘 다 작은 지역에 산다.

11. one of *A* is/was   A의 하나는 ~이다/였다

One of the experiments was conducted in a controlled laboratory.
그 실험들 중 하나는 통제된 실험실에서 진행되었다.

12. in this case   이 경우에는

In this case, problems can arise in these organisms' habitats.
이 경우에는 이 생물들의 서식지에서 문제들이 발생할 수 있다.

13. there are two subcategories of   ~의 두 가지 하위 분류가 있다

There are two subcategories of this theory and understanding them is very important.
이 이론에는 두 가지 하위 분류가 있으며 이것들을 이해하는 것은 아주 중요하다.

14. the example the professor gives is   교수가 드는 예시는 ~이다

The example the professor gives is the way chimpanzees act when in groups.
교수가 드는 예시는 침팬지가 무리에 있을 때 행동하는 방식이다.

15. this is illustrated with   이것은 ~로 설명된다

This is illustrated with not being able to recall past information because of new information.
이것은 새 정보 때문에 과거의 정보를 기억하지 못하는 것으로 설명된다.

Practice

Q4_02

정답 및 해석 | P. 130

>> 주어진 우리말 표현과 같은 뜻이 되도록 빈칸을 채워 보시오.

01. ______________ an experiment, which showed how a frog lays its eggs in water.

이것은 한 실험**으로 설명되었는데,** 이 실험은 개구리가 어떻게 물에 알을 낳는지 보여주었다.

02. ______________ similar to the first one, but ______________ ______________.

두 번째 예시는 첫 번째와 비슷하지만 **더 많은 투자를 필요로 한다.**

03. ______________, this species of bird is ______________ well in water.

이러한 이유로 이 종의 새는 물속에서 **균형을** 잘 **유지할 수 있다.**

04. ______________ how a given area can only support ______________.

강의는 주어진 한 지역이 어떻게 **특정한 개체 수**만 지탱할 수 있는지**에 관한 것이다.**

05. ______________ fish that could be classified with ______________.

뼈 구조로 분류될 수 있는 **두 종류의** 물고기**가 있다.**

06. ______________ mating behavior of bowerbirds.

교수는 바우어새의 짝짓기 행동**의 예시를 든다.**

07. ______________ population fluctuation of ______________.

강의의 주제는 특정 지역의 사슴 개체 수 변동**이다.**

08. ______________ many ways to protect wildlife, ______________.

교수는 자원 봉사 활동을 포함하여 야생 동물을 보호하는 많은 방법**을 설명한다.**

09. ______________, some people heavily focus on ______________.

교수에 따르면, 어떤 사람들은 **제품의 디자인**에 크게 중점을 둔다.

10. ______________ warning coloration's benefits ______ that it ______________ of getting attacked by predators.

경고색 이점**의 한 가지는** 포식자에게 공격 당할 **확률을 낮춘다**는 것**이다.**

Lesson

02 듣기 정리

듣기 정리 전략

교수의 강의를 들으며 주제가 무엇인지, 어떤 예시나 설명이 제시되는지 집중한다. 보통 두 개로 제시되는 예시나 설명을 찾아 짧게 요약하는 연습을 하는 것이 중요하다.

Tip

일반적으로 강의는 주제 유형에 따라 다음과 같이 구성된다.

① 개념 — 개념에 대한 구체적인 설명

↓

② 현상 — 현상의 원인과 결과의 예시

↓

③ 과정 — 과정의 기능을 설명

↓

④ 이론 — 이론을 응용 또는 적용한 예시

노트 정리 예시

듣기 지문

M: One of the most common methods is to hire a celebrity to endorse their products. However, many companies have recently severed endorsement contracts with celebrities and chosen to focus on their products' selling points instead. This trend is due to two phenomena that can severely affect their profit margin: overshadowing and compromising behavior.

The first problem arises when a celebrity is so popular that their fame distracts potential customers from the product that is actually being advertised. For example, many beverage companies hire singers to promote their drinks. However, many companies have come to realize that their sales do not increase enough to justify paying the celebrity. In addition, the singers often see sales of their music increase.

An even more serious situation can arise when a celebrity endorses a product, but their own actions outside of the advertising campaign compromise public perception of the product. Sometimes celebrities publically endorse a product, but they then prove that they do not like or use the product themselves. For example, an athlete may endorse a shoe company, but when he is playing in a game, he wears a different brand of shoes. This is embarrassing to the company, and it reduces people's confidence in their product. Even worse, a celebrity may become involved in an unrelated incident that results in legal problems. This reduces the public's opinion of the celebrity, and it can transfer to the products they endorse.

노트 정리

주제 **a common ad method: hiring a celebrity** 흔한 광고 방법: 유명인 고용하기

problem 1: overshadowing 문제 1: 뒤덮기

- a celebrity's fame distracts customers 유명인의 명성이 소비자들의 주의를 빼앗음
- ex: beverage companies hire singers → sales do not increase / sales of singers' music increase 예시: 음료 회사가 가수를 고용 → 매출 오르지 않음 / 가수의 음반 매출 상승

problem 2: compromising behavior 문제 2: 위태로운 행동

- a celebrity's own action → compromise public perception
  유명인의 행동 → 대중의 인식을 위태롭게 만듦
- ex: an athlete wearing different brand shoes 예시: 다른 브랜드 신발을 신는 운동선수
  a celebrity involved in serious incident 심각한 사건에 연루된 유명인

Practice

>> 다음 강의를 듣고 먼저 아래에 노트 정리를 한 후, 주어진 질문에 답해 보시오.

01

문제 듣기
Q4_03
예시 답변
Q4_04

노트 정리

▶ Question 1: **What is the main idea of the lecture?**

▶ Question 2: **What example(s) does the professor give?**

02

문제 듣기
Q4_05
예시 답변
Q4_06

노트 정리

▶ Question 1: **What is the main idea of the lecture?**

▶ Question 2: **What example(s) does the professor give?**

03

문제 듣기
Q4_07
예시 답변
Q4_08

노트 정리

▶ Question 1: **What is the main idea of the lecture?**

▶ Question 2: **What type of advertising does the professor mention?**

04

문제 듣기
Q4_09
예시 답변
Q4_10

노트 정리

▶ Question 1: **What is the main idea of the lecture?**

▶ Question 2: **What are the two ways of satisfying id through reality principle?**

Lesson

03 정리해서 말하기

말하기 전략

이제 듣기의 내용을 정리한 뒤 말하는 연습을 해 보자.

1. 듣기

강의에서 들리는 모든 것을 필기하려 하면 더 중요한 사항을 놓치게 된다. 핵심적인 사항을 파악하여 키워드 위주로 노트 필기를 하자.

2. 듣기 정리해서 말하기

질문은 보통 강의 내용의 예시를 사용해 설명하라고 지시한다. 20초의 준비 시간 동안에는 노트 필기의 키워드를 바탕으로 말할 내용의 구성과 순서를 정리한 후, 강의의 주제를 먼저 말하면서 시작한다. 마지막에 시간이 남는 경우 강의의 주제를 다시 한 번 요약해주면 좀 더 논리 정연한 인상을 줄 수 있다.

실전 적용 예시

• **강의의 주제 제시**

In the lecture, the professor talks about a common advertising method: hiring a celebrity to endorse a company's product.

강의에서 교수는 흔한 광고 방법에 대해 이야기하는데 그것은 기업의 제품을 홍보하기 위해 유명인을 고용하는 것이다.

• **주요 사항 1 요약**

However, having celebrities promote a company's product can sometimes backfire for the following two reasons. The first one is overshadowing.

그러나 유명인으로 하여금 기업의 제품을 홍보하게 하는 것은 때때로 다음의 두 가지 이유로 인해 역효과를 낳을 수 있다. 첫 번째는 뒤덮기다.

• **주요 사항 1 예시 요약**

An example of overshadowing is when a beverage company hires a singer to promote their drink. After some time, the company finds out that their sales did not increase much, but the singer's music sales did. This is called overshadowing.

뒤덮기의 한 예는 음료 생산 기업이 자사의 음료를 홍보하기 위해 가수를 고용하는 경우다. 얼마간의 시간이 지난 후, 기업은 매출이 그다지 증가하지 않았지만, 그 가수의 음반 매출은 증가했음을 알게 된다. 이것을 뒤덮기라고 부른다.

• **주요 사항 2 요약**

The second problem is compromising behavior by a celebrity.

두 번째 문제는 유명인의 위태로운 행동이다.

• **주요 사항 2 예시 요약**

For instance, when an athlete does not wear the company's shoes that he has been promoting, people will lose confidence in the shoes. Also, a celebrity could do something that results in legal problems. This can seriously harm the company's image, so the company severs its ties with the celebrity after the incident.

예를 들면, 어떤 운동선수가 자신이 홍보하는 기업의 신발을 신지 않을 때, 사람들은 그 신발에 대한 신뢰를 잃을 것이다. 또한 유명인이 법적인 문제로 귀결될 수 있는 어떤 일을 할 수도 있다. 이것은 기업의 이미지를 심각하게 손상할 수 있기 때문에, 기업은 그 사건 이후 그 유명인과의 관계를 끊는다.

Practice 1

>> 다음 대화를 들으며 노트 정리를 완성해 보시오.

01 문제 듣기 Q4_11

노트 정리

주제 cultural diffusion: adopt new culture → spread

예시 1. paper

-

2. acupuncture

-

02 문제 듣기 Q4_12

노트 정리

주제 benefits of trees in cities

예시 1. absorb pollutants

-

2.

-

03 노트 정리

문제 듣기
Q4_13

주제 purchasing a product → what influences the decision?

예시 1.

-

2.

-

-

04 노트 정리

문제 듣기
Q4_14

주제 tool use of animals

예시 1.

-

2.

-

Practice 2

>> 다음 대화를 들으며 노트 정리를 한 후, 주어진 질문에 답해 보시오.

01

문제 듣기 Q4_15

예시 답변 Q4_16

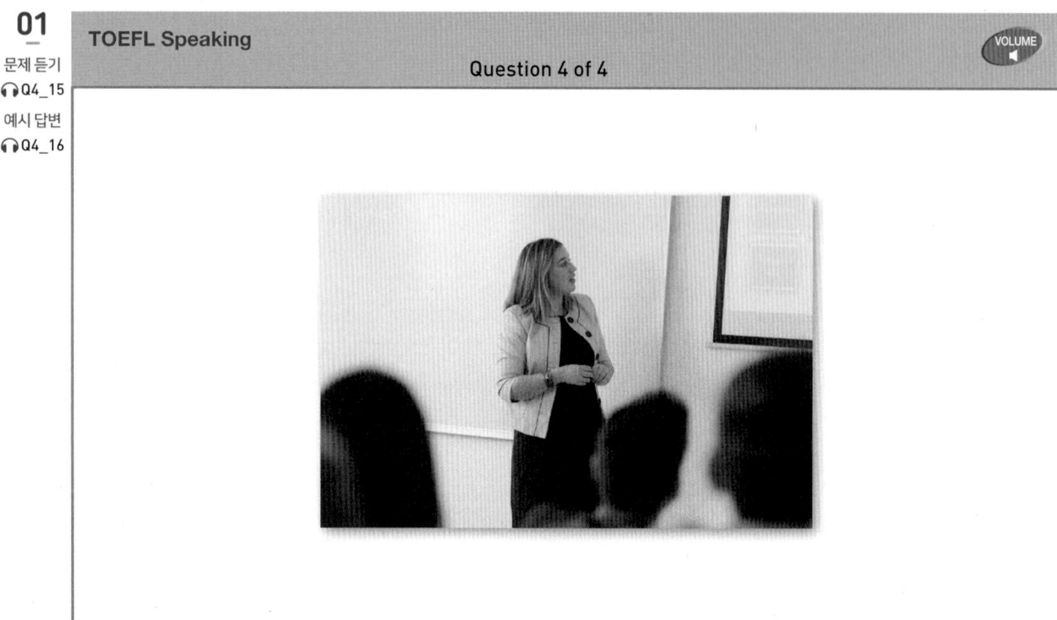

노트 정리

주제 emotional attachment

예시 experiment w. monkeys

2 mothers:

= conclusion:

TOEFL Speaking

Question 4 of 4

Using points and examples from the lecture, explain how warm touch is related to creating parent-child bonds based on the experiment.

PREPARATION TIME
00 : 00 : 20

RESPONSE TIME
00 : 00 : 60

말하기 정리

주제 The lecture deals with emotional attachment as illustrated by an experiment that was conducted using monkeys.

예시 Two groups of baby monkeys were

According to the professor, this shows that

02

문제 듣기
Q4_17
예시 답변
Q4_18

TOEFL Speaking

노트 정리

주제 babies' intellectual abilities

예시 show a doll → place a screen to hide it

show another doll →

baby expects 2 dolls →

= conclusion:

TOEFL Speaking

VOLUME

Question 4 of 4

Using an experiment given in the lecture, explain how babies show their basic intellectual abilities.

PREPARATION TIME
00 : 00 : 20

RESPONSE TIME
00 : 00 : 60

말하기 정리

주제 The lecture is mainly about the intellectual abilities of babies. The professor explains this by giving one experiment as an example.

예시 In the experiment,

After the screen was removed,

Actual Test 1

TOEFL CONTINUE

Speaking Section Directions

In this section of the test, you will be able to demonstrate your ability to speak about a variety of topics. You will answer four questions by speaking into the microphone. Answer each of the questions as completely as possible.

In question one, you will speak about your personal opinion and preference. Your response will be scored on your ability to speak clearly and coherently about the topic.

In questions two and three, you will first read a short text. The text will go away and you will then hear a talk on the same topic. You will then be asked a question about what you read and heard. You will need to combine appropriate information from the text and the talk to provide a complete answer to the question. Your response will be scored on your ability to speak clearly and coherently and to accurately convey information about what you read and heard.

In question four, you will hear part of a lecture. You will then be asked a question about what you heard. Your response will be scored on your ability to speak clearly and coherently and to accurately convey information about what you heard.

You may take notes while you read and listen to the conversation and lectures. You may use your notes to help prepare your response.

Listen carefully to the directions for each question. The directions will not be written on the screen.

For each question, you will be given a short time to prepare your response. A clock will show how much preparation time is remaining. When the preparation time is up, you will be told to begin your response. A clock will show how much response time is remaining. A message will appear on the screen when the response time has ended.

정답 및 해석 | P. 142

문제 듣기 S_AT1_01

예시 답변 S_AT1_02

TOEFL Speaking

Question 1 of 4

If you have a question about an assignment that a professor has given you, would you prefer to speak to the professor via e-mail or in person? Explain.

PREPARATION TIME
00 : 00 : 15

RESPONSE TIME
00 : 00 : 45

문제 듣기 S_AT1_03
예시 답변 S_AT1_04

TOEFL Speaking

Question 2 of 4

Reading Time: 45 seconds

Closing Poetry Writing Courses

Beginning in the fall semester, Regis University will no longer offer poetry writing courses. This is due to the fact that registration numbers are consistently low, and the grading system is too subjective. This has led many students to dispute the scores that they have received in the courses. Students who still wish to take poetry writing classes may take them at Foothills Art Institute. The credits for those classes will be fully transferable and count towards your overall degree.

TOEFL Speaking

Question 2 of 4

TOEFL Speaking

Question 2 of 4

The woman expresses her opinion about the removal of poetry writing courses. State her opinion and explain the reasons she gives for holding that opinion.

PREPARATION TIME
00 : 00 : 30

RESPONSE TIME
00 : 00 : 60

문제 듣기 S_AT1_05
예시 답변 S_AT1_06

TOEFL Speaking

Question 3 of 4

Reading Time: 50 seconds

Plant Communication

In the early 1980s, research showed that various trees might communicate with each other. When insects feed upon trees, they begin producing chemicals to deter them. The scientists observed that trees in the vicinity that were not infested also began to produce the same compounds. They thought that the plants were communicating that they were under attack, which was unprecedented for organisms that lack central nervous systems and are not in physical contact with each other. Their findings met immediate scrutiny and were discounted by much of the scientific community. However, recent research has provided data that supports their assertions.

TOEFL Speaking

Question 3 of 4

TOEFL Speaking

Question 3 of 4

The professor explains how plants communicate with each other by giving some examples. Explain how the examples demonstrate the topic in the reading passage.

PREPARATION TIME
00 : 00 : 30

RESPONSE TIME
00 : 00 : 60

문제 듣기 S_AT1_07
예시 답변 S_AT1_08

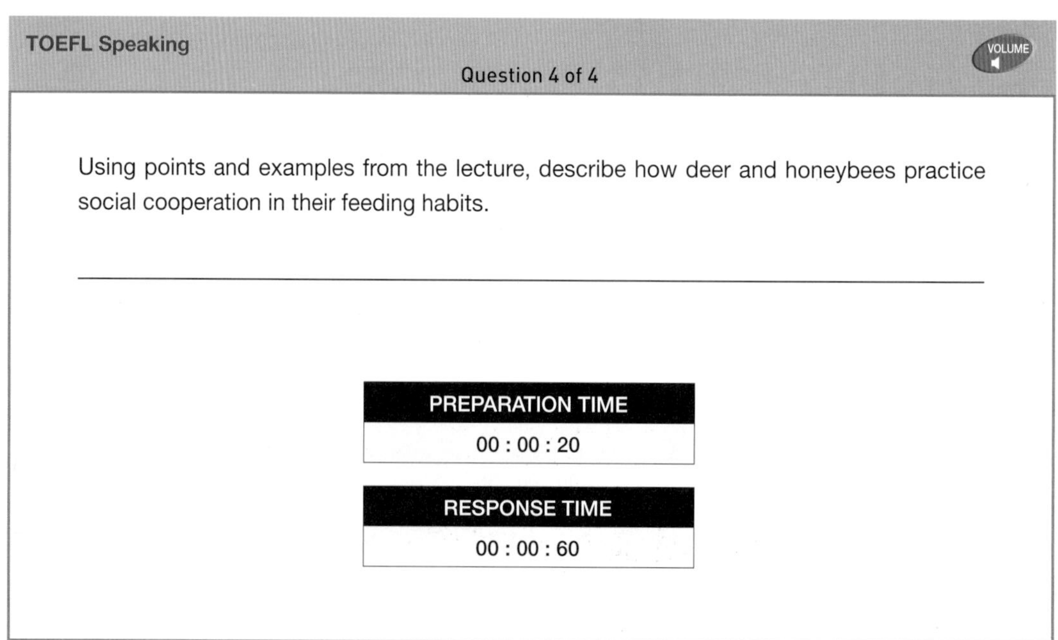

TOEFL Speaking
Question 4 of 4
VOLUME
Using points and examples from the lecture, describe how deer and honeybees practice social cooperation in their feeding habits.
PREPARATION TIME
00 : 00 : 20
RESPONSE TIME
00 : 00 : 60

PAGODA TOEFL 80+ R/L/S/W

Actual Test 2

TOEFL

CONTINUE

Speaking Section Directions

In this section of the test, you will be able to demonstrate your ability to speak about a variety of topics. You will answer four questions by speaking into the microphone. Answer each of the questions as completely as possible.

In question one, you will speak about your personal opinion and preference. Your response will be scored on your ability to speak clearly and coherently about the topic.

In questions two and three, you will first read a short text. The text will go away and you will then hear a talk on the same topic. You will then be asked a question about what you read and heard. You will need to combine appropriate information from the text and the talk to provide a complete answer to the question. Your response will be scored on your ability to speak clearly and coherently and to accurately convey information about what you read and heard.

In question four, you will hear part of a lecture. You will then be asked a question about what you heard. Your response will be scored on your ability to speak clearly and coherently and to accurately convey information about what you heard.

You may take notes while you read and listen to the conversation and lectures. You may use your notes to help prepare your response.

Listen carefully to the directions for each question. The directions will not be written on the screen.

For each question, you will be given a short time to prepare your response. A clock will show how much preparation time is remaining. When the preparation time is up, you will be told to begin your response. A clock will show how much response time is remaining. A message will appear on the screen when the response time has ended.

정답 및 해석 | P. 147

문제 듣기 S_AT2_01

예시 답변 S_AT2_02

TOEFL Speaking

Question 1 of 4

When traveling, many people like to keep a record of their voyage. Others prefer to engage in activities rather than using their time to document the trip. Which do you prefer and why?

PREPARATION TIME
00 : 00 : 15

RESPONSE TIME
00 : 00 : 45

문제 듣기 S_AT2_03

예시 답변 S_AT2_04

TOEFL Speaking

Question 2 of 4

Reading Time: 45 seconds

Greetings students,

As I informed you earlier, I will go to a conference next week, so I will be unable to teach your class. Instead, two of my colleagues have agreed to be guest instructors in my absence. Both are biology professors and active field researchers that spent last summer observing wildlife in two very different climates. You will be able to learn new information from their actual experiences, which should be a nice change of pace from your normal course material. I hope that you enjoy their visits and that you take advantage of this rare opportunity to ask questions of active field researchers.

Sincerely,

Professor Lee

TOEFL Speaking

Question 2 of 4

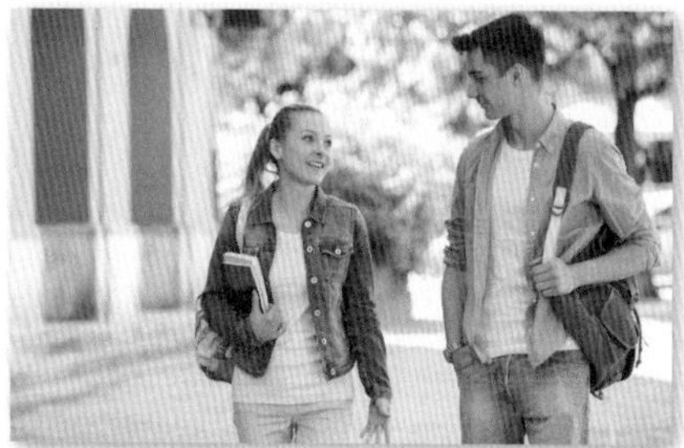

TOEFL Speaking

Question 2 of 4

The woman expresses her opinion about the change in one of her school classes. State her opinion and explain the reasons she gives for that opinion.

PREPARATION TIME
00 : 00 : 30

RESPONSE TIME
00 : 00 : 60

TOEFL Speaking

Question 3 of 4

Reading Time: 50 seconds

Convergent Evolution

Organisms evolve in response to pressures from their environment, and this often results in unique characteristics. However, some adaptations are so useful that unrelated species in different parts of the world develop them in a process called convergent evolution. A prime example of this is flight, an ability which birds, insects, and mammals all have. These animals are unrelated, and they did not learn to fly from one another. They have developed similar body parts that serve the same purpose. The wings of birds, insects, and bats look radically different, but they have evolved to have the same function.

TOEFL Speaking

Question 3 of 4

TOEFL Speaking

Question 3 of 4

The professor explains convergent evolution by giving examples of aardvarks and echidnas. Explain how they demonstrate the topic in the reading passage.

PREPARATION TIME
00 : 00 : 30

RESPONSE TIME
00 : 00 : 60

문제 듣기 S_AT2_07
예시 답변 S_AT2_08

TOEFL Speaking

Question 4 of 4

TOEFL Speaking

Question 4 of 4

In the lecture, the professor describes a number of factors that make TV commercials a powerful medium. Explain what makes TV commercials a powerful medium by using the examples from the lecture.

PREPARATION TIME
00 : 00 : 20

RESPONSE TIME
00 : 00 : 60

PAGODA TOEFL 80+ R/L/S/W

Writing

I. Integrated Task

Lesson 01 노트테이킹

Lesson 02 요약하기

Lesson 03 정리하기

Lesson 04 노트 & 답변 연결하기

II. Academic Discussion Task

Lesson 01 스트레스 관련 주제

Lesson 02 분위기 관련 주제

Lesson 03 사람들과의 관계 관련 주제

Lesson 04 관점의 확장 관련 주제

Lesson 05 조언 관련 주제

Lesson 06 편리함 관련 주제

Lesson 07 시간 활용 관련 주제

III. Actual Tests

Actual Test 1

Actual Test 2

iBT TOEFL® Writing 개요

1. Writing 영역의 특징

Writing 영역의 특징으로는 먼저 2개의 문제가 출제된다는 점을 들 수 있고, 단순히 주어진 주제에 대해 글을 쓰는 아주 기본적인 글쓰기에서 끝나는 것이 아니라, 실제 학업 상황에서 빈번하게 경험하게 되는 읽기, 듣기, 그리고 쓰기가 접목된 통합형 과제(Integrated Task)가 등장한다는 점을 그 특징으로 들 수 있다.

Writing 영역의 주요한 특징은 다음의 4가지로 정리할 수 있다.

1) Writing 영역은 2개의 문제로 구성된다.

첫 번째인 통합형(Integrated Task)은 주어진 지문(Reading Passage)을 3분간 읽고, 약 2~3분 가량의 강의자(Lecturer; Speaker)의 강의(Lecture)를 듣고 난 후, 강의자가 지문에 대해 어떤 주장을 하는지 150~225자의 단어(Words)로 20분 동안 요약(Summary)하여 글쓰기를 하는 문제다.

두 번째 문제는 2023년 7월부터 TOEFL 시험이 개정되면서 추가된 새로운 수업 토론형 과제(Writing for an Academic Discussion Task)다. 기존 독립형 과제(Independent Task)를 대체한 이 새로운 유형의 과제에서 온라인 교실 토론이 등장하는데, 다른 두 학생의 의견을 제시한 후 응시자 자신의 의견을 요구한다. 10분 동안 100자 이상의 단어로 온라인 포럼에서 댓글을 작성하듯이 자신의 의견을 표현하는 문제다.

2) 노트 필기(Note-taking)가 가능하다.

읽고, 듣고, 쓰는 문제에서 노트 필기는 매우 핵심적인 기술이다. 따라서 미리 노트 필기의 기술을 배우고 반복 연습해 두어야 한다.

3) Typing만 가능하다.

수험자가 답안을 작성할 때 컴퓨터를 통한 Typing만 가능하도록 제한되어 있다. (Handwriting 불가) 미리 충분한 속도의 영타가 가능하도록 연습해야 한다. 단, Brainstorming이나 Outline은 종이에 작성할 수 있다.

4) 각 문제에 대한 평가 기준이 다르다.

Writing 영역의 핵심적인 특징 중 하나는 두 문제가 각각 다른 평가 기준(Scoring Rubric)을 가지고 있다는 점인데 고득점을 위해서는 이 평가 기준을 반드시 유념해서 답안을 작성해야 한다.

간단히 말해서 통합형 과제의 평가 기준은 내용적인 측면에 더 많은 강조를 두지만, 수업 토론형 과제의 경우 내용적인 측면과 함께 토론에 대한 연관성과 기여도에 신경을 써야 한다는 것이다.

2. Writing 영역의 문제 유형

ETS가 제시하고 있는 Writing 영역의 문제 유형은 구체적으로 다음과 같다.

1) 통합형 과제(Integrated Task)

읽기와 듣기를 기반으로 요약의 글을 완성하는 유형의 문제로서 작문 능력뿐 아니라 독해력과 청취력도 요구된다.

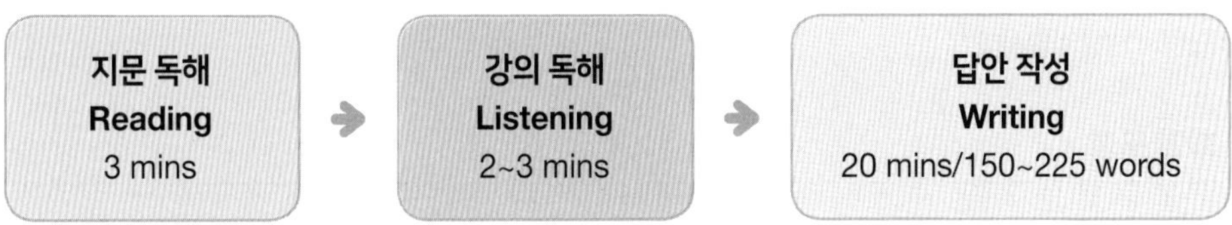

2) 수업 토론형 과제(Writing for an Academic Discussion Task)

주어진 토론 주제에 대해 두 명의 다른 학생의 의견을 읽은 후, 논리적으로 자신의 의견과 이유, 그리고 구체적인 근거를 들어 토론에 기여하는 답안을 작성하는 문제 유형이다. 따라서, 단순히 자신의 생각을 작성하는 능력뿐 아니라 다른 학생들의 의견을 파악하고 토론 주제와 관련성 있는 답변을 구사하는 능력이 요구된다.

I. Integrated Task

Introduction

Integrated Task, 즉 통합형 문제는 지문을 읽은 뒤에 그 지문과 관련된 강의를 듣고 둘의 내용을 통합하는 답변을 요구하는 문제다. 보통 강의와 비슷한 학술적인 내용이 많이 출제되며, 일상생활과 관련된 내용의 비중은 높지 않다. 읽기 지문은 보통 주제에 관한 세 가지 요점을 제시하며, 강의 내용은 앞선 세 가지 요점에 반박하거나 다른 시각을 제시한다. 따라서 읽기 내용의 요점과 듣기 내용의 요점을 잘 파악하고 서로 어떻게 연결되어 있는지 이해해야 답변하기가 수월하다.

화면 구성

TOEFL CONTINUE

Writing based on Reading and Listening Directions

For this task, you will first have three minutes to read a passage about an academic topic. You may take notes on the passage if you wish. The passage will then be removed and you will listen to a lecture about the same topic. While you listen, you may also take notes.

Then you will have 20 minutes to write a response to a question that asks you about the relationship between the lecture you heard and the reading passage. Try to answer the question as completely as possible using information from the reading passage and the lecture. The question does not ask you to express your personal opinion. You will be able to see the reading passage again when it is time for you to write. You may use your notes to help you answer the question.

Typically, an effective response will be 150 to 225 words long. Your response will be judged on the quality of your writing and on the completeness and accuracy of the content. If you finish your response before time is up, you may click on Next to go on to the second writing task.

Now you will see the reading passage for three minutes. Remember it will be available to you again when it is time for you to write. The lecture will begin, so keep your headset on until the lecture is over.

• 안내: 통합형 문제에 관한 설명이 제시된다.

TOEFL Writing VOLUME HELP ? NEXT
Question 1 of 2

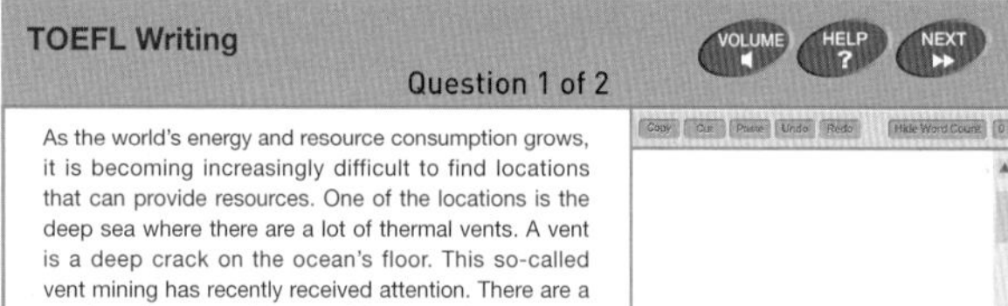

As the world's energy and resource consumption grows, it is becoming increasingly difficult to find locations that can provide resources. One of the locations is the deep sea where there are a lot of thermal vents. A vent is a deep crack on the ocean's floor. This so-called vent mining has recently received attention. There are a number of reasons why vent mining is good.

First, the deep sea has rich metals and minerals. Materials such as gold and iron can be found in enormous supply along these thermal vents. These areas are readily available to humans for harvesting and may even provide larger supplies of metal than land based mines.

• 읽기: 약 250~300단어의 지문이 제시되며 3분의 시간이 주어진다.

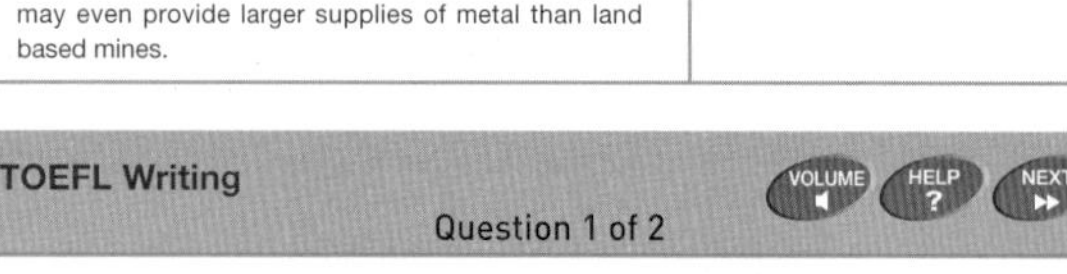

• 듣기: 약 250~300단어의 듣기 강의가 약 2분간 주어진다.

TOEFL Writing Question 1 of 2 VOLUME HELP ? NEXT

Directions : You have 20 minutes to plan and write your response. Your response will be judged on the basis of the quality of your writing and on how well your response presents the points in the lecture and their relationship to the reading passage. Typically, an effective response will be 150 to 225 words.

Questions : Summarize the points made in the lecture you just heard, explaining how they cast doubt on the points made in the reading.

As the world's energy and resource consumption grows, it is becoming increasingly difficult to find locations that can provide resources. One of the locations is the deep sea where there are a lot of thermal vents. A vent is a deep crack on the ocean's floor. This so-called vent mining has recently received attention. There are a number of reasons why vent

Copy Cut Paste Undo Redo Hide Word Count 0

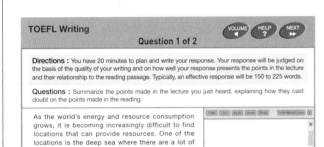

• 쓰기: 화면과 음성으로 질문이 제시된다. 왼쪽 창에는 읽기 지문을 다시 보여주며, 오른쪽 창에 답안을 작성해야 한다. 듣기 강의는 다시 들을 수 없으며, 글쓰기 제한 시간은 20분이다.

Sample Questions 

Summarize the points made in the lecture. Be sure to explain how they oppose the specific points made in the reading passage.

강의에서 제시한 요점을 요약하시오. 읽기 지문의 요점에 대해 강의에서 어떻게 반박하는지 설명하시오.

Learning Strategies

Step 1 읽기 지문이 주어지면 각 문단의 중심 내용을 빠르게 파악하여 노트테이킹한다.

⋯› 읽기 지문은 답변을 작성할 때 다시 볼 수 있다.

Step 2 강의에서는 요점에 관해 어떤 다른 시각을 취하는지 초점을 두고 노트테이킹한다.

⋯› 듣기 강의는 한 번만 들려준다는 점에 유의하고 최대한 많은 정보를 들을 수 있도록 한다.

Step 3 노트테이킹한 내용을 토대로 지문과 강의 내용의 관계를 파악한다.

⋯› 지문에서 제시한 요점에 대해 강의에서 반박하는 경우가 대부분이다.

Step 4 지문과 강의 내용을 연결하여 답변을 작성한다.

⋯› 노트테이킹한 내용을 토대로 지문과 강의 내용을 요약하여 완전한 문장으로 답변을 작성한다. 답변 작성을 완료하면 처음부터 끝까지 훑어보면서 누락된 내용이나 문법적 오류나 오타가 없는지 살펴보며 수정한다.

Lesson

01 노트테이킹

통합형 문제에서 제한된 시간 내에 빠르게 답안을 작성하기 위해서는 읽기 지문과 강의의 관계를 명확히 이해하고 작성한 답안을 여러 번 읽을 수 있는 시간을 벌어야 한다. 그러기 위해서는 차별화된 노트테이킹 기술이 필요하다. 노트테이킹할 때 유념해야 할 전략은 다음과 같다.

1. 간단히 필기한다.

지문이나 강의에서 나오는 내용을 전부 적기도 어려울뿐더러 그럴 필요도 없다. 요점을 파악하고 그 요점을 간단히 빠르게 적는 것이 중요하다. 답변을 작성할 때 노트를 보면서 '이게 이런 내용이었지'하고 이해할 수 있을 정도로만 적으면 된다. 나만 알아볼 수 있으면 된다는 점을 명심하고 최대한 간단히 적자. 필요 없는 수식어는 모두 빼도 내용 이해에 전혀 지장을 주지 않는다. 참고로, 읽기 지문은 답안을 작성하는 20분동안 계속 읽으며 참고할 수 있다.

2. 핵심만 적는다.

답변에 별 도움이 되지 않는 곁가지 내용을 쓰다가 정작 핵심 내용을 놓치는 상황이 발생할 수도 있다. 무엇이 중요한지 파악하여 그 내용을 적는다. 문단의 내용을 요약할 수 있으면 더 좋다. 강의자가 말한 단어를 받아 적는 것이 아니라 강의를 정확히 이해하는 것이 통합형 문제의 핵심이다.

3. 약자와 기호를 사용한다.

익숙한 단어나 표현은 약자로 짧게 줄여 쓰거나 보기 쉽게 기호를 활용하는 것이 시간 절약에 큰 도움이 된다. 앞서 언급한 것처럼 나만 알아보면 되는 노트이므로, 나만의 약자와 기호를 써도 무방하다. 나중에 글을 쓸 때 참고하기 쉽게 한눈에 이해되고 보기 편하게 쓰는 것이 가장 좋다. 영어로 쓰기 편할 때는 영어로, 한글로 쓰기 편할 때는 한글로 쓰면서 노트테이킹하는 것도 빨리 필기할 수 있는 방법이다.

Ex 가격이 오르자 고객이 줄었다.
price ↑ → customer ↓

약자와 기호

약자	단어	약자	단어
bgt	budget	w/ & w/o	with & without
AD	advertisement	esp.	especially
HR	human resources	yr	year
HQ	headquarters	intro	introduction
hr	hour	info	information
min	minute	prof	professor
pls	please	stud	student
ex 또는 e.g.	for example	ppl	people
i.e.	in other words, that is	vs.	in contrast to
etc.	et cetera, and so on	cf.	compare
24/ 7	24 hours a day, seven days a week	est.	established
ASAP	as soon as possible	no.	number
asst.	assistant	Ave.	avenue
bldg.	building	dist.	district
corp.	corporation	ft.	foot, feet
dept.	department	gov.	government, governor
mgmt	management	Inst.	institution
approx.	approximately	pop.	population
appt.	appointment	univ.	university

기호	단어	기호	단어
%	percent	≠	not, different
↑	increase	→	cause, produce, lead to
↓	decrease	←	because of, come from
&	and	〈	smaller, less
–	or	〉	larger, bigger, more
@	at	~	approximately, about
+	moreover, in addition	↔	opposite to
=	is, equal to, refer to	#	number

1. 읽고 노트테이킹

읽기 지문은 스스로 읽는 속도를 조절할 수 있고 답변을 작성하는 공간이 지문 바로 옆에 제공되기 때문에 굳이 노트테이킹이 필요하지는 않다. 답변 작성에 필요한 중요 부분만 몇 단어씩 짧게 적어두면 충분하다. 읽기 지문에서 보통 주제에 관한 세 가지 요점을 제시하므로, 순서대로 번호와 함께 적어두면 보기 편하다.

Example

The deep sea vents are a rich source of metals and minerals that are increasingly difficult to find on land. And materials such as gold and iron can be found in enormous supply along these thermal vents. These areas are readily available to humans for harvesting and may even provide larger supplies of metal than land based mines. In addition, extraction of the minerals from the sea floor sediment would also be much easier than removing them from ore.

노트

주제 deep sea vents = source of metals & minerals → extract

1. ↑ supply than land based mines
2. mineral extraction = easier

위 문단의 주제는 'deep sea vents 근처에서 광물을 추출해야 한다'이다. 따라서 이 문장을 가장 상위 분류로 정리한 뒤에 다음에 따라오는 세부 내용을 차례로 정리한다.

1) 육지에 있는 광맥보다 더 많은 광물을 공급한다는 것
2) 광물 추출이 더 쉽다는 것

이 사실들을 차례로 정리해두면 정보를 한눈에 파악하기 쉽다.

해석 심해 분출구는 육지에서는 점점 더 찾기 힘들어지는 금속과 광물의 풍부한 원천이다. 그리고 금과 철 같은 물질의 엄청난 양이 이 열수 분출구를 따라 발견될 수 있다. 이런 지역은 인간이 채광하기 쉬우며, 육지에 있는 광맥보다 더 많은 금속을 공급할 수도 있다. 또한, 해저 퇴적물에서 광물을 추출하는 것은 광석에서 광물을 분리하는 것보다 훨씬 쉬울 것이다.

Practice

정답 및 해석 | P. 153

>> 다음 지문을 읽고 노트를 완성하시오.

Q1 Many large companies have cafeterias where their employees can eat their lunches. This has many benefits. Employees do not have to use their break to travel to and from restaurants. Thus, they have more time to relax and enjoy their meals. Additionally, they can talk to their coworkers about non-work topics and form closer relationships.

노트

주제 company cafeteria's benefits

1. X waste time finding restaurants → ______________________
2. talk to coworkers → ______________________

Q2 The governments of many countries invest millions of dollars in space exploration every year. However, many editorials have been published that say this is a complete waste of money. Most people do not see any profit gained from space exploration, but they pay for it with their taxes. Not only that, but searching the galaxy for planets that are Earth-like but unreachable is a pointless exercise.

노트

주제 invest $ on space exp. = waste of $

1. no profit gained → ______________________
2. Earth-like planets → ______________________

Q3

Many people choose to take package tours when they go on vacation, but that is not recommended. People on package tours spend most of their time crammed into tour buses, so they cannot enjoy the scenery. Moreover, when they arrive at a tourist attraction, they are hurried through the experience so they cannot really enjoy any aspect of their trip.

노트

주제 package tour → X recommend

1. ______________________ → can't enjoy scenery
2. ______________________ → have to hurry

Q4

Cities that host professional sports teams can receive two major benefits. First, the team's stadium creates hundreds of new jobs, and the ticket sales, refreshments, and team merchandise all bring in revenue to the city. Second, the team brings attention to the city, which can make it more prominent on the national level and attract sports fans and other tourists to the city.

노트

주제 cities hosting pro. sports teams → profit

1. stadium → ______________ → ______________
2. attention to city → ______________________

Q5 Many cultures practice arranged marriage in the past, but that tradition has faded from much of the world. However, some studies indicate that they were more successful than love marriages. For example, the rate of divorce has only increased as arranged marriage has been abandoned. This is because the family is less involved. Moreover, love marriages are often based on passion instead of compatibility, which means that they are destined to fail while arranged marriages are more likely to last.

노트

주제 arranged marriage = better than love m.?

1. ______________________________

2. love m. = passion/arr. m. = compatibility

Lesson 01 Integrated Task

Q6 Although fast food restaurants serve convenient, inexpensive, and tasty meals and snacks, people should not visit these establishments. Fast food poses many health risks. The menu items can cause many health problems due to their high salt and sugar content. Not only that, but they can make people overweight if they eat them too often. They contain a lot of fat and empty calories, which quickly become fat deposits in the body.

노트

주제 don't buy fast food = many health risks

1. ↑ salt & sugar content

2. ______________________________

2. 듣고 노트테이킹

강의는 읽기 지문과 달리 딱 한 번만 들을 수 있기 때문에 노트테이킹이 필수이고 중요성 역시 더 크다. 읽기 지문에서 제시된 요점의 개수만큼(보통 3개) 강의에서도 같은 개수의 요점이 나온다. 정확히 말하면, 읽기 지문에서 제시된 요점들에 관해 강의에서 차례로 반박하거나 다른 의견을 제시한다. 따라서 읽기 지문에서 했던 노트테이킹과 같은 번호를 매칭하며 강의 요점을 적어 두면 나중에 답변을 정리하기가 더 쉽다. 다만 적는 데 집중하다가 뒤에 나오는 내용을 놓치지 않도록 주의해야 한다. 빠르고 간단한 노트테이킹이 가장 중요하다.

Example

I01_EX

Now, first of all, about there being a lot of metal resources near these thermal vents, yes, this is true. But, we don't have any technology that could mine these metals. I mean, first, you need a way to sort the metals from the ocean sediment. This is not possible at the moment; the technology still needs to be developed. And, even if you could sort the metals from the sediment, you would need a way to transport the metals to the surface of the ocean. These technologies just don't exist right now.

노트

주제 It is true that there are lots of metals near thermal vents, but tech X.

1. sort metals from ocean sediment = possible X
2. can't transport metals to ocean surface

위 문단의 주제는 'thermal vents 근처에 metal resources가 많은 것은 사실이나 우리는 이런 금속을 채굴할 수 있는 기술을 갖고 있지 않다'이다. 따라서 이 문장을 가장 상위 분류로 정리한 뒤에 이어서 나오는 세부 내용을 차례로 정리한다.

1) 바다 침전물에서 금속을 분류하는 것은 현재 불가능하다는 것
2) 해수 표면으로 금속을 운반할 기술은 존재하지 않는다는 것

이 사실들을 차례로 정리해두면 정보를 한눈에 파악하기 쉽다.

해석 자, 우선, 이런 열수 분출구 근처에 많은 금속 자원이 있다는 점, 네, 이건 사실입니다. 하지만 우리는 이런 금속을 채굴할 수 있는 기술을 갖고 있지 않아요. 내 말은, 우선 바다 퇴적물에서 금속을 분류할 방법이 필요합니다. 이것은 지금으로서는 불가능해요. 기술을 개발해야 합니다. 그리고 퇴적물에서 금속을 분류할 수 있다 해도, 해수면으로 그 금속을 운반할 방법이 필요할 겁니다. 이런 기술은 현재는 존재하지 않습니다.

Practice

정답 및 해석 | P. 155

>> 다음 강의를 듣고 노트를 완성하시오.

Q1 Listen to the lecture. I01_P01

노트

주제 hiking = beneficial

1. low-impact exercise & fresh air
2. ______________________________

Q2 Listen to the lecture. I01_P02

노트

주제 universal min. wage = bad idea

1. ______________________________
2. take $ from other import. gov't programs

Q3

Listen to the lecture. 🎧 I01_P03

노트

주제 essay @ home = final exam → bad idea

1. do all research on one day – X study
2. ______________________________

Q4

Listen to the lecture. 🎧 I01_P04

노트

주제 doctor resi. program → restructure

1. long shift → ______________________
2. ______________ → ______________________

Q5

Listen to the lecture. I01_P05

노트

주제 world = overpopulated? No

1. ______________________________

2. ______________________________

Q6

Listen to the lecture. I01_P06

노트

주제 ride sharing service = not good

1. backgr. check X sufficient = ______________

2. ______________________________

Lesson
02 요약하기

통합형 문제에서는 읽기 지문의 내용과 강의의 내용을 요약해야 하므로 요약하는 연습이 필수적이다. 앞서 학습한 노트테이킹을 토대로 살을 붙여서 요약문을 작성하는데, 이때 기억해야 할 점은 다음과 같다.

1. 중심 내용 파악하기

앞에서 정리했던 노트테이킹을 보며 지문과 강의의 핵심 내용, 즉 주장하는 내용이 무엇인지를 파악한다. 지문에서는 주제가 제시된 뒤에 그 주제를 뒷받침하는 세부 요점 3개가 나오고, 강의에서는 교수가 '지문의 내용에 동의하지 않는다/내 생각은 다르다'라고 하면서 지문에서 나온 세부 요점 3개에 반박하거나 다른 관점을 제시한다.

Ex 지문의 주장: A는 B이다.
1. A가 B인 첫 번째 이유는 다음과 같다.
2. A가 B인 두 번째 이유는 다음과 같다.
3. A가 B인 세 번째 이유는 다음과 같다.

강의의 주장: A는 B가 아니다./A가 B라는 주장에는 오류가 있다.
1. A가 B가 아닌 첫 번째 이유는 다음과 같다.
2. A가 B가 아닌 두 번째 이유는 다음과 같다.
3. A가 B가 아닌 세 번째 이유는 다음과 같다.

2. 노트테이킹한 내용을 완전한 문장으로 만들기

앞서 적어두었던 노트 필기 내용을 바탕으로 이제 완전한 문장을 만들어본다. 원래 내용과 똑같이 쓰려고 하지 않아도 되고, 내가 아는 단어와 표현을 활용해 풀어서 쓰면 된다. 이를 paraphrasing(다른 말로 바꾸어 표현하기)이라고 하며, 이는 토플의 모든 영역에서 아주 중요한 요소이다. paraphrasing을 할 때는 특정 단어를 같은 뜻을 가진 다른 단어로 바꾸어 쓰거나 주어와 목적어의 자리를 바꾸는 등 다양한 방법으로 새로운 문장을 구성해볼 수 있다.

paraphrasing에 유용한 단어와 표현을 정리해보자.

부정적인, 해로운		긍정적인, 유익한	
worse	~보다 더 나쁜, 안 좋은	better	~보다 더 좋은, 나은
negative	부정적인	positive	긍정적인
harmful	해로운, 유해한	beneficial	유익한, 이로운
detrimental	해로운	effective	효과적인, 실질적인

찬성하다, 동의하다		반대하다, 맞서다	
accept	받아들이다, 수락하다	oppose	반대하다, 겨루다
agree	동의하다	defy	저항하다, 반항하다
comply	동의하다, 응하다	disagree	동의하지 않다, 반대하다
support	지지하다	dispute	반박하다, 이의를 제기하다
approve	찬성하다, 승인하다	disapprove	반대하다, 불만을 나타내다
설명하다		믿다, ~라고 여기다	
explain	설명하다	think	생각하다, 믿다
describe	서술하다, 묘사하다	assume	추정하다, 상정하다
define	정의하다	consider	고려하다, 여기다
illustrate	설명하다, 예증하다	feel	(생각, 느낌이) 들다
clarify	명확히 하다, 분명히 말하다	believe	믿다
주장하다		~하게 하다, 허락하다	
argue	주장하다, 논증하다	let	~하게 하다, 허락하다
assert	주장하다, 확고히 하다	allow	~하게 하다, 허락하다
claim	주장하다, 요구하다	enable	~가 가능하게 하다
contend	주장하다, 겨루다	make it possible to V	~하는 것을 가능하게 하다
야기하다, 기여하다		필요로 하다, 요구하다	
cause	초래하다, 야기하다	need	필요로 하다
contribute	기여하다, ~의 원인이 되다	demand	요구하다
responsible for	~의 원인이 되다	ask	요구하다, 요청하다
generate	발생시키다, 만들어내다	require	필요로 하다, 요구하다
produce	만들어내다, 초래하다	feel necessity for	필요를 느끼다

알아두면 좋은 명사

장점	advantage, benefit, merit, strength	연결	link, connection, association, tie
단점	disadvantage, drawback, weakness, shortcoming	상황	circumstances, surroundings, environment, situation
문제	problem, issue, difficulty, trouble	책무	responsibility, duty, obligation, liability
대안	substitute, alternative, replacement, another option	실수	mistake, error, fault, blunder
이유/근거	reason, grounds, rationale, cause	비용	expense, cost, expenditure, spending

1. 읽고 요약하기

지문을 요약하기 위해서는 핵심 내용을 파악하는 연습을 해야 한다. 긴 문장이나 한 문단을 읽고 핵심이 무엇인지 간단히 정리해보는 연습은 큰 도움이 된다. 이는 질문에 맞는 답변을 하는 데 도움을 주기도 한다. 앞서 학습한 노트테이킹 연습에서 정리했던 주제로 요약하는 연습을 해보자. paraphrasing 기술을 활용하는 것이 좋다.

Example

The deep sea vents are a rich source of metals and minerals that are increasingly difficult to find on land. Materials such as gold and iron can be found in enormous supply along these thermal vents. These areas are readily available to humans for harvesting and may even provide larger supplies of metal than land based mines. Extraction of the minerals from the sea floor sediment would also be much easier than removing them from ore.

노트

주제 deep sea vents = source of metals & minerals → extract

1. ↑ supply than land based mines
2. mineral extraction = easier

Q. According to the passage, what are the advantages of deep sea vent mining?

지문에 의하면, 심해 분출구 채광의 이점은 무엇인가?

위에 적어둔 노트를 보고 완전한 문장으로 바꿔보자.

주제 Deep sea vents are a good source of metals and minerals. Therefore, extracting the minerals from the area would be very beneficial for the following reasons.

1. They can also provide larger supplies than land based mines do.
2. In addition, mineral extraction can be much easier.

해석 심해 분출구는 육지에서는 점점 더 찾기 힘들어지는 금속과 광물의 풍부한 원천이다. 금과 철 같은 물질의 엄청난 양이 이 열수 분출구를 따라 발견될 수 있다. 이런 지역은 인간이 채광하기 쉬우며, 육지에 있는 광맥보다 더 많은 금속을 공급할 수도 있다. 또한, 해저 퇴적물에서 광물을 추출하는 것은 광석에서 광물을 제거하는 것보다 훨씬 쉬울 것이다.

Practice

정답 및 해석 | P. 157

>> 제시된 주제를 참고로 노트를 완성하고, 주어진 질문에 대한 답변을 완성하시오.

Q1 Many people like to drink soft drinks with their meals instead of water. Unfortunately, this is bad for your health in a number of ways. For example, soft drinks contain a lot of sugar and they are very acidic, which means that they can damage your teeth. On top of that, they offer nothing good to your body. They contain very few nutrients so the calories they provide are basically empty. Unneeded calories often lead to weight gain.

노트

주제 soft drinks → bad for health

1. ______________________________

2. ______________________________

Q. According to the passage, why is drinking soft drinks not recommended?

Q2 Avocados are unique fruit that provides many health benefits. One, it is very nutritious and contains important vitamins like B, C, E, and potassium. In addition, avocados are also a rich source of monounsaturated fat, which is very good for the heart and arterial health.

노트

주제 avocado – benefits

1. ______________________________

2. ______________________________

Q. According to the passage, how are avocados beneficial?

Q3

It is a widely held belief that children who begin studying foreign languages early in their life generally reach and maintain a higher level of fluency. Research has proven this idea to be correct for a few reasons. Children appear to have a preexisting mental ability to understand and use grammar easily. Second, they constantly mimic the speech of others, which allows them to adopt new words freely.

노트

주제 study foreign language early – high level

1. ____________________

2. ____________________

Q. According to the passage, why does starting to learn languages early in life allow people to become more fluent?

Q4

Sleep is very beneficial for people's health. First of all, it provides the body with down time to relax and repair itself. That is why sleep is an important part of recovering from an illness. On top of that, it also gives the brain time to process new information and create new mental pathways. This is what happens during dreaming.

노트

주제 benefits of sleeping

1. ____________________

2. ____________________

Q. According to the passage, what are the benefits of sleeping?

Q5 Most school districts rely upon standardized tests to determine what level of academic achievement students have reached. Unfortunately, these tests are flawed for a number of reasons. One is that such tests only measure a small part of cognitive abilities. Another is that some people cannot perform well when tested in this way. Therefore, standardized tests are not a viable way to assess achievement.

노트

주제 standardized test = flawed

1. ______________________

2. ______________________

Q. According to the passage, why are standardized tests flawed?

Q6 Although many students and parents question whether playing team sports at school is necessary, it actually has many benefits for children. Obviously, playing sports provides students with regular exercise, which is important for their health. Team sports also require them to work together toward a common goal. This is a skill that will be very valuable to them throughout their lives.

노트

주제 team sports = beneficial

1. ______________________

2. ______________________

Q. According to the passage, why should students be required to play team sports at school?

2. 듣고 요약하기

읽기 지문과 마찬가지로 강의 내용을 정리한 노트를 보며 완전한 문장으로 만드는 연습을 한다. 읽기 지문에 반박하거나 다른 의견을 제시하는 요점을 잘 파악하여 요약하는 것이 핵심이다. 여기에서도 paraphrasing이 유용하게 쓰인다.

Example

Now, first of all, about there being a lot of metal resources near these thermal vents, yes, this is true. But, we don't have any technology that could mine these metals. I mean, first, you need a way to sort the metals from the ocean sediment. This is not possible at the moment; the technology still needs to be developed. And, even if you could sort the metals from the sediment, you would need a way to transport the metals to the surface of the ocean. These technologies just don't exist right now.

노트

주제 It is true that there are lots of metals near thermal vents, but X tech.

1. sort metals from ocean sediment = X possible
2. can't transport metals to ocean surface

Q. Why does the lecture say deep sea vent mining is not a good idea?

강의는 왜 심해 분출구 채굴이 좋은 생각이 아니라고 하는가?

위에 적어둔 노트를 보고 완전한 문장으로 바꿔보자.

주제 It is true that there are lots of metals near thermal vents, but we simply don't have any technology for this kind of mining.

1. Right now, it is impossible to sort the metals from the ocean sediment.
2. In addition, we don't have any technology for transporting these metals to ocean surface.

해석 자, 우선, 이런 열수 분출구 근처에 많은 금속 자원이 있다는 점, 네, 이건 사실입니다. 하지만 우리는 이런 금속을 채굴할 수 있는 기술을 갖고 있지 않아요. 내 말은, 우선 바다 퇴적물에서 금속을 분류할 방법이 필요합니다. 이것은 지금으로서는 불가능해요. 기술을 개발해야 합니다. 그리고 퇴적물에서 금속을 분류할 수 있다 해도, 해수면으로 그 금속을 운반할 방법이 필요할 겁니다. 이런 기술은 현재는 존재하지 않습니다.

Practice

정답 및 해석 | P. 160

>> 제시된 주제를 참고로 노트를 완성하고, 주어진 질문에 대한 답변을 완성하시오.

Q1 Listen to the lecture. I02_P01

노트

주제 pet ownership = bad for pets

1. ____________________

2. ____________________

Q. According to the passage, why is pet ownership bad for the pets themselves?

Q2 Listen to the lecture. I02_P02

노트

주제 cold weather & catching cold

1. ____________________

2. ____________________

Q. According to the passage, how does cold weather indirectly make people sick?

Q3

Listen to the lecture. I02_P03

주제 Internet's benefits

1. ______________________________

2. ______________________________

Q. According to the passage, what are the benefits of the Internet?

Q4

Listen to the lecture. I02_P04

주제 single-sex schools – drawbacks

1. ______________________________

2. ______________________________

Q. According to the passage, what are the drawbacks of single-sex schools?

Q5

Listen to the lecture. 🎧 I02_P05

노트

주제 lottery – not good

1. ______________________________

2. ______________________________

Q. According to the passage, what are the negative aspects of winning a lottery?

Q6

Listen to the lecture. 🎧 I02_P06

노트

주제 uniform @ work = X good idea

1. ______________________________

2. ______________________________

Q. According to the passage, why is wearing a uniform at work a bad idea?

Lesson

03 정리하기

답변을 작성할 때는 지문과 강의의 요점이 각각 어떻게 연결되어있는지 생각하며 해야 한다.

읽기(지문)		듣기(강의)
주제	⬌	주제 반박
요점 1	⬌	요점 1 반박
요점 2	⬌	요점 2 반박
요점 3	⬌	요점 3 반박

위의 표에 제시된 것처럼 읽기(지문)와 듣기(강의)는 내용이 서로 밀접하게 연결되어있다는 점을 기억하자. 하나의 주제에 대해 읽기에서 먼저 어떤 의견을 제시하면 듣기에서 그 의견에 반박한다. 따라서 지문을 읽으면서 뒤에 나올 강의가 대강 어떤 내용일지 유추가 가능하다. 강의는 결국 지문 내용과 반대이기 때문이다. 다음의 예시를 살펴보자.

공룡이 살던 시대의 거대한 새인 아르젠타비스 마그니피센스는 날지 못했을 것이다.

지문의 도입부에서 위와 같이 주장한다면, 강의의 도입부 주장은 무엇이 될까? 당연히 '이 새가 날 수 있었다/날았을 가능성이 있다'고 주장할 것이다.

이제 다음 문단으로 넘어가 요점 1이 등장한다.

거대한 새인 아르젠타비스 마그니피센스는 날개가 그 몸집에 비례해 엄청나게 길었지만 다리는 생각보다 매우 짧아 날개를 퍼덕이며 날아오르려 하면 땅에 날개가 부딪쳐 날지 못했다. 또한 다리는 짧을 뿐만 아니라 약하고 가늘어서 공중에 뛰어올라 날개를 움직이는 것도 어려웠다.

그렇다면 강의의 요점 1은 무엇일까? 이 내용에 반박하는 내용, 즉 '날개는 그만큼 길지 않았다/다리가 그만큼 짧고 약하지 않았다'는 내용일 수도 있고, 이 새가 이런 약점을 극복하기 위해 취했던 다른 방법이 있었을 거라고 제시할 수도 있다. 그 방법에는 경사진 땅에서 도움닫기를 하거나 날개를 펼친 뒤에 절벽에서 뛰어내리는 방법 등이 있을 수 있다.

요점 1이 마무리되고 다음 문단에서 요점 2가 제시된다.

새가 날기 위해 필요한 가슴 근육을 아르젠타비스 마그니피센스에게서는 잘 찾아볼 수 없다. 이 새의 가슴 근육은 너무 약해 보여서 무게를 지탱하기 어려워 보인다.

그렇다면 강의의 요점 2는 무엇일까? 가슴 근육이 약하지 않았다는 증거를 제시하거나, 약한 가슴 근육을 극복하고 날 만한 다른 방법이 있었을 거라고 설명할 것이다. 이 방법 중 하나는 상승하는 난기류를 타고 날개를 많이 움직일 필요 없이 몇 시간 동안 나는 것이다.

마지막으로 요점 3이 나온다.

아르젠타비스 마그니피센스는 너무 커서 포식자가 몇 없었으므로 날아서 도망칠 필요가 별로 없었고, 그러다가 나는 능력을 잃었을 것이다.

그렇다면 강의의 요점 3은 무엇일까? 이 새를 위협하는 포식자가 분명히 존재했다고 증거를 제시하거나, 새가 날아야 했던 다른 이유를 댈 수도 있다. 즉, 이 새가 사실 죽은 동물을 먹는 새였으며, 죽은 동물을 찾기 위해서는 공중에서 날며 넓은 지역을 둘러봐야 했으므로 비행의 필요성이 분명히 존재했다고 반박할 수 있다.

위의 예시처럼 지문과 강의의 긴밀한 관계를 염두에 두면 내용을 더 쉽게 이해할 수 있을 뿐 아니라 강의에서 어떤 내용이 제시될지도 유추할 수 있고, 더욱 정확한 답변을 할 수 있다.

1. 읽고 정리하기

Example - Reading

As the world's energy and resource consumption grows, it is becoming increasingly difficult to find locations that can provide resources. One source that holds great reserves of minerals is deep sea thermal vents. A vent is a deep crack on the ocean's floor where sea water is heated and filled with minerals. The concept of vent mining has recently received attention, but these are fragile ecosystems with many unique species. Still, there are a number of reasons why vent mining should be carried out.

First, the deep sea vents are a rich source of metals and minerals that are increasingly difficult to find on land. Materials such as gold and iron can be found in enormous supply along these thermal vents. These areas are readily available to humans for harvesting and may even provide larger supplies of metal than land based mines. Extraction of the minerals from the sea floor sediment would also be much easier than removing them from ore.

Secondly, although thermal vents are home to a number of very unique animals that cannot exist elsewhere, we would not have to put those organisms in danger. Much of the minerals from thermal vents can be found as much as two kilometers away from the vent itself. Mining at this distance would not damage these fragile habitats while still yielding the desired resources.

Finally, mineral extraction in the deep sea can be regulated by international law. Many critics say that miners would recklessly mine since it would be very difficult to oversee their operations. But there are many laws and agencies that can regulate mining near the vents. One of these agencies is the International Seabed Authority which was established by the Law of the Sea Convention. This agency ensures that companies follow the strict regulations for ocean mining and do not destroy the environment with their activities.

세계의 에너지와 자원 소비가 증가함에 따라 자원을 제공할 수 있는 장소를 찾는 것이 점점 더 어려워지고 있다. 엄청난 광물 매장량을 보유한 한 원천이 심해의 열수 분출구이다. 분출구는 해저에 있는 깊은 틈으로, 이곳에서는 해수가 데워지고 광물로 가득 차있다. 분출구 채광이라는 개념은 최근에 주목을 받아왔지만, 이곳은 많은 독특한 종들이 서식하는 연약한 생태계이다. 그럼에도 분출구 채광을 해야 하는 많은 이유가 있다.

첫째, 심해 분출구는 육지에서는 점점 더 찾기 힘들어지는 금속과 광물의 풍부한 원천이다. 금과 철 같은 물질의 엄청난 양이 이 열수 분출구를 따라 발견될 수 있다. 이런 지역은 인간이 채광하기 쉬우며, 육지에 있는 광맥보다 더 많은 금속을 공급할 수도 있다. 해저 퇴적물에서 광물을 추출하는 것은 역시 광석에서 광물을 제거하는 것보다 훨씬 쉬울 것이다.

둘째로, 열수 분출구가 다른 곳에서는 존재할 수 없는 아주 독특한 많은 동물들의 서식지라 해도, 이 생물들을 위험에 처하게 할 필요는 없다. 열수 분출구에서 나오는 많은 광물이 분출구에서 2km까지 떨어진 곳에서 발견될 수 있다. 이런 거리에서 채굴하면 이 연약한 서식지에 손상을 입히지 않으면서 원하는 자원을 여전히 산출할 수 있을 것이다.

마지막으로, 심해에서 광물을 채굴하는 것은 국제법으로 규제할 수 있다. 비판하는 사람들 다수는 광부들의 활동을 감독하기가 아주 어렵기 때문에 이들이 무분별하게 채광할지 모른다고 말한다. 그러나 분출구 근처의 채광을 규제할 수 있는 많은 법과 단체가 있다. 이런 단체 중 하나가 국제 해양법 협약에 따라 설립한 국제 해저 기구이다. 이 단체는 기업들이 바다에서 채광할 때 반드시 엄격한 규정을 따르고 채광 활동으로 환경을 파괴하지 않도록 한다.

읽기 노트 예시

주제 deep sea vents mining = advantageous 심해 분출구 채광 = 이점

1. rich source of metals & minerals 금속 & 광물의 풍부한 원천
   - gold & iron available 금 & 철을 구할 수 있음
   - larger supply than land based mines 육지 기반 광산보다 더 많은 공급량
   - extraction much easier 추출이 훨씬 쉬움

2. X danger for animals 동물들에게 위험 X
   - mine far from vents 분출구에서 멀리 떨어져 채굴

3. regulate by int'l law 국제법으로 규제
   - oversee companies, strict regulations 회사들 감독, 엄격한 규제

읽기 지문을 요약할 때는 주제를 맨 위에 쓴 뒤에 주제를 뒷받침하는 내용들을 1, 2, 3의 소제목으로 나열한다. 이 소제목들 아래에 더 작은 세부 사항들을 정리해두면 보기 편하다.

Practice

정답 및 해석 | P. 163

>> 제시된 지문을 읽고 아래의 노트를 완성해보자.

Q1 As the saying goes, "Two heads are better than one." Completing a project as a team is better than doing it alone. Having a group of people divide work can help save time and effort, so many companies and schools focus more on group work. Teamwork brings several benefits.

First, one of the benefits that teamwork brings is that working as a team helps to carry out work more efficiently. A group of people has various abilities. If a team member in a group is skillful at statistics, the group will have expertise in dealing with data. The abilities that each member has help to complete a given task more efficiently.

Second, group work allows team members to come up with various creative ideas. Each team member can talk freely in the process of making a group decision. As various ideas are suggested, there is a high possibility that the group will have creative solutions to problems they have to tackle. For example, when writing an essay, an individual can face limitations in brainstorming for ideas. But a group of people can think of more various and creative ideas than a single individual.

Another benefit of having a group of people tackle a problem is that teamwork can make team members actively participate in the work. This is because team members will feel more responsible for what they do in the group, and they will work harder to achieve positive results. They know that the others are depending on them, so they have more reason to perform.

노트

주제 project: team > alone

1. work more efficiently
   -
2. more creative ideas
   -
3. members actively participate
   -

Q2 Many animals and plants have been imported intentionally or by accident to new areas. These new species transported to new environments often have negative effects. Let us take a look at these negative consequences.

First, a new species always upsets the local ecological balance. A new species is never just added to the native ecosystem. It always competes with some native ecosystems. The damage does not end with the displacement of native competitors as the new species is often unsuitable as food for species further up the food chain. The negative effects thus spread through the whole ecosystem.

Second, the introduction of new species often destroys the local environment. For example, the cane toad, native to South Africa, was introduced to Australia, where it has spread at an alarming speed and has had harmful effects on the local environment. The cane toad, a natural predator, has killed a large number of native species in Australia. In addition to this, its poison sometimes poses a direct threat to children and pets when touched.

Finally, the negative impact caused by the introduction of new species often leads to economic burdens. For example, mesquites, a shrub native to America, were introduced to Africa. After the introduction of mesquites, commonly planted for land restoration and as a source of wood, they started to displace native species in Africa. As a result, African governments are forced to commit economic and bureaucratic resources to control the replacement of native species by mesquites.

노트

주제 new species in new envi. → negative effect

1. upset local ecology's balance
   -
   -
2. destroy local envi.
   -
   -
3. economic burden
   -

Q3 In England before the Industrial Revolution of the late 18th century, manufactured goods such as cloth and thread were produced manually at homes and small workshops. This so-called "putting-out system" developed into the factory system. There are several reasons why the development of the factory system was first made possible in England.

First, the advent of new technologies resulted in the accelerated development of the factory system. The development of steam engines played an especially pivotal role in the spread of the factory system. The introduction of steam engines to factories made it possible to generate a considerable amount of energy that individual workers at home could not create.

Second, the development of the factory system in England was the result of the introduction of property rights. Stable and strict rules of law that protected private property encouraged property holders to develop their property and efficiently allocate resources based on the operation of the market. This, in turn, caused property owners to invest more in new factories.

Finally, this system helped factory owners reduce production costs, especially transportation costs. Before the advancement of the system, raw materials and equipment had been supplied for workers who worked at home. This would have cost business owners considerable amounts of money for transportation. In this case, naturally, they preferred the factory system in which they could reduce the cost of transporting raw materials and goods.

노트

주제 development of factory system in England

1. new technologies
   -
2. intro. of property rights
   -
   -
3. owners: reduce production costs, esp. trans. costs
   -

2. 듣고 정리하기

Example - Listening

 103_EX

We all know there is a definite need to meet the world's demand for mineral resources, and vent mining seems to be one of the best options for collecting these resources. However, I don't think that the reading accurately discusses vent mining. Let's look at the points in the reading, because honestly, they just don't make sense to me.

Now, first of all, about there being a lot of metal resources near these thermal vents, yes, this is true. But, we don't have any technology that could mine these metals. I mean, first, you need a way to sort the metals from the ocean sediment. This is not possible at the moment; the technology still needs to be developed. And, even if you could sort the metals from the sediment, you would need a way to transport the metals to the surface of the ocean. These technologies just don't exist right now.

The second point the author made that mining can be performed two kilometers away from the thermal vents, well, this certainly is not far away enough to guarantee the safety of the ecosystem there. I mean, sure, two kilometers may seem like a large distance, but mining uses some very toxic chemicals that would be very difficult to contain underwater. If the chemicals from the mining actually spread to the ecosystem, the effects might be simply disastrous to the organisms that make their homes at the vents.

Finally, the standards mentioned in the reading only apply to vents that are located within international waters. But, companies would most likely want to mine at vents closer to coastlines. Vents located near these coastlines are not within the jurisdiction of international law. That is, companies would mine in the territorial waters of the country to which the coast belongs. Many of these places have absolutely no form of regulation on vent mining activities, so regulating their activities would be impossible.

광물 자원에 대한 세계의 수요를 맞출 필요가 분명히 있다는 점은 우리 모두 알고 있고, 분출구 채광은 이런 자원을 모으는 데 가장 좋은 선택지 중 하나처럼 보입니다. 하지만 나는 지문이 열수 분출구 채광을 정확하게 논의하고 있다고 생각하지 않아요. 지문의 요점들을 살펴보도록 하죠. 솔직히 저는 이해가 되지 않으니까요.

자, 우선, 이런 열수 분출구 근처에 많은 금속 자원이 있다는 점, 네, 이건 사실입니다. 하지만 우리는 이런 금속을 채굴할 수 있는 기술을 갖고 있지 않아요. 내 말은, 우선 바다 퇴적물에서 금속을 분류할 방법이 필요합니다. 이것은 지금으로서는 불가능해요. 기술을 개발해야 합니다. 그리고 퇴적물에서 금속을 분류할 수 있다 해도, 해수면으로 그 금속을 운반할 방법이 필요할 겁니다. 이런 기술은 현재는 존재하지 않습니다.

채광이 열수 분출구에서 2km 떨어진 곳에서 이루어질 수 있다는 필자의 두 번째 요점은 글쎄요, 이건 분명 그곳 생태계의 안전을 보장하기에 충분히 먼 거리가 아닙니다. 내 말은, 2km가 먼 거리처럼 보일지 모르지만, 채광할 때 매우 유독한 화학 물질을 몇 가지 사용하는데, 이는 물속에서 통제하기가 아주 어려울 겁니다. 만약 채광에 쓰이는 화학 물질이 실제로 생태계에 퍼지면 그 영향은 분출구를 서식지로 삼는 생물들에게 그저 재앙일 수도 있습니다.

마지막으로, 지문에서 언급된 기준은 공해 내에 있는 열수 분출구에만 적용됩니다. 그러나 기업들은 해안선과 더 가까이 있는 분출구에서 채광하고 싶을 겁니다. 이런 해안선 근처에 위치한 분출구들은 국제법의 관할 구역 내에 있지 않아요. 즉, 기업들은 그 해안이 속한 나라의 영해 내에서 채광할 겁니다. 이런 장소들 중 다수는 열수 분출구 채광 행위에 관한 어떤 형태의 규정도 전혀 가지고 있지 않기에 그들의 활동을 규제하는 것은 불가능할 겁니다.

듣기 노트 예시

주제 deep sea vents mining = X advantageous 심해 분출구 채광 = 이점 없음

1. no technology 기술 없음
   - sorting metals 금속 분류
   - transporting them to ocean surface 그것들을 해수면으로 운송

2. X danger for animals? 동물들에게 위험하지 않다?
   - mine far from vents → not enough 분출구에서 먼 곳에서 채광 → 충분하지 않음
   - toxic chemicals can still harm marine species
     유독성 화학 물질이 여전히 해양 종들에게 해를 입힐 수 있음

3. regulate by int'l law? 국제법으로 규제?
   - only apply to int'l waters 공해에만 적용
   - companies mine near coastlines = X jurisdiction
     기업들이 해안선 근처에서 채광 = 관할 구역 없음

읽기 노트와 마찬가지로 강의를 요약할 때 역시 주제를 맨 위에 쓴 뒤에 주제를 뒷받침하는 내용들을 1, 2, 3의 소제목으로 나열한다. 이 소제목들 아래에 더 작은 세부 사항들을 정리해두면 보기 편하다.

Practice

>> 강의를 듣고 아래의 노트를 완성해보자.

Q1

Listen to the lecture. I03_P01

노트

주제 working as a team = not good

1. not efficient
   - ______________________
   - ______________________
2. creative ideas? no
   - ______________________
   - ______________________
3. ppl don't work harder in a group
   - ______________________

Q2

Listen to the lecture. I03_P02

노트

주제 new species in a new envi. cause problems? No

1. disturb ecology? Not really
   - ______________________
2. destroy the natives?
   - ______________________
   - ______________________
3. economic burden?
   - ______________________

Q3

Listen to the lecture. I03_P03

노트

주제 3 reasons for the rise of factory system in England → problems

1. many breakthroughs? no
   - ______________________
   - ______________________
2. property rights X contribute
   - ______________________
3. cost ↓ X
   - ______________________

Q4

Listen to the lecture. I03_P04

노트

주제 hydrogen fuel can replace fossil f. soon? No

1. ______________________
   - the kind of H. used for H. fuel engines is artificial & complicated to make
2. ______________________
   - byproduct = water, true
   - but the process of making that H. requires fossil f. too → pollution
3. ______________________
   - H. fuel engine = platinum = rare & expensive

Lesson

04 노트 & 답변 연결하기

지문(읽기)과 강의(듣기)를 노트테이킹한 내용을 토대로 답변을 작성하는 과정을 살펴보자.

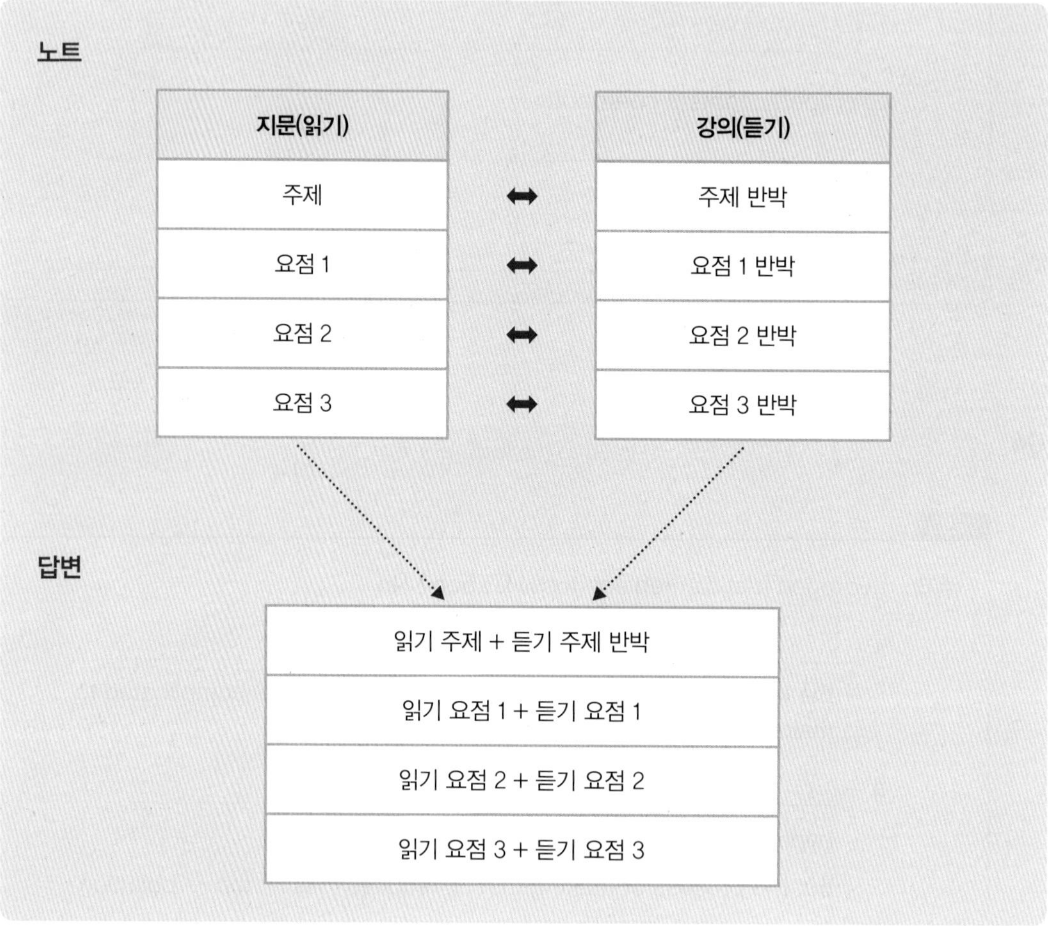

노트

지문(읽기)		강의(듣기)
주제	⟷	주제 반박
요점 1	⟷	요점 1 반박
요점 2	⟷	요점 2 반박
요점 3	⟷	요점 3 반박

답변

읽기 주제 + 듣기 주제 반박
읽기 요점 1 + 듣기 요점 1
읽기 요점 2 + 듣기 요점 2
읽기 요점 3 + 듣기 요점 3

예시 Reading

As the world's energy and resource consumption grows, it is becoming increasingly difficult to find locations that can provide resources. One source that holds great reserves of minerals is deep sea thermal vents. A vent is a deep crack on the ocean's floor where sea water is heated and filled with minerals. The concept of vent mining has recently received attention, but these are fragile ecosystems with many unique species. Still there are a number of reasons why vent mining should be carried out.

First, the deep sea vents are a rich source of metals and minerals that are increasingly difficult to find on land. Materials such as gold and iron can be found in enormous supply along these thermal vents. These areas are readily available to humans for harvesting and may even provide larger supplies of metal than land based mines. Extraction of the minerals from the sea floor sediment would also be much easier than removing them from ore.

Secondly, although thermal vents are home to a number of very unique animals that cannot exist elsewhere, we would not have to put those organisms in danger. Much of the minerals from thermal vents can be found as much as two kilometers away from the vent itself. Mining at this distance would not damage these fragile habitats while still yielding the desired resources.

Finally, mineral extraction in the deep sea can be regulated by international law. Many critics say that miners would recklessly mine since it would be very difficult to oversee their operations. But there are many laws and agencies that can regulate mining near the vents. One of these agencies is the International Seabed Authority which was established by the Law of the Sea Convention. This agency ensures that companies follow the strict regulations for ocean mining and do not destroy the environment with their activities.

노트

주제 deep sea vents mining = advantageous 심해 분출구 채광 = 이점

1. rich source of metals & minerals 금속 & 광물의 풍부한 원천
   - gold & iron available 금 & 철을 구할 수 있음
   - larger supply than land based mines 육지 기반 광산보다 더 많은 공급량
   - extraction much easier 추출이 훨씬 쉬움
2. X danger for animals 동물들에게 위험 X
   - mine far from vents 분출구에서 멀리 떨어져 채굴
3. regulate by int'l law 국제법으로 규제
   - oversee companies, strict regulations 회사들 감독, 엄격한 규제

세계의 에너지와 자원 소비가 증가함에 따라 자원을 제공할 수 있는 장소를 찾는 것이 점점 더 어려워지고 있다. 엄청난 광물 매장량을 보유한 한 원천이 심해의 열수 분출구이다. 분출구는 해저에 있는 깊은 틈으로, 이곳에서는 해수가 데워지고 광물로 가득 차있다. 분출구 채광이라는 개념은 최근에 주목을 받아왔지만, 이곳은 많은 독특한 종들이 서식하는 연약한 생태계이다. 그럼에도 분출구 채광을 해야 하는 많은 이유가 있다.

첫째, 심해 분출구는 육지에서는 점점 더 찾기 힘들어지는 금속과 광물의 풍부한 원천이다. 금과 철 같은 물질의 엄청난 양이 이 열수 분출구를 따라 발견될 수 있다. 이런 지역은 인간이 채광하기 쉬우며, 육지에 있는 광맥보다 더 많은 금속을 공급할 수도 있다. 해저 퇴적물에서 광물을 추출하는 것은 역시 광석에서 광물을 제거하는 것보다 훨씬 쉬울 것이다.

둘째로, 열수 분출구가 다른 곳에서는 존재할 수 없는 아주 독특한 많은 동물들의 서식지라 해도, 이 생물들을 위험에 처하게 할 필요는 없다. 열수 분출구에서 나오는 많은 광물이 분출구에서 2km까지 떨어진 곳에서 발견될 수 있다. 이런 거리에서 채굴하면 이 연약한 서식지에 손상을 입히지 않으면서 원하는 자원을 여전히 산출할 수 있을 것이다.

마지막으로, 심해에서 광물을 채굴하는 것은 국제법으로 규제할 수 있다. 비판하는 사람들 다수는 광부들의 활동을 감독하기가 아주 어렵기 때문에 이들이 무분별하게 채광할지 모른다고 말한다. 그러나 분출구 근처의 채광을 규제할 수 있는 많은 법과 단체가 있다. 이런 단체 중 하나가 국제 해양법 협약에 따라 설립한 국제 해저 기구이다. 이 단체는 기업들이 바다에서 채광할 때 반드시 엄격한 규정을 따르고 채광 활동으로 환경을 파괴하지 않도록 한다.

예시 Listening

I04_EX

We all know there is a definite need to meet the world's demand for mineral resources, and vent mining seems to be one of the best options for collecting these resources. However, I don't think that the reading accurately discusses vent mining. Let's look at the points in the reading, because honestly, they just don't make sense to me.

Now, first of all, about there being a lot of metal resources near these thermal vents, yes, this is true. But, we don't have any technology that could mine these metals. I mean, first, you need a way to sort the metals from the ocean sediment. This is not possible at the moment; the technology still needs to be developed. And, even if you could sort the metals from the sediment, you would need a way to transport the metals to the surface of the ocean. These technologies just don't exist right now.

The second point the author made that mining can be performed two kilometers away from the thermal vents, well, this certainly is not far away enough to guarantee the safety of the ecosystem there. I mean, sure, two kilometers may seem like a large distance, but mining uses some very toxic chemicals that would be very difficult to contain underwater. If the chemicals from the mining actually spread to the ecosystem, the effects might be simply disastrous to the organisms that make their homes at the vents.

Finally, the standards mentioned in the reading only apply to vents that are located within international waters. But, companies would most likely want to mine at vents closer to coastlines. Vents located near these coastlines are not within the jurisdiction of international law. That is, companies would mine in the territorial waters of the country to which the coast belongs. Many of these places have absolutely no form of regulation on vent mining activities, so regulating their activities would be impossible.

노트

주제 deep sea vents mining = X advantageous 심해 분출구 채광 = 이점 없음

1. no technology 기술 없음
   - sorting metals 금속 분류
   - transporting them to ocean surface 그것들을 해수면으로 운송
2. X danger for animals? 동물들에게 위험하지 않다?
   - mine far from vents → not enough 분출구에서 먼 곳에서 채광 → 충분하지 않음
   - toxic chemicals can still harm marine species
     유독성 화학 물질이 여전히 해양 종들에게 해를 입힐 수 있음
3. regulate by int'l law? 국제법으로 규제?
   - only apply to int'l waters 공해에만 적용
   - companies mine near coastlines = X jurisdiction
     기업들이 해안선 근처에서 채광 = 관할 구역 없음

광물 자원에 대한 세계의 수요를 맞출 필요가 분명히 있다는 점은 우리 모두 알고 있고, 분출구 채광은 이런 자원을 모으는 데 가장 좋은 선택지 중 하나처럼 보입니다. 하지만 나는 지문이 열수 분출구 채광을 정확하게 논의하고 있다고 생각하지 않아요. 지문의 요점들을 살펴보도록 하죠. 솔직히 저는 이해가 되지 않으니까요.

자, 우선, 이런 열수 분출구 근처에 많은 금속 자원이 있다는 점, 네, 이건 사실입니다. 하지만 우리는 이런 금속을 채굴할 수 있는 기술을 갖고 있지 않아요. 내 말은, 우선 바다 퇴적물에서 금속을 분류할 방법이 필요합니다. 이것은 지금으로서는 불가능해요. 기술을 개발해야 합니다. 그리고 퇴적물에서 금속을 분류할 수 있다 해도, 해수면으로 그 금속을 운반할 방법이 필요할 겁니다. 이런 기술은 현재는 존재하지 않습니다.

채광이 열수 분출구에서 2km 떨어진 곳에서 이루어질 수 있다는 필자의 두 번째 요점은 글쎄요, 이건 분명 그곳 생태계의 안전을 보장하기에 충분히 먼 거리가 아닙니다. 내 말은, 2km가 먼 거리처럼 보일지 모르지만, 채광할 때 매우 유독한 화학 물질을 몇 가지 사용하는데, 이는 물속에서 통제하기가 아주 어려울 겁니다. 만약 채광에 쓰이는 화학 물질이 실제로 생태계에 퍼지면 그 영향은 분출구를 서식지로 삼는 생물들에게 그저 재앙일 수도 있습니다.

마지막으로, 지문에서 언급된 기준은 공해 내에 있는 열수 분출구에만 적용됩니다. 그러나 기업들은 해안선과 더 가까이 있는 분출구에서 채광하고 싶을 겁니다. 이런 해안선 근처에 위치한 분출구들은 국제법의 관할 구역 내에 있지 않아요. 즉, 기업들은 그 해안이 속한 나라의 영해 내에서 채광할 겁니다. 이런 장소들 중 다수는 열수 분출구 채광 행위에 관한 어떤 형태의 규정도 전혀 가지고 있지 않기에 그들의 활동을 규제하는 것은 불가능할 겁니다.

답변 연결

Reading	Listening
주제 deep sea vents mining = advantageous	deep sea vents mining = X advantageous
1. rich source of metals & minerals - gold & iron available - larger supply than land based mines - extraction much easier	1. no technology - sorting metals - transporting them to ocean surface
2. X danger for animals - mine far from vents	2. X danger for animals? - mine far from vents → not enough - toxic chemicals can still harm marine species
3. regulate by int'l law - oversee companies, strict regulations	3. regulate by int'l law? - only apply to int'l waters - companies mine near coastlines = X jurisdiction

읽기&듣기 연결 → 실제 답변 써보기

도입: Reading과 Listening의 주제

The reading and the lecture both talk about the potential of vent mining. The reading says that there are three reasons why vent mining should be carried out. However, the lecturer argues that the reasons given in the reading are unconvincing.

지문과 강의 둘 다 열수 분출구 채광의 잠재력에 관해 말하고 있다. 지문은 열수 분출구 채광이 시행되어야 하는 세 가지 이유가 있다고 한다. 하지만 강의자는 지문에서 주어진 이유들은 설득력이 없다고 주장한다.

문단 1: Reading의 주장 1과 Listening의 반박

Firstly, the reading states that vent mining is a good idea because there are a lot of precious metals and minerals near thermal vents. Although the lecturer admits that there are a lot of metals at thermal vents, he argues that it is too difficult to get them. This is because we do not have the technology necessary to sort the metals from the sediment at the bottom of the ocean, nor to transport them to the surface of the ocean.

첫째로, 지문은 열수 분출구 근처에 귀금속과 광물이 많이 있기 때문에 열수 분출구 채광이 좋은 생각이라고 말한다. 강의자는 열수 분출구에 많은 금속이 있다는 점은 인정하지만, 그러한 금속을 얻는 것이 너무 어렵다고 주장한다. 왜냐하면 해저 침전물에서 그 금속들을 분리하거나 그것들을 해수면으로 운송하는 데 필요한 기술을 가지고 있지 않기 때문이다.

문단 2: Reading의 주장 2와 Listening의 반박

Secondly, the reading states that vent mining can be done in ways that will not harm marine life near the vents. Much of the minerals are found up to two kilometers away from the vents and their fragile ecosystems. According to the lecture, however, toxic chemicals used in mining are difficult to contain, and they can spread regardless of how far away mining is performed.

둘째로, 지문은 열수 분출구 채광이 분출구 근처의 해양 생물들을 해치지 않는 방법으로 진행될 수 있다고 한다. 많은 광물이 분출구와 그 섬세한 생태계에서 2km까지 떨어진 곳에서 발견된다. 그러나 강의에 따르면, 채굴에 사용되는 유독성 화학 물질은 통제하기 어려우며, 얼마나 멀리서 채굴을 하든 관계없이 확산할 수 있다고 한다.

문단 3: Reading의 주장 3과 Listening의 반박

Thirdly, the reading goes on to say that vent mining in the deep sea can be regulated by international law. However, the lecturer casts doubt on this claim, stating that companies can mine in territorial waters where international law does not apply. This means that international law cannot prevent companies from recklessly extracting metals in the deep sea.

셋째로, 지문은 계속해서 심해의 분출구 채굴이 국제법으로 규제될 수 있다고 말한다. 하지만 강의자는 기업들이 국제법이 적용되지 않는 영해에서 채광할 수 있다고 하며 이러한 주장에 의문을 제기한다. 이는 기업들이 심해에서 금속을 무분별하게 채굴하는 것을 국제법이 막을 수 없다는 의미이다.

어휘 potential n 잠재력, 가능성 | unconvincing adj 설득력이 없는 | precious metal 귀금속 | sediment n 침전물 | the bottom of the ocean 해저 | marine life 해양 생물 | regardless of ~에 관계없이, 상관없이 | regulate v 규제하다, 단속하다 | cast doubt on 의문을 제기하다 | recklessly adj 무분별하게 | extract v 뽑아내다, 채굴하다, 추출하다

Practice

>> 제시된 지문을 읽고 아래의 노트를 완성해보자.

Q1

The top priority for any company is to increase its profits. In order to do so, companies must regularly assess their performance in the market and find new strategies suitable for rapidly changing their economic circumstances. Such strategies often involve releasing new products onto the market, and this can be done in three ways.

One strategy for increasing a company's sales is to develop an entirely new product by using the company's image. For example, if a renowned car company develops a motorcycle, the company can use its popularity to sell the product. Consumers who intend to buy a motorcycle will probably choose this particular motorcycle because of the company's image. Consumers will naturally think that the motorcycles will be just as good as the cars the company produces, so they will buy its motorcycles without any doubt.

The second strategy for raising a company's sales is to make a new version of an existing product. For example, if a soft drink company that is famous for its cola creates a version with an added fruit flavor, the company can easily increase sales. Consumers who love the original cola drink will be inclined to try this variation of the original product. The new cola benefits from both the familiarity that customers have with the old version and their curiosity about the newer one.

The final strategy is to make a partnership with another company. For example, if a company that makes chocolate forms a partnership with an ice cream company, the two companies can easily produce chocolate ice cream products together. In this case, both companies can increase their sales in a short period of time because they both receive a percentage of the new sales of the new chocolate ice cream. The brand images of both companies contribute to those sales.

Listen to the lecture. I04_P01

Reading 노트

주제 ↑ profit by releasing new products, 3 ways

1.
   - consumers buy b/c the comp's image

2.
   - consumers' familiarity & curiosity

3.
   - 2 comps → new product
   - brand images of both comps

Listening 노트

주제 ↑ profit by releasing new products, 3 ways?

1.
   -

2.
   -
   -

3.
   -
   -

노트 & 답변 연결

주제	읽기 The reading and the lecture both talk about strategies companies can use to raise profits by producing new products. 듣기
요점 1	읽기 Firstly, the reading states that 듣기 On the contrary, the lecturer claims that
요점 2	읽기 Secondly, in the reading, the author argues that 듣기 However, the lecturer says that
요점 3	읽기 Thirdly, the reading goes on to say that 듣기 However, the lecturer contradicts this opinion, arguing that

Q2

Intentionally setting a forest fire, called prescribed fire or controlled burning, is widely used in national parks across America. Prescribed fire is widely used because of the benefits that it brings to all of the organisms that live in the forest. However, there are disadvantages far outweigh the benefits of burning forests.

First, in the process of burning forests on a regular basis, many animals are killed. Some argue that animals can escape from the fire. However, what about the young animals that cannot get away from these fires? For example, young birds are not able to fly and therefore will be trapped and die. And even adult animals can become trapped as forest fires spread very rapidly.

Second, like all fires, prescribed fire releases harmful greenhouse gases into the air. The carbon dioxide that is emitted when trees burn is one of the gases that contributes to global warming. As we all know, global warming has a detrimental impact on the planet. For example, global warming makes many areas arid and this harms the forests.

Third, prescribed fire is a waste of time and resources. That is because naturally occurring fire happens in areas where prescribed fire has already been carried out. This happens because of occasional lightning strikes, camping accidents, or just senseless acts of arson. Either way, firefighters and residents must work to put out these fires again, which means that prescribed fire is a waste of time and resources.

Listen to the lecture. I04_P02

Reading 노트

주제 prescribed fire – disadvantages > benefits

1. animals are killed
   -
2.
   - CO_2 → global warming
3.
   - natural fire occurs in the same area anyway → have to put out

Listening 노트

주제 prescribed fire – disadvantages > benefits?

1.
   -

2.
   -

3.
   -

노트 & 답변 연결

주제	읽기 The reading and the lecture both talk about prescribed fire. The article says that such artificial fire leads to several negative consequences. 듣기 However, the lecturer argues that prescribed fire is not as harmful or inefficient as the reading argues.
요점 1	읽기 Firstly, the reading states that 듣기 However, according to the lecturer,
요점 2	읽기 Secondly, in the reading, the author argues that 듣기 In contrast, the lecturer claims that
요점 3	읽기 Thirdly, the reading goes on to say that 듣기 However, the lecturer contradicts this opinion by stating that

II. Academic Discussion Task

Introduction

Academic Discussion Task는 교수의 논제 제시와 논제에 대한 두 학생들의 답변으로 이루어진다. 교수가 논의할 주제를 제시할 때에는, 1) 제시한 주제에 대한 찬성/반대 유형과 2) 자신의 아이디어를 말해야 하는 두 가지 유형으로 나눌 수 있다. 따라서, 주제의 유형에 따라서 답변의 첫 문장, 즉 인트로부터 달라져야 하고, 수험자는 이에 대해 오류 없는 완벽한 문장으로 그에 대한 대비를 철저히 할 필요가 있다.

화면 구성

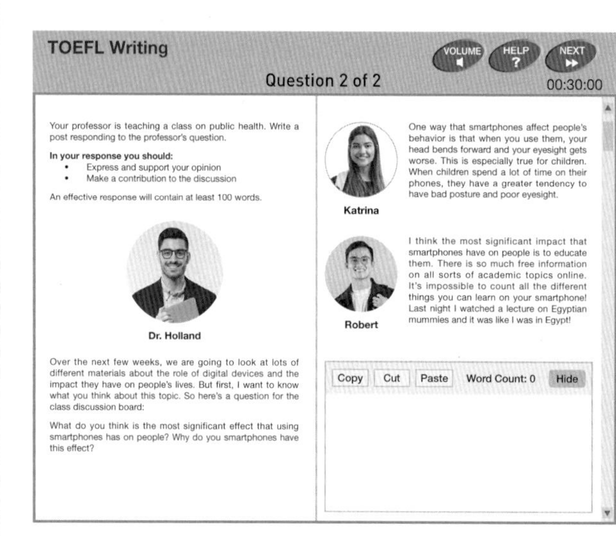

- 교수가 제시한 논제에 대한 토론 참여
- 두 명의 학생이 각자 의견을 제시
- 주어진 논제에 대한 자신의 의견을 간단히 기술 (100단어 / 10분)

Sample Questions

Your professor is teaching a class. Write a post responding to the professor's question.

In your response, you should:

- express and support your opinion
- make a contribution to the discussion

An effective response will contain at least 100 words. You will have 10 minutes to write it.

당신의 교수님께서 강의 중입니다. 교수님의 질문에 답하는 글을 쓰세요.

- 당신의 의견을 표현하고 뒷받침하세요
- 토론에 기여하세요

효과적인 답변은 최소한 100단어를 포함할 것입니다. 당신은 10분 동안 글을 작성할 수 있습니다.

Dr. Springer: Today, we will delve into a thought-provoking topic that centers around government spending. Our focus will be on the question of whether it is important for the

government to allocate funds towards things that are beautiful, rather than solely practical endeavors. In your opinion, should the government spend money on things that are beautiful, not just on those that are practical?
오늘은 정부 지출을 중심으로 한 생각할 여지가 있는 주제에 대해 탐구할 것입니다. 우리의 초점은 정부가 실용적인 노력뿐만 아니라 아름다운 것에 자금을 할당하는 것이 중요한지에 관한 문제입니다. 여러분이 생각하기에, 정부는 실용적인 노력뿐만 아니라 아름다운 것에도 돈을 써야 될까요?

Jeorge: I completely agree with the statement. Investing in aesthetically pleasing projects and initiatives not only enhances the visual appeal of our surroundings but also contributes to the overall well-being and happiness of the population. Beautiful infrastructure, public spaces, and cultural landmarks can attract tourists, boost local economies, and foster a sense of pride among citizens.
이 주장에 완전히 동의합니다. 아름다운 프로젝트와 계획에 투자함으로써 우리 주변의 시각적 매력이 향상되는 것뿐만 아니라 전체적인 웰빙과 시민들의 행복에 기여할 수 있습니다. 아름다운 인프라, 공공 공간 및 문화적 명소는 관광객을 유치하고 지역 경제를 촉진하며 시민들 사이에 자부심을 유발할 수 있습니다.

April: While I appreciate the value of beauty, I believe that practicality should be the primary focus of government spending. Limited resources should be allocated towards addressing pressing issues such as healthcare, education, and infrastructure. Practical investments can directly improve the quality of life and provide essential services to the population, ensuring long-term sustainability and progress.
아름다움의 가치를 고려하긴 하지만, 나는 정부 지출에 있어서 실용성이 주요 관심사여야 한다고 생각합니다. 제한된 자원은 의료, 교육 및 인프라와 같은 긴요한 문제에 할당되어야 합니다. 실용적인 투자는 직접적으로 삶의 질을 높이고 주민들에게 필수적인 서비스를 제공하여 장기적인 지속 가능성과 발전을 보장합니다.

Learning Strategies

Step 1 **교수의 논제를 빠르게 파악한다.**

⋯› 교수의 Discussion Topic은 항상 똑같은 길이가 아니라 때로는 짧게, 혹은 길고 장황하게 제시될 수도 있다. 따라서, 후반부를 중점적으로 보고 빠르고 신속하게 주제 파악을 해야 한다.

Step 2 **두 학생의 포인트를 간단하게 1-2문장으로 파악한다.**

⋯› 토론에 답변하는 두 학생의 의견은 최대한 간단하게 의견(찬성/반대 or 아이디어)만 파악한다. 그 이유는 10분은 답변 작성 시간으로는 정말 짧게 느껴지는 시간이며, 채점관이 중점적으로 보는 부분은 제시된 두 학생의 의견 요약이 아닌 시험 응시자 본인의 개인적 의견과 뒷받침하는 이유이기 때문이다.

Step 3 **시간 관리를 철저히 하여 답변을 작성한다.**

⋯› 답변은 9분 동안 작성하고, 나머지 1분 동안 작성한 내용을 처음부터 끝까지 훑어보면서 누락된 내용이나 문법적 오류나 오타가 없는지 살펴보며 수정한다. 즉, 답변 작성은 9분, 검토는 1분이 필수이다.

고득점 전략 **만점 답변은 약 200단어에 가까운 구체적이고 논리적인 글이다.**

유형 1. 찬성/반대

교수의 Discussion 주제 제시 부분 중 후반부를 보면 주제를 바로 파악할 수 있다.

답변 인트로 문장

From my perspective, both made excellent statements, but I'm on the same page as "토론 참여자들 둘 중 한 명."

예시

Q. **Professor:** Participating in organization or club activities can provide many benefits. Do you agree or disagree?
조직 또는 동아리 활동에 참여하는 것은 많은 이점을 제공할 수 있습니다. 찬성하십니까, 반대하십니까?

Jeorge: agree / **April:** disagree
조지: 동의 / 에이프릴: 반대

A. From my perspective, both made excellent statements, but I'm on the same page as Jeorge.
제 관점에서, 두 사람 모두 훌륭한 주장을 했지만 저는 조지와 같은 생각입니다.

예시처럼 답변 인트로 문장을 이용해서 빈칸을 채워 보자.

Q1 **Professor:** When it comes to spending money, some argue that it is better to invest in something long-lasting, like an expensive piece of jewelry, rather than indulging in short-term pleasures, such as a vacation. What are your thoughts on this matter?

- **Jeorge:** jewelry / **April:** vacation
  April과 같은 의견을 가지고 있는 경우의 인트로 문장을 만들어 보자.

A. ______________________________

____

Q2 **Professor:** Many cities nowadays are devising plans to improve themselves, yet they are unsure of an optimal solution. When it comes to a city's benefit, some argue that the best way to achieve it is by focusing on constructing new buildings rather than preserving nature. What are your thoughts on this matter?

- **Jeorge:** constructing new buildings / **April:** preserving nature

April과 같은 의견을 가지고 있는 경우의 인트로 문장을 만들어 보자.

A. ____

Q3 **Professor:** Some argue that it is more important for parents to spend quality time playing and bonding with their children, rather than focusing solely on academic achievements. What are your thoughts on this statement?

- **Jeorge:** agree / **April:** disagree

Jeorge와 같은 의견을 가지고 있는 경우의 인트로 문장을 만들어 보자.

A. ____

Q4 **Professor:** We often hear the saying "Family should have meals together on a regular basis." What are your thoughts on this statement?

- **Jeorge:** agree / **April:** disagree

Jeorge와 같은 의견을 가지고 있는 경우의 인트로 문장을 만들어 보자.

A. ____

유형 2. 아이디어 말하기

교수의 Discussion 주제 제시 부분 중 후반부를 보면 주제를 바로 파악할 수 있다.

답변 인트로 문장

From my perspective, both made excellent statements, but I would like to add that "자신의 아이디어."

예시

Q. **Professor:** If you had to select just one class to be mandatory for the school's curriculum, which class would you prioritize?
학교 교육과정의 필수 과목으로 딱 한 과목을 선택해야 한다면, 어떤 과목을 우선시하겠습니까?

Jeorge: a class focusing on personal finance / **April:** a class on critical thinking
조지: 개인 금융에 중점을 둔 과목 / 에이프릴: 비판적 사고에 중점을 둔 과목

A. From my perspective, both made excellent statements, but I would like to add that PE class should be mandatory for the school's curriculum.
제 관점에서, 두 사람 모두 훌륭한 주장을 했지만, 저는 학교 교육 과정에 체육 수업이 필수적이어야 한다는 점을 덧붙이고 싶습니다.

예시처럼 답변 인트로 문장을 이용해서 빈칸을 채워 보자.

Q1 **Professor:** People can benefit from traveling all around the world. Tell me one benefit you can gain from world travel.

- **Jeorge:** relieving stress / **April:** meeting different people

  '시야/견문을 확장할 수 있다'란 아이디어로 인트로 문장을 만들어 보자.

A. ______________________________

____

Q2 **Professor:** Please describe a new experience you have had recently that significantly impacted your life. Explain how this experience has influenced your perspective and personal growth.

- **Jeorge:** volunteer program / **April:** internship at a laboratory

'작은 회사에서의 인턴십'이란 아이디어로 인트로 문장을 만들어 보자.

A.

Q3 **Professor:** Which significant scientific breakthrough or technological innovation from the past two centuries would you select as a crucial advancement?

- **Jeorge:** antibiotics / **April:** computer

'인터넷'이란 아이디어로 인트로 문장을 만들어 보자.

A.

Q4 **Professor:** Technology has made the world a better place to live, so please tell me one aspect that impacts your life.

- **Jeorge:** communication / **April:** gaining information

'효과적인 시간 관리'란 아이디어로 인트로 문장을 만들어 보자.

A.

Academic Discussion Task의 답변은 의견을 뒷받침하는 일반적 사실 진술과 구체화 사례로 구성된다.

답변 구조

주제에 해당하는 일반적인 사실 진술 + 해당 진술에 관련된 구체화 사례

1. 일반적 사실 진술

일반적 사실 진술은 답변을 한결 세련되게 다듬어 준다. 사람들이 일반적으로 알고 있는 사실을 풀어내면 글을 보는 채점관과의 공감을 형성할 뿐만 아니라, 글을 더 논리적으로 쓸 수 있다. 지나치게 전문 지식을 쓰면 채점관조차 이해하기 어려울 수 있으니 보편적인 지식으로 의견을 전개하도록 한다.

2. 해당 진술에 연관된 구체화 사례

개인적 경험은 수험자 본인이나 주변 지인들이 겪은 일을 가리킨다. Academic Discussion Task에서는 자기 생각과 경험을 답변에 자유롭게 쓸 수 있으므로, 주제와 경험을 되살려 앞에서 제시한 일반적 사실 진술을 효과적으로 뒷받침하도록 한다.

Example

스프린져 교수
학문적인 연구는 학생들의 미래 성공에 중요하지만, 일부 사람들은 단체나 동아리 활동에 참여하는 것이 동등한 혜택을 제공할 수 있다고 주장합니다. 이 주장에 찬성하십니까, 반대하십니까?

조지
저는 이 주장에 완전히 찬성합니다. 사실, 저는 단순히 학문에 중점을 두는 것보다 단체나 동아리에 참여하는 것이 더 큰 이점을 제공할 수 있다고 믿습니다. 이러한 활동은 학생들에게 사회적 기술을 개발하고 동료 및 전문가와 네트워킹하며 관심 분야에서 실질적인 경험을 얻을 수 있는 기회를 제공할 수 있습니다.

에이프릴
단체나 동아리에 참여하는 것이 가치 있는 경험을 제공할 수 있다고 동의하지만, 학문적인 연구는 여전히 학생들에게 우선순위여야 한다고 생각합니다. 튼튼한 학문적 기반 없이는 추가 교육이나 진로 기회를 추구하기 어려울 수 있습니다. 그러나 동아리나 단체에 참여하는 것은 학문적인 연구를 보완하고 강화할 수 있는 좋은 방법일 수 있습니다.

답변 만들기

일반적 진술 From my perspective, both made excellent statements, but I'm on the same page as Jeorge. Simply put, participating in club activities can contribute to alleviating stress. Nowadays, students often get stressed out from their heavy workloads and the competition with those around them, so they need a pleasant diversion to relax mentally. By spending quality time engaging in enjoyable club activities, they will eventually be able to relax and get back to their work.

구체화 사례 A perfect example of this is a close friend of mine. He used to suffer from a huge workload and pressure. He sometimes stayed up all night getting his work done, so he was basically exhausted physically and mentally. Then one day, he joined an inline hockey club. It truly allowed him to escape from all the stressful matters while engaging in this activity. Thanks to this, he now has a relaxed and confident mental state.

일반적 진술 제 관점으로는, 양쪽 모두 훌륭한 진술을 했지만, 저는 조지와 같은 의견입니다. 간단히 말하면, 동아리 활동에 참여하는 것은 스트레스 완화에 큰 도움을 줄 수 있습니다. 요즈음, 학생들은 과도한 일(공부)과 그들 주변 사람들과의 경쟁 때문에 스트레스를 받고 있어 정신적으로 편안해질 수 있는 즐거운 기분 전환이 필요합니다. 즐길 수 있는 동아리 활동이 주는 깊고 의미 있는 시간을 통해서, 그들은 결국 휴식을 취하고 그들의 일로 돌아가게 될 것입니다.

구체화 사례 이에 대한 완벽한 예시는 내 친한 친구 중 한 명입니다. 그는 너무 많은 일(공부)과 중압감으로 고통받았습니다. 그는 때때로 그의 일을 끝내기 위해 밤을 지새웠습니다. 그래서 그는 완전히 신체적으로나 정신적으로 지쳐 있었습니다. 그러던 어느 날, 그는 인라인 하키 동아리에 가입할 기회를 가지게 되었습니다. 그것은 그가 이 활동에 참여하는 동안에, 모든 스트레스 가득한 일로부터 벗어날 수 있게 해 주었습니다. 이 덕분에, 그는 현재 안정되고 자신감 있는 심리 상태를 가지게 되었습니다.

Lesson 01 스트레스 관련 주제

'예체능 관련 수업, 취미, 여러 가지 사회적 모임, 여행, 동아리 활동' 관련 주제는 일관된 아이디어로 답변을 전개할 수 있다. 사람들과 즐겁게 보내면서, 또한 재충전을 하면서 기분 전환을 하는 것은 모두 '스트레스 해소'와 관련 있는 내용으로 전개할 수 있기 때문이다. 다음의 표현을 익혀둔다면, 별도의 brainstorming 과정 없이도 관련 주제에 대해서 빠르게 정확한 답변을 기술할 수 있다.

01. alleviate stress (= relieve stress)

스트레스를 완화하다

It's a good way to alleviate stress.

그것은 스트레스를 완화할 수 있는 좋은 방법이다.

02. get stressed out from ~

~때문에 스트레스를 받다

I get stressed out from academic matters.

나는 학업과 관련된 일 때문에 스트레스를 받는다.

03. a pleasant diversion

즐거운 여가/기분 전환

Playing with friends can be a pleasant diversion.

친구들과 노는 것은 즐거운 기분 전환이 될 수 있다.

04. quality time

깊고 의미 있는 시간

My best friend and I spend quality time together by having sincere conversations.

내 가장 친한 친구와 나는 진솔한 대화를 나누는 것으로 깊고 의미 있는 시간을 보낸다.

05. suffer from ~

~로 고통을 겪다

He suffers from severe allergies during the spring.

그는 봄철 심한 알레르기로 고통을 겪는다.

06. stay up all night

밤을 지새우다

They stayed up all night watching movies.

그들은 영화를 보느라 밤을 지새웠다.

07. be exhausted 지치다

After working for 8 hours straight, I was completely exhausted.
8시간 동안 쉬지 않고 일한 후, 나는 완전히 지쳐버렸다.

08. escape from ~ ~로부터 탈출하다/ 벗어나다

She needed a vacation to escape from the stress of her work.
그녀는 스트레스를 받는 일에서 벗어나기 위해 휴가가 필요했었다.

09. thanks to ~ ~ 덕분에

Thanks to your help, we were able to complete the project on time.
당신의 도움 덕분에, 우리는 프로젝트를 제시간에 완료할 수 있었다.

10. mental state 심리/정신 상태

Regular exercise can help improve one's mental state.
규칙적인 운동은 사람의 정신 상태를 향상하는 데 도움을 줄 수 있다.

>> 앞에서 학습한 표현들을 활용하여 다음 문장을 영작하시오.

01. 클럽 활동에 참여하는 것은 스트레스를 완화하는 것에 도움을 준다.

02. 그들은 정신적으로 편안해지기 위한 즐거운 기분 전환이 필요하다.

03. 이 덕분에 그는 현재 안정되고 자신감 있는 정신 상태를 가지게 되었다.

Practice

TOEFL Writing

Question 2 of 2

Your professor is teaching a class. Write a post responding to the professor's question.

In your response, you should:

- express and support your opinion
- make a contribution to the discussion

An effective response will contain at least 100 words.
You will have 10 minutes to write it.

Dr. Springer

When it comes to spending money, some argue that it is better to invest in something long-lasting, like an expensive piece of jewelry, rather than indulging in short-term pleasures, such as a vacation. What are your thoughts on this matter?

Jeorge

Personally, I believe that investing in something that lasts, like an expensive piece of jewelry, is a wise decision. Not only does it provide a lasting value, but it can also be seen as an investment that retains or even appreciates in worth over time. Furthermore, owning a valuable piece of jewelry can be a symbol of prestige and accomplishment.

April

While I acknowledge the appeal of long-lasting investments, I believe that spending money on pleasurable experiences, such as a vacation, can be equally valuable. Pleasurable experiences have the potential to create lifelong memories and broaden one's horizons. Additionally, they can contribute to personal growth, cultural understanding, and stress relief, which are all essential aspects of a well-rounded life.

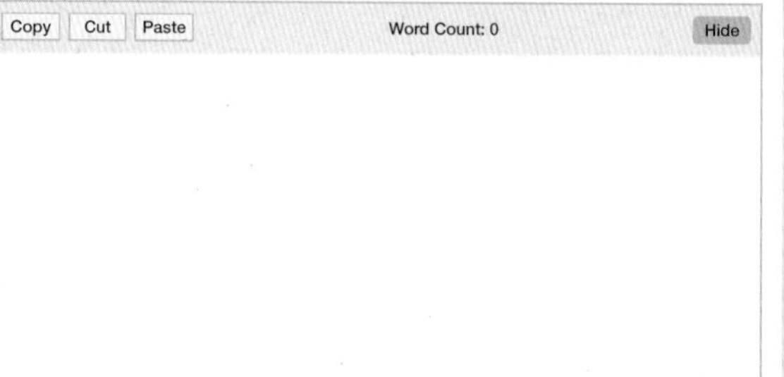

아웃라인

일반적 진술

short-term pleasure: alleviate stress → stressed from work + competition → quality time enjoying short-term pleasure → relax + get back to work

구체화 사례

example → stressed out from work → "family trip" → relaxed mental state

답변 완성하기

일반적 진술

From my perspective, both made excellent statements, but I'm on the same page as

구체화 사례

A perfect example of this is a close friend of mine.

Lesson

02 분위기 관련 주제

'자연 보존, 회사에서의 복장 규율, 학교의 교육과정, 여행, 여러 가지 레저 활동들' 관련 주제는 일관된 아이디어로 답변을 전개할 수 있다. 다양한 활동들에 대한 참여, 각 장소의 분위기에 영향을 받는 것은 모두 'atmosphere의 영향'과 관련 있는 내용으로 전개할 수 있기 때문이다. 다음의 표현을 익혀둔다면, 별도의 brainstorming 과정 없이도 관련 주제에 대해서 빠르게 정확한 답변을 기술할 수 있다.

01. a positive ambiance

긍정적인 분위기

Students can experience a positive ambiance.

학생들은 긍정적인 분위기를 경험할 수 있다.

02. be influenced

영향을 받다

Most students can be influenced by their environment's atmosphere.

대부분의 학생들은 그들의 환경의 분위기에 영향을 받을 수 있다.

03. a lot more important than they might realize

생각(인지)하는 것 이상으로 훨씬 더 중요하다

The influence of the atmosphere is a lot more important than they might realize.

그 분위기의 영향은 그들이 생각(인지)하는 것 이상으로 훨씬 더 중요하다.

04. feel a good atmosphere

좋은 분위기를 느끼다

Students should feel a good atmosphere while they are at school.

학생들은 그들이 학교에 있는 동안에는 좋은 분위기를 느껴야만 한다.

05. competitive and strict

치열하고 엄격한

The workplace used to be very competitive and strict.

그 일터는 매우 치열하고 엄격하곤 했었다.

06. little by little

조금씩

Things changed little by little.

상황이 조금씩 변했다.

07. time and effort

시간과 노력

A lot of time and effort were put into making the city better.
도시를 더 좋게 만들기 위해 많은 시간과 노력이 들어갔다.

08. genuinely appreciate

진심으로 감사해하다

I genuinely appreciate the changed environment.
나는 변화된 환경을 진심으로 감사해하고 있다.

09. top schools with a good reputation

좋은 평판을 가지고 있는 학교들

It made the college one of the top schools with a good reputation.
이는 그 대학을 좋은 평판을 가진 최고의 학교 중 하나로 만들었다.

10. compared to ~

~에 비교해 볼 때

I had a more enjoyable school life compared to my friends.
나는 내 친구들에 비해서 더 즐거운 학교생활을 보냈다.

>> 앞에서 학습한 표현들을 활용하여 다음 문장을 영작하시오.

01. 학생들은 체육 시간 동안 에너지 넘치는 활동에 몰입하면서 긍정적인 분위기를 경험한다.

02. 하지만 교장이 분위기를 바꾸려고 노력한 이후 상황이 조금씩 바뀌었다.

03. 우리 학교의 재학생들은 기분 좋고 활기찬 분위기에 진실로 감사해한다.

Practice

TOEFL Writing

Question 2 of 2

Your professor is teaching a class. Write a post responding to the professor's question.

In your response, you should:

- express and support your opinion
- make a contribution to the discussion

An effective response will contain at least 100 words.
You will have 10 minutes to write it.

Dr. Lucas

When it comes to designing a school's curriculum, there are numerous classes to choose from, each offering its own unique benefits. However, if you had to select just one class to be mandatory for the school's curriculum, which class would you prioritize?

Bobby

Personally, I believe that a class focusing on personal finance and financial literacy should be mandatory for all students. In today's society, financial knowledge is crucial for individuals to navigate the complexities of managing their finances effectively. Such a class would equip students with essential skills like budgeting, saving, and understanding investments, ensuring they have a solid foundation to make informed financial decisions throughout their lives and achieve accomplishments.

Kelly

While I recognize the importance of financial literacy, I would argue that a class on critical thinking and problem-solving should be the mandatory choice. These skills are universally applicable and essential for success in any field. By developing critical thinking abilities, students can learn to analyze and evaluate information, think creatively, and make sound judgments.

Copy | Cut | Paste | Word Count: 0 | Hide

아웃라인

일반적 진술

a positive atmosphere in PE class → influence of the atmosphere: important → students should feel a good atmosphere. → PE: makes students feel more cheerful and energetic

구체화 사례

example → competitive and strict atmosphere in the school → the principal's plan to change the atmosphere → a lot of time and effort to provide enjoyable PE class → positive atmosphere in the school

답변 완성하기

일반적 진술

From my perspective, both made excellent statements, but I would like to add that

구체화 사례

A perfect example of this is the high school that I attended.

Lesson

03 사람들과의 관계 관련 주제

부모와 자식, 교수와 학생, 친구들과 관련된 주제는 일관된 아이디어로 답변을 전개할 수 있다. 주제는 다양할지라도 사람들과의 관계에 관련한 공통점만 있다면 모두 'people과의 관계'와 관련 있는 내용으로 전개할 수 있기 때문이다. 다음의 표현을 익혀둔다면, 별도의 brainstorming 과정 없이도 관련 주제에 대해서 빠르게 정확한 답변을 기술할 수 있다.

01. interact with ~

~와 어우러지다 / 소통하다

She likes to interact with her friends on social media.
그녀는 친구들과 소셜 미디어에서 소통하는 것을 좋아한다.

02. optimal condition

최적의 조건

An optimal condition to improve a relationship can be achieved through sincere conversation.
진중한 대화는 관계를 증진하는 최적의 조건이라고 간주된다.

03. share experiences and emotions

경험과 감정을 공유하다

Close friends often share experiences and emotions with each other.
가까운 친구들은 종종 그들의 경험과 감정을 공유한다.

04. sincere conversation

진중한 대화

He had a sincere conversation about his future plans.
그는 그의 미래 계획에 관한 진중한 대화를 가졌다.

05. drift apart

소원해지다 / 사이가 멀어지다

After going to different colleges, they slowly began to drift apart.
서로 다른 대학교를 다니게 된 이후, 그들은 서서히 사이가 멀어지기 시작했다.

06. have a hard time -ing

~하는 데 힘든 시간을 보내다

They have a hard time interacting with each other.
그들은 서로 소통하는 데 힘든 시간을 보냈다.

07. not just ~ but also ~ 단순히 ~뿐만 아니라 ~도 역시

We played sports not just to entertain ourselves but also to strengthen our friendship.
우리는 단지 즐거워지기 위해서 뿐만 아니라 우리의 우정을 더 강화하기 위해 스포츠를 했다.

08. awkward at first 처음에는 어색한

Meeting new people can be awkward at first.
새로운 사람들을 만나는 것은 처음에는 어색할 수 있다.

09. get close to ~ ~와 가까워지다

It took a long time for him to get close to his friends.
그가 그의 친구들과 가까워지는 데에는 긴 시간이 걸렸다.

10. strong bond 끈끈한 유대/관계

A strong bond was built between them.
그들 사이에 끈끈한 유대가 만들어졌다.

>> 앞에서 학습한 표현들을 활용하여 다음 문장을 영작하시오.

01. 이것은 그들의 관계를 증진하는 최적의 조건을 만든다.

02. 그는 직업 때문에 그의 아들과 소원해졌고, 그들이 소통하는 것을 힘들게 만들었다.

03. 그들 사이에 끈끈한 유대가 만들어지고 발전했다.

Practice

TOEFL Writing

Your professor is teaching a class. Write a post responding to the professor's question.

In your response, you should:

- express and support your opinion
- make a contribution to the discussion

An effective response will contain at least 100 words.
You will have 10 minutes to write it.

Dr. Emilie

Many busy parents struggle to balance their work and family life, and may not have much time to devote to helping their children with schoolwork. Some argue that it is more important for parents to spend quality time playing and bonding with their children, rather than focusing solely on academic achievements. What are your thoughts on this statement?

Oliver

I completely agree with the statement. Spending quality time with your children is essential for building strong relationships and developing their emotional intelligence. Parents who prioritize play-time over academics are sending an important message to their children: that their love and attention are not contingent on academic performance.

Lucy

While I agree that spending quality time with your children is important, I think that academic achievement should not be overlooked. It's important for parents to be involved in their children's education and to provide them with the support they need to succeed in school. This doesn't mean sacrificing play-time, but finding a balance between academic and non-academic activities.

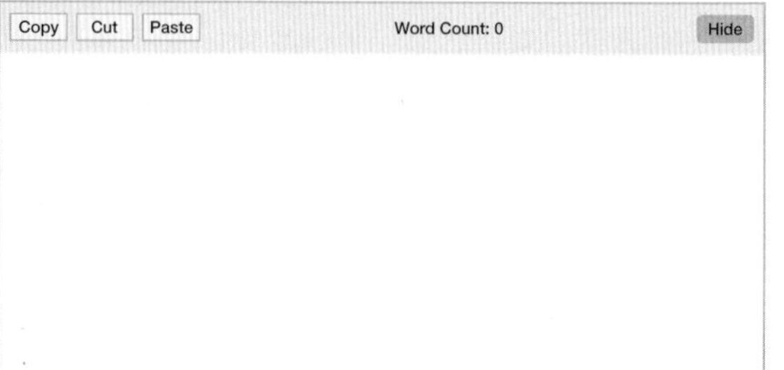

아웃라인

일반적 진술

interaction between parents and children → play together → share experiences and emotions → lead to sincere conversations later

구체화 사례

example → drift apart from his son due to his job → decided to play with his son → awkward and challenging at first → gradually better → a strong bond between father and son

답변 완성하기

일반적 진술

From my perspective, both made excellent statements, but I'm on the same page as

구체화 사례

A perfect example of this is my uncle.

Lesson

04 관점의 확장 관련 주제

'세계 여행, 유학, 새로운 경험, 다양한 친구들과의 교류' 관련 주제는 일관된 아이디어로 답변을 전개할 수 있다. 서로 다른 상황들이지만 다름과 새로움을 통해서 가지고 있지 못했던 것들에 노출이 되고, 그것으로 인한 견문의 확장과 관련 있는 내용으로 전개할 수 있기 때문이다. 다음의 표현을 익혀둔다면, 별도의 brainstorming 과정 없이도 관련 주제에 대해서 빠르게 정확한 답변을 기술할 수 있다.

01. gain inspiration

영감을 얻다

She would often travel to new places to gain inspiration.

그녀는 영감을 얻기 위해 새로운 장소를 여행하곤 했다.

02. broaden perspective

시야/관점을 넓히다

Reading diverse books can broaden your perspective.

다양한 책을 읽는 것은 당신의 시야를 넓힐 수 있다.

03. gain exposure

노출을 얻다 / ~에 노출되다

Working in different countries allows you to gain exposure to diverse cultures.

여러 나라에서 일하는 것은 당신이 다양한 문화에 노출되게 한다.

04. valuable insight

가치 있는 통찰력 / 깨달음

His experience gave him valuable insights into leadership.

그의 경험은 그에게 리더쉽에 관한 가치 있는 통찰력을 주었다.

05. unpredictable situation

예측할 수 없는 상황

Life is full of unpredictable situations.

삶은 예측할 수 없는 상황들로 가득하다.

06. numerous experiences

수많은 경험

Traveling to different countries has provided me with numerous experiences.

여러 국가를 여행하는 것은 나에게 수많은 경험을 제공해 주었다.

07. embrace diversity
다양성을 포용하다/받아들이다

It's essential to embrace diversity in the workplace.
일터에서 다양성을 포용하는 것은 필수적이다.

08. keep distance
거리를 유지하다

She keeps her distance from people she doesn't know well.
그녀는 잘 알지 못하는 사람들에게 거리를 유지한다.

09. open-minded
열려 있는 마음가짐의

Being open-minded is important when discussing new ideas.
열려 있는 마음을 가지는 것은 새로운 아이디어를 논의할 때 중요하다.

10. awkward moment
어색한 순간

The awkward moment during the meeting made everyone uncomfortable.
미팅 도중의 어색한 순간은 모든 사람을 불편하게 만들었다.

>> 앞에서 학습한 표현들을 활용하여 다음 문장을 영작하시오.

01. 전 세계를 여행하는 것은 사람들이 그들의 시야를 넓힐 수 있게 한다.

02. 이것은 그들이 미래에 예측할 수 없는 상황을 헤쳐 나가는 데 필요한 가치 있는 통찰력을 준다.

03. 하지만 다양성을 포용하는 방법을 배우는 것은 흥미진진했다.

Practice

TOEFL Writing

Your professor is teaching a class. Write a post responding to the professor's question.

In your response, you should:

- express and support your opinion
- make a contribution to the discussion

An effective response will contain at least 100 words.
You will have 10 minutes to write it.

Dr. Logan

As we explore the enriching aspects of travel, let's delve into the topic of how people can benefit from traveling from all around the world. We often hear the saying, "People can benefit from traveling from all around the world." What are your thoughts on this statement? Do you believe that travel can provide significant advantages?

Noah

I strongly agree with the statement. Traveling offers a unique opportunity for individuals to broaden their horizons, immerse themselves in different cultures, and gain a deeper understanding of the world. It allows us to break free from our comfort zones, challenge our perspectives, and foster personal growth.

Helen

While I agree that travel can be beneficial, I believe that academic studies should still remain a top priority. Education provides a strong foundation and equips individuals with essential knowledge and skills. However, incorporating travel experiences into one's educational journey can enhance their understanding of diverse cultures and global issues, providing a more holistic and well-rounded education.

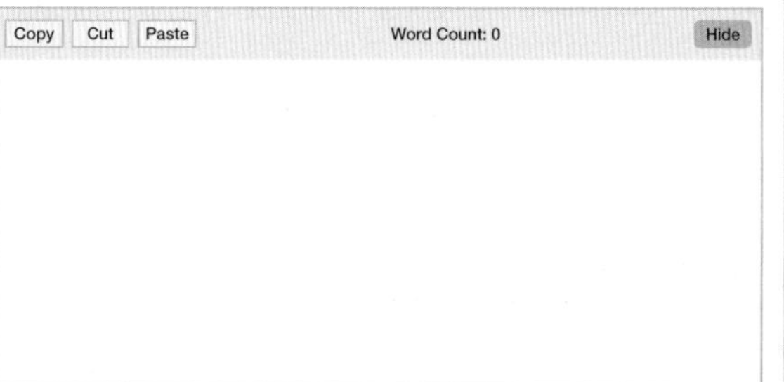

아웃라인

일반적 진술

traveling the world: broaden perspectives → exposure to different matters they haven't experienced before → get valuable insights for the future

구체화 사례

example → a friend who often moved + had numerous experiences → not challenging but exciting to learn how to embrace diversity → traveling all over the world with that friend → me: keeping distance from differences → him: open-minded to everything

답변 완성하기

일반적 진술

From my perspective, both made excellent statements, but I'm on the same page as

구체화 사례

A perfect example of this is a close friend of mine.

Lesson

05 조언 관련 주제

'인턴십, 사회 경험, 자원봉사 활동, 실수를 통한 배움' 관련 주제는 일관된 아이디어로 답변을 전개할 수 있다. 서로 다른 상황이지만 다름과 새로움을 통해서 가지고 있지 못했던 것에 노출이 되고, 그것으로 인한 견문의 확장과 관련 있는 내용으로 전개할 수 있기 때문이다. 다음의 표현을 익혀둔다면, 별도의 brainstorming 과정 없이도 관련 주제에 대해서 빠르게 정확한 답변을 기술할 수 있다.

01. gain a lot of advice 많은 조언을 얻다

Traveling can help you gain a lot of advice.

여행은 많은 조언을 얻는 데 도움이 될 수 있다.

02. a significant impact 지대한 영향

Receiving guidance from my mentor had a significant impact on my decisions.

멘토로부터 지도를 받은 것은 내 결정에 지대한 영향을 미쳤다.

03. valuable advice 가치 있는 조언

She offered me valuable advice on managing stress.

그녀는 스트레스 관리에 관한 가치 있는 조언을 해 주었다.

04. evaluate objectively 객관적으로 평가하다

When giving feedback, it's essential to evaluate objectively for personal growth.

피드백을 줄 때, 개인의 성장을 위해 객관적으로 평가하는 것이 필수적이다.

05. introverted personality 내성적인 성격

For those with an introverted personality, seeking small group interactions can be valuable advice for social growth.

내성적 성격을 가진 사람들에게는 소그룹 상호 작용을 추구하는 것이 사회적 성장을 위한 가치 있는 조언일 수 있다.

06. integrate with new people 새로운 사람들과 어울리다

When starting a new job, the advice to integrate with new people can enhance your professional experience.

새로운 일을 시작할 때, 새로운 사람들과 어울리는 것에 대한 조언은 여러분의 전문적인 경험을 향상시킬 수 있다.

07. learn from real-world experience 실제 경험으로부터 배우다

In pursuing success, valuable advice is to learn from real-world experience.
성공을 추구할 때 소중한 조언은 실제 경험으로부터 배우는 것이다.

08. contemplate matters 문제를 심사숙고하다

When facing challenges, wise advice is to contemplate matters deeply.
도전에 직면했을 때, 현명한 조언은 문제를 심사숙고하는 것이다.

09. practical advice 실용적인 조언

In difficult situations, practical advice can be your guiding light.
어려운 상황에서는, 실용적인 조언이 당신의 길잡이가 될 수 있다.

10. mental growth 정신적인 성장

Seeking diverse experiences contributes to mental growth.
다양한 경험을 추구하는 것은 정신적인 성장에 기여한다.

>> 앞에서 학습한 표현들을 활용하여 다음 문장을 영작하시오.

01. 이러한 경험은 그들이 예측할 수 없는 상황을 헤쳐 나가는 데 실용적이고 가치 있는 조언을 제공한다.

02. 처음에는 새로운 사람들과 어울리고 실제 경험으로부터 배우는 것이 불편하고 힘들었다.

03. 이러한 가치 있는 경험은 나에게 실용적인 조언뿐만 아니라 나의 정신적인 성장에도 기여했다.

Practice

TOEFL Writing

Your professor is teaching a class. Write a post responding to the professor's question.

In your response, you should:

- express and support your opinion
- make a contribution to the discussion

An effective response will contain at least 100 words.
You will have 10 minutes to write it.

Dr. Bliss

I'd like you to share your recent experiences that have had a significant impact on your lives. It's remarkable how diverse experiences can shape our perspectives and contribute to personal growth. So, please describe a new experience you have had recently that significantly impacted your life. Explain how this experience has influenced your perspective and personal growth.

James

Recently, I had the opportunity to participate in a volunteer program in a rural community. This experience has had a profound impact on my life. It exposed me to the realities and challenges faced by underprivileged communities, deepening my empathy and understanding of social issues. Interacting with the locals and working together to improve their living conditions sparked a sense of purpose and a desire to contribute positively to society.

Emma

In contrast, my recent experience was completing a research internship at a prestigious laboratory. This opportunity allowed me to work closely with leading scientists in my field of interest. Through this experience, I gained valuable insights into cutting-edge research and acquired practical laboratory skills. It reinforced my passion for scientific inquiry and provided clarity regarding my career path.

Copy | Cut | Paste | Word Count: 0 | Hide

아웃라인

일반적 진술

advice from experiences → valuable and practical advice for future → through the experiences, evaluate oneself objectively → better life in the future

구체화 사례

example → me: less sociable → live in my own world → internship as a graduation requirement → challenging to learn from the internship opportunity → get used to the situation → got to contemplate a lot of matters → gained advice + mental growth

답변 완성하기

일반적 진술

From my perspective, both made excellent statements, but I would like to add that

구체화 사례

A perfect example of this is my own experience.

Lesson

06 편리함 관련 주제

'발명, 인터넷, 컴퓨터, 여러 과학 기술' 관련 주제들은 일관된 아이디어로 답변을 전개할 수 있다. 언급된 모든 것이 편리함을 제공한다는 내용으로 전개할 수 있기 때문이다. 다음의 표현을 익혀둔다면, 별도의 brainstorming 과정 없이도 관련 주제에 대해서 빠르게 정확한 답변을 기술할 수 있다.

01. provide convenience 편리함을 제공하다

Smartphones provide convenience for quick communication.
스마트폰은 빠른 소통을 위한 편리함을 제공한다.

02. replace traditional offline settings 전통적인 오프라인 환경을 대체하다

Online stores have started to replace traditional offline settings for shopping.
온라인 쇼핑은 전통적인 오프라인 환경을 대체하기 시작했다.

03. unnecessary process 불필요한 과정

Eliminating unnecessary processes enhances convenience.
불필요한 과정을 제거하면 편의성이 향상된다.

04. tedious process 번거로운 과정

Completing paperwork by hand can be a tedious process.
손으로 서류 작업을 완료하는 것은 번거로운 과정일 수 있다.

05. online video chat 온라인 화상 채팅

We had an online video chat with our overseas relatives.
우리는 해외에 사는 친척들과 온라인 화상 채팅을 했다.

06. variety of functions 다양한 기능들

The smartphone offers a variety of functions, making life more convenient.
스마트폰은 다양한 기능을 제공하여 삶을 더 편리하게 만든다.

07. useful features 유용한 기능들

The new software update added many useful features.
새로운 소프트웨어 업데이트는 많은 유용한 기능들을 추가했다.

08. communicate on a daily basis 매일 소통하다

My best friend and I communicate on a daily basis.
나의 친한 친구와 나는 매일 소통한다.

09. travel a long distance 장거리를 이동하다

She had to travel a long distance to attend the conference.
그녀는 학회에 참석하기 위해 장거리를 이동해야 했다.

10. inconvenient offline process 불편한 오프라인 과정

Submitting paper applications can be an inconvenient offline process.
종이 신청서를 제출하는 것은 불편한 오프라인 과정일 수 있다.

>> 앞에서 학습한 표현들을 활용하여 다음 문장을 영작하시오.

01. 이로써 사람들은 불필요하거나 번거로운 과정을 거치지 않게 되었다.

02. 그의 친구가 다른 도시로 이사를 가면서 그는 온라인 화상 채팅 플랫폼에 가입했다.

03. 그가 웹사이트에 접속했을 때, 그것이 유용한 기능을 가지고 있다는 것을 발견했다.

Practice

TOEFL Writing

Your professor is teaching a class. Write a post responding to the professor's question.

In your response, you should:
- express and support your opinion
- make a contribution to the discussion

An effective response will contain at least 100 words.
You will have 10 minutes to write it.

Dr. Ethan

Good day, class. Scientific discoveries and technological innovations have been instrumental in shaping the world as we know it. Today, we'll delve into a captivating question: "Which significant scientific breakthrough or technological innovation from the past two centuries would you select as a crucial advancement?" Let's explore the remarkable achievements that have transformed our lives.

Daniel

Thank you, Professor. When considering significant advancements from the past two centuries, I would definitely pick the discovery of antibiotics. When Alexander Fleming stumbled upon penicillin in 1928, it revolutionized medicine and saved countless lives. The ability to treat bacterial infections transformed healthcare, making surgery safer and preventing deaths from once-fatal diseases.

Judy

I understand the importance of antibiotics, but I'd select the development of the computer. Starting from the 1960s, the computer has changed the way we communicate, work, and access information. It has connected people globally, accelerated research and innovation, and transformed industries. Today, it's an integral part of modern life, driving progress in countless fields.

Copy | Cut | Paste | Word Count: 0 | Hide

아웃라인

일반적 진술

the Internet: provide convenience → communicate with people anytime → replace traditional offline settings → × go through tedious process

구체화 사례

example → cousin's friend moved → signed up for online video chat → useful features to communicate → × travel a long distance in person

답변 완성하기

일반적 진술

From my perspective, both made excellent statements, but I would like to add that

구체화 사례

A perfect example of this is my cousin.

Lesson

07 시간 활용 관련 주제

'계획적인 생활, 인터넷을 이용한 정보 습득, 소통 상황' 관련 주제들은 일관된 아이디어로 답변을 전개할 수 있다. 언급된 모든 것이 시간을 효과적으로, 현명하게 활용할 수 있도록 도와주는 수단 / 방법이라고 전개할 수 있기 때문이다. 다음의 표현을 익혀둔다면, 별도의 brainstorming 과정 없이도 관련 주제에 대해서 빠르게 정확한 답변을 기술할 수 있다.

01. effective time management 효과적인 시간 관리

Effective time management increases productivity.
효과적인 시간 관리는 생산성을 증가시킨다.

02. a considerable amount of time 상당한 시간

She saved a considerable amount of time by using the shortcut.
그녀는 지름길을 이용해서 상당한 시간을 절약했다.

03. utilize time efficiently 효율적으로 시간을 이용하다

Learning to prioritize tasks helps you utilize time efficiently.
작업의 우선순위를 정하는 것을 배우는 것은 시간을 효율적으로 활용하는 데 도움이 된다.

04. at a faster pace 빠른 속도로

She completed the project at a faster pace than expected.
그녀는 예상보다 빠른 속도로 프로젝트를 완료했다.

05. outstanding performance 눈에 띄는 성과

Her dedication and hard work led to outstanding performance.
그녀의 헌신과 고된 노력은 눈에 띄는 성과를 이끌었다.

06. teaching assistant 조교

The teaching assistant managed her time effectively.
조교는 그녀의 시간을 효과적으로 관리했다.

07. go smoothly 부드럽게 흘러가다/진행되다

The meeting didn't go smoothly due to technical issues.
그 모임은 기술적인 이슈 때문에 부드럽게 진행되지 못했다.

08. in advance 미리

She booked her flight tickets in advance to get a discount.
그녀는 할인을 받기 위해서 미리 비행기 표를 예약했다.

09. end up saving time 결국 시간을 절약하다

Using a shortcut on the commute can end up saving time.
통근길에 지름길을 이용하는 것은 결국 시간을 절약할 수 있다.

10. complete on schedule 예정대로 완료하다

She completed the project on schedule.
그녀는 프로젝트를 예정대로 완료했다.

>> 앞에서 학습한 표현들을 활용하여 다음 문장을 영작하시오.

01. 미리 구체적인 계획을 세우는 것은 효과적인 시간 관리에 크게 기여할 수 있다.

02. 구체적인 계획을 갖는 것은 개인들이 더 효율적으로 시간을 활용하는 데 도움이 된다.

03. 그는 상당한 시간을 절약하고, 예정대로 조교 업무를 완료하게 되었다.

Practice

TOEFL Writing

Question 2 of 2

Your professor is teaching a class. Write a post responding to the professor's question.

In your response, you should:

- express and support your opinion
- make a contribution to the discussion

An effective response will contain at least 100 words.
You will have 10 minutes to write it.

Dr. Joanna

It's interesting to see the contrasting viewpoints regarding the benefits of structured plans versus the advantages of being flexible and open to new experiences. Each approach has its merits, and it ultimately depends on individual preferences and circumstances. Some people make a specific plan for their time in advance, while others make instant plans and just go with the flow. Which lifestyle do you prefer?

Justin

Personally, I prefer making specific plans in advance. Having a well-thought-out schedule allows me to prioritize my tasks, manage my time effectively, and stay organized. By planning ahead, I can set clear goals, allocate sufficient time for each activity, and ensure that I make progress towards my objectives. This approach also helps me maintain a sense of discipline and focus, as I have a road map to guide my actions.

Anna

I personally prefer going with the flow. I find that being spontaneous allows me to embrace new opportunities, adapt to unexpected situations, and remain flexible. Sometimes, rigid plans can limit creativity and prevent me from exploring different avenues. By going with the flow, I can seize the present moment, follow my instincts, and embrace serendipity. It allows me to be more open-minded, responsive to changes, and comfortable with uncertainty.

Copy | Cut | Paste | Word Count: 0 | Hide

정답 및 해석 | P. 187

아웃라인

일반적 진술

making specific plan: effective time management → instant plan: time is wasted → specific plan: utilize time efficiently → handle tasks at a faster pace + focus better + outstanding performance

구체화 사례

example → cousin who used to make instant plans + go with the flow → assist professor as T.A. → x enough time for T.A. work → change lifestyle by making specific plans → save time + complete T.A. work on schedule

답변 완성하기

일반적 진술

From my perspective, both made excellent statements, but I'm on the same page as, __________

구체화 사례

A perfect example of this is my cousin, __________

Actual Test 1

TOEFL Writing

Question 1 of 2

In the late 14th century, an unknown poet from the Midlands composed four poems titled *Pearl*, *Sir Gawain and the Green Knight*, *Patience*, and *Cleanness*. This collection of poems is referred to as *Cotton Nero A.x* and the author is often referred to as the Pearl Poet. Up to this day, there have been many theories regarding the identity of this poet, and these are three of the most popular ones.

The first theory is that the author's name was Hugh, and it is based on the *Chronicle of Andrew of Wyntoun*. In the chronicle, an author called Hucheon (little Hugh) is credited with writing three poems, one of which is about the adventures of Gawain. Not only that, but all three poems are written in alliterative verse, as are all four of the poems in *Cotton Nero A.x*. Since they are written in the same style and one poem from each set concerns Gawain, some people contend that all of the *Cotton Nero A.x* poems were written by Hugh.

The second theory is that John Massey was the poet, and it is supported by another poem called *St. Erkenwald* and penmanship. Although the actual authorship of *St. Erkenwald* is unknown, John Massey was a poet who lived in the correct area and time for scholars to attribute it to him. This manuscript was written in very similar handwriting to that of the Pearl Poet, which indicates that one person is likely the author of all five of the poems.

The third theory is that the poems were actually written by different authors from the same region of England. This comes from the fact that there is little linking the poems to each other. Two are concerned with the Arthur legends, but the only link connecting the other two is that they describe the same area of the countryside. They also seem to be written in the same dialect. Taken together, these facts indicate that they were written in the same region, but they probably were not written by the same person.

W_AT1

TOEFL Writing

Question 1 of 2

TOEFL Writing

Question 1 of 2

Directions : You have 20 minutes to plan and write your response. Your response will be judged on the quality of your writing and on how well your response presents the points in the lecture and the relationship to the reading passage. Typically, an effective response will be 150 to 225 words.

Questions : Summarize the points made in the lecture. Be sure to explain how they oppose the specific points made in the reading passage.

In the late 14th century, an unknown poet from the Midlands composed four poems titled *Pearl*, *Sir Gawain and the Green Knight*, *Patience*, and *Cleanness*. This collection of poems is referred to as *Cotton Nero A.x* and the author is often referred to as the Pearl Poet. Up to this day, there have been many theories regarding the identity of this poet, and these are three of the most popular ones.

The first theory is that the author's name was Hugh, and it is based on the *Chronicle of Andrew of Wyntoun*. In the chronicle, an author called Hucheon (little Hugh) is credited with writing three poems, one of which is about the adventures of Gawain. Not only that, but all three poems are written in alliterative verse, as are all four of the poems in *Cotton Nero A.x.* Since they are written in the same style and one poem from each set concerns Gawain, some people contend that all of the *Cotton Nero A.x* poems were written by Hugh.

The second theory is that John Massey was the poet, and it is supported by another poem called *St. Erkenwald* and penmanship. Although the actual authorship of *St. Erkenwald* is unknown, John Massey was a poet who lived in the correct area and time for scholars to attribute it to him. This manuscript was written in very similar handwriting to that of the Pearl Poet, which indicates that one person is likely the author of all five of the poems.

The third theory is that the poems were actually written by different authors from the same region of England. This comes from the fact that there is little linking the poems to each other. Two are concerned with the Arthur legends, but the only link connecting the other two is that they describe the same area of the countryside. They also seem to be written in the same dialect. Taken together, these facts indicate that they were written in the same region, but they probably were not written by the same person.

TOEFL Writing

Question 2 of 2

Your professor is teaching a class. Write a post responding to the professor's question.

In your response, you should:
- express and support your opinion
- make a contribution to the discussion

An effective response will contain at least 100 words.
You will have 10 minutes to write it.

Dr. Michael

Good day, class. As we navigate through the intricacies of resource allocation in universities, a pressing question emerges: "Should universities give the same amount of money to their students' sports activities as they give to their university libraries?" This topic invites us to consider the equilibrium between physical and intellectual development. In the pursuit of a comprehensive discussion, let's explore the dynamics of funding priorities.

Ian

Thank you, Professor. I find merit in the idea that universities should allocate equal funding to sports activities and libraries. While libraries are crucial for academic pursuits, sports play a pivotal role in students' holistic development. Investing in sports fosters physical well-being, teamwork, and a sense of community. These aspects contribute significantly to a student's overall educational experience.

Linda

I appreciate Ian's perspective, but I lean towards a different stance. I believe that universities should prioritize allocating funds based on academic needs rather than equal distribution. Libraries are the heart of academic resources, supporting research, study, and intellectual growth. While sports are valuable for physical well-being, the primary mission of a university is academic excellence. Therefore, a greater allocation to libraries aligns more closely with the core educational mission of universities.

Actual Test 2

TOEFL Writing

Question 1 of 2

Researchers have found that wind turbines kill hundreds of thousands of bats every year. This mostly happens because many migrating bat species fly through areas where wind farms are built, but even non-migrating species are being killed. For this reason, it is important to develop ways to protect bats from wind turbines. Here are three strategies that could help to protect bats.

First, the most basic solution is to avoid building wind turbines in areas where bats are common. Since migrating bats follow the same paths every year, it is easy to figure out where they usually fly and not build in those areas. Bat species that do not migrate usually sleep in caves, and these are also easy to locate and avoid. By carefully researching where bats live and fly, we can build wind farms in areas where they will have little effect on bats.

Second, power companies can protect bats by changing their operating schedules. They can shut down their turbines at night, when bats are most active. If the turbines are not moving, the bats can safely fly around them. This would have little effect on the power companies since the demand for electricity is much lower at night. In fact, one wind power company in the U.S. tested out this method, and they reported far fewer bat deaths with only a tiny loss in annual power generation.

Third, the power companies can use radar to discourage the bats from coming near the turbines. Bats dislike radar waves, which is why they usually avoid areas where radar is used, like airports. So if radar emitters are installed in wind farms and on wind turbines, that will make the bats avoid the area. This method would be ideal, since it keeps the bats safe and allows the wind turbines to operate at any time.

TOEFL Writing

Question 1 of 2

TOEFL Writing

Question 1 of 2

Directions : You have 20 minutes to plan and write your response. Your response will be judged on the quality of your writing and on how well your response presents the points in the lecture and the relationship to the reading passage. Typically, an effective response will be 150 to 225 words.

Questions : Summarize the points made in the lecture. Be sure to explain how they oppose the specific points made in the reading passage.

Researchers have found that wind turbines kill hundreds of thousands of bats every year. This mostly happens because many migrating bat species fly through areas where wind farms are built, but even non-migrating species are being killed. For this reason, it is important to develop ways to protect bats from wind turbines. Here are three strategies that could help to protect bats.

First, the most basic solution is to avoid building wind turbines in areas where bats are common. Since migrating bats follow the same paths every year, it is easy to figure out where they usually fly and not build in those areas. Bat species that do not migrate usually sleep in caves, and these are also easy to locate and avoid. By carefully researching where bats live and fly, we can build wind farms in areas where they will have little effect on bats.

Second, power companies can protect bats by changing their operating schedules. They can shut down their turbines at night, when bats are most active. If the turbines are not moving, the bats can safely fly around them. This would have little effect on the power companies since the demand for electricity is much lower at night. In fact, one wind power company in the U.S. tested out this method, and they reported far fewer bat deaths with only a tiny loss in annual power generation.

Third, the power companies can use radar to discourage the bats from coming near the turbines. Bats dislike radar waves, which is why they usually avoid areas where radar is used, like airports. So if radar emitters are installed in wind farms and on wind turbines, that will make the bats avoid the area. This method would be ideal, since it keeps the bats safe and allows the wind turbines to operate at any time.

TOEFL Writing

Your professor is teaching a class. Write a post responding to the professor's question.

In your response, you should:

- express and support your opinion
- make a contribution to the discussion

An effective response will contain at least 100 words.
You will have 10 minutes to write it.

Dr. Irene

Greetings, class. Today, our focus is on the belief that early exposure to studying abroad is essential for broadening horizons and personal development. The question before us is simple yet profound: Do you agree or disagree with this perspective? Studying overseas at an early age is crucial for evolving as individuals. As we embark on this exploration, let's delve into the dynamics of studying abroad and its potential effects on personal development.

Henry

Thank you, Professor. I wholeheartedly agree with the idea that studying abroad at an early age is crucial for personal development. Experiencing different cultures, meeting diverse people, and navigating unfamiliar environments offer unparalleled opportunities for self-discovery. The challenges and joys of studying abroad shape individuals in ways that traditional education might not.

Lottie

While I acknowledge the benefits Henry highlights, I find myself leaning towards disagreement. Not everyone has the privilege or inclination to study abroad early in life. Moreover, local education can also foster personal development through exposure to diverse perspectives and cultures. The emphasis should be on creating a globally aware curriculum locally, ensuring that all students, regardless of their ability to study abroad, can develop as individuals.

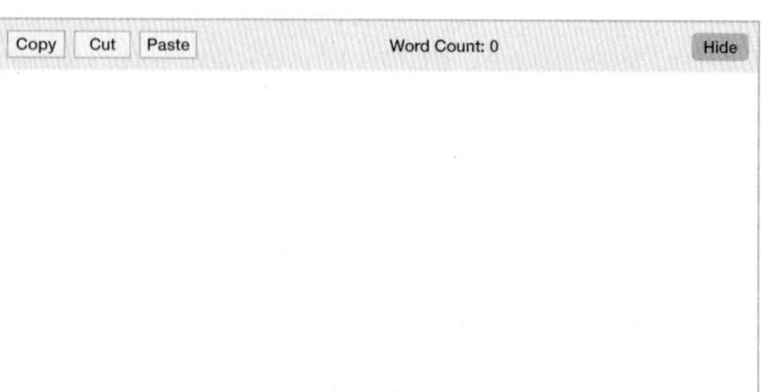

PAGODA TOEFL 80+ R/L/S/W

PAGODA TOEFL 80+ R/L/S/W

PAGODA TOEFL 80+ R/L/S/W

파고다교육그룹 언어교육연구소, 안병남(Bobby Ahn) | 저

PAGODA TOEFL

80+

Reading
Listening
Speaking
Writing

해설서

PAGODA Books

파고다교육그룹 언어교육연구소, 안병남(Bobby Ahn) | 저

PAGODA TOEFL

80+

Reading
Listening
Speaking
Writing

해설서

PAGODA Books

Reading

I. Identifying Details

Lesson 01 Sentence Simplification

본서 I P. 22

Practice

01 A　02 C　03 1. B　2. D　04 1. D　2. B

Practice

본서 I P. 24

01

잉카의 제물

잉카의 성직자들이 아르헨티나의 눈 덮인 산 정상에서 세 명의 어린 아이들을 제물로 바친 지 5세기가 흐른 뒤, 고고학자들은 그들이 거의 완벽한 상태로 얼어 있는 것을 발견했다. 제물이 된 소년의 사체의 약 2피트 위쪽에서 세 개의 작은 라마 조각상이 발견되었다. 잉카인들이 라마 무리의 다산을 보장받고자 하는 의미에서 제물과 함께 라마 조각상을 바쳤으리라고 추측된다. 세 개의 라마 조각상 앞에는 두 개의 남자 조각상이 있었는데, 하나는 금으로, 다른 하나는 국화조개 껍데기로 만들어져 마치 동물들을 이끄는 것을 시사하는 것 같았다. 이 두 개의 남성 조각상은 둘 중 하나를 나타내기 위해서였을 것이다. 자연에서 라마의 주인이라고 믿는 신들, 아마도 산신을 나타내거나, 또는 신에게 바치는 왕족의 동물 무리 관리를 맡은 잉카의 귀족들을 나타내기 위한 것이었을 것이다.

다음 중 지문에 음영 표시된 문장의 핵심 정보를 가장 잘 표현한 문장은? 오답은 문장의 의미를 크게 왜곡하거나 핵심 정보를 누락하고 있다.

Ⓐ 두 개의 작은 조각상은 자연에서 라마의 주인이었던 산신들이나 신들에게 바치는 제물이 될 왕실 동물을 돌보던 잉카의 통치 계급을 상징하는 것으로 생각된다.

Ⓑ 두 조각상은 아마 산을 관장했던 신이나 신에게 속해 있는 라마 무리를 지켰던 잉카 귀족을 보여주는 듯하다.

Ⓒ 조각상 중 하나는 자연에서 라마의 주인이고, 다른 하나는 신에게 바치는 제물이 될 국왕 소유의 라마 무리를 감독하는 잉카의 관리였던 것으로 생각된다.

Ⓓ 작은 남성 조각상들은 보통 자연에서 라마의 주인으로 생각되는 신, 즉 산신이나 혹은 신에게 바치는 제물을 선택했던 잉카의 왕족을 상징한다.

어휘 priest n 성직자, 사제 I miniature n 축소 모형, 미니어처 I figurine n 작은 조각상 I fertility n 생식력, 비옥함 I herd n (짐승)·떼 I deity n 신, 하느님 I oversee v 감독하다 I dedicated adj 전념하는, 헌신적인

02

화산의 종류

사람들은 화산의 생김새에 관해 정형화된 생각을 가지고 있지만 지질학자들은 일반적으로 화산을 네 가지 주요 형태인 분석구, 복식화산, 방패화산, 용암돔으로 분류한다. 가장 인상적인 산 중 일부는 복식화산들인데, 이들은 때때로 성층화산이라고도 불린다. 이들 화산은 일반적으로 주기적인 용암의 흐름과 화산재 및 분석으로 형성된 가파른 경사와 거대한 대칭 원뿔이 특징이다. 그들은 기저 위로 8천 피트 높이만큼 솟을 수 있다. 이런 형태의 화산 중 유명한 예시로 에콰도르의 코토팍시산, 캘리포니아주의 샤스타산, 워싱턴주의 세인트헬렌스산, 일본의 후지산, 오리건주의 후드산이 있다. 대부분의 복식화산들은 정상에 분화구가 있는데, 분화구에는 하나의 중심 열수구나 열수구 군집이 있을 수 있다. 분화구 벽의 틈이나 원뿔의 경사면에 난 틈에서 용암이 흘러나오면서 용암은 그 원뿔을 더 견고하게 만들어주는 거대 늑골의 역할을 하는 암맥과 융기를 형성한다. 화산이 복식화산이라고 간주되기 위한 필수 특징은 구성 물질이 번갈아 층을 이룸으로써 마그마를 지각 내부 깊은 곳으로부터 솟아오르게 하여 갈라진 금과 균열이 생긴 틈을 통해 쏟아져 나오게 하는 관로 체계를 형성하는 것이다.

다음 중 지문에 음영 표시된 문장의 핵심 정보를 가장 잘 표현한 문장은? 오답은 문장의 의미를 크게 왜곡하거나 핵심 정보를 누락하고 있다.

Ⓐ 복식화산의 층 균일성은 마그마를 깊은 곳으로부터 솟아오르게 하는 관로 체계를 형성하게 해준다.

Ⓑ 마그마를 깊은 곳으로부터 솟아오를 수 있게 해주는 관로 체계는 이런 화산 형태에 그 이름을 부여해 준다.

Ⓒ 이런 형태의 화산은 지구 내 깊은 곳으로부터 마그마를 운반하는 여러 다른 물질 층으로 특징지어진다.

Ⓓ 복식화산은 본질적으로 점성이 있는 마그마의 운반을 위한 관로 체계이다.

어휘 stereotypical adj 정형화된, 진부한 I cinder n 분석, 재, 잉걸불 I cinder cone 분석구 I composite adj 합성의 I composite volcano 복식화산 I stratovolcano n 성층화산 I symmetrical adj 대칭적인 I vent n 통풍구, 환기구 I ridge n 산등성이, 산마루 I conduit system 관로 체계, 관로식 I cluster n 무리, 송이 I spill out 넘쳐흐르다, 쏟아져 나오다 I fissure n 길게 갈라진 틈

03

지구 온난화

지구 온난화는 최근 수십 년에 걸쳐 일어났고 계속 일어날 것이라고 예측되는 지표면 근처의 대기와 대양의 평균 온도 상승을 말한다. 지표면 근처의 평균 대기 온도는 지난 세기에 0.74 ± 0.18 ℃ 상승했다. [1] 기후 변화에 관한 정부간 패널(IPCC)은 "20세기 중반 이래 관측된 세계 평균 기온 상승의 대부분은 인간이 발생시킨 온실 가스의 농도 증가 때문일 가능성이 높다"고 결론을 내렸다. 태양의 변화 같은 자연 현상이 화산과 함께 산업화 이전 시대부터 1950년까지 미미한 온난화 효과를 가져왔을지 모르지만, 1950년부터는 소소한 냉각 효과를 가져오고 있다. 이런 기초적 결론은 최소 30여 개의 과학 협회와 과학원으로부터 지지를 받았다. [2] 흥미롭게도 연구 결과에 대한 세계 일류 과학자들의 지지뿐만 아니라 지구 온난화 동향을 뒷받침하는 풍부한 수집 증거에도 불구하고 여전히 이 현상에 관한 견해를 일축하는 사람들이 있다. 그러나 이런 반대자들은 지구 온난화를 줄이기 위한 조치를 취하는 경우 돈을 잃게 되는 특정 이익 집단에 속한 경우가 많다.

1. 다음 중 지문에 음영 표시된 문장의 핵심 정보를 가장 잘 표현한 문장은? 오답은 문장의 의미를 크게 왜곡하거나 핵심 정보를 누락하고 있다.

Ⓐ 한 기후 변화 단체는 20세기 후반에 산업으로부터 배출된 온실 가스가 전 세계 온도 상승을 야기했다고 믿는다.
Ⓑ 한 단체에 따르면, 인간 활동으로 인해 늘어나는 온실 가스 배출량 때문에 20세기 중반부터 전 세계 온도가 상승하고 있다.
Ⓒ 한 단체가 실시한 연구는 지구 온난화가 많은 공장과 기계가 생산되어 사람을 대체하게 된 산업 혁명 때부터 시작되었다고 시사한다.
Ⓓ 한 단체는 20세기 중반의 폭발적 인구 증가 전까지 평균 세계 온도 상승이 일어나지 않았다는 확실한 증거를 제공했다.

2. 다음 중 지문에 음영 표시된 문장의 핵심 정보를 가장 잘 표현한 문장은? 오답은 문장의 의미를 크게 왜곡하거나 핵심 정보를 누락하고 있다.

Ⓐ 세계적으로 저명한 과학자들에 의해 제공된 증거 때문에 지구 온난화를 의심하는 사람들이 있다.
Ⓑ 세계적인 과학자들은 지구 온난화라고 불리는 현상이 존재한다는 것을 증명할 증거를 이미 충분히 수집했다.
Ⓒ 사람들은 심지어 세계적으로 유명한 과학자조차 믿지 않는데 그 이유는 그들이 자신들의 이론에 관한 충분한 증거를 제공하지 못했기 때문이다.
Ⓓ 몇몇 사람들은 많은 뒷받침 증거와 의견들에도 불구하고 지구 온난화에 관해 여전히 의심을 품고 있다.

어휘 intergovernmental adj 정부간의 | anthropogenic adj 인위적인 | endorse v 지지하다 | trend n 동향, 추세 | ample adj 충분한 | dismiss v 묵살하다, 떨쳐 버리다 | naysayer n 반대론자 | curtail v 축소하다, 삭감하다

04

머리 부상

사람들은 때때로 오토바이를 타는 사람들을 위한 헬멧 관련법과 자전거, 인라인 스케이트, 그리고 다른 많은 여가 활동에 헬멧을 필수 장비로 명시한 규정에 대해 불평한다. [1] 헬멧이 불편할 수는 있어도 헬멧의 사용이 장려되는 확실한 이유가 있는데, 아무도 사고가 언제 일어날지 모르고 오토바이와 자전거를 타는 중에 혹은 여가 활동 중에 일어나는 많은 부상이 머리 부상이라는 점 때문이다. 심각한 머리 부상은 뇌 혈관을 손상시켜 두개강에 출혈을 일으킬 수 있다. 혈액이 경뇌막(보호막)과 두개골(머리뼈) 사이에 스며들면 '경막외 출혈'이라는 질환이 생긴다. 혈류가 아래쪽인 경뇌막과 경막하강으로 흘러들면 '경막하 출혈'이라고 한다. [2] 이런 질환의 증상들은 손상된 혈관이 동맥이냐 정맥이냐에 따라 달라지는데, 이유는 동맥의 혈압이 정맥의 혈압보다 높아서 동맥 손상이 정맥 손상보다 더 급격하고 심각한 신경 조직의 뒤틀림을 유발할 수 있기 때문이다. 머리 부상의 특성은 항상 바로 규명할 수 있는 것이 아니기 때문에 빠른 의료 조치를 받는 것이 중요하다.

1. 다음 중 지문에 음영 표시된 문장의 핵심 정보를 가장 잘 표현한 문장은? 오답은 문장의 의미를 크게 왜곡하거나 핵심 정보를 누락하고 있다.

Ⓐ 헬멧을 쓰는 것은 이륜차를 타는 모든 사람들에게 의무사항이어야 하는데 이는 많은 이륜차 운전자가 이륜차를 타다가 머리에 부상을 입기 때문이다.
Ⓑ 이륜차를 타다 넘어지면 주로 머리에 가장 큰 부상을 입기 때문에 잘 만들어진 헬멧이 필수적이다.
Ⓒ 이륜차 운전자들이 이륜차를 탈 때 안전하게 느끼고 즐거운 시간을 가질 수 있도록 편안한 헬멧을 만드는 것이 시급하다.
Ⓓ 자전거 타기와 같은 적극적인 레크리에이션 활동을 할 때는 사고가 날 경우 머리 부상으로 이어질 가능성이 높기 때문에 헬멧을 착용해야 한다.

2. 다음 중 지문에 음영 표시된 문장의 핵심 정보를 가장 잘 표현한 문장은? 오답은 문장의 의미를 크게 왜곡하거나 핵심 정보를 누락하고 있다.

Ⓐ 동맥 손상은 손상된 부위가 심장에 가까운지 여부에 따라 여러 증상을 일으킨다.
Ⓑ 손상된 혈관이 동맥인 경우 동맥의 혈압이 정맥의 혈압보다 높기 때문에 더 심각한 증상이 발생할 수도 있다.
Ⓒ 동맥 손상은 뇌의 신경 조직에 직접적으로 영향을 미치기 때문에 보통 치명적인 증상으로 이어진다.

Ⓓ 신경 질환에서 동맥은 정맥보다 더 중요한데, 그 이유는 동맥의 혈압이 정맥의 혈압보다 높기 때문이다.

어휘 specify v 명시하다 | gear n 기어, 장비 | a host of 다수의 | cerebral adj 뇌의 | cranial cavity 두개강 | dura mater 경뇌막 | cranium n 두개골 | epidural hemorrhage 경막외 출혈 | subdural hemorrhage 경막하 출혈 | vein n 정맥 | artery n 동맥 | distortion n 뒤틀림, 염좌

Lesson 02 Fact & Negative Fact

본서 | P. 28

Practice

01 A 02 C 03 D 04 C

Practice

본서 | P. 30

01

사구

자연 지리학에서 사구는 퇴적이라는 과정으로 형성된 언덕으로 정의하며, 산에서 침식된 모래를 바람이 모래가 많은 지역으로 나를 때 발생한다. 모래가 목적지에 도착할 때 생기는 모양은 사구의 크기뿐 아니라 그 지역의 풍계에 따라 결정되며, 이 두 가지는 기본적으로 사구의 경사진 측면, 즉 사구활주사면의 수와 위치에 영향을 준다. 뿐만 아니라 사구는 그 활주사면의 위치와 수를 기준으로 분류된다. 모든 사구 종류 중에서 신월사구는 비록 지구의 사구 지역에서 적은 비율만을 차지하지만 지구상에 나타나는 사구 모양 중에서는 가장 일반적이다. 이것은 사구의 크기가 상대적으로 작기 때문인데, 세계 최대의 신월사구는 높이가 최대 30m, 길이와 폭이 4km 정도이다. 신월사구는 오목한 측면에 하나의 활주사면이 나타난다. 또한 한 방향에서 불어오는 바람으로 형성되고, 다른 유형의 사구보다 더 빠르고 멀리 이동할 수 있다는 점도 사구에 관한 연구에서 또 한 가지 중요한 사항이다. 다시 언급하지만 이는 신월사구처럼 작은 사구의 고유한 특성이다.

지문에 의하면, 다음 중 신월사구에 관한 내용으로 사실이 아닌 것은 무엇인가?

Ⓐ 아주 작아서 움직임과 모양이 안정적이다.
Ⓑ 가장 자주 발생하는 사구이다.
Ⓒ 다른 종류보다 더 빠르게 이동할 수 있다.
Ⓓ 다른 사구 종류보다 일반적으로 규모가 더 작다.

어휘 physical geography 지학, 자연 지리학 | define v 정의하다 | dune n 사구 | deposition n 퇴적, 퇴적물 | occur v 발생하다 | erode v 침식되다 | destination n 목적지 | slip face 사구활주사면 | steep adj 가파른 | classify v 분류하다 | prevalent adj 일반적인, 널리 퍼져 있는 | comprise v 구성하다, 차지하다 | relatively adv 상대적으로, 비교적 | display v 보이다 | concave adj 오목한 | consideration n 생각, 고려 | inherent adj 내재하는, 고유의 | trait n 특성

02

갈라파고스 제도

갈라파고스 제도는 남아메리카에서 서쪽으로 900km 거리에 위치한 화산섬 제도이다. 이 섬들은 생물체의 진화에 안성맞춤인데 그 이유는 본토에서 너무 멀지도 가깝지도 않은 위치에 있으면서 동물들이 산발적으로만 이동하게 하기 때문이다. 바람과 해류 같은 자연 현상들은 때때로 제도에 있는 섬에 본토 생물들의 일부 개체를 이동시킨다. 만약 이 개체들이 성공적으로 섬 안에서 번식한다면, 이들의 후손은 거기 자리를 잡을 것이다. 섬을 본토와 고립시키는 거대한 바다는 지역적으로 동종의 다른 개체와의 교류를 방해한다. 그러한 이유로 수 세대가 지나면 이 섬의 동물군은 본토의 종과 달라진다. 달라진 동물군의 개체는 차례로 제도에 있는 다른 섬들에 대량 서식하고, 진화 과정을 반복한다. 섬들 사이의 서로 다른 서식지와 도태압(바람직하지 못한 유전형이나 표현형을 제거하는 정도)은 조상이 되는 종들과 더 많은 차이를 낳는다. 예를 들어 갈라파고스 제도에 사는 일명 다윈의 핀치로 알려져 있는 핀치는 폭풍우에 의해 날아온 것으로 여겨졌다. 오랜 시간이 흐르고 수백 세대가 지나고 난 이후 이 핀치들은 15개의 서로 다른 종들로 진화했고, 모두 부리의 크기와 모양이 다르다. 이런 다양한 핀치들은 동일한 조상에서 왔으나 섬마다 눈에 띄게 다른 행동적 특성을 가지고 있는 다른 종들로 분리되었다.

지문에 의하면, 섬에 사는 종들이 본토의 동물군과 다른 이유는

Ⓐ 적이 없어서
Ⓑ 서로간에 강한 사회적 관계를 수립해서
Ⓒ 광대한 바다가 장애물 역할을 해서
Ⓓ 수 세대에 걸쳐 섬에서 진화해서

어휘 sporadically adv 산발적으로 | expanse n 지역, 영역 | impede v 지연시키다, 방해하다 | diverge v 갈라지다, 나뉘다 | colonize v 대량 서식하다, 식민지로 만들다 | foster v 조성하다 | finch n 되새류(부리가 짧은 작은 새) | beak n 부리

03

문명의 발생

여러 출처에서 나온 자료들이 농업의 증거에 관한 명확한 최초의 사례들이 기원전 5천년 경 메소포타미아, 북아프리카, 인도, 중국의 어딘가로 거슬러 올라간다는 것을 보여준다. 분명히 초반에 농업은 식량을 얻는 주된 방법이 아니었고 주로 식량을 얻는 방법이었던 수렵과 채집을 보완하는 역할만 했을 뿐이었다. 곡식 기르기를 시도한 최초의 사람들은 전적으로 곡식 경작만을 통해 스스로 살아갈 만큼 믿을 수 있는 기술이나 지식을 가지고 있지 않았다. 그러나 농업의 획기적인 발전은 강 유역 거주자들이 범람원에 씨앗을 심었을 때 시작되었다. 이것은 사람들이 불규칙적이고 계절적인 비에 의존하기보다 강에서 안정적인 물 공급을 얻게 해 주었다. 이를 통해 유목 생활을 하던 사람들의 무리가 한 곳에 정착하여 사회를 형성할 수 있게 되면서 사람들이 살아가는 방식이 바뀌었다. 식량 유용성의 증가는 인구 확산의 계기가 되었고, 결과적으로 사람들의 요구를 충족시키기 위해 도시 내로 물을 끌어오는 관개를 낳았다. 잉여 농작물로 인해, 정착 농업은 재산권 및 법을 시행할 법률 구조의 발달을 불러왔다. 이것은 또한 더 복잡하고 위계질서가 있는 정부 기관에 대한 개념을 발전시켰다.

지문에 의하면, 조직화된 정부의 발전을 야기한 것은 무엇인가?

Ⓐ 농업에 덜 의존하도록 만든 믿을 만한 사냥 기술
Ⓑ 침입자로부터 수확물을 보호할 필요로 이어진 식량 유용성의 증가
Ⓒ 낚시를 위해 공동체 안으로 끌어들인 수원
Ⓓ 재산권법을 시행할 필요성

어휘 supplement n 보충(물), 추가 | sustain v 살아가게 하다, 지속하게 하다 | nomadic adj 유목의, 방랑의 | trigger v 촉발시키다 | expansion n 확대, 확장 | irrigation n 관개 | surplus n 과잉 | give rise to ~이 생기게 하다 | hierarchical adj 계급에 따른

04

체온 조절

모든 생물체들은 주변 환경에 따른 외부 온도에 영향을 받는다. 주변 환경 온도의 변화는 동물의 체온을 변하게 한다. 그래서 체온을 조절하는 동물의 능력은 극단적 환경에서의 생존에 필수적이다. 그러한 이유로 극도로 추운 기후의 토착 동물들은 체온 조절을 위한 다양한 방법을 발달시켰다. 대다수의 육상 포유류와 새는 두꺼운 털이나 깃털을 길러 열의 흐름을 줄이고 따뜻함을 유지하는 데 필요한 에너지 비용을 낮춘다. 예를 들어, 겨울 털을 갖춘 북극 여우는 따뜻함을 유지하기 위해 신진 대사율을 변화시키지 않고도 영하 50도의 날씨에서도 편하게 앉아있을 수 있다. 동물이 사용하는 또 다른 방법은 혈액의 흐름을 통제하여 열 손실을 막기 위해 말단부 순환을 차단하는 것이다. 알래스카 허스키 개는 38도로 심부 체온을 유지하면서도 사지의 온도는 14도로 유지하고 발바닥은 0도로 유지한다. 그 결과 대부분의 중요한 기관이 있는 몸 중심부의 온도보다 팔다리의 온도를 몇 도 낮춰 열의 손실을 막을 수 있다. 북극곰의 경우 두꺼운 털과 11센티미터에 달하는 지방층, 빛에서 열을 흡수하는 어두운 피부색이 북극곰을 뛰어난 단열 기계로 만든다. 일부 동물은 몸의 열을 보존하기 위해 공 모양으로 몸을 둥글게 하는 등의 행동 적응 방식을 갖고 있다.

지문에 의하면, 추운 지역에서의 삶을 위한 북극곰의 적응 방법으로 언급되지 않은 것은

Ⓐ 두꺼운 지방 조직
Ⓑ 두꺼운 털층
Ⓒ 혈류에 변화를 줘서 추위를 누그러뜨리는 능력
Ⓓ 태양을 흡수하는 피부색

어휘 thermoregulation n 체온 조절 | ambient adj 환경의, 주변의 | fluctuate v 계속 변화하다, 변동을 거듭하다 | extreme adj 극도의, 극심한 | indigenous adj 원산의, 토착의 | plumage n 깃털 | metabolic adj 신진대사의 | forelimb n 앞다리 | dense adj 빽빽한, 조밀한 | peripheral adj 주변의, 지엽적인 | limb n 팔, 날개 | possess v 소유하다

Lesson 03 Vocabulary

본서 | P. 34

Practice

01 1. A 2. C   02 1. B 2. B   03 1. A 2. A   04 1. D 2. B

Practice

본서 | P. 36

01

툰드라

세계의 모든 생물군계들 중에서 툰드라는 가장 춥고 혹독한 환경으로 알려져 있다. 툰드라는 길고 추운 겨울과 매우 짧은 여름을 지닌다. 강수량이 거의 없고, 토지가 척박하며 성장 시기가 짧아서 생물종이 적고 인간 정착지가 거의 없다. 게다가 툰드라는 약 20피트 깊이로 뻗어 있는 영구 동토층이라 불리는 영구적으로 얼어붙은 토양 지층을 가지고 있다. 이러한 환경을 견디기 위해 툰드라의 동식물상은 특별한 적응력을 가

지고 있다. 툰드라에 사는 식물들은 여름에는 녹는 표토에 얕은 뿌리를 내림으로써 살아 남을 수 있고, 동물들은 새끼를 짧은 여름 동안 빨리 낳고 길러내는 식으로 적응해왔다. 툰드라는 서로 다른 두 가지 종류가 있는데, 북극 지방에서 찾을 수 있는 북극 툰드라와 히말라야나 알프스의 가장 높은 봉우리 같은 높고 추운 산의 정상에 위치한 알파인 툰드라다.

1. 지문의 단어 'frigid(추운)'와 의미상 가장 가까운 것은

Ⓐ 추운　Ⓑ 휴면 중인　Ⓒ 존재하는　Ⓓ 끈질긴

2. 지문의 단어 'dwelling(사는)'과 의미상 가장 가까운 것은

Ⓐ 지지하는　Ⓑ 대량 살육하는　Ⓒ 거주하는　Ⓓ 인접하는

어휘 biome n 생물군계 | devoid adj 결여된, ~가 없는 | precipitation n 강수량 | endure v 견디다, 참다 | fauna n 동물군계 | settlement n 정착 | barren adj 불모의, 황폐한 | thaw v 녹다

02

동물의 주기

특정 중요 주기는 일반적으로 동물의 행동을 규제한다. 이러한 순환 주기가 가장 분명하게 드러난 형태 중 하나는 일주율이라고 불리는데, 이것은 24시간을 바탕으로 한 행동 유형을 일컫는다. 이 체내 시계는 배고픔, 수면, 배설 같은 동물의 기초적인 욕구에 영향을 미친다. 일상적 순환과 더불어 동물들은 또한 연 단위로 작용하는 일 년 주기의 리듬으로부터 영향을 받는다. 주로 계절적 변화에 의해 결정되는 동물의 연주율은 동면, 번식, 이주 같은 활동을 하게 만든다. 예를 들면, 겨울의 시작 무렵 얼룩다람쥐들은 그 계절 동안 몹시 추운 온도에 대처하는 가장 좋은 방법으로 동면을 택한다. 몸무게를 두 배로 늘리는 것이 길고 추운 겨울의 전제 조건이므로 동면에 들어가기 전 그들은 평소보다 더 많은 음식을 먹는다.

1. 지문의 단어 'onset(시작)'과 의미상 가장 가까운 것은

Ⓐ 통합　Ⓑ 시작　Ⓒ 업적　Ⓓ 풍부함

2. 지문의 구 'cope with(대처하다)'와 의미상 가장 가까운 것은

Ⓐ 고려하다　Ⓑ 다루다　Ⓒ 지지하다　Ⓓ 지연시키다

어휘 manifestation n 명시, 표명, 징후 | circadian adj 24시간 주기의 | behavioral adj 행동의, 행동에 관한 | drive n 충동, 욕구 | excretion n 배설 | circannian adj 1년 주기의 | operate v 작용하다 | annual adj 연간의, 매년의 | hibernation n 동면, 겨울잠 | onset n 시작, 개시 | frigid adj 몹시 추운, 냉담한 | double v 두 배로 되다, 두 배로 만들다 | dormancy n 휴면, 동면 | consume v 먹다, 소모하다 | prerequisite n 전제 조건, 필수 조건

03

생물 사이의 관계

꽃이 없는 경우에도 많은 식물들이 화외밀선이라는 잎사귀나 줄기에 발달된 구조를 통해 꿀을 분비한다. 이러한 식물은 주로 개미가 많은 열대나 온대 지역에서 발견된다. 그들 중 몇몇 종류는 아미노산을 가지고 있지만, 꿀은 주로 수분과 용해된 당으로 이루어져 있다. 이러한 식물들은 개미를 유인하여 공생하는 방법을 발달시켰다. 개미들은 끈질긴 방어자로, 꿀을 먹는 곤충과 다른 초식동물과 같은 침략자로부터 이 식물을 보호한다. 이러한 종의 식물과 개미는 서로가 없으면 살아갈 수 없다. 매우 활동적인 일개미들은 바쁜 생활 방식을 지원해줄 만한 많은 에너지원을 필요로 한다. 따라서 이 식물들은 화외밀을 제공함으로써 개미들에게 충분한 에너지원을 주면서 그들을 이용한다. 이 호의의 대가로 개미는 귀중한 자원에 대해서 그들과 경쟁을 벌이는 다른 곤충으로부터 그 식물을 보호해주고, 또한 이 식물들의 잎을 먹는 초식동물을 내쫓아 준다.

1. 지문의 단어 'persistent(끈질긴)'와 의미상 가장 가까운 것은

Ⓐ 지속적인　Ⓑ 뒤따르는　Ⓒ 확고한　Ⓓ 배타적인

2. 지문의 단어 'Therefore(따라서)'와 의미상 가장 가까운 것은

Ⓐ 그래서　Ⓑ 그럼에도 불구하고　Ⓒ 게다가　Ⓓ 그 동안

어휘 extrafloral adj 꽃 밖의 | nectary n 꿀샘 | stem n 줄기 | temperate adj 기후가 온화한 | amino acid 아미노산 | compete v 경쟁하다 | exploit v 이용하다 | ward off 물리치다, 피하다

---

04 **직접 새기기**

전통적으로 조각품은 미술가에 의해 진흙으로 빚어진 예비 모형에서 시작되었다. 그 다음 그것들은 돌, 회반죽 또는 청동으로 된 완성품을 최종으로 만들어내는 스튜디오 조수들에게 넘겨졌다. 사실상 조수들이 대체로 원래 작가들보다 조각에 훨씬 능숙했기 때문에 신고전주의 조각가가 나무 망치와 끌을 사용하는 일은 매우 드물었다. 그러나 20세기에 직접 새기기가 중간의 점토 모형을 사용하지 않고도 조각을 만들어내는 새로운 방식으로 출현했다. 기억으로부터 또는 대상 그 자체를 두고 작업을 하면서 한 명의 예술가가 단독으로 조각 작업을 했다. 직접 새기기는 형태를 구성하는 접근법으로서 근대 미술의 돌파구 그리고 원시 예술에서 유래한 기법의 부활로 여겨진다. 직접 새기기 기술의 중요한 측면은 표현 수단의 본질을 보여주려는 예술가의 판단력으로, 작가는 그것이 지닌 매력적인 미적, 조직적인 특성을 드러내기 위해 작업한다. 직접 새기기의 재료와 최종 형태는 종종 모양, 짜임새 혹은 사용된 매개체의 결에서 진화한다.

1. 지문의 단어 'adept(능숙한)'와 의미상 가장 가까운 것은

Ⓐ 빠른 Ⓑ 갑작스러운 Ⓒ 튼튼한 Ⓓ 유능한

2. 지문의 단어 'employed(사용된)'와 의미상 가장 가까운 것은

Ⓐ 모인 Ⓑ 이용된 Ⓒ 고려된 Ⓓ 고용된

어휘 preliminary adj 예비의, 최초의 | finalize v 마무리하다, 완결하다 | plaster n 석고, 회반죽 | mallet n 나무 망치 | chisel v 조각하다, 끌로 새기다 | medium n 수단, 재료, 매개체

Lesson 04 Reference

본서 | P. 40

Practice

01 1. A 2. D   02 1. B 2. D   03 1. C 2. B   04 1. C 2. C

Practice

본서 | P. 42

01 **퀼팅**

퀼팅은 두 겹이나 그 이상의 직물을 함께 바느질하는 과정이며 때때로 그 천들 사이에는 속심이 들어간다. 그것은 처음에는 착용자를 추운 날씨에서 보호하기 위한 옷을 만드는 데 사용되었고, 얼마 동안은 갑옷 패딩(갑옷 속에 입는 누빈 옷)으로 사용되었다. 그러나 화기가 등장하면서 그것은 더 이상 충격을 완화하는 기능을 하지 못했다. 따라서 그 이후 그것은 주로 추운 공기를 피하기 위한 단열 덮개로만 사용되어 왔다. 18세기와 19세기에 퀼팅은 흔히 가족 내 또는 더 큰 지역 사회의 여성과 소녀들을 참여시키는 공동 작업이었다. '퀼트 만드는 모임'은 한 팀이 하나의 퀼트를 공동 작업하는 형태로써 여러 지역 사회에서 중요한 사회적 행사였고, 일반적으로 농업 노동력이 많이 요구되는 시기들의 사이인 농한기에 개최되었다. 퀼트는 주로 결혼식 같은 중요한 일생의 사건을 기념하기 위해 만들어졌다. 이 기간에 여성들은 퀼트를 이용해 사회적 이슈에 대한 그들의 의견을 표현하거나 그들 사이의 사회적 유대감을 강화했다.

1. 지문의 단어 'it(그것)'이 가리키는 것은

Ⓐ 퀼트 Ⓑ 옷 Ⓒ 착용자 Ⓓ 날씨

2. 지문의 단어 'their(그들의)'가 가리키는 것은

Ⓐ 행사들 Ⓑ 지역 사회들 Ⓒ 의식들 Ⓓ 여성들

어휘 sew v 바느질하다, 깁다 | layer n 층, 겹 | pad n 패드, 보호대, 완충대 | armor n 갑옷 | firearm n 화기 | insulating adj 단열을 위한 | communal adj 공동의, 공용의 | quilting bee 퀼트를 만드는 여자들의 모임 | agricultural off-season 농한기 | commemorate v 기념하다 | articulate v 분명히 표현하다, 설명하다 | fortify v 강화하다

02 **반향 위치 측정**

1 ➡ 많은 동물들은 주위의 길을 찾거나 중요한 매일의 일을 수행하기 위해 시각에 의지한다. 그러나 일부 동물은 그들의 시력을 거의 쓸모 없게 하는 빛이 희미하거나 어두운 환경에서 사는 한편, 다른 것들은 좋지 않은 시력을 가지고 있어 장애물을 피하고 먹이를 찾는 데 다른 감각

에 의존해야 한다. 고래, 돌고래, 박쥐, 뾰족뒤쥐 같은 이러한 많은 동물이 반향 위치 측정이라 불리는 기술에 의존한다.

2 ➡ 이런 기술을 사용하는 동물은 짧고 높은 음조의 소리를 낸 뒤 다시 튕겨 오는 소리의 반향을 듣는다. 그런 다음 물체의 크기, 움직임의 방향, 그리고 자신들로부터의 거리를 알아내기 위해 반향을 신중히 해석한다. 소리를 발성하는 순간과 울림이 돌아오는 순간의 시간차는 물체와의 거리를 나타낸다. 그 간격이 길면 길수록 그것도 더 멀리 있다. 반향의 음량은 물체의 크기와 질감을 나타낸다. 실제로 반향 위치 측정은 대단히 효과적이어서, 연구원들은 박쥐가 엄청난 속도로 날면서 얇은 전선을 찾고 피하는 데 그것을 사용하는 것을 관찰했다.

1. **1단락의 단어 'others(다른 것들)'가 가리키는 것은**

Ⓐ 일들 Ⓑ 동물들 Ⓒ 환경들 Ⓓ 감각들

2. **2단락의 단어 'it(그것)'이 가리키는 것은**

Ⓐ 기법 Ⓑ 방향 Ⓒ 거리 Ⓓ 물체

어휘 echolocation n 반향 위치 측정 I dimly adv 어둑하게 I shrew n 뾰족뒤쥐 I emit v 내뿜다 I high-pitched adj (소리가) 아주 높은 I echo n 메아리 I bounce v 튀다, 산란하다 I locate v 찾다 I render v (어떤 상태가 되게) 만들다 I interval n 간격

03 **화산**

1 ➡ 화산은 지각 아래서부터 표면 위로 마그마(매우 뜨거운 용해된 암석)를 분출하기 때문에 어떤 사람들은 화산을 지구의 배관 시스템으로 생각한다. 열점 화산으로 알려진 것들이 대륙 판의 표면 아래에 있는 대단히 활동적인 지점에 위치해 있기는 하지만, 화산 폭발은 대부분 대륙판이나 지질 구조판의 가장자리 근처에서 일어난다. 대개 오래 가지 않는 화산들은 육지에서 이전 화산 분화로부터 비롯된 물질의 축적 결과로 나온 넓고 평평한 화산추 또는 굴뚝과 매우 닮은 분석구를 형성한다. 수면 아래의 화산은 때때로 가파른 기둥을 형성하는데 결국 이것은 해수면을 뚫고 올라와 새로운 섬을 형성하게 된다.

2 ➡ 활화산은 현재 계속 증기 및 여러 종류의 용암과 이산화탄소 같은 가스를 내뿜고 있는 화산이다. 또한 화쇄류(화산암 조각으로 만들어진 흐름)를 만들어 내는데 이는 액화된 뜨거운 가스, 재와 암석이 빠르게 이동하는 강이다. 또한 화산재 이류가 될 수도 있는데 이것은 콘크리트의 농도를 지닌 돌, 진흙, 물의 혼합물로 화산에서 빠른 속도로 강 유역까지 흘러 내린다. 활화산이 있는 지역은 종종 인기 있는 관광 지역이 되는데 이는 그것들이 온천, 간헐천, 머드 포트(진흙이 열 때문에 부글부글 끓는 지점)와 같은 자연의 기적을 포함하고 있기 때문이다. 그러나 불행히도 그곳에는 종종 지진도 일어난다.

3 ➡ 어떤 화산이 활동적인 상태인지 아닌지 말하기는 쉽지 않을 수 있다. 일정 기간 활동을 보여주지 않은 화산들은 휴화산으로 분류되지만 그것들은 경고 없이 다시 분화할 잠재적 가능성이 있다. 영구적으로 멈춘 것으로 여겨지는 다른 것들은 사화산으로 분류된다. 사람들은 사화산이 다시는 폭발하지 않을 것이라고 확신한 나머지 이러한 화산의 분화구 몇 군데에 휴양지를 세우기도 했다.

1. **1단락의 단어 'which(이것)'가 가리키는 것은**

Ⓐ 분석구들 Ⓑ 화산들 Ⓒ 기둥들 Ⓓ 섬들

2. **2단락의 단어 'they(그것들)'가 가리키는 것은**

Ⓐ 강 유역들 Ⓑ 활화산이 있는 지역들 Ⓒ 관광 명소들 Ⓓ 지진들

어휘 plumbing system 배관 시스템 I continental adj 대륙의 I tectonic plate 지각판 I hot spot 열점 (뜨거운 마그마를 분출하는 지역) I cinder n 나무나 석탄이 다 타고 남은 재 I cone n 원뿔 I pillar n 기둥 I lava n 용암 I consistency n 농도, 밀도 I pyroclastic adj 화쇄암의 I fluidize v 유동화하다 I hot spring 온천 I geyser n 간헐 온천 I dormant adj 휴면기의 I deem v ~로 여기다 I resort n 리조트, 휴양지 I crater n 분화구

04 **맨틀**

1 ➡ 지구형 행성의 진화 단계 중 첫 번째는 '분화'이며 이것은 밀도에 따라 구성 요소가 분리되는 것이다. 이 단계에서 더 무거운 물질은 지속적으로 중심부를 향해 가라앉아 단단하고 금속성을 지닌 핵을 형성하며 마침내 상대적으로 얇은 지각으로 둘러싸이게 된다. 현재 지구는 세 개의 주요 층으로 구성되어 있다. 우리가 살고 있는 단단하지만 얇은 층은 일반적으로 지각으로 알려져 있다. 용해된 철로 된 중앙의 구는 핵이다. 그리고 맨틀은 둘 사이에 있는 영역으로 사실상 지구 성분의 2/3를 차지한다. 단단한 지각과 달리 맨틀의 본질은 꽤 유동적이며 밀도가 높은 액체와 비슷하다.

2 ➡ 맨틀은 균일하지 않지만 세 가지 다른 구조적 영역을 지니고 있다. 지각과 맨틀이 만나는 지점에는 다양한 종류의 암석이 마구잡이로 뒤섞여 있다. 맨틀 깊이 들어갈수록 암석은 점차 부드러워지면서 연약권을 만들어낸다. 지각의 지질 구조판을 움직일 수 있게 하는 것이 바로 이

지대이다. 이 연약권 아래는 중간권으로 더 연한 광물질이 결정체로 변하는 곳이며 지표면의 암석 판이 침강하고 중심 핵으로부터 슬래그(액체 상태의 광재)가 맨틀로 융기되는 부분이다. 이 지대는 끊임없이 움직이는 지대이기 때문에 열에너지가 중심 핵에서 상승하거나 가끔 지표면까지 전달되는 두껍고 얇은 지점이 형성된다.

3 ➡ 직접적으로 조사될 수 없기 때문에 맨틀의 나머지 부분에 관해서는 많은 것이 알려져 있지 않다. 오히려 지표면 아래 중간권처럼 깊은 곳에서, 하지만 그보다 더 깊은 곳에서는 일어나지 않는 지진의 지진 측정을 통해 연구된다.

1. **1단락의 구 'the two(둘)'가 가리키는 것은**

Ⓐ 행성 진화와 분화 Ⓑ 물질과 밀도 Ⓒ 지각과 핵 Ⓓ 핵과 맨틀

2. **2단락의 구 'this zone(이 지대)'이 가리키는 것은**

Ⓐ 지각 Ⓑ 맨틀 Ⓒ 연약권 Ⓓ 중간권

어휘 terrestrial adj 지구의 | density n 밀도 | metallic adj 금속성의 | core n 핵, 중심 | relatively adv 상대적으로 | crust n 지각 | flexible adj 유동적인 | uniform adj 획일적인, 통일된 | malleable adj (금속이) 가단성이 있는 | tectonic adj 지질 구조의 | slab n 판 | slag n 슬래그, 광재, 화산암재 | constant adj 불변의, 일정한 | seismic adj 지진의, 지진에 의한

II. Making Inference

Lesson 01 Rhetorical Purpose

본서 | P. 46

Practice

01 C 02 B 03 A 04 C

Practice

본서 | P. 48

01

제조업 지역

제조업 지역은 이전에 중공업과 제조업을 경제의 기반으로 했던 미국의 북동부와 중북부 지역을 말한다. 안타깝게도 1960년대 국제 자유무역 협정의 확대는 강철 같은 중공업 제품을 미국에서 생산하기보다 제3세계 국가들에서 생산한 후 미국으로 수입하는 것이 더 저렴하도록 만들었다. 이는 제조업 지역 전체에 걸친 공장 폐쇄로 이어졌고 그 지역 경제의 몰락을 초래했다. 1969년에 시작된 연이은 불황기에 제조업 일자리는 사라지고 저임금 서비스 일자리로 대체되었다. 그 지역의 새 이름인 녹슨 지역은 산업 시기에 남겨져 녹슬어가는 기계를 일컫는 것이자 그 지역의 전반적인 쇠퇴를 비유적으로 일컫는 말이다.

글쓴이가 제조업 지역 논의에서 '제3세계 국가들'을 언급하는 이유는 무엇인가?

Ⓐ 그 지역의 경제가 취약하다는 것을 보여주기 위해서
Ⓑ 그 지역이 그 영향으로부터 회복될 것임을 보여주기 위해서
Ⓒ 그 지역의 경제가 어떻게 퇴보했는지 설명하기 위해서
Ⓓ 경제에 끼친 영향의 심각함을 나타내기 위해서

어휘 recession n 경기 불황 | rust n 녹 | figurative adj 비유적인 | reference n 언급, 언급 대상

02

시조새

시조새는 일반적으로 새라고 여겨지는 가장 오래된 동물 화석인데 그 이유는 이 새의 깃털이 오늘날의 새의 깃털과 구조와 형태 면에서 매우 흡사하기 때문이다. 사실, 발견된 최초로 알려진 시조새 화석은 이 동물이 가졌던 깃털의 흔적을 확실히 보여준다. 그러나 다른 과학자들은 시조새가 공룡에 더 가까웠다고 믿는데, 왜냐하면 새가 가지고 있지 않은 많은 공룡의 특징을 가지고 있기 때문이었다. 오늘날의 새들과 달리 시조새는 뼈가 있는 긴 꼬리는 물론 작은 이빨을 가지고 있었다. 그들의 세 개의 발가락은 발톱을 가지고 있었고 현존하는 새들의 합쳐진 발가락

과 달리 개별적으로 움직였다. 또한 비행과 연관 있는 골격 구조는 불완전하게 발달한 듯 보이고, 이것은 시조새가 아주 먼 거리를 비행하지는 못했을 것이라는 점을 시사한다. 그래서 이러한 구조들은 비행 목적을 위해 진화한 것이 아닐 수도 있는데, 왜냐하면 새나 비행 능력이 진화하기 전에 이미 공룡에서 그러한 것들이 나타났기 때문이다.

글쓴이가 지문에서 '뼈가 있는 긴 꼬리는 물론 작은 이빨'을 언급하는 이유는 무엇인가?

Ⓐ 시조새가 과학자들의 흥미를 끄는 이유를 설명하기 위해
Ⓑ 공룡과 더 비슷한 특징들의 예시를 제시하기 위해
Ⓒ 시조새가 새였다는 사실을 확증하기 위해
Ⓓ 시조새가 사냥감을 사냥했던 방법을 보여주기 위해

어휘 Archaeopteryx n 시조새 I plumage n 깃털 I bony adj 뼈의, 뼈를 가지고 있는 I bear v 갖다, 지니다 I claw n 발톱

---

03 **유럽의 연료**

영국은 18세기에 심각한 에너지 부족 문제를 경험했다. 그 전에는 나무가 연료의 주요한 공급원이자 필수 건축 재료였다. 그러나 대도시의 인구 증가로 나무의 소비가 상승했고 그 결과 영국뿐만 아니라 유럽 대륙 전반에 걸쳐 빠른 산림 벌채 현상이 나타났다. 산림 벌채의 결과로 공급이 제한되었지만 수요는 지속적으로 상승하여 중요한 주택과 산업을 위한 충분한 목재가 없는 지경까지 이르게 되었다. 게다가 석탄 같은 다른 대체 연료는 기반 시설과 알려져 있던 생산 방법이 제한적이었기 때문에 당시로서는 이용할 수가 없었다. 그래서 정제되지 않은 철을 생산하기 위해 용광로에서 철광석을 태우는 데 목재를 필요로 했던 영국의 제철업은 부족한 나무 공급으로 1790년대에 약화되었다. 당시 오스트리아의 거대한 숲은 이 나라로 하여금 영국이 이미 전에 경험했던 것과 같은 문제에 봉착하기 전까지 수십 년 동안 세계에서 가장 큰 철 생산국이 되는 것을 가능하게 했다.

글쓴이가 지문에서 '오스트리아'를 언급하는 이유는

Ⓐ 패턴이 유럽에서 어떻게 반복되었는지 보여주기 위해서
Ⓑ 나무가 에너지원으로 사용하기에 제일 좋은 재료가 아님을 보여주기 위해서
Ⓒ 그 당시 영국이 얼마나 더 진보했는지를 보여주기 위해서
Ⓓ 당시 왜 제철업이 그렇게 중요했는지를 보여주기 위해서

어휘 deforestation n 산림 벌채 I lumber n 목재 I housing n 주택 I coal n 석탄 I infrastructure n 기반 시설, 기초 시설 I iron industry 제철업 I iron ore 철광석 I decade n 10년

---

04 **화석**

화석은 수천 혹은 수백만 년 전 지구에 살았던 많은 식물과 동물이 남긴 흔적 또는 유해이다. 어떤 화석은 식물과 동물이 죽은 후 보존된 조개껍데기나 뼈처럼 생물체의 단단한 부분이 될 수도 있고, 다른 것은 동물들이 이동하며 남겨놓은 자국이나 흔적이 될 수 있다. 화석의 대부분은 퇴적암에서 발견된다. 그러한 화석은 강, 호수, 늪, 바다의 바닥에 모인 진흙과 모래 아래 빠르게 매립된 식물이나 동물의 유해에서 형성된다. 수천 년이 지나면서 압력이 퇴적물을 바위로 바꾸었다. 동시에 광물이 유해에 스며 유기물을 대체했다. 이것은 결과적으로 그 생물의 돌 복제품을 형성했다. 다른 화석들은 얼음, 타르, 단단한 수액에 통째로 보존된 식물과 동물이다. 예를 들어 작은 벌레나 무척추동물이 나무의 수액 안에 갇히고 시간이 흐르면서 그 수액이 호박으로 변화하면 그것들은 화석화된다. 생물체를 분해하는 박테리아나 곰팡이 같은 분해자가 적은 장소가 화석화에 이상적이다.

지문에서 글쓴이가 '조개껍데기나 뼈'를 언급하는 이유는

Ⓐ 분해자의 존재가 중요함을 강조하기 위해서
Ⓑ 자국이나 흔적 화석과 생물체의 단단한 부분 화석을 대조하기 위해서
Ⓒ 생물의 어떤 부분이 화석이 되는 경향이 있는지를 보여주기 위해서
Ⓓ 굳은 수액 안에서 발견되는 화석의 사례를 보이기 위해서

어휘 myriad n 무수히 많음 I flora n 식물군 I fauna n 동물군 I seashell n 조개껍데기 I sedimentary adj 퇴적물의 I swamp n 늪, 습지대 I tar n 타르 I sap n 수액 I invertebrate n 무척추동물 I scavenger n 죽은 동물을 먹는 동물 I fungi n (fungus의 복수형) 곰팡이 I fossilization n 화석화

본서 | P. 50

Practice

01 D　02 C　03 C　04 C

Practice

본서 | P. 52

01

올림픽의 여성들

그리스 신화에 따르면, 올림픽 경기는 언제나 헤라이아라 불리는 여성들의 축제를 포함했다. 그것은 4년마다 남성들의 축제 직전에 개최되었고 그리스 전역에서 온 소녀들에게 개방되어 있었을 것이다. 세 종류의 도보 경주가 있었는데, 세 가지 연령대별로 각각 하나씩 있었다. 이런 구분은 고대 자료에 정확히 인용되어 있지는 않지만 학자들은 그 범위가 6세부터 18세까지에 달했을 것으로 추측한다. 헤라이아의 우승자들은 남성 경기의 우승자들과 마찬가지로 경기의 모든 참가자들을 대표해 올리브 월계관과 수호신을 위해 도살된 한 마리의 황소 중 일부를 받았다. 헤라이아의 우승자들은 올림픽 성전에 있는 헤라 사원에 자신들의 초상화를 붙였다. 그 초상화들은 오래 전에 사라졌지만 사원 기둥에 그 초상화들이 설치되어 있던 벽면의 움푹 들어간 자리는 여전히 선명하다.

다음 중 지문에서 헤라이아의 우승자들에 관해 추론 가능한 것은 무엇인가?

Ⓐ 일부는 후에 올림픽 우승자들과 결혼했다.
Ⓑ 일부는 후에 종교 교단의 일원이 되었다.
Ⓒ 후세의 소녀들에게 신화적인 여신이 되었다.
Ⓓ 그들의 업적에 대해 높은 존경을 받았다.

어휘 footrace n 도보 경주 | slaughter v 도살하다, 도축하다 | sanctuary n 성소, 성역 | niche n 벽감(벽의 움푹 들어간 곳), 틈새

02

고릴라

영장류 동물학자들은 얼마나 많은 종이 존재하는지 규명하기 위해 다양한 고릴라 개체군 사이의 관계를 지속적으로 연구하고 있다. 최근까지는 마운틴고릴라, 웨스턴로랜드고릴라, 이스턴로랜드고릴라의 세 종이 있다는 데 의견이 일치했었다. 그러나 현재 합의된 바로는 두 종의 고릴라만 존재하며 각각의 종에 두 개의 아종이 있다고 한다. 두 종 중 첫 번째는 웨스턴고릴라인데, 웨스턴로랜드고릴라와 크로스리버고릴라라는 두 아종을 가지고 있다. 두 번째 종은 이스턴고릴라인데, 마운틴고릴라와 이스턴로랜드고릴라라는 두 아종을 가지고 있다. 때때로 브윈디고릴라라고 불리는 또 다른 아종이 이스턴고릴라의 세 번째 추가 아종으로 제안되기도 했지만 이 제안은 영장류 학자들 사이에서 완전히 받아들여지지는 않고 있다.

지문에 따르면 다음 중 동물 종에 관해 추론 가능한 것은 무엇인가?

Ⓐ 한 가지 종에는 항상 두 가지 아종이 있다.
Ⓑ 고릴라 종에 대한 과학적 분류는 결코 바뀐 적이 없다.
Ⓒ 과학자들이 동물 종을 분류하기 위해 이용하는 기준은 시간이 지나면서 바뀔 수 있다.
Ⓓ 영장류 학자들은 최근에 고릴라 종의 분류를 완성했다.

어휘 primatologist n 영장류 동물학자 | subspecies n 아종, 변종 | proposal n 제안, 제의

03

최초의 문명

방랑하던 수렵 채집인들이 언제, 어디서 처음으로 문명 창조를 시작했는지 아무도 정확하게 알아내지 못했다. 명백한 증거는 없지만 일반적으로 문명은 대략 일만 년 전 시작되었고, 그때 사람들이 씨앗을 보존하기 위한 방법으로 우연히 땅에 씨앗을 심었던 것으로 여겨진다. 전에 씨앗을 묻었던 땅 표면을 뚫고 나오는 어린 묘목을 보고 농부들은 놀랐을 것이다. 이것이 농사법 발달에 최초의 박차를 가했고, 이는 결국 작은 지역에 많은 사람들을 살게 할 만큼 충분한 식량 생산을 가능하게 했다. 이런 사실은 역사 기록에서 쉽게 볼 수 있고, 이것은 농사와 최초의 대규모 문명이 거의 동시에 발생했다는 것을 분명하게 보여준다.

지문에 따르면 최초의 농부들에 관해 추론 가능한 것은 무엇인가?

Ⓐ 씨앗을 심기 적절한 땅을 선택하는 방법에 대한 지식이 있었다.

Ⓑ 땅에 모든 씨앗을 저장할 수 있었다.
Ⓒ 최초의 사람들은 우연히 농사짓는 법을 발견했을 가능성이 높다.
Ⓓ 최초의 농부들이 씨앗을 보존하기 시작한 시점이 언제였는지 확실히 알 수 있다.

어휘 embark on ~에 착수하다, 시작하다 I nomadic adj 유목의, 방랑의 I inadvertently adv 무심코, 우연히 I momentum n (일 진행의) 가속도 I contemporaneous adj 동시에 발생하는

04 **나방**

나방은 크기가 엄청나게 다양해서 날개 폭이 4mm에서 거의 300mm에 이른다. 굉장히 종류가 다양해서 극지방의 서식지를 제외하고 모든 지역에서 거주한다. 이들은 나비와 밀접한 관련이 있는 곤충이다. 나비와 마찬가지로 나방의 날개, 몸, 다리는 건드리면 떨어지는 먼지 같은 얇은 비늘로 덮여 있다. 그러나 나비와 나방 사이에는 몇 가지 차이점이 있다. 일부 나방종은 주행성이지만 대부분의 나방은 야행성이다. 나비와 비교했을 때, 그것들은 더 두터운 몸통과 상대적으로 더 작은 날개를 가졌다. 나비는 밝은 색의 날개로 알려진 반면 나방은 주로 숨는 것을 용이하게 해주는 지그재그 무늬가 있는 검은색, 회색, 갈색, 흰색 등의 탁색이다. 또 다른 차이는 더듬이이다. 골프채 모양의 얇은 더듬이를 가지고 있는 나비와 달리 나방은 솜털 같은 더듬이를 가지고 있다. 여기에 더해, 나방은 휴식을 취할 때 날개를 접거나, 몸 주변을 감싸거나 양쪽 측면으로 펼친 채로 있는다.

지문에서 나방에 대해 추론할 수 있는 것은

Ⓐ 보통 매우 넓은 날개 폭을 갖고 있다
Ⓑ 다른 곤충보다 더 연약한 몸을 갖고 있다
Ⓒ 다양한 서식지에서 살 수 있다
Ⓓ 나비와 마찬가지로 보통 주행성이다

어휘 range v ~에서 …에 이르다 I polar adj 북극의, 극지의 I nocturnal adj 야행성의 I stout adj 튼튼한, 통통한 I proportionately adv 비례해서 I antennae n 더듬이 I feathery adj 솜털 같은 I wrap v 싸다

III. Recognizing Organization

Lesson 01 Insertion

본서 I P. 54

Practice

01 A　　02 C　　03 A　　04 D

Practice

본서 I P. 56

01 **증기 기관**

석탄 광산 침수는 18세기에 영국 광부들이 직면한 가장 파괴적인 위험 요소였다. 이 곤경을 마침내 해결한 것은 제임스 와트의 증기기관이었다. 와트의 초기 증기기관은 깊은 광산에서 물을 효과적으로 끌어올렸다. [■A] 그러나 와트는 공장에서 사용할 수 있는 증기기관을 개발하는 데 관심이 있었다. 그의 첫 번째 증기기관은 1776년에 설치되었으며 전 세계적으로 공장 생산 라인의 패러다임에 변화를 가져왔다. [■B] 우선 공장형 증기기관의 출현은 더 많은 생산과 생산 시간 단축을 가능하게 했다. [■C] 게다가 공장의 전력 공급원으로 수력을 필요로 하지 않았기 때문에 공장 건설을 위한 부지가 제한을 덜 받게 되었고, 이는 공장이 어디에나 지어질 수 있게 만들었다. [■D] 마지막으로 증기기관을 가진 공장은 많은 수작업 노동자를 필요로 했으므로 시골에서 확장되고 있는 도심으로 대규모 인구 이동이 있었다. 이 대규모 이동의 영향은 50년 만에 영국을 가내 공업 및 농업 사회에서 공장을 기반으로 한 도시 거주 산업 강국으로 바꾸었다.

지문에 다음 문장이 들어갈 수 있는 위치를 나타내는 네 개의 사각형[■]을 확인하시오.

그러나 와트는 공장에서 사용할 수 있는 증기기관을 개발하는 데 관심이 있었다.

이 문장이 들어가기에 가장 적합한 곳은? [■A]

어휘 devastating adj 대단히 파괴적인 I hazard n 위험 I confront v 맞서다, 정면으로 부딪히다 I address v 다루다 I effectively adv 효과적으로 I predicament n 곤경, 궁지, 어려움 I paradigm n 전형적인 예, 양식 I manual adj 손으로 하는, 육체 노동의 I cottage industry 가내 공업 I agrarian adj 농업의 I powerhouse n 유력 집단

02 **오리온 성운**

젊은 별과 먼지, 기체 더미가 있는 오리온 성운을 바라볼 때 우리가 무질서 가운데서 볼 수 있는 것은 별 공장과 우리 태양계가 초창기에 지녔을 법한 모습이다. [■A] 성운을 구성하는 별들의 나이는 대략 30만 살에서 200만 살이며 별들의 나이치고 매우 젊은 편이다. 비교해 보자면, 우리 태양의 나이는 45억 살이다. [■B] 이런 젊은 별들 중 가장 작은 것은 주로 색이 붉으며 질량이 작다. 이런 작은 별들에 더해 트라페지움을 이루는 네 개의 거대하고 뜨거운 별들이 있다. 트라페지움은 성운에 있는 별 공장의 중심부로 볼 수 있다. 이 네 개의 별 중 가장 큰 오리온자리 세타1C는 우리 태양보다 약 20배쯤 더 크고 약 10만 배쯤 더 밝다. 실은 이 별은 매우 밝아서 성운 전체를 혼자 환하게 비출 수 있다. [■C] 트라페지움의 별들은 자외선을 방출하여 주위에 있는 성운의 먼지와 가스를 밝게 빛나게 한다. 트라페지움 주위 인접 지역에는 성운의 기본 물질이 풍부하기 때문에 수백 개의 더 작은 별로 가득하다. [■D] 별을 형성하는 이런 모든 원료는 이 지역을 우리 은하에서 알려진 그 어느 곳보다도 별들이 가장 빽빽하게 들어찬 무리 중 하나로 만든다.

지문에 다음 문장이 들어갈 수 있는 위치를 나타내는 네 개의 사각형[■]을 확인하시오.

트라페지움의 별들은 자외선을 방출하여 주위에 있는 성운의 먼지와 가스를 밝게 빛나게 한다.

이 문장이 들어가기에 가장 적합한 곳은? [■C]

어휘 nebula n 성운 I amidst prep ~사이에 I infancy n 초기, 유아기 I roughly adv 대략 I reddish adj 불그스름한 I mass n 질량 I trapezium n 사각형 성단 I light up 환하게 만들다 I immediate adj 인접한, 가까이에 있는 I raw adj 날것의, 가공하지 않은 I congest v 혼잡하게 하다, 정체시키다 I cluster n 무리 I galaxy n 은하계

03 **화학의 목적과 연구**

1 ➡ 인류의 삶은 이전에 기록된 인류의 모든 역사에서보다 지난 두 세기 동안 더 많이 바뀌었다. 세계 인구는 1800년 이후 5배 이상 크게 증가했으며 인간의 기대 수명은 질병의 확산을 제어하고, 의약품을 합성하고, 식량 작물의 수확량을 늘릴 수 있는 인류의 능력으로 인해 거의 두 배가 되었다. 인간의 운송 방식은 말타기에서 자동차와 비행기로 바뀌었는데, 이는 석유에서 이용 가능한 에너지를 활용하는 인류의 능력 덕분이다. 우리가 현재 제조하는 많은 제품들은 나무와 금속 대신 세라믹과 중합체로 만들어지며, 이는 자연계에서 발견되는 것과는 다른 특성을 지닌 물질을 만들어낼 수 있는 인류의 능력 덕분이다.

2 ➡ 삶을 변화시키는 이런 각각의 발전은 어떤 식으로라도 직접적으로든 간접적으로든 화학, 즉 물질의 구성, 특성, 변형에 관한 연구를 포함하고 있다. [■A] 화학은 자연계에서 발생하는 변화들의 원인이다. 마찬가지로 화학은 매우 여러 면에서 지난 2백 년 동안 일어난 엄청난 사회적 변화의 원인이기도 하다. [■B] 게다가 화학은 생물체가 어떻게 유전적으로 조절되는지에 관한 세부 내용을 탐구하는 분자 생물학에서 최근 혁명의 핵심에 놓여 있다. [■C] 사실상 오늘날 학식이 있는 사람이라 해도 화학에 관한 최소한의 기본 지식 없이는 우리 주변의 세계를 진정으로 이해할 수 없다. [■D]

지문에 다음 문장이 들어갈 수 있는 위치를 나타내는 네 개의 사각형[■]을 확인하시오.

화학은 자연계에서 발생하는 변화들의 원인이다.

이 문장이 들어가기에 가장 적합한 곳은? [■A]

어휘 previously adv 이전에 I fivefold adj 5배의 I life expectancy 기대 수명 I synthesize v 합성하다 I yield n 산출량 I transportation n 운송 I horseback adj 말을 타고 하는 I harness v 활용하다 I petroleum n 석유 I manufacture v 제조하다 I ceramic n 도자기 I polymer n 중합체 I property n 고유의 성질 I composition n 구성 I transformation n 변형 I profound adj 엄청난, 깊은 I core n 핵심 I revolution n 혁명 I molecular biology 분자 생물학 I ins and outs 자세한 내용 I genetically adv 유전적으로

04 **미국의 혁명주의자들과 그들의 정부 체제**

1 ➡ 영향력 있는 모든 문서와 마찬가지로, 미합중국 헌법의 근본적인 목적은 헌법 구성과 그 후 사람들이 이를 채택하는 과정으로 이어지는 상황과 사건의 연구를 통해서만 밝혀질 수 있다. 먼저 미 헌법이 채택된 시기에 두 개의 큰 당파가 있었음을 기억해야 한다. 한 정당은 정부의 힘과 효율성을 강조했고 다른 정당은 정부의 대중적인 측면을 강조했다.

2 ➡ 물론 영국의 지배적인 존재에 대항하는 반란을 선동하고 혁명가들의 전투적 기질을 높은 수준으로 유지하도록 이끌었던 사람들은 토머스 제퍼슨, 새뮤얼 애덤스, 토머스 페인, 패트릭 헨리와 같은 가장 대담하고 급진적인 사상가들이었다. [■A] 일반적으로 이들은 막대한 자산을

보유한 것도, 풍부한 사업 경험을 가진 것도 아니었다. 그러나 혼돈의 시대에 이들은 사회적 통제보다 개인의 자유를 지속적으로 더 강조했다. [■B] 이들은 귀족 권력에 대항하는 소지주들과 상업 계층들의 시련과 고난의 시기 동안 영국에서 발전했던 인권주의를 극단적으로 밀고 나갔다. [■C] 이러한 상황은 18세기 말 미국의 우세한 경제 상황에 상응하는 것이었다. [■D] 그들은 강한 정부를 군주제와 연관지었기 때문에 최고의 정부는 최소한으로 통치하는 정부라고 믿게 되었다. 이런 다수의 급진주의자들은 모든 정부를, 특히 매우 중앙 집권화된 유형의 정부를 악마의 산물로 보았다. 정부는 단지 약간의 질서 유지에 대한 필요성 때문에 용인되긴 했지만 동시에 지속적인 경계를 통해 최소 수준으로 유지되어야 했다.

지문에 다음 문장이 들어갈 수 있는 위치를 나타내는 네 개의 사각형[■]을 확인하시오.

그들은 강한 정부를 군주제와 연관지었기 때문에 최고의 정부는 최소한으로 통치하는 정부라고 믿게 되었다.

이 문장이 들어가기에 가장 적합한 곳은? [■D]

어휘 influential adj 영향력 있는 | underlying adj 근본적인 | constitution n 헌법 | subsequent adj 그 이후의 | adoption n 채택 | faction n 당파 | stir up 고무하다, 불러 일으키다 | revolt n 반란 | temper n 성질 | dominating adj 지배하는 | radical adj 급진적인 | revolutionist n 혁명론자 | disorder n 혼란 | property n 자산 | to the extreme 극단까지 | consistently adv 지속적으로 | evolve v 발달하다 | doctrine n 원칙 | tribulation n 고난 | trial n 시련 | correspond to ~와 일치하다, ~에 상응하다 | centralized adj 중앙 집권화된 | aristocracy n 귀족 계층 | tolerate v 용인하다 | prevailing adj 우세한 | vigilance n 경계, 조심 | spawn n 산물 | keep ~ to minimum ~를 최소한으로 하다

Lesson 02 Summary

본서 | P. 60

Practice

01 B, E, F　　02 A, C, E　　03 B, D, E　　04 A, C, E

Practice

본서 | P. 64

01

동물의 의사소통

1 ➡ 동물은 지극히 기본적인 청각 의사소통 기술이 있거나 아예 없기 때문에 많은 동물이 시각적 의사소통 방법에 의존한다. 특히 곤충과 새는 매우 정교한 시각적 의사소통 체계를 갖고 있다. 이 시각 체계는 주로 두 개의 다른 범주인 수동적 신호와 능동적 신호에 속하며, 따로 사용되거나 혹은 두 개가 같이 사용될 수도 있다.

2 ➡ 수동적 신호는 동물의 입장에서 아무런 에너지 소비도 필요로 하지 않는다. 이는 수동적 신호가 신체적인 모양의 일부라는 사실에 기인한다. 예를 들어 나비는 다양한 색과 무늬가 있다. 밝은 색의 안점, 줄무늬와 단색으로 나비들은 성과 나이, 종이 무엇인지 알릴 수 있다. 이러한 수동적 신호는 또한 다른 종의 생물들에게 나비가 먹을 수 없다거나 독이 있다는 것을 알려준다. 마찬가지로 나비와 같은 이유로 여러 종류의 새들은 특히 성을 구별하고 번식 활동을 개시하기 위해 여러 색의 무늬를 선보인다.

3 ➡ 능동적 신호 사용은 더 신체적이며, 사용하는 생물체의 에너지를 필요로 한다. 구애와 짝짓기 의식은 능동적 신호가 활기차게 드러나는 영역이다. 몇몇 곤충들은 짝을 유혹하기 위해 복잡한 공중 춤을 춘다. 밤에 개똥벌레들은 생식할 준비가 되어 있거나 이미 생식을 마쳤다는 것을 나타내기 위해 특정한 불빛을 발산한다. 또한 어떤 종의 새는 짝짓기 춤을 춘다. 수컷 초원뇌조는 암컷에게 자기와 짝짓기하도록 확신을 주기 위해 그 주변을 원형으로 뽐내며 걷거나 폴짝폴짝 뛰며 시간을 보낼 것이다. 새들은 또한 침입자의 접근 같은 위험을 무리에 경고하기 위해 날개를 치거나 갑자기 하늘로 날아 오름으로써 능동적인 신호를 사용한다. 이러한 시각적 경고는 빠르게 무리로 퍼지며, 다른 구성원들이 차례로 따라 하게 된다.

지시문: 지문을 간략하게 요약한 글의 첫 문장이 아래에 제시되어 있다. 지문의 가장 중요한 내용을 표현하는 세 개의 선택지를 골라 요약문을 완성하시오. 일부 문장은 지문에 제시되지 않았거나 지문의 지엽적인 내용을 나타내기 때문에 요약문에 포함되지 않는다. ***이 문제의 배점은 2점이다.***

새들과 곤충들은 의사소통을 위해 시각적 수단을 활용한다.

Ⓑ 능동적 신호는 다른 개체에 위험을 경고할 수 있을뿐 아니라 짝짓기하려는 의지와 능력을 보여줄 수 있다.
Ⓔ 수동적 신호는 전달자의 신체적 특징으로 전달된다.
Ⓕ 동물의 의사소통에는 두 개의 시각적 체계가 있다.

Ⓐ 의사소통의 시각적 형태는 매우 명백하다.
Ⓒ 새들은 같은 종에게 수동적 신호를 보내기 위해 매우 정교한 장식을 사용한다.
Ⓓ 개똥벌레는 언어를 표현하는 연속적인 빛의 번쩍임을 이용한다.

어휘 auditory adj 청각의 | sophisticated adj 정교한 | expenditure n 소비 | stripe n 줄무늬 | inedible adj 먹을 수 없는 | mating n 짝짓기 | ritual n 의식 | vigor n 활기, 힘 | intricate adj 복잡한 | airborne adj 공중의 | flock n 무리

---

02 **동물 인지**

1 ➡ 20세기 초반에 동물 심리학은 기본적인 사고 과정을 밝혀내 이후 인간의 발달된 지능을 설명하는 데 사용하고자 하는 실험으로 가득 차 있었다. 행동주의라고 알려진 심리학적 운동에서 유래된 이러한 실험들은 자극과 반응 사이의 관계를 알아내어 특정 행동을 분류하고자 했다. 이러한 실험들의 자료는 동물이 느끼지 않는다고 전제한 정신적, 감정적 상태의 영향은 무시한 채 행동을 과학적으로 설명하기 위해 사용되었다.

2 ➡ 그 후 1950년대 후반에 인지 심리학의 발전은 그것을 인간과 동물 모두의 행동을 설명하기 위한 지배적인 형태로 만들어 주었다. 인지 심리학은 행동주의와는 반대로 행동을 설명했는데 자극과 반응보다는 오히려 내부 상태와 그것의 결과에 대한 영향을 고려했기 때문이었다. 게다가 동물 행동은 인간의 지적인 과정에 대해 알려진 것과 비교하여 분석되었다. 이전에 행동주의자의 실험에 사용된 일반적인 동물은 새, 개, 그리고 쥐였다. 그러나 인지 심리학자들은 원숭이나 유인원 같은 영장류에 연구 초점을 두기로 선택했는데, 이는 이 동물들이 인간과 같이 발달한 변연계를 갖고 있으며 인간과 유전학적으로도 비슷했기 때문이었다. 이 공유된 신경학적 특징은 감정과 동기, 기억에 관련된 감정과 연관되어 있는데 가설적으로 연구자들에게 자신들의 이론을 인간 행동에 적용하는 데 더 합리적인 이유를 제공했다.

3 ➡ 인지 심리학이 동물 인지를 분석하는 표준이 된 이후로 인간 행동과 동물 행동 사이에 많은 유사점이 발견되었다. 동물 인지에 관한 연구는 언어와 기억, 문제 해결 영역에 초점이 맞춰져 왔다. 원숭이들은 인간과 비슷한 단기 기억 현상을 갖고 있다고 밝혀졌지만, 연구가 가장 많이 진척된 부분은 공간 기억과 관련된 연구이다. 동물은 특히 공간적으로 어디에 물체가 위치했는지 기억하는 능력이 있다. 이 현상이 일어나는 가장 대표적인 예는 다람쥐인데, 다람쥐는 먹이를 넓은 범위에 걸친 비밀 장소에 저장한다. 환경의 급격한 변화에도 불구하고 다람쥐는 공간 기억을 사용하여 먹이를 저장한 장소를 능숙하게 기억할 수 있다.

지시문: 지문을 간략하게 요약한 글의 첫 문장이 아래에 제시되어 있다. 지문의 가장 중요한 내용을 표현하는 세 개의 선택지를 골라 요약문을 완성하시오. 일부 문장은 지문에 제시되지 않았거나 지문의 지엽적인 내용을 나타내기 때문에 요약문에 포함되지 않는다. ***이 문제의 배점은 2점이다.***

동물의 사고 과정에 대한 발견은 인간의 인지 작용에 관한 과학적인 통찰력을 제공했다.

Ⓐ 인간의 사고 과정을 이해하려는 초기 시도들은 동물이 행동하는 방식을 분석함으로써 이루어졌다.
Ⓒ 인지 심리학은 심리학자들이 행동을 보고 설명한 방식을 뒤집었고, 실험에서 사용된 동물들마저 변경했다.
Ⓔ 인지 심리학은 주로 기억, 문제 해결, 언어에 주목하여 동물의 행동을 연구하는 데 선호되는 방법이다.

Ⓑ 행동 과학과 연구 기술의 모든 진보에도, 모든 행동을 완벽히 설명하는 것은 여전히 불가능하다.
Ⓓ 원숭이와 유인원은 인간과 대부분 똑같은 유전자 형질과 행동 양식을 공유한다.
Ⓕ 풍경의 커다란 변화는 정확한 공간 기억력을 갖지 않은 동물을 혼란에 빠뜨리고 장소를 인지하지 못하게 할 수 있다.

어휘 cognition n 인지 | be derived from ~에서 파생되다, 유래하다 | stimulus n 자극 | disregard v 경시하다, 무시하다 | predominant adj 우월한, 주된 | primate n 영장류 | ape n 원숭이, 유인원 | limbic adj 대뇌 변연계의 | neurological adj 신경학의 | trait n 특징 | hypothetically adv 가설적으로 | spatial adj 공간의 | radical adj 급격한

---

03 **콜럼버스의 교역**

1 ➡ 크리스토퍼 콜럼버스의 원정대가 카리브해에 도착한 이후 정복자들과 식민지 개척자들의 물결이 아메리카 대륙으로 밀려들었다. 유럽인들은 북미 원주민들과 교류하며 의도적이었든 우연이었든 많은 것을 교환했다. 이런 교환의 상당수는 실물 거래의 형태로 이루어졌다. 긍정적이든 부정적이든 이런 교환은 신세계와 구세계 모두에 극적인 영향을 주었다.

2 ➡ 콜럼버스는 자신의 스페인 후원자들을 위해 카리브해에서 많은 기념품을 가지고 돌아왔다. 그의 본래 임무는 아시아의 향신료 및 다른 풍부한 자원을 위한 새로운 무역 항로를 개척하는 것이었다. 기본적으로 그 임무 완수에는 실패했으나 스페인의 왕과 여왕은 그가 발견한 것에 관심을 보였다. 그 중에는 옥수수, 토마토, 감자, 호박, 초콜릿 등의 새로운 작물이 있었으며, 일부는 후에 유럽인들의 주식이 되었다. 그러나 아메리카 대륙에 대해서 스페인 사람들의 관심을 가장 많이 끌었던 것은 금전적 가치와 희소성을 지닌 금이었다. 스페인 정복자들은 소규모의 군대를 보내어 자신들이 소유권을 주장했던 땅을 탐사하고 그곳의 모든 금을 가져오게 했다. 반면에 유럽인들 또한 많은 농작물을 아메리카에 전해주었는데 가장 중요한 것은 사탕수수와 커피였다. 그들은 또한 닭, 돼지, 소를 포함한 많은 동물들을 가져왔으며 그중 아메리카 원주민들에

게 가장 중요한 존재가 된 동물은 말이었다.

3 ➡ 하지만 이러한 교역에는 부정적인 면도 있었다. 유럽인들은 전쟁과 탄압을 가져왔으나 당시 자신들도 모르는 사이 검이나 총보다 훨씬 더 해로운 것을 전했으니, 바로 신종 질병이었다. 유럽은 때때로 마을 전체를 초토화한 여러 전염병 때문에 수 세기 동안 고통을 받았다. 시간이 흐르며 이러한 전염병 생존자들에게는 이 유행병들에 대한 면역력이 생겼다. 천연두, 인플루엔자, 콜레라, 티푸스, 페스트 등의 질병은 유럽에서도 여전히 심각한 문제였지만 이 질병들이 신세계로 퍼져 나가자 아메리카 원주민들은 초토화되었다. 사망률을 정확히 측정하는 것은 불가능하지만, 외국에서 들어온 질병이 130년 만에 캐나다에서 아르헨티나에 이르기까지 원주민들의 80~90퍼센트를 사망에 이르게 한 것으로 추정된다. 이런 질병들은 정복, 식민지화, 심지어 교역을 위한 짧은 만남을 통해서도 확산되었다. 이후 영국인들이 북아메리카를 식민지화하기 위해 왔을 때에는 아주 적은 수의 지역 주민들만 남아 있었다.

지시문: 지문을 간략하게 요약한 글의 첫 문장이 아래에 제시되어 있다. 지문의 가장 중요한 내용을 표현하는 세 개의 선택지를 골라 요약문을 완성하시오. 일부 문장은 지문에 제시되지 않았거나 지문의 지엽적인 내용을 나타내기 때문에 요약문에 포함되지 않는다. ***이 문제의 배점은 2점이다.***

크리스토퍼 콜럼버스는 신세계를 발견했을 때 유럽과 아메리카 대륙 간 교역의 장을 열었다.

Ⓑ 당시의 가장 중요한 교역품에는 아메리카 대륙에서 나온 금과 유럽에서 온 가축이 포함되어 있었다.
Ⓓ 이런 교환은 양 대륙에 긍정적, 부정적 방식으로 지속적인 영향을 주었다.
Ⓔ 그들의 의도와는 다르게 유럽인들은 원주민 인구의 대부분을 거의 몰살한 질병을 가져왔다.

Ⓐ 원정대의 주 목적은 아시아의 중요한 무역항을 군사력으로 장악하는 것이었으나 그 대륙에 도달하지 못했다.
Ⓒ 스페인 사람들은 중남미 전역에 군대를 보내 금을 찾아오게 했으며 많은 부족들을 정복했다.
Ⓕ 외국산 농작물, 가축, 기술과 재물들이 모두 북미 원주민들과의 사이에 교환되었다.

어휘 expedition n 원정대 I wave n 물결, 집단적 이동 I conqueror n 정복자 I colonist n 식민지 개척자 I interact with ~와 교류하다 I exchange v 교환하다 I intentionally adv 의도적으로 I dramatic adj 극적인 I souvenir n 기념품 I sponsor n 후원자 I trade route 무역로, 항로 I spice n 향신료 I essentially adv 본질적으로 I maize n 옥수수 I staple n 주식 I interest v 관심을 끌다 I sugar cane 사탕수수 I warfare n 전쟁 I oppression n 압제 I plague n 전염병 I immunity n 면역 I devastate v 완전히 파괴하다 I estimate v 추정하다 I conquest n 정복 I colonization n 식민지화 I fraction n 부분, 일부 I inhabitant n 거주자 I military takeover 군부 집권, 군사 쿠데타 I intent n 의도 I wipe out 말살하다, 파괴하다 I livestock n 가축

04

잉카 도로

1 ➡ 13세기에 잉카인들은 페루의 산악 지대에 문명을 처음 세웠다. 잉카 제국은 스페인 사람들이 그 지역을 정복하기 전까지 남미에서 가장 큰 제국이었다. 이 거대한 제국을 연결하여 더 수월하게 통치하기 위해 잉카인들은 당시 아메리카 대륙에서 가장 대규모 교통 체계를 이루었던 도로망을 형성했다. 수도인 쿠스코에서부터 잉카인들은 인접한 여러 문화를 통합했다. 일부는 평화롭게 합류했지만 군사력을 동원해 납득시켜야 했던 경우도 있었다. 잉카인들은 알렉산더 대왕이 자국에서 그랬던 것과 거의 비슷하게 제국 도처에서 잉카 고유의 문화를 강요했다. 잉카인들은 사람들에게 자기들의 언어인 퀘찬을 쓰도록 했으며 무엇보다 잉카의 태양신 인티를 숭배해야 했다. 이와 같이 그들은 체계적인 도로망이 고유의 문화를 유지하고 전파하는 데 도움이 된다고 생각했다.

2 ➡ 잉카의 도로망은 남북으로 이어지는 두 개의 주요 도로로 구성되어 있었으며 이 두 개의 도로는 서로 이어졌고 많은 작은 간선 도로를 통해 외부 지역과도 연결되어 있었다. 서부 도로는 주로 해안 평야를 따라 나 있었지만 사막 지역 근처에 있는 안데스 산맥의 작은 언덕 가까이로 곡선을 이루고 있었다. 동부 도로는 석재로 포장되어 있었으며 폭은 보통 1~3미터 정도로, 안데스 산맥의 높은 산골짜기와 초원을 통과해 나 있었다. 걸어서 하루 거리 간격만큼 떨어져 있는 탐보스라는 휴게소들이 도로를 따라 있었고, 그보다 큰 휴게소는 5~6일 정도의 간격마다 있었다. 여행객들은 그 석조 건물에서 휴식을 취하고 그곳에 보관되어 있는 음식으로 물자를 보충할 수 있었다.

3 ➡ 잉카인들은 바퀴를 개발한 적이 없었으며 말은 이후에 스페인인들에 의해 도입되었는데, 따라서 도로 위의 운송 수단은 사람과 라마였다. 그리하여 도로가 가파른 경사면을 가로지르는 경우 더 편하게 걸을 수 있도록 해주는 긴 층계가 있었다. 모래로 뒤덮인 지역에서는 낮은 벽을 세워 모래가 도로 위로 불어오는 것을 막았다. 그리고 도로가 가파른 지역을 지나가는 곳에는 더 높은 벽을 세워서 사람들이 추락하지 않도록 했다. 전성기 때 도로는 총 4만 킬로미터까지 뻗어나갔다. 하지만 1533년에 스페인이 침입한 이후 이 도로들은 더 이상 유지되지 않았다. 스페인 사람들은 도로의 일부 구간을 뜯어냈고 다른 구간은 그들이 타는 말의 금속 편자 때문에 상태가 악화되었다. 대부분의 도로 체계는 결국 자연적으로 매립되었지만 오늘날 그 도로의 가능한 한 많은 부분을 복구하기 위한 노력이 이루어지고 있다.

지시문: 지문을 간략하게 요약한 글의 첫 문장이 아래에 제시되어 있다. 지문의 가장 중요한 내용을 표현하는 세 개의 선택지를 골라 요약문을 완성하시오. 일부 문장은 지문에 제시되지 않았거나 지문의 지엽적인 내용을 나타내기 때문에 요약문에 포함되지 않는다. ***이 문제의 배점은 2점이다.***

잉카인들은 아메리카 대륙에서 제일 큰 제국을 연결하기 위해 대규모 도로망을 형성했다.

Ⓐ 이 도로 체계에는 제국을 북에서 남으로 가로지르는 두 개의 주요 도로가 있었다. Ⓒ 잉카인들은 이 광범위한 도로망으로 언어와 종교를 전파해 제국을 통합하려고 했다. Ⓔ 잉카인들은 도로를 건설하는 데 큰 정성을 들였으나 그것들은 이후에 유지되지 않았다.

Ⓑ 잉카인들은 알렉산더 대왕의 군사 작전을 본떠 인근의 부족을 정복했다.
Ⓓ 이 도로에는 특별한 휴게소가 있어 여행객들은 그곳에서 식량을 보충하고 밤에 잠을 잘 수 있었다
Ⓕ 오늘날에는 도로를 이전의 상태로 복구하기 위한 보존 활동이 계속 진행되고 있다.

어휘 civilization n 문명 | highland n 산악 지대 | empire n 제국 | vast adj 어마어마한, 방대한 | network of roads 도로망 | transportation system 교통 체계 | incorporate v 통합하다 | neighboring adj 인근의, 인접한 | join v 합류하다 | convince v 설득하다 | military force 군사력 | impose v 강요하다, 부과하다 | worship v 숭배하다 | systematic adj 체계적인 | outlying area 외곽 지역 | connect v 잇다, 연결하다 | make up ~을 이루다 | extensive adj 광범위한 | consist of ~로 구성되다 | curve v 곡선을 이루다 | foothill n 작은 언덕 | grassland n 초원 | pave v (길을) 포장하다 | space v 간격을 두다 | replenish v 보충하다 | steep adj 가파른 | campaign n 군사 작전 | restock v 다시 채우다, 보충하다 | foodstuff n 식량 | underway adj 진행 중인 | restore v 복구하다 | former adj 이전의

Lesson 03 Category Chart

본서 | P. 72

Practice

01 Fungi: A, D, E / Plants: B, F

02 Left: A, G / Right: B, D, E

03 Education: A, D, F / Schooling: B, C

04 Hardwoods: A, D, E / Softwoods: C, G

Practice

본서 | P. 76

01

균류 대 식물

1 ➡ 생명체는 연구를 위해 계(界)라는 광범위하고 기본적인 그룹으로 체계화된다. 균류는 오랫동안 식물계로 분류되었다. 그러다가 과학자들은 균류가 동물과 더 밀접한 관련성이 있긴 하지만 독특한 별도의 생명체라는 사실을 알게 되었다. 이제 균류는 자체 계로 분류되고 있다. 주된 이유는 어떤 균류에게도 엽록소가 없어서 식물과 달리 자체적으로 탄수화물을 합성할 수 없기 때문이다. 균류는 죽은 유기체 찌꺼기나 다른 생명체에서 양분을 얻는다.

2 ➡ 게다가 균류의 세포벽은 식물의 세포벽처럼 섬유소로 구성된 것이 아니라 키틴질이라는 복합당과 같은 중합체로 이루어져 있는데, 이것은 새우, 거미, 곤충의 딱딱한 외골격을 이루고 있는 재질이다. 균류의 세포벽과 식물 세포벽의 화학적 구성의 차이점은 매우 중요한데 그 이유는 자라나는 균사, 즉 균류의 실처럼 생긴 세포 끝에서 균류 자체에는 영향을 미치지 않고 식물의 세포벽을 분해하는 효소를 분비할 수 있기 때문이다.

지시문: 아래 문장들을 알맞게 넣어 다음 표를 완성하시오. 선택지 중 적절한 문장들을 골라 관계된 개념과 연결하시오. 선택지 두 개는 정답이 될 수 없다. ***이 문제의 배점은 3점이다.***

선택지	균류	식물
Ⓐ 엽록소가 없다. Ⓑ 자체적으로 탄수화물을 합성한다. Ⓒ 오직 죽은 유기물에서만 탄수화물을 얻는다. Ⓓ 세포벽이 새우와 곤충의 껍질과 같은 소재를 포함하고 있다. Ⓔ 탄수화물을 합성할 수 없다. Ⓕ 양분을 얻기 위해 엽록소를 이용한다. Ⓖ 식물 세포에 영향을 미치지 않는 효소를 분비하는 균사를 가지고 있다.	Ⓐ Ⓓ Ⓔ	Ⓑ Ⓕ

어휘 kingdom n (생물 분류의) 계 | principal adj 주요한, 주된 | chlorophyll n 엽록소 | synthesize v 합성하다 | cellulose n 섬유소 | polymer n 중합체, 고분자 | enormous adj 막대한, 거대한 | enzyme n 효소

02

뇌의 좌반구와 우반구

1 ➡ 인간의 두뇌는 한 기관이지만 두 개의 반쪽, 즉 반구로 나뉘어 있다. 각각의 반구는 다른 기능을 가졌고 각기 다른 방법으로 정보를 처리한다. 실행되는 일에 따라 한쪽 혹은 다른 한쪽의 반구가 더 지배적이다.

2 ➡ 왼쪽 반구는 세부적인 것에 집중한다. 논리적이고 분석적인 사고를 더 잘 처리한다. 다양한 여러 단계를 거쳐야 하는 조직적 업무를 수행하거나 주변 환경의 특정 부분에 집중하는 것이 필요할 때는 두뇌의 왼쪽 부분이 사용된다. 특징적 기능 중 하나가 상징적 사고인 두뇌의 왼쪽 부분은 사람들이 언어를 해독하여 문자 그대로의, 또는 표면상의 의미를 찾도록 해준다. 그러나 세부적인 것에 집중하는 왼쪽 반구는 보이는 물체들 사이의 관계를 식별하는 능력인 공간 인지에는 적절하지 못하다. 이 일은 세부적인 것에 대한 집중을 덜 요구한다.

3 ➡ 반면 오른쪽 반구는 정보를 더 총체적인 수준에서 처리한다. 이는 장소, 사물, 상황에 관한 총체적 관점을 제공하는 두뇌 부분이다. 오른쪽 반구는 인간 상상력의 중심부이기 때문에 사람들은 창조적 접근을 요구하는, 제한을 두지 않은 업무를 수행할 때 이 반구에 의존한다. 언어를 처리할 때 사람들이 유머나 감정, 은유를 이해하게 하여 함축적 또는 문맥상의 의미를 제공하는 것이 바로 이 오른쪽 반구이다. 더욱이 오른쪽 반구는 공간 지각의 원천으로, 우리가 환경을 3차원적으로 분석하고 거리를 판단할 수 있게 해준다.

지시문: 아래 구절들을 알맞게 넣어 다음 표를 완성하시오. 선택지 중 적절한 구절들을 골라 관계된 개념과 연결하시오. 선택지 두 개는 정답이 될 수 없다. ***이 문제의 배점은 3점이다.***

선택지	좌반구	우반구
Ⓐ 주변 환경의 세부 사항을 알아차리게 해준다	Ⓐ	Ⓑ
Ⓑ 거리를 판단할 수 있게 해준다	Ⓖ	Ⓓ
Ⓒ 꿈을 꾸게 해준다		Ⓔ
Ⓓ 문제를 창조적으로 해결하게 해준다		
Ⓔ 문맥을 파악할 수 있게 해준다		
Ⓕ 해결되어야 하는 문제를 구조화하게 해준다		
Ⓖ 언어를 문자 그대로 이해하게 해준다		

어휘 hemisphere n 반구 I dominant adj 지배적인 I logical adj 논리적인 I analytical adj 분석적인 I concentration n 집중 I decode v 해독하다, 번역하다 I superficial adj 표면상의 I spatial adj 공간의 I discern v 인지하다, 구별하다 I connotative adj 암시적인, 내포하는 I contextual adj 전후 관계상의, 문맥상의 I metaphorical adj 은유적인

03

교육과 학교 교육

1 ➡ 미국에서는 학교가 사람이 교육을 위해 반드시 다녀야 하는 곳이라는 믿음이 흔하다. 그러나 어떤 사람들은 학교에 다니는 것이 아이의 교육을 방해한다고 생각한다. 여기서 제시되는 학교 교육과 교육의 차이점은 중요하다.

2 ➡ 교육은 학교 교육보다 더 광범위하고 포괄적이다. 교육에는 제약이 없다. 교육은 공식적인 학교 교육과 모든 종류의 비공식적 학습을 다 포함한다. 교육 행위자는 훌륭한 조부모, 라디오 대담 프로그램에서 토론을 벌이는 사람들, 다른 아이, 혹은 유명한 학자 등이 될 수 있다. 학교 교육은 여러 가지 면에서 예측 가능한 반면 교육은 자연스럽게 이루어지는 경우가 많다. 예를 들어 낯선 사람과 우연히 나눈 대화를 통해 전에는 잘 알지 못했던 새로운 주제를 접할 수 있다. 사람들은 유아기 때부터 교육을 시작해 죽을 때까지 멈추지 않는다. 이것은 개인이 학교에 가기 전부터 시작되는 평생에 걸친 과정이며, 개인의 일생에서 계속 필수적인 부분이어야 한다.

3 ➡ 반면 학교 교육은 좀 더 형식을 갖춘 구체적인 과정이다. 학교 교육의 일반적 양상은 한 가지 상황이나 다른 것에 따라 거의 달라지지 않는다. 아이들은 똑같은 시간에 등교해 지정된 좌석에 앉으며 성인들에게 교육을 받고, 숙제를 하고 시험을 본다. 알파벳이든 간단한 계산이든, 가르침을 받는 현실의 단편은 대개 교육 과목의 경계에 제약을 받는다. 예를 들어 고등학생들은 지역 사회의 정치적 문제점과 관련한 진실이나 영화 제작자들이 어떤 신기술을 탐색 중인지 등에 관해 배울 가능성은 낮다는 점을 알고 있다. 제도화된 학교 교육에는 명백한 경계가 존재한다.

지시문: 아래 문장들을 알맞게 넣어 다음 표를 완성하시오. 선택지 중 적절한 문장들을 골라 관계된 개념과 연결하시오. 선택지 두 개는 정답이 될 수 없다. ***이 문제의 배점은 3점이다.***

선택지	교육	학교 교육
Ⓐ 태어날 때부터 죽을 때까지 계속된다.	Ⓐ	Ⓑ
Ⓑ 보통 어디에서든 내용이 같다.	Ⓓ	Ⓒ
Ⓒ 결과물을 대부분 예측할 수 있다.	Ⓕ	
Ⓓ 제약이 없다.		
Ⓔ 학업의 연속성을 방해한다.		
Ⓕ 예상하기 어렵고 계획되지 않은 것이다.		
Ⓖ 인간의 발달에 유용하다는 생각은 완전히 무시되어야 한다.		

어휘 interrupt v 방해하다, 중단시키다 I all-inclusive adj 모두를 포함한 I spontaneous adj 자연스러운, 마음에서 우러난 I infancy n 유아기 I integral adj 필수적인, 필요 불가결한 I segment n 부분

04 **경재 대 연재**

1 ➡ 목공과 건축에서 사용되는 나무의 종류는 보통 경재와 연재 두 종류로 나뉜다. 이렇게 분류한 이유는 꽤 명백해 보인다. 일반적으로 경재는 연재보다 더 단단한 경향이 있다. 하지만 항상 그런 것은 아니다. 경재는 확실히 연재보다 밀도가 높지만 모든 경재가 더 단단하지는 않다. 예를 들어 발사나무의 목재는 지구상에서 가장 부드러운 종류의 목재 중 하나이지만 사실 경재로 지정되어 있다. 그래서 이 두 종류의 나무를 제대로 구별하는 것은 더 복잡하다.

2 ➡ 경재와 연재 사이의 진짜 차이점은 목재를 얻은 나무의 종류와 관련이 있다. 경재는 낙엽수로, 매년 가을에 잎을 떨어뜨리고 대체로 껍질이 단단한 씨앗을 맺는 활엽수이다. 이런 나무에는 단풍나무, 오크나무, 벚나무, 마호가니 등이 있다. 연재는 대개 상록수로, 계절에 따라 잎이 지지 않으며 잎이 가늘고 바늘처럼 생겼다. 씨앗은 보통 원뿔형 열매 안에 들어 있으며(이것이 종종 구과 식물이라 불리는 이유이다) 단단한 보호 껍질이 없다. 이 종류에는 특히 소나무, 전나무, 가문비나무, 삼나무 등이 있다.

3 ➡ 이런 두 집단 간의 차이는 모두 외부에서 식별 가능한 것들이지만 가장 중요한 차이점은 안에 있다. 미세한 수준에서 보면 나무들의 구조가 다르다. 연재는 길쭉하고 수직으로 자라는 세포를 가지고 있으며 이 세포들은 힘을 공급하고 수분과 영양분을 나무 전체에 전달한다. 이들은 세포벽을 통해 물질을 전달하는데, 이는 세포벽 내에 물을 함유할 수 있다는 뜻이다. 이 나무들이 일년 내내 초록색을 유지할 수 있는 이유이다. 경재에는 동물의 혈관과 아주 비슷하게 이런 성분을 운반하는 물관이라는 조직이 있다. 이 물관은 나무에 있는 구멍처럼 생겼으며 벽은 도관 요소라는 튼튼한 세포로 만들어져 있다. 벽은 나무에 힘을 추가적으로 공급하고, 벽을 둘러싼 다른 세포는 서로 빽빽하게 모여 나무의 밀도를 더 높여준다. 하지만 겨울에는 기능이 조금 떨어지며 그 때문에 매년 나무의 잎이 지게 된다.

지시문: 아래 구절들을 알맞게 넣어 다음 표를 완성하시오. 선택지 중 적절한 구절들을 골라 관계된 개념과 연결하시오. 선택지 두 개는 정답이 될 수 없다. ***이 문제의 배점은 3점이다.***

선택지	경재	연재
Ⓐ 물과 영양분을 나르는 관 같은 구조를 갖고 있다	Ⓐ	Ⓒ
Ⓑ 보통 고도가 높은 빽빽한 숲에서 자란다	Ⓓ	Ⓖ
Ⓒ 항상 푸른 잎을 지닌 비낙엽성 나무이다	Ⓔ	
Ⓓ 일반적으로 고밀도의 더 단단한 세포를 갖고 있다		
Ⓔ 연 단위로 잎을 떨어뜨린다		
Ⓕ 원뿔형 열매 안에 들어 있는 딱딱한 껍질을 가진 씨앗을 생산한다		
Ⓖ 세포 조직 내에 수분을 저장할 수 있다		

어휘 hardwood n 경재 I softwood n 연재 I woodworking n 목공 I reasoning n 이유, 추론 I grouping n 분류, 그룹으로 나누기 I indeed adv 확실히 I dense adj 고밀도의 I designate v 지정하다 I distinction n 구별 I elaborate adj 복잡한 I discrepancy n 차이, 불일치 I deciduous adj 낙엽성의 I broad-leafed tree 활엽수 I maple n 단풍나무 I oak n 오크나무 I cherry n 벚나무 I mahogany n 마호가니(적색을 띤 목질을 지닌 열대산 활엽수) I seasonally adv 계절에 따라 I foliage n 잎사귀 I cone n 원뿔형 열매 I conifer n 구과 식물, 침엽수 I pine n 소나무 I fir n 전나무 I spruce n 가문비나무 I cedar n 삼나무 I microscopic adj 미세한 I vertically adv 수직으로 I retain v 보유하다 I vessel n (식물의) 물관 I blood vessel 혈관 I pore n 작은 구멍 I vessel element 도관 요소 I tube-like 관 같은 I shed v (잎을) 떨어지게 하다, 떨어뜨리다

Actual Test 1

본서 | P. 80

1. B 2. C 3. C 4. D 5. A 6. B 7. C 8. A 9. B
10. Terrestrial Planets: B, D, E / Jovian Planets: A, F
11. A 12. D 13. C 14. B 15. B 16. C 17. B 18. D 19. C 20. C, E, F

본서 | P. 81

행성의 두 종류

1 ➡ 지구를 포함해 태양계의 모든 행성은 태양 주변에 타원형에 가까운 궤도를 형성하며, 거의 같은 평면에 정렬되어 있다. 태양계 안의 행성이 오직 여덟 개라는 사실을 고려할 때 이들 사이에 얼마나 큰 다양성이 존재하는지 생각해 보면 상당히 놀랍다. 그러나 지난 두 세기에 걸쳐 이웃 행성들에 관해 점점 더 많은 사실들이 밝혀지며 행성들이 크게 두 범주로 분류될 수 있다는 점이 서서히 명확해졌다. 지구형 행성은 고밀도의 암석 물질로 구성된 작은 행성들이고 목성형 행성은 수소 및 헬륨같이 대부분 기체로 이루어진 저밀도의 거대한 행성들이다. 이러한 범주는 행성 분류의 편리한 기준이기도 하지만 태양계가 어떻게 탄생하게 되었는지를 이해하는 데에도 많은 도움을 주는 것으로 증명되었다.

2 ➡ 수성, 금성, 지구, 화성은 지구형 행성이다. '지구형(terrestrial)'이라는 용어는 지구를 의미하는 라틴어 'terra'에서 유래했다. 따라서 이 용어는 이 행성들이 모두 중요한 면에서 지구와 유사하다는 점을 가리키며 실제로도 이들은 몇 가지 공통된 특징을 가지고 있다. 첫째, 이 행성들은 모두 크기가 비슷하고, 더욱 중요한 점은 목성형 행성들보다 훨씬 더 작다는 것이다. 목성형 행성 중 가장 작은 해왕성은 지구형 행성 중에서 가장 큰 지구보다 50배 이상 크다. 또한 지구형 행성은 모두 다른 행성들에 비해 태양에 가깝게 공전한다. 행성 궤도 사이의 거리는 태양에서 멀수록 증가한다. 결과적으로 네 개의 지구형 행성의 궤도는 태양 가까이 몰려 있는 반면 네 개의 외행성은 궤도 사이의 거리가 광대하다. 태양에 더 가까이 있기 때문에 지구형 행성은 태양의 열 에너지로 데워져 있다. 또한 모든 지구형 행성에는 대기가 있는데, 이는 태양열을 보유하는 데 도움이 되고 지구형 행성들의 평균 기온이 더 먼 외행성들에 비해 훨씬 높은 이유를 설명해 준다. 그러나 지구형 행성의 가장 현저한 특징은 그 조밀한 구성이다. 이들의 표면은 주로 규산염암으로 이루어져 있으며 이는 그들이 겪은 험난한 역사를 기록하면서 혜성 충돌로 인한 분화구, 협곡, 산맥, 화산 등이 특징인 이들 행성의 극적인 풍경을 설명해 준다.

3 ➡ 목성, 토성, 천왕성, 해왕성은 목성형(Jovian) 행성이라고 불린다. 이 용어는 주피터라고도 하는 로마신 조브(Jove)의 이름에서 유래한 것으로 따라서 이들 행성과 목성 사이의 유사함을 나타낸다. 네 개의 목성형 행성은 태양계의 거대 행성들로, 지구형 행성들을 작아 보이게 한다. 또한 태양의 온기에서 너무 멀리 떨어진 궤도로 인해 그것들은 모든 행성들 중에서 가장 추운데, 가장 바깥쪽 행성들의 온

1. 1단락에 따르면, 행성 분류에 대해 추론 가능한 것은 무엇인가?
Ⓐ 태양계 내의 행성들을 더 분류하기 위해 더 많은 조사를 할 필요가 없다.
Ⓑ 행성의 밀도와 물질은 그것을 분류하는 데 중요한 역할을 한다.
Ⓒ 우리 태양계는 여덟 개 이상의 집단으로 분류될 수 있다.
Ⓓ 행성 분류는 다른 천체가 어떻게 시작되었는지 설명할 수 있게 해주었다.

2. 2단락의 단어 'retain(보유하다)'과 의미상 가장 가까운 것은
Ⓐ 생산하다
Ⓑ 반영하다
Ⓒ 보유하다
Ⓓ 증가하다

3. 2단락에서 글쓴이가 '해왕성'을 언급하는 이유는 무엇인가?
Ⓐ 지구형 행성들과 목성형 행성들의 구성 성분 차이를 보여주기 위해서
Ⓑ 목성형 행성들은 지구형 행성들보다 더 적절한 곳에 위치해 있다는 증거를 보여주기 위해서
Ⓒ 지구형 행성들이 목성형 행성들에 비해 얼마나 작은지 강조하기 위해서
Ⓓ 지구형 행성들이 목성형 행성들에 비해 태양에 더 가까이 있는 이유를 설명하기 위해서

4. 다음 중 지문에 음영 표시된 문장의 핵심 정보를 가장 잘 표현한 문장은 무엇인가? 오답은 문장의 의미를 크게 왜곡하거나 핵심 정보를 누락하고 있다.
Ⓐ 분화구, 협곡, 산맥, 화산은 바위로 된 표면을 가지고 있는 지구형 행성의 극적인 풍경을 설명해 준다.
Ⓑ 험난한 역사를 가지고 있어서 이 행성들에는 분화구가 있다.
Ⓒ 그래서 분화구, 협곡, 산맥, 화산으로 뒤덮인 이들의 표면은 대부분 규산염암이다.
Ⓓ 바위와 규산염으로 된 표면 때문에 지구형 행성들은 다양한 지형적 특징들로 증명되는 역사적 트라우마의 흔적을 보여준다.

도는 섭씨 영하 200도까지 내려간다. 목성형 행성의 또 한 가지 뚜렷한 특징은 표면이다. 겉으로 보기에는 단단해 보이지만 이들 행성은 대부분 기체로 이루어져 있어 바위투성이인 지구형 행성들과 달리 표면의 윤곽이 뚜렷하지 않다. [■A] 대신 대부분 수소와 헬륨인 대기가 중앙으로 갈수록 더 조밀해져 매우 높은 압력 아래 액체 상태인 내부와 뒤섞여 있다. [■B] 따라서 외부 대기와 내부 표면 사이에 명확한 구분이 없다. 또한 기체 상태인 이 네 개의 거대 행성들을 둘러싼 화려한 고리와 위성이 장관을 이루는 것도 특징이다. [■C] 최대 두 개의 위성을 가지고 있는 지구형 행성과 눈에 띄게 대조적으로 목성은 63개의 위성을 가지고 있다. [■D] 이들 사이의 극적인 차이점을 고려할 때 지구형 행성들이 목성형 행성들과 극단적으로 다른 특징을 가지고 있음은 분명하다.

4 ➡ 목성형 행성과 지구형 행성의 두드러진 차이점은 태양계 탄생 시 그것들이 형성된 방식의 차이점으로 설명된다. 현재의 이론은 태양계가 원래 태양 성운이라는 거대한 회전 구름이었다는 입장을 취하고 있다. 이 구름은 주로 헬륨 및 수소 같은 기체, 그리고 그보다 훨씬 더 적은 양의 고밀도 물질로 이루어져 있었다. 이 구름은 회전하면서 서서히 고밀도 부위가 중심에 모인 원반 형태를 갖추게 되었다. 우리 태양계는 기체가 응축 및 융합되면서 이 구름에서 형성되었다. 기체는 저온과 고압 상태에서 응축한다. 그러나 성운 중심 근처의 조건은 너무 혹독해서 이것이 일어나지 않았다. 그래서 그곳에서 형성된 행성들은 대부분 규소와 금속처럼 녹는점이 높은 혼합물로 이루어졌고, 이 혼합물들의 양이 많지 않았기 때문에 크기가 더 작았다. 이것이 지구형 행성이 되었다. 성운 내의 멀리 떨어진 곳은 조건이 이보다 유리해서 기체가 응축될 수 있었고 중력에 의해 한 곳에 모여 목성형 행성들을 형성할 수 있었다. 이것은 태양계에 존재하는 두 범주의 행성들이 가진 구성 요소, 크기, 밀도 차이를 설명해 준다.

5. 3단락에서 'they(그것들)'가 가리키는 것은

Ⓐ 목성형 행성들
Ⓑ 지구형 행성들
Ⓒ 궤도들
Ⓓ 표면들

6. 3단락에 따르면, 목성형 행성들은 지구형 행성들에 비해서 무엇이 독특한가?

Ⓐ 지구형 행성들이 발달하기 전에 형성되었다.
Ⓑ 주로 가스로 이루어져 있다.
Ⓒ 대기는 주로 수소로 이루어져 있다.
Ⓓ 핵은 상대적으로 단단하다.

7. 4단락에 따르면, 다음 중 우리 태양계에 대해 사실인 것은 무엇인가?

Ⓐ 가스가 압축되면서 만들어졌다.
Ⓑ 융합되기 전에 가스가 압축되어 응축되었다.
Ⓒ 온도가 떨어지고 기압이 올라갈 때 가스는 압축된다.
Ⓓ 중력은 목성형 행성들의 형성에만 역할을 했다.

8. 4단락의 단어 'coalesced(융합되다)'와 의미상 가장 가까운 것은

Ⓐ 결합되다
Ⓑ 정렬되다
Ⓒ 퍼뜨려지다
Ⓓ 팽창되다

9. 지문에 다음 문장이 들어갈 수 있는 위치를 나타내는 네 개의 사각형 [■]을 확인하시오.

따라서 외부 대기와 내부 표면 사이에 명확한 구분이 없다.

이 문장이 들어가기에 가장 적합한 곳은? [■B]

10. **지시문:** 다음 문장들을 알맞게 넣어 다음 표를 완성하시오. 선택지 중 적절한 문장들을 골라 관계된 개념과 연결하시오. 선택지 두 개는 정답이 될 수 없다. 이 문제의 배점은 3점이다.

선택지	지구형 행성들	목성형 행성들
Ⓐ 크기 면에서 이들은 다른 분류에 속한 행성들을 작아 보이게 한다.	Ⓑ	Ⓐ
Ⓑ 다른 분류에 속한 행성들에 비해 작다.	Ⓓ	Ⓕ
Ⓒ 태양의 열에너지에 더 가까이 다가가면서 따뜻해진다.	Ⓔ	
Ⓓ 이 그룹의 행성들은 서로 크기가 비슷하다.		
Ⓔ 암석이 많은 표면을 갖고 있다.		
Ⓕ 위성이 많은 것이 특징이다.		
Ⓖ 이 행성들에서는 가스 공급이 불충분하다.		

어휘 planet ⓝ 행성 | solar system 태양계 | terrestrial adj 지구의 | density ⓝ 밀도 | Jovian adj 목성의 | helium ⓝ 헬륨 | classification ⓝ 분류 | revealing adj 흥미로운 사실을 보여주는 | Mercury ⓝ 수성 | Venus ⓝ 금성 | Mars ⓝ 화성 | indicate ⓥ 암시하다 | Neptune n 해왕성 | orbit n 궤도 v 궤도를 돌다 | immense adj 광대한 | retain v 보유하다 | primarily adv 주로 | silicate n 규산염 | crater n 분화구 | canyon n 협곡 | Jupiter n 목성 | Saturn n 토성 | Uranus n 천왕성 | designate v 명시하다 | outermost adj 가장 바깥의 | conspicuous adj 눈에 띄는 | seemingly adv 겉으로 보기에 | prominent adj 두드러진 | spectacular adj 화려한 | encircle v 에워싸다 | phenomenal adj 비범한, 놀라운 | nebula n 성운 | spin v 돌다 | flatten v 평평하게 하다 | disk n 원반 | condense v 압축/응축하다 | coalesce v 응결하다 | melting point 녹는점 | gravity n 중력

본서 | P. 85

구텐베르크와 금속활자 인쇄

1 ➡ [■A] 활자란 각 기호와 글자를 표현하기 위해 이동 가능한 주조된 금속 조각을 사용하는 인쇄 및 활판 체계를 말한다. [■B] 활자의 발전은 고대 이집트의 목판 인쇄에서 시작되었다. [■C] 8세기 무렵에 중국인들은 문서와 그림으로 가득한 책 전체를 인쇄하는 데 이 기술을 사용했다. 15세기 독일의 인쇄공이자 금세공인이었던 요하네스 구텐베르크는 이후 이것을 더욱 발전시켜 금속활자를 부속물로 이용한 새로운 인쇄 시스템을 도입하여 명성을 얻게 되었다. [■D] 인쇄 기술이 유럽에 도달하기 전에는 책은 수도사들이 손으로 세심하게 따라 써야 했다. 목판 인쇄는 손으로 따라 쓰는 것보다 더 쉽고 더 믿을 만했기 때문에 유럽에 도착했을 때 빠르게 도입되었지만, 속도가 훨씬 더 빠르지는 않았다.

2 ➡ 금속활자가 나오기 전에는 상대적으로 속도가 느린 목판 인쇄로 인쇄가 이루어졌다. 이 고된 작업에서는 인쇄면 각각에 하나의 목판을 이용해 표면에 글자와 그림을 새겨 넣는 과정이 필수적이었다. 그러다 13세기 후반 중국에서 이것이 목판활자로 대체되었다. 덕분에 인쇄공들은 각각의 조각을 끼워 맞춰 단어를 만들 수 있었고, 새로운 면을 인쇄할 때마다 완전히 새로운 이미지를 조각해 넣을 필요가 없어졌다. 생산 시간은 크게 줄어들었으나 나무를 인쇄 도구로 이용하는 데는 여전히 한계가 있었다. 나무는 내구성 있는 재질이었지만 반복적인 인쇄로 압력을 받으면 닳아 없어져서 꽤 자주 교체해야 했다. 게다가 나무에는 자연적인 결과 줄무늬가 있어 글자를 조심스럽게 새겨야 했기 때문에 이것이 글자의 명확성에 영향을 주었고, 생산하는 데 더 많은 시간을 필요로 했다.

3 ➡ 이러한 한계를 극복하기 위해 금속을 이용해 활자를 만들려는 시도가 이루어졌다. 이를 위해 글씨를 새긴 나무 조각을 모래에 눌러 각 글씨나 기호의 음각을 얻었다. 그런 다음 활자를 만들기 위해 청동, 구리, 철, 주석 같은 용융된 금속을 형틀, 즉 주형 안에 부어 넣었다. 이와 같은 금속활자는 요하네스 구텐베르크가 실용적이고 효율적인 인쇄 시스템을 만들기 몇 세기 이전부터 아시아에서 발전해 오고 있었다. 인쇄에 사용되는 각각의 기계적인 부분에 관심을 보였던 발명가들과 달리 구텐베르크는 인쇄와 관련이 있는 모든 부분을 하나로 간주함으로써 그 공정을 다루었다. 그는 금속활자를 제작하기 위한 공정을 개발할 수 있었고 이것은 전에 만들어진 것보다 더 뚜렷한 상을 제작하기 위해 구리 주형을 사용했으므로 이전의 시도들과 차이가 있었다. 게다가 구텐베르크는 인쇄용으로 특별히 제작된 유성 잉크를 새로 개발했다. 이 잉크는 테레빈유, 숯, 호두 기름을 사용해 만들어졌으며 인쇄기에 사용하기 아주 적합한 기름기가 함유된 농도를 갖고 있었다. 마지막으로 그는 올리브 오일과 와인 생산에 사용하는 스크류식 기계와 구조적으로 비슷한 목판 인쇄기를 사용하는 인쇄 기술을 발명했고, 이는 인쇄된 면의 모든 부분에 동일한 압력이

11. 다른 단락들과의 관계에 비추어 1단락의 역할은 무엇인가?

Ⓐ 주제와 그것의 발달에 기여한 사람에 대한 역사적 배경을 소개한다.
Ⓑ 종이 인쇄술 영역에 혁신을 일으켰던 사람의 배경을 제공한다.
Ⓒ 인쇄술에서의 주요 기술적 변화와 활자를 만드는 데 이용된 방법을 설명한다.
Ⓓ 주제와 종이가 인쇄되는 방식에 혁신을 일으켰던 발명품의 결과를 밝혀준다.

12. 2단락에 따르면, 다음 중 인쇄에 사용된 목재의 한계가 아닌 것은 무엇인가?

Ⓐ 비교적 빠르게 마모된다.
Ⓑ 새기는 데 오래 걸린다.
Ⓒ 글자의 가독성에 영향을 끼치는 재질을 갖고 있다.
Ⓓ 어떤 지역에서는 쉽게 구할 수 없다.

13. 3단락에 따르면, 다음 중 구텐베르크의 인쇄술에 대해 사실이 아닌 것은 무엇인가?

Ⓐ 그의 기계에서 나온 인쇄물은 다른 인쇄 기술에 비해 더 선명하고 더 골랐다.
Ⓑ 구텐베르크는 인쇄 전용 잉크를 개발했다.
Ⓒ 구텐베르크는 올리브 오일과 와인 생산에 자신의 기계를 사용했다.
Ⓓ 인쇄물을 만들기 위한 믿을 만한 공정이었다.

14. 4단락에서 'it(그것)'이 가리키는 것은

Ⓐ 인쇄술
Ⓑ 구텐베르크 성경
Ⓒ 활자 공정
Ⓓ 상징

15. 다음 중 지문에 음영 표시된 문장의 핵심 정보를 가장 잘 표현한 문장은 무엇인가? 오답은 문장의 의미를 크게 왜곡하거나 핵심 정보를 누락하고 있다.

Ⓐ 금속활자가 전 세계적으로 많은 사회에 영향을 끼쳤다는 사실은 알려져 있다.
Ⓑ 구텐베르크의 인쇄술은 수백 년간 지속되었고, 전 세계적 문화에 영향을 끼쳤다.
Ⓒ 구텐베르크는 여러 차례 그의 기계를 다시 설계했고, 그 내구성 있는 기계장치가 수 세기에 걸쳐 사용될 수 있게 했다.

작용하게끔 했다. 그 결과 이미지 전체에 잉크가 고르게 분포된 일관된 인쇄물을 얻을 수 있었다.

4 ➡ 구텐베르크의 가장 유명한 도서 인쇄물은 180부가 제작된 구텐베르크 성경이었다. 이 책이 그의 활자 공정으로 인쇄된 첫 번째 책은 아니었지만, 그것은 구텐베르크의 상징일 뿐만 아니라 인쇄서 시대의 시작 역할을 하는 책이다. 이 발명으로 구텐베르크는 여러 세기 동안 지속된 인쇄 시대의 도래를 알렸고, 금속활자의 제작 공정은 오랫동안 바뀌지 않았으며 세계의 거의 모든 사회에 엄청난 영향을 가져왔다. 이것은 주로 금속활자의 높은 내구성 때문이었다. 덕분에 인쇄는 정보를 기록하는 경제적인 방법이 될 수 있었고 인쇄물의 보급을 촉진했다. 실제로 지식층뿐만 아니라 대중도 인쇄물을 접할 수 있게 되면서 금속활자의 효율성은 사회 전반에 영향을 끼쳤다. 확실히 이는 금속활자 사용 초창기에 상류 계층에 대한 위협으로 비추어졌고, 몇몇 사회에서는 정부가 금속활자 인쇄를 정부용으로만 제한하는 법을 만들기도 했다.

5 ➡ 구텐베르크는 글과 이미지를 대량으로 재생산할 수 있는 신뢰할 만하고 효율적인 방법을 만들어냄으로써 르네상스의 정착을 도운 것으로 평가되고 있다. 금속활자 인쇄는 책의 대량 생산을 최초로 가능하게 했고, 뉴스와 정보가 그 어느 때보다 빠르게 유럽 전역으로 퍼졌다. 이는 또한 책을 훨씬 더 싸게 만들어 글을 읽고 쓰는 능력이 빠르게 증가하도록 했다. 사람들은 과거에는 공부할 수 없었을 새로운 아이디어와 주제들에 노출되었다. 실제로 아이디어의 교환이 빠르게 가속화되어 과학 혁명의 시작에 불을 당겼다.

Ⓓ 구텐베르크가 금속활자를 개발할 때 세계 여러 사회에서 그에게 이를 위한 정보를 제공해 주었다.

16. 4단락에 따르면, 다음 중 구텐베르크 성경에 대해 사실인 것은 무엇인가?

Ⓐ 구텐베르크가 새롭게 만들어낸 인쇄 공정을 이용한 첫 번째 인쇄물이었다.
Ⓑ 인쇄 기계를 사용해서 만든 첫 번째 책이었다.
Ⓒ 금속활자와 유성 잉크로 인쇄되었다.
Ⓓ 대부분의 유럽 사회에서 일어난 엄청난 변화의 결과였다

17. 4단락에 따르면, 초기의 금속활자가 상류층 사람들에게 위협으로 여겨진 이유는

Ⓐ 인쇄술이 과거에 그랬던 것보다 훨씬 더 효율적이었기 때문에
Ⓑ 책이 사회의 하층 계급에게도 이용 가능한 것이 되었기 때문에
Ⓒ 책을 출간하는 사람을 규제하는 법안을 만들어야만 했기 때문에
Ⓓ 대중들이 금속활자를 사용하여 책을 인쇄했기 때문에

18. 5단락의 단어 'reliable(신뢰할 만한)'과 의미상 가장 가까운 것은

Ⓐ 평판이 좋은
Ⓑ 괜찮은
Ⓒ 복잡한
Ⓓ 믿을 만한

19. 지문에 다음 문장이 들어갈 수 있는 위치를 나타내는 네 개의 사각형 [■]을 확인하시오.

8세기 무렵에 중국인들은 문서와 그림으로 가득한 책 전체를 인쇄하는 데 이 기술을 사용했다.

이 문장이 들어가기에 가장 적합한 곳은? [■C]

20. 지시문: 지문을 간략하게 요약한 글의 첫 문장이 아래 제시되어 있다. 지문의 가장 중요한 내용을 표현하는 세 개의 선택지를 골라 요약문을 완성하시오. 일부 문장들은 지문에 제시되지 않았거나 지문의 지엽적인 내용을 나타내기 때문에 요약문에 포함되지 않는다. ***이 문제의 배점은 2점이다.***

활자는 역사적 중요성이 매우 큰 인쇄 과정이다.

Ⓒ 인쇄술은 원래 조각된 나무의 전체 판을 사용해서 행했지만 이것이 나중에는 목판활자로 바뀌었다.
Ⓔ 구텐베르크는 금속활자를 부속물로 사용하는 인쇄술을 만들어서 인쇄술의 혁신을 가져왔다.
Ⓕ 구텐베르크의 업적은 정보가 교류되는 속도를 높였으며 영향력이 있는 새로운 움직임들의 도화선이 되었다.

Ⓐ 종이 인쇄는 1400년대 이후로 존재했고 그 기간에 구텐베르크가 잘 알려진 인쇄술을 발달시키기 시작했다.
Ⓑ 목판 활자는 새겨 넣어야 했고 오랜 시간이 걸렸으므로 기능공의 세심한 주의를 필요로 했다.
Ⓓ 금속은 아주 오래가는 재료이기 때문에 인쇄 과정에서 사용되는 자형들을 만드는 데 상당히 유용하다.

어휘 movable adj 움직일 수 있는 | typography n 활판술, 인쇄술 | woodblock n 목판 | goldsmith n 금세공사 | fame n 명성 | implement v 이행하다, 수행하다 | component n 구성 요소 | accomplish v 이룩하다, 성취하다 | arduous adj 힘든 | necessitate v 필요로 하다 |

profoundly adv 깊이, 완전히 | durable adj 내구성 있는, 오래가는 | chisel v 조각하다, 끌로 파다 | bronze n 청동 | copper n 구리 | iron n 철 | tin n 주석 | matrices n (matrix의 복수형) 주형, 형틀 | mold n 거푸집, 주형 | place one's attention on ~에 주의를 기울이다 | turpentine n 테레빈유 | soot n 검댕, 그을음 | uniform adj 동일한 | evenly adv 고르게 | reliable adj 믿을 수 있는 | accelerate v 촉진하다

Actual Test 2

본서 | P. 89

1. C	2. B	3. A	4. C	5. D	6. A	7. C	8. B	9. B	10. A, D, E
11. A	12. C	13. B	14. B	15. B	16. C	17. A	18. D	19. A	20. B, C, D

본서 | P. 90

지진 예측

1 ➡ 지진은 지구에 영향을 미치는 가장 파괴적인 자연 재해 중 하나이고 그것의 예측 불가능한 특성은 그것을 더 심각하게 만든다. 그런 광범위한 파괴에 흔히 동반되는 심각한 인명 손실을 방지하는 데 도움이 될 수 있는 지진 움직임에 대한 정확한 예측은 오랫동안 과학자들의 목표였다. 불행히도 믿을 만한 지진 예측 방법은 아직 알려지지 않았지만 과학자들은 유망한 많은 지진 예측 방법을 계속 연구하고 있으며, 이 방법들은 장기 예측과 단기 예측이라는 두 개의 커다란 범주로 분류된다.

2 ➡ 지진의 장기 예측은 단층대의 특정 분절에 발생한 지진 활동의 역사적 기록을 연구함으로써 이루어진다. 과거 지진이 언제 발생했는지 연대표를 그리고 각 지진의 규모를 기록함으로써 과학자들은 활동 패턴을 만들고 특정 규모의 지진들 사이의 평균 간격을 알아낼 수 있다. 지진 활동 간의 간격을 연구함으로써 그들은 상당한 규모의 지진 사이에 흐른 평균 시간을 알아낼 수 있다. 특정 규모의 지진이 언제 마지막으로 발생했는지에 따라서 그들은 그 다음 것이 언제 발생할지에 대해 어느 정도 알고 추측할 수 있다. 이 방식은 평균치로 이루어지기 때문에 언제 지진이 일어날 가능성이 있는지 예측하는 데에만 사용될 수 있다. 이것은 몇 년에서 몇 십 년이라는 명시된 시간 간격보다 더 정확할 수 없다는 것을 뜻한다.

3 ➡ 단기 예측은 다음 지진이 언제 일어날지 충분히 정확하게 알아내어 인근 지역 사람들을 대피시킬 수 있게 하는 것에 초점을 둔다. 그러기 위해 과학자들은 전조라고 불리는 지난 지진들 직전에 발생한 현상을 연구하는 데 시간을 투자한다. 역사를 통틀어 그 사건들 전에 그 지역에 있었던 생존자들과 과학자들은 다양한 물리적, 화학적 현상을 관찰했다. 쉽게 관찰되는 현상에는 지반 변형과 물의 화학적 성분 변화와 우물과 호수의 수위 변화가 포함된다. 감지하기 위해 정교한 장치를 요구하는 다른 것들은 달라진 지진 활동과 더 직접적으로 관련이 있다. 단층대는 절대로 완전히 안정적이지 않기 때문에 잦은 미진과 지진파가 발생하지만 지진이 임박했을 때 지진파의 속도, 전진이라고 불리는 강한 진동의 빈도와 암석의 전기 저항은 전부 바뀐다.

4 ➡ 이런 많은 전조들을 설명하는 한 가지 이론은 체적팽창 이론이라고 불린다. 단층선에 위치한 암석이 압력 아래서 한계점에 근접하면 체적이 상당히 증가할 수 있다. [■A] 이런 부풀어 오름 또는 팽창

1. 다음 중 지문에 음영 표시된 문장의 핵심 정보를 가장 잘 표현한 문장은 무엇인가? 오답은 의미를 크게 왜곡하거나 핵심 정보를 누락하고 있다.

Ⓐ 감사하게도 과학자들은 지진이 언제 일어날지 예측할 믿을 만한 방법들을 개발해냈으며 이것들은 두 개의 기본 범주로 나뉜다.

Ⓑ 안타깝게도 과학자들은 지진을 장기적으로 정확히 예측하는 어떠한 방법도 발견하지 못할지 모르지만, 단기적 방법은 가능성을 보인다.

Ⓒ 과학자들은 실패할 염려가 없는 지진 예측 방법을 아직 발견하지 못했지만 장기적 예측과 단기적 예측에 맞는 많은 가능성 있는 방법들을 연구하고 있다.

Ⓓ 과학자들은 지진을 예측할 많은 방법들을 개발했지만 이들은 범위가 넓은 장기적 예측에만 쓸모가 있다.

2. 2단락에 따르면, 지진의 장기 예측은 어떻게 이루어지는가?

Ⓐ 한 단층 분절과 그 근처 단층들에서 발생한 비슷한 규모의 지진을 비교함으로써

Ⓑ 지진 활동 패턴에서 확인된 지진 간격을 분석함으로써

Ⓒ 한 단층의 여러 분절에서 발생한 지진의 역사적 연대를 비교함으로써

Ⓓ 모든 지진 사이의 평균적인 시간 간격을 계산함으로써

3. 2단락의 단어 'specified(명시된)'와 의미상 가장 가까운 것은

Ⓐ 정해진

Ⓑ 관찰된

Ⓒ 전형적인

Ⓓ 확고한

4. 3단락에 따르면, 다음 중 지진의 전조 현상이 아닌 것은

Ⓐ 지질의 변화

Ⓑ 암석의 저항력

Ⓒ 단층대의 불안정함

Ⓓ 증가된 지진 활동

이라고 불리는 이것은 암석의 결정체로 된 층 사이의 미세한 균열로 인해 생긴다. [■B] 암석의 약한 알갱이가 분리되면 그 틈으로 지하수가 흘러 들어가 그 틈이 벌어져 있게 만든다. 이것은 암석의 밀도를 바꿔 바위가 지진 에너지를 전달하는 방법을 바꾸고 물 또한 그것의 전기 전도성을 바꾼다. [■C] 팽창이 커다란 바위 층 전역에 발생하면 불가피한 지진 파열이 임박했을 때 지형이 극적으로 변할 수 있다. [■D] 과학자들의 우려를 사고 있는 이런 땅의 융기된 부분 중 한 곳은 샌안드레아스 단층을 따라 로스앤젤레스 근처에 발생했다. 장기 예측이 이 지역에 대규모 지진이 곧 일어날 가능성이 있다고 보여주기 때문에 과학자들은 팜데일 융기라고 불리는 이 특징적인 부분을 앞으로 있을 전조를 감지하기 위해 면밀히 감시하고 있다. 팽창은 지하수 움직임과 우물 또는 호수의 수질에 영향을 미치기도 한다. 물이 암석 균열을 채우면 우물과 호수에 있는 수량이 감소할 수 있다. 암석이 쪼개져서 벌어질 때 가스와 광물이 암석으로부터 방출되면 물의 화학적 성분 또한 바뀔 수 있다. 특히 단층에 압력이 증가할 때 라돈 가스 수치가 물 속에서 증가하는 것으로 보여진다. 진동의 빈도와 강도 또한 증가하는 경향을 보이다가 실제 지진이 일어나기 바로 직전에 급작스럽게 감소한다. 이런 폭풍전야는 물이 암석을 채우기 전에 일시적인 암석 강도의 증가로 야기된다고 여겨진다.

5 ➡ 체적팽창 이론의 현상은 전형적인 일련의 사건들로 정리될 수 있다. 1단계에서는 단층대 한 지역에 압력이 증가한다. 2, 3단계에서는 암석이 팽창하고 미세균열에 물이 차오르면서 팽창의 효과가 느껴진다. 4단계는 대규모 지진이고 5단계는 여진이라고 불리는 추가적인 강진을 흔히 포함하는 큰 지진 후의 여파다. 불행히도 이런 단계들은 모든 지진마다 그 길이가 일정하지는 않으며 전조 현상들은 큰 지진이 일어날 것을 보장하지 않는다. 모든 지진 사건은 제각각 다르기 때문에 전조 현상을 사용해 지진이 언제 일어날지 정확하게 예측하는 것은 매우 힘들다. 예를 들면 1989년에 로마프리타 지진이 발생했을 때 두 번의 규모 5.0의 전진이 15개월과 2개월 전에 앞서 있었고 매번 과학자들은 며칠 이내에 더 강한 지진이 발생할 것이라고 예측했다. 하지만 지진은 일어나지 않았고, 규모 6.9의 지진이 결국 발생했을 때 사람들은 준비되어 있지 않았다. 과학자들은 더 많은 연구와 분석을 통해 체적팽창 이론의 개선이 가능하다고 믿으며 또는 더 나은 새로운 방법이 개발될 수 있다고 생각한다.

5. 3단락의 단어 'imminent(임박한)'와 의미상 가장 가까운 것은

Ⓐ 매우 중요한
Ⓑ 강한 강도의
Ⓒ 짧은 간격으로 발생하는
Ⓓ 곧 일어나려고 하는

6. 글쓴이가 4단락에서 '샌안드레아스 단층'을 언급하는 이유는 무엇인가?

Ⓐ 지형을 변화시키는 전조 현상의 예를 제공하기 위해
Ⓑ 그 지역이 왜 팜데일 융기라고 불리는지 설명하기 위해
Ⓒ 체적팽창 이론의 반례가 되는 지역을 소개하기 위해
Ⓓ 고위험 지역을 파악하는 데에 있어 장기 예측의 효과를 강조하기 위해

7. 4단락에 따르면, 다음 중 물과 관련된 전조 현상에 대해 사실인 것은 무엇인가?

Ⓐ 바위 균열을 채우는 물 속의 라돈 농도는 감소한다.
Ⓑ 지하수 수위의 변화는 전진의 빈도를 증가시킨다.
Ⓒ 바위에서 방출된 광물은 물의 화학적 성분에 변화를 일으킨다.
Ⓓ 수역은 수량의 증가를 보인다.

8. 5단락은 어떻게 조직되어 있는가?

Ⓐ 체적팽창 이론의 개요를 설명하고 지진 예측의 새로운 방법이 왜 발달될 필요가 있는지 이유를 제공한다.
Ⓑ 체적팽창 이론이 어떻게 다섯 단계로 나뉘어져 있는지와 실생활 적용에서의 한계를 설명한다.
Ⓒ 대규모 지진의 진행과 지진 예측이 왜 어려운지 이유를 보여준다.
Ⓓ 전조 현상을 다섯 개의 분명한 범주로 나누고 그들이 어떻게 나타나는지 실제 사례를 제공한다.

9. 지문에 다음 문장이 들어갈 수 있는 위치를 나타내는 네 개의 사각형 [■]을 확인하시오.

암석의 약한 알갱이가 분리되면 그 틈으로 지하수가 흘러 들어가 그 틈이 벌어져 있게 만든다.

이 문장이 들어가기에 가장 적합한 곳은? [■B]

10. **지시문:** 지문을 간략하게 요약한 글의 첫 문장이 아래 제시되어 있다. 지문의 가장 중요한 내용을 표현하는 세 개의 선택지를 골라 요약문을 완성하시오. 일부 문장들은 지문에 제시되지 않았거나 지문의 지엽적인 내용을 나타내기 때문에 요약문에 포함되지 않는다. ***이 문제의 배점은 2점이다.***

정확한 지진 예측은 수년 동안 과학적인 목표였지만 완전히 신뢰할 만한 방법은 아직 발견되지 않았다.

Ⓐ 큰 지진의 단계 순서는 알려졌지만 각 단계의 지속 기간은 동일하지 않아서 예측을 어렵게 만든다.
Ⓓ 땅의 팽창, 증가하는 전진과 수위의 변화와 같은 사건들은 임박한 지진의 지표들이다.
Ⓔ 지진 활동의 연대표를 만듦으로써 과학자들은 비슷한 규모의 지진이 언제 발생할지 예측하는 것을 도와주는 패턴을 찾는다.

Ⓑ 지각 변동의 예 중 하나는 대규모 지진이 곧 발생할 가능성이 있는 샌안드레아스 단층의 팜데일 융기다.
Ⓒ 체적 팽창 이론에서 1단계에서 3단계까지는 각각 4, 5단계로 분류된 큰 지진과 여진을 앞서는 전조 현상들이다.
Ⓕ 로마프리타 지진의 예측은 과학자들이 앞선 전진 후 얼마나 더 있어야 지진이 발생할지를 정확하게 예측하지 못했기 때문에 실패했다.

어휘 devastating adj 대단히 파괴적인 | natural disaster 자연 재해 | unpredictable adj 예측할 수 없는 | seismic event 지진 움직임 | accompany v 동반하다 | destruction n 파괴 | promising adj 유망한, 촉망되는 | seismic activity 지진 활동 | segment n 부분, 한쪽 | fault zone 단층대 | timeline n 연대표 | interval n 간격 | gap n 틈, 공백 | significant adj 중요한, 상당한 | magnitude n 규모 | educated guess 경험에서 우러난 추측 | potential n 가능성 | specified adj 명시된 | focused adj 집중한 | determine v 알아내다, 밝히다 | evacuate v 대피하다 | devote v 전념하다, 바치다 | precursor n 전조 | phenomenon n 현상 | deformation n 변형, 기형 | sophisticated adj 세련된, 정교한 | altered adj 바뀐 | imminent adj 임박한 | seismic wave 지진파 | tremor n 미진, 떨림 | foreshock n 전진 | electrical resistance 전기 저항 | dilatancy model 체적팽창 이론 | fault line 단층선 | breaking point 한계점 | dilation n 팽창 | microcrack n 미세균열 | crystalline adj 결정(질)의, 결정체로 된 | conductivity n 전도성 | inevitable adj 불가피한 | rupture n 파열, 터짐 | uplift n (땅의) 융기 | groundwater n 지하수 | fissure n (암석의) 길게 갈라진 틈 | abruptly adv 갑자기 | impregnate v 스며들게 하다, 포화시키다 | aftermath n 여파 | aftershock n 여진 | precede v 앞서다 | refinement n 개선, 개량

본서 | P. 94

영화의 발달

1 ➡ 영화의 발달은 19세기 중반에 활동 요지경의 발명으로 시작되었다. 화가들은 움직임의 다양한 단계를 보여주는 일련의 그림들, 예를 들자면 커플이 춤추는 그림 같은 것을 그렸다. 이런 그림들은 한 사람이 들여다 볼 수 있는 입구가 있는 원통 안에 넣어졌다. 원통이 적절한 속도로 회전하면 관찰자에게는 원통이 움직이는 대신 실제로 춤추는 사람들이 움직이는 것처럼 보였다. 이런 착시 현상은 파이 현상이라 불리고 이것은 인간이 빠르게 연속으로 일련의 영상을 보면 우리의 눈이 연속 동작을 인지하기 때문에 발생한다. 춤추는 사람들의 그림은 변하지 않지만 우리의 머리는 그것을 움직이는 한 개의 영상으로 보는 방식으로 정보를 처리한다. 1870년대까지 카메라 기술은 예술가인 에드워드 마이브리지가 이 현상을 일련의 카메라를 사용해 모사할 수 있을 정도로 진보했다.

2 ➡ 에드워드 마이브리지는 자연 풍경 사진과 미국 서부의 연구로 유명한 전문 사진가였다. 1872년에 그는 릴런드 스탠퍼드에게서 말의 움직임에 대한 질문을 해결해 달라는 요청을 받았다. 많은 사람들은 말이 빠른 걸음이나 전속력으로 움직일 때 균형을 위해 최소한 한 발굽은 땅에 두고 있다고 믿었다. [■A] 다른 사람들은 말이 특정 시점에서는 네 발굽 모두 공중에 떠 있을 거라고 주장했다. 카메라의 셔터 속도는 마이브리지가 24개를 한 줄로 정렬시켜 말의 움직임을 담아낼 수 있을 정도로 충분히 빨라졌다. [■B] 기수가 말을 타고 시속 36마일 속도로 카메라를 지날 때 그것은 카메라를 작동시키는 트립 와이어를 작동시켰다. [■C] 그 결과로 찍힌 사진들 중 몇몇은 말이 때로는 네 발굽 전부 실제로 공중에 떠 있는 것을 보여줬다. [■D] 마이브리지는 그 사진들을 실루엣으로 변환했고 자신의 설계로 만든 장치에 함께 넣어서 청중이 볼 수 있게끔 스크린에 비추어 첫 영화 전시회를 열었다.

11. 1단락에서 글쓴이가 '파이 현상'을 언급하는 이유는 무엇인가?
Ⓐ 영화를 가능케 한 개념을 설명하기 위해
Ⓑ 인간의 시각적 능력의 다재다능함을 강조하기 위해
Ⓒ 활동 요지경이 왜 원통 형태로 나왔는지를 설명하기 위해
Ⓓ 활동 요지경을 만든 화가들은 분명히 과학자들이었을 거라고 암시하기 위해

12. 2단락의 단어 'converted(변환했다)'와 의미상 가장 가까운 것은
Ⓐ 재현했다
Ⓑ 이동했다
Ⓒ 바꾸었다
Ⓓ 적용했다

13. 2단락에서 마이브리지의 작업에 대해 추론 가능한 것은 무엇인가?
Ⓐ 그는 기수가 말을 특정 속도로 몰 것을 특별히 요청했다.
Ⓑ 카메라들은 단일 렌즈로 여러 장의 사진을 촬영할 만큼 진보하지 않았다.
Ⓒ 그가 움직이는 동물과 작업을 한 것은 처음이었다.
Ⓓ 그는 의도치 않게 동물학 분야에 돌파구를 제공했다.

14. 3단락의 단어 'flexible(유연한)'과 의미상 가장 가까운 것은
Ⓐ 손상되기 쉬운
Ⓑ 구부릴 수 있는
Ⓒ 적응할 수 있는
Ⓓ 뻣뻣한

3 ➡ 영화에 있어 다음으로 큰 혁신은 1880년대 후반에 셀룰로이드 사진 필름과 단일 렌즈로 사진을 연속으로 찍을 수 있는 카메라의 탄생으로 이루어졌다. 유연한 셀룰로이드는 필름 스트립이 카메라에 넣어지는 릴로 감아지는 것을 가능하게 했는데 이것은 몇 초가 아닌 몇 분의 움직임이 촬영되는 것을 가능하게 했다. 마이브리지를 만난 후 토머스 에디슨은 자신만의 영사기와 전시 기구를 개발하기로 결심했다. 그 최종 결과는 필름 스트립을 전구와 렌즈 사이에 통과시키는 키네토스코프였다. 불행히도 키네토스코프는 한번에 한 사람만 사용할 수 있었기 때문에 1894년 뉴욕시에 첫 상업 영화관이 열렸을 때 주인은 기계를 10개 구입해야 했다. 이것이 요구하는 상당한 투자액에도 불구하고 키네토스코프 영화관들은 전국의 주요 도시에 생겨났고 에디슨의 회사는 큰 수익을 거둬들였다.

4 ➡ 키네토스코프가 벌어들이는 수익액 때문에 에디슨은 투사 시스템을 개발해야 할 필요성을 느끼지 않았다. 하지만 다른 회사에 있는 그의 경쟁 상대들은 기계 대 관객 비율 때문에 영화를 더 많은 관객에게 보여주는 것이 훨씬 더 수익성이 있을 거란 것을 인지했다. 많은 기술 혁신이 다른 회사들에서 있었지만 결국 에디슨은 그 결과물인 바이터스코프를 대량생산할 것을 제안받았다. 이 기기는 고휘도 전구를 사용해 영화를 벽이나 천막에 투사했고 그 기술은 수십 년 동안 근본적으로 동일하게 유지되었다. 제작된 가장 초창기의 영화들은 오늘날 기준으로는 단순해 보이지만 그것들은 관중에게 엄청난 영향을 미쳤다. 그것들은 한 시점에서 촬영되었고 아무 수정 없이 한 가지 행위나 사건을 묘사했다. 그것들은 춤, 체육 행사, 자연 풍경, 그리고 유명한 것으로는 기차역에 도착하는 기차를 보여주었다. 기차 영화가 촬영된 각도는 기차가 마치 관객에게 다가오는 것처럼 보이게 했고 스크린과 가깝던 사람들은 두려움으로 좌석에서 달아났다.

5 ➡ 영화의 두 번째 단계는 이야기를 전하기 시작했고 여러 거리와 각도에서 촬영한 다른 장면과 샷을 도입했다. 이런 영화들은 고작 5분에서 10분 길이였는데 이것은 필름 릴이 그만큼의 필름만 수용할 수 있었기 때문이었다. 음향은 기술이 상업적으로 사용 가능해진 1920년대 후반에야 가능해졌다. 그래서 등장인물 간의 대화나 이야기에 대한 설명은 타이틀 카드라고 불리는 글씨가 담긴 빈 스크린을 사용하는 것으로 이루어졌다. 이런 이유로 이 시대의 영화들은 '무성 영화'라고 불리지만 영화관 주인들은 피아노나 오르간 연주자를 고용해 장면들에 보탤 음악을 반주하게 했다. 영화들은 연주되는 음악이 적절하도록 보장하기 위해 보통 준비된 악보와 함께 유통되었고 어떤 영화들은 오케스트라를 고용하는 큰 영화관들을 위해 악보 전부를 갖추었다. 음향 기술이 말소리와 음악과 음향 효과와 함께 사운드 트랙을 포함하기에 적합해지자 영화 스튜디오들은 겉으로 보기에 하룻밤 사이에 '발성 영화'를 제작하는 것으로 변천했다.

15. 다음 중 3단락에서 키네토스코프에 대해 언급되지 않은 것은 무엇인가?

Ⓐ 셀룰로이드 필름을 활용했다.
Ⓑ 렌즈를 통해 몇 분 길이의 필름 스트립을 투사했다.
Ⓒ 한 번에 한 관람자만 허용했다.
Ⓓ 사용을 위해 상당한 재정적 투자를 필요로 했다.

16. 4단락에 따르면, 에디슨이 투사 시스템을 향한 움직임에 늦게 합류한 이유는 무엇인가?

Ⓐ 그의 키네토스코프 장사가 증가된 기기 대 관객 비율로 어려워질 것이었다.
Ⓑ 그는 그의 키네토스코프를 넘어설 더 이상의 혁신이 있을 수 없다고 믿었다.
Ⓒ 그는 더 많은 관객이 더 수익성이 있을 거라는 것을 깨닫는 선견지명이 없었다.
Ⓓ 그의 회사는 투사 시스템을 대량 생산하는 것에 대해 마지막으로 요청을 받은 회사였다.

17. 다음 중 지문에 음영 표시된 문장의 핵심 정보를 가장 잘 표현한 문장은 무엇인가? 오답은 의미를 크게 왜곡하거나 핵심 정보를 누락하고 있다.

Ⓐ 기차 영화는 기차가 충돌할 거라고 관객이 생각하게 만드는 방식으로 촬영되어 관객들은 도망갔다.
Ⓑ 기차 영화는 역으로 다가서는 기차가 잘못된 방향으로 와서 사람들을 치는 모습을 보여주었고 이는 관객이 두려움에 질리게 했다.
Ⓒ 한 영화에 나오는 기차는 엄청나게 빠른 속도로 카메라에 다가오는 모습이 보였고, 이는 관객들의 일부가 겁을 먹게 했다.
Ⓓ 기차 영화는 카메라 앵글이 관객들을 칠 것처럼 보이게 했기 때문에 인기가 아주 많았다.

18. 다음 중 5단락에서 언급되지 않은 것은

Ⓐ 영화가 어떻게 이야기를 전달하는 매체로 등장했는지
Ⓑ 초기 영화에서 상대적으로 정교한 영화 제작 기술의 진보
Ⓒ 발성 영화로의 이행이 일어난 시기
Ⓓ 영화관 주인들이 오케스트라를 위해 악보를 준비한 이유

19. 지문에 다음 문장이 들어갈 수 있는 위치를 나타내는 네 개의 사각형 [■]을 확인하시오.

다른 사람들은 말이 특정 시점에서는 네 발굽 모두 공중에 떠 있을 거라고 주장했다.

이 문장이 들어가기에 가장 적합한 곳은? [■A]

20. 지시문: 지문을 간략하게 요약한 글의 첫 문장이 아래 제시되어 있다. 지문의 가장 중요한 내용을 표현하는 세 개의 선택지를 골라 요약문을 완성하시오. 일부 문장들은 지문에 제시되지 않았거나 지문의 지엽적인 내용을 나타내기 때문에 요약문에 포함되지 않는다. ***이 문제의 배점은 2점이다.***

영화는 19세기 후반과 20세기 초반에 과학적 혁신품에서 주류 오락거리의 형태로 빠르게 발전했다.

Ⓑ 에디슨의 키네토스코프는 그 자체로도 혁신이었지만 또한 처음으로 대중이 짧은 영화들을 오락거리로 소비할 수 있게 해준 것이었다.
Ⓒ 더 많은 관객이 들 경우의 큰 수익성을 감지하고 많은 사람들이 투사 시스템을 개발하는 데 뛰어들었고 바이터스코프를 만들어냈다.
Ⓓ 초기 '무성 영화'들은 '발성 영화'로의 이행이 일어날 때까지 음향의 부재를 타이틀 카드와 라이브 음악 반주를 포함하는 것으로 보충했다.

Ⓐ 마이브리지의 기발한 카메라 설치는 말들이 달릴 때 정말로 네 발굽 모두 공중에 떠 있다는 결론을 제공하도록 해주었다.
Ⓔ 초기 키네토스코프 영화관들은 선불로 상당한 투자를 해야 했지만 그것들에 대한 높은 수요는 그 비용을 상쇄했다.
Ⓕ 움직이지 않는 일련의 그림들을 움직이는 것으로 인지하게끔 하는 파이 현상은 영화 산업에 동력을 제공하는 과학적 돌파구다.

어휘 motion picture 영화 | zoetrope **n** 활동 요지경(통 안의 그림이 움직이는 것처럼 보이는 회전 장치) | cylinder **n** 원통 | optical illusion 착시 현상 | succession **n** 연속, 잇따름 | perceive **v** 감지하다, 인지하다 | advance **v** 전진하다 | replicate **v** 모사하다, 복제하다 | trot **n** 속보 | gallop **n** 질주 | jockey **n** 기수 | trigger **v** 촉발시키다 | activate **v** 작동시키다, 활성화하다 | convert **v** 전환시키다 | project **v** 투사하다, 투영하다 | exhibition **n** 전시 | innovation **n** 혁신 | flexible **adj** 유연한 | apparatus **n** 기구, 장치 | commercial **adj** 상업의 | investment **n** 투자 | launch **v** 개시하다 | reap **v** 거두다, 수확하다 | generate **v** 발생시키다, 만들어 내다 | compel **v** 강요하다, ~하게 만들다 | counterpart **n** (동일한 지위나 기능을 갖는) 상대 | profitable **adj** 수익성이 있는 | mass produce 대량생산하다 | profound **adj** 엄청난, 깊은 | perspective **n** 관점, 시각 | depict **v** 그리다, 묘사하다 | alteration **n** 변화, 개조 | incorporate **v** 포함하다 | character **n** 등장인물 | sheet music 악보 | score **n** 악보 | transition **v** 변천하다, 이행하다 | seemingly **adv** 외견상으로, 겉보기에는

Lesson 01 Main Idea

본서 | P. 104

Practice

Passage 1 B Passage 2 B Passage 3 D Passage 4 B

Practice

본서 | P. 108

Passage 1 Man: Professor | Woman: Student

Listen to part of a conversation between a student and a professor.

W Good afternoon, Professor Norton. Are you busy at the moment?

M Not at all, Bethany, how can I help you?

W I wasn't able to get a copy of the material you gave out in class today. They ran out before they reached my desk.

M I see. Of course you can. I'll get my assistant to make you a copy immediately. Oh, while you are here, I'd like to discuss your paper proposal. Could you spare a few minutes?

W My proposal? Certainly, Professor Norton.

남자: 교수 | 여자: 학생

학생과 교수의 대화를 들으시오.

여 안녕하세요, 노턴 교수님. 지금 바쁘신가요?

남 괜찮아요, 베타니, 무엇을 도와드릴까요?

여 오늘 수업 때 나눠주셨던 자료 복사본을 받지 못했어요. 제 책상에 오기 전에 다 떨어졌거든요.

남 전혀요. 물론 복사본 받을 수 있죠. 지금 내 조교에게 바로 한 부 복사해주라고 할게요. 아, 학생이 여기 왔으니 말인데, 학생의 리포트 제안서에 관해 논의하고 싶네요. 잠깐 시간 좀 낼 수 있나요?

여 제 제안서요? 그럼요, 노턴 교수님.

Q. Why did the student come to see the professor?

(A) To provide the reason why the student missed a class
(B) To ask for a handout that the student did not receive
(C) To discuss ideas for the student's next writing assignment
(D) To talk about an assignment that the student failed to complete

Q. 학생은 왜 교수를 만나러 왔는가?

(A) 학생이 수업에 참석하지 못한 이유를 제시하기 위해
(B) 학생이 받지 못한 프린트물을 요청하기 위해
(C) 학생의 다음 글쓰기 과제를 위한 아이디어를 논의하기 위해
(D) 학생이 완성하지 못한 과제에 대해 이야기하기 위해

어휘 copy n 복사본 | run out 떨어지다, 고갈되다 | assistant n 조교 | immediately adv 즉시, 바로 | discuss v 논의하다 | proposal n 제안서

Passage 2 Man: Professor | Woman: Student

Listen to part of a conversation between a student and a professor.

W Excuse me, professor. Can I speak to you about the school newspaper for a minute?

M Go ahead. What's on your mind?

W Well, I'm having some problems with a student reporter for the sports section. His stories are well written and he is really good at reporting, but he never meets the deadlines. I've spoken to him many times, but he doesn't seem to respond.

M There're some people who just cannot manage their time well enough to submit reports on time. It's difficult to motivate people to make deadlines, but that's your job as an editor.

W What can I do, then?

남자: 교수 | 여자: 학생

학생과 교수의 대화를 들으시오.

여 실례합니다, 교수님. 학교 신문에 대해 잠시 이야기 좀 할 수 있을까요?

남 말해보세요. 무슨 일이죠?

여 저, 스포츠 섹션의 학생 기자와 문제가 좀 있어서요. 그 기자는 기사도 잘 쓰고 보도에도 정말 능숙해요. 하지만 마감일을 지킨 적이 없어요. 제가 여러 번 이야기했지만, 반응이 없어요.

남 제때 보고서를 제출할 만큼 충분히 시간을 잘 관리할 수 없는 사람들이 좀 있죠. 마감일을 맞추도록 동기 부여를 하는 건 어려워요. 하지만 그것이 편집자로서 학생의 역할이죠.

여 그렇다면 제가 뭘 할 수 있을까요?

Q. Why did the student want to speak to the professor?

Ⓐ She needs a new sports reporter for the school newspaper.

Ⓑ She has a problem with the school newspaper's sports reporter.

Ⓒ She wants to become a sports reporter for the school newspaper.

Ⓓ She wants to create a sports section in the school newspaper.

Q. 학생은 왜 교수와 이야기하기를 원했는가?

Ⓐ 학교 신문에 새로운 스포츠 기자가 필요해서

Ⓑ 학교 신문 스포츠 기자와 문제가 있어서

Ⓒ 학교 신문 스포츠 기자가 되고 싶어서

Ⓓ 학교 신문에 스포츠 섹션을 만들고 싶어서

어휘 reporter n 기자 | report v 보도하다 | deadline n 마감 기한 | respond v 반응하다 | manage v 관리하다, ~를 해내다 | submit v 제출하다 | motivate v 동기 부여를 하다 | editor n 편집자

Passage 3 Man: Student | Woman: Housing officer

Listen to part of a conversation between a student and a housing officer.

W Good afternoon. How may I help you?

M I applied for my room to be repainted ages ago, but nothing's been done. I've had all my stuff packed away and boxed up to keep it out of the way of the workmen.

W That's strange. We usually repaint rooms very quickly to avoid inconveniencing people. Let me check the system to see what's happened. Ahh? Ahh... The painter's been around twice, but nobody was home. You didn't check the box on the form to allow access to your room when you were out, so he couldn't get inside.

M Oh, I didn't notice that when I filled out the form. What should I do now?

남자: 학생 | 여자: 기숙사 담당자

학생과 기숙사 담당자의 대화를 들으시오.

여 안녕하세요. 무엇을 도와드릴까요?

남 오래 전에 제 방을 새로 칠해달라고 신청했는데, 아무것도 안 해줘서요. 일하시는 분들에게 방해가 안 되도록 제 짐들을 다 싸서 보관하려고 박스에 담아 치워 놓았어요.

여 이상하군요. 저희는 대개 사람들을 불편하게 만드는 걸 피하기 위해서 페인트칠을 아주 빨리 다시 하거든요. 어떻게 된 일인지 시스템을 확인해 볼게요. 아? 아... 페인트 칠하는 사람이 두 번 갔는데 아무도 없었군요. 학생은 양식상에서 부재중일 때 방에 들어가는 것을 허락하는 빈칸에 표시를 하지 않았어요. 그래서 그가 들어갈 수 없었네요.

남 오, 양식을 작성할 때 그건 알아차리지 못했어요. 그럼 이제 어떻게 해야 하죠?

Q. What are the speakers discussing?

Ⓐ Hiring workmen to repaint the school dormitories

Ⓑ Problems with a painting in a dormitory room

Ⓒ Applying to have a dormitory room repainted

Ⓓ Organizing access to a student's room in order to paint it

Q. 화자들은 무엇에 관해 이야기하고 있는가?

Ⓐ 학교 기숙사 페인트칠을 다시 하기 위해 인부들을 고용하는 것

Ⓑ 기숙사 방에 있는 그림과 관련된 문제

Ⓒ 기숙사 방을 다시 페인트칠하도록 신청하는 것

Ⓓ 학생의 방을 칠하러 들어갈 수 있도록 조정하는 것

어휘 apply v 신청하다, 지원하다 | repaint v 다시 페인트칠하다 | stuff n 물건 | workman n 일꾼, 일하는 사람 | strange adj 이상한 | avoid v 피하다 | inconvenience v 불편하게 하다 | access n 접근, 허용 | notice v 알아차리다

Passage 4 Man: Student | Woman: Registrar

Listen to part of a conversation between a student and a registrar.

M Can I sign up for swimming classes here? I've been looking forward to the opening of the new pool because I've always wanted to learn how to swim. When I heard the pool was

남자: 학생 | 여자: 학적부 직원

학생과 학적부 직원의 대화를 들으시오.

남 여기서 수영 강습을 등록할 수 있나요? 저는 항상 수영을 배우고 싶었기 때문에 새로운 수영장 개장을 고대하고 있었어요. 금요일에 수영장이 개장했다는 소식을 듣고 등록하러 곧장 여기로 온 거예요.

opening on Friday, I came straight over here to sign up.

W You can sign up here, but you know that swimming classes are not free. The pool is free for recreational use, but students who want to take classes have to pay 100 dollars a semester because we have to pay the instructors.

M That's OK. I didn't expect free classes.

Q. What is the conversation mainly about?

Ⓐ Plans to open a new swimming pool on the campus

Ⓑ Registration for swimming classes at the new campus pool

Ⓒ The opening ceremony for an on-campus swimming pool

Ⓓ Hiring swimming instructors for the new campus swimming pool

여 여기서 등록하실 수 있어요. 하지만 수영 강습은 무료가 아닌 것 아시죠. 수영장을 일반적으로 사용하는 것은 무료지만, 우리도 강사료를 지급해야 하기 때문에 강습을 원하는 학생들은 학기당 100달러를 내야 해요.

남 좋아요. 무료 강습을 기대하지는 않았어요.

Q. 대화는 주로 무엇에 관한 것인가?

Ⓐ 캠퍼스에 새로운 수영장을 열기 위한 계획

Ⓑ 새로운 교내 수영장에서 수영 강습 등록

Ⓒ 교내 수영장 개장 기념식

Ⓓ 새로운 교내 수영장에 수영 강사를 고용하는 것

어휘 sign up 신청하다 I recreational adj 오락의, 여가의 I instructor n 강사 I expect v 예상하다

Lesson 02 Details

본서 I P. 110

Practice

Passage 1 D Passage 2 A Passage 3 B Passage 4 C

Practice

본서 I P. 114

Passage 1

Man: Professor I Woman: Student

Listen to part of a conversation between a student and a professor.

M Hello, Cassie, I'm glad you could make it.

W Hello, professor, you said you wanted to discuss my presentation?

M Yes, I think that the topic you have now is just too broad. The causes of the American Civil War are a huge topic, especially for a speech of this length. You should narrow it down a bit more. Instead of all the reasons, maybe you could focus on something like why the poor Southerners supported the conflict.

W Actually, I would really like to focus on the formation of African American units. Why they wanted to fight and the difficulties that they faced.

M That… would also work quite well.

Q. What will the woman do a presentation on?

Ⓐ Reasons that the war was fought

Ⓑ The beginning of the American Civil War

남자: 교수 I 여자: 학생

학생과 교수의 대화를 들으시오.

남 안녕하세요, 캐시, 올 수 있어서 다행이에요.

여 안녕하세요, 교수님, 제 발표에 관해 논의하고 싶다고 하셨죠?

남 그래요, 지금 학생의 주제는 너무 범위가 넓은 것 같아요. 남북 전쟁의 원인들은 엄청나게 큰 주제이고, 이 길이의 발표에는 특히 더 그렇죠. 조금 더 범위를 좁혀야 해요. 모든 이유들에 관해 발표하는 대신, 왜 가난한 남부인들이 갈등을 지지했는지 같은 것에 집중할 수 있죠.

여 사실, 저는 아프리카계 미국인 부대들의 형성에 집중하고 싶어요. 왜 그들이 싸우고 싶어 했는지, 그리고 그들이 마주했던 어려움에 관해서요.

남 그것도... 상당히 괜찮겠네요

Q. 여자는 무엇에 관해 발표할 것인가?

Ⓐ 전쟁이 일어난 이유들

Ⓑ 남북 전쟁의 시작

Ⓒ Why poor Southerners opposed the war
Ⓓ The experiences of African American soldiers

Ⓒ 가난한 남부인들이 전쟁을 반대한 이유
Ⓓ 아프리카계 미국인 군인들의 경험

어휘 discuss v 논의하다 I broad adj 넓은 I American Civil War (미국의) 남북 전쟁 I narrow down ~를 좁히다 I conflict n 갈등 I formation n 형성 I unit n 부대 I difficulty n 어려움 I face v 맞닥뜨리다

Passage 2 Man: Student | Woman: Professor

Listen to part of a conversation between a student and a professor.

M Excuse me, professor. Could I ask you some questions?

W Sure, what do you need to know?

M As you know, I am applying for an overseas internship in France. There are many documents that I need. I have provided a letter of recommendation from my language professor, a certification of my French language skills, and an essay about why I want the position written in French.

W Great, then you just need to submit copies of your transcript and résumé and a completed application form.

M Fantastic, I have all but one of those, and the registrar's office can give me that.

남자: 학생 | 여자: 교수

학생과 교수의 대화를 들으시오.

남 실례합니다, 교수님. 뭔가 여쭤봐도 괜찮을까요?

여 그럼요. 무엇이 알고 싶나요?

남 교수님도 아시겠지만 제가 프랑스의 외국 인턴십에 지원하려고 하는데요. 필요한 서류들이 많아요. 언어 교수님의 추천서, 프랑스어 구사 능력 인증서, 그리고 왜 그 일자리를 원하는지 프랑스어로 쓴 에세이를 보냈어요.

여 훌륭해요. 그러면 이제 학생의 성적 증명서 사본과 이력서, 그리고 작성한 지원서를 제출하기만 하면 돼요.

남 잘됐네요. 그것들 중 하나만 빼고 다 있거든요. 그리고 그건 교무처에서 받을 수 있어요.

Q. What document does the man need to get?

Ⓐ A copy of his transcript
Ⓑ A letter of recommendation
Ⓒ A certificate of his language ability
Ⓓ An essay written in French

Q. 남자는 어떤 서류를 받아야 하는가?

Ⓐ 성적 증명서 사본
Ⓑ 추천서
Ⓒ 언어 능력 인증서
Ⓓ 프랑스어로 쓴 에세이

어휘 apply v 지원하다 I overseas adj 해외의, 외국의 I provide v 제공하다 I letter of recommendation 추천서 I certification n 인증서 I submit v 제출하다 I transcript n 성적 증명서 I résumé n 이력서 I completed adj 작성한, 완성된 I application form 지원서 I fantastic adj 환상적인

Passage 3 Man: University employee | Woman: Student

Listen to part of a conversation between a student and a university employee.

W Excuse me, I need some information about withdrawing from a course.

M Well, then you got here just in time. Today is the deadline for withdrawing from classes. Oh, you do realize that it's too late to get a refund...

W Yeah, I know that. Now I am just worried about protecting my grade point average. This physics course is way more difficult than I thought. I am just not prepared for it.

M That is understandable. Can you give me your student ID number?

W Sure, here is my ID card.

M Great, now let's call up your schedule for this semester.

남자: 대학교 직원 | 여자: 학생

학생과 대학교 직원의 대화를 들으시오.

여 실례합니다, 수강을 취소하는 것에 관한 정보가 필요해서요.

남 음, 그렇다면 학생은 딱 시간에 맞춰 왔네요. 오늘이 수업 취소 마감일이거든요. 아, 그리고 환불을 받기엔 너무 늦었다는 걸 아시죠...

여 네, 알고 있어요. 저는 지금 그저 제 GPA(평점)를 지키는 게 걱정될 뿐이에요. 이 물리학 수업은 제가 생각했던 것보다 훨씬 더 어려워요. 제가 그냥 준비가 안 됐어요.

남 이해해요. 학생증 번호를 주시겠어요?

여 네, 여기 제 학생증이요.

남 좋아요, 그럼 이제 이번 학기 학생의 스케줄을 봅시다.

Q. What does the woman want to do?

Ⓐ Get a refund for a course
Ⓑ Drop a class she cannot handle
Ⓒ Add a class to her schedule
Ⓓ Look up her grade point average

Q. 여자는 무엇을 하고 싶어 하는가?

Ⓐ 수업을 환불받는다
Ⓑ 감당할 수 없는 수업을 취소한다
Ⓒ 일정에 수업을 추가한다
Ⓓ 평점을 알아본다

어휘 withdraw v 철회하다, 취소하다 | deadline n 마감 기한 | realize v 깨닫다 | refund n 환불 | protect v 보호하다 | grade point average (GPA) 평점 | physics n 물리학 | understandable adj 이해할 수 있는

Passage 4 Man: Student | Woman: Professor

Listen to part of a conversation between a student and a professor.

M Sorry I missed class this morning. I had a doctor's appointment. Here is my excuse form.

W Thank you for getting one—many students forget they need to do that. During class today, students chose field trips from the list of art exhibits I provided.

M I was really looking forward to that assignment. What should I do?

W You were not the only student absent, and there are some choices remaining. First, you need to pair up with someone. Then you can choose from what is left.

M OK, then what?

W Then you need to decide how you will divide up the work for your report about the exhibit.

남자: 학생 | 여자: 교수

학생과 교수의 대화를 들으시오.

남 오늘 아침에 수업에 참석하지 못해서 죄송합니다. 검진이 있었어요. 여기 사유서입니다.

여 가져와줘서 고마워요. 많은 학생들이 사유서를 제출해야 한다는 걸 잊어버리죠. 오늘 수업에서 학생들이 내가 제공한 미술 전시회 목록에서 현장 학습을 선택했어요.

남 그 과제를 정말 기대하고 있었어요. 저는 뭘 해야 하죠?

여 결석한 사람은 학생뿐만이 아니고, 남은 선택지들이 몇 개 있어요. 먼저, 누군가와 짝을 지어야 해요. 그 다음에 남은 선택지에서 고를 수 있어요.

남 알겠습니다. 그 다음에는요?

여 그 후에는 그 전시회에 관한 보고서 작업을 어떻게 나눌지 결정해야 해요.

Q. What does the man need to do first?

Ⓐ Visit an art exhibition
Ⓑ Write a report
Ⓒ Locate a partner to work with
Ⓓ Select a destination

Q. 남자는 먼저 무엇을 해야 하는가?

Ⓐ 전시회를 방문한다
Ⓑ 보고서를 작성한다
Ⓒ 함께 작업할 파트너를 찾는다
Ⓓ 목적지를 선택한다

어휘 doctor's appointment 검진, 진료 | excuse form 사유서 | field trip 현장 학습 | assignment n 과제 | absent adj 결석한, 부재의 | pair up 짝을 이루다 | divide v 나누다

Lesson 03 Function & Attitude

본서 | P. 116

Practice

Passage 1 C **Passage 2** C **Passage 3** A **Passage 4** C

Practice

본서 | P. 120

Passage 1 Man: Librarian | Woman: Student

Listen to part of a conversation between a student and a librarian.

남자: 도서관 사서 | 여자: 학생

학생과 도서관 사서의 대화를 들으시오.

M Excuse me, are you aware that the library is closing soon?
W Um, yes. I'm sorry, but these are reference books.
M Oh, I see. You do know that you can photocopy pages from books that you cannot check out. The copy machine is even on this floor.
W Yes, but I will be done soon.
M OK, keep an eye on the time. I have many books to put away before my shift ends.
W Yes, I will do that. Thank you.

남 실례합니다. 도서관이 곧 닫는다는 걸 알고 있나요?
여 음, 네. 죄송해요, 하지만 이건 참고 도서들이에요.
남 아, 그렇군요. 대출할 수 없는 책들은 프린트할 수 있다는 걸 알고 있겠죠. 복사기도 이 층에 있고요.
여 네, 하지만 곧 끝나요.
남 알겠어요. 시간을 엄수하도록 하세요. 일이 끝나기 전에 정리해야 할 책이 많거든요.
여 네, 그럴게요. 감사합니다.

Q. What does the woman mean when she says this:

W I'm sorry, but these are reference books.

Ⓐ The librarian should not bother the student.
Ⓑ The student still has much information to find.
Ⓒ Certain materials cannot be removed from the library.
Ⓓ The copier may damage the books if she uses it.

Q. 여자는 다음과 같이 말하며 무엇을 의미하는가:

여 죄송해요, 하지만 이건 참고 도서들이에요.

Ⓐ 도서관 사서는 학생을 방해해서는 안 된다.
Ⓑ 학생은 아직 찾아야 할 정보가 많다.
Ⓒ 특정 자료들은 도서관에서 대출할 수 없다.
Ⓓ 복사기를 사용하면 복사기가 책을 훼손할 수도 있다.

어휘 aware adj ~을 알고 있는, 인지하는 | reference book 참고 도서 | photocopy v 복사하다

Passage 2 Man: Professor | Woman: Student

Listen to part of a conversation between a student and a professor.

W Professor, you wanted to see me?
M Yes, please have a seat. Were you in class when I assigned your report?
W Me? Of course I was, Professor. I haven't missed any of your lectures. Actually, I was kind of confused by some of the guidelines. They don't correspond with what I learned in my composition class.
M Ah, I see. That is because you are writing a history report. Some of the rules for composing history papers are unique to the subject.
W I'm sorry. If you can explain what I need to change, I would be happy to do so.

남자: 교수 | 여자: 학생

학생과 교수의 대화를 들으시오.

여 교수님, 저를 보길 원하셨다고요?
남 그래요, 앉아요. 내가 리포트 과제를 내줬을 때 학생은 수업에 있었나요?
여 저요? 물론이죠, 교수님. 저는 교수님의 강의를 한 번도 빼먹은 적이 없어요. 사실, 가이드라인 일부가 좀 혼란스럽긴 했어요. 제가 작문 수업에서 배웠던 내용과 일치하지 않거든요.
남 아, 그렇군요. 그것은 학생이 역사 리포트를 쓰고 있기 때문이에요. 역사 리포트 작성에 관한 규칙들 중 일부는 이 과목 특유의 것이죠.
여 죄송합니다. 제가 고쳐야 하는 점을 설명해주실 수 있다면 기꺼이 그렇게 할게요.

Q. Why does the professor say this:

M Were you in class when I assigned your report?

Ⓐ To indicate that the student should change her topic
Ⓑ To emphasize the importance of regular attendance
Ⓒ To suggest that the student wrote her paper incorrectly
Ⓓ To express concern about the student's performance

Q. 교수는 왜 이렇게 말하는가:

남 내가 리포트 과제를 내줬을 때 학생은 수업에 있었나요?

Ⓐ 학생이 주제를 바꿔야 한다고 말하기 위해
Ⓑ 정기적으로 수업에 참석하는 것의 중요성을 강조하기 위해
Ⓒ 학생이 리포트를 잘못 썼다는 점을 시사하기 위해
Ⓓ 학생의 성적에 관해 우려를 표현하기 위해

어휘 assign v 과제를 내주다, 배정하다 | confused adj 혼란스러운, 혼동되는 | correspond v 부합하다, 일치하다 | composition n 작문 | compose v 작성하다, 구성하다 | unique to ~특유의

Passage 3 Man: Radio director | Woman: Student DJ

Listen to part of a conversation between a student DJ and a radio director.

M Sally! Have you heard the news? Your radio show got the highest ratings last semester!

W Oh, really? But how did you find out?

M Well, the station sent out surveys to 500 student listeners, and your show came in number 1 in most categories.

W Fantastic! I never knew I had so many listeners!

M It's good that you're having so much success, but there is one downside.

W What's that?

M They complained that you don't always mention the names of the songs when you play them.

W I know, but it just gets so repetitive.

M That's true, but this is one of our responsibilities. After all, we are in the radio business.

W What should I do?

M I think you need to do two additional things: one, when you come on the air, list the artists and songs you're going to play. Second, put your playlist on the station's website after the show is over.

W That's not too hard. I can do that.

남자: 라디오 감독 | 여자: 학생 DJ

학생 디제이와 라디오 감독의 대화를 들으시오.

남 샐리! 소식 들었어요? 학생의 라디오 쇼가 저번 학기에 가장 높은 평가를 받았어요!

여 오, 정말인가요? 하지만 어떻게 아셨나요?

남 음, 방송국에서 500명의 학생 청취자들에게 설문지를 보냈고 학생의 쇼가 대부분의 카테고리에서 1위를 차지했어요.

여 정말 좋네요! 그렇게 청취자들이 많은 줄 몰랐어요!

남 학생이 이렇게 성공을 거두니 좋지만, 한 가지 부정적인 평가가 있어요.

여 그게 뭔가요?

남 학생이 음악을 틀 때 곡의 이름을 항상 언급하지 않는다고 사람들이 불만을 제기했어요.

여 알아요. 하지만 그건 너무 반복적인 일이 되는 걸요.

남 그건 그래요. 하지만 그게 우리의 책임 중 하나예요. 어쨌든 우린 라디오 업계에서 활동하고 있으니까요.

여 어떻게 해야 할까요?

남 학생이 두 가지를 추가로 해야 한다고 생각해요. 첫째, 라디오 방송을 하게 되면 학생이 틀 곡과 가수들의 목록을 작성하는 거죠. 두 번째로는, 방송이 끝난 뒤 학생의 선곡표를 라디오 방송국의 웹사이트에 올리는 거예요.

여 어렵지 않네요. 할 수 있어요.

Q. What is the woman's attitude about her responsibilities?

Ⓐ She thinks that some tasks are tedious.
Ⓑ She wants the rules to be made clearer.
Ⓒ She is ignoring the man's suggestions.
Ⓓ She feels the changes are unnecessary.

Q. 자신의 책임에 관한 여자의 태도는 어떠한가?

Ⓐ 일부 일이 지루하다고 생각한다.
Ⓑ 규정이 더 명확해지길 원한다.
Ⓒ 남자의 제안을 무시하고 있다.
Ⓓ 변화가 불필요하다고 느낀다.

어휘 rating n 점수, 평가 | survey n 설문지, 설문 조사 | fantastic adj 환상적인 | success n 성공 | downside n 부정적인 면 | complain v 불평하다 | mention v 언급하다 | repetitive adj 반복적인, 반복되는 | responsibility n 책무, 책임 | additional adj 추가의

Passage 4 Man: Student | Woman: Manager

Listen to part of a conversation between a student and a manager.

M Excuse me, are you busy right now? I need to talk to you about the snack bar.

W The snack bar? Is there some sort of problem?

M I wanted to talk to you about the possibility of extending the snack bar hours during midterm exams next week.

W Extending the hours? What exactly did you have in mind?

남자: 학생 | 여자: 관리자

학생과 관리자의 대화를 들으시오.

남 실례합니다. 지금 바쁘세요? 매점에 관해 이야기하고 싶은 게 있어서요.

여 매점이요? 뭔가 문제가 있나요?

남 다음 주 중간고사 기간 동안 매점 운영 시간을 연장하는 가능성에 관해 이야기하고 싶었어요.

여 운영 연장이요? 정확히 어떤 생각을 갖고 있는 거죠?

M Normally, the snack bar closes at 10 o'clock, which is fine during regular weeks, but while midterms are going on, students stay up late and therefore need snacks to keep them going.

W I can certainly understand that. I remember those days! How late were you thinking of extending?

M Could you extend the hours until 1 a.m. during that week? Would that be a problem?

W It definitely will be. You have to remember that the workers at the snack bar are also students like you, and not only do they have to study for their own exams, but they also have to get a good night's sleep before taking their exams.

M I understand that and I can sympathize. But I have this petition that is signed by 100 students who said that they will utilize the snack bar during exam week.

W Hmmm. 100 names, you say? That number may just make it affordable for the snack bar to stay open a couple of hours.

남 보통 매점은 밤 10시에 문을 닫는데, 이건 평상시의 주에는 상관없지만, 중간고사가 치러지는 동안에는 학생들이 늦게까지 깨어 있기 때문에 계속 버티려면 간식이 필요하거든요.

여 그건 확실히 이해할 수 있어요. 그 시절이 기억나네요! 얼마나 늦게까지 연장을 생각하고 있었죠?

남 그 주에는 새벽 1시로 연장해주실 수 있나요? 그게 문제가 될까요?

여 확실히 문제가 되죠. 매점에서 일하는 직원들도 학생과 같은 학생들이라는 것을 기억해야 하고, 그 사람들도 자기 시험을 위해 공부해야 하는 건 물론 시험을 보기 전 잠을 잘 자야 하니까요.

남 이해하고, 공감할 수 있습니다. 하지만 시험 주에 매점을 이용하겠다고 한 학생들 100명이 서명해준 탄원서를 여기 가져왔어요.

여 흠. 100명이라고 했죠? 그 숫자라면 매점이 몇 시간 더 운영될 수 있는 비용이 가능해지겠군요.

Q. What is the woman's opinion of the man's request?

Ⓐ She thinks that it is completely unreasonable.
Ⓑ She wants to help him, but the rules do not allow it.
Ⓒ She believes that she may be able to accommodate him.
Ⓓ She feels that he should be more considerate of other students.

Q. 남자의 요청에 대한 여자의 의견은 무엇인가?

Ⓐ 완전히 말도 안 된다고 생각한다.
Ⓑ 남자를 돕고 싶지만 규정이 허락하지 않는다.
Ⓒ 아마 남자의 요구를 수용할 수 있을 거라고 본다.
Ⓓ 남자가 다른 학생들을 더 배려해야 한다고 느낀다.

어휘 possibility n 가능성 | extend v 연장하다 | exactly adv 정확히 | normally adv 보통 | certainly adv 확실히 | definitely adv 확실히 | sympathize v 공감하다 | petition n 탄원서 | utilize v 이용하다 | affordable adj 감당할 수 있는, 가격이 알맞은

Lesson 04 Connecting Contents

본서 | P. 122

Practice

Passage 1 1. Yes – A, B, D / No – C 2. B

Passage 2 1. Yes – A, C / No – B, D, E 2. D

Practice

본서 | P. 128

Passage 1 Man: Professor | Woman: Student

Listen to part of a conversation between a student and a professor.

W Professor Howell, Do you have a minute?

M Maggie! This is an unexpected surprise! Can I help you with something or did you just want to talk?

W I know, I know. I've had a couple of crucial absences. Still, I would like to talk to you about this research paper.

M Certainly. What would you like to know? Do you have questions about content or procedure?

남자: 교수 | 여자: 학생

학생과 교수의 대화를 들으시오.

여 하웰 교수님, 잠깐 시간 있으세요?

남 매기! 생각지도 못했는데 놀랍군요! 뭐 도와줄 게 있어요, 아니면 그냥 이야기를 하고 싶은 건가요?

여 알아요, 알아요. 제가 중요한 날에 몇 번 결석을 했죠. 그래도 이 학기말 리포트에 관해 이야기를 하고 싶어서요.

남 그럼요. 뭘 알고 싶은가요? 내용에 관한 질문인가요, 아니면 과정에 관한 질문인가요?

W Content. I'm a little confused about the nature of the assignment. Do we only have to observe the test children and then record how they react during the experiment?

M Uh, that's just the tip of the iceberg, I'm afraid. **1(A)** First, you need to go to the library and do as much research as possible on Childhood Behavioral Development. **1(B)** After that, you need to predict certain behavioral patterns based on this research. After that...

W Then, where does the observation come in?

M Oh-oh, you didn't let me finish. **1(D)** I was going to say that after you make your predictions, then you should go and observe the test subjects and see if any of the behavior you observe backs up your research.

W Where on Earth am I supposed to find that many children in such a wide array of ages!

M I'll remind you I went over the procedure on the first day in class in which we discussed this project.

W I'm sorry, but I missed that day because I overslept.

M Oh, I don't have time to go over this with you again, but **2** go see the assistant in the psychology department, and she will go over it in detail.

W I'm sorry again. I'll go and do that immediately.

M That's alright. You just need to pick up the slack for the rest of the term. Anyway, the assistant can provide you with the names and contact information of the parents who have agreed to do the project. You should be able to contact them independently and set up an appointment.

W Thanks again. Sorry for keeping you.

M No problem. See you in class.

여 내용이요. 과제물의 본래 취지가 조금 헷갈려서요. 실험 대상 아이들을 관찰하고 실험 기간 동안 아이들이 어떻게 반응하는지를 기록하기만 하면 되나요?

남 미안하지만 그건 단지 빙산의 일각이에요. **1(A)** 우선, 도서관에 가서 아동 행동 발달에 관해 가능한 한 많이 조사하세요. **1(B)** 그 후에, 이 조사를 기반으로 특정 행동 패턴을 예측해야 돼요. 그리고 나서...

여 그렇다면 어디에서 관찰이 이루어지죠?

남 어어, 내 말이 아직 끝나지 않았어요. **1(D)** 학생이 예측을 한 후에 실험 대상에게 가서 관찰하고 학생이 한 조사를 뒷받침하는 어떤 행동들이 있는지 보라는 얘기를 하려고 했어요.

여 도대체 어디에서 이렇게 방대한 연령대의 아이들을 많이 찾을 수 있나요?

남 이 프로젝트에 관해 이야기했던 수업 첫날에 실험 과정에 대해 살펴봤던 것을 기억하나요?

여 아, 죄송해요. 제가 늦잠을 자서 그 수업을 못 들었어요.

남 오, 지금 학생한테 이걸 다시 이야기해줄 시간은 없지만, **2** 심리학과 조교에게 가면 이걸 자세히 다시 설명해줄 거예요.

여 다시 한번 죄송해요. 지금 바로 가서 그렇게 할게요.

남 괜찮아요. 뒤처진 부분을 학기 나머지 기간 동안 따라잡을 필요가 있어요. 어쨌든, 그 조교가 이 프로젝트에 참여하기로 한 학부모들의 이름과 연락처를 줄 거예요. 학생은 그들과 개별적으로 연락을 한 후 약속을 잡아야 해요.

여 다시 한번 감사합니다. 시간 뺏어서 죄송해요.

남 괜찮아요. 수업 때 봐요.

Lesson 04 Conversations

1. In the conversation, the speakers discuss the requirements of a research paper. Indicate in the table below which of the requirements apply to the student's assignment. Click in the correct box for each phrase.

	Yes	No
(A) Conduct research at the library on Childhood Behavioral Development	✓	
(B) Make predictions about behavioral patterns that may arise	✓	
(C) Locate children to participate in the behavioral study		✓
(D) Observe the test subjects to see if their behavior corresponds with research	✓	

2. Why does the professor mention the assistant in the psychology department?

1. 대화에서 화자들은 학기말 리포트의 필수 조건에 관해 논의한다. 어떤 필수 조건이 학생의 과제에 적용되는지 아래의 표에 표시하시오.

각 구절에 대해 맞는 칸에 표시하시오.

	예	아니오
(A) 도서관에서 아동 행동 발달에 관해 조사하기	✓	
(B) 발생할 수 있는 행동 패턴에 관해 예측하기	✓	
(C) 행동 연구에 참여할 아이들 찾기		✓
(D) 실험 대상의 행동이 조사와 부합하는지 관찰하기	✓	

2. 교수는 왜 심리학과 조교를 언급하는가?

Ⓐ To express how annoyed he is by the student's attitude
Ⓑ To direct the student to someone else who can provide help
Ⓒ To show the student the first step for starting her assignment
Ⓓ To tell the student that he needs to help someone else right now

Ⓐ 학생의 태도에 자신이 얼마나 짜증이 났는지 표현하려고
Ⓑ 도움을 줄 수 있는 다른 누군가에게 학생을 보내려고
Ⓒ 학생에게 과제를 시작하는 첫 단계를 보여주려고
Ⓓ 지금 다른 사람을 도와야 한다고 말하려고

어휘 unexpected adj 예상하지 못한 I crucial adj 중요한 I absence n 결석, 부재 I content n 내용 I procedure n 과정, 절차 I confused adj 혼란스러운, 헷갈리는 I assignment n 과제 I observe v 관찰하다 I record v 기록하다 I react v 반응하다 I experiment n 실험 I iceberg n 빙산 I childhood n 아동기 I behavioral development 행동 발달 I predict v 예측하다 I certain adj 특정한 I subject n (연구·실험) 대상 I back up 뒷받침하다, 지지하다 I array n 집합체, 모음 I discuss v 논의하다 I oversleep v 늦잠 자다 I assistant n 조교 I immediately adv 즉시, 즉각 I pick up the slack (밀린/뒤처진) 일을 처리하다 I contact information 연락처 I independently adv 따로, 개별적으로 I appointment n 약속, 예약

Passage 2

Man: Student | Woman: University employee

Listen to part of a conversation between a student and a university employee.

W Good morning. Do you need help with something?
M Yeah. I think I'm a little lost. Is this the registrar's office?
W Yes, it is.
M Uhhh... I'm not sure if you can, but I do have a question, and I hope you can direct me to someone who can help me.
W I'll do the best I can.
M Well, I was a graduate student and I went here in the early 90's. I graduated from the medical school in 2001. **1(A),(E)** I need my transcripts and a letter of recommendation that are supposed to be here. I heard I could get them online, but when I accessed your website, it said I had to come down here.
W **1(C)** Yes, unfortunately a new federal law prevents us from giving out any private information without checking an ID in person.
M **2** Are you sure? I'm positive that a fellow alumnus was able to upload her transcripts directly to a prospective employer.
W I would seriously doubt that. The law was enacted in 2001 to prevent any sort of identity theft.
M Wow! Is that a fact?
W Let's see if I can help you while you're here. What's your name?
M Scott. Adam Scott.
W And the year of graduation?
M 2001.
W One second please while I access your information. Okay, here you are, Doctor Scott. I have your records.
M Great! Can you give me four copies of the transcripts and three copies of the letter of recommendation?

남자: 학생 | 여자: 대학교 직원

학생과 대학교 직원의 대화를 들으시오.

여 안녕하세요. 도움이 필요하신가요?
남 네, 제가 약간 헤매고 있는 것 같네요. 여기가 학적부 사무실인가요?
여 네, 그래요.
남 어... 도와주실 수 있을지 모르겠는데요, 질문이 있는데 도와줄 수 있는 사람에게 좀 안내해 주셨으면 해요.
여 최선을 다해 보죠.
남 음, 전 대학원 학생이었고 90년대 초에 여길 다녔어요. 2001년에 의과대학을 졸업했고요. **1(A),(E)** 여기 성적증명서와 추천서가 필요해요. 온라인으로 받을 수 있다고 들었는데, 웹사이트에 접속하니 여기로 와야 한다고 되어 있더라고요.
여 **1(C)** 네, 아쉽게도 새로운 연방법 때문에 직접 신분증을 확인하지 않고는 개인 정보를 내주지 못하게 되어 있어요.
남 **2** 확실하신가요? 제 동문 중 한 명이 성적 증명서를 장래의 고용주에게 직접 전송할 수 있었던 걸로 알고 있는데요.
여 그럴 리가요. 모든 종류의 신원 도용을 금하도록 2001년에 법이 제정되었는 걸요.
남 와! 그게 사실이에요?
여 여기 계신 동안 도와드릴 수 있는지 보죠. 성함이 어떻게 되시죠?
남 스캇이요. 아담 스캇이에요.
여 졸업 연도는요?
남 2001년이요.
여 정보를 검색하는 동안 잠시 기다려주세요. 네, 여기 있네요, 스캇 박사님. 기록을 찾았어요.
남 잘됐네요! 성적 증명서 네 장과 추천서 세 장을 주실 수 있나요?

W 1(D) I'm sorry. It takes one working day to process. However, if you show me your ID now, I can mail out your documents tomorrow, and you will get them in 2 to 3 working days.

M Okay. That should be fine. My address is 2456 East Sawgrass Avenue, Kingstree, South Carolina, 29556. Is there any charge for this service?

W None at all, Doctor Scott. 1(B) We mail all of the documents to our alumni free of charge provided the delivery doesn't exceed 10 copies per year.

M Boy! I'm glad I found you!

W Will that be all today?

M It certainly will. Thank you so much for your help.

여 1(D) 죄송하지만 처리하는 데 하루가 걸려요. 하지만 지금 신분증을 보여주시면 서류를 내일 우편으로 보내드릴 수 있어요. 그럼 2~3일 내에 받으실 거예요.

남 네, 좋아요. 제 주소는 2456 동부 서그래스가, 킹스트리, 사우스캐롤라이나주, 29556이에요. 요금을 내야 하나요?

여 전혀 없어요, 스캇 박사님. 1(B) 배송량이 1년에 10부를 넘지 않으면 졸업생에게 모든 서류를 무료로 우편으로 보내고 있어요.

남 와! 제가 담당자를 제대로 만났군요.

여 다른 사항은 없으신가요?

남 네, 도와주셔서 정말 감사합니다.

Lesson 05 Conversations

1. In the conversation, the speakers discuss the process by which documents may be obtained. Indicate in the table below whether each of the following is indicated about that process.

Click in the correct box for each sentence.

	Yes	No
(A) The person must come to the university in person.	✓	
(B) There is a limit to the number of documents that can be obtained.		✓
(C) The person must present a valid identification card.	✓	
(D) The transcripts take a week to process.		✓
(E) The person may access the documents on the university website.		✓

2. Why does the man mention a fellow alumnus?

(A) To tell the woman that she misunderstood him
(B) To show the woman has wrong information
(C) To ask the woman to make an exception
(D) To persuade the woman that she could be wrong

1. 대화에서 화자들은 서류를 받을 수 있는 절차를 논의한다. 다음 각 사항이 그 절차에 나타나 있는 것인지 아래 표에 표시하시오.

각 구절에 대해 맞는 칸에 표시하시오.

	예	아니오
(A) 신청자가 직접 대학에 와야 한다.	✓	
(B) 받을 수 있는 서류의 수량에는 한계가 있다.		✓
(C) 신청자는 유효한 신분증을 제시해야 한다.	✓	
(D) 성적 증명서는 처리하는 데 일주일이 걸린다.		✓
(E) 신청자는 대학교 웹사이트에서 서류에 접근할 수도 있다.		✓

2. 남자는 왜 동문 한 명을 언급하는가?

(A) 여자가 자신의 말을 오해했다고 말하려고
(B) 여자가 잘못된 정보를 갖고 있다는 것을 보이려고
(C) 여자에게 예외를 만들어달라고 부탁하려고
(D) 여자가 틀렸을 수도 있다고 설득하려고

어휘 registrar n 학적부 | direct v 안내하다 | graduate student 대학원생 | transcript n 성적 증명서 | letter of recommendation 추천서 | unfortunately adv 아쉽게도 | prevent v 금지하다, 막다 | private adj 개인의 | alumnus n 졸업생 (pl. alumni) | directly adv 직접, 바로 | prospective adj 장래의, 유망한 | doubt v 의심하다 | enact v 제정하다 | identity theft 신원 도용 | record n 기록 | process v 처리하다 | working day 근무 시간대, 업무일 | exceed v 넘다, 초과하다

Lesson 05 Inference

본서 | P. 130

Practice

Passage 1 A　　Passage 2 C　　Passage 3 C　　Passage 4 A

Passage 1

Man: Professor | Woman: Student

Listen to part of a conversation between a student and a professor.

M Hello, Jessica.

W Hello Professor Reyes, you wanted to speak to me?

M Yes, I read your latest story. You are a very talented writer.

W Thank you, I was pretty proud of that one.

M As well you should be. Have you considered getting it published?

W I would love to get some of my writing published, but I wouldn't know where to start.

M I take it you are unaware of our campus literary magazine.

W No, but I thought it was a poetry magazine.

M Oh, we often publish poetry, but we also accept fiction and essays.

W How do I go about submitting my work?

M If you go on the school website and go to the literature department's page, there is a link to the magazine site. There is an email address that you can send your work to. Just write an email and attach the story to it before you send it.

W What should I say in the email?

M Not much. Just say who you are and give a brief summary of the story. If the editor in chief is interested, she will read the full story. If she wants to publish it, she will contact you.

W OK, that sounds pretty straightforward.

M Oh, but I should warn you. The magazine doesn't pay authors for their work. It doesn't have much funding.

W Oh, that's fine. I would just like to see my work in print.

남자: 교수 | 여자: 학생

학생과 교수의 대화를 들으시오.

남 안녕하세요, 제시카.

여 안녕하세요, 레예스 교수님, 저에게 하실 말씀이 있으시다고요?

남 그래요, 학생의 최근 소설을 읽었어요. 학생은 매우 소질이 뛰어난 작가네요.

여 감사합니다, 저도 그 작품이 상당히 자랑스러워요.

남 자랑스러워해야죠. 혹시 그 소설을 출판하는 걸 생각해 본 적 있나요?

여 제 글의 일부를 정말 출판하고 싶지만, 어디서부터 시작해야 할지 모르겠어요.

남 학생이 우리 학교의 캠퍼스 문학 잡지를 모르는 것 같군요.

여 아닙니다, 하지만 전 그게 시 잡지인 줄 알았어요.

남 오, 우리는 시를 자주 출판하지만 소설과 에세이도 받아요.

여 제 작품을 제출하려면 어떻게 해야 하나요?

남 학교 웹사이트에 들어가서 문학과 페이지로 가면 잡지 사이트 링크가 있어요. 거기에 학생의 작품을 보낼 수 있는 이메일 주소가 있죠. 이메일을 쓰고 보내기 전 작품을 첨부하기만 하면 돼요.

여 이메일에는 뭐라고 써야 하죠?

남 딱히 쓸 건 없어요. 학생이 누구인지 말하고 이야기를 간단히 요약하세요. 만약 편집자가 흥미를 가지면 소설 전체를 다 읽을 거예요. 편집자가 출판하고 싶으면 학생에게 연락할 거고요.

여 알겠습니다, 상당히 간단하네요.

남 아, 하지만 알려줄 게 있네요. 잡지가 작가들에게 돈을 주지는 않아요. 자금이 별로 없거든요.

여 아, 그건 괜찮습니다. 그냥 출판되어 나온 제 작품을 보고 싶어요.

Q. What can be inferred about the professor?

(A) He works on the campus literary magazine.
(B) He often submits stories to the magazine.
(C) He does not think the woman is qualified.
(D) He is a well-known and popular author.

Q. 교수에 관해 무엇을 추론할 수 있는가?

(A) 캠퍼스 문학 잡지 일을 한다.
(B) 잡지에 이야기를 자주 제출한다.
(C) 여자가 자격이 된다고 생각하지 않는다.
(D) 유명하고 인기 많은 작가이다.

어휘 talented adj 재능이 많은 | proud adj 자랑스러워하는, 자랑스러운 | poetry n 시 | straightforward adj 간단한, 쉬운

Passage 2

Man: Student | Woman: Registrar

Listen to part of a conversation between a student and a registrar.

M Hello, can you help me?

남자: 학생 | 여자: 학적부 직원

학생과 학적부 직원의 대화를 들으시오.

남 안녕하세요, 저를 도와주실 수 있으신가요?

W Hopefully, what seems to be your problem?

M I've been trying to register for this class, but it's already full, so I was wondering if you could get me an override, so I can enter the class. If I can't get in, I won't be able to graduate until next spring.

W Well, only professors can give overrides. What was the name of the class?

M Hmm... Reading Strategies 101.

W Reading Strategies? 101? That's a required class for freshmen! Why on Earth did you wait until your senior year to take it?

M I know. I know. It was really foolish of me to wait this long. I wasn't sure if I had to take it or not.

W It's a core class for everyone! The whole student body has to take it! Didn't your academic advisor tell you that?

M He might have. I really don't remember. Is there any way you can help me?

W Your best plan of action is to contact the professor of this class directly.

M I already tried to email Dr. Rickenbacker, but I haven't heard back yet.

W Hmmm... Dr. Rickenbacker is famous for not checking his emails very often.

M What am I going to do then?

W What I would do is tape a note explaining your situation on his office door and leave your phone number so he can get in touch with you.

M Thanks. I'll try that.

W You're welcome. Good luck!

여 그럴 수 있길 바라요. 어떤 문제가 있으신가요?

남 이 강의에 등록하려고 했지만 벌써 인원이 다 차서, 강의에 들어갈 수 있게 추가 등록을 해주실 수 있나 해서요. 수강하지 못하면 내년 봄까지 졸업할 수가 없어요.

여 음, 교수님들만 추가 등록을 해주실 수 있어요. 강의 이름이 뭐였나요?

남 음... 독해 전략 101이에요.

여 독해 전략이요? 101? 그 강의는 신입생 필수 과목이잖아요! 대체 왜 수강하는 걸 4학년이 될 때까지 기다린 거죠?

남 네, 알아요. 이렇게 오래 기다리다니 정말 바보 같은 짓이죠. 그 강의를 들어야 하는지 아닌지 잘 몰랐거든요.

여 그 강의는 모든 학생들의 필수 과목이에요! 학생들 전부 그 과목을 들어야 한다고요. 지도 교수님이 말씀해주시지 않았나요?

남 아마 말씀하셨을 텐데, 생각이 안 나요. 뭐라도 도움을 받을 수 있는 방법이 있을까요?

여 학생이 할 수 있는 제일 좋은 방법은 이 강의를 담당하는 교수님께 직접 연락하는 거예요.

남 벌써 리켄배커 교수님께 이메일을 보냈지만 아직 답을 듣지 못했어요.

여 음... 리켄배커 교수님은 이메일을 그리 자주 확인하지 않는 걸로 유명한데요.

남 그럼 어떻게 해야 하죠?

여 저라면 교수님 연구실 문에 학생의 상황을 설명하는 메모를 붙여놓고 교수님이 연락하실 수 있도록 전화번호를 남기겠어요.

남 감사합니다. 그렇게 해볼게요.

여 천만에요. 행운을 빌어요!

Q. What can be inferred about the student's situation?

Ⓐ His academic advisor didn't tell him he should take the course.
Ⓑ The class always fills up very quickly every semester.
Ⓒ He was not sure if the class was required to graduate.
Ⓓ He already had a full schedule in his freshman year.

Q. 학생의 상황에 대해 무엇을 추론할 수 있는가?

Ⓐ 지도 교수가 이 수업을 들어야 한다고 말해주지 않았다.
Ⓑ 이 수업은 매 학기마다 무척 빨리 마감된다.
Ⓒ 이 수업이 졸업에 필요한지 확신하지 못했다.
Ⓓ 이미 1학년 때 일정이 빡빡했다.

어휘 register v 등록하다 | wonder v 궁금해하다 | get an override 이미 정원이 다 찬 강의에 별도의 요청을 통해 추가 등록하다 | graduate v 졸업하다 | strategy n 전략 | required adj 필수의, 요구되는 | freshman n 1학년생 | senior n 4학년생 | foolish adj 바보 같은 | core adj 중심의, 핵심의 | contact v 연락하다 | directly adv 직접

Passage 3 Man: Housing officer | Woman: Student

Listen to part of a conversation between a student and a housing officer.

W You got a minute, Mr. Franklin?

M Sure, come on in. What can I do for you?

남자: 기숙사 담당자 | 여자: 학생

학생과 기숙사 담당자의 대화를 들으시오.

여 시간 좀 있으세요, 프랭클린씨?

남 네, 들어오세요. 무슨 일인가요?

W My name is Kelly Dumas, and I got a letter from your office, saying that I need to vacate my dorm room as soon as possible. The problem is that I'm leaving for Canada in three months, and I have no other place to go until then. So I was wondering if it would be possible to get an extension for three months.

M What was your name again?

W Kelly Dumas.

M Let's see. Oh, here you are. I see that you've been living in the dorms for three years already. I'm afraid the reason you got the letter in the first place is that the school has a strict policy regarding the maximum length of stay for on-campus housing. I'm sorry, but your time has expired, and you will need to make other arrangements.

W Is there any way you can make an exception this time?

M I'm afraid it's a school housing policy. We need the space for incoming freshmen who apply for dorm rooms, and they usually want as much time as possible to get acquainted with their surroundings.

W It's just that it's so difficult to find a landlord who will give me a three-month lease.

M I can relate to your situation and I sympathize, but try to put yourself in the freshmen's shoes; it's their first time away from home, they're probably a little nervous, so it just wouldn't be fair to make them wait for a dorm room.

W Guess you're right. Do you have any suggestions?

M Well, you're not the first one who has been in this position. You can check with the Student Services Office; they usually have a list of contacts that provide temporary housing.

W Great! That sounds perfect! I'll run over there right now.

M Have a great time on your trip.

여 전 켈리 뒤마라고 하는데, 여기 사무실로부터 가능한 한 빨리 기숙사 방을 비워달라는 편지를 받았어요. 문제는 제가 석 달 후에 캐나다에 가는데 그때까지 머물 곳이 없거든요. 그래서 석 달간 연장이 가능한지 알아보려고요.

남 이름이 뭐라고 했죠?

여 켈리 뒤마요.

남 어디 봅시다. 여기 있네요. 기숙사에서 이미 3년이나 생활했군요. 애당초 편지를 받은 이유는 학교가 기숙사 최대 거주 기간에 엄격한 방침을 가지고 있기 때문이에요. 죄송하지만 기간이 만료됐으니 다른 준비를 해야 해요.

여 이번만 예외로 해주시면 안 될까요?

남 유감스럽지만 학교 기숙사 방침이라서요. 기숙사를 신청하는 신입생들을 위해 방이 필요하고, 신입생들은 대개 주변 환경에 적응하기 위해 가능한 한 많은 시간이 필요하죠.

여 석 달간 집을 빌려줄 집주인을 찾기가 너무 어려워서 그래요.

남 학생의 상황은 이해하고 공감은 되지만 신입생들의 입장에서 생각해보세요. 처음 집을 떠나 다소 불안하기도 할 텐데 기숙사 방을 기다리게 하는 건 합당하지 않잖아요.

여 맞는 말씀이에요. 혹시 뭐 제안할만한 거 있으세요?

남 음, 이런 처지에 있는 사람이 학생이 처음은 아니에요. 학생처에 확인해 보세요. 보통 임시 숙소를 제공해주는 연락처 목록을 갖고 있거든요.

여 좋아요! 그거 좋은 생각이네요! 지금 당장 가봐야겠어요.

남 여행에서 즐거운 시간 보내세요.

Q. What is implied about the school housing policy?

(A) The school housing policy allows some exceptions.
(B) All the freshmen must live in the dormitories.
(C) The school housing policy does not allow any exceptions.
(D) Seniors must leave the dorm immediately after school finishes.

Q. 학교 기숙사 방침에 관해 무엇을 유추할 수 있는가?

(A) 학교 기숙사 방침에서 일부 예외가 허용된다.
(B) 모든 신입생들은 기숙사에서 생활해야 한다.
(C) 학교 기숙사 방침은 예외를 허용하지 않는다.
(D) 4학년들은 학교를 마치는 즉시 기숙사를 나가야 한다.

어휘 vacate v 비우다 | wonder v 궁금해하다 | extension n 연장 | strict adj 엄격한 | policy n 규정 | maximum adj 최대의 | length n 기간, 길이 | expire v 만료되다 | arrangements n 준비, 채비 | exception n 예외 | incoming adj 도착하는, 들어오는 | freshman n 1학년생 | apply v 신청하다, 지원하다 | acquainted with ~에 익숙한, 아는 | surroundings n 환경, 주변 | landlord n 집주인, 임대주 | lease n 임대차 계약 | relate to ~를 이해하다 | situation n 상황 | sympathize v 공감하다, 동정하다 | nervous adj 긴장한 | suggestion n 제안 | temporary adj 임시의

Passage 4 Man: Student | Woman: Administrator

Listen to part of a conversation between a student and an administrator.

남자: 학생 | 여자: 행정 직원

학생과 행정 직원의 대화를 들으시오.

W Hi, there! How can I help you?
M Well, I just got my registration form and it says I'm only registered for three classes, but I need to take five courses this semester.
W Hmm. OK, let me check this for you on the computer. Oh, here's your file. According to the computer, you lost your place in those two courses because you didn't pay your tuition on time.
M That's because I was away on vacation until Monday. I paid my tuition as soon as I got back.
W Well, the deadline was last Friday. At that point, since you hadn't paid, you were removed from the class list to allow other students on the waiting list to enroll in the course.
M I thought I would just be charged a late fee, not kicked out of courses! Is it possible to get back into those courses again?
W Let me check. Some spots in the English class have opened up, but the Asian Studies class is full and has eight students on the waiting list. What would you like to do?
M Please enroll me in the English class and put me on the waiting list for the other course.
W There is also a Chinese History class available. Would you be interested in that class instead of Asian Studies?
M When is the Chinese History class?
W It's on Monday and Wednesday evenings, 7 to 10. What do you think?
M That would work into my timetable well, actually. Sure. Put me in that class, please.
W You're all set. You're back in the English class and also enrolled in Chinese History instead of Asian Studies.
M Thanks for your help!

Q. What does the administrator imply about the Asian Studies class?

Ⓐ It is not likely that the student will get into the class.
Ⓑ The class is not very useful to students with his major.
Ⓒ There are not many people interested in taking it.
Ⓓ The class is usually held in the evening.

여 안녕하세요! 뭘 도와드릴까요?
남 네, 방금 수강신청서를 받았는데 강의가 3개만 등록되어 있다고 나와 있어요. 하지만 전 이번 학기에 5개를 들어야 하거든요.
여 음, 알겠어요. 컴퓨터에서 확인해 볼게요. 아, 여기 학생의 파일이 있네요. 컴퓨터를 보니 학생이 수업료를 제때 내지 않아서 그 두 개의 강의에서 빠진 걸로 나오네요.
남 그건 제가 휴가를 갔다가 월요일에 왔기 때문이에요. 돌아오자마자 수업료를 냈는데요.
여 음, 마감일이 지난주 금요일이었어요. 그 당시에 학생이 수업료를 내지 않았기 때문에 수강 신청 대기자 명단에 있는 다른 학생들이 강의에 등록할 수 있도록 학생을 강의에서 뺀 거예요.
남 저는 강의에서 쫓겨나는 게 아니라 그냥 연체료를 물게 될 거라 생각했어요! 그 수업들을 다시 등록할 수 있을까요?
여 확인해 볼게요. 영어 강의는 몇 자리가 비어 있지만, 아시아학 강의는 인원이 다 찼고 대기자 명단에 8명의 학생이 있네요. 어떻게 하시겠어요?
남 영어 강의는 등록해 주시고, 다른 강의는 대기자 명단에 올려주세요.
여 중국사 강의도 수강이 가능해요. 아시아학 대신 그 강의에 관심 있어요?
남 중국사 강의는 언제 있나요?
여 월요일과 수요일 저녁 7시에서 10시까지네요. 어때요?
남 제 시간표에 맞겠네요. 네, 그 강의에 넣어주세요.
여 다 됐어요. 영어 강의에 다시 등록이 됐고 아시아학 대신 중국사 강의에 등록됐어요.
남 도와주셔서 감사합니다!

Q. 행정 직원은 아시아학 수업에 관해 무엇을 암시하는가?

Ⓐ 학생이 이 수업에 들어갈 것 같지 않다.
Ⓑ 이 수업은 학생과 같은 전공의 학생들에게는 그다지 유용하지 않다.
Ⓒ 이 수업을 듣는 데 관심이 있는 사람들은 많이 없다.
Ⓓ 이 수업은 보통 밤에 진행된다.

어휘 registration n 등록 | tuition n 수업료, 등록금 | deadline n 마감 기한 | enroll v 등록하다 | charge v 요금을 부과하다 | waiting list 대기자 명단 | be all set 준비가 되어있는

Lesson 01 Main Idea

본서 I P. 140

Practice

Passage 1 A   Passage 2 C   Passage 3 C   Passage 4 C

Practice

본서 I P. 144

Passage 1

Woman: Professor

Listen to part of a lecture in a science class.

W Right now, I want to take a look at alternative fuels and how they can possibly help us in the future. Alternative fuels are sources of energy that do not involve the use of oil, coal, natural gas, or propane. They are also usually fuels that are fairly safe for the environment. The primary reason alternative fuels are necessary is that we are quickly using up our oil and coal resources. There just isn't an endless supply of these fuels, and once our supply is depleted, we really need to have an alternative source of energy to power everything. If we do not have this, many of the things that make modern society so convenient, such as cars and other machinery, will be lost. So, let's take a closer look at the different types of alternative fuels that are out there.

여자: 교수

과학 강의의 일부를 들으시오.

여 이제, 대체 연료와 그것이 미래에 우리를 어떻게 도울 수 있는지를 살펴보려 합니다. 대체 연료는 석유, 석탄, 천연 가스와 프로판의 사용을 필요로 하지 않는 에너지원입니다. 그것들은 보통 환경에 상당히 안전한 연료들이기도 합니다. 대체 연료가 필요한 주된 이유는 우리가 석유와 석탄 자원을 빠르게 써 버리고 있다는 것입니다. 이런 연료들은 끝없이 공급되지 않습니다. 그리고 일단 공급량이 고갈되어 버리면, 동력을 공급할 대체 에너지원이 정말로 있어야 합니다. 만약 그런 것이 없다면 자동차와 기타 기계류 같이 현대 사회를 매우 편리하게 해주던 많은 것들이 사라질 것입니다. 그러면, 지금 나와 있는 여러 형태의 대체 연료들을 더 자세히 살펴봅시다.

Q. What is the lecture mainly about?

(A) The importance of alternative fuels
(B) The difficulty of finding an energy source to replace oil
(C) The different types of alternative fuels
(D) Environmental safety

Q. 강의는 주로 무엇에 관한 것인가?

(A) 대체 연료의 중요성
(B) 석유를 대체할 에너지원을 찾는 데 있어서의 어려움
(C) 여러 종류의 대체 연료들
(D) 환경 안전성

어휘 alternative adj 대체의, 대안의 I fuel n 연료 I involve v (필연적으로) 포함하다 I oil n 석유 I coal n 석탄 I natural gas 천연 가스 I propane n 프로판 I primary adj 주된 I resource n 자원 I endless adj 끊임없는 I supply n 공급량 I deplete v 고갈시키다 I convenient adj 편리한

Passage 2

Woman: Professor

Listen to part of a lecture in a history class.

W Hello, everyone. As I'm sure you know, the reason why I'm here today is to talk to you about cliff dwellings. Many of you may be asking yourselves at this point, "What exactly is a cliff dwelling?" Well, a cliff dwelling is a type of housing built by the Pueblo people in the western United States in Utah, Arizona, Colorado, and New Mexico. To be more specific, cliff dwellings are like apartment complexes made of clay and built into the sides of cliffs. Now, why build a

여자: 교수

역사 강의의 일부를 들으시오.

여 안녕하세요. 여러분. 여러분이 알고 있듯이, 오늘 저는 암굴 주거지에 대해서 말하기 위해 이 자리에 있습니다. 여러분 중 다수는 이 시점에서 "암굴 주거가 정확히 뭐지?"라고 질문할 수도 있을 겁니다. 음, 암굴 주거는 미국 서부 지역의 유타주, 애리조나주, 콜로라도주, 뉴멕시코주 등에서 푸에블로족들에 의해 지어진 주거의 한 형태입니다. 더 구체적으로 말하면, 암굴 주거지는 진흙으로 만들어지고

house in the side of a cliff? Well, by doing this, the Pueblo people use the cliffs' overhangs to protect their houses from rain. They need to do this because their houses are made of clay and, as you can imagine, rain can cause quite a bit of damage to a clay structure. In the past, they were also able to use the cliff face to shield themselves from attack. So, let's move on to an examination of the Utah cliff dwellings and why they are especially important to modern anthropologists.

절벽의 측면에 지어진 아파트 단지 같은 것입니다. 자, 왜 절벽의 측면에 집을 지을까요? 이렇게 함으로써, 푸에블로족들은 비로부터 집을 보호하기 위해서 절벽의 돌출 부분을 사용하는 것이죠. 집이 진흙으로 만들어졌기 때문에 이렇게 해야 합니다. 그리고 여러분이 상상할 수 있듯이, 비는 진흙으로 된 건물에 상당한 훼손을 야기할 수 있습니다. 과거에 그들은 또한 공격으로부터 자신들을 지키는 데에 절벽 표면을 이용할 수 있었습니다. 그럼, 이제 유타주 암굴 주거지에 관한 고찰과 그것들이 현대 인류학자들에게 특히 중요한 이유로 넘어가 봅시다.

Q. What is the main idea of the lecture?

Ⓐ How aggression forced the Pueblo to move to a new type of housing

Ⓑ The interest of modern scholars in the Utah cliff dwellings

Ⓒ What cliff dwellings are and why they were helpful to the Pueblo people

Ⓓ Rain and its impact on the Pueblo people's cliff dwellings

Q. 강의의 요지는 무엇인가?

Ⓐ 침략이 어떻게 푸에블로족들로 하여금 새로운 형태의 주거지로 옮겨가도록 했는가

Ⓑ 유타주 암굴 주거지에 대한 현대 학자들의 관심

Ⓒ 암굴 주거지가 무엇이고 왜 그것들이 푸에블로족들에게 도움이 되었는가

Ⓓ 비와 푸에블로족들의 암굴 주거지에 끼친 비의 영향

어휘 cliff n 암굴, 절벽 | dwelling n 주거지, 주거 | exactly adv 정확히 | specific adj 구체적인 | clay n 진흙, 점토 | overhang n 돌출부 | protect v 보호하다 | damage n 훼손, 손상, 피해 | structure n 구조물 | attack n 공격 | examination n 고찰, 조사 | anthropologist n 인류학자

Passage 3

Man: Professor

Listen to part of a lecture in a biology class.

M Good morning. I'd like to start off today by talking about a very unusual type of flower called Rafflesia. The thing that makes it so unusual is that it... well, for one thing, it smells really bad... and, for another, it's really big. If you take a look at this slide, you'll see that the Rafflesia is one huge flower. It can grow to be around a meter in diameter and can weigh as much as 10kg. But from the standpoint of a botanist, the intriguing thing about the Rafflesia is that it doesn't have chlorophyll and it doesn't photosynthesize, and this has caused a lot of debate among botanists about what exactly a plant is. We traditionally thought that plants had to photosynthesize—that it was, um, a defining characteristic of a plant. The Rafflesia, however, defies that theory, and really has very few of the traditional characteristics of a flower. So, if it doesn't photosynthesize, how exactly does the Rafflesia survive?

Well, if you'll take a look at the slide, you'll see that the Rafflesia doesn't have any roots, leaves, stems, or much else for that matter. On the surface, it's just a flower. What's hidden here, however, is that this flower is feeding off of the vine it's attached to. This makes it a parasite, and its host is

남자: 교수

생물학 강의의 일부를 들으시오.

남 안녕하세요. 오늘은 매우 독특한 종류의 꽃인 라플레시아에 관해 이야기하며 시작하고자 합니다. 그 꽃이 매우 독특한 이유는... 음, 한 가지는, 정말 나쁜 냄새가 난다는 것입니다... 그리고 또 다른 이유는 정말 거대하다는 것이죠. 이 슬라이드를 보면, 여러분은 라플레시아가 하나의 거대한 꽃이라는 것을 알 수 있을 겁니다. 이것은 지름이 약 1미터 정도까지 자랄 수 있고 무게가 10kg 정도 나갈 수 있습니다. 하지만 식물학자의 관점에서 보면 라플레시아에 관해 흥미로운 점은 엽록소가 없고 광합성을 하지 않는다는 사실이며, 이는 식물학자들 사이에서 식물이란 정확히 무엇인가에 관해 많은 논쟁을 야기했습니다. 우리는 전통적으로 식물은 광합성을 해야 한다고 생각했습니다. 그것은, 음, 식물을 정의하는 특징이었죠. 하지만 라플레시아는 그 이론을 무시하며 꽃의 전형적인 특징을 거의 가지고 있지 않습니다. 그럼 만약 광합성을 하지 않는다면 라플레시아는 정확히 어떻게 생존할까요?

음, 슬라이드를 보면, 라플레시아는 뿌리, 잎, 줄기 같은 부분을 전혀 갖고 있지 않다는 것을 알 수 있을 겁니다. 겉보기에는 그것은 단지 꽃입니다. 하지

always the same plant, the Tetrastigma. Basically, what the Rafflesia does is it starts as these tiny, uh, filaments inside the Tetrastigma vine. These filaments absorb nutrients and then they grow until they're ready to reproduce, which is when it actually starts to appear outside of the vine as a growth that eventually blooms into the flower that we have been looking at.

What's frustrating about this, though, is that it makes the Rafflesia incredibly difficult to study. We can't really dissect filaments because the Rafflesia's already uncommon and, well, we don't want to risk killing it. But this also means that we can't know as much as we would like about its inner workings. Basically, they're only found in remote parts of Southeast Asia, and even in those places, there aren't a lot of Rafflesias around. They aren't well-protected, and their habitats are being destroyed, which is actually one of the reasons why it's so important for us to study them now—so that we can learn how to sustain them in other, possibly artificial, habitats. The most frustrating thing of all, however, is that even if we're happy just studying the flowers and not the filaments inside the Tetrastigma vine, these flowers start to die after a few days, and that is just not enough time to work with them.

만 여기 감춰져 있는 사실은 이 꽃이 자기가 달라붙어 있는 덩굴들을 먹고 산다는 것입니다. 이것이 그 꽃을 기생 식물로 만드는 것이죠. 그리고 그것의 숙주는 항상 똑같은 식물, 테트라스티그마입니다. 기본적으로 라플레시아가 하는 것은 테트라스티그마 덩굴 안에서 작은 꽃실로부터 시작하는 것입니다. 이 꽃실들은 영양분을 흡수하며 번식할 준비가 될 때까지 성장하는데, 이때부터 실제로 라플레시아의 성장체가 덩굴 밖으로 나와서 보이기 시작하고 이것이 결국 지금 우리가 보는 꽃으로 피어나게 됩니다.

하지만 좌절감을 주는 것은 이것이 라플레시아를 연구하는 것을 엄청나게 어렵게 만든다는 것입니다. 라플레시아는 이미 드물고, 음, 우리는 그것을 죽이는 위험을 감수하고 싶지 않기 때문에 꽃실들을 해부할 수가 없습니다. 하지만 이는 또한 우리가 그것의 내부 활동에 대해서 알아내고 싶은 만큼 알 수 없다는 것을 의미합니다. 기본적으로 그것들은 동남아시아 오지에서만 발견되는데, 그 지역에서조차 라플레시아는 별로 많지 않습니다. 그것들은 잘 보호되지 않고 있으며, 서식지도 파괴되고 있습니다. 그것이 사실은 우리가 그것들을 지금 연구해야 하는 중요한 이유 중 하나입니다. 그래야 우리는 그것들을 다른 곳에서, 가능하다면 인공적인 서식지에서 기르는 방법을 알아낼 수 있습니다. 하지만 그 중에서도 가장 절망적인 것은 비록 우리가 테트라스티그마 덩굴 안의 꽃실 말고 그 꽃만을 연구하는 데 만족한다 하더라도, 이 꽃은 며칠 지나면 죽기 시작하는데 이는 꽃을 연구하기에 충분한 시간이 아니라는 겁니다.

Q. What is the main idea of the lecture?

Ⓐ Tetrastigma and how it sustains the Rafflesia
Ⓑ Photosynthesis and how plants rely on it to survive
Ⓒ Rafflesia and how it differs from most plants
Ⓓ Rafflesia's strong odor and unusual size

Q. 강의의 주제는 무엇인가?

Ⓐ 테트라스티그마와 그것이 라플레시아를 살게 하는 방식
Ⓑ 광합성과, 식물이 생존하기 위해서 광합성에 의존하는 방식
Ⓒ 라플레시아와 그것의 특징이 대부분의 식물들과 어떻게 다른가
Ⓓ 라플레시아의 강한 냄새와 별난 크기

어휘 unusual adj 독특한 I huge adj 거대한 I diameter n 지름 I weigh v 무게가 나가다 I standpoint n 관점 I botanist n 식물학자 I intriguing adj 흥미로운 I chlorophyll n 엽록소 I photosynthesize v 광합성을 하다 I debate n 논쟁 I traditionally adv 전통적으로 I defining adj 정의하는 I survive v 생존하다 I root n 뿌리 I stem n 줄기 I surface n 표면, 외면 I vine n 덩굴, 덩굴 식물 I parasite n 기생 식물 I host n 숙주 I tiny adj 아주 작은 I filament n 꽃실(꽃의 수술을 지지하는 대 부분), 가느다란 실 I absorb v 흡수하다 I nutrient n 영양분 I reproduce v 번식하다 I bloom v 피어나다 I frustrating adj 좌절감을 주는, 짜증 나는 I incredibly adj 엄청나게 I dissect v 해부하다 I risk v 위험을 무릅쓰다 I inner adj 내부의 I habitat n 서식지 I destroy v 파괴하다 I sustain v (생명을) 유지하다 I artificial adj 인공적인

Passage 4

Man: Professor | Woman: Student

Listen to part of a discussion in a geology class.

M I'd like to focus on a very important geological theory: plate tectonics. The basis for the theory is the idea that the Earth's crust, or outer shell, is not one continuous sphere, but is actually broken up into sections, called plates. The mantle, the section of the Earth directly below the crust, is a fluid layer of molten rocks. So it acts as a lubricant enabling the crust plates to slide around and bump into each other. This constant movement results in grinding, compression, and separation at the points where these plates meet, and this causes visible natural phenomena like earthquakes and volcanic eruptions. The crust plates are not all the same. They are divided into two types. Can anyone tell me what those are?

W Oceanic and continental crust plates?

M That's right. We have oceanic plates beneath the oceans and continental plates under the continents. The reason that the distinction between the two is important is that each has very different characteristics. The continental crust, for example, makes up about 40 percent of the earth's solid surface and is usually between 15 and 70 kilometers thick. The oceanic crust, on the other hand, is generally between 5 and 10 kilometers thick, but it is quite a bit denser than the continental crust.

W Does the thickness of a crust plate make such a big difference to the way it behaves that the two types of crusts have to be classified differently?

M Well, it is an important difference, but there is also another, possibly more important difference between the two types of plates. Continental crust is generally older and more stable than oceanic crust. This means that it doesn't move around a great deal. Oceanic plates, on the other hand, are constantly changing and shifting. This often involves the subduction of two plates, but I'm wondering if any of you know what subduction is?

W Well, I wanna say that subduction is when two plates push into each other and one ends up being on top.

M OK, great. That's a very good explanation. Subduction occurs when two tectonic plates begin to push into each other and then one gets pushed under the other. When this happens, rock from the plates is being sent back into the mantle of the Earth, where it is melted down. But if rock is being added to the mantle, where is the excess mass going?

W Umm... Maybe it's coming out through volcanic eruptions?

M That's exactly what happens. The material generated by the oceanic volcanoes is literally being recycled. One plate is pushed below another, and as the lower plate's material

남자: 교수 | 여자: 학생

지질학 수업 중 토론의 일부를 들으시오.

남 저는 판구조론이라는 아주 중요한 지리학적 이론에 초점을 두고 싶습니다. 그 이론의 기초는 지구의 지각 즉, 외부 껍질이 계속 이어지는 하나의 구가 아니라 실제로는 판이라고 불리는 부분들로 분할되어 있다는 생각입니다. 지구 지각의 바로 아래 부분인 맨틀은 녹은 바위로 이루어진 유동층입니다. 그래서 그것은 지각판이 미끄러져서 서로 부딪치도록 해주는 윤활제 같은 역할을 하죠. 이 지속적인 움직임은 판들이 만나는 지점에서 마찰, 압축, 그리고 분리됩니다. 그리고 이것은 지진과 화산 분출과 같은 눈에 보이는 자연 현상들을 야기하기도 합니다. 지각판들이 모두 똑같지는 않습니다. 그것들은 두 가지 형태로 나뉩니다. 그것이 무엇인지 말해볼 사람 있나요?

여 대양과 대륙의 지각판들인가요?

남 맞아요. 대양 아래에는 대양판이, 그리고 대륙 아래에는 대륙판이 있어요. 그 둘을 구별하는 것이 중요한 이유는 각각이 매우 다른 특징을 가지고 있어서입니다. 예를 들면, 대륙판은 지구의 단단한 표면의 약 40%를 구성하고 있고 대개 두께가 15에서 70km죠. 반면에, 대양판은 일반적으로 두께가 5에서 10km이지만 대륙판보다 훨씬 더 밀도가 높아요.

여 지각판의 두께가 두 가지 형태의 판이 다르게 분류되어야 할 만큼 지각판이 움직이는 방식에 그렇게 큰 차이를 가져오나요?

남 음, 중요한 차이죠, 그렇지만 그 두 가지 형태의 판 사이에는 또 다른, 아마도 더 중요한 차이가 있습니다. 대륙판은 대양판보다 대개 더 오래되고 더 안정적입니다. 이는 대륙판이 많이 움직이지 않는다는 것을 의미합니다. 반면에, 대양판은 끊임없이 변화하고 바뀌고 있습니다. 이것은 종종 두 판의 섭입을 수반하는데, 혹시 여러분 중에 섭입이 무엇인지 알고 있는 사람이 있나요?

여 음, 섭입은 두 판이 서로에게 돌진해서 결국은 하나가 위에 놓이게 되는 때가 아닌가 하는데요.

남 네, 맞아요. 아주 좋은 설명입니다. 두 개의 지각 판이 서로에게 돌진하기 시작해서 하나가 다른 하나의 아래로 밀릴 때 섭입이 발생합니다. 섭입이 발생할 때 판에 있던 바위는 지구의 맨틀로 돌려보내지고 거기서 바위는 녹게 됩니다. 그런데 만약 바위가 맨틀에 더해진다면, 그 초과된 분량은 어디로 가게 될까요?

여 음... 아마도 화산 분출을 통해서 나오지 않을까요?

남 정확히 그렇게 되죠. 대양의 화산에 의해 생성된 물질은 말 그대로 재순환되고 있어요. 하나의 판은 다른 하나의 아래로 밀리고, 아래쪽 판의 물질이 지구의 핵으로 가라앉으면서 점점 뜨거워지고 녹아서

Lesson 01 Lectures

sinks toward the Earth's core, it heats up and simply melts to become the same as the rest of the material in the mantle. Then, after this happens, material returns to the surface of the Earth in a volcanic eruption, which completes the perpetual geological cycle of plate tectonics.

맨틀의 나머지 물질들과 똑같아지죠. 그러고 나서 물질은 화산 분출을 통해 지구의 표면으로 돌아옵니다. 이렇게 해서 판구조론의 영구적인 지질학적 순환이 완성되는 것입니다.

Q. What aspect of plate tectonics does the professor mainly discuss?

Ⓐ The formation of tectonic plates
Ⓑ How tectonic plates move
Ⓒ The different types of tectonic plates
Ⓓ How plates are destroyed

Q. 교수는 판구조론의 어떤 측면을 주로 논하는가?

Ⓐ 지각판의 형성
Ⓑ 지각판이 어떻게 움직이는가
Ⓒ 지각판의 다른 형태
Ⓓ 판이 어떻게 파괴되는가

어휘 geological adj 지질학적 | theory n 이론 | plate tectonics 판구조론 | crust n (지구의) 지각, 딱딱한 표면 | continuous adj 이어지는 | sphere n 구, 영역, 층 | mantle n 맨틀 | directly adv 바로 | fluid adj 유동체의 | molten adj 녹은 | lubricant n 윤활유 | enable v ~를 가능하게 하다 | bump into 부딪히다 | constant adj 지속적인 | grinding n 마찰, 연마 | compression n 압축, 압박 | separation n 분리 | visible adj 눈에 띄는 | phenomenon n 현상(pl. phenomena) | earthquake n 지진 | volcanic eruption 화산 분출 | divide v 나누다 | oceanic adj 대양의 | continental adj 대륙의 | distinction n 차이 | solid adj 단단한, 고체의 | surface n 표면 | dense adj 빽빽한, 밀도가 높은 | thickness n 두께 | behave v 움직이다 | classify v 분류하다 | generally adv 일반적으로 | stable adj 안정적인 | shift v 이동하다 | subduction n 섭입대 | explanation n 설명 | occur v 발생하다 | excess adj 초과한 | exactly adv 정확히 | material n 물질, 소재 | literally adv 말 그대로 | recycle v 재순환하다 | core n (지구의) 중심핵, 중심부 | complete v 완성하다 | perpetual adj 영구적인, 영속적인 | cycle n 순환, 주기

Lesson 02 Details

본서 | P. 146

Practice

Passage 1 C　**Passage 2** D　**Passage 3** B　**Passage 4** C

Practice

본서 | P. 150

Passage 1 Woman: Professor

Listen to part of a lecture in an architecture class.

W Okay, let's start off today by talking about adobe clay as it was used by the Native Americans. To begin with, however, we need to distinguish between the Native Americans' use of adobe before and after they were influenced by the Spanish. At first, Native Americans used adobe clay in its, um, pure form—it was just clay and wasn't mixed with anything else. They shaped this clay into balls and then stuck them together to make adobe houses, which worked fairly well for them. However, after the Spanish showed up, they introduced some ideas that worked even better. The first and probably most important of these ideas was for Native Americans to mix the adobe mud with straw, which made the clay stronger. They also learned how to use bricks instead of balls when building their homes. The bricks were

여자: 교수

건축학 강의의 일부를 들으시오.

여 좋아요, 오늘은 미국 원주민들이 사용했던 어도비 점토에 대해 이야기하는 것으로 시작합시다. 그러나 우선 우리는 미국 원주민들의 어도비 사용에 대해 스페인 사람들의 영향을 받기 이전과 이후를 구분할 필요가 있습니다. 처음에 미국 원주민들은 어도비 점토를, 음, 천연의 형태로 사용했습니다. 즉, 단지 점토일 뿐 다른 어떤 것도 섞이지 않은 상태였죠. 그들은 이 점토를 공 모양으로 만든 다음 서로 접착시켜 자신들에게 아주 잘 맞는 어도비 집을 만들었습니다. 하지만 스페인 사람들이 등장한 후, 그들은 훨씬 효율적인 아이디어들을 도입했습니다. 미국 원주민들에게 이런 아이디어 중 첫 번째이자 아마 가장 중요한 것은 어도비 진흙과 짚을 섞는 것이었는데, 이는 점토를 더욱 단단하게 만들었습니

made so that they were less susceptible to rain; they were slanted so that the rain would flow off instead of sitting on top of the bricks. They also made it easier to erect strong structures in general because of their square shape.

다. 또 그들은 집을 지을 때 공 모양 대신 벽돌을 사용하는 법을 배웠습니다. 벽돌은 비의 영향을 덜 받도록 만들어졌는데 비스듬하게 기울어져 있어서 빗물이 벽돌 위에 고이지 않고 흘러내릴 수 있었죠. 또한 벽돌의 네모난 모양 덕분에 견고한 구조를 좀 더 쉽게 세울 수 있게 되었습니다.

Q. According to the professor, what advantage did adobe bricks have over adobe balls in the rain?

Ⓐ They could let rain sit on top of the bricks.
Ⓑ They were flat, which kept the water from soaking in.
Ⓒ They were slanted, which allowed the rain to run off.
Ⓓ They wouldn't roll as much as the adobe balls did.

Q. 교수에 따르면, 비가 올 때 어도비 공에 비해 어도비 벽돌이 가진 장점은 무엇이었는가?

Ⓐ 빗물이 벽돌 위에 고이게 해주었다.
Ⓑ 평평해서 물이 스며들지 않게 해주었다.
Ⓒ 경사가 있어서 빗물이 흘러내리도록 해주었다.
Ⓓ 어도비 공이 굴러갔던 것만큼 굴러가지 않았다.

어휘 adobe clay 어도비 점토 I Native American 미국 원주민 I distinguish v 구분하다 I influence v 영향을 주다 I pure adj 순수한 I shape v 모양을 빚다 I introduce v 도입하다 I straw n 짚 I brick n 벽돌 I susceptible adj 영향을 받기 쉬운, 예민한 I slanted adj 기울어진, 비스듬한 I erect v (똑바로) 세우다

Passage 2

Man: Student | Woman: Professor

Listen to part of a discussion in a psychology class.

W Okay, everyone. Let's start today's class by talking about rewarding children in order to encourage their enjoyment of some activity. This is a topic that has caused a fair amount of debate in recent years. Now, before we start, do you think that rewarding children for participating in an activity such as drawing would be a good idea, even if they already like to draw?

M I think it'd be a good idea. It would keep the kid interested in drawing and make him want to do a good job.

W That's a good answer, and many scientists today agree with it. They say that, if a parent rewards a child for doing a good job or being creative in an activity, it can have a positive effect. At the same time, however, many say that a child shouldn't be rewarded just for doing an activity—he should be rewarded for how well he does the activity. This is how we can keep his interest.

M But... uh... what do you mean by rewarding how well he does? How would a parent determine that?

W Hmm... Well, I think the best thing I can do is to give you a personal example. My daughter likes to read, but she likes to listen to music much more. So I use music to reward her for reading. But your question is about how I do this. Well, I don't just reward her for reading in general. We set goals about which books she should read and how well she should understand them. When she reaches one of these goals, she gets a new album or a pair of concert tickets, which encourages her to read more and also improves her reading ability.

남자: 학생 | 여자: 교수

심리학 강의의 토론 일부를 들으시오.

여 자, 여러분. 오늘은 활동의 재미를 북돋우기 위해 아이들에게 보상을 주는 것에 대한 얘기로 수업을 시작하겠습니다. 최근 들어 상당한 논쟁을 불러일으키고 있는 주제 중 하나이죠. 그럼 시작하기 전에, 여러분은 그림 그리기와 같은 활동에 참여하는 것에 대해 어린이에게 상을 주는 것이 좋은 아이디어라고 생각하나요? 그림 그리는 것을 이미 좋아하는데도 말이에요.

남 저는 좋은 생각이라고 봅니다. 아이들이 그림 그리기에 계속 흥미를 가질 수 있게 해주고, 잘하고 싶게 만들 거예요.

여 좋은 대답이군요. 오늘날 많은 과학자들이 이 의견에 동의하고 있습니다. 그들은 부모들이 아이가 활동 중에 잘한 일이나 독창적인 일에 대해 상을 주면 긍정적인 효과를 나타낼 수 있다고 말합니다. 하지만, 이와 동시에 많은 이들이 아이가 단지 활동을 한 것에 대해서만 보상을 받아서는 안 된다고 말하고 있습니다. 즉, 아이가 그 활동을 얼마나 잘하고 있는가에 대해 보상을 받아야 한다는 겁니다. 이것은 어떻게 하면 아이의 흥미를 유지시킬 수 있는가의 문제이죠.

남 하지만... 음... 아이가 얼마나 잘하느냐에 대해 상을 준다는 것은 어떤 의미인가요? 부모는 어떻게 그것을 결정할 수 있을까요?

여 음... 글쎄, 그것을 설명하기에 가장 좋은 방법은 학생에게 나의 개인적인 예를 하나 들려주는 것일 듯하네요. 내 딸은 독서를 좋아하지만 음악 듣는 것을

훨씬 더 좋아해요. 그래서 나는 독서에 대한 상으로 음악을 사용합니다. 하지만 학생의 질문은 내가 어떻게 이것을 하느냐인데요. 글쎄, 나는 보통 책을 읽는 것 자체에 대해 상을 주지는 않아요. 우리는 딸아이가 어떤 책을 읽어야 하는지, 그리고 얼마나 그 책들을 잘 이해해야 하는지 목표를 정해요. 이런 목표 중 하나에 도달하면 아이는 새로운 앨범이나 콘서트 티켓 두 장을 얻게 되고, 이로써 아이가 독서를 더 많이 하도록 독려하고 아이의 독서 능력을 향상시키게 되죠.

Q. How does the professor reward her daughter for reading?

Ⓐ By giving her extra free time
Ⓑ By buying her more books
Ⓒ By giving her drawing supplies
Ⓓ By buying her music

Q. 교수는 딸이 책을 읽으면 어떻게 상을 주는가?

Ⓐ 추가 자유 시간을 줌으로써
Ⓑ 책을 더 사줌으로써
Ⓒ 그림 용품을 줌으로써
Ⓓ 음악을 사줌으로써

어휘 reward v 보상하다 I encourage v 장려하다 I recent adj 최근의 I participate v 참여하다 I creative adj 창조적인, 독창적인 I positive adj 긍정적인 I determine v 결정하다 I improve v 향상시키다

Passage 3

Man: Professor

Listen to part of a lecture in a biology class.

M Today, I would like to turn our attention to the hydrological cycle, more commonly known as the water cycle, which is the way that water continually circulates on Earth. For the most part, this process is powered by the Sun and requires a great deal of energy. However, there are many entities other than the Sun involved in the process. Just as a way of summarizing the complexity involved here, it's important to note that plants, rivers, oceans, rocks, animals, and even soil particles contribute to water's ability to move about in the hydrological cycle. The primary process of this cycle, however, involves evaporation combined with precipitation. Basically, water tends to always go back to the ocean, which results in the presence of a very large body of water that then rises into the atmosphere through evaporation. The resulting water vapor loses heat as it rises into the air, forms clouds, and returns to the Earth in the form of rain and snow. This completes the cycle, and it is in this way that around 500,000 cubic kilometers of water a year move through the water cycle.

남자: 교수

생물학 강의의 일부를 들으시오.

남 오늘 저는 지구상에서 물이 계속해서 순환하는 방식인 수문 순환, 좀 더 흔히 물의 순환이라고 알려진 과정에 관심을 돌려보려 합니다. 대부분 이 과정은 태양열에 의해 이뤄지며 많은 양의 에너지를 필요로 합니다. 그러나 이 과정에는 태양 외에도 많은 것들이 관련되어 있습니다. 이와 관련된 복잡한 사항들을 요약하자면 한 가지 방법으로 식물, 강, 바다, 바위, 동물, 그리고 토양 입자까지도 수문 순환 내에서 물을 이동하는 데 도움을 준다는 사실에 주목할 필요가 있다는 것입니다. 하지만 이 순환에서 가장 중요한 과정에는 강수와 결합된 증발이 포함됩니다. 기본적으로 물은 항상 바다로 되돌아가려는 경향이 있는데, 그 결과 매우 거대한 수역이 존재하게 되고, 이는 증발을 통해 대기 중으로 올라가게 됩니다. 이 결과로 생긴 수증기는 공기 중으로 올라감에 따라 열을 잃게 되고, 구름을 형성한 다음 비와 눈의 형태로 다시 땅으로 돌아옵니다. 이로써 순환이 완성되고, 이런 방식으로 물의 순환을 통해 1년에 약 5십만 입방 킬로미터의 물이 이동합니다.

Q. According to the professor, what provides most of the energy needed in the water cycle?

Ⓐ Wind
Ⓑ The Sun

Q. 교수에 따르면, 물의 순환에 필요한 에너지의 대부분을 공급하는 것은 무엇인가?

Ⓐ 바람
Ⓑ 태양

Ⓒ Heat from the Earth's core
Ⓓ Energy released when water evaporates

Ⓒ 지구의 중심핵에서 나오는 열
Ⓓ 물이 증발할 때 방출되는 에너지

어휘 attention n 주의, 관심 | hydrological cycle 수문 순환, 물 순환 | commonly adv 흔히, 보통 | continually adv 계속, 지속적으로 | circulate v 순환하다 | require v 필요로 하다 | entity n 독립체 | summarize v 요약하다 | complexity n 복잡함 | soil particle 토양 입자 | contribute v 기여하다 | primary adj 주된 | evaporation n 증발 | combine v 결합하다, 합치다 | precipitation n 강수 | presence n 존재 | atmosphere n 대기 | vapor n 증기 | complete v 끝내다, 완성하다

Passage 4 Man: Professor

Listen to part of a lecture in an astronomy class.

M Actually, today I'm here to talk about the lunar and solar calendars. Most people think that we have only one calendar—the Gregorian solar calendar—but there are really many different calendars out there. For us, the most important one of these "other" calendars is the lunar calendar, which is a calendar based on the phases and movements of the moon. There have been many lunar calendars, but the typical lunar calendar starts each month with a new phase of the moon.

What this means is that a new lunar month starts whenever a new moon, the phase when the moon appears the darkest, occurs.

Okay, so why do we use the Gregorian solar calendar instead of the lunar calendar? Well, a lunar month averages about 29.5 days, and, uh, this is just too short in a way because 12 lunar months will never equal one Earth year. The opposite problem does exist with the Gregorian solar calendar, which is longer than it should be... but we're talking about 26 seconds a year here, and that doesn't really amount to much.

Q. When does a new lunar month start?

Ⓐ When the Moon reaches its fullest point
Ⓑ On the 15th of each month of the Gregorian solar calendar
Ⓒ When the Moon is in its new phase
Ⓓ Approximately half a day before the start of each solar month

남자: 교수

천문학 강의의 일부를 들으시오.

남 사실, 오늘 저는 태음력과 태양력에 대해 이야기하려 합니다. 대부분의 사람들은 우리가 그레고리력이라는 단 하나의 역법을 가지고 있다고 생각하지만, 역법의 종류는 정말 많습니다. 이러한 '다른' 역법들 중 우리에게 가장 중요한 것은 달의 형상과 운행을 기초로 한 태음력입니다. 많은 태음력이 있었지만, 대표적인 태음력은 매달 삭월 단계에서 시작됩니다.

즉, 새로운 음력 달은 달이 가장 어둡게 보이는 단계인 삭월 때마다 시작된다는 것을 의미합니다.

자, 그렇다면 왜 우리는 태음력 대신 그레고리력을 사용할까요? 음, 태음력의 한 달은 평균 29.5일인데, 어, 이러한 방식으로는 12개의 음력 달이 하나의 지구 관측년과 같아지기에는 너무 짧습니다. 이와 반대의 문제가 그레고리력에도 존재하는데, 그레고리력은 지구 관측년보다 더 깁니다... 하지만 이 경우에는 1년에 약 26초가 더 긴 것뿐이고, 이것은 그리 긴 시간이 아니죠.

Q. 새로운 음력 달은 언제 시작되는가?

Ⓐ 보름달이 나타날 때
Ⓑ 그레고리력의 매달 15일
Ⓒ 달이 삭월일 때
Ⓓ 매 양력 달이 시작되기 약 반나절 전

어휘 lunar calendar 태음력 | solar calendar 태양력 | Gregorian solar calendar 그레고리력 | phase n (주기적으로 형태가 변하는 달의) 상 | typical adj 대표적인, 일반적인 | occur v 발생하다 | average v 평균 ~이 되다 | opposite adj 반대의 | exist v 존재하다

Lesson 03 Function & Attitude

본서 | P. 152

Practice

Passage 1 A **Passage 2** C **Passage 3** A **Passage 4** C

Passage 1

Woman: Professor

Listen to part of a lecture in a genetics class.

W Today we will be looking at a new organism in the Eastern United States. Many are referring to this new organism as a "coywolf" because they believe it is a hybrid between coyotes and wolves. But things are often not as simple as they seem. DNA tests have shown that the animals are a mixture of coyotes, wolves, and dogs. These organisms cannot be considered as a fully-formed species because the actual mixture of genes varies depending upon which tests are used and where the samples were taken. In the Northeast, the animals are 60-80 percent coyote, in the central area they are 85 percent dog, and in the Southeast they are over 90 percent coyote. So, no matter the region, the animals have less than 25 percent wolf DNA. It is a well-established fact that domesticated dogs and wolves can interbreed, as people have been making wolf-dog hybrids for decades, and they probably share a common ancestor. Apparently, all three species can interbreed in the wild, although they generally prefer not to, and researchers have been unable to find evidence that these organisms are still actively mating with dogs or wolves. Therefore, some experts have decided that these organisms should be regarded as an emerging species of coyote.

여자: 교수

유전학 강의의 일부를 들으시오.

여 오늘 우리는 미국 동부의 새로운 생물체를 살펴볼 겁니다. 많은 사람들이 이 새로운 생물체를 '코이늑대'라고 부르는데 그 이유는 이 종이 코요테와 늑대의 이종 교배 동물이라고 믿기 때문입니다. 하지만 종종 보이는 것처럼 단순하지 않을 때가 있죠. DNA 테스트는 이 동물이 코요테, 늑대와 개의 이종 교배 동물이라는 것을 보여주었습니다. 어떤 시험이 사용되었고, 어디에서 샘플이 채취되었는지에 따라 유전자의 실제 혼합이 달라지기 때문에 이 종을 완전한 형태의 종이라고 여길 수는 없어요. 동북 지역에서는 60-80퍼센트 코요테이고, 중부에서는 85퍼센트 개, 동남부에서는 90퍼센트 넘게 코요테입니다. 그래서 지역에 관계없이 이 동물은 25퍼센트 이하의 늑대 DNA를 갖고 있어요. 가축화된 개와 늑대가 이종 교배될 수 있다는 것은 확고부동한 사실이며, 사람들은 수십 년이 넘게 늑대와 개의 이종 교배를 해 왔고 이 두 동물은 아마 같은 조상을 공유하고 있을 겁니다. 명백하게, 세 종 모두 일반적으로 그러길 선호하진 않겠지만 야생에서 이종 교배가 가능하며 연구원들은 이 생물체들이 여전히 활동적으로 개나 늑대와 짝짓기를 하고 있다는 것을 보여주는 증거를 찾을 수 없었습니다. 그래서 일부 전문가들은 이 생물체가 최근 나타나기 시작한 코요테의 한 종으로 여겨져야 한다고 결정했습니다.

Q. Listen again to part of the lecture. Then answer the question.

W Many are referring to this new organism as a "coywolf" because they believe it is a hybrid between coyotes and wolves. But things are often not as simple as they seem.

Why does the professor say this:

W But things are often not as simple as they seem.

Ⓐ To imply that people's ideas about the animals may be incorrect

Ⓑ To show that people are mistaking a dog breed for a hybrid

Ⓒ To indicate that coywolf is an inaccurate name for the species

Ⓓ To state that she does not think that it is a new organism at all

Q. 강의를 다시 듣고 질문에 답하시오.

여 많은 사람들이 이 새로운 생물체를 '코이늑대'라고 부르는데 그 이유는 이 종이 코요테와 늑대의 이종 교배 동물이라고 믿기 때문입니다. 하지만 종종 보이는 것처럼 단순하지 않을 때가 있죠.

교수는 왜 이렇게 말하는가:

여 하지만 종종 보이는 것처럼 단순하지 않을 때가 있죠.

Ⓐ 동물에 관한 사람들의 생각이 틀릴 수도 있다는 것을 드러내려고

Ⓑ 사람들이 개를 이종 교배를 위한 동물로 잘못 생각하고 있다는 것을 보여주려고

Ⓒ 코이늑대가 이 종에게 맞지 않는 이름이라는 것을 나타내려고

Ⓓ 이것이 새로운 생물체라고 전혀 생각하지 않는다는 점을 주장하려고

어휘 organism n 생물 | refer to ~라고 부르다, 가리키다 | coywolf 코이늑대 | coyote n 코요테 | wolf n 늑대 | mixture n 혼합물, 혼합체 | consider v 여기다, 고려하다 | gene n 유전자 | vary v 다르다, 달라지다 | domesticated adj 길들여진, 사육된 | interbreed v 이종 교배하다 | decade n 10년 | share v 공유하다 | common adj 공통의 | ancestor n 조상 | apparently adv 명백하게, 분명히 | generally adv 일반적으로 | evidence n 증거 | actively adv 활발하게, 활동적으로 | mate v 짝짓기를 하다 | emerging adj 최근 생겨난, 만들어진

Passage 2 Man: Professor

Listen to part of a lecture in a biology class.

M Today we will continue with our discussion on life in the ocean. People began to survey the ocean floor in the 19th century, but they found only a few microscopic organisms. Of course, their survey methods left much to be desired. Dredging the ocean floor and then raising an unsealed container back to the surface is far from efficient. But they felt that this confirmed their suspicions that the deep ocean was a barren desert almost entirely devoid of life. This belief persisted until the late 1970s when scientists were studying the seafloor near the Galapagos Islands. After plate tectonics theory achieved wide acceptance in the scientific community in the 1950s, geologists predicted that there would be deep-sea vents—places where cold seawater seeps into cracks on the ocean floor, is heated by magma, and rises back through the oceanic crust to create deep-sea hot springs. They weren't entirely sure what they would look like, but they were pretty certain that they must exist.
The survey team at the Galapagos Rift was using a remotely operated still-camera attached to an unmanned submersible to take photographs. They couldn't see the images it recorded until they brought it back up, but they could receive data from its sensors. They noticed a temperature spike in the freezing waters, but they disregarded it as an anomaly. Later that day, as they were reviewing the hundreds of images that the camera took, they were shocked by the ones that corresponded to the temperature spike. They showed a dense bed of clams and mussels in the otherwise empty volcanic plain. A few days later, three people squeezed into a submarine and went down 2,500 meters to the same location. The water was a balmy eight degrees Centigrade and it was filled with minerals that had precipitated out of the vents. They found the same shellfish as well as blind crabs and mouthless tubeworms. Since then some 300 species have been found around deep-sea vents, but their discovery prompted another mystery. With no access to sunlight, how could these animals survive? Where could they be getting their energy from?

Q. Listen again to part of the lecture. Then answer the question.

남자: 교수

생물학 강의의 일부를 들으시오.

남 오늘 우리는 바다에 사는 생명체에 관한 논의를 계속할 겁니다. 사람들은 19세기에 해저를 탐사하기 시작했지만 미세 생물체 몇 개만을 찾아냈을 뿐이었습니다. 물론 탐사 방법들에는 아쉬운 점이 많았습니다. 해저를 훑은 뒤 밀봉되지 않은 컨테이너를 표면으로 다시 끌어 올리는 것은 효율적인 것과 거리가 멀었죠. 하지만 사람들은 이것이 심해가 생명체가 거의 전혀 존재하지 않는 황량한 사막 같을 거라는 의심을 확인해준다고 생각했습니다. 이러한 믿음은 과학자들이 갈라파고스 제도 근처의 해저를 연구하던 1970년대 말까지 지속되었습니다. 1950년대에 판구조론이 과학계에서 널리 인정 받은 뒤 지질학자들은 차가운 해수가 해저에 있는 갈라진 틈으로 들어가 마그마에 의해 데워진 뒤 심해의 온천처럼 해양 지각을 통과해 다시 올라오는 심해 열수구가 있을 것이라고 예측했습니다. 어떻게 생겼을지 완전히 확신할 수는 없었지만 존재하는 건 분명하다고 확신했죠.
갈라파고스 단층에 있던 탐사팀은 사진을 찍기 위해 무인 잠수정에 부착된, 원격으로 작동되는 스틸 카메라를 사용하고 있었습니다. 다시 위로 카메라를 가져오기 전까지는 기록된 이미지를 볼 수 없었지만 센서에서 자료를 받을 수는 있었어요. 엄청나게 차가운 물 가운데서 기온이 급증한 것을 알아차렸지만 이례적인 현상이라 보고 무시했습니다. 그날 늦게, 카메라가 찍은 수백 장의 이미지를 검토하던 중 과학자들은 온도 급증에 부합하는 사진들을 보고 충격을 받았습니다. 그 사진들은 비어 있는 화산 평원에 조개와 홍합이 빽빽히 들어찬 지점을 보여주었습니다. 며칠 뒤 세 명의 사람들이 잠수함 안에 비집고 들어가 2,500미터 아래의 같은 지점으로 내려갔습니다. 수온은 따뜻한 섭씨 8도였고 열수구에서 나온 미네랄로 가득했습니다. 과학자들은 동일한 조개류는 물론 장님 게와 입이 없는 서관충도 발견했죠. 그 이후 약 300개 종들이 심해 열수구 근처에서 발견되었지만 이들의 발견은 또 다른 수수께끼를 불러왔습니다. 햇빛이 없는데 이 동물들은 어떻게 생존할 수 있는 걸까요? 이들은 에너지를 어디에서 얻는 것일까요?

Q. 강의의 일부를 다시 듣고 질문에 답하시오.

Lesson 03 Lectures

M People began to survey the ocean floor in the 19th century, but they found only a few microscopic organisms. Of course, their survey methods left much to be desired.

What does the professor imply by saying this:

M Of course, their survey methods left much to be desired.

Ⓐ The expedition found the only organisms that existed.
Ⓑ The surveyors were not well educated about marine biology.
Ⓒ The techniques that the scientists were using were primitive.
Ⓓ The scientists were using the best technology available to them.

남 사람들은 19세기에 해저를 탐사하기 시작했지만 미세 생물체 몇 개만을 찾아냈을 뿐이었습니다. 물론 탐사 방법들에는 아쉬운 점이 많았습니다.

교수는 다음과 같이 말하며 무엇을 의미하는가?

남 물론 탐사 방법들에는 아쉬운 점이 많았습니다.

Ⓐ 탐사는 존재하던 유일한 생물체를 찾아냈다.
Ⓑ 탐사자들은 해양 생물학에 관해 잘 배우지 못한 사람들이었다.
Ⓒ 과학자들이 사용한 기법들은 원시적인 것이었다.
Ⓓ 과학자들은 당시 가능했던 최고의 기술을 사용하고 있었다.

어휘 continue v 계속하다 | discussion n 토론, 논의 | survey v 조사하다, 살피다 | microscopic adj 미세한 | organism n 생물체 | dredge v 훑다, 건져 올리다 | unsealed adj 밀폐되지 않은 | container n 상자, 통 | surface n 표면 | efficient adj 효율적인 | confirm v 확인해 주다, 확정하다 | suspicion n 의혹, 의심 | barren adj 척박한, 황량한 | desert n 사막 | entirely adv 완전히 | devoid of ~이 없는 | belief n 믿음 | persist v 집요하게 계속하다 | seafloor n 해저 | plate tectonics 판 구조론 | achieve v 달성하다, 성취하다 | acceptance n 받아들임, 수락, 동의 | geologist n 지질학자 | predict v 예측하다 | deep-sea vent 심해 열수구 | crack n 갈라진 곳, 틈 | magma n 마그마 | crust n 지각, 딱딱한 층 | hot springs 온천 | exist v 존재하다 | remotely adv 원격으로, 멀리서 | attach v 부착하다 | unmanned adj 무인의 | submersible n 잠수정 | notice v 알아차리다 | spike n 급등, 급증 | disregard v 무시하다, 묵살하다 | anomaly n 변칙, 이례 | correspond v 일치하다, 부합하다 | dense adj 밀도가 높은 | clam n 조개 | mussel n 홍합 | volcanic plain 화산 평원 | squeeze into 비집고 들어가다 | submarine n 잠수함 | balmy adj 아늑한, 훈훈한 | precipitate v 촉발하다, 치닫게 하다 | shellfish n 조개류, 갑각류 | blind crab 장님 게 | mouthless adj 입이 없는 | tubeworm n 서관충 | discovery n 발견 | prompt v 촉발하다, 유도하다 | mystery n 미스터리, 수수께끼 | access n 접근, 이용 | survive v 생존하다

Passage 3

Woman: Professor

Listen to part of a lecture in a marketing class.

W This week, we are going to look at the market and its role in driving sales. Before we start talking about market-driven companies, though, I will briefly talk about product-driven companies. So, product-driven companies are those which look internally to determine how to boost sales. They may do this by, for example, determining what their customers think of the company's product. This means product-driven companies aren't as concerned with potential customers as they are with keeping their current customers happy.

The thing is, just because one customer wants your product doesn't mean everyone will. If you want your company to grow, you will need to do research. External research is what differentiates a product-driven company from a market-driven company. Market-driven companies pay very close attention to consumer spending habits and work on developing a relationship with new consumers. A market-driven company maintains its competitive edge by converting this market knowledge into innovative products and services.

여자: 교수

마케팅 강의의 일부를 들으시오.

여 이번 주에는 시장과 판매 촉진에 있어 시장의 역할에 대해 살펴볼 겁니다. 하지만 시장 중심 회사들에 대한 이야기를 시작하기 전에, 상품 중심 회사에 관해 간단히 이야기하도록 하겠습니다. 상품 중심 회사는 판매를 촉진하는 방법을 결정하기 위해 내부로 시선을 돌리는 회사들입니다. 예를 들면 고객이 그 회사의 상품을 어떻게 생각하는지 판단함으로써 말이죠. 이는 상품 중심 회사가 현재의 고객을 행복하게 하는 만큼 잠재 고객에게 관심을 두지는 않는다는 의미입니다.

문제는 한 명의 고객이 회사의 상품을 원한다고 해서 모든 사람이 그러지는 않을 거라는 얘기죠. 만약 당신의 회사가 성장하기를 원한다면 조사를 해야만 합니다. 외부 조사가 바로 상품 중심 회사와 시장 중심 회사를 다르게 만드는 부분입니다. 시장 중심 회사들은 소비자의 소비 습관에 매우 깊은 관심을 기울이고 새로운 고객과 관계를 발전시키려고 하죠. 시장 중심 회사는 이 시장 지식을 혁신적인 상품과 서비스로 전환하여 경쟁적 우위를 유지합니다.

Alright? So, let's say you are a market-driven company and you want to know what will get people to buy what you are selling. Basically, the answer is packaging and advertising—both are pretty important. Think about it... packaging is essential because, well, it is a part of our daily lives and we see it all around us. So, it must be eye-catching and appealing, or it won't sell. Advertising, like packaging, must get people's attention, right? Advertising must enable people to make positive associations with a product.
This can be done by using celebrities, attractive models, beautiful beaches, or cute babies, you know, depending on the target market. Advertisers may also use more abstract concepts in their ads such as "speed," "freedom," or "longevity."

알겠죠? 자, 여러분이 시장 중심 회사이고, 무엇이 여러분이 판매하는 물건을 사람들로 하여금 구매하게 하는지 알고 싶어 한다고 합시다. 기본적으로, 답은 포장과 광고이고 둘 다 매우 중요하죠. 생각해 보세요... 포장은 우리 일상 생활의 일부이고 우리 주변 모든 곳에서 보기 때문에 필수적입니다. 그래서 포장은 시선을 끌고 마음을 움직일 수 있어야 하고, 안 그러면 팔리지 않을 겁니다. 포장과 마찬가지로 광고도 사람들의 관심을 끌어야 합니다, 그렇죠? 광고는 사람들이 상품에 관해 긍정적인 연상을 하도록 만들 수 있어야 합니다. 이는 목표 시장에 따라 유명인, 매력적인 모델과 아름다운 해변, 또는 귀여운 아기들을 이용해서 이루어질 수 있죠. 광고주들은 또한 광고에서 '속도', '자유', 또는 '지속성'과 같은 더 추상적인 개념을 사용할 수도 있습니다.

Q. What is the professor's attitude toward product-driven companies?

Ⓐ She feels that their focus is too limited.
Ⓑ She thinks that they should do more internal research.
Ⓒ She believes that they are more successful.
Ⓓ She advises against working for them.

Q. 상품 중심 회사에 관한 교수의 태도는 어떠한가?

Ⓐ 집중 분야가 너무 제한되었다고 본다.
Ⓑ 더 많은 내부 연구를 해야 한다고 생각한다.
Ⓒ 이 회사들이 더 성공적이라고 믿는다.
Ⓓ 이 회사들을 위해 일하는 것을 반대한다.

어휘 role n 역할 | drive v 추진하다, 만들다, 몰아가다 | sales n 판매 | briefly adv 간단히 | product n 제품 | internally adv 내부적으로 | determine v 결정하다 | boost v 신장시키다 | customer n 고객 | potential adj 잠재적인 | current adj 현재의 | grow v 성장하다 | external adj 외부의 | differentiate v 다르게 하다 | attention n 주의, 관심 | spending habit 소비 습관 | develop v 개발하다 | relationship n 관계 | maintain v 유지하다 | competitive adj 경쟁적인 | convert *A* into *B* A를 B로 바꾸다 | knowledge n 지식 | innovative adj 혁신적인 | packaging n 포장 | advertising n 광고 | eye-catching 시선을 잡아 끄는 | appealing adj 매력적인 | positive adj 긍정적인 | association n 연상, 연관 | celebrity n 유명인 | attractive adj 매력적인 | advertiser n 광고주 | abstract adj 추상적인 | concept n 개념 | longevity n 수명, 오래 지속됨

Passage 4

Man: Professor

Listen to part of a lecture in a biology class.

M Cells are the smallest independent metabolic units of life. All organisms are composed of these tiny building blocks of life capable of absorbing and using energy. Though they seem so vital to understanding the basic composition of all organisms, they weren't discovered until the Age of Enlightenment in the Netherlands. It was then that Antonie van Leeuwenhoek improved microscope lens technology and developed microscopes able to make things look 270 times larger.
Well, microscope technology has improved a lot since then, so you'd think we'd know everything by now. But that definitely isn't the case. So far, we've learned that cells contain chromosomes, which means they contain all the genetic information necessary for regulating their functions and for creating new cells. Cells are generally composed

남자: 교수

생물학 강의의 일부를 들으시오.

남 세포는 생명체에서 가장 작은 독립적인 신진대사 단위입니다. 모든 유기체는 에너지를 흡수하고 사용할 수 있는 이 생명의 작은 기초 단위들로 이루어져 있습니다. 세포는 모든 유기체의 기본 구성을 이해하는 데 필수적인 것으로 보이지만 계몽주의 시대가 되어서야 네덜란드에서 발견되었습니다. 그때 안톤 판 레이우엔훅이 현미경 렌즈 기술을 발달시켰고 270배로 확대해서 보여주는 현미경을 개발했죠.
자, 현미경 기술은 그 뒤로 많이 발전했으므로 여러분은 우리가 이제 모든 것을 안다고 생각할 겁니다. 하지만 결코 그렇지 않아요. 지금까지 우리는 세포가 염색체를 가지고 있다는 것을 배웠고 이는 세포가 기능을 조절하고 새로운 세포를 형성하는 데 필요한 모든 유전자 정보를 가지고 있다는 뜻입니다. 세포는 일반적으로 뚜렷하게 다른 12개 요소 중 5

of 5 or more of a total of 12 distinct parts, with no type of cell having all 12. But all cells have plasma membranes and ribosomes. They reproduce and produce protein by means of the ribosomes. And cells can respond to changes in their surroundings and to internal changes. Well, we know all this and more, but it seems as though the more we learn the less we know. You see, as we discover the parts of one thing and learn how they function and interact we learn that those parts have still smaller parts, and those parts have even smaller parts. Every year we learn of new parts like porosomes, which are organelle parts that are invisible without electron microscopes.

개 혹은 그 이상으로 구성되어 있고, 12개 전부를 가진 세포는 없습니다. 하지만 모든 세포는 혈장 세포막과 리보솜을 가지고 있어요. 이들은 리보솜의 도움으로 번식하고 단백질을 생산합니다. 그리고 세포는 주변 환경 변화와 내부 변화에 대응할 수 있습니다. 음, 우리는 이 모든 것과 그 이상을 알고 있지만 더 많이 알수록 더 적게 알게 되는 것 같습니다. 무언가의 일부분을 발견하고 그것들이 어떻게 기능하고 상호 작용하는지 알게 되면서 우리는 그 부분들이 여전히 더 작은 부분을 가지고 있고, 그 부분들이 훨씬 더 작은 부분을 갖고 있다는 것을 알게 됩니다. 전자 현미경 없이는 보이지 않는 세포 기관의 일부인 포로솜 같은 새로운 부분들을 매년 알게 되죠.

Q. What is the professor's opinion about Antonie van Leeuwenhoek?

Ⓐ He feels that he brought the Age of Enlightenment in the Netherlands.
Ⓑ He believes that he is given too much credit in the scientific community.
Ⓒ He thinks that his innovations were integral to the discovery of cells.
Ⓓ He regards him as the first scientist to ever view organic cells.

Q. 안톤 판 레이우엔훅에 관한 교수의 의견은 무엇인가?

Ⓐ 그가 네덜란드에 계몽주의 시대를 불러왔다고 본다.
Ⓑ 과학계에서 너무 과대평가되었다고 믿는다.
Ⓒ 그의 혁신이 세포의 발견에 필수적이었다고 생각한다.
Ⓓ 유기 세포를 본 최초의 과학자로 생각한다.

어휘 independent adj 독립적인 I metabolic adj 신진대사의 I organism n 생물 I composed of ~로 구성된 I absorb v 흡수하다 I vital adj 필수적인 I composition n 구성 I discover v 발견하다 I Age of Enlightenment 계몽주의 시대 I improve v 나아지다, 향상시키다 I microscope n 현미경 I definitely adv 분명히 I chromosome n 염색체 I genetic adj 유전적인 I function n 기능 I plasma membrane 혈장 세포막, 원형질 막 I ribosome n 리보솜 I respond v 대응하다, 반응하다 I surroundings n 주변 환경 I internal adj 내부의 I porosome n 포로솜, 세포 미세공 I organelle n 세포 기관 I invisible adj 보이지 않는, 투명한

Lesson 04 Connecting Contents

본서 I P. 158

Practice

Passage 1 A
Passage 2 D
Passage 3 E - C - B - A
Passage 4 Yes – A, C, D / No – B, E

Practice

본서 I P. 162

Passage 1 Woman: Professor

Listen to part of a lecture in an art history class.

W Surrealism is one of the many art movements that began between the world wars. Like Dadaism, it was a reaction to the horrors of a war led by an incompetent elite class of society. Many of the empires and monarchies that had

여자: 교수

미술사 강의의 일부를 들으시오.

여 초현실주의는 두 차례의 세계 대전 사이에 시작된 많은 미술 운동 중 하나입니다. 다다이즘처럼 사회의 무능한 엘리트 집단이 주도한 전쟁의 참상에 대한 반응이었죠. 세계 대전 전에 세계를 다스렸던 많

governed the world prior to the Great War were deposed or relegated to minor roles in the aftermath. This was in line with the anarchist ideals of the Dadaists, but the surrealists craved order. Their movement emerged during a decade of peace and prosperity, and they were trying to move beyond the wounds from the war. Surrealism was very much a retreat from reality by survivors who did not want to dwell on the past. They focused on exploring the relationship between the conscious and unconscious mind as it was delineated by Sigmund Freud. The great artists of the movement painted in a very traditional style, but they rejected the stark reality of previous art styles in favor of painting dreams as if they were real. They tried to find the meaning in life by exploring the mysteries of the mind and imagination.

은 제국과 군주들이 그 여파로 작은 역할로 물러나거나 좌천되었습니다. 이는 다다이스트들의 무정부주의자 이상과 일치하지만 초현실주의자들은 질서를 갈망했어요. 이들의 운동은 평화와 부흥의 10년 사이 부상했으며 전쟁의 상처를 딛고 나아가려 했습니다. 초현실주의는 과거에 머물고 싶어 하지 않았던 생존자들이 현실에서 도피한 거라고 볼 수 있습니다. 이들은 지그문트 프로이트가 기술한 의식과 무의식 사이의 관계를 탐험하는 데 중점을 두었습니다. 이 운동의 유명한 화가들은 아주 전통적인 양식으로 그림을 그렸지만, 기존 미술 양식이 보여준 냉혹한 현실을 거부하고 꿈을 마치 현실처럼 그리는 것을 선호했습니다. 이들은 정신세계의 신비와 상상을 탐구하는 것을 통해 삶의 의미를 찾으려 노력했습니다.

Q. Why does the professor mention Dadaism in the lecture?

Ⓐ To contrast it with Surrealism as an art form
Ⓑ To illustrate why one movement was more popular
Ⓒ To explain what influenced the creation of surrealism
Ⓓ To compare the techniques that the artists used

Q. 교수는 왜 강의에서 다다이즘을 언급하는가?

Ⓐ 미술 형태로서의 초현실주의와 대조하려고
Ⓑ 왜 한 운동이 더 인기있었는지 설명하려고
Ⓒ 초현실주의의 발현에 영향을 준 것을 설명하려고
Ⓓ 화가들이 사용했던 기법을 비교하려고

어휘 surrealism n 초현실주의 | movement n 운동 | Dadaism n 다다이즘 | reaction n 반응 | horror n 공포, 경악 | incompetent adj 무능한 | empire n 제국 | monarchy n 군주 | govern v 다스리다 | depose v 물러나게 하다, 퇴위시키다 | relegate v 좌천시키다, 강등시키다 | aftermath n 여파, 후유증 | anarchist n 무정부주의자 | ideal n 이상 | crave v 갈망하다, 열망하다 | order n 질서 | emerge v 부상하다, 나타나다 | decade n 10년 | prosperity n 부흥 | wound n 상처 | retreat n 후퇴 | survivor n 생존자 | dwell v 머물다 | explore v 탐사하다, 탐구하다, 살피다 | conscious adj 의식의 | unconscious adj 무의식의 | delineate v 기술하다 | traditional adj 전통적인 | reject v 거부하다 | stark adj 냉혹한 | previous adj 이전의 | mystery n 수수께끼, 신비, 미스터리 | imagination n 상상

Passage 2

Man: Professor

Listen to part of a lecture in an ecology class.

M How many of you remember the Exxon Valdez disaster? Hmm... No one? Well, perhaps you're just a little bit too young, eh? Anyway, today, we'll discuss this sad historical event and its impact on, well, the world, really. In the late 1960s and early 1970s, the United States hoped to decrease the country's dependence on foreign oil by using oil from Alaska. Experts believed that Alaska had the largest oil reserves ever found on the North American continent, so the Trans-Alaskan Pipeline was built in 1977. The Trans-Alaskan Pipeline brought crude oil to the Alaskan coast, and oil tankers brought it south. Well, you know, environmentalists had always protested the pipeline, and in March of 1989 disaster struck when the Exxon Valdez tanker sank near the Alaskan coast. Almost 11 million gallons of oil spilled into Alaska's fragile coastal ecosystem. That was the largest oil spill in U.S. history, and was, obviously, a source of great concern to outraged environmentalists.

남자: 교수

생태학 강의의 일부를 들으시오.

남 여러분 중 엑슨발데스호 참사를 기억하는 사람이 몇 명이나 되죠? 흠... 아무도 없나요? 음, 아마도 여러분 나이가 너무 어리기 때문인가 보군요, 그렇죠? 어쨌든 오늘은 이 안타까운 역사적 사건과 그것이 전 세계에 미친 영향에 대해 논의할 것입니다. 1960년대 후반과 1970년대 초, 미국은 알래스카에서 나는 석유를 사용함으로써 외국산 석유에 대한 국가 의존도를 줄이고자 했습니다. 전문가들은 알래스카가 북미 대륙에서 발견된 것 가운데 가장 큰 원유 매장량을 갖고 있다고 믿었기 때문에 1977년 알래스카 횡단 송유관을 건설하게 됩니다. 알래스카 횡단 송유관은 알래스카 해변으로 원유를 운반했고 유조선이 그 원유를 남쪽으로 운반했습니다. 음, 환경론자들은 줄곧 송유관 사용에 반대했는데, 1989년 3월 엑슨발데스 유조선이 알래스카 해변 가까이에서 침몰하면서 끔찍한 참사가 일어났습니다.

Let me tell you about the cleanup process. First and foremost, it wasn't easy. Among several problems was a setback caused by a storm that spread the oil slick far and wide, onto the long stretch of shoreline and out into the sea. This changed the problem from a large but relatively isolated oil spill to one that overwhelmed the cleanup project. Actually, the storm combined the oil with salt water, creating a mixture that does not burn easily. This prevented the project from using the crude but cost-efficient solution of burning surface oil to remove it from the ocean's surface. Both traditional and non-traditional methods were used to clean up the spill. Since oil is lighter than water, affected beaches were blasted with hot water in order to force the oil back into the water, where it could be skimmed more efficiently. Other efforts included burning oil on the water's surface, using dispersants to scatter it farther into the ocean, and manually cleaning any rocks and animals that were coated with oil. One of the newer and more advanced treatments used was bioremediation. Bioremediation uses a fertilizer that encourages the growth of microbes that actually eat oil. Despite these and other methods, only about 15% of the oil was actually recovered, while umm, a large percentage was burned off, cleaned up, evaporated or dispersed. Still, the ecological impact was devastating. Along about roughly 1,000 miles of shoreline, sea mammal, fish, and bird populations were severely affected. Some affected species are still struggling, and their future remains uncertain even today. And yet, despite the lengthy and disappointing cleanup, things could have been even worse.

거의 천백만 갤런의 석유가 알래스카의 손상되기 쉬운 해안 생태계로 흘러 들어갔습니다. 이는 미국 역사상 가장 규모가 컸던 석유 유출이었고 격분한 환경론자들에게는 분명 아주 큰 걱정거리였습니다.
그 정화 과정에 대해 이야기할게요. 무엇보다도 그 과정은 쉽지 않았습니다. 여러 가지 문제 가운데 석유 기름막을 해변 전체와 바다 속으로 널리 퍼지게 한 폭풍 문제가 있었어요. 양은 많지만 상대적으로 범위가 좁았던 석유 유출을 폭풍은 정화 프로젝트를 압도하는 심각한 문제로 바꾸어 놓게 됩니다. 실제로 폭풍이 석유와 바닷물을 섞이게 해서 쉽게 타지 않는 혼합물이 만들어졌습니다. 이는 정화 프로젝트에서 바다 표면의 석유를 태워 없애는 거칠지만 비용 면에서 효율적인 해결책을 사용할 수 없게 만들었죠.
기존의 방법과 새로운 방법 모두 정화를 위해 사용되었습니다. 기름은 물보다 더 가볍기 때문에 오염된 해변에서는 고온의 물 폭탄을 터뜨려 기름을 다시 바다로 내보냈는데, 이는 더 효과적으로 찌꺼기를 걷어내기 위해서였습니다. 다른 시도는 물 표면의 기름을 태우는 것과 분산제를 사용하여 바다 표면의 기름을 멀리 흩어지게 하는 것, 기름으로 뒤덮인 돌과 동물을 수작업으로 깨끗하게 만드는 것이 있었습니다. 사용된 좀더 새롭고 진보한 방법 중 하나는 생물적 환경 정화였어요. 생물적 환경 정화는 실제로 기름을 먹는 미생물의 성장을 촉진하기 위해 비료를 사용합니다. 이러한 여러 다른 방법에도 불구하고 단지 15퍼센트 정도의 기름만이 회수된 반면, 음, 많은 양의 기름이 연소되고, 정화되고, 증발되고, 또는 흩어졌습니다. 그렇지만 생태학적 여파는 참담했습니다. 대략 천 마일에 달하는 해안에 걸쳐 바다 포유류, 물고기, 새의 개체수가 심각하게 영향을 받았습니다. 일부 오염된 종은 아직까지도 고통을 받고 있으며 그들의 미래는 오늘날까지도 불확실합니다. 하지만 장기화되고 실망스러웠던 정화 과정이었긴 하지만 상황은 더 나빴을 수도 있었습니다.

Q. Why does the professor talk about the different oil clean-up methods?

Ⓐ To classify them into traditional and non-traditional methods
Ⓑ To indicate the scale of the environmental catastrophe
Ⓒ To examine why some were more effective than others
Ⓓ To emphasize the difficulty of cleaning up the Exxon Valdez oil spill

Q. 교수는 왜 각기 다른 기름 정화 방법들에 관해 이야기하는가?

Ⓐ 이들을 전통적 방법과 비전통적 방법으로 분류하기 위해
Ⓑ 이 환경적 재앙의 규모를 나타내기 위해
Ⓒ 왜 어떤 방법은 다른 방법보다 더 효율적이었는지 알아보기 위해
Ⓓ 엑슨발데스호 석유 유출 정화의 어려움을 강조하기 위해

어휘 disaster n 참사, 재앙 | discuss v 논의하다 | historical adj 역사적인 | impact n 영향 | decrease v 줄이다, 감소하다 | dependence n 의존 | foreign adj 외국의 | reserve n 매장량 | continent n 대륙 | Trans-Alaskan Pipeline 알래스카 횡단 송유관 | crude oil 원유 | environmentalist n 환경 운동가 | protest v 항의하다, 반대하다 | fragile adj 손상되기 쉬운, 취약한 | coastal adj 해안의 | ecosystem n 생태계 | concern n 걱정, 우려 | outraged adj 격분한 | cleanup n 정화 | foremost adj 가장 중요한 | setback n 차질 | oil slick 유막 | stretch n 길게 뻗은 지역, 구간 | shoreline n 해안가, 물가 | relatively adv 상대적으로 | isolated adj 고립된, 동떨어진 | overwhelm v 압도하다 | combine v 합치다 | prevent v 막다 | crude adj 거친, 있는 그대로의 | efficient adj 효율적인 | solution n 해결책 | surface adj 표면의 | traditional adj 전통적인 | blast v 폭발시키다, 폭파하다 | skim v 걷어 내다 | dispersant n 분산제 | scatter v 흩다 | manually adv 손으로, 수공으로 | coat v 덮다 | advanced adj 진보한 | treatment n 처리, 치료 | bioremediation n 생물적 환경 정화 | fertilizer n 비료 | encourage v 장려하다 | growth n 성장 | microbe n 미생물 | recover v 되찾다, 회수하다 | evaporate v 증발하다 | disperse v 흩다, 흩어지게 하다 | ecological adj 생태학적 | devastating adj 대단히 파괴적인 | population n 개체수 | struggle v 힘겨워하다 | uncertain adj 불확실한 | lengthy adj 너무 긴, 오랜 | disappointing adj 실망스러운

Passage 3

Man: Professor

Listen to part of a lecture in an American history class.

M Today, I'd like to start off by talking about Tecumseh, a famous Native American who showed a great deal of leadership ability in his life. He was born around 1768 and, consequently, lived during a time of warfare during which the European Americans were trying to take possession of Native American land. Uh, if you don't know what I mean here, you might want to look at the Indian Removal Act of 1830 and its plan to move Native Americans west of the Mississippi. In any case, **(E)** Tecumseh became the chief of the Shawnee tribe in 1789, and he greatly resented the encroachments on Native American land. The movement of American settlers westward increased rapidly **(C)** after the Louisiana Purchase, and **(B)** he tried to bring all of the Native American tribes together in order to form a unified front against the United States. **(A)** He also joined the British in the War of 1812, and, he displayed a great deal of strategic ability before his death in 1813.

Q. The professor described some of the events that occurred during the life of Chief Tecumseh in the lecture. Put those events in the correct order. Drag each answer choice to the space where it belongs. One of the answer choices will not be used.

Ⓐ The Shawnee and other tribes sided with the British in the War of 1812.

Ⓑ Tecumseh tried to rally other Native American Tribes to form a confederacy.

Ⓒ The United States purchased the Louisiana Territory from France.

Ⓓ The Indian Removal Act was passed by the United States government.

Ⓔ Tecumseh became the chief of his tribe, the Shawnee.

남자: 교수

미국 역사 강의의 일부를 들으시오.

남 오늘은 일평생 위대한 지도력을 몸소 보여준 미국 원주민인 티컴세에 대해 이야기해 보도록 합시다. 티컴세는 1768년경 태어나서 유럽계 미국인들이 아메리카 원주민의 땅을 빼앗고자 했던 전쟁 시기에 살았습니다. 음, 제 말을 이해하지 못하겠으면, 아메리카 원주민들을 미시시피주 서부로 이주시키려던 1830년의 인디언 이주법과 그 계획을 보면 좋을 거예요. 어쨌든 **(E)** 티컴세는 1789년 쇼니 부족의 족장이 되었으며 아메리카 원주민의 땅이 침략당하는 것에 분노했습니다. **(C)** 루이지애나주 매입 이후 서쪽으로 향하는 미국 정착민들의 움직임은 급격히 빨라졌고, 그는 미국에 대항하여 **(B)** 통합된 전선을 구축하기 위해 모든 아메리카 원주민 부족을 하나로 모으려고 노력했습니다. **(A)** 그는 또한 1812년 전쟁에서 영국과 손을 잡았고 1813년 세상을 떠나기 전까지 뛰어난 전략적 역량을 보여주었습니다.

Q. 교수는 강의에서 티컴세 족장의 삶에서 일어난 사건 일부를 서술했다. 이 사건들을 올바른 순서로 놓으시오. 각 보기를 알맞은 곳에 끌어다 넣으시오. 보기 중 하나는 사용되지 않는다.

Ⓐ 쇼니와 다른 부족들이 1812년 전쟁 때 영국의 편에 섰다.

Ⓑ 티컴세가 연맹을 형성하기 위해 다른 미국 원주민 부족들을 결집시키려고 했다.

Ⓒ 미국이 프랑스로부터 루이지애나주 영토를 구입했다.

Ⓓ 인디언 이주법이 미국 정부에서 통과되었다.

Ⓔ 티컴세가 자신의 부족인 쇼니의 지도자가 되었다.

1	Ⓔ Tecumseh became the chief of his tribe, the Shawnee.
2	Ⓒ The United States purchased the Louisiana Territory from France
3	Ⓑ Tecumseh tried to rally other Native American Tribes to form a confederacy.
4	Ⓐ The Shawnee and other tribes sided with the British in the War of 1812.

1	Ⓔ 티컴세가 자신의 부족인 쇼니의 족장이 되었다.
2	Ⓒ 미국이 프랑스로부터 루이지애나주 영토를 구입했다.
3	Ⓑ 티컴세가 연맹을 형성하기 위해 다른 미국 원주민 부족들을 결집시키려고 했다.
4	Ⓐ 쇼니족과 다른 부족들이 1812년 전쟁 때 영국의 편에 섰다.

어휘 Native American 미국 원주민 I consequently adv 그 결과, 따라서 I warfare n 전투, 전쟁 I possession n 소유, 차지 I removal n 이동, 이전 I chief n 족장 I tribe n 부족 I resent v 분개하다, 억울해 하다 I encroachment n 침략, 침해 I settler n 정착민 I rapidly adv 급격히 I unify v 통합하다, 통일하다

Passage 4 Woman: Professor

Listen to part of a lecture in an astronomy class.

W Now let's move on to Uranus. It is the seventh planet from the Sun, so **(B)** its orbit lies between Saturn and Neptune. Although it is closer to the Sun than Neptune, its surface temperature is actually colder. In fact, **(C)** it is the coldest planet in our solar system at negative 224 degrees Centigrade. **(E)** Its atmosphere is mostly comprised of hydrogen and helium, but it also contains water, methane, and ammonia. Its high methane content means that the atmosphere reflects blue wavelengths of light, **(D)** giving the planet its smooth blue appearance. Like its neighboring planets, Uranus has a magnetosphere, a ring system, and many moons. What differentiates Uranus from all other planets, however, is its axial tilt. **(A)** Most planets rotate on an axis that is nearly vertical. By comparison, Uranus is lying on its side with its axis pointing toward and away from the Sun.

여자: 교수

천문학 강의의 일부를 들으시오.

여 이제 천왕성으로 넘어갑시다. 천왕성은 태양에서 7번째로 떨어져 있는 행성이기에 **(B)** 궤도가 토성과 해왕성 사이에 놓여 있습니다. 해왕성보다 태양에 가깝지만, 표면 온도는 사실 더 춥죠. 실제로, 천왕성은 섭씨 −224도로 **(C)** 우리 태양계에서 가장 추운 행성입니다. **(E)** 대기는 대부분 수소와 헬륨으로 이루어져 있지만 물과 메탄, 암모니아도 함유하고 있습니다. 높은 메탄 함유량은 대기가 빛의 푸른 파장을 반사하여 **(D)** 행성이 매끄러운 푸른 외형을 가진다는 것을 의미합니다. 이웃에 있는 행성들처럼 천왕성도 자기권과 고리계, 많은 위성을 갖고 있습니다. 그러나 천왕성과 다른 모든 행성들을 구분 짓는 것은 바로 자전축 기울기입니다. **(A)** 대부분의 행성은 거의 수직으로 놓인 축을 중심으로 돕니다. 이에 비해 천왕성은 축이 태양 쪽에서 태양 반대편 쪽으로 향하고 있어 옆으로 누워 있죠.

Q. In the lecture, the professor listed many features of the planet Uranus. Indicate which of the following features are mentioned in the lecture. Click in the correct box for each sentence.

	Yes	No
Ⓐ The planet rotates on a horizontal axis.	✓	
Ⓑ Its orbit lies between Jupiter and Saturn.		✓
Ⓒ Its temperature is the lowest in the solar system.	✓	
Ⓓ The planet looks blue because of its atmosphere.	✓	
Ⓔ Its atmosphere is composed mostly of methane.		✓

Q. 강의에서 교수는 천왕성의 다양한 특징을 열거한다. 다음 중 어느 특징이 강의에서 언급되었는지 표시하시오. 각 문장에 대해 맞는 칸에 표시하시오.

	예	아니오
Ⓐ 이 행성은 수평축을 중심으로 회전한다.	✓	
Ⓑ 이 행성의 궤도는 목성과 토성 사이에 놓여 있다.		✓
Ⓒ 이 행성의 기온은 태양계에서 가장 낮다.	✓	
Ⓓ 이 행성은 대기 때문에 푸른색으로 보인다.	✓	
Ⓔ 행성의 대기는 대부분 메탄으로 구성되어 있다.		✓

어휘 orbit n 궤도 | surface temperature 표면 온도 | solar system 태양계 | atmosphere n 대기 | comprised of ~으로 구성된 | hydrogen n 수소 | helium n 헬륨 | methane n 메탄 | ammonia n 암모니아 | content n 함유량 | reflect v 반사하다 | wavelength n 파장 | appearance n 외형, 생김새 | magnetosphere n 자기권 | moon n 위성 | differentiate v 구분 짓다, 다르게 하다 | axial tilt 자전축 기울기 | rotate v 회전하다 | vertical adj 수직의 | by comparison 그에 비해 | lie v 눕다

Lesson 05 Inference

본서 | P. 164

Practice

Passage 1 C

Passage 2 B

Passage 3 C

Passage 4 D

Practice

본서 | P. 168

Passage 1 Man: Professor

Listen to part of a lecture in an American history class.

M In today's class, I'd like to talk about the history of America's relationship with oil. When I say oil, however, I do not just mean petroleum. I am also talking about whale oil, which was a major source of energy for Americans in the 1700s and 1800s. In these years, it was used to fuel lamps and was very lucrative for businessmen who invested in hunting whales for oil. In fact, by the mid-1800s, America's whaling industry was a huge industry involving over 600 ships and millions of liters of whale oil each year. In spite of this size, however, the whaling industry could not keep up with the United States' growing demands for fuel. America's industrialization and its economic growth were requiring larger amounts of fuel, and, with the advent of petroleum oil, which was less expensive and more easily produced, whale oil started to become obsolete. By the 1900s, petroleum oil had taken over America's fuel market. Americans relied on it for the vast majority of their energy needs, and by the middle of the century, many Americans would have found it hard to live without oil. As we've been learning, however, the possibility of having to live without petroleum is becoming more and more likely. The world's oil supplies are not infinite, and countries are now starting to look to other energy sources to fuel their societies.

Q. What can be inferred about the whaling industry in the United States?

(A) It exported oil products around the world.
(B) It was the largest contributor to the nation's export.
(C) It contributed greatly to the country's economy.
(D) It supported the industrialization of the nation.

남자: 교수

미국 역사 강의의 일부를 들으시오.

남 오늘 수업에서는 미국 역사와 기름의 관계에 대해 이야기하겠습니다. 하지만 제가 말하는 기름이란 단지 석유만을 의미하는 것이 아닙니다. 1700년대와 1800년대 미국인들에게 주요 에너지원이었던 고래 기름도 말하는 겁니다. 이 시기에 고래 기름은 램프에 연료를 공급했고, 기름을 위해 고래 사냥에 투자하는 사업가들은 돈을 굉장히 많이 벌었죠. 사실, 1800년대 중반 미국의 고래 산업은 600개가 넘는 선박을 가진 대규모 사업이었고 매년 수백만 리터의 고래 기름을 생산했습니다. 하지만 이러한 규모에도 불구하고, 고래 산업은 미국의 증가하는 연료 수요를 따라잡을 수가 없었습니다. 미국의 산업화와 경제적 성장은 더 많은 양의 연료를 필요로 하게 되었고, 덜 비싸고 더 쉽게 생산할 수 있는 석유의 출현으로 고래 기름은 쓸모가 없어지기 시작했습니다. 1900년대가 되자 석유는 미국의 연료 시장을 장악하게 되었습니다. 미국인들은 대부분의 에너지 수요를 석유에 의존했고, 20세기 중반이 되자 많은 미국인들이 석유 없이는 생활하기 어렵다는 걸 알게 되었죠. 그러나 우리가 배웠듯이 석유 없이 생활해야 할 가능성이 점점 더 높아지고 있습니다. 세계의 석유 자원은 무한하지 않기 때문에, 여러 나라가 이제 사회에 연료를 공급하기 위한 다른 에너지원을 찾기 시작했습니다.

Q. 미국의 고래 산업에 관해 무엇을 추론할 수 있는가?

(A) 세계 전역에 기름 제품을 수출했다.
(B) 국가 수출에서 가장 큰 기여자였다.
(C) 나라의 경제에 크게 기여했다.
(D) 국가 산업화를 뒷받침했다.

어휘 relationship n 관계 I petroleum n 석유 I whale oil 고래 기름 I fuel v 연료를 공급하다 I lucrative adj 수익성이 좋은 I invest v 투자하다 I industry n 산업 I demand n 수요 I industrialization n 산업화 I economic growth 경제 성장 I require v 필요로 하다, 요구하다 I advent n 출현, 도래 I obsolete adj 쓸모 없는, 구식의 I rely v 의존하다 I vast adj 막대한 I infinite adj 무한한

Passage 2

Woman: Professor

Listen to part of a lecture in a biology class.

W Good morning, everyone. Today I'd like to talk about something that is important to each and every one of you—blood. Blood has so many different aspects. I mean, I could teach a whole semester of classes on blood alone. For example, isn't it interesting that women have 4 to 5 liters of blood while men have 5 to 6 liters in their bodies? And most people carry around a huge number of blood cells every day; we're talking about 25 trillion red blood cells and 50 billion white blood cells! Let's start by talking about the red blood cells, which cause blood to have its red color. They take oxygen from the lungs and circulate it throughout the body. Then they return to the lungs with carbon dioxide that is subsequently pushed out of the body. Next, we have the plasma, which is the watery yellow part of blood. It helps to make blood clot, which helps our wounds stop bleeding and is a very important bodily function. Without this, minor injuries could be much more serious. Then there are the white blood cells. These come from our bone marrow, and they help defend the body against infections and illnesses. If this component of our blood were not present, we would be susceptible to all kinds of things and much more fragile creatures overall.

여자: 교수

생물학 강의의 일부를 들으시오.

여 안녕하세요, 여러분. 오늘은 여러분 모두에게 중요한 것, '혈액'에 대해 이야기해 보도록 하겠습니다. 혈액은 매우 다양한 측면을 지니고 있습니다. 한 학기 강의 전체를 혈액에 대해서만 가르칠 수도 있을 정도죠. 예를 들어, 남자는 몸에 5~6리터의 혈액을 지니고 있는 한편, 여성은 4~5리터를 지니고 있다는 점이 흥미롭지 않습니까? 그리고 대부분의 사람들이 매일 굉장히 많은 수의 혈구를 몸에 지니고 다닙니다. 25조 개의 적혈구와 500억 개의 백혈구를 말하는 거예요! 먼저 혈액이 붉은색을 띠게 하는 적혈구에 대해 이야기합시다. 적혈구는 폐에서 산소를 운반해 몸 전체에 순환시킵니다. 그런 다음 적혈구가 이산화탄소를 가지고 폐로 돌아가면 이산화탄소가 몸 밖으로 배출됩니다. 다음으로는 혈액의 노란색 액체 부분인 혈장이 있습니다. 혈장은 혈액이 응고하도록 해주어 상처가 났을 때 출혈을 멎게 해주는 것으로 몸에서 매우 중요한 기능을 합니다. 혈장이 없으면 조그만 상처도 굉장히 심각해질 수 있어요. 그 다음으로는 백혈구가 있습니다. 백혈구는 우리 골수에서 나오며 감염과 질병으로부터 몸을 방어합니다. 혈액에 이 요소가 없으면 우리는 모든 다양한 것들에 감염되기 쉬워질 것이고 전반적으로 훨씬 더 연약한 생명체가 될 거예요.

Q. What is implied about blood plasma?

Ⓐ It is the main component in blood.
Ⓑ It allows wounds to heal more quickly.
Ⓒ It defends the body against illnesses.
Ⓓ It is a watery yellow fluid produced by the body.

Q. 혈장에 관해 무엇이 암시되었는가?

Ⓐ 피의 주된 요소이다.
Ⓑ 상처가 더 빨리 낫게 해준다.
Ⓒ 질병으로부터 몸을 방어한다.
Ⓓ 몸에서 만들어지는 물 같은 노란 액체이다.

어휘 trillion n 1조 I red blood cell 적혈구 I white blood cell 백혈구 I oxygen n 산소 I lung n 폐 I circulate v 순환하다 I carbon dioxide 이산화탄소 I subsequently adv 그 뒤에, 나중에 I plasma n 혈장 I clot v 응고하다 I wound n 상처 I function n 기능 I injury n 상처 I bone marrow 골수 I defend v 방어하다 I infection n 감염 I illness n 질병 I component n 요소 I susceptible adj 감염되기 쉬운 I fragile adj 연약한

Passage 3

Woman: Professor

Listen to part of a lecture in an environmentology class.

W OK, I'm sure all of you have heard of El Ninõ, which means "little boy" in Spanish by the way, but I don't know how many of you know what El Ninõ really is. It is a change in weather patterns that occurs in the Pacific Ocean around

여자: 교수

환경학 강의의 일부를 들으시오.

여 좋아요, 여러분 모두 스페인어로 '어린 소년'을 의미하는 엘니뇨에 대해 들어봤겠지만, 여러분 중에 실제로 엘니뇨가 무엇인지 아는 사람이 몇 명이나 될지 모르겠군요. 엘니뇨는 매 2년에서 7년마다 남

South America between every two and seven years. This change occurs when water in the Pacific becomes significantly warmer as winds fail to push warm water currents to the west. Now, you may be asking yourself, "What's so bad about warm water?" The answer to this question, however, is complex. One practical problem with it is that it leads to economic problems for many South American fishermen who cannot catch enough fish. On a larger scale, the world's entire weather system changes when El Ninõ occurs. The amount of rainfall in North and South America increases, which can lead to flooding and other problems associated with thunderstorms. In areas of the western Pacific, on the other hand, there is less rainfall, which can lead to droughts and other problems. So, can you see how El Ninõ might affect the lives of millions of people? This has prompted scientists to study weather patterns in greater detail. It has also helped everyday people to realize how small changes in wind and water currents can lead to big problems in the world's weather systems. Now, if you look at the overhead screen, you'll be able to get an even more detailed idea of how air and water currents move throughout the world.

미 부근 태평양에서 발생하는 기후 패턴의 변화입니다. 이 변화는 바람이 난류를 서쪽으로 밀어 보내지 못하게 되면서 태평양의 물이 상당히 더 따뜻해질 때 발생합니다. 자, 여러분은 스스로에게 "물이 따뜻한 게 뭐가 문제지?"라고 물을 수 있을 거예요. 그런데 이 질문에 대한 답은 복잡합니다. 한 가지 실질적인 문제는 많은 남미 어부들이 물고기를 충분히 잡을 수 없게 되는 경제적 문제를 야기한다는 것입니다. 좀 더 넓은 규모로 보면, 엘니뇨가 발생할 경우 세계의 전체 기후 체계가 변화합니다. 북미와 남미의 강우량이 증가하고, 그것은 홍수 및 뇌우와 연관된 기타 문제를 초래할 수 있죠. 한편, 서태평양 지역에서는 강우량이 적어져 가뭄과 다른 문제를 야기할 수 있습니다. 이제 엘니뇨가 어떻게 수백만 명의 삶에 영향을 줄 수 있는지 이해하겠죠? 엘니뇨는 과학자들이 기후 패턴을 더욱 상세히 연구하게 했습니다. 또한 일반 사람들이 바람과 물의 흐름의 작은 변화가 어떻게 세계 기후 체계에 큰 문제를 초래할 수 있는지 깨닫게 해주었습니다. 이제 이 오버헤드 프로젝트 화면을 보면 전 세계적으로 공기와 물의 흐름이 어떻게 이동하는지 훨씬 더 자세히 알 수 있을 거예요.

Q. What can be deduced about El Ninõ from the lecture?

Ⓐ It results in increased rainfall throughout the world.
Ⓑ It contributes to a sharp increase in boating accidents.
Ⓒ It causes natural disasters around the world.
Ⓓ It brings about problems on the Atlantic side of South America.

Q. 강의에서 엘니뇨에 관해 무엇을 추론할 수 있는가?

Ⓐ 전 세계에 강우량 증가를 야기한다.
Ⓑ 보트 사고의 급격한 증가에 일조한다.
Ⓒ 전 세계에 자연 재해를 일으킨다.
Ⓓ 남아메리카의 대서양 쪽에 문제를 일으킨다.

어휘 occur v 발생하다 | significantly adv 상당히 | water current 해류 | complex adj 복잡한 | practical adj 현실적인, 실제의 | economic adj 경제의 | fisherman n 어부 | entire adj 전체의 | rainfall n 강우량 | flooding n 홍수 | associated with ~와 관련된 | thunderstorm n 뇌우 | drought n 가뭄 | affect v 영향을 끼치다 | prompt v 촉발하다 | realize v 깨닫다

Passage 4 Woman: Professor

Listen to part of a lecture in an ecology class.

W Okay, now I would like to move on to a problem that doesn't get much attention in the media but which is still a serious problem. What's going on is that the world's fertile topsoil is slowly disappearing. This is called topsoil-erosion, and it's affecting the entire world right now and making crops more difficult to grow. The consequences of this are obvious, so I'd rather focus on the causes. Most of them involve humans and how they are infringing upon nature, but it is important to remember that erosion occurred long before humans even existed. That is what has produced sea cliffs, certain lakes, and even the Grand Canyon.

여자: 교수

생태학 강의의 일부를 들으시오.

여 자, 이제 미디어에서는 많은 관심을 받지 못하지만 여전히 심각한 문제에 관해 이야기하려고 합니다. 바로 세계의 비옥한 표토가 서서히 사라지고 있다는 것입니다. 이것을 표토 침식이라고 하며 현재 전 세계에 영향을 미치고 있고, 농작물의 성장을 더욱 어렵게 만들고 있습니다. 이에 대한 결과는 명백하기 때문에 원인에 집중하겠습니다. 원인의 대부분이 인간과 인간이 자연을 어떻게 침해하고 있는지와 관련되어 있지만 침식은 인간이 존재하기 오래 전부터 발생했다는 점을 기억하는 것이 중요합니다. 그것은 해식 절벽과 특정 호수들, 심지어 그랜드 캐니언까지 만들었어요.

Lesson 05 Lectures

With that said, humans are speeding up the process of erosion and also hurting themselves through overproduction and overpopulation. They're farming more animals than ever before and doing so in smaller and smaller areas. With more animals present in these spaces, it then becomes possible for the animals to eat up all of the vegetation on a plot of land. After this happens, the soil is left exposed and can be washed or blown away easily. At the same time, high concentrations of animals can compact the soil, which prevents more vegetation from growing in the area.

Humans are also cutting down way too many trees. When they do this and don't try to plant more trees, the soil once again has nothing to protect it or hold it down. It is vulnerable to erosion and can be blown away more easily. We're also farming improperly, which is leading to the same type of problem where plants can't grow on land anymore and then it erodes. But what do I mean by improper farming here? Well, um, certain irrigation methods leave too much salt in the ground, which hinders plant growth. Farmers are also failing to give the soil the time it needs to replenish itself before they plant new crops and overusing fertilizers.

To cut to the chase, farmers are just abusing the land and trying to make it produce more than it should. Humans just aren't looking toward the future. They're trying to get everything now, but they aren't thinking about the consequences of demanding so much from the land they live on. Eventually, this is going to lead to some serious problems in terms of soil erosion and soil infertility.

그 말이 나왔으니 말인데, 인간은 침식 과정을 가속화할 뿐 아니라 과잉 생산과 과잉 인구를 통해 스스로에게 해를 입히고 있습니다. 그 어느 때보다 많은 동물을 사육하고 있으며 점점 더 좁은 공간에서 하고 있죠. 이런 좁은 공간에 동물이 더 많아지면서 그 구역에 있는 초목을 모두 먹어버리는 일이 가능해집니다. 그렇게 되고 나면 토양은 노출된 채 남겨지고 쉽게 씻겨 나가거나 소실될 수 있죠. 동시에 동물들이 밀집해 있으면 토양이 단단하게 다져지고, 이는 그 지역에서 더 이상의 초목이 자라지 못하게 합니다.

또한 인간들은 너무 많은 나무를 베고 있어요. 나무를 베고 더 많은 나무를 심지 않으면 다시 토양을 보호하거나 지탱할 것이 없어지게 됩니다. 침식에 취약해지고 더 쉽게 소실될 수 있죠. 그리고 우리는 부적절하게 경작을 해서 식물이 땅에서 더 이상 자랄 수 없게 하는 동일한 문제를 초래하고 그로 인해 토양은 침식됩니다. 하지만 여기서 부적절한 경작이란 무엇일까요? 음, 어떤 관개 방법은 땅에 너무 많은 염분을 남겨 식물의 성장을 방해합니다. 또한 농부들은 새로운 농작물을 경작하기 전에 땅이 스스로 회복할 수 있는 시간을 주지 않으며, 비료를 남용합니다.

단도직입적으로 말하자면, 농부들은 토지를 남용하고 있으며 적정량 이상으로 더 많이 생산하게 하려 합니다. 인간은 미래를 내다보지 않고 있어요. 지금 당장 모든 것을 얻으려 하지만 자신들이 사는 땅에 많은 것을 요구하고 난 뒤의 결과에 대해서는 생각하지 않죠. 결국 이는 토양 침식과 토양 불모라는 심각한 문제로 이어질 겁니다.

Q. What does the professor imply about current agricultural practices?

Ⓐ Raising large herds of animals compacts the soil.
Ⓑ Too much salt is building up in the soil.
Ⓒ Fertilizers accumulate in the ground water.
Ⓓ Farmers are using up the land that can be farmed.

Q. 교수는 현재의 농업 관행에 관해 무엇을 암시하는가?

Ⓐ 큰 무리의 동물들을 기르는 것은 토양을 다져지게 만든다.
Ⓑ 너무 많은 염분이 토양에 쌓이고 있다.
Ⓒ 비료가 지하수에 축적된다.
Ⓓ 농부들이 경작할 수 있는 땅을 다 고갈시키고 있다.

어휘 attention n 주의, 주목 | fertile adj 비옥한 | topsoil n 표토 | erosion n 침식 | affect v 영향을 주다 | entire adj 전체의 | crop n 작물 | consequence n 결과 | obvious adj 명백한 | cause n 원인 | infringe v 침해하다 | occur v 발생하다 | exist v 존재하다 | sea cliff 해식 절벽 | hurt v 다치게 하다 | overproduction n 과잉 생산 | overpopulation n 인구 과잉 | vegetation n 초목, 식물 | exposed adj 노출된 | blow away 날려버리다 | concentration n 집중 | compact v (단단히) 다지다 | prevent v 막다, 방해하다 | vulnerable adj 취약한 | improperly adv 그릇되게, 틀리게 | erode v 침식되다 | improper adj 부적절한 | irrigation n 관개 | hinder v 저해하다 | growth n 성장 | replenish v 다시 채우다, 보충하다 | overuse v 남용하다 | fertilizer n 비료 | to cut to the chase 본론으로 들어가다 | abuse v 남용하다, 학대하다 | demand v 요구하다 | infertility n 불모

III. Actual Tests

Actual Test 1

본서 | P. 170

Conversation 1	1. B	2. B	3. B	4. A	5. C		
Lecture 1	6. C	7. C	8. A	9. B, D	10. A	11. A	
Conversation 2	1. C	2. A	3. B	4. C	5. B, D		
Lecture 2	6. C	7. A, C, D	8. A	9. D	10. D – B – C – A		11. C
Lecture 3	12. D	13. B	14. D	15. A	16. D	17. B	

Conversation 1

본서 | P. 172

Man: Student | Woman: Librarian

[1-5] Listen to part of a conversation between a student and a librarian.

W Welcome to the library. I'm Judy Wiscot. How may I help you?

M 1 I keep getting these notices from the library telling me that I need to return a book that I checked out for one of my classes.

W Okay. Let's see if we can get to the bottom of this. What's your name and ID number?

M My name is Jim Furyk, and my ID number is 93895.

W All right. Here we are. You checked out *Paradigms and Methodologies in Transactional Behavior*. The book was due two weeks ago. That's why you've been getting return request notices. Is that right?

M Well, it's like this. 2 I'm a senior psychology major, and I was under the impression that seniors were permitted an indefinite extension providing that they needed the materials.

W 2, 3 That's true, but you're forgetting one important condition. While it is true that seniors are allowed to keep books out longer than underclassmen, the seniors must immediately return the books when another student requests the book.

M 3 I don't think I understand why the policy exists in the first place. I mean, if another student can request the book at any time, then the senior doesn't have any guarantee to keep the book! For example, the book that I've checked out is a resource that everybody needs in the psych department, but only seniors depend on it for our final projects that we need in order to graduate. Do you catch my meaning?

남자: 학생 | 여자: 도서관 사서

학생과 도서관 사서의 대화를 들으시오.

여 도서관에 온 걸 환영합니다. 전 주디 위스콧이에요. 어떻게 도와드릴까요?

남 1 제 수업을 위해 대출했던 책을 반납하라는 통지를 도서관에서 계속해서 받고 있어서요.

여 그렇군요. 어떻게 된 일인지 한번 알아보죠. 학생 이름과 학생증 번호가 뭐죠?

남 제 이름은 짐 퓨릭이고 학생증 번호는 93895예요.

여 좋아요. 찾았어요. 〈매매 행태의 범례와 방법론〉이라는 책을 대출했군요. 그 책의 대출 기한이 2주 전이었어요. 그게 바로 학생이 계속해서 반납 통지를 받았던 이유네요. 맞죠?

남 음, 그건 이렇게 된 거예요. 2 저는 심리학 전공 4학년 학생인데 4학년 학생에게는 자료가 필요하다면 무한정 대출 기간을 연장할 수 있게 해주는 줄 알았어요.

여 2, 3 맞아요. 하지만 학생은 한 가지 중요한 조건을 잊었군요. 4학년 학생들이 하급생들보다 더 오랜 기간 책을 대출할 수 있기는 하지만, 다른 학생이 그 책을 대출하기를 원한다면 즉시 해당 도서를 반납해야 해요.

남 3 그럼 애초에 왜 그런 정책이 있는 건지 이해가 안 되네요. 제 말은, 만약 다른 학생이 도서를 어느 때라도 요청할 수 있다면 4학년 학생이 그 책을 계속 볼 수 있도록 보장을 받지 못한다는 거잖아요! 예를 들어, 제가 대출한 책이 심리학과의 모든 학생들에게 필요한 것이긴 하지만 4학년생만 졸업을 위한 최종 프로젝트를 위해 그 책이 꼭 필요하다고요. 제 말 이해하세요?

W 4 Yes, I catch it, but return requests happen less frequently than you might think. Generally, we have plenty of copies of each book, so seniors can keep the books out for the whole semester without anybody missing them.

M I understand, but the number of books the library owns doesn't change my predicament. I still really need this book.

W The rule states that after the return request is satisfied, and the second student is finished with the book, then the library will call the first student to come and pick up the book for a second time.

M That's great service, but again, it doesn't help me at the moment. I have to keep this book in order to pass.

W How about this? Why don't you come back into the office and copy the vital pages on the library's machine free of charge? That way your work won't be interrupted.

M That's very kind of you! Is there any way I'll be able to get the book back soon?

W 5 It will depend on how long the new requester needs to keep the book. Underclassmen get only two weeks for a check out. However, normally, they don't keep the book for that long. If that happens, we'll get the book back to you as soon as possible.

M Great! Thanks so much for your patience. Can I make those copies now?

W Certainly, why don't you come on back, and I'll get somebody to help you.

여 4 네, 무슨 말인지 알아요. 하지만 반납 요청은 학생이 생각하는 것보다 드물게 일어나요. 일반적으로 도서마다 충분히 여러 권을 보유하고 있기 때문에, 4학년 학생들이 다른 학생들의 요구 없이 한 학기 내내 그 도서를 볼 수 있어요.

남 이해가 되긴 하지만, 도서관이 보유하고 있는 도서의 수가 제가 처한 어려운 상황을 바꿔주지는 않는다고요. 전 여전히 이 책이 정말 필요해요.

여 규정에 따르면 도서 반납 요청이 충족되어 두 번째 학생이 이 책을 다 사용하고 나면 도서관에서 첫 번째 학생에게 전화를 걸어 다시 그 책을 대출해 갈 수 있게 해줘요.

남 좋은 제도네요. 하지만 지금 당장은 저에게 도움이 되지 않아요. 수업에 낙제하지 않으려면 이 책이 꼭 필요해요.

여 이렇게 하는 건 어때요? 여기 사무실로 들어와서 중요한 페이지만 무료로 복사해 가는 건 어때요? 그렇게 하면 학생의 학업에 무리가 없을 것 같은데요.

남 정말 친절하시네요! 제가 그 책을 빨리 다시 받아볼 수 있는 방법이 있을까요?

여 5 이 책을 신청한 학생이 얼마나 오랫동안 책을 대출하느냐에 달려 있겠군요. 하급생들은 대출 기간이 2주뿐이에요. 하지만 일반적으로 그렇게 오래 빌리지는 않아요. 만약 그렇다면, 가능한 한 빨리 학생이 책을 다시 대출할 수 있게 해줄게요.

남 좋아요! 양해해 주셔서 감사합니다. 지금 바로 복사할 수 있을까요?

여 물론이에요. 뒤쪽으로 들어오세요. 학생을 도와 줄 사람을 찾아줄게요.

1. Why does the student go to the library?

Ⓐ To check out some materials for a paper he is writing
Ⓑ To find out why he is receiving notices from the library
Ⓒ To inquire about obtaining notes for a psychology lecture
Ⓓ To request a timeline for picking up reserve materials

2. What is a key feature of the library's checkout policy?

Ⓐ Seniors are permitted to keep books out without a time limit.
Ⓑ Seniors are permitted to keep books out longer with some restrictions.
Ⓒ All underclassmen must return books as soon as seniors request them.
Ⓓ Seniors and underclassmen have the same library privileges.

1. 학생은 왜 도서관에 갔는가?

Ⓐ 작성 중인 리포트를 위해 몇 가지 자료를 대출하려고
Ⓑ 왜 자신이 도서관으로부터 계속 통지를 받고 있는지 알아보려고
Ⓒ 심리학 수업 노트를 얻는 것에 대해 문의하려고
Ⓓ 예약 자료를 가져갈 일정을 요청하려고

2. 도서관 대출 정책의 주요 특징은 무엇인가?

Ⓐ 4학년생들은 기간 제한 없이 책을 대출할 수 있다.
Ⓑ 4학년생들은 약간의 제약과 함께 책을 좀 더 오래 대출할 수 있다.
Ⓒ 4학년생이 책을 요청하는 즉시 모든 하급생들은 그 책을 반납해야 한다.
Ⓓ 4학년생과 하급생들은 도서관에서 똑같은 권리를 갖는다.

3. **Listen again to part of the conversation. Then answer the question.**

> W That's true, but you're forgetting one important condition. While it is true that seniors are allowed to keep books out longer than underclassmen, the seniors must immediately return the books when another student requests the book.
> M I don't think I understand why the policy exists in the first place.

What does the student imply when he says this:

> M I don't think I understand why the policy exists in the first place.

Ⓐ He does not comprehend the rules of the book return policy.
Ⓑ He is irritated about the ineffective book return policy.
Ⓒ He thinks the policy regarding a senior extension is unfair.
Ⓓ He believes that the library should lengthen the policy time.

4. **What is true about the return request?**
Ⓐ It is something that does not happen that often.
Ⓑ It guarantees a semester-long checkout for seniors.
Ⓒ It requires students to fill out a form.
Ⓓ It has to be fulfilled within a week.

5. **What is the likely outcome of the conversation?**
Ⓐ The student will be allowed to keep the book until the completion of his project.
Ⓑ The student will no longer be able to check books out from the library.
Ⓒ The student will return the book but receive it back sooner than thought.
Ⓓ The student will not utilize the services of the library any longer.

3. 대화의 일부를 다시 듣고 질문에 답하시오.

> 여 맞아요. 하지만 학생은 한 가지 중요한 조건을 잊었군요. 4학년 학생들이 하급생들보다 더 오랜 기간 책을 대출할 수 있기는 하지만, 다른 학생이 그 책을 대출하기를 원한다면 즉시 해당 도서를 반납해야 해요.
> 남 그럼 애초에 왜 그런 정책이 있는 건지 이해가 안 되네요.

학생은 다음과 같이 말하며 무엇을 의미하는가:

> 남 그럼 애초에 왜 그런 정책이 있는 건지 이해가 안 되네요.

Ⓐ 도서 반납 정책의 규칙을 이해하지 못한다.
Ⓑ 비효율적인 도서 반납 정책에 짜증이 났다.
Ⓒ 4학년생의 대출 기간 연장과 관련한 정책이 불공평하다고 생각한다.
Ⓓ 도서관이 정한 기간을 늘려야 한다고 생각한다.

4. 도서 반납 요청에 관해 옳은 것은 무엇인가?
Ⓐ 그다지 자주 일어나지 않는 일이다.
Ⓑ 4학년생에게 한 학기 내내 대출을 보장한다.
Ⓒ 학생들이 양식을 작성하도록 요구한다.
Ⓓ 1주일 내에 이행되어야 한다.

5. 이 대화의 결과는 어떠하겠는가?
Ⓐ 학생이 프로젝트를 끝낼 때까지 책을 가지고 있는 것이 허용될 것이다.
Ⓑ 학생은 이제 더 이상 도서관에서 책을 대출할 수 없게 될 것이다.
Ⓒ 학생은 책을 반납하겠지만 생각했던 것보다 더 빨리 다시 돌려받게 될 것이다.
Ⓓ 학생은 더 이상 도서관 서비스를 이용하지 않을 것이다.

어휘 notice n 통지, 알림 | check out (책을) 대출하다 | paradigm n 전형적인 예, 양식 | methodology n 방법론 | transactional behavior 매매 행태 | psychology n 심리학 | under the impression ~라고 생각한 | permit v 허락하다 | indefinite adj 무기한의, 정해져 있지 않은 | extension n 연장 | material n 자료 | condition n 조건 | underclassman n 하급생 | immediately adv 즉시 | policy n 규정 | guarantee n 보장 | resource n 출처, 자료 | graduate v 졸업하다 | generally adv 일반적으로 | predicament n 곤경, 궁지 | satisfy v 만족하다, 충족하다 | interrupt v 방해하다 | patience n 인내

Actual Tests Actual Test 1

Man: Professor

[6-11] Listen to part of a lecture in an astronomy class.

M **6** Let's start today's lecture by talking about Pluto, the planet we know the least about in our solar system, but are learning more about day by day. In fact, when I say planet I'm actually wrong. In 2006, the official status of Pluto was changed from planet to dwarf planet. A dwarf planet is like a planet except for one thing, its gravity isn't strong enough to clear the area around it, so it shares its neighborhood with other objects. But, Pluto used to be considered the 9th planet, the furthest planet from the Sun, and the smallest planet in our solar system—until 2006 when it was reclassified. **7** In fact, Pluto is so remote and so small that it wasn't until 1930 that it was even discovered, quite by accident. You see, there was this mathematical model that said the gravity of an as-yet-undiscovered planet must be influencing Neptune's orbit. So, a team of astronomers got busy trying to track down this mysterious 9th planet. And they found one. But, strangely, the calculations that had started their search turned out to be wrong. So, I guess that if it hadn't been for that lucky little miscalculation, we might still not know about the existence of Pluto. And although we know that it exists, we don't have much information about it. **8** Even with today's best telescope, the Hubble, we can only get very low quality, fuzzy pictures of Pluto.

So, like I said, information about Pluto is constantly changing. But, we do know that it's composed mostly of rock and ice and its orbit around the Sun isn't like the other planets'. Their orbits are all circular, but Pluto's orbit isn't a circle; it's an oval—sort of a "squashed circle shape". That means that at some points in its orbit it gets closer to the Sun—closer than Neptune, in fact. And at other times, it is very far away from the Sun. **9(B)** We also know that Pluto has a thin atmosphere of nitrogen, carbon monoxide, and methane. But there's something really strange about its atmosphere. Normally, Pluto is a chilly minus 270 degree Celsius. But when the planet is on the part of its orbit that takes it farthest away from the Sun, it gets even colder.

남자: 교수

천문학 강의의 일부를 들으시오.

남 **6** 명왕성에 대한 이야기로 오늘의 수업을 시작해 봅시다. 명왕성은 우리 태양계 행성 중에서 우리가 알고 있는 바가 가장 적지만 서서히 더 알아가고 있는 행성이죠. 사실, 행성이라고 말하는 것은 잘못된 것입니다. 2006년에 명왕성의 공식적인 지위는 행성에서 왜행성으로 바뀌었습니다. 왜행성은 한 가지를 빼고는 행성과 같은데, 그 한가지는 중력이 그 주변 지역에 아무것도 존재하지 못하게 할 만큼 세지 않기 때문에 다른 물체와 그 주변을 공유한다는 점입니다. 하지만 명왕성은 2006년에 새롭게 분류되기 전까지 아홉 번째 행성이자 태양으로부터 가장 먼 행성, 우리 태양계에서 가장 작은 행성으로 여겨져 왔습니다. **7** 실제로, 명왕성은 너무 멀리 있고 크기도 너무 작아서 1930년이 되어서야 발견되었고, 그것도 거의 우연에 의해서였어요. 무슨 말이냐 하면, 아직 발견되지 않은 행성의 중력이 해왕성의 궤도에 영향을 주고 있다는 수학적 모델이 있었습니다. 따라서 천문학자들로 구성된 팀이 이 신비로운 아홉 번째 행성을 추적하기 위해 바삐 움직였습니다. 그리고 하나를 찾아냈죠. 그러나 이상하게도, 그들로 하여금 조사를 착수하게 했던 계산은 틀린 것으로 밝혀졌습니다. 그러니 그런 우연한 작은 계산 착오가 없었더라면 우리는 여전히 명왕성의 존재에 대해 모르고 있지 않을까 생각합니다. 그리고 비록 명왕성이 존재한다는 것은 알지만, 그에 대한 정보는 많지가 않아요. **8** 오늘날 최상의 망원경인 허블 망원경으로 보아도 명왕성의 영상은 아주 질이 떨어지고 흐릿합니다.

따라서 제가 말한 것처럼, 명왕성에 대한 정보는 끊임없이 바뀌고 있습니다. 그러나 우리는 명왕성이 대부분 암석과 얼음으로 구성되어 있으며 태양을 도는 궤도가 다른 행성들의 궤도와는 다르다는 것은 알고 있습니다. 다른 행성들의 궤도는 모두 원형이지만, 명왕성의 궤도는 원형이 아니고 타원형, 일종의 '눌린 원형'입니다. 이 말은 궤도의 어떤 지점에서 명왕성은 태양과 더 가까워진다는 말이며, 실제로 해왕성보다 더 태양과 가까워집니다. 또 다른 지점에서는 태양과 매우 멀리 떨어지게 되죠. **9(B)** 우리는 또한 명왕성이 질소, 일산화탄소, 그리도 메탄으로 된 얇은 대기를 갖고 있다는 것을 알고 있습니다. 그러나 그 대기와 관련해 정말 이상한 것이 있어요. 일반적으로 명왕성은 섭씨 영하 270도로 매우 춥습니다. 하지만 이 행성이 궤도상 태양으로부터 가장 먼 곳에 왔을 때는 더 차가워집니다.

9(D) During that time, most of the atmosphere freezes and falls to the surface as frost and snow. We're talking about the whole planet hidden under a thick blanket of snow! Once frozen, it doesn't thaw again for hundreds of years until Pluto swings back closer to the Sun.

It's interesting; most of what we do know about Pluto has only been learned since the late 1970s through observation from Earth alone. And we've basically done all of the research we can do from here. To find out more about the dwarf planet, we need close-up observation. **10, 11** That's why NASA sent an unmanned robot-probe, called New Horizons, to fly by Pluto and take readings and images of the surface. It was launched in January 2006, and it reached Pluto on July 14, 2015. It reached Pluto at the time when it was warmer, so its atmosphere wasn't in frozen form. You can understand why that's important, right? If the whole planet was covered in a thick layer of snow, it would obviously make the ground impossible to see. They needed to get there before the snow season started again in order to get some good pictures of the surface. For researchers like me, this is really exciting! I've been studying Pluto for almost 20 years now and have no idea what it really looks like.

9(D) 이 시기 동안, 대기의 대부분이 얼어서 서리나 눈으로 표면에 떨어지게 됩니다. 행성 전체가 두꺼운 눈의 층에 덮여 가려지는 거예요! 일단 얼면, 태양에 더 가까워지는 지점에 이르기 전까지 수백 년 동안 다시 녹지 않습니다.

흥미로운 점은 우리가 명왕성에 대해 알고 있는 대부분은 1970년대 후반에 와서야 지구에서만 이뤄진 관측을 통해 알려진 것이라는 사실입니다. 그리고 우리는 지구상에서 할 수 있는 모든 연구는 기본적으로 다 했어요. 그 왜행성에 대해 더 알기 위해서는 근접 관찰이 필요합니다. **10, 11** 이것이 NASA가 명왕성 주변을 돌며 표면의 관찰 자료와 이미지를 얻기 위해 뉴호라이즌스라는 이름의 무인 로봇 탐사선을 보낸 이유입니다. 이 탐사선은 2006년 1월에 발사되었고, 2015년 7월 14일에 명왕성에 도착했습니다. 탐사선은 명왕성이 좀 따뜻해서 대기가 얼어 있지 않았던 시기에 그곳에 도착했습니다 왜 그것이 중요한지 알 수 있죠? 만약 행성 전체가 두꺼운 눈 층으로 덮여 있다면 땅 표면을 보는 것이 당연히 불가능할 겁니다. 표면을 잘 보여줄 사진을 찍기 위해 탐사선은 눈 내리는 계절이 시작되기 전에 그곳에 도착해야 했습니다. 저 같은 연구자들에게는 이것이 얼마나 흥미로운지 몰라요! 제가 명왕성을 지금까지 거의 20년 동안 연구했는데 실제로 어떻게 생겼는지는 알지 못하니까요.

6. What is the topic of this lecture?

Ⓐ Pluto and its constantly-changing position in the solar system

Ⓑ Pluto and the space agencies that are fighting to reach it first

Ⓒ The characteristics of Pluto and the ongoing process of learning about it

Ⓓ Pluto and the type of spacecrafts that have explored there

7. What does the professor imply about the discovery of Pluto?

Ⓐ The mistake was not very important to the discovery of Pluto.

Ⓑ Pluto exists only as a mathematical possibility.

Ⓒ Pluto was only discovered because of a mistake.

Ⓓ We know about Pluto only because of its influence on Neptune's orbit.

6. 강의의 주제는 무엇인가?

Ⓐ 명왕성과 태양계에서 계속 변하는 명왕성의 위치

Ⓑ 명왕성과 그곳에 먼저 도착하려고 다투는 항공 우주국들

Ⓒ 명왕성의 특징과 그것을 연구하려는 지속적인 과정

Ⓓ 명왕성과 명왕성을 탐사해온 우주선의 종류

7. 교수는 명왕성의 발견에 관해 무엇을 암시하는가?

Ⓐ 그 실수는 명왕성의 발견에 그다지 중요하지 않았다.

Ⓑ 명왕성은 수학적 가능성으로만 존재한다.

Ⓒ 명왕성은 실수 때문에 발견되었다.

Ⓓ 우리는 해왕성의 궤도에 미치는 명왕성의 영향 때문에 명왕성을 안다.

8. **How does the professor account for the fact that so little is known about Pluto?**

Ⓐ Pluto cannot be seen clearly even with our best telescope.
Ⓑ Pluto is large and is located very far from Earth.
Ⓒ Pluto has only been observed from other planets.
Ⓓ Pluto has a circular orbit, which makes it invisible for long periods.

9. **What does the professor say are the characteristics of Pluto's atmosphere?** Choose 2 answers.

Ⓐ It is not affected by Pluto's orbit.
Ⓑ It is composed of methane, carbon monoxide, and nitrogen.
Ⓒ It is very stable.
Ⓓ It stays frozen for hundreds of years at a time.
Ⓔ The snow and ice covering Pluto melts spontaneously.

10. **Listen again to part of the lecture. Then answer the question.**

> M That's why NASA sent an unmanned robot-probe, called New Horizons, to fly by Pluto and take readings and images of the surface. It was launched in January 2006, and it reached Pluto on July 14, 2015. It reached Pluto at the time when it was warmer, so its atmosphere wasn't in frozen form. You can understand why that's important, right?

Why does the professor say this:

> M You can understand why that's important, right?

Ⓐ He thinks that the students can understand based on what he has already said.
Ⓑ He thinks that the students couldn't possibly understand why it is important.
Ⓒ He thinks that the students already knew why the probe is important.
Ⓓ He thinks the students will find this boring because they already know a lot about it.

11. **What will the professor probably talk about next?**

Ⓐ He will go on to discuss the New Horizons mission in more detail.
Ⓑ He will move to a discussion about Mars and the Hubble telescope.
Ⓒ He will talk about the possibility of humans living on Pluto.
Ⓓ He will discuss the costs and benefits of space exploration.

8. **교수는 명왕성에 대해 알려진 바가 적다는 사실을 어떻게 설명하고 있는가?**

Ⓐ 명왕성은 우리가 갖고 있는 최고 수준의 망원경을 통해서도 또렷하게 볼 수 없다.
Ⓑ 명왕성은 거대하고 지구로부터 매우 멀리 떨어져 있다.
Ⓒ 명왕성은 다른 행성에서만 관찰되어 왔다.
Ⓓ 명왕성은 원형 궤도를 갖고 있어 오랜 기간 동안 눈에 띄지 않는다.

9. **교수가 말한 명왕성 대기의 특징은 무엇인가?**

두 개를 고르시오.

Ⓐ 명왕성 궤도에 영향을 받지 않는다.
Ⓑ 메탄과 일산화탄소, 질소로 구성되어 있다.
Ⓒ 매우 안정되어 있다.
Ⓓ 한 번에 수백 년 동안 언 상태로 유지된다.
Ⓔ 명왕성을 덮은 눈과 얼음은 갑자기 녹는다.

10. **강의의 일부를 다시 듣고 질문에 답하시오.**

> 남 이것이 NASA가 명왕성 주변을 돌며 표면의 관찰 자료와 이미지를 얻기 위해 뉴호라이즌스라는 이름의 무인 로봇 탐사선을 보낸 이유입니다. 이 탐사선은 2006년 1월에 발사되었고, 2015년 7월 14일에 명왕성에 도착했습니다. 탐사선은 명왕성이 좀 따뜻해서 대기가 얼어 있지 않았던 시기에 그곳에 도착했습니다. 왜 그것이 중요한지 알 수 있죠?

교수는 왜 이렇게 말하는가:

> 남 왜 그것이 중요한지 알 수 있죠?

Ⓐ 교수는 학생들이 그가 이미 이야기한 바에 근거해 이해할 수 있을 거라고 생각한다.
Ⓑ 교수는 학생들이 그것이 왜 중요한지 아마도 이해하지 못할 거라 생각한다.
Ⓒ 교수는 학생들이 그 탐사선이 왜 중요한지 이미 알고 있었다고 생각한다.
Ⓓ 교수는 학생들이 그것에 대해 이미 많이 알고 있기 때문에 지루해할 것이라고 생각한다.

11. **교수는 다음에 무엇을 언급하겠는가?**

Ⓐ 뉴호라이즌스호 임무에 대해 좀 더 자세하게 논의를 계속할 것이다.
Ⓑ 화성과 허블 망원경에 대한 논의로 넘어갈 것이다.
Ⓒ 명왕성에서 인간이 거주할 가능성에 대해 언급할 것이다.
Ⓓ 우주 탐사 비용과 그 이익에 관해 논의할 것이다.

어휘 solar system 태양계 | status n 지위, 상태 | dwarf planet 왜행성 | neighborhood 이웃 | reclassify v 재분류하다 | remote adj 외딴 | discover v 발견하다 | by accident 우연히, 사고로 | mathematical adj 수학의 | gravity n 중력 | influence v 영향을 주다 | astronomer n 천문학자 | track down 추적하다 | mysterious adj 신비한 | strangely adv 이상하게 | calculation n 계산 | miscalculation n 계산 착오 | existence n 존재 | telescope n 망원경 | quality n 질, 품질 | fuzzy adj 흐릿한 | constantly adv 계속, 지속적으로 | composed of ~로 구성된 | orbit n 궤도 | circular adj 원형의 | oval adj 타원형의 | squash v 짓누르다 | atmosphere n 대기 | nitrogen n 질소 | carbon monoxide 일산화탄소 | methane n 메탄 | chilly adj 쌀쌀한, 추운 | freeze v 얼어붙다 | surface n 표면 | frost n 서리 | thick adj 두꺼운 | swing v 빙 돌다, 휙 움직이다 | observation n 관찰 | unmanned adj 무인의 | obviously adv 명백히

Conversation 2

본서 | P. 178

Man: Cafeteria manager | Woman: Student

[1-5] Listen to part of a conversation between a student and a cafeteria manager.

W Hi. Can you tell me where I can find the manager?

M Yes, you've found the right person.

W Oh. Good. I need to speak to you about something. I was interested in....

M 2 Is this about the job? Because the position has been filled, we don't have any other opportunities at the moment. Why don't you come back when it's not the lunch rush?

W Whoa! I think you misunderstood me. 1 I don't know anything about a job opening; I was here to inquire about taking the baking class I read about in the student bulletin.

M Oh! That's different. I'm terribly sorry. I've been a little overwhelmed with all the traffic in here asking about the job positions lately. I've never seen it like this! What exactly are you interested in?

W Well, it's like this. 3 My friend Emily, who is on the soccer team, broke her leg playing in the regionals last week. She was in traction at the hospital for a few days, and now she's back in the dorm resting.

M Ouch! I'm very sorry to hear that.

W 3 Anyway, she's been down in the dumps because of it, so I thought I would bake her a cake to try to cheer her up. She absolutely loves cakes, but I never learned to bake one.

M That's very kind of you. You're a good friend. Is there anything we can do for her?

W Thanks. She just sits in bed all day, upset that she can't play soccer anymore. Plus it's her birthday next week. Do you think you can help me out?

M Definitely! Let me explain how this works. The cooking class goes over three days starting early next week. On Monday, there is a brief orientation followed by a simple explanation of what constitutes a cake. Then, the instructor explains all the cooking tools that are needed to make a cake.

W Hmmm. Sounds like that might be a little tedious. Can I skip that day and come on Tuesday?

남자: 구내 식당 매니저 | 여자: 학생

학생과 구내 식당 매니저의 대화를 들으시오.

여 안녕하세요. 매니저가 어디 있는지 아세요?

남 네, 전데요.

여 오. 잘됐네요. 드릴 말씀이 좀 있어서요. 제가 관심 있는 게 있는데....

남 2 일자리 때문인가요? 사람이 충원되어서 지금은 더 이상 자리가 없어요. 바쁜 점심 시간 말고 다른 때 오시겠어요?

여 와, 오해하신 것 같네요. 1 구직에 대해선 모르고요. 저는 학생 게시판에서 본 제빵 수업 수강과 관련해서 궁금한 게 있어서 왔어요.

남 아! 그거라면 상황이 다르죠. 정말 미안해요. 최근에 일자리 때문에 사람들이 너무 많이 와서 주체를 못 할 정도였거든요. 이 정도로 몰려온 건 처음이어서요! 정확히 무엇에 관심이 있으신 거죠?

여 음, 그게요. 3 제 친구 에밀리가 축구 팀에서 뛰고 있는데 지난주에 지역 경기에서 뛰다가 다리가 부러졌어요. 며칠 동안 병원에서 골절 견인치료를 받다가 지금은 기숙사로 돌아와서 쉬고 있어요.

남 저런! 정말 유감이네요.

여 3 어쨌든 그것 때문에 의기소침해 있어서 그 친구를 위해 케이크를 하나 구워줄까 해서요. 친구가 케이크를 굉장히 좋아하는데, 전 케이크 굽는 것을 배운 적이 없거든요.

남 정말 사려 깊군요. 좋은 친구네요. 그 친구를 위해서 저희가 해드릴 수 있는 일이 있을까요?

여 감사합니다. 에밀리는 그냥 하루 종일 침대에 앉아 있어요. 축구를 더 이상 못한다는 사실에 괴로워하면서요. 게다가 다음 주가 생일이에요. 절 도와주실 수 있을까요?

남 그럼요! 어떻게 진행되는지 설명해 드릴게요. 요리 수업은 다음 주 초에 시작해서 3일 동안 진행돼요. 월요일에는 짧은 오리엔테이션을 한 후 케이크가 무엇으로 구성되는지에 대해 간단히 설명할 거예요. 그런 뒤 선생님이 케이크를 만드는 데 필요한 요리 도구를 전부 설명해요.

여 흠. 약간 지루할 것처럼 들리는데요. 그날은 건너뛰고 화요일에 와도 되나요?

M Bear with me. The reason we teach that part is that... so students understand the common language needed to communicate with the instructor.

W I guess that makes sense. What happens on Tuesday? Do we actually get to bake a cake in this class?

M Of course! On Tuesday, the class will choose the type of cake, learn how to mix ingredients and finally do some baking. Then, on the last day, students will learn how to use decorating tools and techniques. **4** It should be perfect for helping out your friend.

W **4** You sold me! How can I sign up? Are there any fees?

M You are a student here, right? If you're a student of this university, then all charges are covered under the student activity fee you pay every semester. Can I get your name?

W Sure. I'm Lauren Billings. Student ID number 935085. Do I need to bring anything?

M B-i-l-l-i-n-g-s. Okay. Got it. **5(B), (D)** Yes, as far as what to bring, you're going to need an apron because we just don't have enough to spare in the kitchen, and some clothes you don't mind getting dirty. But as far as all kitchen utensils like spatulas or beaters, they will be provided. Great. OK. We'll see you on Monday. The class starts right here in the kitchen at 8 o'clock sharp. Anything else?

W No, that will do it. Thanks. I'll see you on Monday.

남 제 말을 들어보세요. 우리가 그 부분을 가르치는 이유는... 학생들이 선생님과 대화할 때 주로 필요한 언어를 이해할 수 있게 하려는 거예요.

여 말이 되네요. 화요일에는 어떤 일을 해요? 수업 시간에 실제로 케이크를 굽게 되나요?

남 물론이죠! 화요일 수업 시간에 케이크의 종류를 선택하고, 어떻게 재료를 섞을지를 배우고, 마지막으로 케이크를 구워요. 그런 다음 마지막 날에 학생들은 장식 도구를 사용하는 법과 기술을 배우게 될 겁니다. **4** 친구를 돕는 데 완벽할 거예요.

여 **4** 들어야겠어요! 어떻게 등록할 수 있나요? 돈을 내야 하나요?

남 여기 학생이죠, 맞죠? 이 대학교 학생이면 모든 비용은 매 학기 내는 활동비에 포함되어 있어요. 이름을 알려주시겠어요?

여 그럼요. 로렌 빌링스입니다. 학생증 번호는 935085이에요. 제가 가져와야 하는 것이 있을까요?

남 B-i-l-l-i-n-g-s. 네, 됐습니다. **5(B), (D)** 네, 준비물에 대해서라면, 여기 주방에 앞치마 여분이 충분하지 않기 때문에 앞치마가 필요할 거고, 더러워져도 되는 옷을 가져오세요. 하지만 주걱이나 거품기 같은 주방용품은 전부 제공될 겁니다. 좋아요. 됐어요. 그럼 월요일에 뵙겠습니다. 수업은 정각 8시에 바로 여기 주방에서 시작합니다. 또 필요한 게 있으세요?

여 아뇨, 다 된 것 같아요. 감사합니다. 월요일에 뵐게요.

1. Why does the student go to see the cafeteria manager?

Ⓐ To make a complaint about the quality of the food
Ⓑ To apply for a vacant work position at the cafeteria
Ⓒ To ask about information involving a baking class
Ⓓ To substitute a working shift for a sick friend

2. What is the man's attitude at the beginning of the conversation?

Ⓐ He is trying to show that he is too busy to talk at the moment.
Ⓑ He is implying that the student is not qualified for the job.
Ⓒ He is stating that the cooking class has filled up.
Ⓓ He is wondering if the woman filled the lunch order.

3. What made the student want to register for the cooking class?

Ⓐ She wants to improve her cooking skills because she lives alone.
Ⓑ She wants to learn to bake a cake to cheer up her injured friend.

1. 학생은 왜 구내 식당 매니저를 보러 가는가?

Ⓐ 음식의 질에 대해서 불평하려고
Ⓑ 구내 식당의 빈 일자리에 지원하려고
Ⓒ 제빵 수업에 대한 정보를 물어보려고
Ⓓ 아픈 친구를 위해 근무를 대신하려고

2. 대화 초반에 남자의 태도는 어떠한가?

Ⓐ 지금 너무 바빠서 말할 시간이 없다는 것을 보여주려고 한다.
Ⓑ 학생이 일할 자격이 안 된다는 것을 암시하고 있다.
Ⓒ 요리 수업이 다 찼다고 이야기하고 있다.
Ⓓ 여자가 점심 식사를 주문했는지 궁금해하고 있다.

3. 학생이 요리 수업에 등록하고 싶어 하게 된 계기는 무엇인가?

Ⓐ 혼자 살기 때문에 요리 실력을 키우고 싶어 한다.
Ⓑ 다친 친구를 기쁘게 해주려고 케이크 굽는 법을 배우고 싶어 한다.

Ⓒ She is trying to impress her parents, who are coming to visit.
Ⓓ She is considering changing her major to the culinary arts.

Ⓒ 자신을 보러 오는 부모님을 감동시키려고 한다.
Ⓓ 자신의 전공을 조리로 바꾸는 것을 고려 중이다.

4. Listen again to part of the conversation. Then answer the question.

M It should be perfect for helping out your friend.
W You sold me! How can I sign up? Are there any fees?

Why does the student say this:

W You sold me! How can I sign up? Are there any fees?

Ⓐ She is excited that she got a job working at the cafeteria.
Ⓑ She is angry because she thinks the manager overcharged her.
Ⓒ She is very happy because the class will be beneficial to her.
Ⓓ She is upset at the man because he gave away her spot in the class.

4. 대화의 일부를 다시 듣고 질문에 답하시오.

남 친구를 돕는 데 완벽할 거예요.
여 들어야겠어요! 어떻게 등록할 수 있나요? 돈을 내야 하나요?

학생은 왜 이렇게 말하는가:

여 들어야겠어요! 어떻게 등록할 수 있나요? 돈을 내야 하나요?

Ⓐ 구내 식당에서 일자리를 구해서 신이 났다.
Ⓑ 매니저가 돈을 더 받았다고 생각해서 화가 나 있다.
Ⓒ 수업이 자신에게 유익할 것이라고 생각해서 매우 기뻐한다.
Ⓓ 남자가 수업의 자기 자리를 다른 사람에게 주었다고 생각해서 화가 나 있다.

5. What are two items that the student needs to bring to the cooking class? Choose 2 answers.

Ⓐ Spatula
Ⓑ Apron
Ⓒ Beater
Ⓓ Old clothes

5. 학생이 요리 수업에 가지고 와야 할 두 가지 물건은 무엇인가? 두 개를 고르시오.

Ⓐ 주걱
Ⓑ 앞치마
Ⓒ 거품기
Ⓓ 낡은 옷

어휘 position n 자리 | opportunity n 기회 | misunderstand v 오해하다 | inquire v 묻다 | bulletin n 게시판 | overwhelmed adj 압도된 | traffic n (사람들의) 혼잡함 | exactly adv 정확히 | regionals n 지역 대회 | traction n (골절 치료의) 견인 | down in the dump 우울해하는 | absolutely adv 절대적으로 | upset adj 언짢은 | definitely adv 명백히, 분명히 | explanation n 설명 | constitute v ~를 구성하다, ~이 되다 | tedious adj 지루한 | common adj 일반적인, 흔한 | communicate v 소통하다 | ingredient n 재료 | decorate v 꾸미다 | sign up 등록하다 | spare v 나누어주다, 빌려주다 | utensil n 기구, 도구 | spatula n 주걱, 뒤집개 | beater n 거품기, 먼지떨이

Lecture 2

본서 | P. 180

Man: Student | Woman: Professor

[6-11] Listen to part of a discussion in a marine biology class.

W Hello everyone. 6 Let's start out today by talking about our little friends, the crustaceans. Who can tell me what a crustacean is?

M It's an underwater animal that has a hard shell and a body with three main parts, like... crabs, lobsters, and uh... shrimp.

W Right, thank you. 6 But, remember, not all crustaceans live only in the water. Some live on land too, which brings

남자: 학생 | 여자: 교수

해양 생물학 수업 중 토론의 일부를 들으시오.

여 모두 안녕하세요. 6 오늘은 먼저 우리의 작은 친구 갑각류에 대해서 이야기해 봅시다. 갑각류가 무엇인지 말해볼 사람 있나요?

남 딱딱한 껍데기와 세 부분의 몸체로 되어 있는, 일종의... 게, 가재, 어... 그리고 새우와 같은 수중 동물입니다.

여 맞습니다, 고마워요. 6 하지만 기억해야 할 것은 모든 갑각류가 물속에서만 살지는 않는다는 것입니

me to what I wanted to talk about today, our neighbor, the fiddler crab. If you go down to the harbor when the tide is out, you'll probably notice these tiny balls of mud in little piles; there are usually lots of them. Well, believe it or not, they are actually a sign that these cute little crabs, Uca Pugnax, are nearby. Let me write that up here for you. **7(A)** OK, like a lot of other small crabs, these fiddler crabs feed by scooping up mud and using their mouths to sort out the edible material, like algae, fungus, or decaying plant and animal matter, that sort of thing. So, those balls you see are actually "leftovers" from the crab, if you know what I mean.
7(C) If you look closely, you'll see a little hole in the mud. That's where their burrow is, their home. A burrow is a tunnel that the crabs dig into the mud. They can be up to a foot deep and may connect to other tunnels. This is so they can have more than one entrance and escape from predators like fish, raccoons, water birds, and so on. Safety is one of the reasons why the crab never goes too far from its home.
Another reason they stay near their burrows is because they live in what's called the intertidal zone—an area that is covered by water at high tide. **7(D)** To keep their homes dry during high tide, they roll up a ball of mud and use it to plug the entrances before the water comes in, so that they have a tiny pocket of air to breathe until the water goes down. But when the tide is out, you'll see them out searching for food again.
OK, so here's a picture of the little guy. This one's probably about two inches or so across and fully grown, by the way. **8** The first thing you'll probably notice is that one of his front claws is huge, like a giant pair of scissors—I mean, it's huge relative to the size of the rest of the body. That tells us he's an adult male. The females' claws are smaller and the same size. **9** You might wonder what this huge claw the male has is used for. It looks too big to be useful. But, I'll give you a hint. You can see this sort of thing in other creatures, too, like goliath beetles, walruses, rhinos, bulls. Anyone?

M Well, you said they eat mud, so it's obviously not for hunting. Is it related to fighting other crabs?

W You're getting warmer. It isn't for feeding, certainly. They use it, first of all, to defend their homes from other males that might be around. Usually they just make a rattling sound to warn other crabs not to come near, but they might fight sometimes. It's not too serious though, more like arm

다. 어떤 것은 육지에서도 사는데, 오늘 이야기하고자 하는 우리의 이웃인 농게도 그러합니다. 썰물일 때 항구로 내려가면 아마도 작은 퇴적물 속에 조그만 진흙 공들이 있는 것을 볼 수 있을 겁니다. 보통 그런 것들이 굉장히 많죠. 뭐, 믿기 힘들지 몰라도, 그것들은 이 작고 귀여운 게인 습지 농게가 가까이에 있다는 뜻입니다. 여기에 이름을 써줄게요. **7(A)** 자, 다른 작은 게들처럼 이 농게는 진흙을 퍼 올려서 그 속의 조류, 균류, 부패된 식물과 동물질같이 먹을 만한 것들을 입으로 골라내면서 먹습니다. 그래서 여기 보이는 공들은, 제 말이 무슨 뜻인지 이해한다면, 사실 게들의 '먹고 남은 찌꺼기'입니다.
7(C) 가까이서 보면 진흙 속에 작은 구멍이 보일 겁니다. 그곳이 그들의 집인 굴이 있는 곳입니다. 굴은 게들이 진흙을 파서 만든 터널입니다. 그것들은 깊이가 1피트 정도이고 다른 터널들과 연결되어 있을 수 있습니다. 이것은 입구를 한 개 이상 두어서 물고기, 너구리, 물새 등의 포식자로부터 도망칠 수 있게끔 하기 위한 것입니다. 안전은 게가 집으로부터 너무 멀리 나가지 않는 이유 중 하나예요.
굴 가까이에서 지내는 또 다른 이유는, 그것들이 만조일 때 물에 의해 덮이는 부분인 조간대라고 불리는 곳에 살기 때문입니다. **7(D)** 만조일 때 집을 마른 상태로 유지하기 위해 그들은 물이 들어오기 전에 진흙공을 만들어서 입구를 막는데, 이렇게 하면 물이 빠질 때까지 숨을 쉴 수 있는 작은 공기 주머니를 갖게 되죠. 하지만 썰물일 때 게들이 다시 밖으로 나와서 먹이를 찾는 것을 볼 수 있을 거예요.
자, 여기 이 작은 녀석의 사진을 보세요. 약 2인치 정도 될 텐데, 참고로 말하면 완전히 자란 겁니다. **8** 첫 번째로 눈에 띄는 것이 아마도 앞 집게발 하나가 마치 거대한 가위처럼 아주 크다는 점일 겁니다. 제 말은, 몸의 나머지 부분의 크기에 비해서 크다는 거죠. 이걸로 이 게가 다 큰 수컷이라는 것을 알 수 있습니다. 암컷의 집게발은 더 작고 크기가 같습니다. **9** 수컷이 지닌 커다란 집게발이 어디에 쓰이는지 아마 궁금할 겁니다. 쓸모가 있기에는 너무 커 보이죠. 하지만 힌트를 드릴게요. 이런 것은 골리앗 풍뎅이, 바다코끼리, 코뿔소, 황소와 같은 다른 동물에서도 볼 수 있습니다. 어디 한번 대답해볼 사람 있나요?

남 음, 농게들이 진흙을 먹는다고 했으니까 분명 사냥을 위한 것은 아니겠고, 다른 게들과 싸우는 것과 연관이 있는 건가요?

여 거의 근접했어요. 먹는 데 사용하는 건 아닌 게 확실하죠. 첫째로, 집게발을 사용하여 주위에 돌아다니는 다른 수컷들로부터 집을 방어합니다. 보통은 다른 게들이 다가오지 못하도록 경고하기 위해서 그냥 덜거덕거리는 소리를 내지만, 때로는 싸울 수도 있습니다. 그렇다고 굉장히 심각한 싸움은 아니

wrestling. 11 The other purpose of this over-sized claw is to attract females. During the breeding period, all of the males try to find a mate. They all stand at the edge of their burrows and as females return from foraging during low tide, they move among the males and "check them out", almost like it's a crab singles bar. Each male tries to impress the females by waving his large claw and if a female likes what she sees, she'll choose him. Now, let's take a look at the life cycle of the fiddler crab.

고, 그냥 팔씨름 같은 것이에요. 11 특대 크기 집게발의 또 다른 목적은 암컷의 관심을 끄는 것입니다. 번식 기간에 모든 수컷은 짝을 찾으려고 합니다. 그것들은 모두 굴 끝에 서 있고, 암컷들은 간조 때 먹이를 찾으러 다니다 돌아와서는, 수컷들 사이를 돌아다니면서 마치 독신 게들이 모이는 술집인 것처럼 누구를 선택할지 '훑어봅니다'. 수컷들은 모두 커다란 집게발을 흔들며 암컷의 관심을 끌려고 하고, 암컷은 만약 맘에 드는 것을 발견할 경우 그 수컷을 선택합니다. 이제 농게의 생애 주기에 대해 알아봅시다.

6. What is the discussion mainly about?

Ⓐ The life cycle of the fiddler crab
Ⓑ The role of the fiddler crab in its local ecosystem
Ⓒ The fiddler crab's features and patterns of behavior
Ⓓ The dating rituals of the fiddler crab

7. What are the main characteristics of fiddler crabs mentioned by the professor? Choose 3 answers.

Ⓐ They filter their food from mud.
Ⓑ They are most active during high tide.
Ⓒ They live in networks of small tunnels.
Ⓓ They breathe air.
Ⓔ Their main food is small birds and fish.

8. According to the professor, how can male and female crabs be differentiated?

Ⓐ Female fiddler crabs' claws are both the same size, whereas the males' aren't.
Ⓑ Female fiddler crabs remain in their burrows more than males do.
Ⓒ Female fiddler crabs look for food in the intertidal region, while males don't.
Ⓓ Both male and female fiddler crabs wave their claws during dating.

9. What does the professor infer when she talks about goliath beetles and walruses?

Ⓐ Male fiddler crabs have the same body parts as these creatures.
Ⓑ Male fiddler crabs have structures that look very similar to the structures of these organisms.
Ⓒ The behavior of male fiddler crabs is similar to these creatures.
Ⓓ The enlarged claw of male fiddler crabs has a function similar to body parts of these creatures.

6. 토론은 주로 무엇에 대한 것인가?

Ⓐ 농게의 생애 주기
Ⓑ 지역 생태계에 있어서 농게의 역할
Ⓒ 농게의 특징과 행동 패턴
Ⓓ 농게의 데이트 의식

7. 교수가 언급한 농게의 주요 특징은 무엇인가? 세 개를 고르시오.

Ⓐ 진흙으로부터 먹잇감을 걸러낸다.
Ⓑ 만조일 때 가장 활동적이다.
Ⓒ 연결되어 있는 작은 터널들 속에서 산다.
Ⓓ 공기로 숨을 쉰다.
Ⓔ 주식은 작은 새들과 물고기다.

8. 교수에 따르면, 수컷과 암컷 게들을 어떻게 구별할 수 있는가?

Ⓐ 암컷 농게의 집게발은 둘 다 같은 크기인데 수컷의 집게발은 그렇지 않다.
Ⓑ 암컷 농게는 수컷보다 굴에 더 오래 있는다.
Ⓒ 암컷 농게는 조간대에서 음식을 찾지만, 수컷은 그러지 않는다.
Ⓓ 수컷과 암컷 농게 모두 짝짓기하는 동안 집게발을 흔든다.

9. 교수는 골리앗풍뎅이와 바다코끼리에 관해 말하며 무엇을 암시하는가?

Ⓐ 수컷 농게들은 이런 동물들과 동일한 신체 부위를 가지고 있다.
Ⓑ 수컷 농게들은 이런 생물들과 무척 비슷하게 보이는 구조를 가지고 있다.
Ⓒ 수컷 농게의 행동은 이런 동물들과 유사하다.
Ⓓ 수컷 농게의 커다란 집게발은 이런 동물들의 신체 부위와 비슷한 기능을 가지고 있다.

10. Put the following words in the same order as the professor used when talking about the characteristics of the crabs.

Ⓐ Mating Behavior
Ⓑ Habitat
Ⓒ Body Structure
Ⓓ Feeding Behavior

1	Ⓓ Feeding behavior
2	Ⓑ Habitat
3	Ⓒ Body Structure
4	Ⓐ Mating behavior

11. Listen again to part of the discussion. Then answer the question.

> W The other purpose of this over-sized claw is to attract females. During the breeding period, all of the males try to find a mate. They all stand at the edge of their burrows and as females return from foraging during low tide, they move among the males and "check them out", almost like it's a crab singles bar.

Why does the professor say this:

> W ..., almost like it's a crab singles bar.

Ⓐ To help students understand that crabs mate very often during their lifetime
Ⓑ To demonstrate ways that females behave and ways that males try to get their attention
Ⓒ To add humor and interest and give students a vivid image that they will more easily remember
Ⓓ To help students see that crabs behave strangely during breeding season

10. 다음 단어들을 교수가 게들의 특징에 관해 이야기하며 사용한 순서대로 놓으시오.

Ⓐ 짝짓기 행동
Ⓑ 서식지
Ⓒ 신체 구조
Ⓓ 섭식 행동

1	Ⓓ 섭식 행동
2	Ⓑ 서식지
3	Ⓒ 신체 구조
4	Ⓐ 짝짓기 행동

11. 토론의 일부를 다시 듣고 질문에 답하시오.

> 여 특대 크기 집게발의 또 다른 목적은 암컷의 관심을 끄는 것입니다. 번식 기간에 모든 수컷은 짝을 찾으려고 합니다. 그것들은 모두 굴 끝에 서 있고, 암컷들은 간조 때 먹이를 찾으러 다니다 돌아와서는, 수컷들 사이를 돌아다니면서 마치 독신 게들이 모이는 술집인 것처럼 누구를 선택할지 '훑어봅니다'.

교수는 왜 이렇게 말하는가:

> 여 ... 마치 독신 게들이 모이는 술집인 것처럼

Ⓐ 게들이 일생 동안 무척 자주 짝짓기를 한다는 것을 학생들이 이해하도록 돕기 위해서
Ⓑ 암컷들이 행동하는 방식과 수컷들이 암컷들의 관심을 끌려고 하는 방식을 예를 들어가며 설명하기 위해서
Ⓒ 유머와 흥미를 더하고 학생들에게 기억하기 더 쉽도록 생생한 이미지를 주기 위해서
Ⓓ 게들이 번식 기간에 이상하게 행동하는 것을 학생들이 알도록 돕기 위해서

어휘 crustacean n 갑각류 I underwater adj 수중의, 물속의 I crab n 게 I lobster n 가재 I shrimp n 새우 I fiddler crab 농게 I harbor n 항구 I tide n 조수, 밀물과 썰물 I notice v 알아차리다 I mud n 진흙 I pile n 더미 I scoop up 뜨다, 퍼 올리다 I sort out 걸러내다 I edible adj 먹을 수 있는 I algae n 조류, 말 I fungus n 균류 I decay v 부패하다 I leftover n 찌꺼기, 남은 것 I burrow n 굴 I tunnel n 터널 I entrance n 입구 I escape v 탈출하다 I raccoon n 너구리 I safety n 안전 I intertidal zone 조간대 I plug v 막아 넣다 I claw n (게 등의) 집게발 I walrus n 바다코끼리 I rhino n 코뿔소 I bull n 황소 I defend v 방어하다 I rattle v 달가닥거리다 I warn v 경고하다 I arm wrestling 팔씨름 I attract v (주의·흥미를) 끌다 I breeding n 번식 I mate n 짝 I forage v 먹이를 찾다 I wave v 흔들다

Woman: Professor

[12-17] Listen to part of a lecture in a psychology class.

W Welcome class. How many of you want to repeat everything I say, word-for-word, over and over again? Does that sound like fun? Well, this is the type of learning that is used in a teacher-centered classroom, and it is called rote learning. This is probably how your parents learned when they were children. And believe it or not, this early method of educating students survives in many classrooms even in these modern times.

So, the tradition of rote learning in schools began centuries ago. **13** In this setting, students who could memorize information, even without making any intellectual associations with the material, were considered intelligent and educated. However, this concept of intelligence had no practical basis, only proving that a student could cooperate in a passive learning environment. **12** In light of this, progressive educators began appearing in the 19th century, and an American named John Dewey would come to represent a new way of looking at how children were educated.

John Dewey is famous for not only his efforts in educational reform but also his work in philosophy and psychology. His philosophies were somewhere between Plato's society-centered thinking and Rousseau's emphasis on the individual. He felt that individuals were only meaningful if they were a fixed part of a society and that society's only importance was the existence of its individual members. Indeed, his philosophical ideas had a direct influence on his educational theories. These were based on the learning of skills and knowledge that students could apply to their lives as both individuals and members of the community. So, to make his theories a reality, he founded the University Laboratory School, now known as the Dewey School, in 1896. With curricula based on hands-on learning, the name of the school was quite appropriate. Of course, this school starkly contrasted the long-established 19th-century institutions.

Before John Dewey... umm, educational theorists, believing repetition led to skill, applied this basic concept to classroom instruction. They felt that children should be educated by learning facts memorized through repetition. Now, this method allowed students to learn information rapidly, especially data unrelated to their existing knowledge, like a vocabulary word from a foreign language. This was considered an advantage since it made the classroom an efficient learning center, with the added

여자: 교수

심리학 강의의 일부를 들으시오.

여 안녕하세요 여러분. 여러분 중 몇 명이나 제가 말하는 모든 것을, 토씨 하나 빠뜨리지 않고, 몇 번이고 반복해서 따라 말하고 싶습니까? 재미있을 것 같나요? 음, 이것은 교사 중심 수업에서 사용되는 학습 유형이고, 암기 학습이라 불립니다. 이것은 아마도 여러분의 부모님이 어렸을 때 학습한 방법일 것입니다. 그리고 믿기 힘들겠지만, 이러한 초기 교수법은 요즘과 같은 현대에도 많은 교실에서 행해지고 있습니다.

학교의 암기 학습의 전통은 몇 세기 전에 시작되었습니다. **13** 이러한 학습 환경 하에서는, 자료에 대해 아무런 지적 연상을 하지 않고서도 학습 내용을 외울 수 있었던 학생들은 똑똑하고 교육을 잘 받은 것으로 간주되었습니다. 그러나 이런 식의 지능이라는 개념은 실제적인 근거를 갖추고 있지 않았고, 오로지 학생이 수동적인 학습 환경에서도 협조적일 수 있다는 것을 증명할 뿐이었습니다. **12** 이런 관점에서 19세기에 진보적인 교육자들이 출현하기 시작했고, 존 듀이라는 미국인은 아이들이 어떻게 교육을 받는지를 바라보는 새로운 방식을 제시하게 되었습니다.

존 듀이는 교육 개혁에 있어서의 노력뿐 아니라 철학과 심리학에 있어서의 성과로도 유명합니다. 그의 철학은 플라톤의 사회 중심적인 생각과 루소의 개인에 대한 강조 사이 어딘가에 있었습니다. 그는 개인은 사회의 고정된 부분일 때만 의미가 있고 사회의 유일한 중요성은 개별 구성원들이 존재한다는 사실뿐이라고 느꼈습니다. 실제로 그의 철학 사상은 그의 교육 이론에 직접적인 영향을 미쳤습니다. 이는 학생들이 개인이자 공동체의 일원으로서 자신들의 삶에 적용할 수 있는 기술과 지식의 학습에 기반을 둔 것이었습니다. 그래서 자신의 이론을 현실화하기 위해서 그는 1896년에 지금은 듀이가 학교로 알려진 대학 실험 학교를 설립했습니다. 직접 해보는 학습에 기반을 둔 교과 과정을 볼 때 그 학교의 이름은 꽤 적절했습니다. 물론 이 학교는 설립된 지 오래된 19세기의 학원들과는 완전히 달랐습니다.

존 듀이 이전의... 음, 교육 이론가들은 반복이 기술로 이어진다고 믿고 교실 수업에 이 기본 개념을 적용했습니다. 그들은 아이들이 반복을 통해서 암기된 사실을 학습하는 방식으로 교육받아야 한다고 느꼈습니다. 자, 이 방법은 학생들이 지식을, 특히 기존의 지식과 연관이 없는 외국어 단어와 같은 지식을 빠르게 학습하도록 했습니다. 이것은 교실을 효율적인 학습 센터로 만들었고, 교사들에게는 특

bonus that it didn't require much expertise on the part of instructors. However, what Dewey felt was necessary for classrooms was opposite to the typical classroom conditions. He believed that students should use reasoning to learn and that this skill was to be acquired by experiential learning. So he would recommend a class take a field trip to learn about a location or a science experiment be carried out by students with the teacher only supervising. Also, he felt books were necessary, but they had the less important role of supplementing students' activities.

And... well... central to Dewey's classrooms was the belief that people learn by working in a social environment, seeing how their educational efforts are relevant to everyday life. Furthermore, he liked to highlight the relationship between doing an activity not considered academic, like sewing, cooking, or carpentry, and the diverse academic subjects covering these activities. So by teaching children how to cook, he believed they could learn how to add and subtract when measuring recipe quantities, how to manage time when creating a meal, and also how to cooperate and work with others. This activity would be supplemented with books and materials when necessary, but the real advantage was that students could see and enjoy the outcome of their efforts. You see... Dewey was trying to create people that had real-world knowledge, developed social skills, an advanced intellect, and professional ability.

Now in your opinion, which type of class would you prefer to take? Would you prefer to have your nose buried in a history book, learning facts, or would you prefer to be making delicious foods while covering the subjects applicable to the process? OK, if you are old like me, then maybe you would prefer to have your nose buried in a book! But seriously, most people would prefer Dewey's method. It's only natural that people prefer active learning. **15, 16** For example, my son attends a public school, but I can see that the way he learns fits Dewey's style of teaching. At home, he always plays with wooden toy blocks. He builds all kinds of structures, only to break them down and build them all over again. By doing this, he's developing his knowledge of geometry first hand and in a natural setting. And what I like is that he's having fun while learning.

For the rest of the week, we are going to be looking at some more of Dewey's methods for creating a learner-centered classroom, which, of course, should not be a quiet place.

별한 전문적 기술을 요하지 않는다는 추가적인 보너스로 인해 장점으로 간주됐습니다. 하지만 듀이가 교실에 필요하다고 느낀 것은 전통적인 교실 상황에 반대되는 것이었습니다. 그는 학생들이 학습하는 데 있어서 추론을 사용해야 하며, 이 기술은 경험적인 학습에서 습득된다고 믿었습니다. 그래서 수업 시간에 어떤 장소에 관해서 배우기 위해 현장학습을 가거나, 교사는 감독만 하는 가운데 학생들이 과학 실험을 하도록 권고했습니다. 또한 그는 책은 필요하지만, 학생들의 활동을 보완해주는 데 덜 중요한 역할을 맡고 있다고 생각했습니다.

그리고... 음... 듀이 교실의 중심이 되는 것은 사람들이 자신의 교육적 노력이 어떻게 일상 생활과 관련이 있는지를 보면서 사회적 환경 속에서 일을 함으로써 배운다는 믿음이었습니다. 더 나아가, 그는 바느질, 요리, 목공과 같은 학문적이지 않은 활동과 이러한 활동을 다루는 다양한 학문적인 주제들 사이의 관계도 강조하고 싶어했습니다. 그래서 아이들에게 요리하는 방법을 가르침으로써 아이들이 조리 시 양을 측정할 때 더하기와 빼기를 배우고, 식사를 준비하면서 시간을 관리하는 방법을 배우고, 그리고 다른 사람들과 협동해서 일하는 방법을 배울 수 있다고 믿었습니다. 이 활동은 필요할 때 책과 자료들로 보충될 수 있지만, 진짜 장점은 학생들이 자신들의 노력의 결과를 보고 즐길 수 있다는 것이었습니다. 아시겠죠... 듀이는 실제 세상의 지식, 발달된 사회적 기술, 높은 지적 능력, 그리고 전문적인 능력을 가진 사람들을 만들어내려고 노력한 것입니다.

자, 여러분 생각에는 어떤 종류의 수업을 받고 싶나요? 역사책에 코를 파묻고 사실들을 배우는 게 나을까요, 아니면 맛있는 음식을 만들면서 그 과정에 응용할 수 있는 주제들을 배우는 게 나을까요? 좋아요, 만약 여러분이 저처럼 나이가 들었다면 책에 코를 박는 것을 선호할지도 모르죠! 하지만 사실 대부분의 사람들은 듀이의 방법을 선호할 겁니다. 사람들이 활동적인 학습을 선호하는 것은 자연스러운 일입니다. **15, 16** 예를 들어, 제 아들은 공립학교를 다니지만 그 아이가 배우는 방식은 듀이 방식의 교수법입니다. 집에서 아이는 항상 나무로 된 장난감 블록을 가지고 놉니다. 온갖 종류의 구조물을 짓고, 다시 무너뜨리고, 또다시 짓습니다. 이렇게 함으로써 아이는 직접적으로, 그리고 자연스러운 환경에서 기하학 지식을 발달시킵니다. 그리고 제 마음에 드는 점은 아이가 배우는 동안 즐거워한다는 것입니다.

이번 주 남은 시간 동안 학습자 중심의 교실 환경을 형성하는 듀이의 방법들에 대해서 좀 더 알아볼 텐데, 물론 이러한 교실은 조용한 곳이 아니겠죠.

17 Students should be interacting and working toward their goals cooperatively. In accordance with this, I won't be lecturing to you. I will be giving handouts with some of Dewey's key methods along with projects you will be using to develop classroom curricula. Just remember, doing equals learning.

17 학생들은 서로 영향을 주고받고 목표를 향해서 협력해 나가야 합니다. 이에 따라, 저는 강의를 하지 않겠습니다. 듀이의 주요 방법들에 대한 프린트물과 함께 수업 교과 과정을 발전시켜 나가기 위해 여러분이 활용하게 될 프로젝트를 나눠주겠습니다. 이것만 기억하세요. 행하는 것이 배우는 것입니다.

12. What is the lecture mainly about?

Ⓐ Using cooking to learn about other things
Ⓑ John Dewey's personal life
Ⓒ Reforms in rote-learning techniques
Ⓓ A revolutionary development in education

13. What does the professor say about memorization?

Ⓐ It's a critical part of student-centered learning.
Ⓑ It's not a useful indicator of practical intelligence.
Ⓒ It can be used in any classroom situation.
Ⓓ It cannot be influenced by repetition.

14. How is the lecture organized?

Ⓐ The spokesperson gives a biographical account of a prominent figure in 20th-century education.
Ⓑ The professor shows students feedback received from a class that used a learner-centered style.
Ⓒ The teacher introduces an alternative form of education followed by its pros and cons.
Ⓓ The instructor discusses a traditional teaching method before presenting John Dewey's alternative.

15. According to the professor, what does her son do to learn about geometry?

Ⓐ He uses toys to construct different things.
Ⓑ He breaks his toys into pieces.
Ⓒ He attends a public school taught by Dewey.
Ⓓ He practices making buildings outside in nature.

16. What is the professor's attitude toward her son's playing with wooden blocks?

Ⓐ She is disappointed that he has to use toys to learn a subject taught in schools.
Ⓑ She likes the structures he creates with the wooden toy blocks.
Ⓒ She feels that his public school should use this type of learning in its classrooms.
Ⓓ She is happy he is enjoying himself while naturally learning about geometry.

12. 강의는 주로 무엇에 관한 것인가?

Ⓐ 다른 것에 대해 배우기 위해서 요리를 이용하는 것
Ⓑ 존 듀이의 사생활
Ⓒ 기계적인 학습 기법의 개혁
Ⓓ 교육에 있어 혁신적인 발달

13. 교수는 암기에 대해서 무엇이라고 말하는가?

Ⓐ 학생 중심의 학습에 있어서 중요한 부분이다.
Ⓑ 실용적 지식의 유용한 지표가 아니다.
Ⓒ 어떤 교실 상황에서도 사용될 수 있다.
Ⓓ 반복에 의해서 영향을 받을 수 없다.

14. 강의는 어떻게 구성되어 있는가?

Ⓐ 교수는 20세기 교육의 주요 인물에 대해서 전기식으로 설명을 한다.
Ⓑ 교수는 학생들에게 학습자 중심의 방식을 사용한 수업에서 얻은 피드백을 보여준다.
Ⓒ 교수는 교수법의 대안을 설명하고, 이어서 그것에 대한 찬반 양론을 개진한다.
Ⓓ 교수는 존 듀이의 대안을 설명하기 전 전통적인 교수법에 관해서 논한다.

15. 교수에 의하면, 교수의 아들은 무엇을 하면서 기하학에 대해서 배우는가?

Ⓐ 장난감을 사용해서 다양한 것들을 만든다.
Ⓑ 장난감을 산산조각 낸다.
Ⓒ 듀이가 가르치는 공립학교에 다닌다.
Ⓓ 자연 속에서 건물 짓는 것을 연습한다.

16. 아들이 나무 블록을 가지고 노는 것에 대한 교수의 태도는 어떠한가?

Ⓐ 학교에서 가르친 것을 배우는 데 장난감을 사용해야 한다는 것에 실망하고 있다.
Ⓑ 아들이 장난감 나무 블록으로 만드는 구조물을 좋아한다.
Ⓒ 아들이 다니는 공립학교에서 수업 시간에 이런 종류의 학습법을 사용해야 한다고 생각한다.
Ⓓ 기하학을 자연스럽게 배우면서 그것을 즐기고 있다는 데 기뻐한다.

17. **Listen again to part of the lecture. Then answer the question.**

W Students should be interacting and working toward their goals cooperatively. In accordance with this, I won't be lecturing to you.

Why does the professor say this:

W In accordance with this, I won't be lecturing to you.

Ⓐ Since the students are already cooperating with each other, the professor doesn't want to do any lecturing in the next class.

Ⓑ Since she lectures during the class, the students will be listening to her rather than cooperatively working toward their goals together.

Ⓒ Since each student is already in charge of achieving his or her goals, the professor feels it is unnecessary to do any lecturing.

Ⓓ Since listening isn't necessary in a learner-centered class, the professor feels it doesn't need to be practiced in the next class.

17. 강의의 일부를 다시 듣고 질문에 답하시오.

여 학생들은 서로 영향을 주고받고 목표를 향해서 협력해 나가야 합니다. 이에 따라, 저는 강의를 하지 않겠습니다.

교수는 왜 이렇게 말하는가:

여 이에 따라, 저는 강의를 하지 않겠습니다.

Ⓐ 학생들이 이미 서로 협력하고 있으므로 교수는 다음 수업 시간에 더 이상 강의하고 싶지 않다.

Ⓑ 교수가 수업 시간에 강의를 하면 학생들은 목표를 향해서 함께 협력하기보다는 교수의 말을 들을 것이다.

Ⓒ 학생들 각자가 이미 목표 달성의 책임을 지고 있어서 교수는 강의를 할 필요가 없다고 느낀다.

Ⓓ 학습자 중심의 수업에서 듣기는 필요하지 않기 때문에 교수는 다음 수업시간에 듣기를 연습할 필요가 없다고 느낀다.

어휘 repeat v 반복하다 | rote learning 암기 학습, 기계적 학습 | survive v 살아남다, 생존하다 | tradition n 전통 | intellectual adj 지능적인 | association n 연관, 연상 | educated adj 교육을 받은 | concept n 개념 | practical adj 실질적인 | cooperate v 협력하다 | passive adj 수동적인 | progressive adj 진보적인, 혁신적인 | represent v 보이다 | reform n 개혁, 개선 | philosophy n 철학 | psychology n 심리학 | emphasis n 강조 | individual n 개인 | meaningful adj 의미 있는 | existence n 존재 | theory n 이론 | knowledge n 지식 | apply v 적용하다 | reality n 현실 | curricula n 교육 과정 | hands-on 직접 해보는, 실천하는 | appropriate adj 적절한 | starkly adv 완전히 | contrast v 대조를 이루다 | established adj 수립된, 정립된 | institution n 기관, 관습 | repetition n 반복 | advantage n 이점 | expertise n 전문성 | opposite adj 반대의 | typical adj 전형적인, 일반적인 | reasoning n 추론, 추리 | acquire v 습득하다 | experiential adj 경험상의 | recommend v 추천하다 | experiment n 실험 | supervise v 감독하다 | supplement v 보완하다, 보충하다 | relevant adj 관련이 있는 | highlight v 강조하다 | academic adj 학문의 | sewing n 바느질 | carpentry n 목공일 | diverse adj 다양한 | subtract v 빼다 | measure v 측정하다 | quantity n 수량 | outcome n 결과 | develop v 발달시키다 | advanced adj 진보한, 발달한 | professional adj 직업적인, 전문적인 | prefer v 선호하다 | bury v 묻다 | attend v 다니다, 참석하다 | geometry n 기하학 | interact v 상호 작용하다 | in accordance with ~에 따라서 | lecture v 강의하다 | handout n 프린트물 | method n 방법 | equal v ~와 같다

Actual Test 2

본서 | P. 184

Conversation 1	1. D	2. B	3. C	4. D	5. C	
Lecture 1	6. B	7. B	8. A, C	9. A	10. D	11. A
Conversation 2	1. C	2. B	3. A, C	4. D	5. D	
Lecture 2	6. C	7. A	8. A	9. C	10. C	11. D
Lecture 3	12. C	13. B	14. B	15. C	16. A	17. C

Conversation 1

본서 | P. 186

Man: Student | Woman: Resident assistant

[1-5] Listen to part of a conversation between a student and a resident assistant.

M Excuse me. Are you the head resident assistant?

W Yes, I'm Jane Kirkpatric, the head R.A. How can I be of assistance?

M Well, Ms. Kirkpatric. **1** I'm having a serious problem with my roommate. You see, I'm a morning person, that is, I wake up early and do my work and run errands first thing in the morning.

W **1** I see. Does this somehow conflict with your roommate's schedule?

M **1** You better believe it! He always stays up late, plays his music so loud we have had complaints from other students, and he even brings his friends over in the middle of the night.

W What do you have in mind? I've been working here a long time, and I've seen these situations many times before.

M Well, I think the logical solution is for one of us to move out or to exchange with another roommate, don't you think?

W **2** Well, when students go away to college, they need to learn to fend for themselves without their parents' involvement. Unfortunately, part of that experience is learning to resolve differences by yourself without having to appeal to an authority.

M You don't think I've tried? Just to give you an example of what I'm talking about. He agreed to meet me here 15 minutes ago, but he didn't bother to show up! How do you suggest I deal with that amount of irresponsibility?

W OK, I think I understand why you're upset. I'll tell you what I can do. There are a couple of options. The first is to submit your request to the Dean of Students, but to be honest, he tends to ignore these manners unless a serious violation has occurred.

M Doesn't sound very promising. You said there was a second choice?

W **3** Well, the other option is a better solution, but generally really hard to bring about. If you could find someone who is willing to switch rooms with you or your roommate, then you can move.

M Why didn't you say so before? I took the liberty of lining up someone, and I have a friend of mine who is ready to move in!

W **3, 4** Hold on just a minute. We need to get three signatures plus your own to facilitate the move. You need signatures from your current roommate, the new roommate, and the new roommate's current roommate. Do you get that?

남자: 학생 | 여자: 기숙사 조교

학생과 기숙사 조교의 대화를 들으시오.

남 실례합니다. 혹시 기숙사 수석 조교이신가요?

여 네, 기숙사 수석 조교 제인 커크패트릭입니다. 어떻게 도와드릴까요?

남 그게, 커크패트릭씨. **1** 제가 룸메이트와 심각한 문제가 있어서요. 저는 아침형 인간이라 일찍 일어나서 숙제를 하고 볼일을 아침에 먼저 처리하거든요.

여 **1** 그렇군요. 그게 룸메이트의 스케줄과 잘 맞지 않나요?

남 **1** 말도 마세요! 그 애는 항상 늦게까지 자지도 않고 음악을 너무 크게 틀어서 다른 학생들에게 불만을 사고 있어요. 그리고 심지어 한밤중에 친구들을 기숙사로 데려와요.

여 어떻게 할 생각인가요? 나는 여기서 오랫동안 일하면서 이런 경우를 전에 많이 봐왔어요.

남 제 생각으로는 우리 중 하나가 나가거나 룸메이트를 바꾸는 것이 이치에 맞는 해결책일 것 같아요, 안 그래요?

여 **2** 글쎄요, 학생들이 대학에 갈 때는 부모님의 관여 없이 자립하는 법을 배울 필요가 있어요. 안됐지만, 학교 당국에 호소하지 않고 학생 스스로 의견차를 해결하는 법을 배우는 것도 그런 경험의 일부예요.

남 제가 노력을 안 했다고 생각하세요? 제 말을 이해하실 수 있도록 한 가지 예를 들어드릴게요. 그 애는 여기서 저랑 15분 전에 만나기로 했어요. 하지만 나타나지도 않고 있잖아요! 그 정도로 무책임한 애를 제가 어떻게 더 상대해야 할까요?

여 알았어요, 왜 학생이 화가 났는지 알 것 같네요. 제가 해 드릴 수 있는 일들을 말해 볼게요. 두 가지 선택지가 있어요. 첫 번째는 학장님께 요청서를 제출하는 방법인데, 하지만 솔직히 말해 그분은 심각한 위반 행위가 아니면 이런 문제들은 무시하시는 경향이 있어요.

남 그리 잘될 것 같지 않네요. 두 번째 대안도 있다고 하셨죠?

여 **3** 음, 다른 대안은 더 좋은 해결책이긴 한데 대개 실행하기가 정말 어려워요. 학생이 만약 학생 본인이나 학생의 룸메이트와 방을 기꺼이 바꿔줄 사람을 찾는다면 그때는 방을 옮길 수 있어요.

남 왜 이제서야 그 말씀을 하세요? 제가 임의로 사람들을 좀 알아봤는데 바로 이사 올 수 있는 친구가 있어요!

여 **3, 4** 잠시만 기다려봐요. 방 이동을 가능하게 하기 위해서는 학생의 서명 외에도 세 사람의 서명이 더 필요해요. 현재 룸메이트, 새 룸메이트, 그리고 새 룸메이트의 현재 룸메이트의 서명이요. 알아들으셨나요?

M 4 I sure do. It shouldn't be a problem. All of the parties involved know each other, and in fact, we have discussed this type of scenario in the past.

W You'd better make sure you get it in writing. Just focus on getting those signatures. People have a way of making agreements without following through sometimes.

M 5 Boy, you can say that again! I'll get to work on that right away on getting the paperwork started. Is that all there is to it?

W That's the first step. After that, you need to bring the signed form back here, and I'll approve it. After that, you need to settle on a convenient time for everybody to move, which sounds like it might be a problem considering the different schedule you and your roommate are on?

M Believe me, when I get all of those signatures, I will stay up late, pack, and then move!

W Well, this looks like it will work out for everyone's best benefit. I'm glad we are able to accommodate you.

M You're glad!

남 4 그럼요. 그건 문제도 안 되죠. 관련된 모든 애들이 서로 알고 있고 또 사실상 과거에 이런 종류의 이야기를 논의한 적이 있어요.

여 학생은 서명을 서면으로 받아야 해요. 서명들을 받는 것에만 초점을 맞추세요. 사람들은 종종 동의는 해놓고 실제로 이에 따르지 않는 경향이 있어요.

남 5 정말 그래요! 지금 당장 서류작업을 시작할게요. 그게 다인가요?

여 그건 첫 번째 단계예요. 그 후에 서명한 서류를 여기로 다시 가져오면 제가 승인을 할게요. 그러고 나서, 이사하기에 모두가 편한 때를 정하면 되는데, 학생과 학생 룸메이트의 스케줄이 그렇게 다르니 문제가 되지 않겠어요?

남 염려 마세요. 서명을 다 받으면 밤늦게까지 짐을 싸서 이사할 거예요.

여 이게 모두를 위해 가장 좋은 방법인 듯 하네요. 학생을 도울 수 있어 다행이에요.

남 그렇군요!

1. What is the conversation mainly about?

Ⓐ The speakers are discussing a problem with the dormitory lease.
Ⓑ The speakers are debating the benefits of living in the dorm.
Ⓒ The speakers are wondering where a late student is.
Ⓓ The speakers are trying to resolve a roommate issue.

2. What is implied about the school's policy toward student problems in the dorms?

Ⓐ The school has very strict regulations regarding students' behavior.
Ⓑ The school would prefer that students solve problems on their own.
Ⓒ The school never permits students to change rooms in mid-semester.
Ⓓ The school allows students to change rooms at any point in the year.

3. What does the housing officer tell the student to do?

Ⓐ She insists that the student solve the problem on his own with the roommate.
Ⓑ She directs the student to take up the problem with the Dean of Students.
Ⓒ She suggests that the student gather the signatures needed to change rooms.
Ⓓ She advises the student to coordinate schedules with the roommate.

1. 대화는 주로 무엇에 관한 것인가?

Ⓐ 화자들은 기숙사 임대 문제에 대해 논의하고 있다.
Ⓑ 화자들은 기숙사에 사는 이점에 대해 논쟁하고 있다.
Ⓒ 화자들은 늦은 학생이 어디 있는지 의아해하고 있다.
Ⓓ 화자들은 룸메이트 문제를 해결하고자 애쓰고 있다.

2. 기숙사에서 학생이 겪는 문제들에 대한 학교의 정책에 관해 무엇이 암시되었는가?

Ⓐ 학교는 학생의 행동에 관해 매우 엄격한 규정을 가지고 있다.
Ⓑ 학교는 학생 스스로 문제를 해결하는 것을 선호한다.
Ⓒ 학교는 학생이 학기 중에 방을 바꾸는 것을 절대로 허용하지 않는다.
Ⓓ 학교는 학생들이 연중 어느 때라도 방을 바꾸는 것을 허용하고 있다.

3. 기숙사 직원은 학생에게 무엇을 하라고 말하는가?

Ⓐ 혼자 힘으로 룸메이트와 문제를 해결하라고 주장한다.
Ⓑ 학장에게 문제를 제기하라고 지도한다.
Ⓒ 방을 바꾸는 데 필요한 서명을 모으라고 제안한다.
Ⓓ 룸메이트와 스케줄을 조정해보라고 충고한다.

4. **What does the student say about the R.A.'s second suggestion?**
Ⓐ He is concerned about his new roommate's current roommate.
Ⓑ He believes it will be effective since he already got their signatures.
Ⓒ He is worried since he needs to persuade a few people.
Ⓓ He thinks it can work out very well since he already knows what to do.

5. **Listen again to part of the conversation. Then answer the question.**

M Boy, you can say that again! I'll get to work on that right away on getting the paperwork started. Is that all there is to it?

What does the student mean when he says this:

M Boy, you can say that again!

Ⓐ The student would like the R.A. to repeat the instructions.
Ⓑ The student is upset he has to do the appropriate paperwork.
Ⓒ The student understands the signatures are most important.
Ⓓ The student doubts that he will be able to get all the signatures.

4. **학생은 기숙사 조교의 두 번째 제안에 관해 무엇이라고 말하는가?**
Ⓐ 새 룸메이트의 현재 룸메이트에 관해 걱정한다.
Ⓑ 이미 서명들을 받았기 때문에 효과적일 것이라고 믿는다.
Ⓒ 몇 사람을 설득해야 해서 걱정하고 있다.
Ⓓ 이미 어떻게 해야 할지 알고 있으므로 잘 될 거라고 생각한다.

5. **대화의 일부를 다시 듣고 질문에 답하시오.**

남 정말 그래요! 지금 당장 서류작업을 시작할게요. 그게 다인가요?

학생은 다음과 같이 말하며 무엇을 의미하는가:

남 정말 그래요!

Ⓐ 조교가 설명을 반복해줄 것을 원한다.
Ⓑ 적절한 서류 업무를 해야 한다는 것에 화가 나 있다.
Ⓒ 서명이 가장 중요하다는 것을 이해한다.
Ⓓ 모든 서명을 받을 수 있을지 의구심이 든다.

어휘 resident assistant 기숙사 조교 | assistance n 도움 | serious adj 심각한 | errand n 할 일, 심부름 | conflict v 상충(상반) 되다, 갈등을 초래하다 | complaint n 불만 | situation n 상황 | logical adj 논리적인 | solution n 해결책 | exchange v 바꾸다 | fend for 자립하다, 혼자 힘으로 하다 | involvement n 관여, 개입 | unfortunately adv 안타깝게도 | experience n 경험 | resolve v 해결하다 | appeal v 호소하다, 간청하다 | authority n 권위, 권위자, 당국 | irresponsibility n 무책임함 | submit v 제출하다 | request n 요청 | ignore v 무시하다 | violation n 위반 | occur v 발생하다 | generally adv 일반적으로 | switch v 바꾸다 | liberty n 자유 | signature n 서명 | facilitate v 가능하게 하다 | party n 당사자 | agreement n 동의 | approve v 승인하다 | convenient adj 편리한 | accommodate v 수용하다

Lecture 1

본서 | P. 188

Man: Student | Woman: Professor

[6-11] Listen to part of a discussion in a history class.

W Yesterday, we were discussing the many Neolithic circles that have been found throughout Europe. Like Stonehenge, it is thought that many of these acted as celestial calendars that allowed people to calculate the seasons. **6** One such circle was found in Germany, and it is called the Goseck circle. It was not made with large stones like many other circles, so it lay undiscovered for a long time. Even more

남자: 학생 | 여자: 교수

역사 수업 중 토론의 일부를 들으시오.

여 어제 우리는 유럽 전역에서 발견된 많은 신석기 시대 원형 유적들에 대해 이야기했습니다. 스톤헨지처럼 이들 중 많은 수가 사람들로 하여금 계절을 계산하도록 도와주는 천체 달력의 역할을 한 것으로 보입니다. **6** 이러한 원형 유적들 중 하나는 독일에서 발견되었는데, 고섹 원형 유적이라고 불리죠. 다른 많은 원형 유적들처럼 거대한 돌들로 만들어지지 않

recently, something truly remarkable was discovered not far from that site: a portable celestial calendar called the Nebra sky disk. Made of bronze inlaid with gold, the disk is about 30 centimeters across and weighs a little over two kilograms. The bronze disk has a bluish-green patina, and the gold inlay depicts the sun and or moon, and a field of stars. There are also three arcs of gold that were added later. **7** Its actual age has not been ascertained yet.

M Excuse me professor, where exactly was it found?

W In Saxony-Anhalt, Germany, about 60 kilometers west of the city of Leipzig. It was found in a prehistoric structure at the summit of a 252 meter hill in the Ziegelroda Forest. The hill is referred to as the Mittelberg, which means "central hill", and the area shows signs of human habitation dating back to the Neolithic period, including around 1,000 burial sites of the barrow type. **8(A)** From the small structure, one can view the sun set behind the tallest peak of the Harz Mountains, the Brocken, on the solstices. Since the site has such a clear astrological association, and the disk depicts celestial objects, it was quickly proposed that it was some form of calendar.

9 The disk was discovered in 1999 by treasure hunters and not archaeologists, so its authenticity was extremely questionable, and some people still think it is a forgery. The authorities heard about its existence and managed to arrange a trap to acquire it from its then owner in 2002. They eventually followed the trail back to the men who discovered it and other artifacts, who arranged to receive reduced sentences by leading the authorities to the site. They found traces that proved the items had indeed been buried there, but that did not prove their authenticity. However, microphotography has revealed marks from corrosion that could not be forged.

M What other artifacts did they find?

W **10** There were two swords, two axe heads, a chisel, and some bracelets; all bronze. These were quite important, because they allowed the scientists to determine approximately when the disk had been buried. The style of the weapons is consistent with the second millennium BCE, and they found a piece of birch bark in the site that they carbon dated to about 1600 BCE. But, that only tells us when it was buried, not when the disk was made.

았기 때문에 오랜 시간 동안 발견되지 않은 채로 남아 있었습니다. 그 지역으로부터 멀지 않은 곳에서 더 최근에 정말로 놀라운 것이 발견되었어요. 네브라 하늘 원반이라고 불리는 이동식 천체 달력이 바로 그것이죠. 청동으로 만들어져 금으로 무늬가 새겨져 있는 이 원반은 지름이 30센티미터 정도이며 무게는 2킬로그램이 약간 넘습니다. 이 청동 원반은 청록빛의 동록을 가지고 있으며 금으로 새겨진 상감은 해 혹은 달, 그리고 별무리를 묘사합니다. 나중에 추가된 세 개의 금으로 된 호도 있어요. **7** 이 원반의 실제 연도는 아직 확인되지 않았습니다.

남 실례합니다, 교수님. 이 원반은 정확히 어디에서 발견되었나요?

여 라이프치히시에서 서쪽으로 60킬로미터 떨어진 독일의 작센안할트주에서 발견되었어요. 지겔로다숲에 있는 252미터 높이의 언덕 정상에 있던 선사 시대 구조물 안에서 발견했죠. 이 언덕은 미텔베르크라고 불리는데, '중앙 언덕'이라는 뜻이며, 이 지역은 약 1,000여개의 고분 유형 매장터를 포함해 신석기 시대까지 거슬러 올라가는 인간의 거주 흔적들을 보여주고 있습니다. **8(A)** 이 작은 구조에서 하지점과 동지점에 하르츠산의 가장 높은 봉우리인 브로켄 뒤로 해가 지는 것을 볼 수 있죠. 이 부지가 명확한 점성술적 연관성을 보여주고, 원반이 천체를 묘사하고 있어서 이 원반이 달력의 한 유형이라는 가정이 금세 생겨났습니다.

9 이 원반은 고고학자들이 아닌 보물을 찾는 사람들에 의해 1999년에 발견되어서 진품인지가 극히 의심스러웠으며 어떤 이들은 여전히 이 원반이 위조품이라고 믿고 있어요. 당국에서는 이 원반의 존재에 대해 듣고 2002년에 당시 주인으로부터 이 원반을 되찾기 위한 덫을 설치하게 되었습니다. 결국 이 원반과 다른 유물들을 발견한 한 남자를 추적할 수 있었고, 이것들을 발견한 곳으로 당국을 데려간다면 감형을 해주기로 했죠. 실제로 이 물건들이 그곳에 묻혀 있었다는 것을 증명하는 흔적은 찾았지만, 그것이 이 유물들이 진품인지는 증명해주지 않았죠. 그러나 현미경 사진은 위조될 수 없는 부식 흔적을 찾아냈습니다.

남 그들이 발견한 다른 유물들은 무엇이었나요?

여 **10** 두 개의 검, 두 개의 도끼 머리, 끌과 몇 개의 팔찌들이 있었어요. 모두 청동으로 만든 것들이었죠. 이것들은 꽤 중요한데, 그 이유는 이 유물들이 과학자들로 하여금 네브라 하늘 원반이 대략 언제쯤 묻혔는지 밝히도록 해주었기 때문입니다. 무기 양식은 기원전 2천 년경으로 일정하며, 그 현장에서 자작나무 껍질 조각 하나를 발견해 탄소 연대 측정을 했는데 기원전 1600년경의 것으로 밝혀졌습니다. 그러나 이는 원반이 언제 묻혔는지를 말해줄 뿐, 언제 만들어졌는지는 알려주지 않죠.

It was clearly added to over time, and it was a very important object, so it was probably used for many generations before it was laid in the ground.

8(C) On the disk, there is a cluster of dots that resembles the constellation of Pleiades, and other dots have been correlated to other constellations, stars, and planets. Using the gold arcs on opposite sides, the disc could be used to measure where the sun sets on the winter and summer solstices. This means it could be used as a solar calendar that they could correlate to the lunar cycle to predict when to plant and harvest crops. **11** If it is authentic, it would be the oldest discovered portable object used for this purpose. Its composition is also significant, as the copper came from Austria, and the tin and some of the gold came from Cornwall, England, which means that its makers traded extensively.

시간이 지난 뒤 매장된 것이 분명하며, 매우 중요한 물건이었기 때문에 아마 땅에 묻히기 전 수 세대에 걸쳐 사용되었을 겁니다.

8(C) 원반에는 플레이아데스 성단의 성좌를 연상하게 하는 점의 무리들이 있으며 다른 점들은 다른 성좌, 별, 그리고 행성들과 연관되어 있습니다. 서로 맞은편에 있는 금으로 새겨진 호를 이용해서 이 원반은 동지점과 하지점에 태양이 어디에서 질지 측정하는 데 사용되었을 수 있습니다. 이 말은 언제 작물을 경작하고 추수할지를 예측하기 위한 태음 주기와 연관 짓기 위해 이 원반이 양력 달력으로 사용되었을 가능성이 있다는 의미입니다. **11** 만약 이 원반이 진품이라면 이 용도를 위해 만들어진, 발견된 것들 중 가장 오래된 이동식 물체가 될 겁니다. 원반의 구성 요소 역시 중요한데, 구리가 오스트리아에서 왔으며 주석과 금 약간이 영국의 콘월에서 왔다는 점을 봤을 때 이들의 제작자들이 광범위하게 교역했다는 것을 보여주기 때문이죠.

6. What is the discussion mainly about?

Ⓐ The time-consuming process of excavating the Nebra sky disk
Ⓑ The interesting discovery that was made in Germany
Ⓒ The lives of people who lived during the Neolithic period
Ⓓ The astrological observances made with an ancient calendar

7. What is true about the Nebra sky disk?

Ⓐ It was invented for ritual purposes.
Ⓑ Its age has yet to be discovered.
Ⓒ It was made of gold, bronze, and silver.
Ⓓ Its diameter is about one meter.

8. Why did scientists assume that the Nebra sky disk was some form of calendar? Choose 2 answers.

Ⓐ The area that it was found is deeply related with astrology.
Ⓑ The numbers carved on the disk showed similarities with today's calendar.
Ⓒ There are some celestial bodies portrayed on the surface of the disk.
Ⓓ People during the Neolithic period had already been using calendars.

6. 토론은 주로 무엇에 대한 것인가?

Ⓐ 오랜 시간이 걸린 네브라 하늘 원반 발굴 과정
Ⓑ 독일에서 있었던 흥미로운 발견
Ⓒ 신석기 시대에 살았었던 사람들의 삶
Ⓓ 고대 달력으로 행해진 점성술 관찰

7. 네브라 하늘 원반에 관해 옳은 것은 무엇인가?

Ⓐ 의식을 치를 목적으로 발명되었다.
Ⓑ 그 연대가 아직 밝혀지지 않았다.
Ⓒ 금, 청동, 그리고 은으로 만들어졌다.
Ⓓ 지름이 약 1미터이다.

8. 과학자들은 왜 네브라 하늘 원반이 일종의 달력이라고 가정하였는가? 두 개를 고르시오.

Ⓐ 그것이 발견된 지역이 천문학과 깊은 관련이 있었다.
Ⓑ 원반에 새겨진 숫자들이 오늘날의 달력과 유사점들을 보여주었다.
Ⓒ 원반 표면에 몇몇 천체들이 묘사되어 있다.
Ⓓ 신석기 시대 사람들은 이미 달력을 사용하고 있었다.

9. What can be inferred about the Nebra sky disk and other artifacts?

Ⓐ Their original burial site cannot solely prove their authenticity.

Ⓑ There are various ways to prove that they were forged.

Ⓒ They were almost sold to another country by the hunters.

Ⓓ Their existence proved the widespread use of iron in the region.

10. Why does the professor mention a piece of birch bark?

Ⓐ To show the interesting use of trees during the Neolithic period

Ⓑ To emphasize the importance of small objects for a burial ritual

Ⓒ To introduce another important discovery from the Bronze Age

Ⓓ To explain how scientists discovered the burial date of the artifacts

11. Why does the professor say this:

> W If it is authentic, it would be the oldest discovered portable object used for this purpose. Its composition is also significant, as the copper came from Austria, and the tin and some of the gold came from Cornwall, England, which means that its makers traded extensively.

Ⓐ He is telling the students that many things still need to be revealed.

Ⓑ He sees the difficulty of determining whether the disk is authentic or not.

Ⓒ He finds it interesting to see the earliest trade route of mankind.

Ⓓ He is excited that the authenticity of the disk was finally made certain.

9. 네브라 하늘 원반과 다른 유물들에 관해 무엇을 추론할 수 있는가?

Ⓐ 이들이 원래 묻혀 있던 장소 자체가 이들이 진품이라는 것을 증명하지는 못한다.

Ⓑ 이들이 위조되었다는 것을 증명할 방법들이 많이 있다.

Ⓒ 사냥꾼들에 의해 다른 나라로 거의 팔릴 뻔했다.

Ⓓ 이들의 존재는 그 지역에서의 광범위한 철 사용을 증명했다.

10. 교수는 왜 자작나무 껍질 한 조각을 언급하는가?

Ⓐ 신석기 시기의 흥미로운 나무 사용을 보여주려고

Ⓑ 매장 의식에서 작은 물건들의 중요성을 강조하려고

Ⓒ 청동기 시대에 있었던 또 다른 중요한 발견을 소개하려고

Ⓓ 과학자들이 어떻게 유물들의 매장 시기를 밝혀냈는지 설명하려고

11. 교수는 왜 이렇게 말하는가:

> 여 만약 이 원반이 진품이라면 이 용도를 위해 만들어진, 발견된 것들 중 가장 오래된 이동식 물체가 될 겁니다. 원반의 구성 요소 역시 중요한데, 구리가 오스트리아에서 왔으며 주석과 금 약간이 영국의 콘월에서 왔다는 점을 봤을 때 이들의 제작자들이 광범위하게 교역했다는 것을 보여주기 때문이죠.

Ⓐ 밝혀져야 할 것들이 여전히 많이 있다고 학생들에게 말하고 있다.

Ⓑ 원반이 진품인지 아닌지를 결정하는 것의 어려움을 안다.

Ⓒ 인류 최초의 무역로를 보게 되어 흥미를 느낀다.

Ⓓ 원반이 진품이라는 것이 마침내 확인되어서 흥분했다.

어휘 Neolithic adj 신석기 시대의 | circle n 둥글게 (원을 그리며) 모여 있는 것들 | celestial adj 하늘의, 천체의 | calculate v 계산하다 | remarkable adj 놀라운 | portable adj 이동이 쉬운, 휴대 가능한 | disk n 동그랗고 납작한 판 | inlaid adj 세공을 한, 무늬를 새긴 | weigh v 무게가 ~이다 | patina n (금속의 표면에 생기는) 녹청 | inlay n 상감, 상감 세공 재료 | depict v 묘사하다 | arc n 호, 활 모양 | ascertain v 알아내다, 확인하다 | prehistoric adj 선사 시대의 | summit n 정상, 절정 | habitation n 거주, 주거 | date back to ~까지 거슬러 올라가다 | barrow n 무덤, 고분 | peak n 정상 | solstice n 지점(하지점과 동지점) | astrological adj 점성술의 | association n 연관성, 관련, 연계 | treasure hunter 보물 찾는 사람 | archaeologist n 고고학자 | authenticity n 진품, 진짜임 | questionable adj 의심스러운, 미심쩍은 | forgery n 위조된 물건 | authority n 당국 | existence n 존재 | trap n 덫, 함정 | artifact n 공예품, 인공 유물 | reduce v 감소시키다 | sentence n 형벌, 형, 선고 | microphotography n 현미경 사진 | corrosion n 부식 | axe n 도끼 | chisel n 끌 | bracelet n 팔찌 | bronze n 청동 | approximately adv 거의, 근사치의 | consistent adj 한결같은, 일관된 | millennium n 천 년 | birch bark 자작나무 껍질 | carbon date 탄소 연대를 측정하다 | generation n 세대 | cluster n 무리 | dot n 점 | constellation n 별자리, 성좌 | correlate v 연관성이 있다 | measure v 측정하다 | lunar cycle 태음 주기 | predict v 예측하다 | plant v 경작하다 | harvest v 추수하다 | composition n 구성 | tin n 주석 | trade v 교역하다, 무역하다 | extensively adv 광범위하게

Man: Registrar | Woman: Student

[1-5] Listen to part of a conversation between a student and a registrar.

M Next in line, please. Yes, how may I help you?

W 1 I need to register for a class, and I normally use the registrar's website, but I kept getting locked out of the system when I tried to book a class this morning.

M All right. Sounds like a problem we can fix. Which course were you trying to enroll in?

W 1 I was trying to get into Political Science 255. Study of North American Politics. I wanted Tuesday-Thursday afternoon class, but the system wouldn't let me get into the section I wanted.

M Ah, I can see why. All of the sections of that particular class have been filled up.

W Oh no! But that class is a prerequisite for all 300-level classes. I have to take it in order to graduate on time!

M 2 If it was so important to you, why did you wait to the last minute to register? You were allowed to register as far back as June! You're not a freshman; you should know that there are only a certain number of spaces available for each class.

W I don't understand that if these courses always fill up, why don't they open more sections?

M I couldn't really tell you that. It could have something to do with the availability of the professors. They can work only a limited number of hours per week.

W What am I going to do? If I can't take the class this semester, that will throw my timetable off for the rest of my college career!

M 3(A) Have you thought about taking summer classes? Many students make up classes that they can't take during the regular year in the summer. Plus, the class sizes are smaller and professors are usually more laid back.

W Yeah. I know that, but I normally need to work full time during the break to make tuition for the rest of the year. Are there any other options?

M Well, the best I can do is to put you on the waiting list. That means we put you on an overflow list and you wait to see if anybody drops the class you want.

W Hmm... That doesn't give me much of a chance. What are the chances that somebody or a bunch of people are going to drop?

M Well, that all depends. A lot of times people drop classes at the beginning of the semester, then we take replacements on a first come, first served basis.

W OK. Is there any way you can check and see what my position on the list is?

남자: 학적부 직원 | 여자: 학생

학생과 학적부 직원의 대화를 들으시오.

남 다음 분 오세요. 네, 무엇을 도와드릴까요?

여 1 수업에 등록하려고 하는데요. 평소에는 온라인 상으로 등록을 했는데, 오늘 아침에 등록하려고 하니까 등록 시스템에 접속이 되지 않았어요.

남 알겠어요. 우리가 해결할 수 있는 문제인 것 같군요. 어떤 수업에 등록을 하려고 했죠?

여 1 북미 정치학 수업인 정치학 255에 등록하려고 했어요. 화요일과 목요일 오후 수업을 원했는데, 시스템상으로 제가 원하는 시간대에 접근할 수 없었어요.

남 아, 왜 그런지 알겠어요. 그 수업의 모든 시간대가 이미 마감되었네요.

여 아, 이런! 그 수업은 300단계 수업을 듣기 위한 선수 과목이에요. 제때 졸업을 하려면 그 수업을 들어야만 해요!

남 2 만일 그렇게 중요한 수업이었다면, 왜 등록을 마지막 순간까지 기다렸나요? 6월부터 등록할 수 있었는데 말이죠! 신입생도 아니니 각 수업마다 등록할 수 있는 수가 정해져 있다는 것을 알았을 텐데요.

여 이해가 안 돼요. 만일 이 수업이 항상 마감된다면 좀 더 많은 시간대의 수업을 열어야 하는 것 아닌가요?

남 그렇게 말하기엔 곤란한 부분이 있어요. 그건 교수님들이 시간이 되는지 여부와 관련이 있거든요. 그 분들은 매주 정해진 만큼의 시간만 일할 수 있어요.

여 그럼 전 어떻게 해야 하나요? 이번 학기에 그 수업을 들을 수 없다면, 앞으로 남은 제 학사 일정이 모두 엉망이 될 거예요!

남 3(A) 여름 계절 학기 수업을 들을 생각은 해봤어요? 많은 학생들이 정규 학기 동안 들을 수 없던 수업을 여름에 보충하거든요. 그리고 수업 정원이 더 적고 교수님들도 대개 더 여유가 있으세요.

여 네. 그건 알지만, 전 방학 동안 보통 남은 학기의 수업료를 벌기 위해 하루 종일 일해야 하거든요. 다른 방법은 없나요?

남 글쎄, 제가 할 수 있는 최선의 방법은 학생을 대기자 명단에 넣는 거예요. 다시 말해 초과 인원 명단에 이름을 넣고 다른 누군가가 학생이 원하는 수업을 취소하기를 기다리는 거죠.

여 흠... 가능성이 별로 없겠군요. 한 명이나 아니면 여러 명이 한꺼번에 수업을 취소할 가능성은 얼마나 되죠?

남 글쎄요, 상황에 따라 달라요. 많은 경우 학생들이 학기 초에 수업을 취소하는데, 그럼 저희가 선착순으로 대체 인원을 뽑아요.

여 알겠어요. 제가 명단 상에서 몇 번째에 있는지 확인해주실 수 있는 방법이 있나요?

M Sure. What was the name of that class again? Political Science 255? And, which section were you looking for?

W That's right, Polly-Sci, section C. That's a Tuesday-Thursday afternoon class, but I could be flexible with other sections if that would help the possibility of me getting into that class.

M 4 Hmmm. I'm sorry to say that it doesn't look very good. The section you're looking for actually has the fewest students on the waiting list with 27. All the other sections have far more.

W 4 That doesn't sound like much of a chance. Probably the only way to get in is right near the final withdrawal deadline. And by that time, I'll have missed most of the course!

M 3(C) Oh, have you considered auditing the class? What you can do is go to class, listen to the lectures, and that way you'll be familiar with all the class work. Then, when a regular spot opens up in the class, you can just slide in and you won't have missed anything!

W Hey! That sounds pretty good! Do I need to get special permission or something to audit a class?

M Hang on just a second! Before you get too excited, you have to consider how you're going to attend the political seminars at City Hall during the course. Usually, those meetings have limited spaces, and they are reserved for regular students only. I'll tell you what. 5 Why don't you talk this through with Professor Peterson. She's usually very helpful to students. She may have the ability to get you a spot in the seminars if you promise to always attend.

W 5 Hmm... Sounds a little complicated, with a lot of variables. But, if that's the best we can do, I'll talk with Professor Peterson. Thanks for helping me out.

남 물론이죠. 수업의 이름이 뭐라고 했죠? 정치학 255? 그리고, 어떤 시간대의 수업을 듣고 싶다고 했죠?

여 맞아요. 정치학, C섹션 수업이에요. 화요일–목요일 오후 수업이요. 그런데 만일 제가 수업에 등록할 수 있는 가능성이 높아진다면 다른 시간대도 괜찮아요.

남 4 흠. 유감이지만 상황이 좋아 보이지는 않네요. 사실 학생이 원하는 시간대의 수업에 대기자 수가 가장 적지만, 그래도 27명이에요. 다른 시간대에는 훨씬 더 많은 대기자가 있고요.

여 4 가능성이 많지 않아 보이네요. 아마 등록할 수 있는 유일한 방법은 취소 마감일이 다 되어야 나오겠네요. 그때쯤이면 전 그 수업의 대부분을 듣지 못했을 테고요!

남 3(C) 아, 수업을 청강하는 것은 생각해봤나요? 수업에 가서 강의를 들으면 돼요. 그런 방식으로 모든 수업 내용에 익숙해질 수 있어요. 그러고 나서, 정규 수업 인원에 여유가 생기면, 정식으로 수업에 들어갈 수 있고 수업 내용을 하나도 놓치지 않을 수 있죠!

여 와! 좋은 생각이에요! 수업을 청강하려면 특별히 받아야 하는 허가나 다른 어떤 것이 있나요?

남 잠깐만 기다려봐요! 너무 기뻐하기 전에, 이 수업 동안 시청에서 열리는 정치학 세미나에 참여할 수 있는 방법을 생각해봐야 해요. 대개 그 모임은 자리가 한정되어 있는데, 정규 학생들 전용이거든요. 이렇게 해보세요. 5 피터슨 교수님께 이 문제에 관해 이야기해 보세요. 그 교수님은 학생들에게 도움을 많이 주시거든요. 만일 학생이 빠지지 않고 출석한다고 약속한다면 교수님께서 세미나에 자리를 마련해주실 수 있을 거예요.

여 5 음... 변수가 많고 약간 복잡해 보이네요. 하지만 그 방법이 할 수 있는 최선이라면 피터슨 교수님께 말씀 드릴게요. 도와주셔서 감사합니다.

1. Why does the student go to the registrar's office?

Ⓐ She wants to check an error on her tuition bill.
Ⓑ She needs to pay a political seminar fee.
Ⓒ She wants to sign up for a required class.
Ⓓ She has signed up for the wrong class.

2. What is the man's attitude toward the student at the beginning of the conversation?

Ⓐ He is annoyed by the fact that the student could not register the class herself.
Ⓑ He is puzzled why the student took so long to register for the class.

1. 왜 학생은 학적부 사무실을 찾아가는가?

Ⓐ 수업료 고지서의 오류에 관해 확인하길 원한다.
Ⓑ 정치학 세미나 수업료를 지불해야 한다.
Ⓒ 필수 과목 수업에 등록하려고 한다.
Ⓓ 잘못된 수업에 등록했다.

2. 대화 초반에 학생에 대한 남자의 태도는 어떠한가?

Ⓐ 학생이 스스로 수업을 등록하지 못한다는 사실에 짜증이 나 있다.
Ⓑ 학생이 왜 수업을 등록하기까지 이렇게 오래 걸렸는지 의아해 한다.

Ⓒ He is irritated that the student is taking so long to complete the registration.
Ⓓ He is not sure if the class is really important for the student.

3. What suggestions does the registrar give to the student?
Choose 2 answers.
Ⓐ He suggests that the student make up the course in the summer.
Ⓑ He suggests that the student get an override from the professor.
Ⓒ He suggests that the student try to audit the class and wait.
Ⓓ He suggests that the student take the class at a different university.

4. Listen again to part of the conversation. Then answer the question.

> M Hmmm. I'm sorry to say that it doesn't look very good. The section you're looking for actually has the fewest students on the waiting list with 27. All the other sections have far more.
> W That doesn't sound like much of a chance. Probably the only way to get in is right near the final withdrawal deadline. And by that time, I'll have missed most of the course!

What does the student mean when she says this:

> W That doesn't sound like much of a chance.

Ⓐ She thinks the idea doesn't sound necessary.
Ⓑ She does not understand why there are so many people on the list.
Ⓒ She thinks she will get into the course soon in the semester.
Ⓓ She thinks that she will not be admitted into the class this semester.

5. What will the student most likely do?
Ⓐ Find an open spot to audit the required course
Ⓑ Visit City Hall to sign up for the political seminar
Ⓒ Go and see Professor Peterson regarding her grade
Ⓓ Visit Professor Peterson's office to ask for help

Ⓒ 학생이 등록을 마치는 데 너무 오래 걸려 짜증이 나 있다.
Ⓓ 이 수업이 학생에게 정말로 중요한지 확신하지 못한다.

3. 학적부 직원은 학생에게 어떤 제안을 하는가?
두 개를 고르시오.
Ⓐ 학생에게 여름 학기 동안 수업을 보충하라고 제안한다.
Ⓑ 학생에게 교수님으로부터 정원 외 등록을 허락 받으라고 제안한다.
Ⓒ 학생에게 수업을 청강하며 기다리라고 제안한다.
Ⓓ 학생에게 다른 대학에서 수업을 들으라고 제안한다.

4. 대화의 일부를 다시 듣고 질문에 답하시오.

> 남 흠. 유감이지만 상황이 좋아 보이지는 않네요. 사실 학생이 원하는 시간대의 수업에 대기자 수가 가장 적지만, 그래도 27명이에요. 다른 시간대에는 훨씬 더 많은 대기자가 있고요.
> 여 가능성이 많지 않아 보이네요. 아마 등록할 수 있는 유일한 방법은 취소 마감일이 다 되어야 나오겠네요. 그때쯤이면 전 그 수업의 대부분을 듣지 못했을 테고요!

학생은 다음과 같이 말하며 무엇을 의미하는가:

> 여 가능성이 많지 않아 보이네요.

Ⓐ 그 아이디어가 필요한 것 같지 않다고 생각한다.
Ⓑ 명단에 그렇게 많은 사람이 올라가 있는 이유를 이해하지 못한다.
Ⓒ 학기 중 곧 그 수업에 등록할 수 있을 것이라고 생각한다.
Ⓓ 이번 학기에 그 수업에 등록할 수 없을 것이라고 생각한다.

5. 학생은 다음에 무엇을 할 것 같은가?
Ⓐ 필수 과목을 청강하기 위해 가능한 자리를 찾는다
Ⓑ 정치 세미나에 등록하기 위해 시청을 방문한다
Ⓒ 성적과 관련해 피터슨 교수를 찾아간다
Ⓓ 도움을 요청하기 위해 피터슨 교수의 사무실을 방문한다

어휘 register v 등록하다 | normally adv 보통 | get locked out (밖에 있는 채로) 잠겨서 들어가지 못하다 | fix v 바로잡다, 고치다 | enroll v 등록하다 | political science 정치학 | particular adj 특정한 | prerequisite n 필수 과목, 선행 필수 요건 | graduate v 졸업하다 | availability n (이용, 사용) 가능성 | limited adj 제한된 | timetable n 시간표 | regular adj 정규의 | laid back adj 편한, 느긋한 | tuition n 등록금 | overflow n 정원 초과, 흘러 넘침 | replacement n 대체 | flexible adj 유동적인 | possibility n 가능성 | withdrawal n 철회 | audit v 청강하다 | slide in 미끄러져 들어가다 | permission n 허락 | reserve v 따로 남겨 두다, 예약하다 | helpful adj 도움이 되는, 유용한 | attend v 참석하다 | complicated adj 복잡한 | variable n 변수

Man: Professor

[6-11] Listen to part of a lecture in a biology class.

M OK, 6 I ran out of time yesterday, so I didn't get a chance to explain how plants create new plants, which is what we call plant reproduction. So today I want to detail how seed plants actually reproduce. As you know, a seed grows into a plant, but after this, the plant must reproduce to extend its species. For this, 6 it uses its reproductive organs in a process called pollination, which can occur in two ways: through self-pollination or cross-pollination.

So what is pollination? Basically, it's the transfer of pollen from a flower's stamen to either its stigma or that of another flower. This fertilizes the plant, allowing it to develop seeds. Now, to better understand the process, it will help if we look at the structure of a plant, which has both male and female parts. 7 The stamen is the male portion of a plant, and it produces a sticky yellow powder called pollen. It's the powder that covers your car, making it yellow each spring. And there's also a female part to plants, called the pistil, the top of which has a sticky area known as the stigma.

As I said, there are a few ways plants can be pollinated, and they both have their benefits and drawbacks. Self-pollination occurs when a plant's pollen is transferred from its stamen to its own stigma, and cross-pollination occurs when a plant's pollen reaches the stigma of a different plant from its species. Therefore, pollination only occurs within a species, so an apple tree can't pollinate a cherry tree, for example. Now, the benefits of self-pollination are that only one self-pollinating plant is needed to reproduce, but with this comes some problems. Since the new plants are composed of the same genetic material, they can all be killed by the same disease. And if a plant makes a genetic adaptation, it can't pass this benefit on to others of its species. Cross-pollinating plants don't suffer from this. They can pass any helpful genetic changes on to other plants quickly. However, a pollinator, which transfers pollen from plant to plant in the form of insects, mammals, or wind, must be present for this to occur.

Pollinators' work is done by accident. What I mean is that they don't intentionally pollinate flowers. They are all at the flower to get food in the form of pollen or nectar. And

남자: 교수

생물학 강의의 일부를 들으시오.

남 좋아요. 6 어제는 시간이 부족해서 어떻게 식물이 새로운 식물을 만들어내는지, 소위 식물의 번식에 대해 설명할 기회가 없었어요. 그래서 오늘은 종자 식물들이 실제로 어떻게 번식을 하는지 자세히 설명하겠습니다. 여러분도 알다시피 종자는 성장해서 식물이 되고, 이후에는 종을 확산시키기 위해 번식을 해야 합니다. 이를 위해, 6 식물은 수분이라 불리는 과정에서 번식 기관을 이용하는데, 이러한 수분은 두 가지 방법으로 발생합니다. 자가 수분과 타화 수분이 바로 그것입니다.

그렇다면 수분이란 무엇일까요? 기본적으로 수분은 꽃 수술에서 암술머리로 또는 다른 꽃의 암술머리로 꽃가루를 이동시키는 것을 말합니다. 이것은 식물을 수정시켜 씨앗이 자라날 수 있도록 합니다. 이제 이 과정을 좀 더 잘 이해하기 위해, 수술과 암술을 모두 가진 식물의 구조를 살펴보면 도움이 될 것입니다. 7 수술은 식물의 수컷 부분으로, 꽃가루라고 불리는 끈적거리는 노란색 가루를 만들어냅니다. 매년 봄 여러분의 자동차를 뒤덮어 노랗게 만드는 가루죠. 그리고 식물에는 암술이라고 불리는 암컷 부분도 있는데, 이것의 꼭대기에는 암술머리라고 불리는 끈적거리는 부분이 있습니다.

이미 말한 대로 식물들이 수분을 할 수 있는 방법이 몇 가지 있는데, 각각 장점과 단점을 가지고 있습니다. 자가 수분은 한 식물의 꽃가루가 수술에서 자신의 암술머리로 전달될 때 일어나며, 타화 수분은 한 식물의 꽃가루가 같은 종의 다른 식물의 암술머리로 전달될 때 일어납니다. 따라서 수분은 같은 종 내에서만 일어나기 때문에, 예를 들어, 사과나무는 체리나무와 수분할 수 없는 것입니다. 자가 수분의 장점은 번식을 위해 하나의 자가 수분 식물만이 필요하다는 것인데, 여기에는 몇 가지 문제점이 따라붙습니다. 새로운 식물들이 동일한 유전 물질들로 구성되기 때문에 같은 질병으로 전부 죽을 수 있다는 것입니다. 그리고 만일 한 식물이 이에 유전적으로 적응을 한다고 해도, 이를 같은 종의 다른 식물들에게 전달할 수 없습니다. 타화 수분 식물들은 이런 문제를 겪지 않습니다. 그들은 도움이 되는 유전적 변화를 다른 식물들에게 빨리 전달할 수 있습니다. 하지만, 이를 위해서는 곤충이나 포유동물, 그리고 바람과 같이 꽃가루를 식물과 식물 사이에 전달하는 수분 매개체가 있어야만 합니다.

수분 매개체의 활동은 우연히 이루어집니다. 의도적으로 꽃들을 수분시키는 것이 아니라는 말이죠. 그들은 꽃가루나 꿀 형태로 되어 있는 먹이를 얻

since pollen is sticky, it sometimes sticks to their bodies and gets transferred when the pollinator visits another plant and accidentally drops some of the pollen on the flower's stigma. The most successful flower cross-pollinators are moths, bees, butterflies, and hummingbirds. **8** However, wind can also function as a pollinator, mainly cross-pollinating grasses like corn. In fact, it's easy to identify plants that use the wind for pollination. They don't have bright colors or flower petals because they don't need to visually attract animal pollinators. As you can assume, wind doesn't direct pollen too precisely, so it doesn't lend itself well to pollinating flowers. But for vast areas that need pollen scattered throughout, I don't know of a better pollinator.

In the last century, animal pollinator numbers have decreased, yet orchard and field sizes have steadily increased. And for the last twenty years, pollination management has become an important issue in farming. By understanding a crop's pollination needs, growers can significantly improve not only the production but also the quality of the crop. **9** For example, in the United States, blueberry producers bring in vast numbers of honeybees to act as pollinators in their fields. Although these bees are not as effective as the bees native to the area, they make up for inefficiency with sheer numbers. Of course, when the plants are out of season, there is a massive decline in the honeybee population. But the farmers are able to bring more bees to the area again in the next season while still being able to make money from their work.

10, 11 Well, that's it for pollination. But what happens after a plant is fertilized? Well, please read pages 80-110 tonight so you can get some background information on tomorrow's class. **11** And there's an important question I would like you to tell me the answer to tomorrow. Is the tomato a fruit or a vegetable?

기 위해 꽃에 접근합니다. 그리고 꽃가루는 끈적거리기 때문에 때때로 그것들의 몸에 붙게 되고, 그것들이 다른 식물에게 가서 그 꽃의 암술머리에 우연히 꽃가루를 떨어뜨리면서 꽃가루가 전해지는 것입니다. 가장 좋은 타화 수분 매개체는 나방, 벌, 나비, 그리고 벌새입니다. **8** 하지만 바람도 수분 매개체 역할을 할 수 있는데, 주로 옥수수와 같은 식물을 타화 수분시킵니다. 사실, 수분을 하는 데 바람을 이용하는 식물을 식별하는 것은 쉬운 일입니다. 이들은 수분 매개체인 동물들을 시각적으로 끌어들일 필요가 없기 때문에 밝은 색이나 꽃잎을 가지고 있지 않습니다. 여러분이 추측할 수 있는 대로 바람은 꽃가루를 정확하게 인도할 수 없기 때문에 꽃을 수분시키는 데에는 적합하지 않습니다. 그러나 사방에 꽃가루가 흩어져야 하는 방대한 지역에서는 이보다 더 나은 수분 매개체를 찾기 어렵죠.

지난 세기에 수분 매개체 역할을 하는 동물의 수는 감소해왔지만, 과수원과 밭의 규모는 꾸준히 증가해왔습니다. 그리고 지난 20년 동안 수분을 관리하는 것은 농업에 있어 중요한 문제가 되었죠. 농작물의 수분 필요성을 이해함으로써 경작자들은 생산량을 증대할 뿐만 아니라 작물의 품질도 향상시킬 수 있습니다. **9** 예를 들어, 미국에서 블루베리 농사를 짓는 사람들은 수분 매개체로 활동할 수 있도록 대량의 꿀벌을 밭으로 데려왔습니다. 비록 이 벌들은 그 지역 토종 벌들보다 효과적이지는 않지만, 많은 수만으로도 이러한 비효율성을 보완했습니다. 물론 식물을 기르는 기간이 지나고 나면 꿀벌 수가 엄청나게 줄어들겠지요. 하지만 농부들은 다음 철에 더 많은 벌들을 데려올 수 있을 것이고 여전히 작물로 수익을 거둘 수 있습니다.

10, 11 음, 이것으로 수분에 대한 이야기를 마치도록 하죠. 그런데 식물이 수분된 뒤에는 어떤 일이 일어날까요? 내일 수업에 대한 배경 지식을 좀 얻을 수 있도록 오늘 밤에 80~110페이지를 읽도록 하세요. **11** 내일 여러분이 제게 답을 해야 할 중요한 질문이 하나 있습니다. 토마토는 과일일까요, 채소일까요?

6. What is the topic of the lecture?

Ⓐ Self-pollination and how plants do it
Ⓑ The way farmers can make more money
Ⓒ The different ways plants create new plants
Ⓓ Cross-pollination and what makes it happen

7. What does the professor say about pollen?

Ⓐ It is commonly seen in the springtime.
Ⓑ It makes all flowers yellow in color.
Ⓒ It is helpful for protecting flowers.
Ⓓ It is the male portion of a plant.

6. 강의의 주제는 무엇인가?

Ⓐ 자가 수분과 식물들이 그것을 하는 방법
Ⓑ 농부들이 더 많은 돈을 벌 수 있는 방법
Ⓒ 식물이 새로운 식물을 만들어내는 다양한 방법
Ⓓ 타화 수분과 그것을 발생하게 하는 것

7. 교수는 꽃가루에 관해 뭐라고 말하는가?

Ⓐ 일반적으로 봄철에 볼 수 있다.
Ⓑ 모든 꽃들을 노랗게 만든다.
Ⓒ 꽃을 보호하는 데 도움을 준다.
Ⓓ 식물의 수컷 부분이다.

8. **What is the professor's attitude toward wind as a pollinator of large areas?**
Ⓐ He feels the wind is the best for them.
Ⓑ He thinks the wind is better for flowers.
Ⓒ He wants more information.
Ⓓ He isn't sure the wind is strong enough to be effective.

9. **How can honeybees be compared to the bees native to the area?**
Ⓐ They are less expensive than native bees.
Ⓑ They are larger than native bees.
Ⓒ They aren't as efficient at pollinating as native bees.
Ⓓ They pollinate plants faster than native bees.

10. **Listen again to part of the lecture. Then answer the question.**

> M Well, that's it for pollination. But what happens after a plant is fertilized? Well, please read pages 80-110 tonight so you can get some background information on tomorrow's class.

Why does the professor say this:

> M But what happens after a plant is fertilized?

Ⓐ To develop ideas for discussion in the next class
Ⓑ To talk about how pollination fertilizes plants
Ⓒ To inform students what they will be reading about for homework
Ⓓ To describe the process that creates new plants

11. **How does the professor conclude the lecture?**
Ⓐ By assigning homework and reviewing the lecture
Ⓑ By answering questions about pollination
Ⓒ By telling students to read about vegetables
Ⓓ By giving a homework assignment and asking a question

8. **넓은 지역의 수분 매개체로서의 바람에 관한 교수의 태도는 어떠한가?**
Ⓐ 바람이 최선의 방법이라고 생각한다.
Ⓑ 바람이 꽃들에게 더 낫다고 생각한다.
Ⓒ 더 많은 정보를 필요로 한다.
Ⓓ 바람이 효과적일 만큼 강한지 확실치 않다.

9. **꿀벌은 그 지역의 토종 벌과 어떻게 비교되는가?**
Ⓐ 토종 벌보다 덜 비싸다.
Ⓑ 토종 벌보다 더 크다.
Ⓒ 수분시킬 때 토종 벌만큼 효율적이지 못하다.
Ⓓ 토종 벌보다 식물들을 더 빨리 수분시킨다.

10. **강의의 일부를 다시 듣고 질문에 답하시오.**

> 남 음, 이것으로 수분에 대한 이야기를 마치도록 하죠. 그런데 식물이 수분된 뒤에는 어떤 일이 일어날까요? 내일 수업에 대한 배경 지식을 좀 얻을 수 있도록 오늘 밤에 80~110페이지를 읽도록 하세요.

교수는 왜 이렇게 말하는가:

> 남 그런데 식물이 수분된 뒤에는 어떤 일이 일어날까요?

Ⓐ 다음 수업의 토론에 관한 생각을 진전시키려고
Ⓑ 수분이 식물을 어떻게 수정시키는지 이야기하려고
Ⓒ 학생들에게 과제로 읽게 될 내용을 알려주려고
Ⓓ 새로운 식물을 만드는 과정을 설명하려고

11. **교수는 강의를 어떻게 마무리하는가?**
Ⓐ 과제를 주고 강의를 복습하면서
Ⓑ 수분에 관한 질문에 답하면서
Ⓒ 학생들에게 채소에 관해 읽어보라고 말하면서
Ⓓ 과제를 주고 질문을 하면서

어휘 reproduction n 번식 | seed n 씨앗 | extend v 확장하다, 넓히다 | organ n 기관 | pollination n 수분 | occur v 발생하다 | self-pollination n 자가 수분 | cross-pollination n 타화 수분 | transfer n 이동, 전이 | pollen n 꽃가루 | stamen n 수술 | stigma n 암술머리 | fertilize v 수정하다 | structure n 구조 | sticky adj 끈적거리는 | pistil n 암술 | benefit n 장점, 이점 | drawback n 단점 | genetic adj 유전의 | disease n 질병 | adaptation n 적응 | suffer v 고통 받다 | insect n 곤충 | mammal n 포유류 | by accident 우연히, 사고로 | intentionally adv 의도적으로 | nectar n (꽃의) 꿀 | moth n 나방 | hummingbird n 벌새 | function v 기능하다 | identify v 식별하다 | visually adv 시각적으로 | attract v 끌어들이다, 유인하다 | lend v 주다, 부여하다 | vast adj 막대한 | scatter v 흩어지다, 뿌리다 | decrease v 감소하다 | orchard n 과수원 | steadily adv 꾸준히 | significantly adv 크게 | inefficiency n 비능률 | sheer adj (크기나 양을 강조하여) 순전한 | massive adj 거대한 | population n 개체수

Man: Student | Woman: Professor

[12-17] Listen to part of a discussion in a business class.

W Hello again! So, last week we were talking about marketing. 12 Today, we are going to look closer at one of the parts of marketing, advertising. Many people seem to think that "marketing" and "advertising" are the same, but they're not. Advertising is simply one of the many parts of marketing. So, what exactly is advertising then? 13 It is techniques and practices used to inform the public about something in order to get them to respond in a certain way. Confusing? Well, let me put it this way... it's a type of communication with a controlled message, for a purpose.

For over 2,000 years, advertising has been used to inform, educate, and motivate people about issues like AIDS and the environment, um... political beliefs, religious recruitment, and so on. Most commonly, though, advertisers are looking for profit... and advertising can be expensive! Believe it or not, the average cost of a single 30-second commercial spot during the Super Bowl is, like, 2.7 million dollars! If you bought a laptop for a thousand dollars, you could buy 2,700 laptops for the same price it costs to have a 30-second commercial during the Super Bowl... wow, huh?

M Excuse me, professor, you said 2.7 million dollars? Isn't that crazy? Why would a company spend millions of dollars on 30 seconds of advertising?

W Well, that's a great question, 12 and it gets us into what I really wanted to talk about, the 4 M's of advertising. Let me talk about that for a second, and I think you will find the answer, okay?

M Sure, thanks.

W So, last week we talked about the 4 P's of marketing, right? Place, product, price, and promotion. 12 Now, let's look at the 4 M's of advertising... the four most important factors companies consider when trying to plan successful advertisements: market, media, money, and message. 14 OK, first... market. Companies do research on consumers and try to figure out who their target consumer is and what the need is for the product. They think about the age and gender of who will buy their product. Knowing who to attract is very important. If a company is trying to sell diapers, its target audience would be mothers. And, to determine the need for the product, they look at results from phone surveys or mail in questionnaires, because it's usually the mothers who answer them.

남자: 학생 | 여자: 교수

경영학 수업 중 토론의 일부를 들으시오.

여 안녕하세요! 지난 시간에는 마케팅에 관해 이야기했죠. 12 오늘은 마케팅의 한 부분인 광고에 대해 자세히 살펴볼 겁니다. 많은 사람들이 '마케팅'과 '광고'를 같은 것으로 생각하는 것 같아요. 하지만 그렇지 않습니다. 광고는 마케팅의 많은 부분 중 하나일 뿐이죠. 그럼, 광고란 정확히 무엇을 말할까요? 13 대중이 특정 방식으로 반응하도록 만들기 위해서 어떤 것에 관한 정보를 주는 데 사용된 기술이나 행위를 말합니다. 복잡한가요? 음, 이렇게 이야기해 볼 수 있어요... 광고란 어떤 목적을 위해 통제된 메시지를 전달하는 소통 형식이라고 말이죠.

2천 년이 넘는 시간 동안 광고는 사람들에게 AIDS나 환경과 같은 문제들, 음... 정치 이념, 종교 집단의 모집 등에 관한 정보를 주고, 교육을 시키고, 동기를 부여하는 데 사용되어 왔습니다. 물론 일반적으로 광고주는 이윤을 추구하며... 광고에는 많은 비용이 들 수 있습니다! 믿기 힘들겠지만, 슈퍼볼 중계방송 동안 방영되는 30초짜리 상업 광고 하나에 평균 2백7십만 달러의 비용이 들어갑니다! 만일 여러분이 천 달러짜리 노트북을 산다면, 슈퍼볼을 중계할 때 방영되는 30초짜리 광고에 드는 비용으로 2천7백 대의 노트북을 살 수 있는 겁니다... 대단하죠, 정말?

남 잠시만요 교수님, 2백7십만 달러라고 하셨어요? 너무 심하지 않나요? 왜 기업은 30초짜리 광고에 수백만 달러를 소비하는 거죠?

여 음, 좋은 질문이에요, 12 그리고 제가 오늘 말하려고 하는 광고의 4M과 관련이 있어요. 조금만 이야기하면 그 답을 찾을 수 있을 거예요, 괜찮죠?

남 물론이죠, 감사합니다.

여 자, 지난주에 마케팅의 4P에 대해서 이야기했죠? 위치, 상품, 가격, 그리고 홍보. 12 이제 광고의 4M에 대해서 알아봅시다... 이건 성공적인 광고를 기획할 때 기업이 고려해야 하는 네 가지 중요한 요소로서, 시장, 매체, 비용, 그리고 메시지를 말합니다. 14 자, 우선... 시장에 대해서 얘기해 봅시다. 기업은 소비자에 대해 조사를 하고, 목표 소비자가 누구인지, 상품에 대해 어떤 수요가 있는지를 알아내려 노력합니다. 기업은 누가 물건을 구입할 것인지 그 성별과 연령에 대해 생각합니다. 누구를 끌어모아야 할지 아는 것은 매우 중요합니다. 만일 기업이 기저귀를 판매하려고 하면, 목표 대상은 어머니들일 것입니다. 그리고 상품에 대한 수요를 파악하기 위해 전화 설문이나 우편 설문의 결과를 조사할 것입니다. 왜냐하면 그 질문에 답변을 주는 사람은 대개 어머니일 테니 말이죠.

OK, the second M is media. Media is the way that the company will present the message, like, uh... commercials, magazines, internet popups, and you know, stuff like that. **15** So, they calculate which form of media will be most successful. Like... if a company is selling teaching supplies to young teachers in their 20s or in their early 30s, ads should be put into magazines for young teachers, not for old ones, right? They want to use the right media for their target consumer.

M So, in the Super Bowl, the target consumer would be uh... sports fans? And they use commercials during the Super Bowl because so many sports fans watch it?

W Exactly! Because... think of the products: beer, sports drinks and soda, chips, cars... products that average, young to middle-aged people want. **16** And, to answer the other question about why they should spend millions of dollars for those ads, let's look at the third M... money. Companies ask themselves, "Will the cost of the advertisement be a good investment?" So, advertisers have to consider the right time for ads. For instance, ads for sports items in weekend magazines aren't so good because their target consumers tend to go on weekend retreats or leaves, not read magazines. But... to put an ad on during the Super Bowl, worldwide... that's like... well, I'm sure it's over a hundred million viewers just in the U.S.! Do you think it's worth it?

M Yeah, I guess so! That's a lot of people!

W Definitely. Once the company has looked at the other three parts, they have to come up with a way to promote the product that is interesting and memorable, and think about what kind of message it sends... the fourth M, the message. Here's a funny example for you: when a soup shop owner gave out socks to customers for a sales promotion, total sales decreased instead of increased because customers associated the soup with feet. And who wants soup that reminds them of smelly feet? Bad message, right? So, they have to find the right message. **17** OK, so who can tell me again what the 4M's of advertising are?

자, 두 번째 M은 매체입니다. 매체는 상업 광고, 잡지, 인터넷 팝업 등과 같이 기업이 메시지를 전달하는 방식을 말합니다. **15** 따라서 기업은 어떤 형태의 매체가 가장 효율적일지 계산합니다. 만일 기업이 20대나 30대 초반의 젊은 선생님들에게 강의에 필요한 용품을 팔려고 한다면, 광고는 나이든 선생님이 아니라 젊은 선생님을 대상으로 하는 잡지에 게재되어야 합니다. 맞죠? 기업은 목표로 하는 소비자에 맞게 매체를 사용하기를 원합니다.

남 그럼, 슈퍼볼에서 목표로 하는 소비자는 어... 스포츠 팬들이겠네요? 그리고 기업은 많은 스포츠 팬들이 그것을 볼 테니까 슈퍼볼이 방영되는 기간 동안 상업 광고를 하고요?

여 그렇죠! 왜냐하면... 상품을 생각해 보세요. 맥주, 스포츠 음료, 탄산 음료, 감자칩, 자동차... 젊은이들부터 중년들까지 보통 사람들이 좋아하는 품목들이죠. **16** 그리고 왜 기업이 광고비로 수백만 달러를 써야 하는지에 대한 답을 얻기 위해 세 번째 M인... 비용에 대해 알아봅시다. 기업은 다음과 같이 스스로에게 묻습니다. "광고에 들이는 비용이 좋은 투자가 될까?" 그래서 광고주들은 광고를 하기에 적합한 시기를 고려해야 합니다. 예를 들어, 스포츠 용품 광고가 주말 잡지에 실리는 것은 좋지 않습니다. 왜냐하면 그 제품들의 목표 소비자들은 주말에 잡지를 읽지 않고 여행을 가거나 놀러 가는 경향이 있기 때문입니다. 하지만 슈퍼볼이 방영되는 동안 광고를 하면, 전 세계적으로... 그건 마치... 음, 미국에서만도 분명 수억 명의 시청자들이 있을 겁니다! 그럴 만한 가치가 있다는 생각이 드나요?

남 네, 그럴 것 같아요! 그건 정말 많은 수의 사람들이니까요!

여 분명 그렇죠. 일단 회사가 이러한 세 가지 부분을 고려한 뒤에는 흥미롭고 기억에 남는 상품 홍보 방법을 생각해내야 하며, 어떤 메시지를 전달할지에 대해서도 생각해야 합니다. 바로 네 번째 M인 메시지입니다. 여기 재미있는 예가 있어요. 수프 가게 주인이 판매 홍보를 위해 손님들에게 양말을 나눠주었을 때, 총 매출은 증가하지 않고 오히려 감소했습니다. 손님들이 수프와 발을 연결해서 생각했기 때문입니다. 냄새 나는 발을 떠오르게 하는 수프를 누가 좋아할까요? 잘못된 메시지죠? 그래서 기업은 올바른 메시지를 찾아야 합니다. **17** 자, 그럼 누가 광고의 4M이 무엇인지 다시 말해볼 수 있을까요?

12. What aspects of advertising is the professor mainly discussing?

Ⓐ The costs and benefits of advertising

Ⓑ The types of messages that companies try to send through advertisements

12. 교수는 광고의 어떤 면을 주로 이야기하고 있는가?

Ⓐ 광고의 비용과 장점

Ⓑ 기업이 광고를 통해 전달하고자 하는 메시지의 유형

Ⓒ The main elements companies must consider when planning advertisements
Ⓓ The four types of advertising media

13. Listen again to part of the discussion. Then answer the question.

> W It is techniques and practices used to inform the public about something in order to get them to respond in a certain way. Confusing? Well, let me put it this way... it's a type of communication with a controlled message, for a purpose.

Why does the professor say this:

> W Confusing? Well, let me put it this way...

Ⓐ She does not think the students need another definition.
Ⓑ She wants to give a definition that is a little easier to understand.
Ⓒ She feels like the students should be able to understand the first definition.
Ⓓ She's trying to say that the first definition is not confusing.

14. What is the market in the 4 M's of advertising?

Ⓐ The method used to show the advertisements
Ⓑ Who will buy the product and how much they need it
Ⓒ The number of people who will see the TV commercial
Ⓓ The style the company uses to make the ad

15. According to the professor, how is market related to media?

Ⓐ Market and target consumers are more important than the media form.
Ⓑ The media that is chosen is more important than the market.
Ⓒ The target customer must be established before determining which form of media to use.
Ⓓ The media message should be chosen first, then companies can decide whom to target.

16. Why is time important in terms of the third M, 'money'?

Ⓐ It gets the most viewership and maximizes the number of potential consumers.
Ⓑ It reminds existing consumers of a certain product again to purchase.
Ⓒ It can estimate the number of people who watch the Super Bowl.

Ⓒ 광고를 기획할 때 기업이 고려해야 하는 주된 요소들
Ⓓ 광고 매체의 4가지 유형

13. 토론의 일부를 다시 듣고 질문에 답하시오.

> 여 대중이 특정 방식으로 반응하도록 만들기 위해서 어떤 것에 관한 정보를 주는 데 사용된 기술이나 행위를 말합니다. 복잡한가요? 음, 이렇게 이야기해 볼 수 있어요... 광고란 어떤 목적을 위해 통제된 메시지를 전달하는 소통 형식이라고 말이죠.

교수는 왜 이렇게 말하는가:

> 여 복잡한가요? 음, 이렇게 이야기해볼 수 있어요...

Ⓐ 학생들이 단어의 다른 정의를 필요로 한다고 생각하지 않는다.
Ⓑ 이해하기 더 쉬운 정의를 말해주려고 한다.
Ⓒ 학생들이 첫 번째 정의를 이해해야 한다고 생각한다.
Ⓓ 첫 번째 정의가 복잡하지 않다고 말하려 한다.

14. 광고의 4 M에서 시장은 무엇인가?

Ⓐ 광고를 보여주기 위해 사용되는 방법
Ⓑ 누가 상품을 구입할 것이며 그것을 얼마나 필요로 하는지
Ⓒ 텔레비전 광고를 보는 사람들의 수
Ⓓ 기업이 광고를 만드는 데 사용하는 방식

15. 교수에 따르면, 시장은 매체와 어떻게 관련되었는가?

Ⓐ 시장과 목표 소비자는 매체의 형태보다 더 중요하다.
Ⓑ 선택된 매체는 시장보다 더 중요하다.
Ⓒ 사용할 매체를 결정하기 전에 목표 소비자가 정해져야 한다.
Ⓓ 매체의 메시지가 먼저 결정되어야 하고, 기업은 그 뒤에 누구를 목표로 할지 정할 수 있다.

16. 시간은 왜 세 번째 M인 '돈'의 개념에서 중요한가?

Ⓐ 가장 많은 시청자를 모으며 잠재 고객의 수를 최대화한다.
Ⓑ 기존 고객에게 다시 구매할 특정 상품을 상기시킨다.
Ⓒ 슈퍼볼을 보는 사람들의 수를 추산할 수 있다.

Ⓓ It attracts different groups of people who can affect a company's sales.

Ⓓ 회사의 영업에 영향을 주는 다양한 무리의 사람들을 끌어들인다.

17. How does the professor conclude the discussion?

Ⓐ By repeating the main topic of the lecture

Ⓑ By giving several examples of the main topic

Ⓒ By asking the students if they can remember something

Ⓓ By reminding the students the most important example of the lecture

17. 교수는 어떻게 토론을 마무리하는가?

Ⓐ 강의의 주제를 반복하면서

Ⓑ 주제의 몇 가지 예시들을 들면서

Ⓒ 학생들에게 무언가를 기억할 수 있는지 물으면서

Ⓓ 강의에서 가장 중요한 예시를 상기시키면서

어휘 marketing n 마케팅 | advertising n 광고 | exactly adv 정확히 | technique n 기법, 기술 | practice n 행위, 관행 | inform v 알리다 | respond v 반응하다 | confusing adj 혼란스러운, 헷갈리는 | communication n 소통 | controlled adj 통제된 | purpose n 목적 | educate v 교육하다 | motivate v 동기를 부여하다 | environment n 환경 | political adj 정치적인 | belief n 신념 | religious adj 종교적인 | recruitment n 모집 | profit n 이익, 이윤 | average cost 평균 비용 | commercial n 광고 | promotion n 홍보 | factor n 요인 | consider v 고려하다 | consumer n 소비자 | attract v 끌어들이다 | diaper n 기저귀 | determine v 알아내다 | result n 결과 | questionnaire n 설문지 | calculate v 계산하다 | investment n 투자 | retreat n 휴양(여행), 은둔, 피난 | promote v 홍보하다 | memorable adj 기억할 만한 | decrease v 감소하다 | associate *A* with *B* A와 B를 연결하다, 연관 짓다 | smelly adj 냄새 나는

Speaking

I. Independent Task　Q1. 선택 말하기

Lesson 01 표현 익히기

Practice 1

본서 | P. 208

01. The old software ran very slowly whereas the new one seems to work at lightning speed.
02. I heard that the weather will be very different from today's weather.
03. Meanwhile, he decided to stop by a coffee shop while waiting for his friend to arrive.
04. I can still introduce him to you even though I don't know him as well as Bryan does.
05. Eventually, we decided to drop the project since we were short on materials.
06. In short, they need funding from the government to continue their research.
07. I could notice that he was sick since his face was unlike his usual one.
08. Despite having a difficult time, she tried to be patient with her new project.
09. After I ran into my old high school teacher, I thought the world is a small place after all.
10. In the meantime, we started to develop a new plan for the construction project.
11. Although it looks small, you will be able to see the kitchen area is in fact quite spacious.
12. At the bus station, I noticed that people waiting for the bus were dressed similarly.
13. After a 20-minute long pause, the match was able to begin at last.
14. The store clerk said that shops in the area do not accept credit cards unless otherwise noted.
15. However, it was announced that schools in the district will cancel classes for a snow day.
16. The meeting went on for an extra 30 minutes until both parties finally came to an agreement.
17. Since the road is currently under construction, everybody needs to make a detour.
18. I want to look at things on the positive side instead of just complaining about them.

Practice 2

본서 | P. 214

01. I don't mind going anywhere for my vacation as long as it is a quiet place.
02. Personally, I think the author's first book was more interesting than his most recent one.
03. I suppose I can spare some time to mow the lawn to help my parents.
04. I enjoy working out at the gym late at night because there is hardly anyone there.
05. I would rather choose a small bag than a big one since it is easy to carry around.
06. I'm more interested in astronomy since I liked watching stars when I was young.
07. After two weeks of practice, I was totally prepared for the public speech.
08. I agree with the idea partially because I have something better to suggest.
09. I prefer the second applicant because he is more experienced.

10. I like this house better than the first one because its backyard is much bigger.

11. I'm going to say I agree with the first statement because I grew up in a small city.

12. That is not necessarily true because enough evidence shows the result.

13. I need to know exactly when the performance starts to see if he is available.

14. What I mean is the company is going to spend more money on research and development.

Lesson 02 이유 제시하기

Practice

본서 P. 217

01

Students at many high schools are required to take art classes like music or painting in addition to academic courses, while others are not. Which do you think is better and why? Give reasons and examples to support your opinion.

많은 고등학교에서 학생들이 필수적으로 학교 수업에 더해 음악이나 미술 같은 예능 수업을 들어야 하는 반면, 그렇지 않은 학생들도 있다. 어느 쪽이 더 낫다고 생각하며 그 이유는 무엇인가? 당신의 의견을 뒷받침할 수 있는 이유와 예시를 제시하시오.

노트 정리 예시

선택 should be required

이유 1. help them become creative thinkers

예시·설명·근거
- creativity is an essential skill
- can be applied to any subject

2. allow for self-expression

예시·설명·근거
- explore their mind
- gain self-esteem

필수가 되어야 함

1. 창의적인 생각을 하는 사람이 되게 도와줌
- 창의력은 필수적인 기술임
- 어떤 분야에도 적용될 수 있음

2. 자기 표현을 할 수 있게 해줌
- 자신의 정신 세계를 탐구함
- 자부심을 갖게 됨

어휘 require v 요구하다 | creative adj 창의성 있는 | creativity n 창의력 | essential adj 필수적인 | apply v 적용하다 | self-expression n 자기 표현 | explore v 탐구하다, 탐험하다 | self-esteem n 자부심, 자존감

02

Do you agree or disagree with the following statement? Video games can actually be beneficial to children. Please include specific examples in your explanation.

당신은 다음 진술에 동의하는가 아니면 동의하지 않는가? 비디오 게임은 사실 아이들에게 도움이 될 수 있다. 구체적인 예시를 포함해 설명하시오.

노트 정리 예시

선택 agree

이유 1. improve many skills

예시·설명·근거
- visual skill, problem solving, creativity
- accomplish many different objectives

2. enjoy competition

예시·설명·근거
- world is a relay of competitions
- experience winning and losing in games

동의함

1. 여러 가지 기술을 향상시켜줌
- 시각적 기술, 문제 해결, 창의력
- 여러 가지 다른 목표들을 달성함

2. 경쟁을 즐기게 해줌
- 세상은 경쟁의 연속
- 게임을 통해 이기고 지는 것을 경험함

어휘 beneficial adj 이익이 되는 I improve v 향상시키다 I visual adj 시각의 I problem solving 문제 해결 I creativity n 창의성, 창의력 I accomplish v 이루다, 성취하다 I objective n 목적, 목표 I competition n 경쟁 I relay n 릴레이

03

While attending university, some students only take classes that focus on the specific career path they have chosen, whereas others prefer to take a wide variety of courses that provide them with broader knowledge. Which do you think is better and why?

대학교를 다니는 동안, 어떤 학생들은 그들이 선택한 특정한 진로에 초점을 맞춘 강의만 수강하는 반면, 다른 학생들은 좀 더 폭넓은 지식을 제공하는 다양한 분야의 강의를 수강한다. 당신은 어느 쪽이 더 낫다고 생각하며 그 이유는 무엇인가?

노트 정리 예시

선택 wide variety of courses — 다양한 분야의 강의

이유 1. people are not sure at first — 1. 처음엔 확신이 서지 않음

예시·설명·근거

- chance to find out what they are passionate about — 자기가 열정을 느끼는 분야를 찾아낼 기회

2. open up many opportunities — 2. 많은 기회를 만들어 줌

예시·설명·근거

- stay competitive → obtain knowledge in various fields — 경쟁력을 유지함 → 여러 분야에서 지식을 쌓음
- utilize many different skills — 여러 가지 다른 기술을 활용하게 됨

어휘 attend v (학교에) 다니다 I specific adj 특정한, 구체적인 I career path 진로 I variety n 다양함 I broad adj 폭넓은 I knowledge n 지식 I passionate adj 열정적인 I opportunity n 기회 I competitive adj 경쟁력 있는 I field n 분야 I utilize v 활용하다, 이용하다

04

Do you agree or disagree with the following statement? Students should gain some experience in a field before they can complete a degree in it.

당신은 다음 진술에 동의하는가 아니면 동의하지 않는가? 학생들은 한 분야에서 학위를 따기 전에 실제 현장에서 경험을 쌓아야 한다.

노트 정리 예시

선택 agree — 동의함

이유 1. better prepared in the workplace — 1. 업무 현장에 대한 준비를 더 잘하게 됨

예시·설명·근거

- already have experiences — 이미 경험을 갖고 있음
- capable in dealing with different situations — 다양한 상황에 대처할 수 있음

2. test whether to pursue the particular field — 2. 특정 분야를 계속 밀고 나갈지 시험해볼 수 있음

예시·설명·근거

- before it is too late — 너무 늦기 전에
- save time and money → switch major — 시간과 돈을 절약함 → 전공을 변경함

어휘 experience n 경험 I complete v 완수하다, 끝내다 I degree n 학위 I prepare v 준비하다 I situation n 상황 I pursue v 추구하다, 밀고 나가다 I particular adj 특정한 I field n 분야 I switch v 바꾸다 I major n 전공

Lesson 03 문장으로 말하기

Practice

본서 P. 220

01

For academic success, some students like to take courses online. Others prefer to study in traditional courses on campus. Which do you prefer and why? Include details and examples to support your explanation.

학업적 성공을 위해 어떤 학생들은 온라인 수업을 듣는 것을 좋아한다. 다른 학생들은 학교에서 전통적인 방식의 수업을 듣는 것을 선호한다. 당신은 어느 쪽을 선호하며 그 이유는 무엇인가? 당신의 설명을 뒷받침할 수 있는 세부 사항과 예를 포함하시오.

예시 답변

I think I'd have to say that I prefer to take online courses.
The first reason is because it's very convenient. To be more specific, online courses provide me with easy access. If there's any computer device with an Internet connection, I can easily access my online lectures anywhere and anytime.
Another reason is that it's also economical. For example, a few years ago, I had a chance to take some online courses. Back then, I had to work and study at the same time, so I thought taking online courses would be pretty convenient. I realized that it was not only convenient but also more economical in terms of lower tuition fees and the time that I saved since I didn't physically have to go to school. So, for these reasons, I prefer to take online courses.

어휘 traditional adj 전통적인 | convenient adj 편리한 | access n 접근, 이용 | device n 장치 | connection n 연결 | lecture n 강의 | economical adj 경제적인 | realize v 깨닫다 | tuition fee 등록금 | physically adv 물리적으로

02

Would you rather study in a large class or a small class? Explain your answer and include details and examples to support your explanation.

당신은 규모가 큰 수업에서 공부하는 것을 선호하는가 아니면 작은 수업에서 공부하는 것을 선호하는가? 당신의 설명을 뒷받침할 수 있는 세부 사항과 예를 포함해 답변하시오.

예시 답변

I would rather study in a small class.
That's because there is a lot more individual attention from the professor in a small class. I've taken large classes before, and the professor didn't even know my name. I think it makes a class a lot better when the teachers know a little bit about the students.
Also, in a small class, students have more chances to participate in the class. For example, they can ask questions and get involved in class discussions, which can definitely help students to develop strong communication skills. This will eventually add to their whole learning experience at school.

어휘 individual adj 개인의 | attention n 관심, 집중 | participate v 참여하다 | discussion n 논의, 토론 | definitely adv 확실히, 분명히 | communication skill 의사소통 능력 | eventually adv 결국 | experience n 경험

03

Some universities require first-year students to live on campus in dormitories. Other universities allow first-year students to live off-campus. Which policy do you think is better for first-year students and why? Include details and examples to support your explanation.

어떤 대학교에서는 1학년 학생들이 교내 기숙사에서 살 것을 요구한다. 다른 대학교에서는 1학년 학생들이 학교 밖에서 사는 것을 허용한다. 당신은 어떤 정책이 1학년 학생들에게 더 낫다고 생각하며 그 이유는 무엇인가? 당신의 설명을 뒷받침할 수 있는 세부 사항과 예를 포함하시오.

예시 답변

I think that, for first-year students, it's much better to live on campus in a dorm.
The main reason is that it can help them fit in at the university. Since they're on campus, it's easier to make new friends. They can also get involved in clubs or group activities more easily.
Another good reason is that it is less stressful to live in a dorm because there are no chores to take care of. If it's their first time living alone, it could be really stressful as they would have to do the cooking and cleaning all by themselves. Living in a dorm, they wouldn't have as many domestic responsibilities.

어휘 dormitory(dorm) n 기숙사 I stressful adj 스트레스가 많은 I chore n 심부름, 해야 할 일 I domestic adj 집안의, 가정의 I responsibility n 책임

04

Would you rather organize a trip yourself or take a trip organized by a tour company and why? Include details and examples to support your explanation.

당신은 스스로 여행을 계획하겠는가 아니면 여행사에서 기획한 여행을 가겠는가, 그리고 그 이유는 무엇인가? 당신의 설명을 뒷받침할 수 있는 세부 사항과 예를 포함하시오.

예시 답변

I would rather organize a trip myself than take a trip organized by a tour company.
That is because I like to be spontaneous when on vacation, and I like to be able to change my plans if I hear of something new or better than my original plan. For example, if I visited a new city, and found out that there was a festival I had not expected, I would rather go there than stick to my original plans.
But if I were with a tour company, I would probably have to give up going to that festival and follow their plans. So, if I organize a trip myself, I don't have to be restricted by time, and I might enjoy my trip more.

어휘 organize v 계획하다, 조직하다 I spontaneous adj 즉흥적인 I original adj 원래의 I festival n 축제 I expect v 예상하다 I stick to 고수하다 I restrict v 제한하다

II. Integrated Task Q2. 읽고 듣고 말하기: 대학 생활

Lesson 01 표현 익히기

Practice 본서 P. 229

01. One reason is that the funding should be used to purchase new equipment.

02. I believe that student tutors will be able to help other students well.

03. I have to do some additional research at the library in order to finish my essay.

04. According to the announcement, the school festival will feature some local musicians.

05. It is beneficial to the freshmen students who are not familiar with the university yet.

06. He suggests that cutting the budget will be a bad move for the university.

07. She disagrees with the idea that students need more equipment at the gym.

08. Therefore, as of May 1st, renovations of parking lot A will begin.

09. He thinks the change is a good idea because it will provide cleaner air.

10. It is unnecessary to require everyone to attend the seminar.

Lesson 02 읽기 정리

Practice

본서 | P. 231

01

읽기 지문&해석

Dear Editor,

The center of our campus is currently taken up by a large parking lot, which detracts from the university as a whole. I propose that this parking lot be removed and replaced with a park. Since all of the administration buildings have their own small parking lots, and large parking lots have been built both north and south of campus for student use, I think that the central lot has become unnecessary. Replacing the asphalt with grass and trees would not only make the area more aesthetically pleasing, it would also make the air cleaner.

- Clara Bowes

편집자님께,

우리 학교 중앙은 현재 커다란 주차장이 차지하고 있는데, 이는 전체적인 대학교의 모습에서 동떨어져 있습니다. 저는 이 주차장을 없애고 공원으로 대체하는 것을 제안합니다. 모든 행정 건물에는 각기 작은 주차장이 있고, 학생들이 사용하도록 교정 북쪽과 남쪽에 모두 커다란 주차장들이 지어져 있으므로 중앙 주차장은 불필요해졌다고 생각합니다. 아스팔트를 풀과 나무로 바꾸는 것은 이 구역을 더 미학적으로 만족스럽게 만들어 줄 뿐만 아니라 공기도 더 깨끗하게 해 줄 것입니다.

– 클라라 보우스

노트 정리 예시

주제 remove central parking lot → change to park
- central one = unnecessary
- park = clean air

중앙 주차장 없애기 → 공원으로 바꾸기
– 중앙 주차장 = 필요 없음
– 공원 = 깨끗한 공기

▶ Question: What does the student propose?

학생은 무엇을 제안하는가?

예시 답변

The student proposes the university remove the central parking lot and change it to a park because the central parking lot is unnecessary. In addition, the park will provide cleaner air.

학생은 대학이 중앙 주차장을 없애고 공원으로 바꿀 것을 제안하는데, 그것은 중앙 주차장이 필요 없기 때문이다. 게다가 공원은 더 깨끗한 공기를 제공할 것이다.

어휘 currently adv 현재 | detract v 가치가 떨어지다, 주의를 딴 데로 돌리다 | remove v 없애다 | replace v 대체하다 | administration n 행정 | aesthetically adv 미학적으로 | pleasing adj 만족스러운, 즐거운

02

읽기 지문&해석

Dormitories and Classrooms Renovation

Due to the recent increase in complaints regarding cold dormitory rooms and classrooms, the university's board of directors has decided to renovate many buildings on campus. As heating costs have risen, we will be replacing the windows in some buildings and upgrading the climate control systems in others. To take full advantage of warm weather, this process will begin in April and continue through the summer. Classes in affected buildings will have to be relocated, and a list of

기숙사와 교실 보수 공사

추운 기숙사 방과 교실에 관한 불만 사항이 최근 늘었기 때문에 대학교 이사회에서는 교내 많은 건물들을 보수 공사하기로 결정했습니다. 난방비가 상승했기 때문에 일부 건물에 있는 창문을 교체하고, 다른 건물에는 실내 온도 조절 시스템을 업그레이드할 것입니다. 따뜻한 날씨를 충분히 이용하기 위해 이 과정은 4월에 시작되어 여름 내내 계속될 예정입니다. 영향을 받는 건물에서 진행되는 수업들은 장소를 옮길 것이

affected courses can be found on the university website. The dormitory improvements will not begin until June, so student accommodations will be unaffected.

며, 영향을 받는 수업들의 목록은 대학교 웹사이트에서 볼 수 있습니다. 기숙사 개선 작업은 6월까지는 시작되지 않을 것이므로 학생들 숙소는 영향을 받지 않을 것입니다.

노트 정리 예시

주제 dorm/classroom renov.
- heating cost: replace windows/upgrade climate control system
- class: relocate/dorm: students won't be affected

기숙사/교실 보수 공사
– 난방비: 창문 교체/실내 온도 조절 시스템 업그레이드
– 수업: 이동/기숙사: 학생들 영향 없음

▶ Question: **What has the university's board of directors decided to do?**

대학교 이사회는 무엇을 시행하기로 결정했는가?

예시 답변

The university is going to renovate dormitories and classrooms. They are going to replace windows and upgrade climate control systems. Therefore, classes will have to relocate. However, since dormitory improvements start later, students living in the dormitory will not be affected.

대학은 기숙사와 교실의 보수 공사를 할 것이다. 창문을 교체하고 실내 온도 조절 시스템을 업그레이드할 것이다. 따라서 수업들은 장소를 옮겨야 한다. 하지만 기숙사 개선 작업은 나중에 시작하므로 기숙사에 사는 학생들은 영향을 받지 않을 것이다.

어휘 dormitory n 기숙사 | renovation n 보수 공사, 수리 | recent adj 최근의 | increase n 증가 | complaint n 불평, 불만 사항 | board of directors 이사회 | replace v 대체하다 | climate n 기후 | affect v 영향을 주다 | relocate v 장소를 옮기다 | improvement n 개선 (작업), 개량, 향상 | accommodation n 숙소, 시설, 거처

03

읽기 지문&해석

Car Rental Program on Campus

The president of the university announced today that the school has formed a partnership with the car rental agency near campus on 8th Street. Since the campus is located on the east side of town, it is a long way for students to go downtown for shopping or entertainment. It is also difficult to travel outside of the city for weekend trips. This new partnership will help students move around more easily. Students will still have to pass the customary requirements to rent a vehicle, but if they present their university ID, they will receive a 50% discount on any rental.

교내 자동차 대여 프로그램

대학교 총장이 오늘 학교 근처 8번가에 있는 자동차 대여점과 제휴를 체결했다고 발표했습니다. 학교가 도시 동쪽에 자리 잡고 있기 때문에 학생들이 쇼핑이나 여흥을 위해 시내까지 가는 데 오래 걸립니다. 또한 주말 여행을 위해 도시 밖으로 나가는 것도 어렵습니다. 이 새로운 제휴는 학생들이 좀 더 쉽게 돌아다닐 수 있도록 도와줄 것입니다. 학생들은 차량을 빌리기 위해서 관례적인 필수 요건을 만족시켜야 하지만, 학생증을 제시할 경우 모든 대여에서 50퍼센트 할인을 받게 될 것입니다.

노트 정리 예시

주제 univ. partnership with car rental agency
- easy to go to downtown & travel outside of city
- univ. ID = 50% discount

대학교와 자동차 대여점의 제휴
– 시내 나가기 & 도시 밖으로 여행하기 쉬움
– 학생증 = 50퍼센트 할인

▶ Question: **What has the university announced?**

대학교 측은 무엇을 발표했는가?

예시 답변

The university has announced that they have formed a partnership with a car rental agency. This will make going to downtown and traveling outside of the city easier. Students need to present their school ID to get a 50 percent discount.

대학교 측은 자동차 대여점과 제휴를 맺었다고 발표했다. 이는 시내로 가는 것과 도시 밖으로 나가는 것을 더 쉽게 해줄 것이다. 학생들은 50퍼센트 할인을 받으려면 학생증을 제시해야 한다.

어휘 rental n 대여 I announce v 발표하다 I partnership n 제휴, 협력, 파트너십 I entertainment n 여흥, 놀이 I customary adj 관례적인 I requirement n 필수 요건 I vehicle n 차량 I discount n 할인

Lesson 03 듣기 정리

Practice

본서 I P. 235

01

듣기 지문&해석

M So, this young woman thinks that the central parking lot should be replaced with green space. Do you think this is a good idea? Many people park there, you know.

W As she pointed out, there are plenty of other places to park. The lecture halls and other school facilities are within walking distance whether you park north or south of campus.

M That's true. It's pretty unnecessary.

W Yes, there would be less traffic in the central area of the campus, so the air would be cleaner.

남 그래서 이 젊은 여성은 중앙 주차장이 녹지로 대체되어야 한다고 생각하는 거네. 넌 이게 좋은 생각이라고 생각하니? 많은 사람들이 그곳에 주차를 하잖아.

여 그녀가 지적했듯이 주차할 다른 곳들이 많아. 교정 북쪽에 주차를 하든 남쪽에 하든 강의실과 다른 학교 시설은 모두 걸어갈 수 있는 거리에 있어.

남 그건 맞아. 상당히 불필요해.

여 그래, 학교 중심부의 교통량이 더 적어질 테니까 공기가 더 깨끗해질 거야.

노트 정리 예시

주제 central parking lot → replace with green space
woman: agree
- buildings are in walking distance from n/s parking lots
- less traffic in central campus area = clean air

중앙 주차장 → 녹지로 대체
여자: 동의함
– 건물들이 북쪽/남쪽 주차장에서 걸어갈 수 있는 거리에 있음
– 학교 중심부의 교통량이 적어짐 = 깨끗한 공기

▶ Question: **What does the woman think? Why does she think that way?**

여자는 뭐라고 생각하는가? 왜 그렇게 생각하는가?

예시 답변

The woman agrees with the idea that the central parking lot needs to be replaced with green space. First, people can use north and south parking lots as campus buildings are all within walking distance. Second, this will reduce the traffic in the central area, which will make the air cleaner.

여자는 중앙 주차장이 녹지로 대체되어야 한다는 의견에 동의한다. 먼저, 사람들은 학교 건물들이 모두 걸어갈 수 있는 거리에 있으므로 북쪽과 남쪽 주차장을 이용할 수 있다. 두 번째로, 이는 중심부의 교통량을 줄여 공기를 더 깨끗하게 해줄 것이다.

어휘 replace v 대체하다 I point out 가리키다, 지적하다 I facility n 시설

02

듣기 지문&해석

M Did you see the announcement regarding the renovations?
W I think it's a great idea and long overdue.
M Really? It sounds like a big inconvenience to me. Dormitories and classrooms will be closed, and classes will be relocated...
W You need to read this more carefully. It says that the dormitory renovations will not begin until after the semester is over. That means that the students will be gone. We will be back at home.
M Oh, I guess so. But, the lecture hall renovations will begin in April.
W That will inconvenience some people, but it will help them in the long run. Some of those classrooms are frigid in the winter. I have to keep my coat on when I am inside!

남 보수 공사에 관한 공지 봤니?
여 내가 보기엔 참 좋은 생각이고, 진작 했어야 하는 일인 것 같아.
남 그래? 나는 크게 불편할 것 같은데. 기숙사와 강의실이 폐쇄될 거고 수업은 다른 곳으로 옮겨질 거고…
여 이걸 좀 더 자세히 읽어봐. 기숙사 보수 공사는 학기가 끝나기 전까지는 시작하지 않는다고 되어 있어. 그건 학생들이 이미 떠난 후라는 뜻이야. 우리는 집에 돌아가 있을 거라고.
남 아, 그러네. 그래도 강의실 보수 공사는 4월에 시작되잖아.
여 그건 어떤 사람들에게는 불편이 될 수 있겠지만 장기적으로 보면 도움이 될 거야. 일부 강의실은 겨울에 정말 추워. 안에 있을 때도 코트를 입고 있어야 한다고!

노트 정리 예시

주제 renovation → dorms & classrooms close
woman: good idea!
- dorm renovations will begin after semester is over, does not affect students
- classrooms are so cold, renovation is good for the long run

보수 공사 → 기숙사 & 강의실 폐쇄
여자: 좋은 생각!
– 기숙사 보수 공사는 학기가 끝난 뒤 시작됨, 학생들에게 영향 안 줌
– 교실이 너무 추움, 보수 공사는 장기적으로 좋음

▶ Question: **What does the woman think? Why does she think that way?**

여자는 뭐라고 생각하는가? 왜 그렇게 생각하는가?

예시 답변

The woman thinks the renovations of dormitories and classrooms are a good idea. First, dormitory renovations will start only after the semester is over, so students are not going to be affected. Second, this will help students in the long run since the classrooms are indeed really cold.

여자는 기숙사와 교실 보수 공사가 좋은 생각이라고 생각한다. 먼저, 기숙사 보수 공사는 학기가 끝난 뒤에야 시작해서 학생들은 영향을 받지 않을 것이다. 두 번째로, 교실이 실제로 정말 춥기 때문에 이는 학생들에게 장기적으로 도움이 될 것이다.

어휘 overdue adj 진작 했어야 할, 이미 늦어진 | inconvenience v 불편하게 하다 n 불편함 | relocate v 장소를 옮기다, 이전하다 | carefully adv 주의 깊게 | frigid adj 몹시 추운

03

듣기 지문&해석

M According to the notice, the philosophy department is going to start providing breakfast for the students for their monthly meetings. It is at 9 A.M., so I usually don't have time for breakfast.
W Well, I often skip breakfast. The food they offer at the cafeteria on Saturday morning is terrible.

남 공지에 따르면, 철학과에서 월례 모임에 참석한 학생들에게 아침 식사 제공을 시작할 거래. 오전 9시라서 난 보통 아침 식사를 할 시간이 없거든.
여 음, 나는 자주 아침을 걸러. 토요일 아침에 구내 식당에서 제공하는 음식은 정말 끔찍하거든.

M True, but the food at the meeting should be good. They are going to get local restaurants to cater the events starting next month.

W That sounds nice, but wouldn't that be expensive?

M No, not really. The notice says that there will be no fee to attend. I guess they worked out some kind of deal with the restaurants.

남 맞아. 그렇지만 모임의 음식은 괜찮을 거야. 다음 달부터 행사의 음식을 제공하기 위해 지역 레스토랑들이 케이터링을 하게 할 거거든.

여 그거 괜찮은데, 하지만 비싸지 않을까?

남 그렇지는 않아. 공지에서 참석비가 없을 거라고 했으니까. 내 생각에는 학부에서 레스토랑들과 뭔가 협의를 했을 것 같아.

노트 정리 예시

주제 philosophy dept. → provide breakfast for monthly meeting
man: good idea
- food will be good
- no fee to pay

철학과 → 월례 모임에 아침 식사 제공
남자: 좋은 생각
– 음식이 맛있을 것이다
– 돈을 내지 않아도 된다

▶ Question: **What does the man think? Why does he think that way?**

남자는 뭐라고 생각하는가? 왜 그렇게 생각하는가?

예시 답변

The man thinks the philosophy department's decision to provide breakfast at their monthly meetings is a good idea. First, the food will be good since it will be from local restaurants. Second, students do not need to pay a fee to attend the meeting.

남자는 월례 모임에서 아침 식사를 제공한다는 철학과의 결정이 좋은 생각이라고 생각한다. 먼저, 음식은 지역 레스토랑에서 오는 것이므로 맛있을 것이다. 두 번째로, 학생들은 모임에 참가하기 위해 돈을 낼 필요가 없다.

어휘 notice n 공지 I philosophy n 철학 I provide v 제공하다 I monthly adj 매월의 I offer v 제공하다 I terrible adj 끔찍한 I cater v (사업으로 행사에) 음식을 공급하다 I fee n 비용 I attend v 참석하다 I deal n 거래, 협정

04

듣기 지문&해석

M This student is suggesting that we have this year's graduation ceremony outdoors. He suggested that we have the ceremony in front of Merchant Hall.

W Oh? Does he give any reasons?

M Yes, he says that the campus's beautiful buildings will be nice for the ceremony. He also mentioned that the gymnasium it is usually held in isn't big enough.

W I see. But, you don't seem to think that sounds like a good idea.

M No, not really. I don't think that the people in the audience will pay any attention to their surroundings once the event gets started. They will be focused on the speeches and the students. Besides, this year's graduating class is smaller than last year's. So, there won't be as many people there to watch the ceremony.

W Oh, I didn't realize that this year's class was that much smaller.

남 이 학생은 올해 졸업식을 야외에서 하자고 제안하고 있어. 졸업식을 머천트홀 앞에서 해야 한다고 제안했어.

여 오? 그가 이유를 말했니?

남 응, 학교의 아름다운 건물들이 졸업식에 좋을 거라고 했어. 또한 보통 졸업식이 열리는 체육관이 충분히 크지 않다고 언급했어.

여 그렇구나. 하지만 너는 이게 좋은 생각이라고 보지 않는 것 같네.

남 맞아, 그렇게 생각하지 않아. 나는 객석에 있는 사람들이 행사가 시작되면 주변에 관심을 두지 않을 거라고 생각해. 연설과 학생들에게 집중할 거야. 게다가 올해 졸업하는 학생 수는 작년보다 더 적어. 그래서 졸업식을 볼 사람들이 그만큼 많지 않을 거야.

여 아, 난 올해 졸업하는 학생들이 훨씬 더 적다는 건 몰랐어.

노트 정리 예시

주제 graduation ceremony → outdoors man: not a good idea - people will not care about the buildings - this year's graduation class is smaller	졸업식 → 야외 남자: 좋은 생각 아님 – 사람들은 건물에 신경 쓰지 않을 것임 – 올해의 졸업생 수는 더 적음

▶ Question: **What does the man think? Why does he think that way?**

남자는 뭐라고 생각하는가? 왜 그렇게 생각하는가?

예시 답변

The man thinks having a graduation ceremony outdoors is not a good idea. This is because people will not care about the buildings once the ceremony starts, and this year's graduation class is smaller than last year's.

남자는 야외에서 졸업식을 하는 것이 좋은 생각이 아니라고 생각한다. 왜냐하면 사람들은 졸업식이 시작되면 건물에 신경을 쓰지 않을 것이고, 올해의 졸업생 수는 작년보다 더 적기 때문이다.

어휘 graduation ceremony 졸업식 | mention ⓥ 언급하다 | pay attention to ~에 주의를 기울이다 | surroundings ⓝ 주변, 환경 | focus on ~에 집중하다 | speech ⓝ 연설 | realize ⓥ 깨닫다

05

듣기 지문&해석

W Hey, you know that car rental agency over on 8th Street? Have you ever rented a car there? According to this article in the school newspaper, they are going to offer discounts to university students. They started a partnership with our university.

M That sounds like yet another way for the university to get more money out of us.

W That's not the impression that I got. This says that the agency will give a 50 percent discount to any student who presents their student ID. They still have to qualify as a safe renter just like anyone else, though.

M Really? That's a big discount!

W Yes, and I think it's a really good idea. Think about when we want to go downtown to run errands or watch a movie. We always have to ride the bus. That takes so long that we only have enough time to go to 2 or 3 shops.

여 저기, 8번가에 있는 자동차 대여점 알지? 거기서 차 빌려본 적 있어? 학교 신문 기사에 따르면, 그 회사가 학교 학생들에게 할인을 제공할 거래. 우리 대학교랑 그 회사가 제휴를 시작했어.

남 학교가 우리한테서 돈을 더 뜯어내려는 또 다른 방법처럼 들리는데.

여 내가 받은 느낌은 그렇지 않아. 기사에 따르면 학생증을 제시하는 학생 누구에게나 50퍼센트 할인을 해준다고 되어 있어. 다른 사람들처럼 안전한 운전자 자격을 지녀야겠지만.

남 정말? 그건 진짜 큰 할인인데!

여 맞아, 그리고 나는 이게 정말 좋은 아이디어라고 생각해. 볼일이 있거나 영화를 보기 위해 시내에 나가야 할 때를 생각해 봐. 항상 버스를 타야 하지. 너무 오래 걸려서 상점 두세 군데밖에 갈 시간이 없어.

노트 정리 예시

주제 car rental agency → partnership with univ. woman: good idea! - 50% discount - going to downtown: bus takes so long	자동차 대여점 → 대학교와 제휴 여자: 좋은 생각! – 50퍼센트 할인 – 시내 가기: 버스는 너무 오래 걸림

▶ Question: **What does the woman think? Why does she think that way?**

여자는 뭐라고 생각하는가? 왜 그렇게 생각하는가?

예시 답변

The woman thinks the idea of the university, forming a partnership with a car rental agency, is a good idea. Because this will offer students a 50 percent discount, and going to downtown by bus takes a long time.

여자는 대학이 자동차 대여점과 제휴를 맺은 것이 좋은 생각이라고 생각한다. 왜냐하면 이는 학생들에게 50퍼센트 할인을 제공할 것이며, 버스로 시내에 가는 것은 너무 오래 걸리기 때문이다.

어휘 rent ⓥ 대여하다 I article ⓝ 기사 I discount ⓝ 할인 I impression ⓝ 인상 I present ⓥ 제시하다, 보이다 I qualify ⓥ 자격을 얻다, 유적격자가 되다 I errand ⓝ 할 일, 심부름

06

듣기 지문&해석

M Did you read the school newspaper today? A student is against the rule prohibiting beverages in the campus library. I think she is right. There are no water fountains in the library, and I often feel thirsty when I study there. Not only that, but she also points out that having coffee, tea, or some other drinks with caffeine is helpful when studying.

W I agree with that as well, but the student union building is next to the library. You can go to the cafeteria in that building. It's right there. And let's not forget the real reason why drinks are banned from the library. If a drink gets spilled, it could ruin a book, and some of the books in the library are very rare.

M Yes, but we aren't children, are we? The letter also points that out. The students are responsible adults.

W You cannot guarantee that. Accidents happen to everyone, no matter how mature they are. I still support the library's rule. If you need a drink, go outside.

남 오늘 학교 신문 읽었니? 어떤 학생이 학교 도서관에서 음료수를 금지하는 것에 반대하고 있어. 나는 그녀가 옳다고 생각해. 도서관에 식수대가 없고, 나는 거기서 공부할 때 자주 목이 말라. 그뿐 아니라, 그 학생은 커피나 차, 아니면 카페인이 들어 있는 다른 음료를 마시는 것은 공부할 때 도움이 된다는 점을 지적하고 있어.

여 나도 그 점에 동의해. 하지만 학생 회관이 도서관 옆에 있잖아. 그 건물에 있는 구내식당에 가면 돼. 바로 옆이니까. 그리고 도서관에서 음료가 금지된 진짜 이유를 잊으면 안 돼. 만약 음료를 엎지르면 책을 망가뜨릴 수도 있는데, 도서관에 있는 책 일부는 매우 진귀한 것들이야.

남 그래, 그렇지만 우리는 애들이 아니잖아? 편지도 그 점을 지적하고 있어. 학생들은 책임감 있는 성인들이야.

여 그건 보장할 수 없어. 사람들이 아무리 성숙해도 사고는 누구에게나 일어나니까. 나는 여전히 도서관의 규정을 지지해. 만약 마실 것이 필요하면 밖에 나가면 돼.

노트 정리 예시

주제 beverage in the campus library
woman: not a good idea
- cafeteria right outside
- accidents happen to everyone

학교 도서관 내의 음료
여자: 좋은 생각이 아님
– 구내식당이 바로 밖에 있음
– 사고는 누구에게나 일어남

▶ Question: **What does the woman think? Why does she think that way?**

여자는 뭐라고 생각하는가? 왜 그렇게 생각하는가?

예시 답변

The woman does not think being able to drink beverages in the library is a good idea. First, there is a cafeteria right next to the library. Second, spilling a drink could ruin a book and accidents can happen to anyone.

여자는 도서관 안에서 음료를 마실 수 있는 것은 좋은 생각이 아니라고 생각한다. 먼저, 도서관 바로 옆에 구내식당이 있다. 두 번째로, 음료를 쏟으면 책을 망가뜨릴 수 있고 사고는 누구에게나 일어날 수 있다.

어휘 prohibit v 금지하다 | beverage n 음료 | water fountain 식수대 | point out 지적하다 | caffeine n 카페인 | spill v 쏟다 | ruin v 망가뜨리다 | rare adj 진귀한, 보기 힘든 | guarantee v 보장하다 | mature adj 성숙한 | support v 지지하다

Lesson 04 정리해서 말하기

Practice 1

본서 | P. 240

01

읽기 지문&해석

Recreation Center Renovations

We are sorry to announce that the Recreation Center will be closed for the summer session, from June 1st to September 15th, for renovations. It has been more than ten years since the facility was built, and since then, the student population has expanded. The current Recreation Center is no longer able to accommodate the increasing number of students on campus, so the plans will include the expansion of the pool, gym, and weight room as well as the purchase of new weight and cardio machines. We apologize for any inconvenience this may cause you, and we hope to see you all in September!

레크리에이션 센터 보수 공사

보수 공사 때문에 6월 1일부터 9월 15일까지 여름 학기 동안 레크리에이션 센터가 폐쇄된다는 사실을 알려드리게 되어 유감스럽게 생각합니다. 이 시설이 건설된 지 10년이 넘었고, 그 이후로 학생 수가 늘어났습니다. 현재의 레크리에이션 센터는 학교의 증가하는 학생 수를 더 이상 수용할 수가 없으므로, 새 중량 운동 기구 및 심근 강화 운동 기구의 구입뿐만 아니라, 수영장, 체육관 및 체력 단련실의 확장 계획이 있습니다. 불편을 끼쳐드리는 점 죄송하게 생각하며, 9월에 모두 뵙기를 희망합니다!

어휘 renovation n 보수 공사, 수리 | expand v 확장되다 | no longer 더 이상 ~ 않는 | accommodate v 수용하다 | increase v 증가하다, 늘어나다 | weight room 체력 단련실 | weight n 역기 등의 중량 운동 기구 | cardio n 심장 강화 운동 | apologize v 사과하다

읽기 – 노트 정리 예시

주제 recreation center renovations
- close Jun 1 ~ Sep 15 for renovations
- expansion: pool, gym, etc.

레크리에이션 센터 보수 공사
– 6월 1일~9월 15일까지 보수 공사를 위해 폐쇄
– 확장: 수영장, 체육관 등

Now listen to two students talking about the announcement.

이제 공지에 대해 이야기하는 두 학생의 대화를 들으시오.

듣기 지문&해석

M They've got to be joking! The gym is going to be closed all summer?

W Yeah, they're expanding the pool and gymnasium. They said the facilities have gotten too small and there isn't enough equipment for the number of students.

M What? That doesn't make any sense. I use the gym all the time, and there are hardly any people there. And I've never had to wait in line for any of the equipment... even in the morning when it's the busiest. It doesn't need to be expanded at all!

W Hmm, I see your point, but still, they are buying new equipment. The facilities are getting a little old. Aren't they?

M No, they are not that old. In fact, there's nothing wrong with the current facilities at all. The equipment in the weight room is still in good shape. And there's nothing really wrong with the gym or the pool.

남 농담이겠지! 여름 내내 체육관을 닫는다고?

여 그래, 수영장과 체육관을 확장한대. 학생 수에 비해 시설이 너무 작아졌고, 운동 기구도 충분하지 않다는 거야.

남 뭐라고? 말도 안 돼. 나는 체육관을 항상 이용하는데 사람들이 거의 없어. 어떤 기구도 줄 서서 기다린 적이 없어… 심지어 가장 붐비는 아침에도 말이야. 확장할 필요가 전혀 없어!

여 흠, 무슨 말인지는 알겠지만, 그래도 새로운 기구를 구입하려고 하던데. 시설이 좀 낡았잖아. 안 그래?

남 아니, 그렇게 낡지 않았어. 사실, 현재 시설에는 전혀 문제가 없어. 체력 단련실의 운동 기구들은 아직 상태가 좋아. 그리고 체육관과 수영장도 전혀 잘못된 것이 없고 말이야.

W Well, but I guess the school wants to do something about it, though.
M All they need to do is clean them up a bit and repaint them. I think it's a waste of money to make those renovations and buy new equipment.

여 음, 그래도 학교가 뭘 좀 해보고 싶나 보네.
남 청소 좀 하고 페인트칠만 다시 하면 돼. 보수 공사를 하고 새 기구를 사는 건 돈 낭비 같아.

어휘 gymnasium n 체육관 I facility n 시설 I make sense 이치에 맞다, 말이 되다 I hardly adv 거의 ~ 않다 I wait in line 줄 서서 기다리다 I in good shape 상태가 좋은 I there's nothing wrong with ~에 아무 문제도 없다 I a waste of money 돈 낭비

듣기 – 노트 정리 예시

의견 man: no

이유 1. no need for expansion
- always go to the gym, hardly anyone there
2. no need for new equipment
- they are all quite new

남자: 반대

1. 확장할 필요 없음
– 항상 체육관에 감, 사람이 거의 없음
2. 새로운 기구 필요 없음
– 전부 상당히 새 것임

02

읽기 지문&해석

Announcement on the Removal of TV in the Cafeteria

Please be advised that the large LCD TV in the main cafeteria at Raleigh House will be moved to the Recreation Center at the end of this month. The first reason brought up was that quite a few students have meetings and study in the cafeteria, and the noise from the television disturbs them. Also, the cafeteria is an important place to talk and get to know one another. Having the LCD TV in the cafeteria interferes with this. Therefore, to help build relationships among students, we have decided to move the TV to the Recreation Center on the third floor. For further information, please contact the Housing Committee.

구내식당 TV 제거 공지

롤리 기숙사 메인 구내식당의 대형 LCD TV가 이달 말에 레크레이션 센터로 옮겨진다는 것을 알려드립니다. 제기된 첫 번째 이유는 꽤 많은 학생들이 구내식당에서 모임을 가지거나 공부를 하는데 텔레비전 소리가 방해가 된다는 것입니다. 또한 구내식당은 대화를 하고 서로를 알아가기 위한 중요한 장소입니다. 구내식당에 LCD TV가 있으면 이런 것에 방해가 됩니다. 따라서 우리는 학생들 사이의 교류를 돕기 위해 TV를 3층의 레크리에이션 센터로 옮기기로 결정했습니다. 좀 더 상세한 정보를 얻으려면 기숙사 위원회로 연락 바랍니다.

어휘 be advised that ~를 숙지하시오 I quite a few 상당수의 I disturb v 방해하다 I get to know 알게 되다 I interfere v 방해하다 I build relationships 관계를 쌓다 I contact v 연락하다 I committee n 위원회

읽기 – 노트 정리 예시

주제 remove TV from cafeteria
- TV noise = disturb students who meet & study
- students should talk & get to know

구내식당에서 TV 제거
– TV 소음 = 모임 & 공부하는 학생들 방해
– 학생들은 서로 대화 & 알아가야 함

Now listen to two students talking about the announcement from the Housing Committee.

이제 기숙사 위원회 공지에 대해 이야기하는 두 학생의 대화를 들으시오.

듣기 지문&해석

M Did you read that they're going to get rid of the TV in the cafeteria?
W That's a good idea, I guess.

남 구내식당에서 TV를 없앨 거라는 공지 읽었니?
여 그건 좋은 생각 같아.

M Come on, we need some place to just relax, don't we? We're all so busy with school work and studying. In the cafeteria, we should be able to just relax and watch TV if we want to.

W Yeah, you've got a point. I suppose it's good to have a place to just relax.

M Exactly! Since we're all adults here, we can make our own decisions about how to spend our time. If you want to talk, talk. If you want to watch TV and relax, you should be able to do that, too.

W But people who want to study would definitely have a hard time concentrating because of the TV noise.

M People who want to study should go to the library or the study hall. That's what those places are for.

W Okay, but what about the point about the TV interfering with people getting to know one another?

M I think that point makes no sense at all. In fact, I believe TV can be a really helpful tool to make friends with others or break the ice. When students meet other people for the first time and don't have common things to talk about, they can make conversation by talking about what's being shown on the TV.

W Hmm, I guess I've never thought of it from that perspective.

남 저기, 우린 그냥 휴식을 취할 장소가 필요해, 그렇지 않아? 모두들 학교 과제와 공부로 굉장히 바빠. 구내식당에선 원할 때 그냥 좀 쉬면서 TV를 볼 수 있어야 해.

여 그래, 네 말도 일리가 있어. 내 생각에도 단순히 쉴 수 있는 공간이 필요한 것 같아.

남 내 말이! 우린 모두 성인이기 때문에 시간을 어떻게 쓸지에 대해 스스로 결정할 수 있어. 대화를 하고 싶으면 대화를 해. TV를 보며 쉬고 싶으면 그렇게 할 수도 있어야 해.

여 하지만 공부하고 싶어하는 사람들은 분명 TV 소음 때문에 집중하기가 힘들 거야.

남 공부하고 싶은 사람들은 도서관이나 자습실에 가면 되지. 거기가 공부를 하기 위한 장소잖아.

여 그래, 하지만 TV가 사람들이 서로를 알아가는 데 방해가 된다는 거에 대해선 어떻게 생각해?

남 내 생각에 그건 전혀 말이 안 되는 것 같아. 사실, TV는 친구를 사귀고 서먹한 분위기를 깨뜨리는 데 정말 유용한 도구라고 생각해. 학생들이 다른 사람들을 처음 만나서 이야기할 공통된 화제가 없을 때 TV에서 방송되는 것을 보며 대화를 할 수 있거든.

여 음, 그런 관점으로 생각해 본 적은 없었네.

어휘 get rid of 없애다, 제거하다 I be busy with ~하느라 바쁘다 I make one's decision 결정을 내리다 I have a hard time -ing ~하는 데 어려움을 겪다 I that's what *A* is for 그걸 위해서 A가 있다 I make friends with others 다른 이들을 사귀다, 친해지다 I break the ice 서먹한 분위기를 깨다 I common adj 공통의 I make conversation 대화하다, 잡담하다 I perspective n 관점, 시각

듣기 – 노트 정리 예시

의견 man: no

이유 1. ppl just want to relax
- meet & study ppl should go somewhere quiet

2. TV is useful
- ppl can talk about what's on TV: break ice

남자: 반대

1. 사람들은 그저 휴식을 취하고자 함
– 모임 & 공부하는 사람들은 조용한 곳으로 가야 함

2. TV는 유용함
– 사람들은 TV에서 방송되는 것에 대해 이야기할 수 있음: 서먹한 분위기 깨기

Practice 2

본서 P. 242

01

The university is making an announcement regarding construction work in one of its parking lots. You will have 50 seconds to read the announcement. Begin reading now.

대학교가 주차장 한 곳의 공사에 관한 공지를 하고 있다. 공지를 읽는 데 50초가 주어진다. 이제 읽기 시작하시오.

읽기 지문&해석

Parking Lot Under Construction

All parking permit holders should be aware that Lot C, located next to the Registrar's Office, will be closed for construction.

주차장 공사 중

모든 주차 허가증 소지자들에게 학적부 사무실 옆에 위치한 C주차장이 공사를 위해 폐쇄함을 알려드립니

With the increase in enrollment over the past five years, the number of people parking in the lot has also increased dramatically. To increase capacity, the university is planning to build a four-story parking garage on the site of Parking Lot C from the beginning of August until the end of October. While the parking lot is under construction, Lot C permit holders can park in any of the other parking lots on campus.

다. 지난 5년 동안 재학생 수가 증가하면서 그 주차장을 이용하는 사람 수 또한 급격히 증가했습니다. 수용량을 늘리기 위해 대학에서는 8월 초부터 10월 말까지 C주차장 자리에 4층짜리 주차장을 지을 계획입니다. 주차장이 공사 중인 동안 C주차장 허가증 소지자들은 캠퍼스의 다른 주차장 어느 곳에든 주차할 수 있습니다.

어휘 under construction 공사 중인 I be aware that (of) ~를 알다/인지하고 있다 I next to ~ 옆에 I enrollment n 등록 I over the past five years 지난 5년 동안 I the number of ~의 수 I dramatically adv 급격히 I four-story adj 4층의 I parking garage 주차장 I site n 위치, 장소, 현장

읽기 - 노트 정리 예시

주제 parking lot under construction (next to Registrar's office)
- 4-story parking garage
- construction Aug~Oct

주차장 공사 중 (학적부 사무실 옆)
– 4층짜리 주차장
– 8~10월에 공사

Now listen to two students talking about the announcement.

이제 공지에 대해 이야기하는 두 학생의 대화를 들으시오.

듣기 지문&해석

M Oh, no way! They're not seriously going to close the parking lot, are they?

W Yup, it looks like it… for three months starting next week.

M What are they thinking?

W Well, it'll be good to have a new parking garage, won't it? I don't know about you, but it takes me forever to find a spot. Sometimes, I'm even late for class.

M For sure, we need more parking spaces, but come on! August and September? Those are the busiest months for registration. Everyone wants to park near the Registrar's Office. Why couldn't they have done it earlier in the summer when there is less traffic on campus?

W I guess you've got a point. But we can park in the other lots, right? It won't be that bad.

M No way! All of the other lots are already full all the time. With all of the extra cars from Lot C wanting to park in them, we'll never get a spot. I guess I'll just start riding my bike to school in the fall.

남 오, 말도 안 돼! 정말로 주차장을 폐쇄하지는 않겠지, 그렇지?

여 그럴 것 같은데… 다음 주부터 석 달 동안.

남 대체 무슨 생각이지?

여 음, 새 주차장이 생기면 좋을 거야, 안 그래? 네 경우는 모르겠지만 난 주차할 자리를 찾는 데 시간이 굉장히 오래 걸려. 가끔은 수업에 늦기도 해.

남 물론 주차 공간이 더 필요하긴 해. 하지만 8월과 9월이라니! 등록 때문에 제일 바쁜 달이잖아. 모두들 학적부 사무실 가까이에 주차하기를 원해. 왜 학교가 덜 붐비는 초여름에 하지 않은 걸까?

여 네 말이 일리가 있긴 해. 하지만 다른 주차장에 주차할 수 있잖아, 그렇지? 그리 나쁘지 않을 거야.

남 그렇지 않아! 다른 주차장들은 이미 항상 붐벼. C주차장의 모든 차들까지 거기에 주차하려 들면, 우린 절대 자리를 찾지 못할 거야. 가을엔 학교에 그냥 자전거를 타고 다녀야겠네.

어휘 seriously adv 진지하게, 진심으로, 심각하게 I spot n 자리 I be late for ~에 늦다 I for sure 물론, 확실히 I parking space 주차 공간 I registration n 등록 I all the time 항상 I ride a bike 자전거를 타다

듣기 - 노트 정리 예시

의견 man: not a good idea

이유 1. Aug & Sep are the busiest months
2. other parking lots are already full

남자: 좋은 생각이 아님

1. 8월 & 9월은 가장 바쁜 달
2. 다른 주차장은 이미 만원임

The man expresses his opinion about the announcement by the Facilities Management Department. State his opinion and explain the reasons he gives for holding his opinion.

남자는 시설 관리부 공지에 대한 자신의 의견을 표현하고 있다. 그의 의견에 대해 서술하고 그렇게 생각하는 이유가 무엇인지 설명하시오.

예시 답변

The man is opposed to the university's plan to close Lot C to build a new parking garage in the busiest months. For one thing, many students park in that lot during the registration period because it is right next to the Registrar's Office. But they won't be able to do that because it will be closed during that period. Also, he thinks that it will be very hard to park in the other parking lots. There are already very few spots, and with Lot C closed, there will be even fewer spots left. He thinks that he won't be able to get a spot during construction. That's why he is against the plan.

남자는 가장 바쁜 달에 새 주차장을 짓기 위해 C주차장을 폐쇄한다는 대학교 측의 계획에 반대한다. 우선, 그 주차장이 학적부 사무실 바로 옆에 있기 때문에 많은 학생들이 등록 기간 동안 그 주차장에 주차한다. 하지만 그 주차장이 그 기간 동안 폐쇄될 것이기 때문에 그렇게 할 수 없을 것이다. 또한 그는 다른 주차장에 주차하는 것이 매우 어려울 것이라고 생각한다. 이미 자리가 거의 없고, C주차장이 문을 닫은 상태에서는 남은 자리가 훨씬 더 적을 것이다. 그는 공사 중에 자리를 잡을 수 없을 것이라고 생각한다. 그래서 그는 그 계획에 반대한다.

02

The university is making an announcement regarding an annual orientation. You will have 45 seconds to read the announcement. Begin reading now.

대학교가 연례 오리엔테이션에 관한 공지를 하고 있다. 공지를 읽는 데 45초가 주어진다. 이제 읽기 시작하시오.

읽기 지문&해석

School of Engineering Orientation

Welcome back from the summer break! Once again, the faculty of the School of Engineering will be hosting its annual orientation activities; but this year, due to students' complaints, there will be a few changes. In previous years, the faculty hosted a barbeque and a hiking trip on the first weekend in September. This year, however, the events are scheduled for Wednesday, September 20th, between noon and 4 o'clock. Additionally, students can choose which of the planned events they wish to attend. Students may sign up for the preferred activity on the webpage of the School of Engineering by noon on the 19th.

공과 대학 오리엔테이션

여름 방학이 끝나고 돌아오신 것을 환영합니다! 다시 한 번 공과 대학에서 연례 오리엔테이션 행사를 주최합니다. 그러나 올해에는 학생들의 불만에 의해 몇 가지 변경 사항이 있습니다. 예년에는 9월 첫째 주말에 바비큐 파티와 하이킹 여행을 개최했습니다. 하지만 올해는 행사가 9월 20일 수요일 정오에서 4시 사이로 일정이 잡혔습니다. 또한 학생들은 계획된 행사 중 참석하고 싶은 행사를 선택할 수 있습니다. 학생들은 공과 대학 웹페이지에서 19일 정오까지 원하는 활동을 등록하면 됩니다.

어휘 engineering n 공학 I faculty n 학부, 학과 I due to ~ 때문에 I complaint n 불평, 불만 사항 I host v 주최하다 I additionally adv 또한, 게다가 I sign up for 등록하다

읽기 – 노트 정리 예시

주제 school of engineering orientation
- change 1: time - noon to 4
- change 2: students can choose the events they want

공과 대학 오리엔테이션
- 변화 1: 시간 – 정오에서 4시
- 변화 2: 학생들은 원하는 행사를 선택할 수 있음

Now listen to two students talking about the announcement.

이제 공지에 대해 이야기하는 두 학생의 대화를 들으시오.

듣기 지문&해석

M Hey, did you hear about orientation this year?
W Yeah, it was a smart move switching it to a Wednesday.
M Oh, you think so? I couldn't understand why they changed it. Don't most people have more free time on the weekend?
W Not at the beginning of term. We're all running around doing so many different things—buying books, registering for classes, getting set up with our housing. We really need the time on the weekend to do those things. If you lose your pace at the beginning, it kinda continues to the end. You remember? We actually talked about this last semester!
M Yeah, I remember! And that's true. It was a bit of a hassle to go to orientation on the weekend last year.
W Not only that, I'm also really happy that students get to choose their activity. Last year, we had to go to the barbeque and go hiking. The hiking was so boring, but I didn't have any choice.
M Yeah. I remember that. I am happy that we have an option in the activities too. I'd probably want to go to the barbeque, but I can do without the hiking.
W I'm with you! I don't want to waste time doing stuff I'm not interested in. Just have some food and take off.
M Maybe we could do something together after the barbeque.
W That sounds good.

남 올해 오리엔테이션 얘기 들었어?
여 응, 수요일로 바꾼 건 현명한 처사야.
남 어, 그렇게 생각하니? 난 왜 바꿨는지 이해가 안 돼. 대부분의 사람들이 주말에 더 시간이 많지 않아?
여 학기 초엔 그렇지 않아. 모두들 책 사고, 수강 신청하고, 숙소를 마련하는 등 많은 일을 하느라 바쁘게 돌아다녀. 그런 일들을 하려면 정말로 주말에 시간이 필요해. 만약 처음에 속도를 맞춰 가지 못하면, 끝까지 그렇게 되잖아. 기억나? 우리 지난 학기에 이거 이야기했잖아!
남 응, 기억나! 맞아. 작년엔 주말에 오리엔테이션 가느라 정신이 없었어.
여 그뿐 아니라, 학생들이 활동을 선택할 수 있다는 것도 좋아. 작년엔 바비큐와 하이킹을 가야 했잖아. 하이킹은 정말 지루했지만 선택의 여지가 없었지.
남 그래. 기억나. 나도 활동에 선택 사항이 있어서 좋아. 나는 아마 바비큐는 가고 싶을 것 같은데, 하이킹은 가지 않을 거야.
여 나도 그래! 관심 없는 일을 하며 시간을 낭비하고 싶지 않아. 음식만 좀 먹고 자리를 뜨자.
남 바비큐 끝나고 우리끼리 뭔가를 할 수도 있을 거야.
여 그거 좋은 생각이다.

어휘 smart move 현명한 처사 I switch v 바꾸다 I at the beginning of term 학기 초에 I run around 돌아다니다 I register for a class 수강 신청하다 I housing n 숙소, 집 I lose pace 속도를 잃다(보조를 맞추지 못하다) I hassle n 곤란한 일, 난국 I do not have any choice 선택의 여지가 없다 I probably adv 아마 I do without ~없이 지내다/해내다 I waste v 낭비하다 I stuff n 일, 것 I take off 가버리다

듣기 – 노트 정리 예시

의견 woman: a good idea
이유 1. everyone is really busy, good to change the time
2. don't have to waste time on something you don't like

여자: 좋은 생각임
1. 모두가 정말 바쁨, 시간을 바꾸기 잘했음
2. 하고 싶지 않은 일에 시간을 낭비할 필요 없음

The woman gives her opinion about the announcement. State her opinion and explain the reasons she gives for holding that opinion.

여자는 공지에 대한 자신의 의견을 말하고 있다. 그녀의 의견에 대해 서술하고 그렇게 생각하는 이유가 무엇인지 설명하시오.

예시 답변

According to the reading passage, the orientation schedule for the engineering department has been changed from the weekend to Wednesday, and students may choose their own activities. The woman in the dialogue thinks that this is a really good idea. She gives two reasons. First of all, she says that students are really busy on the weekend at the beginning of the semester because they have to do so many things, such as buying books and registering for classes. Secondly, she

읽기 지문에 따르면, 공과 대학 오리엔테이션 일정이 주말에서 수요일로 변경되었으며, 학생들이 직접 활동을 선택할 수도 있다. 대화에서 여자는 이것이 정말 좋은 아이디어라고 생각한다. 그녀는 두 가지 이유를 제시한다. 우선, 그녀는 학생들이 책을 사고 수업에 등록하는 것과 같은 많은 것들을 해야 하기 때문에 학기 초에는 주말에 정말 바쁘다고 말한다. 둘째로, 그녀는 학생들이 이제 그들의 활동에 선택권을 가질 수

mentions that it's good that students now have a choice in their activities. They are not forced to do something they don't want. So, for these reasons, she thinks this whole change is a really great idea.

있는 것이 좋다고 언급한다. 그들은 원하지 않는 것을 강제로하는 것이 아니다. 그래서 이런 이유들로, 그녀는 이 모든 변화가 정말 좋은 아이디어라고 생각한다.

III. Integrated Task Q3. 읽고 듣고 말하기: 대학 강의

Lesson 01 표현 익히기

Practice 본서 | P. 251

01. There's another example of how two organisms benefit from each other.

02. The professor explains it is almost impossible to distinguish the insect from a tree branch.

03. We can observe how this theory works in a laboratory setting.

04. The professor gives an example of business forecasting in the lecture.

05. A common example is how this animal behaves when threatened by a predator.

06. According to the reading, a placebo effect can happen to anyone.

07. The lecture is mainly about psychological strategies called defense mechanisms.

08. The second example is the Notothenioidei fish, which inhabits the Antarctic.

09. Another type of cultural change is what we saw in the Philippines.

10. The professor talks about her personal experience to show the process of learning new information.

Lesson 02 읽기 정리

Practice 본서 | P. 253

01

읽기 지문&해석

The Principle of Allocation

For all organisms, their ultimate purpose is to reproduce. However, many are unable to obey this most primal of directives. Their time and resources are limited, so they must allocate their energy to the most important task at that time. This is called the principle of allocation. Organisms have other basic needs, like finding food, locating shelter, and migrating. When food is scarce, they have less energy to put towards reproduction, which can consume much time and energy. This does not apply to many insects that only mate once during their brief lifetimes. However, species that can potentially mate many times must favor their own survival over potential offspring.

분배 원리

모든 생물에게 있어서 궁극적 목적은 번식하는 것이다. 그러나 많은 생물이 이러한 가장 원초적인 명령에 따를 수가 없다. 그들의 시간과 자원은 한정되어 있어서 그들은 당시에 가장 중요한 과업에 에너지를 분배해야만 한다. 이것은 분배 원리라고 불린다. 생물체들은 먹이를 찾고, 주거지를 찾고, 이주하는 것과 같은 다른 기본적인 욕구를 가지고 있다. 먹이가 적을 경우, 많은 시간과 에너지를 소모시킬 수 있는 번식 활동에 쏟을 에너지가 부족하다. 짧은 생 동안 오직 한 번만 짝짓기하는 많은 곤충들에게 이것은 적용되지 않는다. 하지만 잠재적으로 여러 번 짝짓기할 수 있는 종들은 잠재적인 자손보다는 자신의 생존을 우선해야 한다.

어휘 principle n 원리, 원칙 | allocation n 할당, 분배 | ultimate adj 궁극적인 | reproduce v 번식하다 | primal adj 태고의, 원초적인 | directive n 지시, 명령 | allocate v 분배하다, 할당하다 | put towards 주다 | reproduction n 번식 | potentially adv 잠재적으로 | favor *A* over *B* B보다 A를 선호하다 | potential adj 잠재적인 | offspring n 자식, 새끼

노트 정리 예시

주제 the principle of allocation - how organisms allocate time & resource to the most important task - e.g. finding food & mating	분배 원리 – 생물들이 시간 & 자원을 가장 중요한 일에 분배하는 방법 – 예) 먹이 찾기 & 짝짓기

▶ Question: **What is the principle of allocation?** | **분배 원리란 무엇인가?**

예시 답변

The principle of allocation is how organisms allocate their time and resources to the most important task at that time. The most important tasks include finding food and mating.	분배 원리는 생물들이 자신의 시간과 자원을 그 시점에서 가장 중요한 일에 분배하는 방법이다. 가장 중요한 일들에는 먹이 찾기와 짝짓기가 포함된다.

02

읽기 지문&해석

Synomones	시노몬
One means of communication utilized in nature is the use of scent compounds. These typically take two forms: pheromones, which are chemical signals used to communicate with other members of the same species, and allelochemicals, which are used for interspecies communication. One type of allelochemicals called synomones benefit both organisms, and they are an intense area of study. One example is when plants that are being eaten release scent compounds to attract predators like parasitic wasps that prey upon the insects attacking them.	자연에서 사용되는 의사소통 방법 중 하나는 향기 화합물을 사용하는 것이다. 이것은 보통 두 가지 형태를 띠는데, 같은 종의 다른 구성원과 소통하기 위해 사용되는 화학적 신호인 페로몬과 서로 다른 종 사이의 소통에 사용되는 이종감응물질이다. 이종감응물질의 한 종류인 시노몬은 두 생물 다에게 이익을 주며 열정적으로 연구되고 있다. 한 예시는 먹히게 된 식물이 자신을 공격하는 곤충을 먹이로 삼는 기생 말벌 같은 포식자를 끌어들이기 위해 향기 화합물을 내보내는 것이다.

어휘 utilize v 이용하다 | scent n 향기 | compound n 화합물 | typically adv 보통, 일반적으로 | allelochemical n 이종감응물질 | interspecies adj 서로 다른 종 사이의, 이종 간의 | intense adj 열정적인, 치열한, 진지한 | parasitic adj 기생하는 | wasp n 말벌

노트 정리 예시

주제 synomones - allelochemicals: interspecies communication - benefit both organisms	시노몬 – 이종감응물질: 서로 다른 종 사이의 의사소통 – 두 생물체 모두에게 이익

▶ Question: **According to the passage, what are synomones?** | **지문에 따르면, 시노몬이란 무엇인가?**

예시 답변

Synomones are a type of scent chemicals, which are used for interspecies communication. Through synomones, both organisms benefit from the communication.	시노몬은 서로 다른 종 사이의 의사소통에 이용되는 향기 화학물의 한 종류다. 시노몬을 통해 두 생물 모두 의사소통에서 이익을 얻는다.

03

읽기 지문&해석

Adaptive Reuse

Adaptive reuse is the practice of repurposing buildings to fulfill a new role, often preserving the exterior shell of the building while renovating the interior. In many cases, these buildings would have been demolished to make room for the construction of an entirely new structure. However, some buildings have great historical and societal value which leads the community to save them. If a building is still structurally sound, and the site is ecologically viable, then it may become a candidate for adaptive reuse. The buildings that are typically treated in this manner are industrial buildings like factories and power plants, political buildings like palaces and courthouses, and community buildings like churches and schools.

건물의 전용

건물의 전용은 새로운 목적을 위해 건물을 다른 역할에 맞게 고치는 관행인데, 종종 건물의 뼈대는 보존하고 내부를 수리한다. 많은 경우 이러한 건물들은 완전히 새로운 구조물의 건설을 위한 공간 마련을 위해 철거되었을 것이다. 그러나 어떤 건물들은 중요한 역사적 사회적 가치를 지니고 있기 때문에 지역 주민들이 보존하게 된다. 건물이 여전히 구조적으로 견고하고 그 현장이 생태학적인 면에서 유지 가능하다고 간주되면, 그것은 건물의 전용의 후보가 될 수도 있다. 이런 방식으로 다루어지는 건물들은 보통 공장이나 발전소 같은 공업 건물들, 궁전이나 법원 같은 정치적 건물들, 그리고 교회나 학교 같은 지역 사회 건물들이다.

어휘 adaptive reuse 건물의 전용 I practice n 관행 I repurpose v 다른 목적에 맞게 고치다 I fulfill v 이행하다, 완수하다 I preserve v 보존하다 I exterior adj 외부의 I interior n 내부 I demolish v 철거하다, 무너뜨리다 I construction n 건설 I entirely adv 완전히 I ecologically adv 생태학적으로 I viable adj 생존 가능한, 실행 가능한 I industrial adj 산업의 I power plant 발전소 I courthouse n 법원

노트 정리 예시

주제 adaptive reuse
- repurpose buildings to fulfill a new role
- preserve exterior, renovate interior
- e.g. factories, power plants, palaces, courthouses…

건물의 전용
– 새로운 역할을 위해 건물을 다른 용도에 맞게 고침
– 외부는 보존, 내부는 수리
– 예) 공장, 발전소, 궁전, 법원…

▶ Question: **What is adaptive reuse?**

건물의 전용이란 무엇인가?

예시 답변

Adaptive reuse is the practice of repurposing buildings to fulfill a new role and often preserves the exterior and renovates the interior. Typical examples include factories, power plants, palaces, courthouses, etc.

건물의 전용은 새로운 목적을 위해 건물을 다른 역할에 맞게 고치는 관행이며 종종 건물의 외부를 보존하고 내부를 수리한다. 대표적인 예로 공장과 발전소, 궁전, 법원 등이 있다.

Lesson 03 듣기 정리

Practice

본서 | P. 257

01

듣기 지문&해석

M According to the principle of allocation, animals capable of reproducing more than once in their lifetime must divide their energy between feeding and mating. This means that some species must forego feeding altogether during their mating season. Elephant seals are large carnivores with very few predators, so they usually do not have to

남 분배 원리에 따르면, 일생에 한 번 이상 번식 가능한 동물들은 먹이 섭취와 짝짓기에 에너지를 나눠야 합니다. 이는 일부 종들은 짝짓기철 동안 먹이 섭취를 아예 포기해야 한다는 의미예요. 코끼리바다물범은 포식자 수가 아주 적은 커다란 육식동물이기에 많은 에너지를 먹이 섭취에 쏟지

devote much energy to feeding. That is important because when mating season comes, they have little time to feed. Almost all of a male elephant seal's energy is used to fight to determine dominance and claim territory. The dominant bulls must defend their females against other males, so they cannot leave them unguarded. Therefore, they must remain in their territory, which prohibits them from feeding for months at a time.

않아도 됩니다. 짝짓기 철이 오면 먹이를 먹을 시간이 적기 때문에 이는 중요하죠. 수컷 코끼리바다물범의 거의 모든 에너지가 지배를 결정하고 영역을 주장하기 위해 싸우는 데 사용됩니다. 지배적인 수컷은 다른 수컷에 대항해 암컷을 지켜야 하기에 지켜지지 않은 채로 놔둘 수 없죠. 따라서 자기 영역에 있어야만 하고, 이 때문에 때로는 몇 달간 먹이 섭취를 못 하기도 합니다.

어휘 allocation n 배분, 할당 | reproduce v 번식하다 | feeding n 먹이 섭취, 먹이 먹기 | mating n 짝짓기 | forego v 포기하다 | elephant seal 코끼리바다물범 | carnivore n 육식동물 | predator n 포식자 | devote v 바치다 | dominance n 지배 | territory n 영역 | bull n (동물의) 수컷 | unguarded adj 지켜지지 않는 | prohibit v 막다, 금하다

노트 정리 예시

주제 principle of allocation

예시 - animals can reproduce more than once in lifetime divide energy between mating and feeding
- elephant seals: cannot feed during mating season, must fight with other males for females

분배 원리

– 평생 한 번 이상 번식하는 동물들은 먹이 섭취와 짝짓기 사이에 에너지를 나눠야 함
– 코끼리바다물범: 짝짓기철에는 먹이 섭취 못 함, 암컷을 놓고 다른 수컷들과 싸워야 함

▶ Question: **What does the principle of allocation say about certain animals?**

분배 원리는 특정 동물들에 대해 뭐라고 말하는가?

예시 답변

The principle of allocation says that animals that can reproduce more than once in a lifetime need to divide their energy between feeding and mating. Elephant seal males cannot feed during their mating season because they must constantly fight other males for the females.

분배 원리는 평생 한 번 이상 번식할 수 있는 동물은 먹이 섭취와 짝짓기 사이에 에너지를 나누어야 한다고 말한다. 코끼리바다물범의 수컷은 암컷을 놓고 다른 수컷들과 계속 싸워야 하기 때문에 짝짓기철에 먹이를 먹지 못한다.

02

듣기 지문&해석

W When studying synomones, scientists have observed that clownfish appear to be innately protected by specific species of sea anemones. They have also found that these fish recognize the appropriate anemone species by chemicals that the anemone emits. Young fish cannot defend themselves, so they begin to search for an anemone to call home within 7 to 10 days of hatching. The strong attraction that these anemones have for the fish has been studied in a laboratory setting. Scientists extracted mucus from the anemones that contained a scent chemical. When they released it into tanks containing different kinds of fish, the species that were observed with such anemones in the wild were attracted to the scent.

여 과학자들은 시노몬을 연구하며 흰동가리가 선천적으로 특정 종의 말미잘로부터 보호를 받는다는 점을 관찰했습니다. 그들은 또한 흰동가리가 말미잘이 내뿜는 화학 물질을 통해 적절한 말미잘을 알아본다는 것을 알아냈습니다. 어린 물고기는 스스로를 방어할 수 없으므로 부화하고 7~10일 안에 집으로 삼을 만한 말미잘을 찾기 시작합니다. 이러한 말미잘이 흰동가리에게 미치는 강력한 끌어당김은 실험실에서 연구되었습니다. 과학자들은 향기 화학 물질을 가지고 있는 말미잘에게서 점액을 추출했습니다. 과학자들이 그것을 다양한 종류의 물고기들이 있는 탱크에 방출하자 야생에서 이 말미잘과 함께 있는 것이 관찰되었던 종의 물고기들이 그 냄새에 이끌렸습니다.

어휘 synomone n 시노몬 | clownfish n 흰동가리 | innately adv 선천적으로 | sea anemone 말미잘 | appropriate adj 적절한 | chemical n 화학 물질 | emit v 내뿜다, 방출하다 | hatching n 부화 | extract v 추출하다 | mucus n 점액 | release v 방출하다 | in the wild 야생에서

노트 정리 예시

주제 synomones	시노몬
예시 clownfish & sea anemone - clownfish is protected by anemones - fish recognize anemone by its chemicals	흰동가리와 말미잘 – 흰동가리가 말미잘에게 보호받음 – 물고기가 말미잘의 화학 물질로 말미잘을 알아봄

▶ **Question: What is the example of synomones?** | 시노몬의 예는 무엇인가?

예시 답변

The example of synomones is clownfish and sea anemones. Clownfish are protected by sea anemones, and the fish recognize an anemone by the chemical it emits.

시노몬의 예는 흰동가리와 말미잘이다. 흰동가리는 말미잘에 의해 보호받으며, 말미잘이 내뿜는 화학 물질로 말미잘을 인식한다.

03

듣기 지문&해석

M For cities that have existed for a long period of time, it is not unusual for buildings to outlive their usefulness. They have to be torn down, and new structures replace them. However, many older buildings are valued by the community for their historical or societal value. Sometimes these buildings are renovated on the inside and used for entirely different purposes. This practice is called adaptive reuse, and one example of this is the Tate Gallery in London. This building began life as the Bankside Power Station, which supplied electricity to London for nearly 30 years. After a decade of disuse, it was faced with demolition, but a TV documentary led to its being saved and converted into a museum of modern art.

남 오랫동안 존재해온 도시들의 경우, 건물들이 유용성이 다할 때까지 살아남는 것은 특이한 일이 아닙니다. 이 건물들은 해체되어야 하며 새 구조물이 그것들을 대체합니다. 그러나 많은 오래된 건물들은 역사적 또는 사회적 가치 때문에 지역 사회에서 소중하게 여겨집니다. 때때로 이런 건물들은 내부가 개조되고 전혀 다른 목적을 위해 사용되죠. 이런 관행은 건물의 전용이라고 불리는데, 이것의 한 예가 런던의 테이트 미술관입니다. 이 건물은 원래 거의 30년간 런던에 전기를 공급한 뱅크사이드 발전소였습니다. 이 건물은 10년간 사용되지 않다가 철거를 맞이하게 되었지만, 한 TV 다큐멘터리가 건물을 살리고 현대 미술관으로 탈바꿈하도록 이끌었습니다.

어휘 exist v 존재하다 | outlive v 오래 존재해서 ~을 잃다 | usefulness n 유용성 | structure n 구조물 | replace v 대체하다 | value v 소중하게 여기다 n 가치 | historical adj 역사적인 | societal adj 사회적인 | renovate v 보수 공사를 하다 | entirely adv 완전히 | practice n 관행 | adaptive adj 적응하는 | power station 발전소 | electricity n 전기 | decade n 10년 | disuse n 사용되지 않음 | demolition n 철거, 파괴 | convert v 개조하다, 바꾸다

노트 정리 예시

주제 adaptive reuse	건물의 전용
예시 - new purpose → keep exterior, renovate inside - Tate Gallery in London	– 새로운 목적 → 외부 유지, 내부 수리 – 런던의 테이트 미술관

▶ **Question: What is the example of adaptive reuse?** | 건물 전용의 예는 무엇인가?

예시 답변

Adaptive reuse is renovating a building for a new purpose, often the exterior is kept and the interior is renovated. One example of this is the Tate Gallery in London. It was an unused power station that was going to be destroyed.

건물의 전용은 새로운 목적을 위해 건물을 보수하는 것이며 종종 외부는 유지하고 내부를 수리한다. 이것의 한 예는 런던의 테이트 미술관이다. 이곳은 철거될 예정이었던 사용되지 않는 발전소였다.

04

듣기 지문&해석

W Wolves are very social animals that form packs that consist of a breeding pair, called alphas, and their offspring. The wolves within a pack have a strict social order, and the subordinate members use appeasement behavior to avoid physical conflict. Wolves do not rule by violence, but by limiting access to resources. Wolves hunt together and share their food, but the alphas get to feed first. They will gorge themselves on meat for their pups and take pieces of the animal away to feed on later at their leisure. If another wolf wants to feed, it will put its head close to the ground and flatten its fur to its body. This shows that it does not want to fight, and the leader may ignore it entirely, snarl at it to make it wait, or put its mouth around the animal's nose without biting. This is not a threatening gesture; it merely shows that the leader accepts the other animal's acknowledgment of its leadership.

여 늑대들은 알파라 불리는 하나의 번식 쌍과 그들의 새끼들로 구성되는 무리를 이루는 매우 사회적인 동물입니다. 무리 안의 늑대들은 엄격한 사회 질서를 가지며, 하위 구성원들은 물리적 충돌을 피하기 위해 유화 행동을 합니다. 늑대들은 폭력을 통해서가 아니라 자원에 대한 접근을 제한하는 방식으로 지배합니다. 늑대들은 함께 사냥하고 먹이를 나누지만 알파들이 제일 먼저 먹습니다. 그들은 새끼들을 위해 고기를 잔뜩 먹고, 남은 조각은 나중에 여유 있게 먹기 위해 가지고 갑니다. 만약 다른 늑대가 먹이를 먹기 원하면, 그 늑대는 머리를 땅 가까이 대고 털을 몸에 납작하게 붙일 것입니다. 이는 그 늑대가 싸우기를 원치 않는다는 것을 보여줍니다. 우두머리는 그 늑대를 완전히 무시할 수도 있고, 기다리게 하기 위해 으르렁댈 수도 있고, 아니면 그 늑대의 코 주변을 물지는 않고 입을 댈 수도 있습니다. 이는 위협하는 행동이 아니며, 단순히 그 늑대가 우두머리의 리더십을 인정한다는 사실을 우두머리가 받아들인다는 것을 보여주는 것입니다.

어휘 pack n 동물의 무리 | consist of ~로 구성되다 | breeding pair 함께 새끼를 기르는 한 쌍의 동물 | social order 사회 질서 | subordinate adj 하위의 | physical conflict 물리적 충돌 | limit v 제한하다 | access n 접근 | resource n 자원 | gorge v 게걸스레 먹다 | pup n 새끼 | flatten v 납작하게 하다 | fur n 털 | snarl v 으르렁거리다 | threatening adj 위협하는 | acknowledgment n 인정, 승인

노트 정리 예시

주제 appeasement behavior

예시 - wolves (alphas & offspring)
- alphas feed first → other wolves acknowledge leadership by putting head close to the ground, flatten fur = don't want to fight = get food

유화 행동

- 늑대 (알파와 새끼들)
- 알파들이 먼저 먹이를 먹음 → 다른 늑대들이 땅에 머리를 가까이 대거나 털을 납작하게 해서 리더십을 인정 = 싸우기 싫음 = 먹이를 얻음

▶ **Question: What is the example of appeasement behavior?**

유화 행동의 예는 무엇인가?

예시 답변

The example of appeasement behavior is shown through wolves. There are alphas and their offspring in the group. Alphas feed first, and other wolves get food by showing they don't want to fight through putting their heads close to the ground and flattening their fur.

유화 행동의 예는 늑대를 통해 볼 수 있다. 무리에는 알파들과 이들의 새끼들이 있다. 알파들이 먼저 먹이를 먹으며, 다른 늑대들은 머리를 땅에 가까이 대고 털을 납작하게 함으로써 싸우기 싫다는 모습을 보여 먹이를 얻는다.

05

듣기 지문&해석

M As we discussed earlier, many animals behave like young animals so that dominant members of their group will be nice to them. Today we will be looking at a slightly different version of this called agonistic buffering. There is a type of monkey called macaques that have a unique form of this behavior. Macaques live throughout Asia and in parts of northern Africa, and there are many different species. However, they are all quite intelligent and have a complex social structure. The males and females all help to raise the young monkeys, even if they are not the parents. These monkeys have a female-dominated society apart from the alpha male. So, the males often fight over dominance. In order to keep the peace, the subordinate males will often take a baby away from a female and carry it over to a more dominant male.

남 우리가 전에 이야기했듯이, 많은 동물들은 어린 새끼처럼 행동해서 그들 집단의 우세한 동물들이 자신들에게 잘해주도록 합니다. 오늘 우리는 이러한 행동의 약간 다른 형태인 투쟁 완화라 불리는 것에 대해 알아볼 겁니다. 이러한 행동의 독특한 형태를 보이는 마카크라는 원숭이가 있습니다. 마카크 원숭이는 아시아 전역과 북부 아프리카 일부 지역에 서식하며 많은 다양한 종이 있습니다. 그러나 그들은 모두 상당히 똑똑하며 복잡한 사회 구조를 가지고 있습니다. 수컷과 암컷은 모두 부모가 아니더라도 새끼 원숭이들을 기르는 것을 돕습니다. 이 원숭이들은 우두머리 수컷을 제외하고는 암컷 중심의 사회를 가지고 있습니다. 그래서 수컷들은 종종 지배권을 두고 싸움을 합니다. 평화를 유지하기 위해, 하위 수컷들은 암컷에게서 새끼를 빼앗아서 더 우위에 있는 수컷에게 데리고 갑니다.

어휘 behave v 행동하다 I dominant adj 지배하는, 우세한 I slightly adv 약간 I agonistic adj 투쟁적인 I buffering n 완화, 완충 I intelligent adj 똑똑한 I complex adj 복잡한 I raise v 기르다 I dominance n 지배, 우세 I subordinate adj 하위의

노트 정리 예시

주제 agonistic buffering

예시 - macaque monkeys
- males fight over dominance → subordinate males bring a baby → peace

투쟁 완화

– 마카크 원숭이
– 수컷들이 지배권을 두고 싸움 → 하위 수컷들이 아기를 데려옴 → 평화

▶ Question: What is the example of agonistic buffering?

투쟁 완화의 예는 무엇인가?

예시 답변

One example of agonistic buffering can be seen from macaque monkeys. When males fight over dominance, subordinate males take a baby from a female and bring it to a more dominant male to keep the peace.

투쟁 완화의 한 예는 마카크 원숭이에게서 볼 수 있다. 수컷들끼리 지배권을 두고 싸울 때, 하위 수컷들은 평화를 지키기 위해 암컷에게서 아이를 빼앗아 더 우위의 수컷에게 데려간다.

06

듣기 지문&해석

W In this age of social media, people often feel overwhelmed by the amount of information they receive. This is called information overload, and in many cases, it can have disastrous results, especially in business. For example, my friend was screening applicants for a management position in his main store. It was an attractive position, so he received many applications, and he couldn't check them all. For that reason, he just selected the ones that had the

여 이 소셜 미디어의 시대에 사람들은 받아들이는 정보의 양에 압도될 때가 많습니다. 이는 정보 과다라고 불리며 많은 경우, 특히 비즈니스에서 끔찍한 결과를 낳을 수도 있습니다. 예를 들면, 제 친구는 자신의 본점에서 일할 관리직 지원자들을 가려내고 있었습니다. 그것은 매력적인 자리여서 친구는 많은 지원서를 받았고, 전부 확인할 수가 없었습니다. 그런 이유로 나열된 경력이 가장 좋은

Q3. Lesson 03 Integrated Task

best experience listed. Unfortunately, since he didn't take the time to check the references they had given, he ended up hiring someone who wasn't actually qualified.	사람들만 뽑았습니다. 안타깝게도, 그들이 제출한 추천서를 확인하는 데 시간을 들이지 못했기 때문에 친구는 결국 실제로는 자격이 없는 사람을 뽑고 말았습니다.

어휘 overwhelmed adj 압도된 I overload n 과다, 과부하 I disastrous adj 처참한, 형편없는 I result n 결과 I screen v 적절한지 확인하다, 가려내다 I applicant n 지원자 I management n 관리 I attractive adj 매력적인 I application n 지원서 I select v 선택하다 I unfortunately adv 안타깝게도, 불행히도 I reference n 추천서, 추천인 I end up -ing 결국 ~하게 되다 I qualify v 자격을 갖추다

노트 정리 예시

주제 information overload	정보 과다
예시 - professor's friend was reviewing applications for a position - too many → didn't have time → ended up hiring not qualified person	– 교수의 친구가 일자리 지원서를 검토함 – 너무 많음 → 시간 없음 → 자격 안 되는 사람을 뽑게 됨

▶ Question: **How does the professor explain the concept of information overload?**

교수는 정보 과다의 개념을 어떻게 설명하고 있는가?

예시 답변

The professor explains the concept of information overload by talking about her friend. He was reviewing applications for a position. Since he received too many, he didn't have time to look at all of them. So he just picked the ones who had the best experience and ended up selecting a person who was not really qualified.	교수는 자신의 친구에 관해 이야기하며 정보 과다의 개념을 설명한다. 그는 한 일자리를 위한 지원서를 검토하고 있었다. 너무 많이 받아서 전부를 볼 시간이 없었다. 그래서 그냥 가장 좋은 경력을 가진 사람들을 뽑았고, 결국 실제로는 자격이 없는 사람을 뽑고 말았다.

Lesson 04 정리해서 말하기

Practice 1

본서 I P. 262

01

읽기 지문&해석

The Peak-End Rule	**피크엔드 법칙**
When people are asked to describe certain events that have happened in their lives, a psychological phenomenon termed as the peak-end rule often comes into play. The peak-end rule states that a person is most likely to focus on the highlights or the last parts of his or her experience and discard virtually all other information when describing the event as a whole. The main reason is that people have a tendency to recall their experiences with ease when strong, either negative or positive, emotions are attached to them. Minor emotions and information are often disregarded in the process of remembering and describing the overall experience of the event.	사람들이 본인의 삶에서 일어난 특정한 일들을 기술해 달라고 요청받을 때, 피크엔드 법칙이라고 불리는 심리학적 현상이 흔히 일어난다. 피크엔드 법칙은 어떤 사건의 전체를 설명할 때, 사람이 본인 경험의 중요한 부분 혹은 마지막 부분에만 집중하고 사실상 나머지 다른 정보는 다 버리는 경향을 말한다. 주된 이유는 사람들이 부정적이든, 긍정적이든 강한 감정이 결부되어 있을 때 경험을 더 쉽게 기억하는 경향이 있다는 것이다. 중요하지 않은 감정들이나 정보는 사건의 전체적 경험을 기억하고 기술하는 과정에서 흔히 묵살된다.

어휘 psychological phenomenon 심리학적 현상 | term [v] 이름 붙이다 | come into play 활동하기 시작하다 | be likely to ~하기 쉽다, ~할 가능성이 있다 | discard [v] 버리다 | virtually [adv] 사실상 | as a whole 전체로써 | have a tendency to ~하는 경향이 있다 | recall [v] 상기시키다 | with ease 쉽게 | attached to ~에 부착된 | minor [adj] 주요하지 않은, 가벼운 | disregard [v] 묵살하다 | in the process of ~의 과정에서

읽기 – 노트 정리 예시

주제 The Peak-End Rule	피크엔드 법칙
- remembering something → focus on highlights/last parts of experience	– 뭔가를 기억해냄 → 경험의 중요 부분/마지막 부분에 집중
- tendency to recall something with strong emotions	– 강한 감정이 결부된 것을 기억하는 경향

Now listen to part of a lecture on this topic in a psychology class.

이제 이 주제에 대한 심리학 강의의 일부를 들으시오.

듣기 지문&해석

W Um… Memory is often unreliable. This is because of what is called the peak-end rule. We tend to filter certain parts of an event and focus on the parts that made a strong impression on us. In remembering the event as a whole, we often end up remembering only the highlights or peaks of the event rather than remembering the rest of the event as well.

Let me give you a few examples. My family took a road trip a couple of years ago, and we wanted to visit this famous restaurant. Anyway, on the way there, we realized there was something wrong with the directions, and we ended up getting lost. It took a really long time for us to finally find the restaurant. When we eventually got to the place, we realized why the restaurant had such a good reputation; the food and service was just perfect. The restaurant was impeccable! Our entire experience at that restaurant was just amazing! And when we were asked about the trip later on, my family rarely mentioned any other parts of the trip and only talked about how great that restaurant was. Everybody in my family thought it was a good trip just because of this restaurant.

Here's another example. My friend and I once watched this movie together. As we were watching, the movie was pretty boring for the most part. Then all of a sudden, there were several dramatic turns of events in the second half of the movie, and there was a really great action scene towards the end of the movie. Because of these parts of the movie, we both thought the movie was great overall. This is how we remember things based on the peak-end rule.

여 음… 기억은 종종 믿을 만한 것이 못 됩니다. 이것은 피크엔드 법칙이라고 불리는 것 때문이죠. 우리는 사건의 특정 부분들을 여과하고 우리에게 강한 인상을 남긴 것들에만 집중하는 경향이 있습니다. 전체로써 사건을 기억하는 데 있어서 우리는 사건 전체의 나머지까지도 다 기억하기보다는 가장 중요한 부분이나 최고의 부분을 기억하는 데에만 그칠 때가 많습니다.

몇 가지 예를 들어보겠습니다. 우리 가족은 몇 년 전에 자동차 여행을 가서 이 유명한 레스토랑을 방문하고 싶었습니다. 그런데 거기 가는 길에 길 안내가 뭔가 잘못되었다는 것을 깨달았고 결국 길을 잃게 되었습니다. 그 레스토랑을 찾는 데 정말 오래 걸렸습니다. 마침내 그곳에 도착했을 때 그 레스토랑이 그런 명성을 얻은 이유가 있다는 것을 깨달았습니다. 음식과 서비스가 정말 완벽했어요. 레스토랑은 흠잡을 데가 없었습니다! 그 레스토랑에서의 전체 경험은 정말 좋았습니다! 나중에 그 여행에 대해서 질문을 받았을 때 우리 가족은 그 여행의 다른 부분에 대해서는 거의 언급하지 않고 그 레스토랑이 얼마나 좋았는지에 대한 이야기만 했습니다. 우리 가족은 오로지 이 식당 때문에 그 여행이 좋았다고 생각했던 것입니다.

또 다른 예가 있습니다. 제 친구랑 저는 전에 어떤 영화를 함께 보았습니다. 영화는 대부분 정말 재미가 없었습니다. 그런데 갑자기 영화 후반부에 극적인 반전 몇 개가 있었고, 영화 끝부분으로 갈수록 정말 좋은 액션 장면이 있었습니다. 영화의 이 부분 때문에 우리 둘 다 영화가 전체적으로 좋았다고 생각했습니다. 이것이 우리가 피크엔드 법칙에 기반하여 사물을 기억하는 방식입니다.

어휘 unreliable [adj] 신뢰할 수 없는 | filter [v] 여과하다 | make an impression on somebody ~에게 인상을 주다 | end up -ing (결국) ~하는 상태로 끝나다 | highlight [n] 가장 중요한(흥미로운) 부분 | peak [n] 절정, 최고점 | road trip (장거리) 자동차 여행 | reputation [n] 명성 | impeccable [adj] 흠잡을 데 없는 | all of a sudden 갑자기 | dramatic turn of events 극적인 반전

Q3. Lesson 04 Integrated Task

듣기 – 노트 정리 예시

예시 1. family trip
- good restaurant → remember the trip as a good one

2. movie
- mostly not interesting, but last part was good → think movie was good

1. 가족 여행
– 좋은 레스토랑 → 여행이 좋았다고 기억함

2. 영화
– 대체로 재미없었지만, 끝부분이 좋았음 → 영화가 좋았다고 생각

02

읽기 지문&해석

Fixed Action Patterns

In the animal kingdom, there are some species that show fixed action patterns, which are complex instinctive behavior produced in response to specific stimuli. One important aspect is that the response is normally elicited by a set of perceptions, such as shapes, color combinations, or specific smells, rather than by specific objects in the environment. Another important feature is that, once started, a fixed action pattern does not stop until the entire action sequence is completed. Even if the stimulus is no longer present, the organism would still show the same behavioral pattern since it is a kind of reflex response.

고정적 행동 양식

동물계에는 고정적 행동 양식, 즉 특정 자극에 반응하여 생기는 복합적인 본능적 행동 양식을 보여주는 몇몇 종들이 있다. 한 가지 중요한 점은 이 반응이 보통 주변 환경 내의 특정 대상보다는 모양이나 색상 조합, 특정 냄새 같은 일련의 지각 작용에 의해 유발된다는 점이다. 또 다른 주요 특성은 이러한 고정 행동 양식은 일단 시작되면 전체 연속 행동이 완료될 때까지 멈추지 않는다는 점이다. 자극이 더 이상 존재하지 않더라도 그 생물은 여전히 똑같은 행동 양식을 보일 텐데, 이는 그것이 일종의 반사 반응이기 때문이다.

어휘 fixed adj 고정된 I instinctive adj 본능적인 I in response to ~에 반응하여 I stimulus n 자극 (pl. stimuli) I aspect n 양상, 면 I elicit v 끌어내다, 도출하다 I perception n 지각, 인식 I sequence n 연속적 사건들, 순서, 차례 I present adj 존재하는 I reflex n 반사

읽기 – 노트 정리 예시

주제 Fixed Action Patterns
- specific stimuli → show fixed action pattern
- elicited by a set of perceptions such as shapes and color
- does not stop until the entire action sequence is completed

고정적 행동 양식
– 특정 자극 → 고정적 행동 양식을 보임
– 모양이나 색깔 같은 일련의 지각 작용에 의해 유발됨
– 전체 연속 행동이 완료될 때까지 멈추지 않음

Now listen to part of a lecture on this topic in a biology class.

이제 이 주제에 대한 생물학 강의의 일부를 들으시오.

듣기 지문&해석

M Some organisms have instinctive behaviors called fixed action patterns. Don't get this confused with habitual behaviors in humans. Of course, similar kinds of recurring behaviors can be exhibited by human beings, but they're different from animals'. What I am talking about is animal behaviors that are completely fixed that the animals cannot even attempt to quit or change.

One thing about fixed action patterns is that they are triggered by a stimulus, like a specific color combination or a smell, and not by a specific object. Take the stickleback

남 일부 유기체는 고정적 행동 양식이라는 본능적 행동을 지니고 있습니다. 이것을 인간에게서 일어나는 습관적 행동과 혼동하지 말기 바랍니다. 물론, 비슷한 종류의 반복적으로 일어나는 행동이 인간에게서도 발견되기는 하지만, 연속된 행동 전체가 완료될 때까지 계속되도록 프로그램이 짜여 있거나 고정된 게 아니라는 점에서 동물의 행동과는 다릅니다. 제가 말하는 것은 완전히 고정된 행동이라서 동물들이 그것들을 없애거나 바꾸려는 시도조차 할 수 없는 동물들의 행동입니다.

fish for example. Every spring, the belly of the male stickleback turns bright red, and it becomes very territorial. When this happens, the male stickleback will attack any other male that comes into the area. But what's interesting is that if you put anything red near this stickleback, even if it looks nothing like a fish, the fish is going to become aggressive. Therefore, in essence, it's the color, and not the sight of another male stickleback, that triggers the behavior.

Another important aspect of a fixed action pattern is that once it is triggered, it will continue to the end. A well-known example of this is a graylag goose. If the graylag goose sees that one of its eggs has fallen out of the nest, it will instinctively roll the egg back into the nest with its beak. However, if you show it the egg and then take it away right in front of its eyes, the goose will still go through that action sequence and roll an imaginary egg back to its original place. Once the sight of the displaced egg triggers its rolling behavior, the removal of the egg from its sight cannot make the goose stop its action since it's a reflex behavior. The action pattern continues to the end once it has started.

고정적 행동 양식에 관한 한 가지 사실은 그 행동 양식이 특정 대상이 아니라 특정 색상 조합이나 냄새와 같은 자극에 의해 유발된다는 점입니다. 큰가시고기를 예로 들어봅시다. 매년 봄에 수컷 큰가시고기는 배가 밝은 적색으로 변하고 영역 보호적 습성을 강하게 갖게 됩니다. 이렇게 되면 수컷 큰가시고기는 자기 영역에 들어오는 다른 모든 수컷을 공격합니다. 그러나 흥미로운 점은 이 큰가시고기 근처에 붉은 색의 아무 물체, 물고기처럼 보이지도 않는 물체를 놓아둔다고 할지라도 큰가시고기는 공격적으로 변합니다. 그러므로 본질적으로 그런 행동을 유발하는 것은 다른 수컷 큰가시고기의 모습이 아니라 바로 색깔입니다.

고정적 행동 양식의 또 다른 중요한 면은 일단 행동이 유발되면 그 행동이 끝까지 계속된다는 점입니다. 이것의 잘 알려진 예는 회색기러기입니다. 회색기러기는 자신의 알 중 하나가 둥지 밖으로 떨어지는 것을 볼 경우 본능적으로 부리로 알을 굴려 원래 둥지로 되돌립니다. 하지만 만약 당신이 회색기러기에게 알을 보여주고 바로 눈앞에서 사라지게 해도, 회색기러기는 여전히 같은 동작을 연속으로 행할 것이며, 상상의 알을 원래의 장소로 다시 굴릴 것입니다. 알의 위치가 이탈된 것 을 보고 굴리는 행동이 시작이 되었지만 알이 없어지는 것을 보아도 회색기러기는 그 동작을 멈추지 못합니다. 왜냐하면 그것은 반사 행동이기 때문입니다. 행동 양식은 일단 시작되면 끝까지 계속됩니다.

어휘 organism n 유기체, 생물 | action pattern 행동 양식 | recurring adj 되풀이하여 발생하는 | attempt v 시도하다 | trigger v 촉발하다 | combination n 조합 | stickleback n 큰가시고기 | territorial adj 세력권을 주장하는 | in essence 본질적으로 | well-known adj 잘 알려진 | graylag goose 회색기러기 | beak n 부리 | take away 가져가다 | reflex behavior 반사 행동

듣기 – 노트 정리 예시

예시 1. stickleback fish
- male's body turns red → attack other males in their territory → attack anything red

2. graylag goose
- roll egg back into the nest → still do the same thing even if the egg disappears

1. 큰가시고기
- 수컷의 몸이 붉게 변함 → 영역 내 다른 수컷을 공격 → 모든 붉은 것을 공격

2. 회색기러기
- 알을 둥지로 다시 굴려옴 → 알이 사라져도 같은 행동을 계속함

Practice 2

본서 P. 264

01

Read the passage about polygamy. You will have 45 seconds to read the passage. Begin reading now.

다혼에 대한 지문을 읽으시오. 지문을 읽는 데 45초가 주어진다. 이제 읽기 시작하시오.

읽기 지문&해석

Polygamy

In the animal kingdom, different types of mating patterns have evolved in order to maximize the chance of increasing the number of young. The most common type among animals is called polygamy, where one male or female mates with two or more other partners at the same time. Within this multiple-partner mating system, the fittest animals have more partners than those with relatively less power or dominance. In a general zoological sense, polygamy can be categorized as either polygyny or polyandry. In polygyny, a male mates with more than one female; whereas in polyandry, one female partners with several males.

다혼

동물계에서는 새끼의 수를 늘릴 수 있는 가능성을 극대화하기 위해 다양한 유형의 짝짓기 방식이 발달해왔다. 동물들 사이에서 가장 보편적인 짝짓기 방식은 다혼이라고 하며 한 마리의 수컷 또는 암컷이 동시에 둘 이상의 짝과 짝짓기하는 것이다. 이처럼 상대가 여럿인 짝짓기 체계에서는 적자인 동물이 상대적으로 힘이 약하거나 덜 우세한 동물들보다 더 많은 짝을 갖는다. 일반적인 동물학적 의미에서 다혼은 일부다처 혹은 일처다부로 분류될 수 있다. 일부다처에서는 한 수컷이 하나 이상의 암컷과 짝을 맺는 반면, 일처다부에서는 한 암컷이 여러 수컷과 짝을 맺는다.

어휘 polygamy n 다혼 | animal kingdom 동물계 | mating pattern 짝짓기 유형 | maximize v 극대화하다 | mate with ~와 짝짓기하다 | at the same time 동시에 | fit adj 적합한 | relatively adv 상대적으로 | dominance n 우세, 지배 | zoological adj 동물학의 | categorize v 분류하다 | polygyny n 일부다처 | polyandry n 일처다부 | whereas conj (앞의 것과 대조하여) 반면에

읽기 – 노트 정리 예시

주제 polygamy
- very common in animal kingdom
- one male/female mates with two or more partners
- polygyny: male & several females
  polyandry: female & several males

다혼
– 동물계에서 매우 흔함
– 한 수컷/암컷이 둘 혹은 그 이상의 상대와 짝짓기함
– 일부다처: 수컷 & 여러 암컷들
  일처다부: 암컷 & 여러 수컷들

Now listen to part of a lecture on this topic in a zoology class.

이제 이 주제에 대한 동물학 강의의 일부를 들으시오.

듣기 지문&해석

W Okay, class, as you all know, there are many different types of mating patterns in the animal kingdom. Yesterday, we went over monogamy which can be defined as the practice or condition of having only one mate during a breeding season. Today, we are going to talk about polygamy, which involves having more than one mate of the opposite sex to reproduce with.

A common form of polygamy is called polygyny. This is where one male mates with two or more females. This type of mating pattern is particularly common in males that establish their own dominance in order to provide adequate food and protection for the females in their group. A good example of this can be seen in elephant seals. During the mating season, male elephant seals can be observed fighting against each other on beaches for breeding rights. The male elephant seals that prove to be the strongest form their own harems of more than twenty female elephant seals. In this process, the weaker males are excluded from breeding altogether.

Another type of polygamy is called polyandry, which is

여 좋아요. 여러분, 다들 잘 알다시피 동물계에는 여러 가지 많은 종류의 짝짓기 유형이 있습니다. 어제 우리는 번식기에 오로지 하나의 짝만 가지는 관행 혹은 상태로 정의될 수 있는 단혼을 살펴보았습니다. 오늘은 번식을 위해 하나 이상의 이성 짝을 갖는 다혼에 관해 이야기하겠습니다.

다혼의 흔한 형태 중 하나는 일부다처라고 불립니다. 이것은 한 마리의 수컷이 둘 혹은 그 이상의 암컷과 짝을 짓는 것입니다. 이런 종류의 짝짓기 패턴은 자기 무리의 암컷들에게 적당한 음식과 보호를 제공하기 위해 자기만의 영역을 확립하려는 수컷에게서 특히 흔하게 발견됩니다. 이러한 일부다처의 좋은 예는 코끼리바다물범에게서 볼 수 있습니다. 짝짓기 철에 코끼리바다물범이 번식을 위해 해변에서 서로 싸우는 것을 관찰할 수 있습니다. 가장 강하다고 입증된 수컷 코끼리바다물범은 보통 20마리 이상의 암컷 코끼리바다물범으로 이루어진 자신의 무리를 형성합니다. 이 과정에서 약한 수컷들은 번식에서 완전히 배제됩니다.

the mating pattern where females breed with two or more males. This is rather uncommon and is typically seen in species in which the male is involved in raising the young. A good example of this is the jacana bird. The female jacana is very aggressive and is fifty percent heavier than the male. Once the female lays eggs, the male assumes responsibility for incubating and raising the chicks. The female then goes off to find a new mate and lay more eggs.

또 다른 종류의 다혼은 일처다부라고 불리며 암컷이 둘 혹은 그 이상의 수컷과 교배하는 짝짓기 패턴입니다. 이것은 다소 보기 드문 경우로, 보통 수컷이 새끼를 키우는 종들에서 볼 수 있습니다. 일처다부의 좋은 예로 물꿩이 있습니다. 암컷 물꿩은 매우 공격적이며 수컷보다 몸이 50퍼센트나 더 무겁습니다. 암컷이 알을 낳으면 수컷이 알을 품고 새끼를 기르는 책임을 맡습니다. 그리고 나면 암컷은 새로운 수컷을 찾아 떠나 알을 더 낳습니다.

어휘 monogamy n 단혼 | define v 정의하다 | mate n 짝 | breeding season 번식기 | reproduce v 번식하다 | adequate adj 충분한, 적당한 | harem n 암컷의 무리 | exclude v 배제하다, 차단하다 | aggressive adj 공격적인 | lay eggs 알을 낳다 | assume v (책임/임무를) 맡다 | incubate v (알을) 품다 | chick n 새끼 새, 병아리

듣기 – 노트 정리 예시

예시 1. polygyny: elephant seal
- strongest male with many females, weak ones are excluded

2. polyandry: jacana bird
- male raises young, female leaves to mate again

1. 일부다처: 코끼리바다물범
– 가장 강한 수컷과 여러 암컷들, 약한 수컷들은 배제됨

2. 일처다부: 물꿩
– 수컷이 새끼를 키우고, 암컷은 다시 짝짓기하러 떠남

The professor talks about polygamy in the animal kingdom. Use the examples from the lecture to explain what the types of polygamy are and how they benefit organisms that practice them.

교수는 동물계에서의 다혼에 대해 이야기하고 있다. 강의에 나온 예시를 이용하여 다혼의 종류는 무엇이고 다혼이 어떻게 그것을 행하는 생물들에게 이득이 되는지 설명하시오.

예시 답변

The professor talks about two different forms of polygamy by describing the mating patterns of elephant seals and jacana birds. The elephant seal's mating pattern is an example of polygyny. The male elephant seal mates with more than one female elephant seal. Males fight with each other to determine which of them has the chance to mate with the females. The dominant male may then mate with up to twenty female seals. The jacana bird, on the other hand, is completely the opposite. Its mating pattern is called polyandry. The female jacana bird mates with two or more males. Once the female lays eggs, the male takes care of the chicks. Then, the female leaves to find a new partner to have more eggs.

교수는 코끼리바다물범과 물꿩의 짝짓기 유형을 설명하면서 두 가지 형태의 다혼에 대해 이야기한다. 코끼리바다물범의 짝짓기 유형은 일부다처의 한 예다. 수컷 코끼리바다물범은 한 마리 이상의 암컷 코끼리바다물범과 짝짓기를 한다. 수컷들은 그들 중 누가 암컷과 짝짓기할 수 있는 기회를 갖는지 결정하기 위해 서로 싸운다. 그리고 우월한 수컷은 최대 20마리의 암컷 바다물범과 짝짓기를 할 수 있다. 반면에 물꿩은 완전히 그 반대다. 물꿩의 짝짓기 유형은 일처다부라고 불린다. 암컷 물꿩은 둘 혹은 그 이상의 수컷과 짝짓기를 한다. 암컷이 알을 낳으면 수컷이 새끼들을 돌본다. 그리고 나서 암컷은 더 많은 알을 낳기 위해 새로운 짝을 찾아 떠난다.

02

Read the passage about film techniques. You will have 50 seconds to read the passage. Begin reading now.

영화 촬영 기법에 대한 지문을 읽으시오. 지문을 읽는 데 50초가 주어진다. 이제 읽기 시작하시오.

읽기 지문&해석

Film Techniques	영화 촬영 기법
In filmmaking, various camera shots are used to give viewers a better comprehension of the film's story. One of the shots often used is called an "establishing shot." Usually shown at the beginning of the movie, it gives viewers general ideas about the whole movie, so it provides the basic context or background information. There is another type called a "bridging shot," which makes a smooth transition between two different scenes. If there is a jump or a break in the flow of a story, perhaps in time or place, a bridging shot can be inserted to cover the gaps between those disconnected scenes, helping viewers to avoid any confusion.	영화를 제작할 때, 영화 내용에 대한 보는 이의 이해를 돕기 위해 다양한 카메라 숏이 사용된다. 자주 사용되는 숏 중 하나는 '설정 숏'이다. 주로 영화 앞부분에 보여지는 이 숏은 보는 이에게 영화 전체에 관한 전반적인 것들을 알려주며, 따라서 기본적 상황이나 배경 정보를 담고 있다. 또 다른 종류는 '연결 숏'으로, 서로 다른 두 가지 장면 사이를 매끄럽게 연결한다. 영화에서 시간이든 장소든 이야기가 진행되는 와중에 건너뛰는 장면이나 흐름이 끊어지는 부분이 있을 경우, 이러한 끊어진 장면들의 틈을 메워서 보는 이들이 혼란을 느끼는 것을 막기 위해 연결 숏이 삽입될 수 있다.

어휘 various adj 다양한 I shot n 숏(영화에서 한 번의 연속 촬영으로 찍은 장면) I viewer n 보는 이, 관람자 I context n 맥락, 전후 I bridge v 연결하다, 다리를 놓다 I smooth adj 매끄러운 I transition n 이행, 장면 전환 I jump n 급격한 변화(이동) I flow n 흐름 I insert v 삽입하다 I cover the gap 틈새를 막다 I disconnected adj 끊어진 I confusion n 혼란

읽기 – 노트 정리 예시

주제 film techniques - establishing shot = gives general idea about the movie - bridging shot = smooth transition between two different scenes	영화 촬영 기법 – 설정 숏 = 영화에 대한 전반적인 것들을 알려줌 – 연결 숏 = 서로 다른 두 장면 사이를 매끄럽게 연결

Now listen to part of a lecture on this topic in a film studies class.	이제 이 주제에 대한 영화학 강의의 일부를 들으시오.

듣기 지문&해석

M Well, in filmmaking, there are some techniques or shots that filmmakers use in order to deliver a long story within a short amount of time. One of the shots that are often used is called the "establishing shot." This is particularly used at the beginning of a movie, giving the viewers a general idea about the whole movie. Let's suppose that at the start of a movie, you see a scene that shows many tall buildings, skyscrapers, some kind of old-fashioned-looking cars, and signs on the streets. And even, perhaps, there is a wider view of a dark and gloomy-looking city. With all of these details in the first scene of a movie, what kind of things would you assume about the whole movie? Of course, the movie takes place somewhere in a big city sometime in the past, right? And you might also assume that it's more of a grim and mysterious movie, rather than a happy and positive movie, just because of the shot that you saw in the beginning. Um... there's another shot called, the "bridging shot." This is a special shot that filmmakers use in order to connect two disconnected scenes. Let's say there is a character	남 음, 영화를 제작할 때 짧은 시간 안에 긴 이야기를 전달하기 위해 제작자들이 사용하는 몇 가지 기술이나 장면들이 있습니다. 자주 사용되는 장면 중 하나는 '설정 숏'이라고 불리는 것입니다. 이 장면은 특히 영화 초반에 사용되고, 보는 이들에게 영화 전체의 전반적인 점을 말해줍니다. 영화가 처음 시작할 때, 높은 건물들, 마천루, 구식 자동차들, 거리의 간판들을 보여주는 장면을 본다고 가정해 봅시다. 그리고 더 나아가 좀 어둡고 음울해 보이는 도시 전경이 나올 수도 있겠죠. 영화 첫 장면에서 보여주는 이런 모든 세부 사항들을 합하면 영화 전체에 대해 어떤 추정을 할 수 있을 것 같나요? 물론, 이 영화는 큰 도시 어딘가에서 과거의 어떤 시간을 배경으로 할 겁니다, 그렇죠? 그리고 처음에 봤던 장면 때문에 아마 행복하고 긍정적인 영화라기보다는 뭔가 좀 암울하고 미스터리한 분위기의 영화일 거라고 생각할 겁니다. 음… '연결 숏'이라고 불리는 또 다른 숏도 있습니다. 이것은 영화 제작자들이 두 개의 끊어진 장

who was a young boy in the first scene, and you see him as a grown man in the next scene. Obviously, there is a break or jump in the story. You were probably expecting more of a linear story in the movie, right? In this case, simply showing the two scenes together will cause confusion for the viewers and make it difficult for them to assume that it is the same character. So, the filmmaker could insert a scene that shows, perhaps, calendar pages suggesting how much time has passed between the two scenes. This makes a smooth transition, closing the gaps between the two different scenes, right? Then the audience would assume that the young boy and the grown-up person are the same character, only older in the latter scene.

면을 잇는 데 이용하는 특별한 숏입니다. 예를 들어, 어떤 인물이 첫 번째 장면에서는 어린 남자아이였는데 다음 장면에서는 성인으로 나온다고 합시다. 이는 분명히 이야기가 끊어지거나 건너뛴 것입니다. 여러분은 아마 영화 속에서 좀 더 선형으로 이어지는 이야기를 기대하고 있었을 겁니다. 그렇죠? 이 경우에는 단순히 두 장면을 같이 보여주는 것은 보는 이들을 혼란스럽게 하고 두 사람이 같은 인물이라고 추정하는 것을 어렵게 할 겁니다. 그래서 영화 제작자는 달력 같은 것을 보여주는 장면을 삽입해서 두 장면 사이에 시간이 얼마나 지났는지 암시할 수 있을 겁니다. 이것은 서로 다른 두 장면 사이의 틈을 메우면서 장면 전환이 매끄럽게 이루어지게 만듭니다. 그렇죠? 그러면 관객은 그 어린아이와 성인이 같은 인물이고 그저 뒤의 장면에서 더 나이가 들었을 뿐이라고 생각할 수 있을 겁니다.

어휘 suppose v 가정하다, 생각하다 | old-fashioned adj 구식의 | gloomy-looking adj 우울해 보이는 | assume v 추정하다 | take place 일어나다 | grim adj 암울한, 음침한 | latter adj 후자의

듣기 – 노트 정리 예시

예시 1. establishing shot
- often seen at the beginning
- old, dark, gloomy-looking city → taking place in the past/grim & mysterious

2. bridging shot
- a young boy → a grown man
- transition = insert a calendar pages scene

1. 설정 숏
– 종종 초반에 나옴
– 오래되고, 어둡고, 우울해 보이는 도시 → 과거 배경/암울하고 미스터리함

2. 연결 숏
– 어린 남자아이 → 성인 남성
– 장면 전환 = 달력 장면 삽입

The professor is discussing two different shots used in filmmaking. Using points and examples given in the lecture, describe these shots and how they are used.

교수는 영화 제작에 쓰이는 두 가지 서로 다른 숏에 대해 이야기하고 있다. 강의에서 주어진 요점과 예시를 이용하여 이 숏들과 이것들이 어떻게 쓰이는지에 대해 서술하시오.

예시 답변

The lecture is about two types of special shots that are often used in filmmaking. First, the professor talks about the establishing shot which gives background information for a whole movie in the beginning scene of the movie. He gives an example of a movie that shows skyscrapers, old-styled cars and street signs, and a gloomy, mysterious atmosphere at the start. In this case, people can guess that the entire movie has the background of a big city in the past, and it is a somewhat gloomy, mysterious type of movie. As for the second type, the professor talks about the bridging shot that connects two different scenes. For example, if there is discontinuity in a story because of the time passed between two scenes, filmmakers may use a shot of calendar pages to show there has been some passage of time involved.

이 강의는 영화 제작에 자주 사용되는 두 종류의 특별한 숏에 관한 것이다. 먼저, 교수는 영화의 시작 장면에서 영화 전체에 대한 배경 정보를 제공하는 설정 숏에 대해 이야기한다. 그는 마천루, 구식 자동차와 거리의 간판, 그리고 시작부터 암울하고 미스터리한 분위기를 풍기는 영화의 예를 든다. 이 경우 영화 전체가 과거의 대도시를 배경으로 하며, 다소 암울하고 미스터리한 종류의 영화라는 것을 짐작할 수 있다. 두 번째 유형의 경우, 교수는 서로 다른 두 가지 장면을 연결하는 연결 숏에 대해 이야기한다. 예를 들어, 두 장면 사이에 흘러간 시간 때문에 이야기가 단절되는 경우, 영화 제작자들은 달력 숏을 사용하여 시간이 어느 정도 흘러갔음을 보여줄 수 있다.

IV. Integrated Task Q4. 듣고 말하기: 대학 강의

Lesson 01 표현 익히기

Practice

본서 P. 273

01. This is illustrated with an experiment, which showed how a frog lays its eggs in water.

02. The second example is similar to the first one, but it requires more investment.

03. For these reasons, this species of bird is able to maintain its balance well in water.

04. The lecture is about how a given area can only support a certain population.

05. There are two types of fish that could be classified with their bone structures.

06. The professor gives an example of mating behavior of bowerbirds.

07. The lecture's main idea is population fluctuation of deer in a certain area.

08. The professor explains many ways to protect wildlife, including volunteering activities.

09. According to the professor, some people heavily focus on the design of a product.

10. One of warning coloration's benefits is that it reduces the chance of getting attacked by predators.

Lesson 02 듣기 정리

Practice

본서 P. 276

01

듣기 지문&해석

W One of the most important factors in marketing a beverage is the container in which it will be sold. Like any other feature of a product, packaging naturally changes over time.

For example, let's take a look at the milk industry. For many years, milk was sold and delivered in glass bottles. They were the best choice because they could easily be washed and reused and did not affect the flavor of the milk. But, glass bottles have some serious problems. Glass breaks easily when dropped, so bottles have to be thick in order to be strong. Unfortunately, that makes them expensive, but there were few other options. One answer was to use cardboard containers, which are cheap but not very strong. Then plastic became easier to make and extremely cheap. Plastic bottles are both light and strong whether their walls are thick or thin, so they were a much better choice. Glass bottles and cardboard containers are still used by many companies, but plastic has become very common.

여 음료 마케팅에서 가장 중요한 요소들 중 하나는 그 음료가 팔리게 될 용기입니다. 제품의 다른 특징과 마찬가지로 포장은 시간에 따라 자연스럽게 변화합니다.

예를 들어 우유 산업을 한 번 살펴보죠. 오랫동안 우유는 유리병에 담겨 판매되고 배달되었습니다. 유리병은 세척과 재사용이 쉽고 우유의 맛에 영향을 끼치지 않았기 때문에 최선의 선택이었습니다. 하지만 유리병에는 몇 가지 심각한 문제점이 있습니다. 유리는 떨어지면 쉽게 깨져서, 튼튼하게 하기 위해서는 병이 두꺼워야 합니다. 불행히도 이는 병을 비싸게 만들었지만, 몇 가지 다른 선택의 여지가 있었습니다. 한 가지 해결책은 판지로 된 용기를 사용하는 것이었는데 이건 저렴하지만 별로 튼튼하지가 않습니다. 그 다음에 플라스틱 생산이 쉬워지고 매우 저렴해졌습니다. 플라스틱 병은 두껍든 얇든 가볍고 내구성이 좋아서 훨씬 더 나은 선택이었습니다. 여전히 많은 회사들이 유리병과 판지로 된 용기를 사용하고 있지만 이제는 플라스틱이 아주 흔해졌습니다.

어휘 factor n 요인, 요소 I beverage n 음료 I container n 용기, 통 I feature n 특징 I packaging n 포장, 포장재 I naturally adv 자연스럽게 I industry n 산업 I reuse v 재사용하다 I affect v 영향을 주다 I unfortunately adv 안타깝게도 I cardboard n 판지 I extremely adv 극히, 대단히 I common adj 흔한

노트 정리 예시

주제 marketing a beverage: packaging change 1. glass bottles: break easily, too thick → expensive 2. cardboard: cheap, not strong 3. plastic: cheap & strong	음료 마케팅: 포장 변화 1. 유리병: 쉽게 깨짐, 너무 두꺼움 → 비쌈 2. 판지: 저렴함, 튼튼하지 못함 3. 플라스틱: 저렴하고 튼튼함

▶ Question 1: **What is the main idea of the lecture?** 강의의 주제는 무엇인가?

▶ Question 2: **What example(s) does the professor give?** 교수는 어떤 예를 들고 있는가?

예시 답변

1. The main idea of the lecture is one factor of marketing a beverage, which is packaging. 2. The professor gives examples of glass, cardboard, and plastic as packaging materials.	1. 강의의 주제는 음료 마케팅의 한 요소인 포장이다. 2. 교수는 유리와 판지, 플라스틱을 포장재의 예로 든다.

02

듣기 지문&해석

M In many cases, adult insects are already dead by the time their eggs hatch, which makes parental supervision impossible. However, this does not mean that they do not make an effort to provide for their young. In fact, some flying insects sometimes go to great lengths to ensure that their children are met by a feast when they are born.
Butterflies often can only eat one or two plant species, and even those that can consume many still have plants that they prefer over others. So, it is not surprising that butterflies are very selective about where they lay their eggs. Female butterflies explore their environment to locate the best leaves for their young to feed upon. They determine whether a plant is suitable by scents that they can recognize. They typically lay their eggs on young leaves to avoid toxins and high up to avoid accidental consumption by herbivores and predation by ants. They must also keep the degree of shade, humidity, and temperature in mind.

남 많은 경우 곤충의 성충은 알이 부화할 때쯤이면 이미 죽어 있는데 이는 부모의 감독을 불가능하게 만듭니다. 그러나 이것은 곤충들이 새끼를 돌보려는 노력을 하지 않는다는 뜻은 아닙니다. 실제로 일부 날아다니는 곤충들은 새끼들이 태어났을 때 풍부한 먹이를 맞이할 수 있도록 아주 먼 거리를 여행하기도 합니다.
나비는 흔히 하나 혹은 두 가지의 식물 종만 섭취할 수 있고, 다양한 종류의 식물을 섭취할 수 있는 종도 다른 것보다 선호하는 식물이 있습니다. 따라서 나비가 알을 낳는 곳을 조심스럽게 고르는 것은 놀라운 일이 아닙니다. 암컷 나비는 새끼가 먹기에 가장 좋을 것 같은 잎을 찾기 위해 주변 환경을 탐색합니다. 나비는 자신이 식별할 수 있는 냄새로 어떤 식물이 적합한지 아닌지 알아냅니다. 나비는 보통 독소를 피하기 위해 어린 나뭇잎에 알을 낳고, 초식동물에게 우연히 먹히거나 개미에게 먹히는 일을 피하기 위해 높은 곳에 알을 낳습니다. 그들은 또한 그늘의 정도, 습도, 그리고 온도를 염두에 두어야 합니다.

어휘 hatch v 부화하다 I parental supervision 부모의 감독 I feast n 진수성찬, 잔치, 연회 I consume v 먹다, 마시다, 소모하다 I selective adj 조심해서 고르는 I locate v 정확한 위치를 찾다 I suitable adj 적합한, 알맞은 I scent n 냄새, 향기 I typically adv 보통 I toxin n 독소 I accidental adj 우연한 I consumption n 소비, 섭취 I herbivore n 초식동물 I predation n 포식 I shade n 그늘 I humidity n 습도

노트 정리 예시

주제 insects dead before eggs born → prepare feast for young e.g. butterflies: carefully select place to lay eggs (degree of shade, humidity, temperature…)	곤충들은 알이 부화하기 전에 죽음 → 새끼들을 위해 풍부한 먹이를 준비 예시) 나비: 알 낳을 곳을 조심스럽게 고름 (그늘의 정도, 습도, 온도…)

▶ Question 1: **What is the main idea of the lecture?** 강의의 주제는 무엇인가?

▶ Question 2: **What example(s) does the professor give?** 교수는 어떤 예를 들고 있는가?

예시 답변

1. The main idea of the lecture is how some flying insects prepare a feast for their young before they hatch.
2. The example the professor talks about is butterflies.

1. 강의의 주제는 일부 날아다니는 곤충이 어떻게 새끼가 부화하기 전에 풍부한 먹이를 준비하는지에 대한 것이다.
2. 교수가 말하는 예시는 나비다.

03

듣기 지문&해석

W When a company decides to release a new product, it must first decide how to advertise that item based upon the current market situation. The market may already have many examples of that product available, or they may be introducing an entirely new product.
When a healthy market already exists, most companies prefer to engage in secondary or selective demand advertising. In this type of advertising, the company assumes that the public already has a working understanding of the product. So, it will focus its energy on differentiating its product or service from others that exist in the market. For example, cell phone makers usually advertise what features make their models better than those of other companies. This often involves features like memory, wireless service, screen size and clarity, ease of use, battery life, etc. Their goal is to convince customers that their cell phone is the best one available.

여 기업은 새로운 제품을 출시하기로 결정할 때 우선 현재 시장 상황에 기초해 어떻게 그 제품을 광고할 것인지 결정해야 합니다. 시장에는 출시하려는 제품이 이미 다양한 종류로 존재할 수도 있고, 아니면 완전히 새로운 제품을 소개하게 될 수도 있습니다.
건강한 시장이 이미 존재한다면 대부분의 기업은 2차적 또는 선택적 수요 광고를 선호합니다. 이러한 종류의 광고에서 기업은 대중이 이미 제품에 대한 실용적인 이해를 하고 있다고 가정합니다. 그래서 기업은 자사의 제품이나 서비스를 시장에 존재하는 다른 것들과 차별화하는 데 에너지를 집중할 것입니다. 예를 들면, 휴대전화 생산자들은 보통 어떠한 특징이 다른 회사 제품보다 자사 제품을 더 낫게 하는지에 관해 광고합니다. 이는 흔히 메모리와 무선 서비스, 화면 크기와 해상도, 사용의 편리함, 배터리 수명 등의 특징을 포함합니다. 이들의 목표는 소비자에게 자사 휴대전화가 구할 수 있는 것들 중 최고라고 설득하는 겁니다.

어휘 release v 출시하다 I product n 제품 I advertise v 광고하다 I based upon ~에 기초하여 I current adj 현재의 I situation n 상황 I introduce v 소개하다, 도입하다 I entirely adv 완전히 I exist v 존재하다 I engage in ~에 관여하다/참여하다 I secondary adj 이차적인, 부차적인 I selective demand 선택적 수요(특정 브랜드에 대한 수요) I assume v 가정하다 I public n 대중 I differentiate v 차별화하다 I wireless adj 무선의 I clarity n 선명함, 해상도 I convince v 설득하다

노트 정리 예시

주제 company releases a new product → advertising: current market situation - not an entirely new product → already have many products → secondary or selective advertising	회사에서 신제품을 출시함 → 광고: 현재 시장 상황 – 완전히 새로운 상품은 아님 → 이미 많은 상품이 있음 → 2차적 또는 선택적 수요 광고

▶ Question 1: **What is the main idea of the lecture?**

강의의 주제는 무엇인가?

▶ Question 2: **What type of advertising does the professor mention?**

교수는 어떤 종류의 광고를 언급하는가?

예시 답변

1. The main idea of the lecture is how a company advertises their product when releasing a new product.
2. The professor talks about secondary or selective advertising, which is used when the market already has many products.

1. 강의의 주제는 회사가 새 제품을 출시할 때 그들이 제품을 광고하는 방법이다.
2. 교수는 시장에 이미 제품이 많이 있을 때 사용되는 2차적 또는 선택적 수요 광고에 대해 이야기한다.

04

듣기 지문&해석

M The reality principle is how our mind strives to satisfy the id in socially acceptable and realistic ways. As we lose interest in socially acceptable activities through repetition, our id drives us to perform other less acceptable ones. To avoid such behavior, we develop a part of our personality that weighs the pros and cons of an activity and decides whether to act upon that impulse or to delay or disallow it altogether.

Two ways to ensure that socially acceptable activities continue to satisfy the id are by adjusting the frequency of the activity and adding variety to it. If we repeat the same activity in a regular pattern, it soon becomes boring. By waiting to perform that activity and doing it irregularly, we increase our anticipation, which in turn increases our pleasure when we actually do it. For example, if you really like ice cream, you should only eat it occasionally and not on a regular basis, which will make the ice cream taste even better. Injecting variety into the experience can also intensify our pleasure, so eating ice cream in different locations or trying new flavors should help.

남 현실원칙은 이드(id)를 사회적으로 용인되고 현실적인 방법들로 만족시키기 위해 우리의 생각이 분투하는 방식입니다. 반복을 통해 사회적으로 용인되는 행위에 대한 흥미를 잃으면 우리의 이드는 덜 받아들여지는 행위를 하도록 우리를 몰고 갑니다. 그러한 행동을 피하기 위해 우리는 어떤 행동의 장점과 단점을 따져보는 성격을 개발하고, 그러한 충동을 실행에 옮길 것인지, 아니면 연기하거나 완전히 인정하지 않을지 결정합니다.
사회적으로 용인되는 활동으로 계속 이드를 충족하는 두 가지 방법은 그 활동의 빈도를 조절하는 것과 활동에 다양성을 부여하는 것입니다. 같은 활동을 규칙적인 패턴으로 반복하면 곧 지루해지죠. 그 활동을 하는 것을 기다리고 불규칙적으로 함으로써 우리는 우리의 기대감을 증가시키고, 결과적으로 실제 그 활동을 할 때의 만족감을 증가시킵니다. 예를 들어, 여러분이 아이스크림을 정말 좋아한다면 아이스크림을 가끔, 그리고 불규칙적으로 먹어야 합니다. 이렇게 함으로써 아이스크림을 훨씬 더 맛있게 즐길 수 있을 것입니다. 경험에 다양성을 주입하는 것 또한 우리의 만족감을 높일 수 있으므로 다른 장소에서 아이스크림을 먹거나, 새로운 맛을 먹어보는 것도 도움이 될 겁니다.

어휘 reality principle 현실원칙 | strive v 분투하다 | acceptable adj 용인되는, 받아들일 수 있는 | repetition n 반복 | personality n 인격, 성격 | weigh v 따져보다, 저울질하다 | pros and cons 장단점 | act upon ~에 따라 행동하다 | disallow v 허용하지 않다 | adjust v 조절하다, 조정하다 | frequency n 빈도 | irregularly adv 불규칙적으로 | anticipation n 예측, 기대 | in turn 결과적으로 | occasionally adv 가끔 | on a regular basis 정기적으로, 규칙적으로 | inject v 주입하다 | intensify v 강화하다

노트 정리 예시

주제 reality principle (satisfy id in socially acceptable & realistic ways) → repetition → socially acceptable behavior X
- change frequency of the activity
- add variety to the activity

현실원칙 (사회적으로 용인되고 현실적 방법으로 이드를 충족시킴) → 반복 → 사회적으로 용인되는 행위 X
- 활동 빈도 바꾸기
- 활동에 다양성 더하기

▶ Question 1: What is the main idea of the lecture?

▶ Question 2: What are the two ways of satisfying id through reality principle?

강의의 주제는 무엇인가?

현실원칙을 통해 이드를 충족시키는 두 가지 방법은 무엇인가?

예시 답변

1. The professor talks about how we get tired of an activity through repetition. Reality principle kicks in to satisfy our id in a socially acceptable and realistic way.
2. There are two ways. One is to change the frequency of the activity, and the other is to add variety to the activity.

1. 교수는 우리가 어떻게 반복을 통해 어떤 행동을 지겹게 느끼게 되는지에 대해 말한다. 현실원칙은 이드를 사회적으로 용인되고 현실적인 방법으로 충족시키기 위해 개입한다.
2. 두 가지 방법이 있다. 하나는 활동의 빈도를 바꾸는 것이고, 다른 하나는 활동에 다양성을 더하는 것이다.

Lesson 03 정리해서 말하기

Practice 1

본서 | P. 280

01

Now listen to part of a lecture in an anthropology class.

이제 인류학 강의의 일부를 들으시오.

듣기 지문&해석

W Today, let's talk about one of the important concepts in anthropology, which is called cultural diffusion. As you all know, whenever groups of people come into contact, as they have throughout recorded history, they're bound to influence each other. And aspects of culture such as behaviors, ideas, materials, technology spread from one society to another. When a group or members of a group are exposed to the new culture; they adopt some aspects of that culture, and, from there, it spreads to the rest of their society.

Paper is a good example of cultural diffusion. It was originally developed by the Chinese in the second century BCE. At that time, other societies were writing on other materials, like papyrus or bamboo, but those were not as practical as paper made from wood pulp. So, as countries learned about it and learned how to make it, it spread quickly from China to Korea, and then to Japan. Later, it spread to the Middle East and India, and then, it spread to the West. I mean, this was very important technology, and it made a huge impact on all of the cultures that adopted it.

Another example of cultural diffusion is acupuncture. As a part of medical procedure, the Chinese have been using needles to treat illnesses for thousands of years. During the procedure, various sizes of needles, typically made of stainless steel, are inserted into different parts of the human body. This technique is especially well known for its effectiveness in treating certain medical problems, such

여 오늘은 인류학에서 중요한 개념 중 하나인 문화 확산이라고 불리는 것에 관해 이야기하도록 합시다. 여러분 모두 알다시피, 기록된 역사를 통해 늘 그래왔듯이 사람들의 집단은 접촉을 할 때마다 반드시 서로에게 영향을 미치게 됩니다. 이 과정에서 행동과 생각, 물질, 기술과 같은 문화의 측면들은 한 사회에서 다른 사회로 퍼져나가게 됩니다. 집단이나 집단의 구성원들이 새로운 문화에 노출되면 그들은 그 문화의 일부 측면을 받아들이게 되고, 거기서부터 그 문화는 그 사회의 나머지 부분으로 퍼집니다.

종이는 문화 확산의 좋은 예입니다. 종이는 기원전 2세기에 중국인들이 처음으로 개발했습니다. 그 당시 다른 사회에서는 파피루스나 대나무 같은 다른 재료에 글을 썼지만 그것들은 목재 펄프로 만든 종이만큼 실용적이지 않았습니다. 그래서 여러 나라들이 종이에 대해 알게 되고 종이를 만드는 방법을 배우게 되자 종이는 중국에서 한국으로, 그리고 일본으로 빠르게 퍼져나갔습니다. 그 뒤 종이는 중동과 인도로 퍼져나간 다음 서양으로 퍼져나갔습니다. 종이는 아주 중요한 기술이었고, 종이를 받아들인 모든 문화에 아주 큰 영향을 주었습니다.

문화 확산의 다른 예는 침술입니다. 의료 방법의 일환으로 중국인들은 수천 년 동안 병을 치료하기 위해 바늘을 사용했습니다. 시술하는 동안 주로 스테인리스 강철로 만들어진 다양한 크기의

as headaches or chronic pain. So these techniques have spread throughout Asia and are widely used. Since about the 1940s, many western countries have begun to adopt Chinese acupuncture. It's obviously gaining much more acceptance in many countries nowadays, but Westerners still haven't really accepted the exact traditional Asian medical system because it is so different from the Western system.

바늘이 몸의 다양한 부분에 삽입됩니다. 이 기술은 특히 두통이나 만성적인 통증 같은 질환을 치료하는 데 아주 효과적인 것으로 유명합니다. 그래서 이 기술은 아시아 전역으로 퍼져나갔고, 널리 사용되고 있습니다. 1940년대쯤부터 서양의 많은 나라들은 중국의 침술을 받아들이기 시작했습니다. 분명 요즘은 많은 나라에서 침술이 훨씬 더 많이 받아들여지고 있지만, 서양인들은 여전히 아시아의 전통적인 의료 체계 그대로를 실질적으로 수용하지는 않고 있는데, 그것이 서양의 체계와 너무 다르기 때문입니다.

어휘 anthropology n 인류학 | cultural diffusion 문화 확산 | come into contact 접촉하다 | recorded history 기록된 역사 | be bound to ~할 수밖에 없다 | aspect n 면, 양상 | spread v 퍼지다 | be exposed to ~에 노출되다 | adopt v 채택하다 | BCE (before the Common Era) 기원전 | bamboo n 대나무 | wood pulp 목재 펄프 | make an impact on ~에 영향을 미치다 | acupuncture n 침술 | medical procedure 의료 절차 | needle n 바늘 | treat v 치료하다 | illness n 질병 | stainless adj 녹슬지 않는, 스테인리스로 만든 | insert v 삽입하다 | well known 잘 알려진 | effectiveness n 효과 | chronic adj 만성적인 | widely adv 널리 | obviously adv 분명히 | gain acceptance 받아들이다 | nowadays adv 요즘

노트 정리 예시

주제 cultural diffusion: adopt new culture → spread

예시 1. paper
- origin: China → Asian countries → Middle East & India → West

2. acupuncture
- origin: China → Asian countries → West

문화 확산: 새로운 문화 받아들임 → 전파

1. 종이
– 기원: 중국 → 아시아 국가들 → 중동과 인도 → 서양

2. 침술
– 기원: 중국 → 아시아 국가들 → 서양

02

Now listen to part of a lecture in a biology class.

이제 생물학 강의의 일부를 들으시오.

듣기 지문&해석

M Last week in class, we covered how beneficial trees can be for the planet, and we also discovered some of the economic benefits of forests. Today, I'd particularly like to talk about the benefits of urban forests. Most of us are already well aware of the great advantage of trees in cities because they obviously provide us with shade and beautify the landscape. Well, these are, of course, great benefits, but they offer more than that. And, I'd like to talk about two of them.

One great benefit of the trees is absorbing many pollutants in the atmosphere of the cities. Among the many pollutants commonly found in the cities, trees can particularly remove much of the carbon dioxide. And since carbon dioxide is considered a direct cause of global warming and causes a lot of damage to the Earth as well as humans, I'd have to say that trees in urban areas play an extremely important role. Trees naturally require a significant amount of carbon

남 지난주 수업에서 우리는 나무가 지구에 얼마나 이로울 수 있는지에 대해서 다뤘고, 또한 산림의 몇몇 경제적 이점에 대해 배웠습니다. 오늘은 특별히 도시 산림의 이점에 대해 말하려고 합니다. 우리 대부분은 이미 도시에서 나무가 갖는 커다란 이점을 잘 알고 있습니다. 우리에게 그늘을 제공하고 주변 풍경을 아름답게 하기 때문이죠. 물론 이러한 것들도 큰 이점이긴 합니다만 나무는 그 이상을 제공합니다. 그 중 두 개를 이야기하겠습니다.

나무의 큰 이점 하나는 도시의 대기에서 많은 오염원을 흡수하는 것입니다. 도시에서 주로 발견되는 많은 오염원 중에서도 나무는 특히 다량의 이산화탄소를 제거할 수 있습니다. 이산화탄소는 지구 온난화의 직접적인 원인으로 여겨지며 인간뿐 아니라 지구에 많은 피해를 끼치기 때문에 도심지의 나무가 극히 중요한 역할을 한다고 할 수

dioxide for their survival and generate a great amount of oxygen in return. Therefore, cities can maintain fairly clean air even though there is a significant amount of harmful gases produced every day.
The other benefit of trees in urban spaces is that they help control the water flow. Trees help reduce urban runoff and erosion by storing water and breaking the force of rain as it falls. When it rains, it's easier for cities to be flooded. Since many of their structures are made of concrete and steel, they cannot absorb water at all. So, controlling the amount and rate of rainfall at a mild level is extremely important to the cities. But thanks to the trees, the runoff on the city surfaces can be controlled and moves at a much slower pace because rain falls on the leaves of trees first before it reaches the ground. And after the rain reaches the ground, the water flow can be controlled once again because the roots of the trees absorb and hold on to much of the water naturally absorbed by the ground. Due to their major roles in controlling pollution and water flow, many cities are investing in planting more trees.

있죠. 나무는 생존을 위해 자연적으로 상당한 양의 이산화탄소를 필요로 하고, 대신 엄청난 양의 산소를 발생시킵니다. 그러므로 매일 상당한 양의 해로운 기체가 생산됨에도 불구하고 도시는 꽤나 깨끗한 공기를 유지할 수 있는 겁니다.
도시 지역에서 나무의 또 다른 이점은 유수를 조절하는 데 도움을 준다는 겁니다. 나무는 물을 저장하고 빗물이 떨어지는 힘을 약화시켜 도시 지역의 유수와 침식을 줄입니다. 비가 오면 도시는 홍수가 나기 쉽습니다. 많은 건물들이 콘크리트와 강철로 만들어졌기 때문에 물을 전혀 흡수하지 못합니다. 그래서 강수량과 강수 비율을 약하게 조절하는 것이 도시에 특히 중요합니다. 하지만 나무 덕분에 도시 지면에 흐르는 빗물이 조절되고 훨씬 더 느린 속도로 흐르는 거죠. 비가 지면에 떨어지기 전에 나무의 잎에 먼저 떨어지기 때문입니다. 그리고 빗물이 지면에 떨어지고 나면 유수는 다시 한 번 조절될 수 있는데, 이는 나무의 뿌리가 땅에 자연스럽게 흡수된 물의 상당량을 흡수하고 저장하기 때문입니다. 오염과 물의 흐름을 조절하는 나무의 중요한 역할 때문에 많은 도시들이 더 많은 나무를 심는 데 투자하고 있습니다.

어휘 beneficial adj 이로운, 유익한 | urban adj 도시의 | a great advantage 커다란 이점 | shade n 그늘 | beautify v 아름답게 하다 | landscape n 풍경 | pollutant n 오염원 | atmosphere n 대기 | carbon dioxide 이산화탄소 | direct adj 직접적인 | cause n 원인 | generate v 생성하다 | oxygen n 산소 | in return 대신에 | water flow 유수 | runoff n 유수, 땅 위로 흐르는 물 | erosion n 침식 | store v 저장하다 | break the force 힘을 약화시키다 | flood n 홍수 v 홍수가 나다, 범람하다 | absorb v 흡수하다 | mild adj 약한, 가벼운, 온화한 | extremely adv 아주 | ground n 지표면 | hold on to 계속 보유하다, 꽉 잡다, 지키다 | invest v 투자하다

노트 정리 예시

주제 benefits of trees in cities

예시 1. absorb pollutants
- esp. carbon dioxide → generate oxygen

2. control water flow
- runoff on city surface → reach tree first before falling on the ground & roots of the trees absorb water

도시에 있는 나무의 이점

1. 오염원을 흡수함
– 특히 이산화탄소 → 산소를 발생시킴

2. 유수를 조절함
– 도시 지면에 흐르는 빗물 → 땅에 떨어지기 전에 나무에 먼저 도달함 & 나무 뿌리가 물을 흡수함

03

Listen to part of a lecture in a business class.

이제 경영학 강의의 일부를 들으시오.

듣기 지문&해석

W When a consumer has to choose between two products, what factors influence the decision? If the purchaser has to select between two products that cost the same, which one do you think he will buy? It is most likely that the purchasers will choose the higher quality product since the price is identical. But what does it mean for a product to

여 소비자가 두 가지 상품 중 선택을 해야 할 때 결정에 영향을 미치는 요인이 무엇일까요? 만약 가격이 같은 두 가지 상품 중 구매자가 선택을 해야 한다면 어떤 것을 구입할 거라고 생각하나요? 가격이 동일하기 때문에 품질이 더 좋은 상품을 선택할 가능성이 높겠죠. 하지만 제품이 고품질로

be considered high-quality? Business analysts lay out two major factors for quality: reliability and features.
Reliability is described as the quality of well-functioning products that last for a reasonable period of time without needing repairs. For example, if a car or any other vehicle does not function as well as expected by consumers and needs repairs too soon, the product can be defined as unreliable. So, it used to be that the reliability of a product was the key deciding factor in a consumers' purchase. I mean, don't get me wrong: the reliability is still an important factor these days, but because of the high standards of manufacturing lines in many countries, almost all vehicles are considered highly reliable and are often warranted for a substantial amount of time by their current manufacturers.
So, if the reliability is not the deciding factor anymore, what is it then? Features! The extra features that make the car more special and fancy are the ones that consumers consider these days. The extra features may not be necessary for the product to be used, but they have become essential for consumerism. Examples of features include but are not limited to remote keyless entry, a sunroof, air conditioning, built-in GPS navigation, a rear-seat DVD player, and mp3 compatible stereos. Since reliability is guaranteed pretty much equally with high manufacturing standards across the world, people review features when comparing products. This is why manufacturers today provide various features when releasing new lines of products.

여겨진다는 게 무슨 의미일까요? 경영 분석가들은 품질에 관한 두 가지 주요 요인을 제시합니다. 신뢰성과 특성입니다.
신뢰성은 수리할 필요 없이 합리적인 기간 동안 잘 기능하는 제품의 품질이라고 묘사됩니다. 예를 들어, 만약 자동차나 다른 어떤 차량이 소비자가 기대하는 것만큼 잘 작동하지 않고, 너무 금세 수리를 필요로 한다면 이 제품은 신뢰할 수 없다고 정의될 수 있죠. 그래서 제품의 신뢰성이야말로 소비자의 구매에 결정적인 요인이 되곤 했습니다. 오해하진 마세요, 신뢰성은 오늘날에도 여전히 중요한 요소지만, 많은 나라의 제조 라인이 높은 기준을 갖고 있기 때문에 거의 모든 차량들은 매우 신뢰할 수 있는 것으로 여겨지며, 현재 제조사가 상당히 오랜 기간 동안 품질 보증을 합니다.
그래서 만약 신뢰성이 더 이상 결정적 요인이 아니라면 무엇이 결정적 요인일까요? 특성입니다! 차를 더 특별하고 멋지게 하는 추가 특성들이야말로 요즘 소비자들이 고려하는 것이죠. 이러한 추가적 특성들은 제품을 사용하는 데 필수적인 것은 아닐지 모르지만 소비에는 필수적인 것이 되었습니다. 특성의 예에는 차량 원격 조종 장치, 선루프, 에어컨, 내장형 GPS 내비게이션, 뒷좌석 DVD 플레이어, 그리고 mp3 호환 스테레오가 포함되며, 이뿐만이 아닙니다. 신뢰성은 세계 전역에서 높은 제조 기준으로 거의 동일하게 보장되므로 사람들은 제품을 비교할 때 특성을 살피죠. 그래서 오늘날 제조사들은 새 제품 라인을 출시할 때 다양한 특성을 제공합니다.

어휘 purchaser n 구매자 | it is likely that ~할 것 같다 | identical adj 동일한 | analyst n 분석가 | lay out 펼치다 | reliability n 신뢰성 | feature n 특징 | well-functioning adj 기능을 잘하는 | reasonable adj 합리적인, 적당한 | vehicle n 차량, 탈것 | define v 정의하다 | deciding factor 결정적인 요인 | high standard 높은 기준 | manufacturing line 제조 라인 | substantial amount of time 상당한 시간 | consumerism n 소비, 소비지상주의 | remote keyless entry 차량 원격 조종 장치(열쇠 없이 차 문을 원격으로 열고 닫을 수 있는 시스템) | sunroof n 선루프(자동차의 개폐식 지붕) | rear adj 뒤의, 후방의 | compatible adj 호환이 되는 | across the world 전 세계에

노트 정리 예시

주제 purchasing a product → what influences the decision?

예시 1. reliability
- function well, last long: cars

2. features
- more important than reliability
- many features of cars

상품 구매하기 → 결정에 영향을 미치는 것은 무엇인가?

1. 신뢰성
– 잘 작동하고, 오래감: 자동차

2. 특성
– 신뢰성보다 더 중요함
– 차의 다양한 특성들

04

Listen to part of a lecture in a zoology class.

이제 동물학 강의의 일부를 들으시오.

듣기 지문&해석

M Researchers once thought that only human beings used tools. In fact, that was an important characteristic particular to humans—something that made us different from animals and distinguished our behavior as intelligent. But more recently, this idea has changed. Since in the early 1960s, researchers have observed animals using tools as well. So, that has really challenged the way we think of ourselves as distinct from animals, or at least unique in terms of our intelligence. However, it's very important how we define "tool" in this context. We can talk about two different types of definitions: a broad definition and a narrow definition.

First, according to the broad definition, a tool can be anything that is used to perform a task. Its shape doesn't have to be changed or transformed under this definition. Let me give you an example. When elephants feel their backs are itchy, they sometimes find and pick up branches and use them to scratch their backs. So, in this case, even though there isn't any change in or transformation of the object, it can still be said that elephants exhibit tool use because they use the branches as tools to perform the task of scratching their backs.

By the narrow definition, though, a tool is something from the environment that is changed or adapted in order to perform a task. That is, a tool is something that is made and transformed for a purpose. But, surprisingly, there are a few animals that exhibit tool use even according to this narrow definition. Chimps have been seen stripping the leaves off of branches to make tools for catching termites. Sometimes they even chew the end to make it narrower so it can fit inside the opening of the termites' nest. They're adapting something that they've found in their environment for a specific use, and that is clearly tool use. Most researchers feel that it shows they have some form of intelligence.

남 학자들은 한때 인간만 도구를 사용한다고 생각했습니다. 사실 이 점은 인간에게 특별히 나타나는 중요한 특징으로서, 인간을 동물과 다르게 만들어주었고 사람의 행동이 지능적인 특징을 갖게 해주었습니다. 하지만 최근에 이러한 생각이 바뀌었습니다. 1960년대 초부터 학자들은 마찬가지로 도구를 사용하는 동물들을 관찰했습니다. 그래서 우리 스스로가 동물과 구별된다는 생각, 혹은 최소한 지능이라는 점에서는 유일무이하다는 생각에 이의가 제기되었습니다. 그러나 이 맥락에서 '도구'를 어떻게 정의하느냐가 아주 중요합니다. 넓은 정의와 좁은 정의, 두 종류로 말할 수 있습니다.

먼저 넓은 의미로 볼 때 도구는 어떤 일을 수행할 때 사용되는 어떤 것이든 될 수 있습니다. 이 정의에 따르면 도구의 형태는 변화하거나 변형될 필요가 없습니다. 예시를 드리겠습니다. 코끼리는 등이 가렵다고 느낄 때 때로 나뭇가지를 찾아 집어 들고 등을 긁는 데 사용합니다. 그러므로 이 경우 도구에 어떠한 변화나 변형이 없지만 등을 긁는 일에 사용하는 도구로 나뭇가지를 썼기 때문에 여전히 코끼리도 도구를 사용한다고 말할 수 있습니다.

하지만 좁은 의미에서 보면 도구는 주변 환경으로부터 가져와서 어떤 일을 수행하기 위해 변형되거나 개조된 것입니다. 즉, 도구는 어떠한 목적으로 만들어지거나 변형된 것입니다. 그러나 놀랍게도 이 좁은 개념을 따르더라도 도구 사용을 보여주는 몇몇 동물들이 있습니다. 침팬지는 나뭇가지에서 잎을 떨어뜨려 흰개미를 잡는 도구를 만듭니다. 심지어 나뭇가지 끝을 씹어서 흰개미 집의 입구에 집어넣기 알맞도록 더 가늘게 만들기도 합니다. 그들이 특정 용도를 위해 주변 환경에서 찾은 무언가를 변형했기에 이는 분명히 도구 사용입니다. 대부분의 학자들은 이러한 도구 사용이야말로 침팬지에게 지능이 있음을 보여준다고 생각합니다.

어휘 characteristic n 특징 | distinguish v 구별하다, 구분하다 | observe v 관찰하다 | the way we think of ~를 생각하는 방식 | distinct adj 뚜렷한, 구분이 되는 | unique adj 독특한 | in terms of ~라는 점에서 | intelligence n 지능 | context n 상황, 맥락 | definition n 정의 | transform v 변형시키다 | itchy adj 가려운 | pick up 줍다 | branch n 나뭇가지 | scratch v 긁다 | in this case 이 경우에 | exhibit v 보여주다 | tool use 도구 사용 | perform v 수행하다 | adapt v 개조하다, 적응하다 | strip off ~을 벗기다 | termite n 흰개미 | chew v 씹다 | fit v ~에 맞추다

노트 정리 예시

주제 tool use of animals

예시 1. broad definition: adaptation X
- elephants: use a branch to scratch

동물의 도구 사용

1. 넓은 정의: 개조 X
– 코끼리: 긁는 데 나뭇가지를 사용함

2. narrow definition: adaptation O
- chimps: use a branch to catch termites

2. 좁은 정의: 개조 O
– 침팬지: 흰개미를 잡기 위해 나뭇가지를 사용함

Practice 2

본서 P. 282

01

Now listen to part of a lecture in a psychology class.

이제 심리학 강의의 일부를 들으시오.

듣기 지문&해석

W Today, I'd like to focus on how babies develop an emotional attachment to their mothers. As you all know, developing an emotional attachment in infancy is really important for one's life because it determines the social and emotional development of that person. Then, how does a baby develop this attachment bond with its caregiver?
It is a pretty well-known fact that babies have an emotional attachment to their mother, who feeds them. People have usually thought that the most essential factor in the creation of this emotional relationship and sense of attachment is the act of feeding. So, it has been thought that babies become attached to whoever feeds them. However, a study has shown that babies actually respond more to the warm and loving touch rather than the food itself. This has implications for emotional development in raising children, showing the importance for children to bond with parents through touch.
Now let's look at the experiment that was conducted during the study in more detail. The research involved an experiment using monkeys as subjects. In this experiment, baby monkeys were divided into groups, and the researchers observed how these monkeys responded. They basically placed two different replacement mothers among the monkeys. One of the fake mothers was made from soft material while the other was bare, made only from metal wire, but both mothers contained food. The researchers let the baby monkeys play without any instruction or guidance. Interestingly, during the experiment, the researchers found that monkeys preferred to spend time with the soft cloth mother rather than the bare metal wire mother. Even when the bare metal wire mother contained more food, the baby monkeys responded in the same way and spent more time with the soft material mother. Thus, it was shown that the baby monkeys favored touch over food.

여 오늘은 어떻게 아기들이 엄마에게 감정적 애착을 갖게 되는지에 초점을 맞춰보겠습니다. 여러분들도 모두 아시다시피 유아기에 감정적 애착을 발달시키는 것은 한 사람의 사회적, 정서적 발달을 결정하기 때문에 그 사람의 인생에 정말 중요한 일입니다. 그렇다면 어떻게 아기는 돌보는 사람과 이런 애착 관계를 갖게 될까요?
아기가 자신에게 젖을 주는 엄마에게 감정적 애착을 가지고 있다는 것은 잘 알려진 사실입니다. 사람들은 보통 이러한 감정적 관계와 애착심 생성에 가장 중요한 요소는 젖을 주는 행위라고 생각해 왔습니다. 그래서 아기들이 젖을 주는 사람이면 누구든 애착을 갖게 된다고 생각해 왔습니다. 하지만 한 연구 결과가 아기는 실제로 음식 자체보다 따뜻하고 애정이 깃든 접촉에 반응한다는 것을 보여주었습니다. 이것은 아이 양육에서 감정 발달에 영향을 미치며, 아이들이 촉감을 통해 부모와 결속되는 것의 중요성을 보여줍니다.
이제 그 연구 중 수행한 실험을 더 자세히 살펴봅시다. 연구에는 원숭이를 대상으로 한 실험이 포함되었습니다. 이 실험에서 새끼 원숭이들을 그룹으로 나누고 연구자들은 이들이 어떻게 반응하는지 관찰했습니다. 연구원들은 기본적으로 두 개의 대체 어미 원숭이를 원숭이들 사이에 두었습니다. 가짜 어미 원숭이 하나는 부드러운 재료로 만들어졌고 다른 하나는 옷을 입히지 않은 철사로만 만들어졌지만 두 어미 모두 먹이를 갖고 있었습니다. 연구원들은 새끼 원숭이들에게 아무런 지시나 지도를 하지 않고 놀게 두었습니다. 흥미롭게도 실험 동안 학자들은 원숭이들이 옷을 입히지 않은 철사 어미보다 부드러운 천으로 된 어미와 더 많은 시간을 보낸다는 사실을 알게되었습니다. 심지어 옷을 입히지 않은 철사 어미에게 더 많은 음식이 있을 때도 새끼 원숭이들은 같은 방식으로 반응했고 부드러운 천으로 된 어미와 더 많은 시간을 보냈습니다. 따라서 새끼 원숭이들이 먹이보다 촉감을 더 선호한다는 점이 드러났습니다.

This was an important study as it showed for the first time that baby monkeys are not only interested in food. Rather, they are attracted by touch and warmth. With this experiment, many child psychologists concluded that babies are more attracted to a warm, loving touch than food or the action of feeding, and develop special bonds with their mothers through touch.

이 연구는 새끼 원숭이들이 먹이에만 흥미가 있는 것이 아니라는 점을 처음으로 보여주었기 때문에 중요한 연구였습니다. 오히려 원숭이들은 촉감과 따뜻함에 더 끌렸습니다. 이 실험으로 많은 아동 심리학자들이 아기들은 음식이나 음식을 먹여주는 행동보다는 따뜻하고 애정 있는 촉감에 더 끌리며, 촉감을 통해 엄마들과 특별한 유대감을 발전시킨다는 결론을 내렸습니다.

어휘 emotional attachment 감정적 애착 I infancy n 유아기 I bond n 유대, 결속 I caregiver n 돌보는 사람 I feed v 먹이다 I sense of attachment 애착심 I implication n 암시 I bond with 유대 관계를 형성하다 I conduct v (실험 등을) 수행하다 I in detail 상세히 I involve v 포함하다 I subject n (실험) 대상, 주제 I place v 두다 I replacement n 대체(물) I fake adj 가짜의 I bare adj 헐벗은 I metal wire 철사 I contain v 가지다 I instruction n 지시 I guidance n 안내, 지도 I favor v 호의를 가지다 I child psychologist 아동 심리학자

노트 정리 예시

주제 emotional attachment
예시 experiment w. monkeys
2 mothers: soft material & metal wire (both had food)
baby monkeys preferred soft mother
= conclusion: food < touch & warmth, maybe humans too

감정적 애착
원숭이 실험
두 어미: 부드러운 소재와 철사 (둘 다 먹이를 갖고 있음)
새끼 원숭이들은 부드러운 어미를 선호함
= 결론: 먹이 〈 촉감과 따뜻함, 아마 사람도 그러할 것임

Using points and examples from the lecture, explain how warm touch is related to creating parent-child bonds based on the experiment.

강의에서 주어진 요점과 예시를 이용하여 따뜻한 촉감이 부모 자식 간 유대 관계 형성과 어떻게 관련되어 있는지 실험에 근거하여 설명하시오.

말하기 정리 예시

The lecture deals with emotional attachment as illustrated by an experiment that was conducted using monkeys.
Two groups of baby monkeys were exposed to two replacement mothers, one made of a soft material, the other made of bare metal wire. Both mothers contained food and were able to feed the babies. The experiment showed that the babies preferred to spend time with the soft mother rather than the metal mother.
According to the professor, this shows that the baby monkeys were not only attracted by food but that they also craved touch and warmth. So, it can be concluded that warmth and softness and not food alone contribute to the creation of bond attachment between monkey mothers and babies, and perhaps, therefore, in humans too.

강의는 원숭이를 이용한 실험으로 설명된 감정적 애착을 다룬다.
두 그룹의 새끼 원숭이들이 두 마리의 대체 어미에게 노출되었는데, 한 마리는 부드러운 재료로 만들어졌고, 다른 한 마리는 옷을 입히지 않은 철사로 만들어졌다. 두 어미 모두 먹이를 갖고 있었고 새끼들에게 먹이를 줄 수 있었다. 이 실험은 새끼들이 금속 어미보다 부드러운 어미와 시간을 보내는 것을 더 좋아한다는 것을 보여주었다.
교수에 따르면, 이것은 새끼 원숭이들이 먹이에만 이끌린 게 아니라, 촉감과 따뜻함을 갈망했다는 것을 보여준다. 그래서 먹이뿐만 아니라 따뜻함과 부드러움이 원숭이 어미들과 새끼들 사이의 유대감 형성에 영향을 주며, 그리고 아마도 인간에게도 영향을 미친다고 결론지을 수 있다.

02

Now listen to part of a lecture in a psychology class.

이제 심리학 강의의 일부를 들으시오.

듣기 지문&해석

M Scientists have recently learned an interesting thing about the intellectual abilities of babies. They believe that children as young as five months old acquire basic arithmetic comprehension such as addition. There is, in fact, evidence of babies recognizing that one plus one equals two and not one. Obviously, we came to this conclusion from an observational study because of the limitations of babies to communicate verbally.

So, let me explain this with one experiment... um... An experiment was conducted in which a doll was presented on a table for the baby to see. After a few moments, the researcher placed a screen in front of the doll so that there was a barrier between the baby and the doll. The baby could no longer see the doll but could sense that there was a doll behind the screen. Well, with the baby watching, the researcher placed a second doll behind the screen resulting in what should have been a total of two dolls. But the researcher took one away secretly.

Then the researcher removed the screen so that the baby could see the doll again. Not knowing that the researcher has secretly taken away one of the dolls, the baby expected to see two dolls. However, since what the baby saw was not two but only one, the baby was very surprised. Well, the surprised reaction of the baby was analyzed based on its eye movements.

Generally, when a baby is surprised by something such as a loud bang or sudden flash of lights, it focuses on the source of the surprise by staring at it. And in the experiment, the baby did exactly the same thing. Since the number of dolls that the baby saw was different from what it had expected, the baby stared at the table. And this experiment indicates that babies are, in fact, able to count to this basic number.

남 과학자들은 최근 아기들의 지적 능력에 관해 재미있는 점을 발견했습니다. 이들은 생후 5개월밖에 안 된 아기가 덧셈 같은 기본적인 계산 능력을 습득할 수 있다고 생각합니다. 그리고 실제로 아기들이 1 더하기 1이 1이 아니라 2라는 것을 인지한다는 증거가 있습니다. 분명히 아기는 언어로 소통하는 것에 한계가 있기 때문에 관찰 연구를 통해 이 결론에 도달했습니다.

자, 그럼 이것을 하나의 실험을 가지고 설명하겠습니다… 음… 한 실험에서는 탁자 위에 아기가 볼 수 있도록 인형을 한 개 놓고 실험을 진행했습니다. 잠시 후에 연구자는 그 인형 앞에 가리개를 두어 아기와 인형 사이에 장애물이 있도록 만들었습니다. 그 아기는 더 이상 인형을 볼 수 없었으나 가리개 뒤에 인형이 있다는 것은 알 수 있었습니다. 아기가 보고 있을 때 연구자는 두 번째 인형을 가리개 뒤에 두어 인형이 전부 두 개가 되도록 만들었습니다. 하지만 연구자는 몰래 하나를 치웠어요.

그런 다음 연구자는 가리개를 치워 아기가 인형을 다시 볼 수 있게 했습니다. 연구자가 몰래 인형 하나를 치운 줄 몰랐던 아기는 두 개의 인형을 볼 것으로 예상했습니다. 하지만 아기가 본 것은 두 개가 아니라 하나였기에 아기는 매우 놀랐습니다. 음, 아기의 놀란 반응은 눈 움직임에 기반하여 분석했습니다.

일반적으로 아기는 큰 소리나 갑작스러운 섬광 같은 것에 놀랐을 때 그것을 계속 응시함으로써 놀라게 한 근원에 집중합니다. 그리고 이 실험에서 아기는 정확히 그렇게 했습니다. 아기가 보았던 인형의 숫자가 기대했던 것과 달랐기 때문에 탁자를 응시했던 것입니다. 이 실험은 사실 아기들이 기본적인 계산을 할 수 있다는 것을 보여줍니다.

어휘 acquire v 습득하다 | arithmetic n 산수, 계산 | comprehension n 이해 | addition n 덧셈 | come to a conclusion 결론에 도달하다 | observational study 관찰 연구 | limitation n 한계 | verbally adv 말로, 구두로 | conduct v 행하다 | screen n 칸막이, 가리개 | barrier n 장애물, 장벽 | take away 없애다 | bang n 쾅 하는 소리 | flash of light 섬광 | focus on ~에 집중하다 | source n 원천, 근원 | stare at ~을 응시하다 | indicate v 나타내다, 보여주다 | count v 계산하다, (숫자를) 세다

노트 정리 예시

주제 babies' intellectual abilities

예시 show a doll → place a screen to hide it
show another doll → secretly take away
baby expects 2 dolls → see only 1 doll → surprised
= conclusion: babies can count

아기들의 지적 능력

인형 하나를 보여줌 → 숨기기 위해 가리개를 둠
다른 인형을 보여줌 → 몰래 치움
아기는 인형 2개를 예상 → 인형 1개만 봄 → 놀람
= 결론: 아기들은 계산을 할 수 있음

Using an experiment given in the lecture, explain how babies show their basic intellectual abilities.

강의에서 주어진 실험을 이용하여 아기들이 어떻게 기본적인 지적 능력을 보여주는지 설명하시오.

말하기 정리 예시

The lecture is mainly about the intellectual abilities of babies. The professor explains this by giving one experiment as an example.
In the experiment, a baby was shown a doll on the table, and after a moment, the researcher placed a screen between the baby and a doll. While the baby was still watching, a researcher placed another doll on the table. However, one of the dolls was secretly taken away behind the screen.
After the screen was removed, the baby looked surprised. This is because the baby was expecting to see two dolls. This experiment demonstrates that babies are in fact able to do basic counting.

강의는 주로 아기들의 지적 능력에 관한 것이다. 교수는 한 가지 실험을 예로 들어 이를 설명한다.
실험에서 아기에게 탁자 위에 놓인 인형을 보여주고, 잠시 후 연구자가 아기와 인형 사이에 가리개를 설치했다. 아기가 아직 쳐다보고 있는 동안, 연구원은 또 다른 인형을 탁자 위에 놓았다. 그러나 그 인형들 중 하나는 가리개 뒤에서 몰래 치워졌다.
가리개가 치워진 후 아기는 놀란 표정을 지었다. 이는 아기가 인형 두 개를 볼 것으로 예상했기 때문이다. 이 실험은 사실 아기들이 기본적인 계산을 할 수 있다는 것을 보여준다.

V. Actual Test

Actual Test 1

본서 | P. 286

Question 1

If you have a question about an assignment that a professor has given you, would you prefer to speak to the professor via e-mail or in person? Explain.

교수가 내준 과제에 대해 의문 사항이 있다면, 당신은 교수에게 이메일로 이야기하는 것과 직접 이야기하는 것 중 어느 것을 선호하겠는가? 설명하시오.

예시 답변

If I have a question about an assignment that a professor has given me, I would prefer to speak to the professor in person. I have two reasons to support this idea. First, if the professor is busy, it could take days or weeks to receive his reply. Since there is a deadline for an assignment, it is important to have my questions answered as soon as possible. Second, when I am communicating with my professor via e-mail, I have to send another e-mail if follow-up questions come to mind. Instead, I can ask all of these questions if I speak to him in person. These are the reasons why I would prefer to speak to a professor in person.

만약 교수님이 내주신 과제에 대해 질문이 생기면, 나는 교수님에게 직접 이야기하는 것을 선호할 것이다. 이 의견을 뒷받침할 두 가지 이유가 있다. 첫째, 교수님이 바쁘면, 답장을 받을 때까지 며칠 혹은 몇 주가 걸릴 수도 있다. 과제에는 마감기한이 있기 때문에, 내 질문에 대한 답을 최대한 빨리 받는 것이 중요하다. 둘째, 이메일로 대화를 하면, 후속 질문이 생각났을 때 이메일을 또 보내야 한다. 대신, 교수님과 직접 대화를 하면 이 모든 질문들을 물어볼 수 있다. 이것이 내가 교수님과 직접 이야기하는 것을 선호하는 이유이다.

어휘 assignment n 과제 | via e-mail 이메일로 | in person 직접, 몸소 | follow-up adj 후속의, 뒤따르는 n 후속 조치, 후속 기사

Question 2

Read the notice on the registration page about poetry classes. You will have 45 seconds to read. Begin reading now.

수강 신청 페이지에 있는 시 수업에 관한 공지를 읽으시오. 읽는 데 45초가 주어진다. 이제 읽기 시작하시오.

읽기 지문&해석

Closing Poetry Writing Courses

Beginning in the fall semester, Regis University will no longer offer poetry writing courses. This is due to the fact that

시 쓰기 수업 폐강

가을 학기부터 레지스 대학교에서는 시 쓰기 수업을 더 이상 제공하지 않을 것입니다. 이는 등록자 수가

registration numbers are consistently low, and the grading system is too subjective. This has led many students to dispute the scores that they have received in the courses. Students who still wish to take poetry writing classes may take them at Foothills Art Institute. The credits for those classes will be fully transferable and count towards your overall degree.

지속적으로 적기 때문이며, 성적 산출 시스템이 너무 주관적이기 때문입니다. 이로 인해 많은 학생들이 자기가 강의에서 받은 점수에 대해 이의를 제기했습니다. 여전히 시 쓰기 수업을 듣고 싶은 학생들은 풋힐스 예술학교에서 수업을 들을 수 있습니다. 그 수업의 학점은 전부 인정이 되며 여러분의 전체적인 학위 취득(을 위한 학점)에 포함될 것입니다.

어휘 registration number 등록자 수 I consistently adv 지속적으로 I grading system 성적 산출 시스템 I subjective adj 주관적인 I credit n 학점 I transferable adj 전환 가능한

Now listen to two students as they discuss the notice.

이제 공지에 대해 논의하는 두 학생의 대화를 들으시오.

듣기 지문&해석

M Hello, Clarice. What's wrong?
W Hi, Bill. I don't want to talk about it.
M Are you sure?
W Did you see the notice on the registration page about poetry classes?
M Poetry classes... oh, yeah. Yes, I did. Are they really going to close them all?
W They aren't just closing them. They are completely removing them from the course catalog. They will never be taught here again.
M Do you know why they made that decision?
W They said that there are too few students, which means that they think they are a waste of money... typical university attitude towards the arts and humanities. Of course, the classes are small. They're meant to be so the students can get the attention and feedback they need for their work. The senior seminar classes are all small, so are they going to remove them as well?
M I doubt it, those are required courses. But, didn't the notice say something about classes at Foothills Art Institute?
W Yes, they said that students can take classes there and receive credit for them here. Which is very nice of FAI, they don't have to do that.
M I guess they want to help out artists as much as they can.
W Unlike our school... but FAI is so far away. I mean, it isn't even in the same city.
M Doesn't the subway go there?
W No, at least, not yet it doesn't. They are extending the line, but the station won't open for a year or more. So, students would have to take buses, which only go there once an hour. Otherwise, they have to have their own transportation.
M And most students don't have cars.
W Exactly. It's really unfair.

남 안녕, 클라리스. 무슨 일이야?
여 안녕, 빌. 별로 이야기하고 싶지 않아.
남 확실해?
여 수강 신청 페이지에 있는 시 수업에 관한 공지 봤니?
남 시 수업이라… 아, 응, 그래, 봤어. 정말 시 수업이 전부 폐강되는 거야?
여 그냥 폐강하는 정도가 아니야. 시 수업들을 강의 카탈로그에서 완전히 빼버리는 거야. 이곳에서 그 수업들이 다시 개설되는 일은 없을 거야.
남 학교 측이 왜 그런 결정을 내렸는지 아니?
여 학생 수가 너무 적대, 그건 학교에서 시 수업들이 돈 낭비라고 생각한다는 뜻이지… 예술과 인문학에 대한 전형적인 대학교 측의 태도야. 물론, 그 수업들은 규모가 작아. 학생들이 자신들의 작품에 필요한 관심과 피드백을 받기 위해서는 수업 규모가 작을 수밖에 없어. 4학년 세미나 수업들도 모두 규모가 작아. 그러면 그런 수업들도 다 없애겠다는 거야?
남 그렇지는 않겠지. 그 수업들은 필수 과목들이잖아. 그런데 공지에서 풋힐스 예술학교의 수업에 대해 뭔가 이야기하지 않았어?
여 그래, 학생들이 그곳에서 수업을 듣고 우리 학교에서 학점을 받을 수 있다고 했지. 풋힐스 예술학교에서 배려를 많이 한 거지, 그럴 필요가 없는데.
남 그들이 할 수 있는 만큼 예술가들을 도와주고 싶은가 봐.
여 우리 학교와는 다르게 말이지… 하지만 풋힐스 예술학교는 너무 멀어. 내 말은, 그 학교는 심지어 같은 도시에 있지도 않아.
남 지하철이 거기까지 가지 않아?
여 안 가, 적어도 아직은 안 가. 지하철 노선을 연장하고는 있지만 지하철이 개통되려면 일 년 이상은 걸릴 거야. 그래서 학생들은 버스를 타야 하는데 버스는 한 시간에 한 대만 운행해. 아니면 알아서 교통편을 마련해야 하지.

남 그리고 대부분의 학생들은 차를 가지고 있지 않지.
여 맞아. 이건 정말 불공평해.

어휘 humanities n 인문학 | extend v 연장하다 | unfair adj 불공평한

Now get ready to answer the question.

The woman expresses her opinion about the removal of poetry writing courses. State her opinion and explain the reasons she gives for holding that opinion.

이제 질문에 답하시오.

여자는 시 쓰기 수업을 없애는 것에 대해 자신의 의견을 표현하고 있다. 그녀의 의견에 대해 서술하고 그렇게 생각하는 이유가 무엇인지 설명하시오.

예시 답변

The reading passage explains that the school's poetry writing classes are being closed. It states that students can take the same courses at another university. However, the woman does not think this is a good idea. First, she says that removing the classes just because there are too few students does not make sense. Like all senior seminar classes, they are small because students need attention and feedback on their work. Second, she talks about the inconvenience of taking the same courses at the Foothills Art Institute. Since the school is located in another city, it takes a long time to get there, and the bus from the woman's school only goes there once an hour, which makes it even more inconvenient.

읽기 지문은 학교의 시 쓰기 수업이 폐강된다고 설명한다. 지문은 학생들이 다른 대학에서 같은 수업을 들을 수 있다고 말한다. 하지만 여자는 이것이 좋은 아이디어라고 생각하지 않는다. 첫째, 그녀는 학생이 너무 적다는 이유만으로 수업을 없앤다는 것은 말이 되지 않는다고 이야기한다. 다른 모든 4학년 세미나 수업들처럼, 학생들이 그들 작품에 대한 관심과 피드백을 필요로 하기 때문에 수업 규모가 작다. 둘째, 그녀는 풋힐스 예술학교에서 같은 수업을 듣는 것의 불편함에 대해 이야기한다. 그 학교가 다른 도시에 위치해 있기 때문에 그곳에 가려면 오랜 시간이 걸리고, 여자가 다니는 학교에서 그곳에 가는 버스는 한 시간에 한 대밖에 없어서 훨씬 더 불편하다.

Question 3

Now read the passage about plant communication. You have 50 seconds to read the passage. Begin reading now.

이제 식물의 의사소통에 관한 지문을 읽으시오. 지문을 읽는 데 50초가 주어진다. 이제 읽기 시작하시오.

읽기 지문&해석

Plant Communication

In the early 1980s, research showed that various trees might communicate with each other. When insects feed upon trees, they begin producing chemicals to deter them. The scientists observed that trees in the vicinity that were not infested also began to produce the same compounds. They thought that the plants were communicating that they were under attack, which was unprecedented for organisms that lack central nervous systems and are not in physical contact with each other. Their findings met immediate scrutiny and were discounted by much of the scientific community. However, recent research has provided data that supports their assertions.

식물의 의사소통

1980년대 초에 연구는 다양한 나무들이 서로 소통할 수 있다는 것을 보여주었다. 곤충들이 나무를 먹을 때, 나무들은 곤충을 막기 위해 화학 물질들을 만들어 내기 시작한다. 과학자들은 해충의 피해를 입지 않은 주변의 나무들 역시 같은 화합물을 만들어낸다는 것을 관찰하였다. 그들은 식물들이 공격을 받고 있다고 소통하는 것이라 생각했는데, 이는 중앙 신경체계를 가지고 있지 않고, 서로 물리적으로 접촉이 없는 생물체들에게는 전례가 없는 것이었다. 그들의 발견은 즉각적으로 철저한 검토 대상이 되었고, 대부분의 과학 단체로부터 무시당했다. 그러나 최근의 연구에서 그들의 주장을 뒷받침하는 자료가 제시되었다.

어휘 deter v 단념시키다, 그만두게 하다 | vicinity n 부근, 인근 | infest v 해충이 해치다, 해충이 들끓다 | compound n 화합물, 혼합물, 복합체 | be under attack 공격을 받고 있다 | unprecedented adj 전례 없는 | scrutiny n 정밀 조사, 철저한 검토 | discount v 무시하다, 무가치한 것으로 치부하다 | assertion n 주장, (권리 등의) 행사

Now listen to part of a lecture in a biology class.

이제 생물학 강의의 일부를 들으시오.

듣기 지문&해석

W Plants possess a variety of ways in which they can fight against organisms that attack and feed upon them. For example, many types of trees exude large amounts of sap when they are damaged by insects. This sap envelops some of the attackers, suffocating them. Many other plants produce chemicals that make them less nutritious, unpalatable, and even toxic to the insects that feed upon their leaves.

One scientist was studying Sitka willows and how they will alter the nutritional value of their leaves when they become infested by tent caterpillars. In a laboratory setting, he fed leaves from infested willows to caterpillars, and the worms that ate them grew more slowly than those that ate leaves from undamaged trees. However, he noticed that the leaves from undamaged trees in the lab also provided inferior nutrition to the caterpillars. He interpreted this to mean that the infested willows were emitting some kind of signal that the undamaged willows were responding to chemically in advance of predation. This was received with a great deal of skepticism.

A decade later, another scientist was studying sagebrush, which produces an airborne chemical called methyl jasmonate when it is attacked. The scientist thought that the chemical was being used to deter the insects from feeding, but it proved far more significant. He placed damaged leaves from sagebrush plants into airtight containers with tomato plants, and the tomatoes began pumping out their own defensive chemicals which affect insects' digestion. He believes that this not only confirms that plants can communicate in times of crisis, but that they can also communicate across species.

여 식물들은 그들을 공격하고 먹이로 삼는 생물에 대항해 싸우는 다양한 방법들을 가지고 있습니다. 예를 들면, 많은 종류의 나무들은 곤충들에 의해 피해를 받으면 많은 양의 수액을 분출합니다. 이러한 수액은 공격자들을 감싸서 질식시킵니다. 많은 다른 식물들은 스스로를 영양분이 적어지게 하고, 덜 맛있게 만들며, 자신의 잎을 먹는 곤충들에게 독성이 있기까지 한 화학 물질들을 만들어냅니다.

한 과학자는 시트카버드나무와 그것이 천막 벌레나방 유충의 피해를 입으면 어떻게 영양적 가치를 변화시키는지에 대해 연구했습니다. 실험실 환경에서 그는 충해를 입은 버드나무 잎을 유충들에게 먹였고, 그것을 먹은 유충들은 충해를 입지 않은 잎을 먹은 유충들보다 더 느리게 성장했습니다. 하지만 그는 실험실의 충해를 입지 않은 나무의 잎도 유충들에게 열등한 영양분을 제공한다는 것을 알아차렸습니다. 그는 이것이 충해를 입은 버드나무들이 피해를 입지 않은 나무들로 하여금 충해를 입기 전에 미리 화학적으로 반응하게 하는 어떤 신호를 보내고 있는 것이라고 해석했습니다. 이 연구는 매우 회의적으로 받아들여졌습니다.

십 년 후, 다른 과학자가 공격을 받으면 메틸 자스모네이트라는 공기로 운반되는 화학 물질을 분비하는 산쑥을 연구했습니다. 그 과학자는 그 화학 물질이 곤충이 그것을 먹는 것을 막는 데 사용된다고 생각했지만, 그보다 훨씬 더 중요한 것으로 증명되었어요. 그는 손상된 산쑥의 잎을 토마토와 함께 밀폐된 용기에 두었는데, 토마토가 곤충의 소화에 영향을 주는 방어적 화학 물질을 뿜어내기 시작했습니다. 그는 이것이 식물들이 위기의 순간에 소통할 수 있을 뿐만 아니라 종을 뛰어넘어 소통할 수 있다는 것이 사실임을 보여준다고 생각합니다.

어휘 exude v (액체나 냄새를) 흘리다 | sap n 수액 | suffocate v 질식시키다 | unpalatable adj 맛없는, 입에 안 맞는 | nutritional adj 영양상의 | emit v 내다, 내뿜다 | predation n 포식 | skepticism n 회의, 의심 | airborne adj 공기로 운반되는 | airtight adj 밀폐된 | digestion n 소화, 소화력

Now get ready to answer the question.

이제 질문에 답하시오.

The professor explains how plants communicate with each other by giving some examples. Explain how the examples demonstrate the topic in the reading passage.

교수는 몇 가지 예를 들어 식물들이 어떻게 서로 소통하는지 설명하고 있다. 예시들이 지문의 주제를 어떻게 입증하는지 설명하시오.

예시 답변

The professor explains the ways plants communicate with each other by giving a few examples. The first example was an experiment done with Sitka willows. The scientist testing this theory noticed that the caterpillars that ate damaged Sitka willow leaves grew more slowly. However, he soon discovered that the caterpillars that ate the leaves of undamaged trees were provided with inferior nutrition as well, which shows the connection between damaged and undamaged trees. The second experiment was done using damaged leaves from sagebrush plants and tomato plants. When the damaged leaves from sagebrush plants were placed into airtight containers with tomato plants, the tomatoes began pumping out their own defensive chemicals. This test confirmed that plants can also communicate across species.

교수는 몇 가지 예를 들어 식물들이 서로 소통하는 방법에 대해 설명한다. 첫 번째 예는 시트카버드나무로 한 실험이다. 이 이론을 시험한 과학자는 충해를 입은 시트카버드나무 잎을 먹은 유충들이 더 느리게 자랐다는 것을 알아차렸다. 그러나 그는 곧 충해를 입지 않은 나무의 잎을 먹은 유충들 또한 열등한 영양분을 제공받았다는 것을 발견했으며, 이는 충해를 입은 나무와 입지 않은 나무 사이의 연결점을 보여준다. 두 번째 실험은 충해를 입은 산쑥의 잎과 토마토를 가지고 한 것이다. 손상된 산쑥의 잎을 토마토와 함께 밀폐된 용기에 두었을 때, 토마토가 방어적 화학 물질을 뿜어내기 시작했다. 이 실험은 식물들이 종을 뛰어 넘어서도 소통할 수 있다는 것이 사실임을 보여주었다.

Question 4

Now listen to part of a lecture in a zoology class.

이제 동물학 강의의 일부를 들으시오.

읽기 지문&해석

M Many species of animals live in social groups of varying complexity. Some only form groups for short periods of time, while others live their entire lives as members of tight groups. Many of these groups are based upon their need to cooperate to survive. This is why examples of social cooperation often revolve around a species' feeding habits. In order for animals to successfully find and safely eat food, they often have to cooperate.

A very basic example of this can be seen with deer. When they are feeding alone, deer must constantly be on the lookout for predators like wolves and mountain lions. This means that an individual animal cannot concentrate on eating, so it can only eat small amounts of food at a time. But when deer graze in groups, the animals will sort of take turns eating and being on the lookout. The animals will gather plants for a while, and then look around while chewing their food. This means that a few deer are always looking around for danger while the others graze.

On the other hand, honeybees live in very complex, cooperative groups. Honeybees live in hives that contain thousands of individuals, and every action is done for the good of the whole group. When one worker bee discovers food, it will return to the hive to tell its sisters. It communicates through a special dance that has repeated body movements. These movements tell the others what direction the food is in and how far away it is. This allows the bees to go there as a group and bring back a large amount of food. They share the food according to the group's needs, so the hive can be nourished effectively.

남 많은 종의 동물들은 가지각색의 복잡한 사회적 무리에서 생활합니다. 어떤 동물들은 잠시 동안만 무리를 짓는 반면, 다른 동물들은 강한 유대를 지닌 무리의 구성원으로 전 생애를 살아갑니다. 이러한 무리들 중 많은 수는 생존을 위한 협력의 필요성에 기반하고 있습니다. 사회적 협동의 예들이 종종 그 종의 먹이 섭취 습성을 중심으로 돌아가는 이유가 바로 이것입니다. 동물들은 성공적으로 먹이를 찾고 안전하게 먹기 위해 자주 협력해야 합니다.

이것의 가장 기본적인 예는 사슴에게서 찾아볼 수 있습니다. 사슴은 혼자서 먹이를 먹을 때, 늑대나 퓨마와 같은 포식자들을 항상 경계해야 합니다. 이는 그 한 마리는 먹이를 먹는 것에 집중하지 못해서, 한 번에 적은 양의 먹이만을 먹을 수 있다는 것을 뜻합니다. 하지만 사슴이 무리를 지어 먹이를 먹을 때, 이들은 번갈아 가며 먹고 망을 봅니다. 사슴들은 잠깐 풀을 모으고, 그다음에 풀을 씹어 먹으면서 주변을 둘러보죠. 이것은 다른 사슴들이 풀을 뜯는 동안 몇 마리의 사슴들은 항상 위험을 살피고 있다는 의미입니다.

한편, 꿀벌은 매우 복잡하고 협력적인 무리를 이뤄 삽니다. 꿀벌은 수천 마리가 모여 있는 벌집에서 생활하고, 모든 행동은 무리 전체의 이익을 위해 행해집니다. 한 마리의 일벌이 먹이를 발견하면, 그 벌은 다른 벌들에게 소식을 전하기 위해 벌집으로 돌아옵니다. 벌은 몸 동작을 반복하는 특별한 춤을 통해 의사소통을 합니다. 이러한 움직임은 다른 벌들에게 먹이가 어느 방향에 있고 얼마나 멀리 있는지 알려줍니다. 이 행동은 벌들이 무리로 그곳에 가서 많은 양의 먹이를 가져올 수 있도록 해줍니다. 벌들은 벌집 전체가 효율적으로 영양분을 공급받을 수 있도록 무리의 필요에 따라 먹이를 나눕니다.

어휘 varying adj 가지각색의 I complexity n 복잡성 I cooperate v 협력하다 I feeding habit 먹이 섭취 습성 I on the lookout 망을 보고, 경계하여 I mountain lion 퓨마 I graze v 풀을 뜯다 I take turns -ing 교대로 ~하다 I hive n 벌집 I nourish v 영양분을 공급하다

Now get ready to answer the question.

Using points and examples from the lecture, describe how deer and honeybees practice social cooperation in their feeding habits.

이제 질문에 답하시오.

강의에서 제시된 요점과 예시를 이용하여 사슴과 꿀벌이 먹이 섭취 습성에서 어떻게 사회적 협력을 하는지 서술하시오.

예시 답변

The professor describes how animals use social cooperation to survive by giving two examples. First, he describes how deer cooperate when feeding. When they graze in groups, they take turns eating and being on the lookout. As a result, a few deer are always looking around for danger while the others graze safely. Second, he describes how honeybees cooperate when they bring and share food. When an individual worker bee discovers food, it returns to the hive to tell its sisters the location of the food through a special dance. This allows the bees to go there as a group and bring back a large amount of food. They share the food according to the group's needs.

교수는 동물들이 생존하기 위해 어떻게 사회적 협력을 이용하는지 두 가지 예를 들어 설명한다. 첫째, 그는 사슴이 먹이를 먹을 때 어떻게 협력하는지 묘사한다. 사슴은 무리를 지어 풀을 뜯을 때, 번갈아 가며 먹고 망을 본다. 결과적으로 다른 사슴들이 안전하게 풀을 뜯는 동안, 항상 몇 마리의 사슴은 망을 본다. 둘째, 그는 꿀벌이 먹이를 가져오고 나눌 때 어떻게 협력하는지 설명한다. 한 마리의 일벌이 먹이를 발견하면, 그 벌은 벌집으로 돌아와 특별한 춤을 통해 다른 일벌들에게 먹이의 위치를 알린다. 이는 벌들이 무리로 그곳에 가서 많은 양의 먹이를 가지고 올 수 있도록 해준다. 그들은 무리의 필요에 따라 먹이를 나눈다.

Actual Test 2

본서 | P. 292

Question 1

When traveling, many people like to keep a record of their voyage. Others prefer to engage in activities rather than using their time to document the trip. Which do you prefer and why?

많은 사람들은 여행을 할 때 그들의 여행을 기록하는 것을 좋아한다. 다른 사람들은 여행을 기록하는 데 시간을 쓰기보다는 활동하는 것을 선호한다. 당신은 어떤 것을 선호하며 그 이유는 무엇인가?

예시 답변

I prefer to engage in activities rather than document my trip when traveling. First, I can engage in certain activities only in a special place. For example, exploring a gorgeous reef is possible only in Australia. So, missing out on that activity would be equal to not going on the trip at all. Second, I can broaden my mind and experience more. To be specific, I can visit museums and historic places to learn about the country's culture. For these reasons, I prefer to engage in activities rather than document my trip when traveling.

나는 여행할 때 여행을 기록하기보다는 활동을 하는 것을 선호한다. 우선, 나는 특별한 곳에서만 할 수 있는 특정 활동을 할 수 있다. 예를 들어, 아름다운 암초를 탐험하는 일은 호주에서만 가능하다. 그래서 그런 활동을 놓치는 일은 여행을 아예 안 간 것이나 다름없을 것이다. 둘째, 여행을 통해 마음을 넓힐 수 있고 더 많이 경험할 수 있다. 구체적으로 말하자면, 나는 그 나라의 문화에 대해 배우기 위해 박물관이나 역사적 명소를 가 볼 수 있다. 이러한 이유들로 나는 여행을 할 때 여행을 기록하기보다는 활동을 하는 것을 선호한다.

어휘 keep a record 기록하다 | voyage n 여행 | engage in activities 활동을 하다 | document v 기록하다 | explore v 탐험하다 | gorgeous adj 아주 아름다운/멋진 | reef n 암초 | miss out on ~를 놓치다 | broaden v 넓히다

Question 2

Read an e-mail from the professor. You will have 45 seconds to read. Begin reading now.

교수가 보내온 이메일을 읽으시오. 읽는 데 45초가 주어진다. 이제 읽기 시작하시오.

읽기 지문&해석

Greetings students,

As I informed you earlier, I will go to a conference next week, so I will be unable to teach your class. Instead, two of my colleagues have agreed to be guest instructors in my absence. Both are biology professors and active field researchers that spent last summer observing wildlife in two very different climates. You will be able to learn new information from their actual experiences, which should be a nice change of pace from your normal course material. I hope that you enjoy their visits and that you take advantage of this rare opportunity to ask questions of active field researchers.

Sincerely,

Professor Lee

학생 여러분 안녕하세요.

전에 공지한 바와 같이, 제가 다음 주에 학회에 참석하게 되어 수업을 할 수 없게 되었습니다. 대신 동료 두 명이 제가 없는 동안 초대 강사가 되어주기로 했습니다. 두 사람 모두 생물학 교수이며, 지난 여름을 각기 매우 다른 기후의 야생 생태계를 연구하는 데 보낸 활발한 현장 연구원들입니다. 여러분은 그들의 실제 경험에서 새로운 정보를 배울 수 있을 것이며, 이는 여러분의 정규 수업 내용에서 벗어난 좋은 변화가 될 것입니다. 여러분이 초대 강사들의 방문을 즐기고, 현장 연구원들에게 질문할 수 있는 이 귀한 기회를 활용하기 바랍니다.

리 교수

어휘 conference n 학회 | field researcher 현장 연구원 | change of pace 기존의 방법을 바꿈, 기분 전환

Now listen to two students as they discuss the e-mail.

이제 이메일에 대해 논의하는 두 학생의 대화를 들으시오.

듣기 지문&해석

M Did you check your e-mail this afternoon?

W Yes, I did, and I think I know which message you are going to ask me about.

M You don't sound pleased.

W No, I am not. I understand that our professors have to attend conferences, but I don't like the fact that she invited guest lecturers to take her place. I think that they should just reschedule the class.

M Wouldn't that be really inconvenient?

W I don't think most of the students would mind as long as she told us in advance. We could attend lectures by other professors that teach the same course, or she could arrange extra evening sessions for next week. The students would have enough time to rearrange their own schedules, or they could arrange to copy a classmate's notes.

M I guess so, but I think having guest lecturers is a great idea. It would be something new for many of the students. Most of our professors haven't been out in the field for many years. We can also learn about recent research from them.

W Yes, we could, but do the students need all of the extra work? We already have so much course material to cover.

M Um, extra work would not be good. But I doubt that

남 오늘 오후에 이메일 확인했어?

여 응, 했어, 그리고 네가 어떤 메시지에 대해 물어보려는지 알 것 같아.

남 넌 별로 좋아하는 것 같지 않은데.

여 응, 맞아. 교수님들이 학회에 참석해야 하는 건 이해하지만, 교수님이 자기를 대신해서 초대 강사들을 불렀다는 건 싫어. 그냥 수업 시간을 변경해야 한다고 생각해.

남 그렇게 하면 정말 불편하지 않을까?

여 교수님이 미리 알려주기만 한다면 대부분의 학생들은 괜찮다고 생각할 것 같아. 우리가 같은 과목을 가르치는 다른 교수님들의 강의를 들을 수도 있고, 아니면 교수님이 다음 주에 추가로 저녁에 수업을 정할 수도 있어. 학생들은 자신의 스케줄을 조정할 충분한 시간이 있을 거고, 아니면 다른 학생의 필기를 복사할 수도 있지.

남 그런 것 같아, 하지만 나는 초대 강사들이 오는 건 정말 좋은 아이디어라고 생각해. 많은 학생들에게 새로운 경험이 될 거야. 우리 교수님들 대부분은 몇 년간 현장에 나가지 못하셨었어. 우리는 초대 강사들에게서 최근의 연구에 대해서도 배울 수 있을 거야.

information from the guest lecturers will show up on any of our tests.

W Even if that is true, we don't have enough time to cover all of our regular material. And any of the information from our long reading list could be on the test.

M I understand how you feel, but I am still looking forward to the guest lecturers.

여 그래, 그럴 수 있지. 하지만 학생들이 추가 공부가 필요할까? 우리는 이미 다뤄야 할 수업 내용이 너무 많아.

남 음, 추가 공부는 별로 좋지 않겠네. 하지만 초대 강사들로부터 듣게 될 정보가 시험에 나올 거라고는 생각하지 않아.

여 그게 사실이라 하더라도, 우리는 정규 교재를 전부 다룰 시간이 부족해. 그리고 긴 도서 목록에 있는 정보는 어떤 것이든 시험에 나올 수가 있어.

남 네 기분은 이해하지만, 나는 여전히 초대 강사들이 기대돼.

어휘 take someone's place 누군가를 대신하다 I reschedule v 일정을 변경하다 I in advance 미리, 사전에 I rearrange v 조정하다, 배열을 바꾸다 I doubt v 염려하다

Now get ready to answer the question.

The woman expresses her opinion about the change in one of her school classes. State her opinion and explain the reasons she gives for that opinion.

이제 질문에 답하시오.

여자는 자신의 학교 수업 중 한 과목의 변경에 대한 자신의 의견을 표현하고 있다. 그녀의 의견에 대해 서술하고 그렇게 생각하는 이유가 무엇인지 설명하시오.

예시 답변

According to the e-mail, the professor has invited guest instructors to teach her classes. The woman does not think it is a good idea. First, she explains that the professor should reschedule the class instead of inviting guests. This is because the students wouldn't mind as long as she announces the changes in advance. Second, she says that the students don't need extra work because they already have too much regular material to cover. Even if the information from the guest lecturers doesn't show up on the test, students will be losing time to study the regular material. For these reasons, the woman does not think it is a good idea.

이메일에 따르면, 교수는 자신의 수업을 가르칠 초대 강사들을 초청했다. 여자는 이것이 좋은 아이디어라고 생각하지 않는다. 첫째, 그녀는 교수가 강사들을 초대하는 대신 수업 시간을 변경해야 한다고 설명한다. 왜냐하면 수업 변경을 미리 공지하기만 한다면 학생들은 별로 상관하지 않을 것이기 때문이다. 둘째, 그녀는 학생들이 이미 다뤄야 할 정규 자료가 너무 많기 때문에 추가적인 공부가 필요하지 않다고 말한다. 초대 강사들이 주는 정보가 시험에 나오지 않는다 하더라도, 학생들은 정규 자료를 공부할 시간이 없을 것이다. 이러한 이유들로 여자는 그것이 좋은 아이디어라고 생각하지 않는다.

Question 3

Read the passage about the convergent evolution. You will have 50 seconds to read the passage. Begin reading now.

수렴 진화에 관한 지문을 읽으시오. 지문을 읽는 데 50초가 주어진다. 이제 읽기 시작하시오.

읽기 지문&해석

Convergent Evolution

Organisms evolve in response to pressures from their environment, and this often results in unique characteristics. However, some adaptations are so useful that unrelated species in different parts of the world develop them in a process called convergent evolution. A prime example of this is flight, an ability which birds, insects, and mammals all have. These animals are unrelated, and they did not learn to fly from one another. They have developed similar body parts

수렴 진화

생명체들은 환경으로부터의 압력에 대한 반응으로 진화하며, 이는 종종 독특한 특징들로 귀결된다. 그러나 어떤 적응들은 매우 유용하여 세계의 여러 다른 지역의 관계없는 종들도 수렴 진화라 불리는 과정에서 그러한 적응들을 발달시킨다. 이것의 주된 예는 비행인데, 조류, 곤충, 그리고 포유류 모두가 갖는 능력이다. 이 동물들은 연관되어 있지 않고, 나는 법을 서로에게서 배우지도 않았다. 그들은 같은 목적을 수행하는 비

that serve the same purpose. The wings of birds, insects, and bats look radically different, but they have evolved to have the same function.

슷한 신체 기관들을 발달시켰다. 새, 곤충, 그리고 박쥐의 날개는 매우 다르게 생겼지만, 같은 기능을 갖도록 진화했다.

어휘 convergent evolution 수렴 진화 I in response to ~에 응하여 I adaptation n 적응, 적응 형태 I flight n 비행 I radically adv 철저히, 근본적으로

Now listen to part of a lecture in a biology class.

이제 생물학 강의의 일부를 들으시오.

듣기 지문&해석

M Convergent evolution can be observed throughout the natural world, and many species that evolved in total isolation from one another possess similar structures that perform the same tasks. One common category for convergent evolution is in feeding. Many species are insectivores, but some very different organisms have developed similar traits to aid them in eating their preferred food.

For example, aardvarks of Africa and echidnas of Australia both have a similar diet which largely consists of ants and termites. Although they do bear a superficial physical resemblance, they are actually quite distinct species. Fully grown adult aardvarks' lengths are usually between 100 and 130cm and typically weigh between 50 and 80kg. On the other hand, echidnas are much smaller in size; their body lengths are usually between 30 and 50cm, weighing no more than 10kg at most. Aardvarks have thinly scattered coarse hairs and thick skin on their bodies that protect them from attacks to some extent. However, echidnas have long and tough protective spines, and when in danger, they curl up in a ball for defense. Even more importantly, echidnas are members of the rare egg-laying mammals known as the monotremes, unlike aardvarks that give birth to live young. Despite these many differences, these animals share similar adaptations that allow them to eat the same prey. Aardvarks feed upon ants and termites utilizing their heavy front claws to tear into hives and a long, sticky tongue to lap up the insects. The echidnas of Australia also possess a long sticky tongue that they use to lick up insects whose home they have torn open with their strong front claws, but the similarities really end there. So, as you can see, these genetically and geographically separate organisms have all evolved the same traits to feed upon the same prey. They are prime examples of convergent evolution.

남 수렴 진화는 자연계 전체에서 관찰할 수 있으며, 서로로부터 완전히 고립된 상태에서 진화한 많은 종들이 동일한 일을 수행하는 유사한 구조를 지니고 있습니다. 수렴 진화의 흔한 범주 하나는 먹이 섭취입니다. 많은 종들은 곤충을 먹는데, 매우 다른 생물체들이 자신들이 좋아하는 먹이를 먹는 것을 돕는 유사한 특징들을 발전시켰습니다.

예를 들면, 아프리카의 땅돼지와 호주의 바늘두더지는 둘 다 주로 개미와 흰개미로 구성되는 비슷한 식단을 가지고 있습니다. 그들은 피상적인 신체적 유사성을 가지고 있기는 하지만, 실제로 매우 다른 종입니다. 다 자란 어른 땅돼지의 길이는 보통 100~130센티미터이며, 50~80킬로그램의 무게가 나갑니다. 반면, 바늘두더지는 크기가 훨씬 더 작습니다. 그들의 몸길이는 보통 30~50센티미터이고, 무게는 기껏해야 10킬로그램을 넘지 않습니다. 땅돼지는 얇게 흩어져 있는 거친 털과 공격으로부터 어느 정도는 보호해 주는 두꺼운 피부를 가지고 있습니다. 하지만 바늘두더지는 길고 튼튼한 보호용 가시를 가지고 있으며, 위험에 빠졌을 때 방어를 위해 공처럼 몸을 둥글게 맙니다. 훨씬 더 중요하게, 바늘두더지는 새끼를 낳는 땅돼지와는 다르게 단공류동물이라고 알려진 알을 낳는 흔치 않은 포유류입니다. 이 많은 차이점들에도 이 동물들은 같은 먹이를 먹게 해주는 비슷한 적응점들을 공유합니다. 땅돼지는 개미와 흰개미를 먹이로 하는데, 육중한 앞 발톱을 사용하여 개미굴을 뚫고, 길고 끈적한 혀로 곤충을 핥아먹습니다. 호주의 바늘두더지 역시 길고 끈적한 혀를 가지고 있는데, 그것으로 곤충을 핥아 먹는 데 사용하며, 강한 앞 발톱으로 곤충의 둥지를 찢어 엽니다. 하지만 유사점은 거기서 끝이 납니다. 그래서 여러분이 보다시피, 이렇게 유전적, 지리적으로 분리된 생물체들이 같은 먹이를 먹기 위해 비슷한 특징을 진화시킨 것입니다. 그들은 수렴 진화의 주요한 예입니다.

어휘 isolation n 고립 I category n 범주 I insectivore n 식충 동물 I trait n 특성 I aardvark n 땅돼지 I echidna n 바늘두더지 I termite n 흰개미 I superficial adj 피상적인 I resemblance n 유사점, 닮음 I at most 기껏해야 I thinly scattered 얇게 흩어진 I coarse adj 거친 I curl up 몸을 동그랗게 말다, 웅크리다 I monotreme n 단공류동물 I claw n 발톱 I sticky adj 끈적거리는 I lap up 핥다 I tear open 찢어 열다 I genetically adv 유전적으로 I geographically adv 지리적으로 I prime adj 주요한

Now get ready to answer the question.

이제 질문에 답하시오.

The professor explains convergent evolution by giving examples of aardvarks and echidnas. Explain how they demonstrate the topic in the reading passage.

교수는 땅돼지와 바늘두더지의 예를 들어 수렴 진화에 대해 설명하고 있다. 그들이 지문의 주제를 어떻게 입증하는지 설명하시오.

예시 답변

The reading passage explains the convergent evolution. This term describes the process where unrelated species develop similar unique features as a result of having to adapt to environments that are alike. To illustrate this concept more clearly, two animals are compared in the listening section. Aardvarks and echidnas are two distinct animals that are found in separate geographical areas. Aardvarks' skins are thick and are covered with tough hair, while echidnas have sharp spines but are much smaller in size. Most importantly, aardvarks give birth to their offspring and echidnas lay eggs instead. Above all these different characteristics, aardvarks and echidnas have one thing in common: their diet. Because of this factor, both aardvarks and echidnas developed long sticky tongues and heavy front claws to dig up ants and termites. This is the one unique trait that these two distinct animals converged upon.

읽기 지문은 수렴 진화를 설명하고 있다. 이 용어는 관련되어 있지 않은 종들이 비슷한 환경에 적응해야 했던 결과로써 유사한 독특한 특징을 발전시키는 과정을 말한다. 이 개념을 더 명확히 설명하기 위해, 두 동물이 듣기 부분에서 비교된다. 땅돼지와 바늘두더지는 분리된 지리학적 영역에서 발견되는 뚜렷이 다른 동물들이다. 땅돼지의 피부는 두껍고 거친 털로 덮여있는 반면, 바늘두더지는 날카로운 가시를 가지고 있지만, 크기가 훨씬 더 작다. 가장 중요한 것은, 땅돼지는 새끼를 낳고, 바늘두더지는 대신 알을 낳는다. 이런 모든 다른 특징들 위에, 땅돼지와 바늘두더지는 한 가지 공통점을 갖는데, 그것은 그들이 먹는 음식이다. 이 요인 때문에 땅돼지와 바늘두더지 둘 다 개미와 흰개미를 파내기 위해 길고 끈적한 혀와 강한 앞 발톱을 발달시켰다. 이것이 뚜렷이 다른 이 두 가지 동물이 수렴한 독특한 특징이다.

Question 4

Now listen to part of a lecture in a business class.

이제 경영학 강의의 일부를 들으시오.

읽기 지문&해석

W Today, we will look at how TV commercials appeal to customers. TV commercials are a powerful medium that incorporates sound and images to convey their message. This allows them to influence far more people than print or radio advertising can.
Take this magazine advertisement for a Caribbean vacation package for example. Sure, it shows lovely images, but it is ultimately forgettable. Now, take a radio commercial. A pleasant female voice is telling what the island resort offers. But, we don't have images to associate with the words, so they wouldn't stick in your mind either. But, when we put the two together in a commercial, they become a powerful tool. The narrator's voice acts as bullet points in an outline, focusing on specific images that you are being shown, thereby fixing them in your memory. So, after you walk away from the television or computer screen, you are still thinking about the resort and its many perks.
Of course, there are other factors at play here as well. TV commercials are often paired with programs that have particular demographics. Daytime programming often consists of dramas and talk shows, which are programs

여 오늘은 TV 광고가 소비자에게 어떻게 어필하는지에 관해 살펴보겠습니다. TV 광고는 메시지를 전달하기 위해 소리와 이미지를 통합하는 강력한 매체입니다. 이는 TV 광고가 활자 광고나 라디오 광고가 할 수 있는 것보다 훨씬 더 많은 사람들에게 영향을 미칠 수 있게 합니다.
카리브해 지역으로의 휴가에 대한 이 잡지 광고를 예로 들어 보도록 하죠. 물론 이 광고는 멋진 이미지들을 보여주지만, 궁극적으로 잊혀집니다. 이제 라디오 광고를 들어보죠. 기분 좋은 여성의 목소리가 섬의 리조트가 제공하는 것들을 얘기합니다. 하지만 그 단어들과 연결시킬 이미지가 없기 때문에 여러분의 마음에 남아 있지 않게 될 것입니다. 그러나 그 두 가지를 광고에서 결합하면 그것들은 강력한 도구가 됩니다. 내레이터의 목소리는 여러분이 보고 있는 특정 이미지에 집중하며 전체 윤곽에서 중요 항목 역할을 하고, 따라서 여러분의 기억에 각인을 시키죠. 그래서 여러분이 TV나 컴퓨터 화면 앞에서 떠난 후에도 여러분은 그 리조트와 그것의 많은 특전들에 대해 생각합니다.

that housewives typically watch. So, the commercials that are on are chosen to appeal to that demographic as well. They advertise cleaning products, clothing stores, and other stereotypically feminine things. Not only that, but they will often present the same things differently depending on the perceived audience. So, if the Caribbean resort commercial were on during the daytime, it would focus on the aspects of the resort that they think appeal to women. If it were on during a sporting event broadcast, it would focus on the exciting activities that men could enjoy at the resort. Similar tactics are used with print advertisements, but TV commercials are much more effective.

물론 여기에는 다른 요인들도 같이 작용합니다. TV 광고는 종종 특정한 인구층을 갖는 방송들과 짝이 지어집니다. 낮 방송들은 가정주부들이 흔히 시청하는 프로그램들인 드라마와 토크쇼로 자주 이루어집니다. 따라서 방송되는 TV 광고들은 그러한 인구층의 관심을 끌기 위해 선택됩니다. 그들은 세제, 옷 가게, 그리고 다른 전형적으로 여성적인 것들을 광고합니다. 그뿐 아니라, 시청자들에 따라 종종 같은 것들을 다르게 보여줍니다. 그래서 만약 카리브해의 리조트 광고가 낮 시간에 방송되면, 여성들이 매력을 느낄 것이라고 생각되는 리조트의 면들에 집중할 것입니다. 만약 그것이 스포츠 경기 중계 시간에 방송된다면, 남성들이 리조트에서 즐길 수 있는 흥미로운 활동들에 초점을 맞출 것입니다. 비슷한 전략들은 활자 광고에도 사용되지만, TV 광고가 훨씬 더 효과적입니다.

어휘 appeal to 관심을 끌다, 호소하다 I medium **n** 매체, 수단 I incorporate **v** 일부로 포함하다, 통합시키다 I Caribbean **adj** 카리브해의 **n** 카리브해 지역 I pleasant **adj** 기분 좋은, 즐거운 I associate **v** 연상하다, 연관 짓다 I narrator **n** 서술자, 내레이터 I bullet point 중요 항목 I outline **n** 윤곽 I perk **n** 특전 I demographics **n** 인구 통계 (자료) I stereotypically **adv** 진부하게, 틀에 박혀서 I perceived **adj** 인지된 I tactic **n** 전략, 전술

Now get ready to answer the question.

In the lecture, the professor describes a number of factors that make TV commercials a powerful medium. Explain what makes TV commercials a powerful medium by using the examples from the lecture.

이제 질문에 답하시오.

강의에서 교수는 TV 광고를 강력한 매체로 만드는 여러 가지 요인들을 설명한다. 무엇이 TV 광고를 강력한 매체로 만드는지 강의의 예를 사용하여 설명하시오.

예시 답변

In the lecture, the professor talks about a number of factors that make TV commercials a powerful medium. First, TV commercials are more remembered by the viewers because they incorporate both visual and auditory stimuli. Secondly, depending on the demographics of the TV viewers at certain times of day, the type of commercials vary. During the daytime, commercials that contain products that are more appealing to housewives are usually on TV. Also, if there is a commercial which will be aired on different channels, depending on the TV programming it follows, the commercial will emphasize different aspects of the product. For example, if a sporting event broadcast is on a channel, the commercial will highlight features that are more appealing to men than women.

강의에서 교수는 TV 광고를 강력한 매체로 만드는 여러 가지 요인들에 대해 이야기한다. 첫째, TV 광고가 시각적, 청각적 자극 둘 다를 포함하기 때문에 보는 사람들이 기억하기 더 쉽다. 둘째, 하루 중 특정 시간대 TV 시청자들의 인구 구성에 따라 광고의 종류가 달라진다. 낮 시간에는 가정주부들이 더 관심을 가질 만한 상품을 포함한 광고들이 주로 방송된다. 또한, 만약 어떤 광고가 여러 다른 채널에서 방송된다면, 광고 전에 나오는 방송 프로그램에 따라 광고는 상품의 다른 면을 강조하게 될 것이다. 예를 들어, 어떤 채널에서 스포츠 경기가 방송되면, 광고는 여성들보다는 남성들이 더 매력을 느끼는 특징을 강조할 것이다.

Writing

I. Integrated Task

Lesson 01 노트테이킹

1. Practice 본서 P. 307

Q1

Many large companies have cafeterias where their employees can eat their lunches. This has many benefits. Employees do not have to use their break to travel to and from restaurants. Thus, they have more time to relax and enjoy their meals. Additionally, they can talk to their coworkers about non-work topics and form closer relationships.

많은 대기업들은 직원이 점심을 먹을 수 있는 구내식당을 갖추고 있다. 여기에는 많은 이점이 있다. 직원들은 식당을 찾아 왔다 갔다 하는 일에 휴식 시간을 쓸 필요가 없다. 따라서 쉬면서 식사를 즐길 시간이 더 있다. 또한, 동료들과 일이 아닌 주제에 관해 이야기하며 더 친밀한 관계를 쌓을 수도 있다.

노트

주제 company cafeteria's benefits
1. X waste time finding restaurants → relax & enjoy meal
2. talk to coworkers → closer relationships

회사 구내식당의 이점
1. 식당을 찾는 데 시간 낭비 X → 휴식 & 식사 즐김
2. 동료들과 이야기 → 더 친밀한 관계

어휘 cafeteria n 구내식당 | employee n 직원 | break n 휴식 시간 | relax v 휴식을 취하다, 쉬다 | additionally adv 추가적으로 | coworker n 동료 | relationship n 관계

Q2

The governments of many countries invest millions of dollars in space exploration every year. However, many editorials have been published that say this is a complete waste of money. Most people do not see any profit gained from space exploration, but they pay for it with their taxes. Not only that, but searching the galaxy for planets that are Earth-like but unreachable is a pointless exercise.

많은 나라의 정부에서 매년 우주 탐사에 수백만 달러를 투자한다. 그러나 이것이 완전히 돈 낭비라고 말하는 많은 사설들이 게재되었다. 대부분의 사람들이 우주 탐사에서 어떤 이윤도 찾지 못하고 있지만, 이를 위해 자신들의 세금으로 돈을 내고 있다. 그뿐 아니라 지구와 비슷하지만 도달할 수 없는 행성을 은하계에서 찾는 것은 무의미한 일이다.

노트

주제 invest $ on space exp. = waste of $
1. no profit gained → tax wasted
2. Earth-like planets → can't go anyway

우주 탐사에 돈 투자 = 돈 낭비
1. 얻는 것 없음 → 세금 낭비됨
2. 지구와 같은 행성 → 어차피 못 감

어휘 invest v 투자하다 | exploration n 탐사 | editorial n 사설 | publish v 게재하다, 출간하다, 출판하다 | complete adj 완전한 | profit n 이윤 | tax n 세금 | galaxy n 은하계 | unreachable adj 도달할 수 없는 | pointless adj 무의미한, 할 가치가 없는

Q3

Many people choose to take package tours when they go on vacation, but that is not recommended. People on package tours spend most of their time crammed into tour buses, so they cannot enjoy the scenery. Moreover, when they arrive at a tourist attraction, they are hurried through the experience so they cannot really enjoy any aspect of their trip.

많은 사람들이 휴가를 갈 때 패키지여행을 선택하지만 그건 추천할 만하지 않다. 패키지여행을 하는 사람들은 관광버스에 구겨 넣어진 채 대부분의 시간을 보내기 때문에 풍경을 즐길 수가 없다. 게다가 관광지에 도착하면 서둘러서 관광해야 하기 때문에 여행의 어떤 측면도 진정 즐길 수 없다.

노트

주제	package tour → X recommend 1. spend time in the bus → can't enjoy scenery 2. tourist att. → have to hurry	패키지 여행 → 추천 안 함 1. 버스에서 시간 보냄 → 경치 못 즐김 2. 관광지 → 서둘러야 함

어휘 recommend v 추천하다 | cram into ~에 쑤셔 넣다 | scenery n 풍경 | tourist attraction 관광지, 관광 명소 | experience n 경험 | aspect n 측면, 양상

Q4

Cities that host professional sports teams can receive two major benefits. First, the team's stadium creates hundreds of new jobs, and the ticket sales, refreshments, and team merchandise all bring in revenue to the city. Second, the team brings attention to the city, which can make it more prominent on the national level and attract sports fans and other tourists to the city.

프로 스포츠팀을 유치하는 도시들은 두 가지 중요한 이익을 얻을 수 있다. 첫 번째로, 팀의 경기장이 수백 개의 새로운 일자리를 창출하고, 티켓 판매와 간식, 팀 상품 등이 모두 도시에 수익을 가져온다. 두 번째로, 팀이 도시에 대한 관심을 불러일으켜 국가적으로 이 도시를 더 유명하게 할 것이고, 스포츠 팬들과 다른 관광객들을 도시로 끌어들일 것이다.

노트

주제	cities hosting pro. sports teams → profit 1. stadium → create many jobs → revenue 2. attention to city → sports fans & tourists visit	프로 스포츠팀 유치 도시 → 이익 1. 경기장 → 많은 일자리 창출 → 수익 2. 도시에 관심 → 스포츠 팬 & 관광객 방문

어휘 host v 주최하다, 주인 노릇을 하다 | professional adj 프로의, 전문적인, 직업의 | refreshment n 가벼운 음식 | revenue n 수익 | prominent adj 중요한, 유명한 | national adj 국가의 | attract v 끌다, 끌어들이다

Q5

Many cultures practice arranged marriage in the past, but that tradition has faded from much of the world. However, some studies indicate that they were more successful than love marriages. For example, the rate of divorce has only increased as arranged marriage has been abandoned. This is because the family is less involved. Moreover, love marriages are often based on passion instead of compatibility, which means that they are destined to fail while arranged marriages are more likely to last.

많은 문화가 과거에 중매 결혼을 했지만, 그 전통은 세계 많은 지역에서 점차 사라졌다. 그러나 일부 연구는 중매 결혼이 연애 결혼보다 더 성공적이었음을 보여준다. 예를 들어, 이혼율은 사람들이 중매 결혼을 그만둔 후 증가하기만 했다. 왜냐하면 가족이 덜 관여되었기 때문이다. 게다가 연애 결혼은 두 사람의 화합 대신 열정에 자주 기반하는데, 이는 중매 결혼이 오래 지속될 가능성이 높은 반면 연애 결혼은 실패할 수밖에 없다는 의미다.

노트

주제	arranged marriage = better than love m.? 1. divorce ↑ after arr. m. was abandoned 2. love m. = passion/arr. m. = compatibility	중매 결혼 = 연애 결혼보다 낫다? 1. 중매 결혼 그만둔 후 이혼 증가 2. 연애 결혼 = 열정/중매 결혼 = 화합

어휘 practice v 행하다, 실천하다 | arranged marriage 중매 결혼 | tradition n 전통 | fade v 사라지다 | successful adj 성공적인 | rate of divorce 이혼율 | abandon v 그만두다, 버리다 | be involved 관계되다, 연루되다 | passion n 열정 | compatibility n 적합성, 화합성 | be destined to ~할 운명이다, ~할 수밖에 없다 | fail v 실패하다

Q6

Although fast food restaurants serve convenient, inexpensive, and tasty meals and snacks, people should not visit these establishments. Fast food poses many health risks. The menu items can cause many health problems due to their high salt and sugar content. Not only that, but they can make people

패스트푸드 식당은 편리하고 값이 싸며 맛있는 식사와 간식을 제공하지만, 사람들은 이러한 가게에 가면 안 된다. 패스트푸드는 많은 건강상의 위험을 일으킨다. 메뉴에 있는 제품들이 높은 염분과 당분 함유량 때문에 건강 문제를 야기할 수 있다. 그뿐 아니라 너무 자주 먹으면 사람들

overweight if they eat them too often. They contain a lot of fat and empty calories, which quickly become fat deposits in the body.

을 과체중으로 만들 수도 있다. 지방 과다에 영양 없는 빈 칼로리가 많이 들어있는데, 이것은 체내에서 금세 지방으로 축적된다.

노트

주제 don't buy fast food = many health risks 1. ↑ salt & sugar content 2. overweight = fat & empty calories	패스트푸드를 사면 안 됨 = 많은 건강 문제 1. 높은 염분 & 당분 2. 과체중 = 지방 & 빈 칼로리

어휘 convenient adj 편리한 | tasty adj 맛있는 | establishment n 시설, 점포 | pose v 제기하다 | risk n 위험 | content n 함유량 | overweight adj 과체중인 | contain v 함유하다, ~이 들어있다 | fat n 지방 | fat deposit 지방 축적

2. Practice

본서 | P. 311

Q1

I would like to suggest hiking as a great hobby with many benefits. First, it is obviously good for people to get low-impact exercise and fresh air. In addition, walking alone or with friends in the forest is very relaxing and a great way to alleviate stress.

나는 하이킹이 많은 이점이 있는 훌륭한 취미라고 생각합니다. 먼저, 하이킹은 사람들이 충격이 적은 운동을 하고 신선한 공기를 마시는 데 분명 좋습니다. 또한 혼자 또는 친구들과 숲을 걷는 것은 마음을 아주 느긋하게 해주며, 스트레스를 완화하기에 매우 좋은 방법입니다.

노트

주제 hiking = beneficial 1. low-impact exercise & fresh air 2. walking in the forest = relaxing & get rid of stress	하이킹 = 이로움 1. 충격이 적은 운동 & 신선한 공기 2. 숲에서 걷기 = 휴식 & 스트레스 없애줌

어휘 obviously adv 분명히, 명백히 | low-impact adj 충격이 적은, 영향을 덜 미치는 | relaxing adj 편한, 마음을 느긋하게 해주는 | alleviate v 완화하다, 덜다

Q2

As you read, some people think that a universal minimum wage is a good idea, but I think it would do much more harm than good. Many people would rather not work at all if they would still get paid. It would also take money away from other important government programs.

읽은 것처럼 어떤 사람들은 보편적인 최저 시급이 좋은 생각이라고 생각하지만, 나는 장점보다는 단점이 더 많다고 생각해요. 많은 사람들이 여전히 돈을 받게 된다면 일을 하지 않으려 할 것입니다. 이는 또한 다른 중요한 정부 프로그램을 위한 자금을 빼앗을 거예요.

노트

주제 universal min. wage = bad idea 1. ppl X work – still get paid 2. take $ from other import. gov't programs	보편적 최저 시급 = 안 좋은 생각 1. 사람들이 일을 안 함 – 여전히 돈 받음 2. 정부의 다른 중요한 프로그램을 위한 돈을 빼앗음

어휘 universal adj 보편적인 | minimum wage 최저 시급

Q3

Some professors like to give their students essays to write at home as their final exam, but I don't think that is a good idea. First, it allows the students to do all of their research on one day instead of studying like they should. Second, an exam is supposed to make the students perform under pressure, and

일부 교수들은 기말시험으로 학생들이 집에서 리포트를 써 오게 하는 것을 좋아하지만 나는 그것이 좋은 생각이라고 보지 않아요. 먼저, 이는 학생들이 해야만 하는 공부를 하게 하는 대신 하루에 자료 조사를 전부 하게 만듭니다. 두 번째로, 시험은 학생들이 중압감을 느끼면서 치러

writing an essay at home does not give students that kind of pressure at all.

야 하는 것이며, 집에서 리포트 쓰기는 학생들에게 그러한 압박을 전혀 주지 않습니다.

노트

주제 essay @ home = final exam → bad idea
1. do all research on one day – X study
2. exam = should perform under pressure

집에서 리포트 = 기말시험 → 안 좋은 생각
1. 하루 만에 자료 조사 – 공부 안 함
2. 시험 = 중압감을 느끼며 치러야 함

어휘 be supposed to ~해야 하다, ~하기로 되어있다 I perform v 해내다, 실시하다 I pressure n 압박

Q4

Now, I believe that doctor residency programs are valuable, but they need to be restructured. First, the residents are required to work very long shifts that make mistakes much more likely. Second, the extreme stress of working in that environment can permanently damage their health.

나는 의사 레지던트 프로그램이 가치 있다고 믿지만, 그 프로그램은 개혁해야 합니다. 먼저, 레지던트들은 교대 근무 시간이 매우 길어 실수할 가능성이 훨씬 커집니다. 둘째로, 그런 환경에서 일하는 극한의 스트레스가 그들의 건강을 영구적으로 해칠 수 있습니다.

노트

주제 doctor resi. program → restructure
1. long shift → chance of mistakes ↑
2. extreme stress → permanent health damage

의사 레지던트 프로그램 → 개혁
1. 긴 근무 시간 → 실수 가능성 높아짐
2. 극한의 스트레스 → 영구적인 건강 손상

어휘 residency program (의사) 레지던트 프로그램 I restructure v 개혁하다, 구조를 조정하다 I shift n 교대 근무 시간 I extreme adj 극단적인 I permanently adv 영구적으로 I damage v 손상을 입히다

Q5

Even though many people believe that the world is overpopulated, this is not the case for the following reasons. First, the world's natural resources will be sufficient for the current population since people are putting more efforts into sharing them properly. Second, although the populations of some nations are increasing, many others are actually shrinking.

많은 사람이 세계가 인구 과잉이라고 믿지만, 그것은 다음의 이유로 사실이 아닙니다. 먼저, 세계의 천연자원은 사람들이 자원을 적절히 공유하기 위해 더 많은 노력을 하고 있으므로 현재의 인구에 충분할 겁니다. 두 번째로, 일부 국가의 인구가 늘고 있기는 하지만 다른 많은 나라들의 인구는 사실 줄고 있습니다.

노트

주제 world = overpopulated? No
1. natural resources: sufficient if shared properly
2. many nations' pop. ↓

세계 = 인구 과잉? 아니다
1. 천연자원: 제대로 공유하면 충분함
2. 많은 나라의 인구가 줄어듦

어휘 overpopulated adj 인구 과잉의 I natural resource 천연자원 I sufficient adj 충분한 I population n 인구 I properly adv 적절히 I shrink v 줄어들다

Q6

Despite their popularity, ride sharing services are not a great idea. For one thing, the services cannot do thorough background checks on the drivers that want to participate, so it can be dangerous for the passengers. For another thing, the drivers themselves are not paid much, so they tend to be very picky about where they will drive.

그 인기에도 불구하고 차량 공유 서비스는 좋은 생각이 아닙니다. 한 이유로, 이 서비스는 참여하고 싶어 하는 운전자의 신원 조회를 철저하게 할 수 없기 때문에 승객에게 위험할 수도 있어요. 다른 이유로, 운전자들이 돈을 많이 받지 못하기 때문에, 목적지에 관해 아주 까다로운 경향이 있습니다.

노트

주제 ride sharing service = not good 1. backgr. check X sufficient = dangerous 2. drivers X paid much → picky about location	차량 공유 서비스 = 안 좋음 1. 신원 조회 불충분 = 위험 2. 운전자들 돈 많이 못 받음 → 목적지에 대해 까다로움

어휘 popularity n 인기 | ride sharing service 탈것(차량) 공유 서비스 | thorough adj 철저한 | background check 신원 조사 | participate v 참여하다, 참가하다 | passenger n 승객 | picky adj 까다로운

Lesson 02 요약하기

1. Practice

본서 P. 317

Q1

Many people like to drink soft drinks with their meals instead of water. Unfortunately, this is bad for your health in a number of ways. For example, soft drinks contain a lot of sugar and they are very acidic, which means that they can damage your teeth. On top of that, they offer nothing good to your body. They contain very few nutrients so the calories they provide are basically empty. Unneeded calories often lead to weight gain.

많은 사람들이 식사할 때 물 대신 청량음료를 마시는 걸 좋아한다. 안타깝게도 이는 많은 이유에서 건강에 좋지 않다. 예를 들어, 청량음료는 당이 많이 함유되어 있고 산성이 강해 치아에 손상을 입힐 수 있다. 게다가 몸에 좋은 점이 하나도 없다. 영양가는 거의 없어서 이들이 제공하는 칼로리는 기본적으로 빈 칼로리이다. 불필요한 칼로리는 흔히 체중 증가로 이어진다.

노트

주제 soft drinks → bad for health 1. sugar and acid → damage teeth 2. nutrition X/empty calories → gain weight	청량음료 → 건강에 나쁨 1. 당분과 산성 → 치아 손상 2. 영양가 없음/빈 칼로리 → 체중 증가

Q. According to the passage, why is drinking soft drinks not recommended?

지문에 따르면, 청량음료를 마시는 것은 왜 권고되지 않는가?

First, soft drinks are bad for your health because they are full of sugar and acid. They can damage your teeth. In addition, they contain very little nutrition and are mostly empty calories that can make people gain weight if they regularly drink them.

먼저, 청량음료는 당과 산 성분으로 가득해서 건강에 나쁘다. 치아에 손상을 입힐 수 있다. 그리고 영양분은 거의 함유하고 있지 않고 대부분 빈 칼로리라 자주 마시면 살이 찌게 한다.

어휘 soft drink 청량음료 | unfortunately adv 안타깝게도 | a number of 많은 | contain v 함유하다, 포함하다, ~가 들어있다 | sugar n 설탕, 당 | acidic adj 산성의 | damage v 손상을 입히다 | on top of that 게다가, 그뿐 아니라 | nutrient n 영양분 | basically adv 기본적으로 | unneeded adj 불필요한 | weight n 체중 | gain n 증가 v 늘리다

Q2

Avocados are unique fruit that provides many health benefits. One, it is very nutritious and contains important vitamins like B, C, E, and potassium. In addition, avocados are also a rich source of monounsaturated fat, which is very good for the heart and arterial health.

아보카도는 많은 건강상의 이점을 제공하는 독특한 과일이다. 한 가지 이점으로 이 과일은 영양분이 아주 많으며 비타민 B, C, E 같은 중요 비타민과 칼륨을 함유하고 있다. 게다가, 아보카도는 불포화 지방도 많이 함유하고 있는데, 이는 심장과 동맥 건강에 아주 좋다.

노트

주제 avocado – benefits 1. important vitamins & potassium 2. fat = good for heart	아보카도 – 이점 1. 중요한 비타민 & 칼륨 2. 지방 = 심장에 좋음

Q. According to the passage, how are avocados beneficial?

지문에 따르면, 아보카도는 어떻게 이로운가?

Avocados are very nutritious and contain many important vitamins. Also, they contain a lot of fat that is good for the heart.

아보카도는 영양분이 아주 많으며 중요한 비타민을 많이 함유하고 있다. 또한, 심장에 좋은 지방이 많이 들어 있다.

어휘 unique adj 독특한 I nutritious adj 영양가가 있는 I potassium n 칼륨 I monounsaturated fat 불포화 지방 I arterial adj 동맥의

Q3

It is a widely held belief that children who begin studying foreign languages early in their life generally reach and maintain a higher level of fluency. Research has proven this idea to be correct for a few reasons. Children appear to have a preexisting mental ability to understand and use grammar easily. Second, they constantly mimic the speech of others, which allows them to adopt new words freely.

조기에 외국어를 공부하기 시작하는 아이들은 일반적으로 더 높은 수준의 유창함에 도달하고 유지한다는, 널리 퍼진 믿음이 있다. 연구는 이 생각이 몇 가지 이유로 옳다고 증명했다. 아이들은 쉽게 문법을 이해하고 사용하는 기존의 정신적 능력을 갖춘 것으로 보인다. 두 번째로, 아이들은 다른 사람들의 말을 계속 따라 하며, 이는 새로운 단어를 자유롭게 쓰게 해 준다.

노트

주제 study foreign language early – high level
1. innate ability to learn grammar
2. repeat what others say

일찍 외국어 공부 – 높은 수준
1. 선천적인 문법 학습 능력
2. 다른 사람들이 하는 말 반복

Q. According to the passage, why does starting to learn languages early in life allow people to become more fluent?

지문에 따르면, 일찍 언어 공부를 시작하는 것은 왜 사람들을 더 유창하게 만드는가?

First, children have an innate ability to learn grammar. Second, they repeat what they hear others say.

먼저, 아이들은 선천적인 문법 학습 능력을 갖고 있다. 두 번째로, 아이들은 다른 사람들이 하는 말을 듣고 반복한다.

어휘 generally adv 일반적으로 I fluency n 유창함 I correct adj 옳은 I pre-existing adj 이미 존재하는 I grammar n 문법 I constantly adv 계속, 지속적으로 I mimic v 흉내 내다, 따라 하다 I adopt v 쓰다, 취하다, 채택하다

Q4

Sleep is very beneficial for people's health. First of all, it provides the body with down time to relax and repair itself. That is why sleep is an important part of recovering from an illness. On top of that, it also gives the brain time to process new information and create new mental pathways. This is what happens during dreaming.

잠은 사람의 건강에 매우 이롭다. 먼저, 몸이 쉬고 치유할 휴식 시간을 준다. 그래서 잠은 병에서 회복하는 데 중요한 부분이다. 또한, 잠은 뇌가 새 정보를 처리하고 새로운 정신 경로를 만들 시간을 준다. 이것이 꿈을 꾸는 동안 일어나는 일이다.

노트

주제 benefits of sleeping
1. body = time to relax & repair
2. process new info - dreaming

수면의 이점
1. 신체 = 쉬고 치유할 시간
2. 새 정보 처리 – 꿈

Q. According to the passage, what are the benefits of sleeping?

지문에 따르면, 잠의 이점은 무엇인가?

Sleep helps your body to relax and repair itself. It helps you to recover when you are sick. In addition, dreaming helps your mind to deal with new data.

잠은 몸이 쉬고 자신을 보수하는 것을 돕는다. 아플 때 회복하는 것을 돕는다. 그리고 꿈은 정신이 새로운 정보를 처리하는 것을 돕는다.

어휘 beneficial adj 이익이 되는 | down time 휴식 시간 | relax v 쉬다 | repair v 회복하다, 치료하다 | recover v 회복하다 | illness n 병 | process v 처리하다 | pathway n 진로, 경로

Q5

Most school districts rely upon standardized tests to determine what level of academic achievement students have reached. Unfortunately, these tests are flawed for a number of reasons. One is that such tests only measure a small part of cognitive abilities. Another is that some people cannot perform well when tested in this way. Therefore, standardized tests are not a viable way to assess achievement.

대부분의 학군은 학생들이 어떤 수준의 학문적 성과에 도달했는지 알아내기 위해 표준화된 시험에 의존한다. 안타깝게도, 이 시험들은 몇 가지 이유로 결함이 있다. 하나는 이 시험들이 인지 능력의 작은 부분만을 측정한다는 점이다. 또 다른 점은 일부 사람들은 이런 방식으로 시험을 보면 능력을 잘 발휘할 수가 없다는 점이다. 따라서 표준화된 시험은 성과를 평가하기에 실용적인 방법이 아니다.

노트

주제 standardized test = flawed
1. only test a small part of mental ability
2. some ppl are bad at test taking

표준화된 시험 = 결함
1. 지적 능력의 작은 부분만 시험
2. 어떤 사람들은 시험을 잘 못 봄

Q. According to the passage, why are standardized tests flawed?

지문에 따르면, 표준화된 시험은 왜 결함이 있는가?

For one thing, standardized tests only test a small part of mental ability. For another thing, they do not account for people who are bad at test taking. Hence, they are not a good way to assess academic achievement.

우선, 표준화된 시험은 인지 능력의 작은 부분만 시험할 뿐이다. 또한, 시험을 잘 못 보는 사람들을 설명해주지 못한다. 따라서, 학업 성과를 평가하기에 좋은 방법이 아니다.

어휘 school district 학군 | standardized adj 표준화된 | determine v 알아내다 | academic adj 학문적인 | achievement n 성취, 달성 | unfortunately adv 불행히도 | flawed adj 결함이 있는 | measure v 측정하다 | cognitive adj 인지의 | viable adj 실행 가능한, 실용적인 | assess v 평가하다

Q6

Although many students and parents question whether playing team sports at school is necessary, it actually has many benefits for children. Obviously, playing sports provides students with regular exercise, which is important for their health. Team sports also require them to work together toward a common goal. This is a skill that will be very valuable to them throughout their lives.

많은 학생과 부모가 학교에서 팀 스포츠를 하는 것이 필요한지 아닌지에 대해 의문을 품지만, 사실 이는 아이들에게 많은 이점을 준다. 분명, 스포츠를 하면 규칙적으로 운동을 하게 되는데, 이는 건강에 중요하다. 팀 스포츠는 또한 공통된 목표를 향해 학생들이 함께 노력하게 한다. 이는 살아가는 동안 무척 소중히 여기게 될 능력이다.

노트

주제 team sports = beneficial
1. make students exercise
2. work together → achieve tasks = life skill

팀 스포츠 = 이로움
1. 학생들이 운동하게 함
2. 함께 노력함 → 목표 이룸 = 삶의 기술

Q. According to the passage, why should students be required to play team sports at school?

지문에 따르면, 왜 학생들은 학교에서 팀 스포츠를 해야 하는가?

First, playing team sports regularly makes students exercise. Second, it forces them to work together with people they don't know well to achieve a task. This is a life skill that they need.

첫 번째로, 팀 스포츠를 규칙적으로 하면 학생들은 운동하게 된다. 두 번째로, 이것은 학생들이 과업을 달성하기 위해 잘 모르는 사람들과 협력하게 한다. 이는 학생들에게 필요한 삶의 기술이다.

어휘 question v 의문을 갖다 | obviously adv 분명히, 확실히 | regular adj 정기적인, 규칙적인 | common adj 공통의 | valuable adj 가치 있는 | throughout prep 쭉, 내내

2. Practice

본서 P. 321

Q1

Let's take a critical look at pet ownership. Many people talk about the advantages this can have for people, but it has many disadvantages for the animals themselves. People buy pets to keep them company at home, but that often means that the animals spend most of the day alone. Loneliness can affect animals, too. People also say that owning pets teaches responsibility, but people often do the bare minimum to take care of their pets. Feeding and cleaning up after an animal is important, but they need exercise and socialization as well.

반려동물 소유를 비판적인 시각으로 봅시다. 많은 사람들이 이것이 사람에게 주는 이점에 관해 이야기하지만, 사실 동물에게는 단점이 많아요. 사람들은 집에서 함께하기 위해 반려동물을 구입하지만, 그것은 그 동물들이 거의 온종일 혼자 보내야 한다는 뜻일 때가 많습니다. 외로움은 동물들에게도 영향을 줄 수 있어요. 사람들은 또한 반려동물을 소유하는 것이 책임감을 가르쳐준다고 하지만 사람들은 반려동물을 돌보는 데 가장 기본적인 최소한의 일만 하는 경우가 많습니다. 동물에게 먹이를 주고 용변을 치워 주는 것도 중요하지만 동물은 운동과 사회화 또한 필요로 해요.

노트

주제 pet ownership = bad for pets
1. alone most of the day → lonely
2. ppl don't do much → pets don't get things they need

반려동물 소유 = 반려동물에게 나쁨
1. 거의 온종일 혼자 있음 → 외로움
2. 사람들이 많은 일을 안 함 → 반려동물이 필요한 것을 얻지 못함

Q. According to the passage, why is pet ownership bad for the pets themselves?

지문에 따르면, 왜 반려동물 소유는 반려동물에게 나쁜가?

First, the pets are often left alone most of the day, which makes them feel lonely. Next, people don't do much to take care of their animals, so pets don't get things that they need.

첫 번째로, 반려동물은 거의 온종일 혼자 남겨질 때가 많아서 외롭다. 다음으로, 사람들은 동물을 돌보기 위해 그다지 많은 일을 하지 않아서 반려동물은 필요한 것을 얻지 못한다.

어휘 critical adj 비판적인 | ownership n 소유 | company n 동반자, 벗 | loneliness n 외로움 | affect v 영향을 주다 | responsibility n 책임, 책임감 | bare adj 가장 기본적인 | minimum n 최소 한도 | feed v 먹이를 주다 | socialization n 사회화

Q2

I want to address a common misconception about catching colds. Many people think that being exposed to cold, wet weather can make you sick, but that is only an indirect factor. The common cold is caused by a virus, so weather does not cause the illness. However, such weather does weaken the immune system, which makes it easier for a virus to infect a person. In addition, the cold virus is passed between people quite easily, and cold weather often makes people stay inside. The more people you have in an enclosed space, the easier it is to spread disease.

저는 감기에 걸리는 것과 관련된 흔한 오해를 짚어 보려고 합니다. 많은 사람들이 춥고 습한 날씨에 노출되는 것이 사람을 병들게 한다고 생각하지만, 이는 간접 요인에 불과해요. 평범한 감기는 바이러스 때문에 야기되는 것이라 날씨가 병을 불러오진 않습니다. 하지만 이러한 날씨가 면역 체계를 약화시켜 바이러스에 더 쉽게 감염되게 하죠. 또한, 감기 바이러스는 사람들 사이에서 쉽게 전염되고, 추운 날씨는 사람들이 자주 실내에 머물도록 합니다. 닫힌 공간에 사람이 더 많을수록 질병이 퍼지기는 더 쉽죠.

노트

주제 cold weather & catching cold
1. weaken immune system → easy to get sick
2. ppl stay inside w. others → easy to catch cold

추운 날씨 & 감기 걸림
1. 면역력 약화 → 병들기 쉬워짐
2. 사람들이 다른 이들과 실내에 있음 → 감기 걸리기 쉬워짐

Q. According to the passage, how does cold weather indirectly make people sick?

지문에 따르면, 추운 날씨는 간접적으로 어떻게 사람들을 아프게 만드는가?

First, cold weather can weaken your immune system, which makes it easier to get sick. Second, it makes people stay inside with other people, making it easier to catch a cold.

첫 번째로, 추운 날씨는 면역 체계를 약화시킬 수 있는데, 그러면 병들기 쉬워진다. 두 번째로, 사람들이 다른 사람과 실내에 있게 하므로 감기에 걸리기 더 쉬워진다.

어휘 address v 다루다, 이야기하다 I common adj 흔한, 평범한 I misconception n 오해, 잘못된 생각 I catch (a) cold 감기에 걸리다 I expose v 노출하다 I indirect adj 간접적인 I weaken v 약화시키다 I immune system 면역 체계 I infect v 감염시키다 I enclosed adj 닫힌 I disease n 질병

Q3

The Internet may have its drawbacks, but its intended purposes far outweigh any negative aspects. First, it facilitates communication in a way that no other method can rival. It allows people to send a message to anyone with Internet access anywhere in the world at any time. Furthermore, it allows people to access information quickly and easily. Before it existed, one had to talk to an expert or go to a library.

인터넷은 단점이 있을 수도 있지만, 겨냥하는 목표는 모든 부정적인 면보다 더 큽니다. 먼저, 인터넷은 그 어떤 방법도 필적할 수 없는 방식으로 소통을 가능하게 해요. 언제든, 세계 어느 곳에 있든 인터넷 접속이 가능한 누구에게나 메시지를 보낼 수 있게 해 줍니다. 게다가, 사람들이 정보를 빠르고 쉽게 이용할 수 있게 해요. 인터넷이 존재하기 전에 사람들은 전문가와 이야기하거나 도서관에 가야만 했습니다.

노트

주제 Internet's benefits
1. communicate w/o restrictions & limit
2. access info quickly & easily

인터넷의 이점
1. 제한 & 한계 없이 소통
2. 빠르고 쉽게 정보를 얻음

Q. According to the passage, what are the benefits of the Internet?

지문에 따르면, 인터넷의 이점은 무엇인가?

First, it allows people to communicate without restrictions. Second, it allows people to access information quickly and easily.

먼저, 인터넷은 사람들이 제한 없이 소통하게 해준다. 두 번째로, 사람들이 정보를 빠르고 쉽게 얻도록 해준다.

어휘 drawback n 단점 I intended adj 의도된 I purpose n 목적 I outweigh v ~보다 더 크다 I negative adj 부정적인 I facilitate v 가능하게 하다, 용이하게 하다 I rival v 필적하다, 경쟁하다 I instantly adv 즉시 I furthermore adv 뿐만 아니라, 더욱이 I exist v 존재하다 I expert n 전문가

Q4

Now, many people believe that boys and girls benefit from attending single-sex schools, but the actual data does not back up this claim. Research has shown that students that attend single-sex schools do not perform any better on tests than their counterparts at regular schools. Not only that, but the researchers stated that the children who attend co-ed schools are much better at socializing with members of the other gender. So, single-sex schools may actually be hindering their social development.

많은 사람들이 남자와 여자가 한쪽의 성만으로 구성된 학교에 다니면 이점이 있다고 믿지만, 실제 자료는 이 주장을 뒷받침하지 않습니다. 연구자들은 공학이 아닌 학교에 다니는 학생들이 일반 학교에 다니는 상대편 학생들보다 시험 결과가 더 좋은 건 아니라는 점을 보여주었습니다. 그뿐 아니라, 연구자들은 남녀공학에 다니는 학생들이 반대 성별의 학생들과 더 잘 어울린다고 주장했어요. 그래서 공학이 아닌 학교가 사실 학생들의 사회적 발달에 방해가 될 수도 있다는 겁니다.

노트

주제 single-sex schools – drawbacks
1. students don't perform better
2. prevents learning to socialize

한 성별만 다니는 학교 – 단점
1. 학생들이 더 좋은 성적을 받지 않음
2. 사회화 학습을 방해함

Q. According to the passage, what are the drawbacks of single-sex schools?

지문에 따르면, 한 성별만 있는 학교들의 단점은 무엇인가?

Research has shown that students at single-sex schools do not get a better education. It also showed that it prevents them from learning to socialize properly.

연구는 한 성별만 있는 학교에 다니는 학생들이 더 나은 교육을 받지 못한다는 것을 보여주었다. 또한, 학생들이 제대로 사회화하는 법을 배우지 못하게 한다는 점을 보여주었다.

어휘 attend v (학교 등을) 다니다 I single-sex adj 한쪽 성만을 위한 I back up 뒷받침하다 I claim n 주장 I counterpart n 대응 관계에 있는 사람(것), 상대 I co-ed adj 남녀 공학의 I socialize v 어울리다, 사귀다 I hinder v 방해하다, 저해하다 I development n 발달

Q5

Many people play the lottery because they think it will make their life perfect. However, in many cases it has had the opposite effect. First of all, when you win a large amount of money, the government will take a huge chunk out of it in taxes. Second, since many lotteries require the winner to publicly receive their prize, everyone knows that you have won. So, people will constantly be asking you for money.

많은 사람들이 복권이 삶을 완벽하게 만들어주리라는 생각으로 복권을 삽니다. 하지만 많은 경우 복권은 반대의 효과를 불러오죠. 먼저, 큰 액수에 당첨되면 정부가 그중 상당액을 세금으로 떼어갈 겁니다. 두 번째로, 대다수는 복권 당첨자가 공개적으로 상금을 수령하도록 요구해서 모두가 당첨자를 알게 됩니다. 그래서 사람들이 항상 당첨자에게 돈을 요구할 거예요.

노트

주제 lottery – not good
1. win → pay a lot in tax
2. get prize publicly → ppl will ask for $

복권 – 안 좋음
1. 당첨 → 세금을 많이 냄
2. 공개적으로 수령 → 사람들이 돈을 달라고 할 것

Q. According to the passage, what are the negative aspects of winning a lottery?

지문에 따르면, 복권에 당첨되는 것의 부정적인 측면은 무엇인가?

First, lottery winners will have to pay a lot of their money in taxes. Second, lottery winners often have to get their prize publicly, so many people will ask them for money.

먼저, 복권 당첨자들은 상당액을 세금으로 내야만 한다. 두 번째로, 복권 당첨자들은 공개적으로 상금을 타야 하는 경우가 많으므로 많은 사람들이 이들에게 돈을 달라고 할 것이다.

어휘 lottery n 복권 I opposite adj 반대의 I chunk n 상당히 많은 양 I tax n 세금 I publicly adv 공개적으로 I prize n 상금 I constantly adv 계속, 지속적으로

Q6

Many people believe that people should have to wear a uniform or obey a dress code at their work. However, a recent study has shown that this is actually a bad idea. The typical clothing that men and women wear to look professional is often uncomfortable, which can distract them from doing their work. In addition, being forced to conform to a standard can stifle people's creativity, so their work will be lower in quality.

많은 사람들이 직장에서 제복을 입거나 복장 규정을 따라야 한다고 믿습니다. 하지만 최근의 연구는 이것이 사실 안 좋은 생각이라는 것을 보여주죠. 전문적으로 보이기 위해 남성과 여성이 입는 일반적인 옷은 불편할 때가 많으며, 이는 일하는 데 방해가 될 수 있습니다. 또한, 기준에 순응하라고 강요받는 것은 사람들의 창조성을 억누를 수 있어서 작업의 질이 저하될 거예요.

노트

주제 uniform @ work = X good idea
1. uncomfortable = hard to work
2. forced to conform → make ppl less creative

직장에서 제복 = 안 좋은 생각
1. 불편 = 일하기 힘듦
2. 순응을 강요 → 사람들을 덜 창의적으로 만듦

Q. According to the passage, why is wearing a uniform at work a bad idea?

지문에 따르면, 직장에서 제복을 입는 것은 왜 안 좋은 생각인가?

First, the clothing that people usually wear for work is often uncomfortable, which makes it hard to work. Second, being forced to conform can make people less creative.

먼저, 사람들이 일하기 위해 보통 입는 옷은 불편할 때가 많으며 이는 일을 하기 어렵게 한다. 두 번째로, 순응하도록 강요받는 것은 사람들의 창의성을 떨어뜨린다.

어휘 uniform n 제복, 교복 | obey v 따르다 | dress code 복장 규정 | recent adj 최근의 | typical adj 일반적인 | professional adj 전문직의 | uncomfortable adj 불편한 | distract v 방해하다 | conform v 순응하다 | stifle v 억누르다, 억압하다 | creativity n 창조성

Lesson 03 정리하기

1. Practice

본서 | P. 327

Q1

As the saying goes, "Two heads are better than one." Completing a project as a team is better than doing it alone. Having a group of people divide work can help save time and effort, so many companies and schools focus more on group work. Teamwork brings several benefits.

옛말에도 있듯 '백지장도 맞들면 낫다.' 팀으로 하나의 과제를 완성하는 것은 혼자 하는 것보다 낫다. 한 무리의 사람들에게 일을 나누게 하면 시간과 노력을 절약할 수 있기에 많은 기업과 학교가 그룹 활동에 더 초점을 맞춘다. 팀 활동은 여러 이점을 가져다준다.

First, one of the benefits that teamwork brings is that working as a team helps to carry out work more efficiently. A group of people has various abilities. If a team member in a group is skillful at statistics, the group will have expertise in dealing with data. The abilities that each member has help to complete a given task more efficiently.

먼저, 팀워크가 주는 장점 중 하나는 팀으로 협력하는 것이 일을 더 효율적으로 하도록 돕는다는 것이다. 한 집단의 사람들은 다양한 능력을 갖추고 있다. 만약 그룹의 구성원 중 한 명이 통계학에 능숙하다면 그 그룹은 자료를 처리하는 데 전문성을 갖게 된다. 각 구성원이 가진 능력은 주어진 업무를 더 효율적으로 완수하게 돕는다.

Second, group work allows team members to come up with various creative ideas. Each team member can talk freely in the process of making a group decision. As various ideas are suggested, there is a high possibility that the group will have creative solutions to problems they have to tackle. For example, when writing an essay, an individual can face limitations in brainstorming for ideas. But a group of people can think of more various and creative ideas than a single individual.

두 번째로, 그룹 활동은 팀 구성원이 다양하고 창의적인 아이디어를 떠올리게 해 준다. 그룹이 결정을 내리는 과정에서 팀 구성원 각자가 자유롭게 이야기할 수 있다. 다양한 생각들이 제안되기 때문에 그룹은 해결해야 할 문제에 대한 창의적인 해결 방안을 얻을 가능성이 높다. 예를 들면, 논문을 쓸 때 한 개인은 아이디어를 떠올리는 데 한계에 부딪힐 수 있다. 하지만 한 무리의 사람들은 한 명의 개인보다 더 다양하고 독창적인 아이디어를 생각해 낼 수 있다.

Another benefit of having a group of people tackle a problem is that teamwork can make team members actively participate in the work. This is because team members will feel more responsible for what they do in the group, and they will work harder to achieve positive results. They know that the others are depending on them, so they have more reason to perform.

한 무리의 사람들에게 문제를 해결하게 하는 또 다른 이점은 팀 구성원이 적극적으로 활동에 참여하게 할 수 있다는 것이다. 왜냐하면 팀 구성원들은 그 그룹에서 자신들이 하는 일에 더 많은 책임감을 느낄 것이고, 긍정적인 성과를 내기 위해 더 열심히 작업할 것이기 때문이다. 다른 사람들이 의지하고 있다는 것을 알기 때문에 잘해야 하는 이유가 더 있는 것이다.

노트

주제 project: team > alone
1. work more efficiently
   - each individual has different abilities
2. more creative ideas
   - various ideas are suggested → creative solutions
3. members actively participate
   - more responsibility → work harder

프로젝트: 팀 〉 혼자
1. 더 효율적으로 일함
   – 개인이 서로 다른 능력을 갖추고 있음
2. 더 창의적인 아이디어
   – 다양한 아이디어 제시 → 창의적 해결책
3. 팀원들이 적극적으로 참여
   – 더 많은 책임감 → 더 열심히 일함

어휘 Two heads are better than one. 백지장도 맞들면 낫다. | complete [v] 완료하다, 끝마치다 | save time and effort 시간과 노력을 줄이다 | focus on ~에 초점을 맞추다 | carry out 수행/이행하다 | be skillful at ~에 능숙하다 | statistics [n] 통계, 통계 자료 | expertise in ~에 대한 전문 지식 | deal with 다루다, 처리하다, 해결하다 | come up with ~을 떠올리다, 생각해내다 | tackle [v] 해결하다 | face limitations in ~하는 데 한계에 부딪히다 | brainstorm for ideas (여러 가지) 아이디어를 생각해내다 | participate [v] 참여하다 | achieve [v] 달성하다, 해내다 | perform [v] (일, 과제 등을) 해내다

Q2

Many animals and plants have been imported intentionally or by accident to new areas. These new species transported to new environments often have negative effects. Let us take a look at these negative consequences.

First, a new species always upsets the local ecological balance. A new species is never just added to the native ecosystem. It always competes with some native ecosystems. The damage does not end with the displacement of native competitors as the new species is often unsuitable as food for species further up the food chain. The negative effects thus spread through the whole ecosystem.

Second, the introduction of new species often destroys the local environment. For example, the cane toad, native to South Africa, was introduced to Australia, where it has spread at an alarming speed and has had harmful effects on the local environment. The cane toad, a natural predator, has killed a large number of native species in Australia. In addition to this, its poison sometimes poses a direct threat to children and pets when touched.

Finally, the negative impact caused by the introduction of new species often leads to economic burdens. For example, mesquites, a shrub native to America, were introduced to Africa. After the introduction of mesquites, commonly planted for land restoration and as a source of wood, they started to displace native species in Africa. As a result, African governments are forced to commit economic and bureaucratic resources to control the replacement of native species by mesquites.

많은 동식물이 의도적으로 혹은 우연히 새로운 지역으로 반입된다. 새로운 환경으로 옮겨진 이러한 새로운 종들은 흔히 부정적인 영향을 미친다. 이러한 부정적인 결과를 살펴보자.

첫 번째로, 새로운 종은 항상 지역 생태계의 균형을 깨뜨린다. 새로운 종은 고유한 생태계에 단순히 추가되는 것이 결코 아니다. 그것은 항상 일부 생태계와 경쟁한다. 새로운 종은 흔히 먹이 사슬 위에 있는 종에게 먹이로 적합하지 않기에 피해는 현지 경쟁자의 대체로 끝나지 않는다. 따라서 부정적인 영향은 생태계 전체로 퍼지게 된다.

두 번째로, 새로운 종의 유입은 지역 환경을 파괴하는 경우가 많다. 예를 들면, 원래 남아프리카에 서식하는 사탕수수 두꺼비가 호주에 유입되었고, 이곳에서 놀라운 속도로 퍼져 지역 환경에 해로운 영향을 끼치게 되었다. 자연 포식자인 사탕수수 두꺼비는 호주에서 많은 재래종을 죽였다. 이뿐 아니라 이 두꺼비의 독은 때때로 아이나 애완동물과 접촉할 때 직접적인 위협이 되기도 한다.

마지막으로 새로운 종의 유입으로 인한 부정적인 영향은 종종 경제적 부담으로 이어진다. 예를 들면, 미국이 원산지인 관목의 일종인 메스키트가 아프리카로 유입되었다. 토지 복원을 위해, 그리고 목재의 원천으로서 흔히 심는 메스키트의 유입 이후 이들은 아프리카의 재래종을 대체하기 시작했다. 그 결과 아프리카 정부들은 메스키트로 인한 재래종의 교체를 통제하는 데 경제적, 관료적 자원을 투입해야 한다.

노트

주제 new species in new envi. → negative effect

1. upset local ecology's balance
   - compete w/ natives
   - mess up the food chain → upset whole eco.
2. destroy local envi.
   - new species kill native species
   - poisonous ones can even harm humans
3. economic burden
   - gov'ts have to invest money to control the spread of new species

새 환경의 새로운 종 → 부정적 영향

1. 지역 생태계 균형 무너뜨림
   - 토착종들과 경쟁
   - 먹이 사슬 망가뜨림 → 생태계 전체를 무너뜨림
2. 지역 환경 파괴
   - 새 종이 토착종을 죽임
   - 독이 있는 것들은 인간도 해칠 수 있음
3. 경제적 부담
   - 정부가 새 종의 확산을 통제하기 위해 돈을 투자해야 함

어휘 intentionally [adv] 의도적으로 | by accident 우연히 | transport [v] 이동시키다, 옮기다 | consequence [n] 결과 | upset [v] 뒤엎다, 망치다 | native ecosystem 재래 생태계, 고유 생태계 | compete [v] 경쟁하다 | displacement [n] (제자리에서 쫓겨난) 이동, 대체 | further up 더 위쪽의 | food chain 먹이 사슬 | cane toad 사탕수수 두꺼비 | alarming [adj] 놀라운, 걱정스러운 | native species 재래종 | in addition to ~뿐

만 아니라 | pose a threat 위협이 되다 | mesquite n 메스키트(콩과 식물의 일종) | shrub n 관목 | restoration n 회복, 복구 | commit v (시간, 돈 등을) 쓰다 | bureaucratic adj 관료의, 관료주의적인

Q3

In England before the Industrial Revolution of the late 18th century, manufactured goods such as cloth and thread were produced manually at homes and small workshops. This so-called "putting-out system" developed into the factory system. There are several reasons why the development of the factory system was first made possible in England.

First, the advent of new technologies resulted in the accelerated development of the factory system. The development of steam engines played an especially pivotal role in the spread of the factory system. The introduction of steam engines to factories made it possible to generate a considerable amount of energy that individual workers at home could not create.

Second, the development of the factory system in England was the result of the introduction of property rights. Stable and strict rules of law that protected private property encouraged property holders to develop their property and efficiently allocate resources based on the operation of the market. This, in turn, caused property owners to invest more in new factories.

Finally, this system helped factory owners reduce production costs, especially transportation costs. Before the advancement of the system, raw materials and equipment had been supplied for workers who worked at home. This would have cost business owners considerable amounts of money for transportation. In this case, naturally, they preferred the factory system in which they could reduce the cost of transporting raw materials and goods.

18세기 후반 산업혁명 이전의 영국에서 천이나 섬유 같은 제조 상품은 집이나 작은 작업장에서 수작업으로 생산되었다. 이러한 소위 '선대제'라고 불리는 것이 공장제로 발달했다. 공장제가 영국에서 처음으로 가능했던 데에는 몇 가지 이유가 있다.

첫째, 새로운 기술의 출현이 공장제의 발전을 가속화하는 결과를 가져왔다. 증기 기관의 발달이 공장제 확산에 특히 중추적 역할을 했다. 증기 기관의 공장 도입으로 집에서 개개인의 근로자들이 만들 수 없었던 상당한 양의 에너지가 만들어질 수 있었다.

두 번째로, 영국에서 공장제의 발달은 사유 재산권 도입의 결과였다. 사유 재산을 보호해 주는 안정적이고 엄격한 법 규정은 재산을 가진 사람들이 재산을 늘리고 시장의 운용에 기초해 자원을 효율적으로 배분하도록 장려했다. 이것은 결과적으로 재산을 가진 사람들이 새로운 공장에 더 많이 투자하게 했다.

마지막으로, 이러한 시스템은 공장 소유주가 생산 비용, 특히 운송비를 줄이도록 도와주었다. 이 시스템의 발전 이전에는 원자재와 장비가 집에서 일하는 노동자들에게 공급되었다. 이것이 사업주에게 상당한 운송 비용을 초래했을 것이다. 이러한 상황에서 이들은 자연스럽게 원자재와 상품을 운송하는 비용을 줄일 수 있는 공장제를 선호했다.

노트

주제 development of factory system in England
1. new technologies
   - steam engines: huge energy generation
2. intro. of property rights
   - protect property holders
   - invest more in new factories
3. owners: reduce production costs, esp. trans. costs
   - cost for transp. raw materials & equipment ↓

영국의 공장 시스템 발달
1. 새로운 기술
   – 증기 기관: 엄청난 에너지 생산
2. 사유 재산권 도입
   – 사유 재산 소유자를 보호
   – 새 공장에 더 투자
3. 소유주: 생산 비용, 특히 운송비 절감
   – 원자재 & 장비 운송 비용 줄임

어휘 manufactured a 제조된, 생산된 | cloth n 옷감, 천 | thread n 실, 섬유 | manually adv 수동으로, 수작업으로 | workshop n 작업장 | advent n 출현 | accelerate v 가속화하다 | play a role 역할을 하다 | pivotal adj 중추적인 | spread n 확산, 전파 | considerable adj 상당한 | property n 재산, 자산, 부동산 | stable adj 안정적인, 안정된 | strict adj 엄격한 | private property 사유 재산 | allocate v 배분/할당하다 | in turn 결과적으로 | transportation n 운송, 교통 | advancement n 발달 | raw material 원자재

Lesson 03 Integrated Task

Q1

Okay, class. Yes, I know "Two heads are better than one." It seems right to argue that teamwork leads to better results, but in fact there are more problems that people fail to notice when working together as a team. These problems far outweigh the benefits. Let me explain.

자, 여러분. 네, 저는 '백지장도 맞들면 낫다.'라는 말을 알고 있습니다. 팀 활동이 더 나은 결과를 가져다준다고 주장하는 것이 옳은 것처럼 보이지만, 사실 사람들이 팀을 이뤄 일할 때 보지 못하는 문제점이 더 있습니다. 이러한 문제점들은 이점들보다 훨씬 더 많죠. 설명하도록 하겠습니다.

Contrary to the reading's claim that teamwork helps people to work more efficiently, a group of people takes more time to do a project. This is because all of the group members have to reach a consensual agreement. Each member has to adjust their schedule to decide when they are going to meet. This is pretty time-consuming.

팀 활동이 사람들이 일을 더 효율적으로 하도록 도와준다는 지문의 주장과는 반대로 한 그룹의 사람들이 어떤 프로젝트를 하는 데에는 시간이 더 걸립니다. 그룹 구성원들 모두가 합의점에 도달해야 하기 때문이죠. 언제 만날지 결정하기 위해 팀원들 각자 일정을 조정해야 해요. 이건 꽤 시간이 걸리는 일입니다.

Second, the reading indicates that teamwork will help team members come up with creative ideas. But in reality, this is not true. The reason for this is that one or two influential people in a group will dominate the group's decision making process. Thus, group members will be forced to follow the ideas that the leader suggests.

두 번째로, 지문은 팀 활동이 팀의 구성원들이 창의적인 아이디어를 생각해내도록 도와준다고 말합니다. 하지만 이것은 사실이 아니에요. 그 이유는 한 그룹에서 영향력 있는 한두 명이 그 그룹의 의사 결정 과정을 장악할 것이기 때문입니다. 그러므로 그룹의 구성원들은 리더가 제안하는 생각을 따를 수밖에 없을 거예요.

Finally, I do not think group work will make members work harder. This is because of the free rider problem. The free riding problem in a group makes it more difficult for the group to produce efficient results. Humans are selfish. They will gladly reap the good results other teammates have produced rather than exert themselves. Eventually, this free riding problem will make all team members reluctant to participate actively in any work. No one will work hard in a situation in which someone next to them just sits back and relaxes.

마지막으로, 나는 구성원들이 그룹 활동이라고 해서 더 열심히 할 것으로 생각하지 않아요. 왜냐하면 무임승차자 문제 때문이죠. 한 그룹 내의 무임승차 문제는 그 그룹이 효율적인 성과를 내는 것을 더 어렵게 합니다. 인간은 이기적이에요. 자신이 노력하기보다는 팀의 다른 구성원들이 만들어낸 좋은 결과를 기꺼이 거둡니다. 결국 이러한 무임승차 문제는 모든 팀 구성원들이 어떤 활동이든 적극적으로 참여하는 것을 꺼리게 할 겁니다. 옆에 있는 누군가가 그저 편히 앉아서 쉬고 있는 상황에서는 누구도 열심히 일하지 않을 거예요.

노트

주제 working as a team = not good
1. not efficient
   - always have to reach an agreement
   - time-consuming
2. creative ideas? no
   - 1 or 2 ppl will lead the group
   - other ppl have to follow leaders
3. ppl don't work harder in a group
   - a free rider → everyone will lose motivation

팀으로 일하는 것 = 안 좋음
1. 효율적이지 않음
   – 항상 합의에 이르러야 함
   – 시간이 걸림
2. 창의적 아이디어? 아니다
   – 한두 사람이 무리를 이끌 것
   – 다른 사람들은 리더를 따라야 함
3. 사람들은 무리에서 더 열심히 일하지 않는다
   – 무임승차자 → 모두가 의욕을 잃을 것

어휘 fail to ~하지 못하다, ~하는 데 실패하다 | outweigh v ~보다 더 크다 | consensual adj 합의하는, 합의에 의한 | adjust v 조절하다, 조정하다 | time-consuming adj (많은) 시간이 걸리는 | come up with 생각해내다, 떠올리다 | influential adj 영향력 있는 | dominate v 압도하다, 지배하다 | free riding 무임승차 | selfish adj 이기적인 | reap v 거두다, 수확하다 | exert oneself 노력하다 | reluctant adj 꺼리는, 망설이는

Q2

Some species that have been introduced to new regions of the world are believed to cause harm. However, new species do not

세계의 새로운 지역에 유입된 일부 종은 피해를 야기하는 것으로 여겨집니다. 하지만 새로운 종이 반드시 해로운 영

necessarily cause only bad effects. Rather, depending on what specific aspects you look at, the impact of the introduction of new species can be interpreted differently.

향만 야기하는 것은 아니에요. 오히려 어떤 특정 관점으로 보는지에 따라 새로운 종 유입의 영향은 다르게 해석될 수 있습니다.

First, the argument that the introduction of new species disturbs the ecological balance seems to be quite exaggerated. The introduction of some species makes a great contribution to local communities without upsetting the local ecological balance. For example, a new type of wheat was introduced to Kansas because of favorable conditions for wheat production, and it resulted in high-yield production. This has made it possible to supply a large quantity of wheat as an essential food source for animals as well as humans.

첫 번째로, 새로운 종의 유입이 생태계의 균형을 어지럽힌다는 주장은 상당히 과장된 것으로 보입니다. 일부 종의 유입은 그 지역의 생태적 균형을 깨뜨리지 않고 지역 사회에 크게 기여할 수 있어요. 예를 들면, 밀 생산에 적합한 조건 때문에 캔자스 주에 유입된 새로운 종류의 밀은 높은 생산량이라는 결과를 가져왔습니다. 이는 인간뿐 아니라 동물에게도 중요한 식량 원천으로 많은 양의 밀 공급을 가능하게 했어요.

Second, although it can be argued that some introduced new species would degrade the overall quality of the environment, the impact of a new species depends on which part of the environment you look at. For instance, the cane toad was initially introduced for the biological control of agricultural pests, and it has successfully reduced the number of garden insects and rats. As a result, the introduction of that new species has in some ways helped the local environment.

두 번째로, 새로 유입된 일부 종이 전체적인 환경의 질을 저하시킬 거라고 주장할 수는 있겠지만, 새로운 종의 영향은 환경의 어떤 부분을 볼 것인가에 달려 있습니다. 예를 들면, 사탕수수 두꺼비는 처음에 농작물 해충들의 생물학적 통제를 위해 도입되었으며 정원의 곤충과 쥐의 개체 수를 성공적으로 감소시켰어요. 그 결과, 이 새로운 종의 도입은 지역 환경에 어느 정도 도움을 주었습니다.

Finally, as for economic burdens brought about by the introduction of new species, their impact also depends on which part of the economy you look at. For example, economic burdens that mesquites cause should be compared with the benefits that they generate. This is because they serve as a source of valuable products such as firewood and high-quality timber. Therefore, given that these economic benefits have a significant effect on local economies, the economic burdens they cause should be reconsidered.

마지막으로, 새로운 종의 유입으로 야기된 경제적 부담의 경우, 그들의 영향 또한 경제의 어떤 부분을 보는가에 달렸습니다. 예를 들면, 메스키트가 초래하는 경제적 부담은 그것이 창출한 이점과 비교되어야 해요. 왜냐하면 그것이 장작이나 양질의 목재 등 가치 있는 생산물의 원천 역할을 하기 때문입니다. 따라서, 이러한 경제적 이익이 지역 경제에 중대한 영향을 미치는 것을 고려할 때, 이들이 일으킨 경제적 부담은 재검토되어야 합니다.

노트

주제 new species in a new envi. cause problems? No

1. disturb ecology? Not really
   - can contribute to local comm. (e.g. ↑ yield production)
2. destroy the natives?
   - No. e.g. = cane toad ↓ # of insects and rats
   - can be helpful to local envi.
3. economic burden?
   - they can also generate benefits

새 환경에서 새 종이 문제를 야기한다? 아니다

1. 생태계 교란? 그렇지 않다
   – 지역 사회에 일조할 수 있음(예: 생산량 높아짐)
2. 토착종 파괴?
   – 아니다. 예 = 사탕수수 두꺼비가 곤충, 쥐 숫자를 감소시킴
   – 지역 환경에 도움을 줄 수 있음
3. 경제적 부담?
   – 이윤도 창출할 수 있음

어휘 species n 생물의 종 | not necessarily 반드시 ~는 아닌 | aspect n 관점, 측면 | interpret v 해석하다 | disturb v 어지럽히다 | exaggerate v 과장하다 | contribution n 기여, 이바지 | wheat n 밀 | favorable adj 적합한, 유리한 | degrade v (질적으로) 저하시키다, 저해하다 | initially adv 처음에 | pest n 해충 | serve as ~로서 역할을 하다 | firewood n 장작 | timber n 목재 | given that ~을 고려하면 | significant adj 중대한, 상당한 | reconsider v 다시 생각/검토하다

Q3

Okay, class, I'd like to continue to discuss the emergence of the factory system in the beginning of the Industrial Revolution. Now,

좋아요, 여러분, 산업 혁명 초기의 공장제 출현에 관해 이야기를 계속하겠습니다. 자, 주말 동안 읽으라고 여러분에

the article that I gave you to read over the weekend seems to imply that there were three strong factors that affected the rise of the factory system in England, but in fact, um, there are some problems… well, with the reasons mentioned in the reading.

게 준 글은 영국에서 공장제의 발달에 영향을 미친 세 가지 강력한 요인들이 있다고 암시하는 것처럼 보이지만, 사실, 음, 지문에서 언급된 이유에는… 몇 가지 문제점이 있어요.

First of all, contrary to the suggestion of the reading, there were not many noticeable breakthroughs. For example, steam engines were not used that much because the engines often broke down and had a high risk of explosion. So at that time, workers used almost the same machines that they used before and kept the same manufacturing process, with several fellow workers at home or at a small workshop.

먼저, 지문이 제시하는 내용과는 반대로 주목할 만큼 획기적인 발전은 많지 않았습니다. 예를 들면, 증기 기관은 엔진이 자주 고장 났고 폭발의 위험이 컸기 때문에 그렇게 많이 사용되지 않았어요. 그래서 당시 노동자들은 전에 쓰던 것과 거의 같은 기계를 사용했고, 몇 명의 동료 노동자들과 집이나 작은 작업장에서 같은 제조 과정을 고수하며 일했습니다.

Second, property rights introduced by the English government are generally thought of as a main factor in the creation of the factory system. However, property rights do not necessarily contribute to the rise of a factory system. For example, we could hardly find the advancement of the system in Germany even though the government made a great effort to protect individual property rights.

두 번째로, 영국 정부가 도입한 재산권은 일반적으로 공장제 탄생의 중요한 요소로 여겨집니다. 하지만 재산권은 딱히 공장제의 성공에 기여하지 않아요. 예를 들면, 독일 정부는 개인의 재산권을 지키기 위해 엄청난 노력을 기울였지만, 독일에서는 공장제의 발전을 찾아보기 어렵습니다.

Finally, yes, it is true that factory owners could reduce the costs of transporting raw materials and goods. But they had to spend the same amount of money on managing their factories as they saved. For instance, they had to build a factory and hire someone who could supervise the factory laborers.

마지막으로, 네, 공장 소유주가 원자재와 상품의 운송 비용을 줄일 수 있었던 것은 사실이에요. 하지만 아낀 돈을 공장을 관리하는 데 써야만 했습니다. 예를 들면, 공장을 짓거나 공장 근로자들을 감독하는 누군가를 고용해야만 했죠.

노트

주제 3 reasons for the rise of factory system in England → problems

1. many breakthroughs? no
   - steam engine → not used much
   - workers used same machines
2. property rights X contribute
   - German gov't did the same → nothing really happened
3. cost ↓ X
   - had to spend same $ for managing factories

영국 공장 시스템 성공의 세 가지 이유 → 문제점들

1. 획기적인 발전 많음? 아니다
   – 증기 기관차 → 많이 사용되지 않음
   – 노동자들은 같은 기계 사용
2. 재산권이 기여 X
   – 독일 정부도 똑같이 함 → 아무 일도 일어나지 않음
3. 비용 절감 X
   – 공장 관리에 그만큼의 비용을 써야 했음

어휘 emergence n 출현, 도래 I rise n 성공, 상승, 증가 I noticeable adj 주목할 만한, 주요한 I breakthrough n 획기적인 변화, 발전 I break down 망가지다 I explosion n 폭발 I property rights 재산권 I contribute to ~에 기여하다 I advancement n 발전 I make a great effort to ~에 큰 노력을 기울이다 I transport v 운송하다 I raw material 원자재, 원료 I good n 재화(상품) I manage v 운영하다, 관리하다 I supervise v 감독하다, 감시하다

Q4

Okay, class. Yes, I know hydrogen is a cleaner energy source than fossil fuels, but the article is simply too optimistic about the possibility that hydrogen fuel will replace fossil fuels anytime soon. I think the possibility seems very low. Let's look at the key points discussed in the reading.

자, 여러분. 그래요, 수소가 화석 연료보다 깨끗한 에너지라는 것은 알지만, 지문은 수소 연료가 화석 연료를 조만간 언제든 대체할 것이라는 가능성에 그저 너무 긍정적입니다. 저는 그 가능성이 매우 낮다고 생각해요. 지문에서 논의된 요점들을 살펴봅시다.

Even though it is true that hydrogen gas is renewable and very abundant, the kind of hydrogen that is used in hydrogen

수소 가스가 재생할 수 있고 매우 풍부하다는 것은 사실이지만, 수소 연료 엔진에 사용되는 종류의 수소는 매우

fuel engines is highly artificial and requires a very complicated process to create. The gas is processed into a liquid state that must be kept at a constant temperature of -253 degrees Celsius in specially designed containers. This means it is very hard to create hydrogen that can be used as an energy source because generating this liquid form is very complex.

인공적이고 만드는 데 아주 복잡한 과정을 필요로 합니다. 이 기체는 특별히 고안된 용기에서 섭씨 영하 253도의 일정한 온도로 유지되어야 하는 액체 형태로 처리되죠. 이는 이러한 유형의 액체 형태를 만드는 일이 매우 복잡하기 때문에 에너지원으로 사용될 수 있는 수소를 만드는 것은 매우 어렵다는 뜻입니다.

Next, the article mentions pollution. Yes, it is true that the only byproduct generated when using hydrogen as an energy source is water. But, the article fails to discuss the process used to create that type of hydrogen. In order to create the liquid hydrogen used in fuel cells, a very large amount of fossil fuels, such as coal, must be burned. So, you see that, even though no pollution is given off when hydrogen is used for energy, there is a lot of pollution added to the atmosphere when generating it.

다음으로, 지문은 오염을 언급합니다. 그래요, 수소를 에너지원으로 사용할 때 만들어지는 유일한 부산물이 물이라는 것은 사실입니다. 하지만 지문은 그러한 유형의 수소를 만드는 데 사용되는 과정을 논의하지 않아요. 연료 전지에 사용되는 액체 수소를 만들기 위해서는 석탄 같은 매우 많은 양의 화석 연료를 태워야 합니다. 그래서 수소가 에너지로 사용될 때는 아무런 오염물을 배출하지 않는다고 해도 수소를 만들어 낼 때는 대기가 크게 오염된다는 걸 알 수 있죠.

And last, I can't see why the reading would say that hydrogen fuel cell engines will become more cost-effective. These engines require platinum. As you all know, platinum is a very rare and very expensive metal. Without platinum, the engines used in hydrogen fuel cells cannot complete the chemical reactions to achieve energy creation. So, without this very expensive metal, these engines can't make the energy move a vehicle.

그리고 마지막으로, 저는 왜 수소 연료 전지 엔진이 비용 대비 효과가 더 클 것이라고 지문에서 말했는지 이해할 수 없군요. 이러한 엔진에는 백금이 필요합니다. 여러분 모두 알다시피, 백금은 매우 희귀하고 아주 비싼 금속입니다. 백금 없이는 수소 연료 전지에 사용되는 엔진이 에너지를 생성시키는 위한 화학 반응을 온전히 일으킬 수 없어요. 그래서 이 비싼 금속이 없으면 이러한 엔진은 자동차를 움직이게 만드는 에너지를 생성해 낼 수 없습니다.

노트

주제 hydrogen fuel can replace fossil f. soon? No

1. not that simple
   - the kind of H. used for H. fuel engines is artificial & complicated to make
2. No pollution?
   - byproduct = water, true
   - but the process of making that H. requires fossil f. too → pollution
3. cost effective?
   - H. fuel engine = platinum = rare & expensive

수소 연료가 곧 화석 연료를 대체? 아니다

1. 그렇게 간단하지 않음
   - 수소 연료 엔진에 사용되는 수소는 인공적 & 만들기 복잡함
2. 오염 없음?
   - 부산물 = 물, 사실
   - 그러나 그 수소를 만드는 과정에서도 화석 연료가 사용됨 → 오염
3. 비용 효율적?
   - 수소 연료 엔진 = 백금 = 귀함 & 비쌈

어휘 optimistic adj 낙관적인, 긍정적인 | renewable adj 재생 가능한 | abundant adj 풍부한 | artificial adj 인공적인, 인위적인 | complicated adj 복잡한 | liquid adj 액체의 | state n 상태 | constant adj 지속적인, 일정한 | designed adj 고안된, 만들어진 | container n 용기, 그릇 | byproduct n 부산물 | fail to ~하지 못하다 | coal n 석탄 | give off 발산하다, 내뿜다 | cost-effective adj 비용 효율적인 | platinum n 백금 | rare adj 드문, 희귀한 | chemical reaction 화학 반응

Lesson 04 노트 & 답변 연결하기

Practice

본서 | P. 338

Q1 Reading

The top priority for any company is to increase its profits. In order to do so, companies must regularly assess their performance in the market and find new strategies suitable for rapidly changing their economic circumstances. Such strategies often involve

어떤 기업이든 최우선순위는 이익을 증대하는 것이다. 그러기 위해 기업들은 시장에서 거둔 성과를 정기적으로 평가하고, 그들의 경제적 상황을 빠르게 변화시키기에 알맞은 새로운 전략을 찾아야 한다. 이러한 전략들에는 시장에

releasing new products onto the market, and this can be done in three ways.

새 제품을 출시하는 것이 흔히 포함되며, 이는 세 가지 방법으로 행할 수 있다.

One strategy for increasing a company's sales is to develop an entirely new product by using the company's image. For example, if a renowned car company develops a motorcycle, the company can use its popularity to sell the product. Consumers who intend to buy a motorcycle will probably choose this particular motorcycle because of the company's image. Consumers will naturally think that the motorcycles will be just as good as the cars the company produces, so they will buy its motorcycles without any doubt.

회사의 매출을 올리는 한 가지 전략은 회사의 이미지를 이용하여 아예 새로운 제품을 개발하는 것이다. 예를 들어, 유명한 자동차 회사가 오토바이를 개발하면 그 회사는 제품을 판매하기 위해 회사의 인기를 이용할 수 있다. 오토바이를 사려고 하는 소비자들은 아마도 그 회사의 이미지 때문에 이 특정 오토바이를 선택할 것이다. 소비자들은 그 회사에서 생산하는 자동차만큼 그 오토바이 역시 좋을 거라고 자연스럽게 생각할 것이기에 의심하지 않고 오토바이를 구매할 것이다.

The second strategy for raising a company's sales is to make a new version of an existing product. For example, if a soft drink company that is famous for its cola creates a version with an added fruit flavor, the company can easily increase sales. Consumers who love the original cola drink will be inclined to try this variation of the original product. The new cola benefits from both the familiarity that customers have with the old version and their curiosity about the newer one.

회사의 매출을 증가시키는 두 번째 전략은 기존 제품의 새로운 버전을 만드는 것이다. 예를 들어, 만약 콜라로 유명한 청량음료 회사가 과일 맛이 추가된 버전의 콜라를 만든다면 그 회사는 쉽게 매출을 올릴 수 있다. 원래의 콜라를 좋아하는 소비자들이 원래 제품의 다른 버전인 이 제품을 마셔보고 싶어 할 것이다. 새 콜라는 소비자들이 기존 버전에 대해 가진 익숙함과 새 제품에 대한 호기심 둘 다에서 덕을 본다.

The final strategy is to make a partnership with another company. For example, if a company that makes chocolate forms a partnership with an ice cream company, the two companies can easily produce chocolate ice cream products together. In this case, both companies can increase their sales in a short period of time because they both receive a percentage of the new sales of the new chocolate ice cream. The brand images of both companies contribute to those sales.

마지막 전략은 다른 회사와 제휴를 맺는 것이다. 예를 들어, 만약 초콜릿을 생산하는 어떤 회사가 아이스크림 회사와 제휴를 맺는다면 두 회사는 쉽게 같이 초콜릿 아이스크림 제품을 생산할 수 있다. 이 경우 두 회사가 새 초콜릿 아이스크림의 판매에서 오는 수익의 일부를 가져가게 되므로 두 회사 모두 짧은 기간에 매출을 증가시킬 수 있다. 두 회사의 브랜드 이미지가 매출에 기여한다.

어휘 priority n 우선순위 | profit n 이윤 | regularly adv 정기적으로 | assess v 평가하다 | strategy n 전략 | suitable adj 적합한 | release v 출시하다 | entirely adv 완전히 | renowned adj 유명한 | popularity n 인기 | intend v 의도하다 | particular adj 특정한 | consumer n 소비자 | doubt n 의심 | existing adj 기존의, 존재하는 | flavor n 맛 | variation n 변형 | familiarity n 익숙함, 낯익음 | curiosity n 호기심 | partnership n 제휴, 동업 | percentage n 수익의 일부 | contribute v 기여하다, 일조하다

Listening

Okay, class. Today, I am going to talk about different ways that companies try to expand their product lines. The article I gave to you yesterday introduced three common strategies that companies often use, but I do not think such strategies always bring benefits. In fact, those strategies often cause companies serious problems. Let me explain.

자, 여러분. 오늘은 회사가 제품군을 확장하는 다른 방법들에 관해 이야기하겠습니다. 어제 여러분에게 준 글은 기업들이 자주 사용하는 세 가지 흔한 전략을 소개하지만, 나는 그 전략들이 항상 이익을 가져온다고 생각하지는 않아요. 사실, 그 전략들은 기업에게 자주 심각한 문제를 야기합니다. 설명하도록 하죠.

The first strategy that the reading mentions is creating an entirely new product that the company will market using its existing positive image. But, this strategy can have the opposite effect and harm its image instead. For example, what if the motorcycles mentioned in the reading turn out to be not as good as the company's cars? Then the car company's image will be damaged, and this will end up lowering the sales of its cars as well as the motorcycles.

지문이 언급하는 첫 번째 전략은 그 기업이 기존에 가진 긍정적 이미지를 이용해서 광고할 아예 새로운 제품을 만드는 겁니다. 하지만 이 전략은 반대의 효과를 불러 이미지를 훼손할 수 있어요. 예를 들어, 만약 지문에서 언급된 오토바이가 이 회사의 자동차만큼 좋지 않다면 어떻게 될까요? 그러면 자동차 회사의 이미지가 손상을 입을 것이고, 이는 결국 오토바이 매출뿐 아니라 자동차 매출까지 하락하게 할 겁니다.

Next, making a new version of an existing product may seem effective at first glance. But this strategy can actually cause a company to lose its long-time loyal customers. For example, the soft drink company mentioned in the reading developed a new version of an existing cola drink. Consumers who have bought the original cola drink for a long time may doubt the quality of the drink that they have trusted. They may think the company made the new fruit flavored version because the quality of the original cola drink declined. These consumers may not purchase the original product or the new version.

Lastly, let's talk about a partnership between two companies. Forming a partnership is a very dangerous strategy because one partner could violate the deal. The ice cream company mentioned in the reading may decide to steal the chocolate company's recipe to make chocolate ice cream products on its own. This would result in undesirable consequences for the chocolate company, and it could lead to an expensive legal battle.

다음으로, 기존 제품의 새로운 버전을 만드는 것은 언뜻 보면 효율적으로 보일지 모릅니다. 하지만 이 전략은 사실 기업이 오래된 충성 소비자들을 잃게 할 수도 있어요. 예를 들어, 지문에서 언급된 청량음료 회사는 기존 콜라 제품의 새 버전을 개발했습니다. 오랫동안 원래의 콜라를 구매했던 소비자들은 자신들이 믿었던 음료의 품질에 의심을 가질 수 있어요. 원래 콜라의 품질이 하락해서 새 과일맛 버전을 만들었다고 생각할지도 모릅니다. 이 소비자들은 원래 제품도, 새 버전도 구매하지 않을 수 있어요.

마지막으로, 두 기업의 제휴에 관해 이야기합시다. 제휴를 맺는 것은 한 파트너가 거래를 위반할 수도 있기 때문에 매우 위험한 전략입니다. 지문에서 언급된 아이스크림 회사가 직접 초콜릿 아이스크림 제품을 만들기 위해 초콜릿 회사의 제조법을 훔치기로 결심할 수도 있어요. 이는 초콜릿 회사에 원치 않는 결과를 야기할 것이고, 큰 비용이 드는 법적 싸움으로 이어질 수 있습니다.

어휘 expand v 확장하다 | article n 글, 기사 | introduce v 소개하다 | opposite adj 반대의 | harm v 해를 끼치다 | effective adj 효과적인 | loyal adj 충성스러운 | decline v 하락하다, 쇠퇴하다, 감소하다 | violate v 위반하다, 어기다 | deal n 거래, 협정 | steal v 훔치다 | undesirable adj 원하지 않는, 바람직하지 않은 | consequence n 결과 | legal adj 법적인, 법의

Reading 노트

주제 ↑ profit by releasing new products, 3 ways

1. develop an entirely new pro. by using the comp's image
   - consumers buy b/c the comp's image
2. new v. of existing pro.
   - consumers' familiarity & curiosity
3. partnership w. another comp.
   - 2 comps → new product
   - brand images of both comps

새 제품을 출시하여 이익 증대하기, 3가지 방법

1. 회사의 이미지를 이용해 완전히 새로운 제품 개발
   – 소비자가 회사 이미지 때문에 구매
2. 기존 제품의 새로운 버전
   – 소비자의 익숙함 & 호기심
3. 다른 회사와의 제휴
   – 두 회사 → 새 제품
   – 두 회사의 브랜드 이미지

Listening 노트

주제 ↑ profit by releasing new products, 3 ways?

1. develop an entirely new pro. by using the comp's image?
   - new product not as good? → hurt the company's image and lower the sales of existing pro.
2. new v. of existing pro.?
   - comp. might lose long-time customers
   - they will think the original one's quality is ↓
3. partnership w. another comp.?
   - one partner could violate the deal
   - lead to expensive lawsuit

새 제품을 출시하여 이익 증대하기, 3가지 방법?

1. 회사의 이미지를 이용해 완전히 새로운 제품 개발?
   – 새 제품이 전처럼 좋지 않으면? → 회사의 이미지를 훼손하고 기존 제품 매출을 하락시킴
2. 기존 제품의 새로운 버전?
   – 회사가 오래된 고객을 잃을 수 있음
   – 기존 제품의 품질이 떨어졌다고 생각할 것
3. 다른 회사와의 제휴?
   – 한 파트너가 거래를 깰 수도 있음
   – 값비싼 소송으로 이어짐

노트 & 답변 연결

주제

읽기 The reading and the lecture both talk about strategies companies can use to raise profits by producing new products. The reading says that there are three strategies that companies can use.

듣기 However, the lecturer argues that the strategies can also have very negative results.

지문과 강의 모두 새 제품을 만들어 이익을 증대하기 위해 기업들이 이용할 수 있는 전략에 관해 이야기한다. 지문은 회사들이 이용할 수 있는 세 가지 전략이 있다고 말한다.

하지만 강의자는 그 전략들이 아주 부정적인 결과를 불러올 수도 있다고 주장한다.

요점 1

읽기 Firstly, the reading states that making a new product by using the company's positive image is a good strategy. The author gives the example of a car company producing motorcycles and relying on the company image for sales.

듣기 On the contrary, the lecturer claims that if the quality of the motorcycles proves to be not as good as the cars it makes, the company can end up damaging its image instead. And eventually, the company's sales will drop significantly.

먼저, 지문은 기업의 긍정적 이미지를 이용해 새 제품을 만드는 것이 좋은 전략이라고 주장한다. 필자는 오토바이를 생산하고 판매를 위해 회사의 이미지에 의존하는 한 자동차 회사의 예시를 든다.

그와 반대로, 강의자는 만약 오토바이의 품질이 이 회사에서 만드는 자동차만큼 좋지 않은 것으로 밝혀질 경우 회사는 오히려 스스로의 이미지에 손상을 입힐 수 있다고 주장한다. 그리고 결국 회사의 매출은 크게 감소할 것이다.

요점 2

읽기 Secondly, in the reading, the author argues that making a new version of an existing product is a good strategy. He provides the example of a soft drink company producing a new version of its popular cola.

듣기 However, the lecturer says that making a new version may cause the company to lose its loyal customers. Consumers who have trusted the soft drink company may think that the company developed the new fruit flavored version because the quality of the original cola declined. This means that the company cannot sell the original product or the new version.

두 번째로, 지문에서 필자는 기존 제품의 새 버전을 만드는 것이 좋은 전략이라고 주장한다. 그는 인기 많은 콜라의 새 버전을 만든 한 청량음료 회사의 예를 제시한다.

그러나, 강의자는 새로운 버전을 만들 경우 기업이 충성 고객들을 잃을 수도 있다고 한다. 그 청량음료 회사를 신뢰했던 소비자들은 원래 콜라의 품질이 떨어졌기 때문에 새로운 과일 맛 버전을 개발했다고 생각할 수도 있다. 이는 이 회사가 원래 제품도, 새 버전도 판매할 수 없다는 의미다.

요점 3

읽기 Thirdly, the reading goes on to say that forming a partnership is a good strategy. For example, a chocolate company can establish a partnership with an ice cream company to increase sales.

듣기 However, the lecturer contradicts this opinion, arguing that this strategy is very dangerous because one partner might break the deal. The ice cream company could steal the chocolate company's know-how for making chocolate and sell their own chocolate ice cream products. This could cause an expensive legal fight.

세 번째로, 지문은 이어서 제휴를 맺는 것이 좋은 전략이라고 말한다. 예를 들어, 한 초콜릿 회사에서 판매량 증가를 위해 아이스크림 회사와 제휴를 맺을 수 있다.

하지만 강의자는 이 의견에 반박하며 한 파트너가 거래를 깰 수도 있기 때문에 아주 위험한 전략이라고 주장한다. 아이스크림 회사에서 초콜릿 회사가 초콜릿을 만드는 노하우를 훔쳐 스스로 초콜릿 아이스크림 제품을 판매할 수도 있다. 이는 비용이 많이 드는 법적 싸움을 야기할 수 있다.

어휘 negative adj 부정적인 I positive adj 긍정적인 I significantly adv 상당히, 크게 I establish v 설립하다, 수립하다 I contradict v 반박하다, 부인하다, 모순되다

Q2 Reading

Intentionally setting a forest fire, called prescribed fire or controlled burning, is widely used in national parks across America. Prescribed fire is widely used because of the benefits that it brings to all of the organisms that live in the forest.

However, there are disadvantages far outweigh the benefits of burning forests.

First, in the process of burning forests on a regular basis, many animals are killed. Some argue that animals can escape from the fire. However, what about the young animals that cannot get away from these fires? For example, young birds are not able to fly and therefore will be trapped and die. And even adult animals can become trapped as forest fires spread very rapidly.

Second, like all fires, prescribed fire releases harmful greenhouse gases into the air. The carbon dioxide that is emitted when trees burn is one of the gases that contributes to global warming. As we all know, global warming has a detrimental impact on the planet. For example, global warming makes many areas arid and this harms the forests.

Third, prescribed fire is a waste of time and resources. That is because naturally occurring fire happens in areas where prescribed fire has already been carried out. This happens because of occasional lightning strikes, camping accidents, or just senseless acts of arson. Either way, firefighters and residents must work to put out these fires again, which means that prescribed fire is a waste of time and resources.

'지정 화재' 또는 '통제 소각'이라고 불리는, 고의로 낸 산불은 미국 전역의 국립 공원에서 널리 활용되고 있다. 지정 화재는 숲에 사는 모든 생물에게 가져다주는 이점 때문에 널리 활용되고 있다. 그러나 숲을 태우는 것의 이점을 훨씬 넘어서는 단점들이 있다.

첫째로, 정기적으로 숲을 태우는 과정에서 많은 동물이 죽는다. 어떤 사람들은 동물들이 그 불을 피할 수 있다고 주장한다. 하지만 이러한 불에서 도망칠 수 없는 어린 동물들은 어떤가? 예를 들면, 어린 새들은 날 수가 없어 갇혀서 죽게 될 것이다. 그리고 심지어 다 자란 동물도 산불이 아주 빠르게 퍼지기 때문에 갇힐 수 있다.

둘째로, 모든 불과 마찬가지로 지정 화재는 공기 중으로 해로운 온실가스를 방출한다. 나무가 타면서 방출되는 이산화탄소는 지구 온난화에 일조하는 가스 중 하나다. 우리 모두 알고 있듯이 지구 온난화는 지구에 해로운 영향을 끼친다. 예를 들어, 지구 온난화는 많은 지역을 메마르게 하고 이는 숲에 해를 끼친다.

세 번째로, 지정 화재는 시간과 자원 낭비다. 왜냐하면 지정 화재가 이미 행해진 장소에서는 자연적으로 발생하는 화재가 일어나기 때문이다. 이는 가끔 일어나는 낙뢰나 캠핑 사고, 몰상식한 방화 행위 때문에 발생한다. 어떤 식으로든 소방관과 주민들을 이 불을 다시 진화하기 위해 애써야 하는데, 이는 지정 화재가 시간과 자원 낭비라는 뜻이다.

어휘 intentionally adv 의도적으로, 고의로 | prescribed adj 미리 정해진, 지정의 | outweigh v ~보다 더 크다 | on a regular basis 정기적으로 | trap v 가두다 | spread v 퍼지다 | release v 방출하다 | emit v 내뿜다 | detrimental adj 해로운, 유해한 | arid adj 건조한, 메마른 | lightning strike 낙뢰 | senseless adj 몰상식한, 지각없는, 무분별한 | arson n 방화 | put out (불 등을) 끄다

Listening

The reading states that prescribed fire is not beneficial for various reasons. However, the arguments are not convincing because prescribed fire isn't as harmful or inefficient as the reading says. Let me explain.

The point in the reading about trapping animals is way off. For a certain period of time during the year, animals reproduce and raise their young. Prescribed fires can be executed during the months when animals don't breed and there wouldn't be any offspring to worry about. All that has to be considered is to make the timing of the fire coincide with the time of the year when animals are not reproducing.

Another point made in the reading is that carbon dioxide from the smoke will pollute the air, but this is also a false statement. Carbon dioxide released into the air from fires is absorbed by nearby vegetation. Plants normally take in carbon dioxide during photosynthesis. Moreover, the young plants that grow after the

지문은 지정 화재가 여러 이유에서 이롭지 않다고 주장합니다. 하지만 지정 화재가 지문이 말하는 것만큼 해롭거나 비효율적이지 않기 때문에 이 주장은 설득력이 없어요. 설명하겠습니다.

동물들이 갇히는 것에 관한 지문의 주장은 완전히 잘못되었습니다. 한 해의 일정 기간 동안 동물들은 새끼를 낳고 기릅니다. 지정 화재는 동물들이 새끼를 낳지 않아서 걱정할 만한 새끼 동물들이 없는 달에 시행될 수 있어요. 유일하게 고려해야 할 점은 동물들이 번식하지 않는 그 시기와 화재 시점이 맞아떨어지게 하는 겁니다.

지문의 또 다른 주장은 연기에서 나오는 이산화탄소가 공기를 오염시킨다는 것이지만, 이 또한 틀린 주장입니다. 산불로 인해 공기 중으로 방출되는 이산화탄소는 근처의 식물들에 흡수돼요. 식물들은 보통 광합성을 하면서 이산화탄소를 흡수합니다. 게다가 화재 이후 자라는 어린 식물 또한 대기로부터 잉여 이산화탄소를 흡수하기에 지문에

fire also absorb the excess carbon dioxide from the air, so there won't be as much pollution as was stated in the reading.

서 말하는 것만큼의 오염은 없을 거예요.

Finally, I don't think prescribed fire is a waste of time and resources. Natural fires that happen after would be less intense due to prescribed fire. This is because prescribed fire decreases the possibility of great forest fires by eliminating the excess dead shrubs or trees on the forest floor. So people will not need to allocate much time and money to trying to put out these fires.

마지막으로, 나는 지정 화재가 시간과 자원 낭비라고 생각하지 않습니다. 지정 화재 뒤에 일어나는 자연발생적 화재는 지정 화재 때문에 정도가 덜합니다. 왜냐하면 지정 화재가 숲 바닥에 남아 있던 죽은 관목과 나무를 제거하여 큰 산불의 가능성을 낮추기 때문이죠. 그래서 사람들은 이러한 불을 끄는 데 많은 시간과 돈을 할애하지 않아도 됩니다.

어휘 inefficient adj 비효율적인 I reproduce v 생식하다, 번식하다 I execute v 실행하다 I breed v 새끼를 낳다 I offspring n 자손, (동물의) 새끼 I coincide with ~와 동시에 일어나다 I pollute v 오염시키다 I absorb v 흡수하다 I vegetation n 식물, 초목 I photosynthesis n 광합성 I excess adj 잉여의, 여분의, 초과한 I intense adj 극심한, 강렬한 I eliminate v 제거하다 I shrub n 관목 I allocate v 할당하다, 할애하다

Reading 노트

주제 prescribed fire – disadvantages > benefits
1. animals are killed
   - can't escape easily
2. harmful greenhouse gas
   - CO_2 → global warming
3. waste of time & resources
   - natural fire occurs in the same area anyway → have to put out

지정 화재 – 단점 〉 장점
1. 동물들이 죽음
   – 쉽게 탈출 못 함
2. 해로운 온실가스
   – 이산화탄소 → 지구 온난화
3. 시간 & 자원 낭비
   – 자연발생적 화재가 같은 지역에서 일어남 → 불을 꺼야 함

Listening 노트

주제 prescribed fire – disadvantages > benefits?
1. animals are killed?
   - set fire when animals are not reproducing
2. harmful greenhouse gas?
   - CO_2 → absorbed by nearby vegetation
3. waste of time & resources?
   - natural fire = easy to put out since prescribed f. clears forest floor

지정 화재 – 단점 〉 장점?
1. 동물들이 죽음?
   – 동물들이 번식하지 않는 시기에 불을 놓음
2. 해로운 온실가스?
   – 이산화탄소 → 근처 식물에 흡수됨
3. 시간 & 자원 낭비?
   – 자연발생적 화재 = 지정 화재가 숲 바닥을 깨끗하게 정리하므로 끄기 쉬움

노트 & 답변 연결

주제

읽기 The reading and the lecture both talk about prescribed fire. The article says that such artificial fire leads to several negative consequences.
듣기 However, the lecturer argues that prescribed fire is not as harmful or inefficient as the reading argues.

지문과 강의 둘 다 지정 화재에 대해서 말한다. 지문은 그런 인위적인 화재가 몇 가지 부정적인 결과를 가져온다고 말한다.
하지만 강의자는 지정 화재가 지문이 주장하는 만큼 해롭거나 비효율적이지 않다고 주장한다.

요점 1

읽기 Firstly, the reading states that prescribed fire kills animals in the forest like young animals that cannot escape from the flames.
듣기 However, according to the lecturer, prescribed fire can be implemented during the months when animals don't breed.

첫째로, 지문은 지정 화재가 불길에서 탈출할 수 없는 어린 동물들과 같은 숲속의 동물들을 죽인다고 말한다.

그러나 강의자의 말에 따르면, 지정 화재는 동물들이 번식하지 않는 시기에 시행될 수 있다. 이는 지정 화

This means that prescribed fire would not kill many animals, nor would it be dangerous to young animals in particular.	재가 많은 동물들을 죽이지 않을 뿐만 아니라, 특히 어린 동물들에게 위험하지 않을 거라는 의미다.

요점 2

읽기 Secondly, in the reading, the author argues that prescribed fire releases harmful gases, such as carbon dioxide, which pollutes the air. 듣기 In contrast, the lecturer claims that the carbon dioxide that is released by fires is absorbed by nearby vegetation. He goes on to say that the young plants that grow after the fire also absorb the carbon dioxide in the atmosphere.	두 번째로, 지문에서 저자는 지정 화재가 대기를 오염시키는 이산화탄소 등의 해로운 가스를 배출한다고 주장한다. 이와 반대로 강의자는 화재에서 방출되는 이산화탄소가 근처의 식물에 흡수된다고 주장한다. 강의자는 이어서 화재 뒤에 자라나는 어린 식물들 또한 대기 중의 이산화탄소를 흡수한다고 말한다.

요점 3

읽기 Thirdly, the reading goes on to say that prescribed fire is a waste of time and resources because fires occur naturally or intentionally in areas where prescribed fire has already been implemented. 듣기 However, the lecturer contradicts this opinion by stating that people will spend less money and time on extinguishing these fires. According to the lecture, the fires will be less intense because materials on the forest floor that can make fires intense, like dead trees, have been eliminated beforehand by prescribed fire.	세 번째로, 지문은 이어서 지정 화재가 이미 시행된 지역에서도 화재는 자연적으로나 의도적으로 일어나기 때문에 지정 화재는 시간과 자원 낭비라고 말한다. 하지만 강의자는 사람들이 이러한 화재를 진압하기 위해 돈과 시간을 덜 쓸 것이라고 말하며 이 의견을 반박한다. 강의에 따르면 화재를 키울 수 있는 죽은 나무 같은 숲속 바닥의 물질들이 지정 화재로 미리 제거되었기 때문에 화재 규모가 덜할 것이다.

어휘 implement v 이행하다, 시행하다 | extinguish v (불을) 끄다 | beforehand adv 전에, 미리

II. Academic Discussion Task

유형 1. 찬성/반대

본서 | P. 344

Q1

Professor: When it comes to spending money, some argue that it is better to invest in something long-lasting, like an expensive piece of jewelry, rather than indulging in short-term pleasures, such as a vacation. What are your thoughts on this matter?	**교수:** 돈을 쓸 때, 어떤 사람들은 비싼 보석 같은 오래가는 것에 투자하는 것이 휴가처럼 단기적인 즐거움에 빠져들기보다 나은 것이라고 주장합니다. 이에 대한 여러분의 생각은 무엇인가요?

어휘 when it comes to ~에 관한 한 | invest in ~에 투자하다 | indulge v 빠져들다 | short-term pleasure 단기의 기쁨

Jeorge: jewelry / **April:** vacation	**조지:** 보석 / **에이프릴:** 휴가
A. From my perspective, both made excellent statements, but I'm on the same page as April.	**A.** 제 관점에서, 두 사람 모두 훌륭한 주장을 했지만 저는 에이프릴과 같은 생각입니다.

Q2

Professor: Many cities nowadays are devising plans to improve themselves, yet they are unsure of an optimal solution.	**교수:** 요즘 많은 도시가 스스로를 개선하기 위한 계획을 세우고 있지만, 최선의 해결책을 모르고 있습니다. 도시

When it comes to a city's benefit, some argue that the best way to achieve it is by focusing on constructing new buildings rather than preserving nature. What are your thoughts on this matter?

의 이익에 관해서는 새로운 건물을 건설하는 데 중점을 두는 것이 자연을 보존하는 것보다 더 나은 방법이라고 주장하는 사람들도 있습니다. 여러분은 이에 대해 어떻게 생각하시나요?

어휘 devise v 고안하다 I argue v 언쟁하다 I unsure of ~ 에 확신이 없는 I preserve v 보존하다

Jeorge: constructing new buildings / **April:** preserving nature

A. From my perspective, both made excellent statements, but I'm on the same page as April.

조지: 새로운 건물을 건설하는 것 / **에이프릴:** 자연을 보존하는 것

A. 제 관점에서, 두 사람 모두 훌륭한 주장을 했지만 저는 에이프릴과 같은 생각입니다.

Q3

Professor: Some argue that it is more important for parents to spend quality time playing and bonding with their children, rather than focusing solely on academic achievements. What are your thoughts on this statement?

교수: 어떤 사람들은 부모가 자녀의 학업 성취에만 집중하기 보다 자녀와 깊고 의미 있는 시간을 보내고 유대감을 형성하는 것이 더 중요하다고 주장합니다. 여러분은 이 주장에 대해 어떻게 생각하시나요?

어휘 quality time 깊고 의미 있는 시간 I bond n 유대 I solely adv 오로지 I achievement n 성취

Jeorge: agree / **April:** disagree

A. From my perspective, both made excellent statements, but I'm on the same page as Jeorge.

조지: 찬성 / **에이프릴:** 반대

A. 제 관점에서, 두 사람 모두 훌륭한 주장을 했지만 저는 조지와 같은 생각입니다.

Q4

Professor: We often hear the saying "Family should have meals together on a regular basis." What are your thoughts on this statement?

교수: "가족은 정기적으로 함께 식사를 해야 한다."는 말을 종종 듣습니다. 이 주장에 대한 여러분의 생각은 무엇인가요?

어휘 meal n 식사 I regular adj 규칙적인 I on a regular basis 정기적으로

Jeorge: agree / **April:** disagree

A. From my perspective, both made excellent statements, but I'm on the same page as Jeorge.

조지: 찬성 / **에이프릴:** 반대

A. 내 관점에서, 두 사람 모두 훌륭한 주장을 했지만 저는 조지와 같은 생각입니다.

유형 2. 아이디어 말하기

본서 I P. 346

Q1

Professor: People can benefit from traveling all around the world. Tell me one benefit you can gain from world travel.

교수: 사람들은 전 세계 여행에서 혜택을 얻을 수 있습니다. 전 세계 여행에서 얻을 수 있는 혜택 중 하나를 말해 보세요.

어휘 benefit v ~에서 득을 보다 I enable v 가능케 하다 I broaden v 확장하다 I perspective n 관점, 식견

Jeorge: relieving stress / **April:** meeting different people

A. From my perspective, both made excellent statements, but I would like to add that traveling all over the world enables them to broaden their perspectives.

조지: 스트레스를 완화하는 것 / **에이프릴:** 다양한 사람들을 만나는 것

A. 제 관점에서, 두 사람 모두 훌륭한 발언을 했지만, 전 세계를 여행하는 것이 그들의 관점을 넓힐 수 있다는 것을 덧붙이고 싶습니다.

Q2

Professor: Please describe a new experience you have had recently that significantly impacted your life. Explain how this experience has influenced your perspective and personal growth.

교수: 최근에 겪은 새로운 경험 중에 당신의 삶에 큰 영향을 미친 것에 대해 설명해 주세요. 이 경험이 여러분의 시각과 개인적인 성장에 어떤 영향을 미쳤는지 설명하세요.

어휘 significantly adv 상당히 크게 I impact n 영향 I growth n 성장 I laboratory n 실험실

Jeorge: volunteer program / **April:** internship at a laboratory

조지: 자원봉사 프로그램 / **에이프릴:** 실험실에서의 인턴십

A. From my perspective, both made excellent statements, but I would like to add that the internship at a small company had a significant impact on my life.

A. 제 관점에서, 두 사람 모두 훌륭한 발언을 했지만, 작은 회사에서의 인턴십이 제 삶에 큰 영향을 미쳤다는 것을 덧붙이고 싶습니다.

Q3

Professor: Which significant scientific breakthrough or technological innovation from the past two centuries would you select as a crucial advancement?

교수: 지난 200년 동안 중요한 과학적 발견이나 기술적 혁신 중에서 어떤 것을 중요한 발전으로 선택하겠습니까?

어휘 breakthrough n 획기적 발전 I crucial adj 중대한, 결정적인 I antibiotic n 항생제, 항생 물질 I by far 단연코

Jeorge: antibiotics / **April:** computer

조지: 항생제 / **에이프릴:** 컴퓨터

A. From my perspective, both made excellent statements, but I would like to add that the Internet would be the most important technological invention by far.

A. 제 관점에서, 두 사람 모두 훌륭한 발언을 했지만, 제가 추가하고 싶은 것은 인터넷이 현대에 가장 중요한 기술 발명이라는 것입니다.

Q4

Professor: Technology has made the world a better place to live, so please tell me one aspect that impacts your life.

교수: 기술은 세상을 더 좋은 곳으로 만들었다는 점에서, 여러분의 삶에 영향을 미치는 한 가지 측면을 말씀해 주세요.

어휘 aspect n 측면 I gain v 얻다 I contribute v 기여하다 I management n 관리

Jeorge: communication / **April:** gaining information

조지: 소통 / **에이프릴:** 정보를 얻는 것

A. From my perspective, both made excellent statements, but I would like to add that technology can contribute to effective time management.

A. 제 관점에서, 두 사람 모두 훌륭한 발언을 했지만, 제가 덧붙이고 싶은 것은 기술이 효과적인 시간 관리에 기여할 수 있다는 것입니다.

Lesson 01 스트레스 관련 주제

본서 I P. 351

01. Participating in club activities can contribute to alleviating stress.

02. They need a pleasant diversion to relax mentally.

03. Thanks to this, he now has a relaxed and confident mental state.

Practice

본서 I P. 352

Your professor is teaching a class. Write a post responding to the professor's question.

당신의 교수님께서 강의 중입니다. 교수님의 질문에 답하는 글을 쓰세요.

In your response, you should:

- express and support your opinion
- make a contribution to the discussion

An effective response will contain at least 100 words.
You will have 10 minutes to write it.

Dr. Springer: When it comes to spending money, some argue that it is better to invest in something long-lasting, like an expensive piece of jewelry, rather than indulging in short-term pleasures, such as a vacation. What are your thoughts on this matter?

Jeorge: Personally, I believe that investing in something that lasts, like an expensive piece of jewelry, is a wise decision. Not only does it provide a lasting value, but it can also be seen as an investment that retains or even appreciates in worth over time. Furthermore, owning a valuable piece of jewelry can be a symbol of prestige and accomplishment.

April: While I acknowledge the appeal of long-lasting investments, I believe that spending money on pleasurable experiences, such as a vacation, can be equally valuable. Pleasurable experiences have the potential to create lifelong memories and broaden one's horizons. Additionally, they can contribute to personal growth, cultural understanding, and stress relief, which are all essential aspects of a well-rounded life.

- 당신의 의견을 표현하고 뒷받침하세요
- 토론에 기여하세요

효과적인 답변은 최소한 100단어를 포함할 것입니다.
당신은 10분 동안 글을 작성할 수 있습니다.

스프린져 교수: 돈을 쓸 때, 어떤 사람들은 비싼 보석과 같이 오래가는 물건에 투자하는 것이 휴가와 같은 단기적인 즐거움에 빠지는 것보다 나은 것이라고 주장합니다. 이 문제에 대한 당신의 생각은 무엇인가요?

조지: 개인적으로 저는 오랫동안 가치가 유지되는 비싼 보석과 같은 것에 투자하는 것이 현명한 결정이라고 생각합니다. 이것은 지속적인 가치를 제공할 뿐만 아니라 시간이 지남에 따라 가치를 유지하거나 더 높아질 수 있는 투자로도 볼 수 있습니다. 더구나 소중한 보석을 소유하는 것은 명예와 성취의 상징이 될 수 있습니다.

에이프릴: 오래 지속되는 투자의 매력을 인정하면서도 저는 휴가와 같은 즐거운 경험에 돈을 쓰는 것이 동등하게 가치 있을 수 있다고 믿습니다. 즐거운 경험은 평생 기억을 만들고 시야를 넓힐 수 있는 잠재력이 있습니다. 더불어 이러한 경험은 개인적인 성장, 문화적 이해, 스트레스 해소에 기여할 수 있으며, 이는 모두 균형 잡힌 삶의 필수적인 측면입니다.

어휘 long-lasting adj 오래 지속되는 | indulge v 빠져들다 | prestige n 명성 | acknowledge v 인정하다 | lifelong adj 일생의 | horizon n 시야, 지평선 | well-rounded life 균형 잡힌 삶

아웃라인

일반적 진술

short-term pleasure: alleviate stress → stressed from work + competition → quality time enjoying short-term pleasure → relax + get back to work

구체화 사례

example → stressed out from work → "family trip" → relaxed mental state

단기적인 즐거움: 스트레스 완화 → 일과 경쟁으로부터의 스트레스 → 단기적인 즐거움을 즐기는 값진 시간 → 편안해지고 + 다시 일로 돌아갈 수 있음

예시 → 일 때문에 스트레스를 받음 → 가족 여행 → 편안해진 정신 상태

예시 답변

일반적 진술

From my perspective, both made excellent statements, but I'm on the same page as April. Simply put, experiencing short-term pleasures can contribute to alleviating stress. Nowadays, people often get stressed out from their heavy workloads and the competitions with those around them, so they need a pleasant diversion to relax mentally. By spending quality time on short-term pleasures such as vacations, they will eventually

제 관점에서는 두 사람 모두 훌륭한 주장을 했지만, 저는 에이프릴과 동일한 견해를 가지고 있습니다. 간단히 말해 단기적인 즐거움을 경험하는 것은 스트레스 해소에 기여할 수 있습니다. 요즘 사람들은 무거운 업무 부담과 주변 사람들과의 경쟁에서 스트레스를 받는 경우가 많아서, 정신적으로 편안해질 수 있는 즐거운 기분 전환이 필요합니다. 휴가와 같은 단기적인

be able to relax and get back to their work.

즐거움에 깊고 의미 있는 시간을 보내면 결국에는 휴식을 취하고 업무로 돌아갈 수 있을 것입니다.

구체화 사례

A perfect example of this is a close friend of mine. He used to suffer from a heavy workload and its pressure. He sometimes stayed up all night getting his work done, so he was basically exhausted physically and mentally. Then one day, he got to have a chance to take a family trip, and it truly allowed him to escape from all the stressful matters while enjoying the trip. Thanks to this, he now has a relaxed and confident mental state.

이에 대한 완벽한 예시는 제 친한 친구 중 한 명입니다. 그는 무거운 업무 부담과 압박으로 고통받았습니다. 그는 때때로 일을 끝내기 위해 밤을 새워야 했기 때문에 신체적으로나 정신적으로 완전히 지쳤었습니다. 그러던 어느 날, 그는 가족 여행을 떠날 기회를 얻었고, 이 여행을 즐기면서 모든 스트레스에서 벗어날 수 있었습니다. 이로 인해 그는 이제 편안하고 자신감 있는 정신 상태를 가지고 있습니다.

Lesson 02 분위기 관련 주제

본서 | P. 355

01. Students experience a positive ambiance while engaging in energetic activities during PE class.

02. However, things changed little by little after the school principal tried to change the atmosphere.

03. The current students at my school genuinely appreciate the cheerful and energetic atmosphere.

Practice

본서 | P. 356

Your professor is teaching a class. Write a post responding to the professor's question.

In your response, you should:
- express and support your opinion
- make a contribution to the discussion

An effective response will contain at least 100 words.
You will have 10 minutes to write it.

당신의 교수님께서 강의 중입니다. 교수님의 질문에 답하는 글을 쓰세요.

- 당신의 의견을 표현하고 뒷받침하세요
- 토론에 기여하세요

효과적인 답변은 최소한 100단어를 포함할 것입니다.
당신은 10분 동안 글을 작성할 수 있습니다.

Dr. Lucas: When it comes to designing a school's curriculum, there are numerous classes to choose from, each offering its own unique benefits. However, if you had to select just one class to be mandatory for the school's curriculum, which class would you prioritize?

루커스 교수: 학교 교육 과정을 설계할 때는 각각이 특유한 이점을 제공하는 다양한 수업이 있습니다. 그러나 학교 교육 과정의 필수 과목으로 딱 한 과목을 선택해야 한다면 어떤 과목을 우선시하겠습니까?

Bobby: Personally, I believe that a class focusing on personal finance and financial literacy should be mandatory for all students. In today's society, financial knowledge is crucial for individuals to navigate the complexities of managing their finances effectively. Such a class would equip students with essential skills like budgeting, saving, and understanding investments, ensuring they have a solid foundation to make informed financial decisions throughout their lives and achieve accomplishments.

바비: 개인적으로 저는 모든 학생들에게 개인 금융과 금융 이해력에 중점을 둔 수업이 필수적이라고 생각합니다. 현대 사회에서 재무 지식은 각 개인이 자신의 재무를 효과적으로 관리하기 위한 복잡성을 다루는 데 중요합니다. 이러한 수업은 학생들에게 예산 편성, 저축, 투자 이해와 같은 필수 기술을 제공하여 평생 정보에 입각한 재무 결정을 내릴 수 있는 견고한 기반을 갖도록 보장합니다.

Kelly: While I recognize the importance of financial literacy, I would argue that a class on critical thinking and problem-solving should be the mandatory choice. These skills are universally applicable and essential for success in any field.

켈리: 금융 이해력의 중요성을 인정하지만 저는 비판적 사고와 문제 해결력에 중점을 둔 수업이 필수 선택이 되어야 한다고 주장하겠습니다. 이러한 기술은 보편적으로 적용 가능하며 모든 분야에서 성공하는 데 필수적입니다. 학생들이 비판적 사고 능력을 개발함으로써 정보를 분석하고 평가하며 창의적으로 생각하고 적절한 판단을 내릴 수 있게 됩니다.

By developing critical thinking abilities, students can learn to analyze and evaluate information, think creatively, and make sound judgments.

어휘 numerous adj 다수의 I mandatory adj 의무적인 I navigate v 다루다, 항해하다 I complexity n 복잡성 I equip v 익히게 하다, 갖추다 I ensure v 보장하다, 확보하다 I accomplishment n 성취

아웃라인

일반적 진술

a positive atmosphere in PE class → influence of the atmosphere: important → Students should feel a good atmosphere. → PE: make students feel more cheerful and energetic

체육 수업의 긍정적 분위기 → 분위기의 영향 : 중요함 → 학생들은 좋은 분위기를 느껴야만 한다. → 체육 수업: 학생들을 활기차게 만들어 줄 수 있다는 점 강조

구체화 사례

example → competitive and strict atmosphere in the school → the principal's plan to change the atmosphere → a lot of time and effort to provide enjoyable PE class → positive atmosphere in the school

예시 → 치열하고 엄격한 학교의 분위기 → 분위기를 쇄신하려는 학교장의 계획 → 즐길 수 있는 체육 수업을 제공하기 위한 많은 시간과 노력 투자의 과정 → 긍정적으로 변화된 학교의 분위기

예시 답변

일반적 진술

From my perspective, both made excellent statements, but I would like to add that PE class should be a mandatory part of the school curriculum. Essentially, students experience a positive ambiance while engaging in energetic activities during PE class. This is primarily because most students can be influenced by the atmosphere in their surroundings. The impact of the atmosphere is a lot more important than they might realize. Therefore, students should feel a positive atmosphere while they are at school. PE class simply makes students feel so cheerful and energetic that they have a more enjoyable school life.

제 관점에서는 두 사람 모두 훌륭한 주장을 했지만, 저는 체육 수업이 학교 교육 과정의 필수 과목이어야 한다고 생각합니다. 기본적으로 학생들은 체육 수업에서 활기찬 활동에 참여하면서 긍정적인 분위기를 경험합니다. 이는 대부분의 학생들이 주변 환경의 분위기에 영향을 받을 수 있기 때문입니다. 분위기의 영향은 그들이 생각하는 것보다 훨씬 더 중요합니다. 따라서 학생들은 학교에서 긍정적인 분위기를 느껴야 합니다. 체육 수업은 학생들이 정말로 기분 좋고 활기찬 느낌을 갖게 만들어 더 즐거운 학교생활을 할 수 있게 합니다.

구체화 사례

A perfect example of this is the high school I attended. The school used to be very competitive and strict. However, things changed little by little after the school principal tried to change the atmosphere. A lot of time and effort were put into making the school curriculum better with more enjoyable PE classes. Now, the current students at my school genuinely appreciate the cheerful and energetic atmosphere. The school has also gained a good reputation that students want to be accepted into.

이에 대한 완벽한 예시는 제가 다녔던 고등학교입니다. 학교는 이전에 매우 치열하고 엄격했습니다. 그러나 교장이 분위기를 변화시키기 위해 노력한 후에 조금씩 변화가 일어났습니다. 더 즐거운 체육 수업으로 교육 과정을 개선하기 위해 많은 시간과 노력이 들어갔습니다. 이제 우리 학교의 재학생들은 즐겁고 활기찬 분위기에 진심으로 감사하고 있습니다. 학교는 또한 학생들이 입학하고 싶어 하는 좋은 평판을 얻었습니다.

Lesson 03 사람들과의 관계 관련 주제

본서 I P. 359

01. It creates an optimal condition for improving their relationship.

02. He used to drift apart from his son due to his job, making it challenging for them to interact.

03. A strong bond was built and developed between them.

Practice

본서 | P. 360

Your professor is teaching a class. Write a post responding to the professor's question.

In your response, you should:

- express and support your opinion
- make a contribution to the discussion

An effective response will contain at least 100 words.
You will have 10 minutes to write it.

Dr. Emilie: Many busy parents struggle to balance their work and family life, and may not have much time to devote to helping their children with schoolwork. Some argue that it is more important for parents to spend quality time playing and bonding with their children, rather than focusing solely on academic achievements. What are your thoughts on this statement?

Oliver: I completely agree with the statement. Spending quality time with your children is essential for building strong relationships and developing their emotional intelligence. Parents who prioritize play-time over academics are sending an important message to their children: that their love and attention are not contingent on academic performance.

Lucy: While I agree that spending quality time with your children is important, I think that academic achievement should not be overlooked. It's important for parents to be involved in their children's education and to provide them with the support they need to succeed in school. This doesn't mean sacrificing play-time, but finding a balance between academic and non-academic activities.

당신의 교수님께서 강의 중입니다. 교수님의 질문에 답하는 글을 쓰세요.

- 당신의 의견을 표현하고 뒷받침하세요
- 토론에 기여하세요

효과적인 답변은 최소한 100단어를 포함할 것입니다.
당신은 10분 동안 글을 작성할 수 있습니다.

에밀리 교수: 많은 바쁜 부모들은 직장과 가정생활을 균형 있게 유지하는 데 어려움을 겪으며, 아이들의 공부를 돕는 데 많은 시간을 할애하기 어려울 수 있습니다. 어떤 사람들은 부모가 아이들과 놀고 유대감을 형성하며 깊고 의미 있는 시간을 보내는 것이 학업 성취에만 중점을 두는 것보다 더 중요하다고 주장합니다. 이에 대한 여러분의 의견은 무엇인가요?

올리버: 그 주장에 완전히 동의합니다. 아이들과 깊고 의미 있는 시간을 보내는 것은 강한 관계를 형성하고 그들의 정서 지능을 발전시키기 위해 중요합니다. 학업보다 놀이를 우선시하는 부모들은 중요한 메시지를 자녀들에게 전달하고 있습니다. 즉, 그들의 사랑과 관심은 학업 성취에 달려있지 않다는 것입니다.

루시: 아이들과 깊고 의미 있는 시간을 보내는 것이 중요하다는 데 동의하지만, 학업 성취를 간과해서는 안 된다고 생각합니다. 부모는 자녀 교육에 참여하고 학교에서 성공하기 위한 지원을 제공하는 것이 중요합니다. 이는 놀이 시간을 희생하는 것이 아니라 학문과 비학문 활동 간의 균형을 찾는 것을 의미합니다.

어휘 balance v 균형을 유지하다 | devote v 헌신하다 | quality time 깊고 의미 있는 시간 | emotional intelligence 정서 지능 | prioritize v ~에 우선순위를 매기다 | contingent adj (~을) 조건으로 하는 | overlook v 간과하다

아웃라인

일반적 진술

interaction between parents and children → play together → share experiences and emotions → lead to sincere conversations later

부모와 자식 사이에서의 소통 → 같이 놀면서 어울림 → 경험들을 함께하고 감정들을 공유함 → 진지한 대화들을 나눌 수 있는 기회

구체화 사례

example → drift apart from his son due to his job → decided to play with his son → awkward and challenging at first → gradually better → a strong bond between father and son

예시 → 일 때문에 아들과의 관계가 소원함 → 아들과 같이 노는데 더 많은 시간을 보내기로 결정 → 처음에는 어색하고 힘들었음 → 점차 나아짐 → 아빠와 아들 사이에서의 끈끈한 유대가 생기게 됨

예시 답변

일반적 진술

From my perspective, both made excellent statements, but I'm on the same page as Oliver. Essentially, parents can truly interact with their children while playing together, creating an optimal condition for improving their relationship. This is mainly because, when they play together, they have more opportunities to share various experiences and emotions. These shared experiences can possibly lead to sincere conversations later on.

제 관점에서는 두 사람 모두 훌륭한 주장을 했지만, 저는 올리버와 의견이 일치합니다. 기본적으로 부모는 함께 놀면서 자녀와 진정한 상호 작용을 할 수 있으며, 이는 관계 향상을 위한 최적의 상태를 만들어 낼 수 있습니다. 이는 주로 함께 놀 때 다양한 경험과 감정을 공유할 수 있는 더 많은 기회가 있기 때문입니다. 이러한 공유된 경험은 나중에 진정한 대화로 이어질 수 있습니다.

구체화 사례

A perfect example of this is my uncle. He used to drift apart from his son due to his job, making it challenging for them to interact. Then, one day, he decided to go hiking with his son at least once a week, not just to maintain his health but also to improve their relationship. At first, it seemed awkward and challenging for them to get close to each other, but it gradually improved. His son slowly opened up to him, and a strong bond was built and developed between them.

이에 대한 완벽한 예시는 제 삼촌입니다. 그는 직업 때문에 아들과 멀어져 상호 작용하기 어려웠습니다. 그러던 어느 날, 그는 건강을 유지하기 위해서 뿐만 아니라 관계를 개선하기 위해 매주 적어도 한 번 아들과 등산하기로 결정했습니다. 처음에는 서로 가까워지기가 어색하고 어려웠지만, 점차 나아졌습니다. 그의 아들은 천천히 그에게 마음을 열고, 그들 사이에 강한 유대가 형성되고 발전했습니다.

Lesson 04 관점의 확장 관련 주제

본서 | P. 363

01. Traveling all over the world enables people to broaden their perspectives.

02. This provides them with valuable insights that are needed as they navigate unpredictable situations in the future.

03. However, it was exciting to learn how to embrace diversity.

Practice

본서 | P. 364

Your professor is teaching a class. Write a post responding to the professor's question.

In your response, you should:
- express and support your opinion
- make a contribution to the discussion

An effective response will contain at least 100 words.
You will have 10 minutes to write it.

Dr. Logan: As we explore the enriching aspects of travel, let's delve into the topic of how people can benefit from traveling from all around the world. We often hear the saying, "People can benefit from traveling from all around the world." What are your thoughts on this statement? Do you believe that travel can provide significant advantages?

Noah: I strongly agree with the statement. Traveling offers a unique opportunity for individuals to broaden their horizons, immerse themselves in different cultures, and gain a deeper understanding of the world. It allows us to break free from

당신의 교수님께서 강의 중입니다. 교수님의 질문에 답하는 글을 쓰세요.

- 당신의 의견을 표현하고 뒷받침하세요
- 토론에 기여하세요

효과적인 답변은 최소한 100단어를 포함할 것입니다.
당신은 10분 동안 글을 작성할 수 있습니다.

로건 교수: 여행의 풍부한 측면을 탐험하는 동안, 세계 각지에서 여행하는 것이 어떻게 사람들에게 이로움을 줄 수 있는지에 대한 주제를 살펴보겠습니다. "사람들은 세계 각지에서 여행함으로써 이로움을 얻을 수 있다."는 말을 종종 듣습니다. 이 주장에 대한 여러분의 생각은 무엇인가요? 여행이 상당한 이점을 제공할 수 있다고 생각하시나요?

노아: 저는 그 주장에 강력히 동의합니다. 여행은 개인들이 시야를 넓히고 다양한 문화에 몰두하며 세계를 더 깊이 이해할 수 있는 독특한 기회를 제공합니다. 여행은 편안한 지역에서 벗어나 우리의 관점을 의

our comfort zones, challenge our perspectives, and foster personal growth.

심하고 개인적인 성장을 촉진하는 기회를 제공합니다.

Helen: While I agree that travel can be beneficial, I believe that academic studies should still remain a top priority. Education provides a strong foundation and equips individuals with essential knowledge and skills. However, incorporating travel experiences into one's educational journey can enhance their understanding of diverse cultures and global issues, providing a more holistic and well-rounded education.

헬렌: 여행이 유익할 수 있다는 데는 동의하지만, 학문적인 연구가 여전히 최우선 사항이어야 한다고 생각합니다. 교육은 강력한 기초를 제공하며, 필수적인 지식과 기술을 개인에게 제공합니다. 그러나 여행 경험을 자신의 교육 여정에 통합하면 다양한 문화와 세계적인 문제에 대한 이해를 향상시킬 수 있어 더 전체적이고 균형 있는 교육을 제공할 수 있습니다.

어휘 significant adj 중요한 | immerse v 몰두하다 | comfort zone 편안함을 주는 상황 | foundation n 기초, 기반 | incorporate v 통합하다 | diverse adj 다양한 | holistic adj 종합적인

아웃라인

일반적 진술

traveling the world : broaden perspectives → exposure to different matters they haven't experienced before → get valuable insights for the future

전세계를 여행하는 것: 관점/시야의 확장 → 이전에 경험해 보지 않았던 다른 것들에 대한 노출 → 미래를 위해 필요한 가치 있는 통찰을 얻게 됨

구체화 사례

example → a friend who often moved + had numerous experiences → not challenging but exciting to learn how to embrace diversity → traveling all over the world with that friend → me: keeping distance from differences → him: open-minded to everything

예시 → 자주 이사를 다니고 수많은 경험을 겪었던 한 친구 → 많은 곳을 돌아다니면서 다양성을 포용하는 법을 배우게 되어 매우 즐거웠음 → 그 친구와의 세계 여행 → 나: 다름에 대해 거리를 둠 → 그 친구: 모든 것들에 대한 열려 있는 태도

예시 답변

일반적 진술

From my perspective, both made excellent statements, but I'm on the same page as Noah. Simply put, traveling all over the world enables people to gain inspiration and broaden their perspectives. While traveling to different places, people gain exposure to many different matters they haven't experienced before. This provides them with valuable insights that are needed as they navigate unpredictable situations in the future.

제 시각에서 두 분 모두 훌륭한 주장을 하셨다고 생각하지만, 저는 노아와 동일한 견해를 가지고 있습니다. 간단히 말씀드리면, 전 세계를 여행하는 것은 사람들이 영감을 얻고 시야를 넓히는 것을 가능케 만든다고 생각합니다. 다양한 장소를 여행하면서 사람들은 이전에 경험하지 못한 많은 다양한 문제에 노출되게 됩니다. 이는 미래에 예측할 수 없는 상황에서 필요한 귀중한 통찰력을 제공한다고 생각합니다.

구체화 사례

A perfect example of this is a close friend of mine, whose father was a diplomat traveling the world. Due to his father's job, he often moved and had numerous experiences. He said that, even though it was challenging to lead such a lifestyle, it was exciting to learn how to embrace diversity. In fact, while traveling all over the world with him, I kept my distance from different people, whereas he was open-minded toward people from various backgrounds because he had experienced similar situations before. Furthermore, there were no uncomfortable or awkward moments between him and others.

이에 대한 완벽한 사례로 언급할 수 있는 것은 제 친한 친구인데, 그의 아버지는 세계를 여행하는 외교관이셨습니다. 그의 아버지의 직업 때문에 자주 이사를 다니면서 다양한 경험을 쌓았습니다. 그는 이러한 생활 방식이 도전적이었지만, 다양성을 포용하는 법을 배우는 것은 흥미로웠다고 말했습니다. 실제로 그와 함께 전 세계를 여행하면서 저는 다른 사람들과 거리를 두었지만, 그는 이전에 비슷한 상황을 경험했기 때문에 다양한 배경을 가진 사람들에게 열린 마음을 가졌습니다. 더 나아가 그와 다른 사람들 사이에 불편하거나 어색한 순간은 전혀 없었습니다.

Lesson 05 조언 관련 주제

본서 | P. 367

01. These experiences provide them with practical and valuable advice as they navigate unpredictable situations.

02. Initially, it was uncomfortable and challenging for me to integrate with new people and learn from real-world experience.

03. This valuable experience not only provided me with practical advice but also contributed to my mental growth.

Practice

본서 | P. 368

Your professor is teaching a class. Write a post responding to the professor's question.

In your response, you should:
- express and support your opinion
- make a contribution to the discussion

An effective response will contain at least 100 words.
You will have 10 minutes to write it.

Dr. Bliss: I'd like to share your recent experiences that have had a significant impact on your lives. It's remarkable how diverse experiences can shape our perspectives and contribute to personal growth. So, please describe a new experience you have had recently that significantly impacted your life. Explain how this experience has influenced your perspective and personal growth.

James: Recently, I had the opportunity to participate in a volunteer program in a rural community. This experience has had a profound impact on my life. It exposed me to the realities and challenges faced by underprivileged communities, deepening my empathy and understanding of social issues. Interacting with the locals and working together to improve their living conditions sparked a sense of purpose and a desire to contribute positively to society.

Emma: In contrast, my recent experience was completing a research internship at a prestigious laboratory. This opportunity allowed me to work closely with leading scientists in my field of interest. Through this experience, I gained valuable insights into cutting-edge research and acquired practical laboratory skills. It reinforced my passion for scientific inquiry and provided clarity regarding my career path.

당신의 교수님께서 강의 중입니다. 교수님의 질문에 답하는 글을 쓰세요.

- 당신의 의견을 표현하고 뒷받침하세요
- 토론에 기여하세요

효과적인 답변은 최소한 100단어를 포함할 것입니다.
당신은 10분 동안 글을 작성할 수 있습니다.

블리스 교수: 여러분의 삶에 큰 영향을 미친 최근 경험을 나누고 싶습니다. 다양한 경험이 어떻게 우리의 관점을 형성하고 개인적인 성장에 기여할 수 있는지 놀랍습니다. 그러니 최근에 겪은 여러분의 삶에 큰 영향을 미친 새로운 경험을 설명해 주세요. 이 경험이 어떻게 여러분의 관점과 개인적인 성장에 영향을 미쳤는지 설명해 주세요.

제임스: 최근에 저는 시골 지역에서 자원봉사 프로그램에 참여할 기회가 있었습니다. 이 경험이 제 삶에 깊은 영향을 미쳤습니다. 이것은 빈곤한 지역이 직면하는 현실과 어려움을 접하게 되었고 사회 문제에 대한 제 공감과 이해가 깊어졌습니다. 현지 주민들과 소통하며 그들의 생활 조건을 개선하기 위해 협력하는 경험은 저에게 목적감과 사회에 긍정적으로 기여하고자 하는 열망을 일깨웠습니다.

에마: 대조적으로, 제 최근 경험은 명성 있는 연구실에서 연구 인턴십을 완료한 것이었습니다. 이 기회를 통해 저는 제가 관심을 가지고 있는 분야에서 선도적인 과학자들과 밀접하게 협력할 수 있었습니다. 이 경험을 통해 저는 최첨단 연구에 대한 소중한 통찰력을 얻었으며 실질적인 실험실 기술을 습득했습니다. 이는 저의 과학적 탐구에 대한 열정을 강화하고 제 진로에 대한 명확성을 부여했습니다.

어휘 significant adj 중요한 | shape v ~을 형성하다 | volunteer n 자원봉사자 | profound adj 깊은, 심오한 | rural adj 시골의 | underprivileged adj 불우한 | prestigious adj 명성 있는

아웃라인

일반적 진술

advice from experiences → valuable and practical advice for future → through the experiences, evaluate oneself objectively

경험들로부터 얻는 조언 → 미래를 위한 가치 있고 실용적인 조언 → 그러한 경험들을 통해서, 자신들을 객관

→ better life in the future

적으로 평가하게 됨 → 미래에 더 나은 삶을 가지게 됨

구체화 사례

example → me: less sociable → live in my own world → internship as a graduation requirement → challenging to learn from the internship opportunity → get used to the situation → got to contemplate a lot of matters → gained advice + mental growth

예시 → 나: 사회성이 결여되어 있었음 → 나만의 세계에서 살고 있었음 → 졸업 요구조건으로서 인턴십을 해야만 함 → 인턴십 기회로부터 배우는 것은 처음에 굉장히 힘들었음 → 상황에 익숙해지게 됨 → 많은 것들에 대해 깊이 생각하게 되는 기회를 가지게 됨 → 조언과 정신적 성장을 얻게 됨.

예시 답변

일반적 진술

From my perspective, both made excellent statements, but I would like to add that the internship at a small company had a significant impact on my life. In essence, people can gain a lot of advice from their work experience. It's obvious that these experiences provide them with practical and valuable advice as they navigate unpredictable situations. Through these moments, people have the opportunity to evaluate themselves objectively, leading to a better life in the future.

제 시각에서 두 분 모두 훌륭한 발언을 하셨다고 생각하지만, 저는 작은 회사에서의 인턴 경험이 제 삶에 상당한 영향을 끼쳤다는 점을 덧붙이고 싶습니다. 본질적으로 사람들은 직무 경험을 통해 많은 조언을 얻을 수 있습니다. 이러한 경험은 예측할 수 없는 상황에서 실질적이고 가치 있는 조언을 제공합니다. 이러한 순간을 통해, 사람들은 객관적으로 자기 자신을 평가할 수 있는 기회를 얻게 되어 미래에 더 나은 삶을 살아갈 수 있게 됩니다.

구체화 사례

A perfect example of this is my own experience. I used to be naive and less sociable due to my introverted personality. This led me to isolate myself from others and live in my own world. Then, one day, I had an internship experience as a graduation requirement. Initially, it was uncomfortable and challenging for me to integrate with new people and learn from real-world experience. However, as I became accustomed to it, I started to contemplate matters I hadn't considered before. This valuable experience not only provided me with practical advice but also contributed to my mental growth.

완벽한 예시로는 제 자신의 경험이 있습니다. 예전에는 내성적인 성격으로 인해 순진하고 사회성이 부족한 편이었습니다. 이로 인해 저는 다른 사람들로부터 저를 고립시키고 저만의 세계에 머무르곤 했습니다. 그런데 어느 날, 졸업 요건으로 인턴 경험을 하게 되었습니다. 처음에는 새로운 사람들과 어울리고 현실 경험을 통해 배우는 것이 불편하고 어려웠습니다. 그러나 익숙해지면서 저는 이전에 생각하지 못한 문제를 고찰하게 되었습니다. 이 소중한 경험은 실질적인 조언뿐만 아니라 저의 정신적인 성장에도 기여하였습니다.

Lesson 06 편리함 관련 주제

본서 | P. 371

01. Thanks to this, people don't have to go through any unnecessary or tedious processes.

02. When his friend moved to another city, he signed up for an online video chat platform.

03. When he visited the website, he found it had useful features.

Practice

본서 P. 372

Your professor is teaching a class. Write a post responding to the professor's question.

In your response, you should:

- express and support your opinion
- make a contribution to the discussion

An effective response will contain at least 100 words.
You will have 10 minutes to write it.

당신의 교수님께서 강의 중입니다. 교수님의 질문에 답하는 글을 쓰세요.

- 당신의 의견을 표현하고 뒷받침하세요
- 토론에 기여하세요

효과적인 답변은 최소한 100단어를 포함할 것입니다.
당신은 10분 동안 글을 작성할 수 있습니다.

Dr. Ethan: Good day, class. Scientific discoveries and technological innovations have been instrumental in shaping the world as we know it. Today, we'll delve into a captivating question: "Which significant scientific breakthrough or technological innovation from the past two centuries would you select as a crucial advancement?" Let's explore the remarkable achievements that have transformed our lives.

에단 교수: 안녕하세요, 여러분. 과학적 발견과 기술 혁신은 우리가 아는 세계를 형성하는 데 중요한 역할을 해왔습니다. 오늘은 매혹적인 질문에 대해 논의해 보겠습니다: "지난 200년 동안의 중요한 과학적 발견 또는 기술 혁신 중 어떤 것을 중요한 발전으로 선택하겠습니까?" 우리 삶을 변화시킨 놀라운 성취를 살펴보죠.

Daniel: Thank you, Professor. When considering significant advancements from the past two centuries, I would definitely pick the discovery of antibiotics. When Alexander Fleming stumbled upon penicillin in 1928, it revolutionized medicine and saved countless lives. The ability to treat bacterial infections transformed healthcare, making surgery safer and preventing deaths from once-fatal diseases.

다니엘: 감사합니다, 교수님. 지난 200년 동안의 중요한 발전을 고려할 때, 저는 확실히 항생물질의 발견을 선택하겠습니다. 1928년 알렉산더 플레밍이 페니실린을 우연히 발견한 것은 의학을 혁신하고 무수한 생명을 구했습니다. 세균 감염을 치료할 수 있는 능력은 수술을 더 안전하게 만들고 예전에는 치명적이었던 질병으로 인한 사망을 예방했습니다.

Judy: I understand the importance of antibiotics, but I'd select the development of the computer. Starting from the 1960s, the computer has changed the way we communicate, work, and access information. It has connected people globally, accelerated research and innovation, and transformed industries. Today, it's an integral part of modern life, driving progress in countless fields.

주디: 항생물질의 중요성을 이해하지만, 저는 컴퓨터의 발전을 선택할 것입니다. 1960년대부터 컴퓨터는 우리의 의사소통, 업무, 정보 접근 방식을 바꿨습니다. 이는 전 세계적으로 사람들을 연결하고, 연구와 혁신을 가속하며, 산업을 변형시켰습니다. 오늘날 이는 현대 생활에서 불가결한 부분으로, 무수한 분야에서 진보를 이끌고 있습니다.

어휘 breakthrough n 돌파구 | innovation n 혁신 | advancement n 발전, 진보 | stumble upon ~을 우연히 발견하다 | once-fatal disease 한때 치명적이었던 질병 | access n 접근 | integral adj 불가결한 | countless adj 무수한

아웃라인

일반적 진술

the Internet: provide convenience → communicate with people anytime → replace traditional offline settings → × go through tedious process

인터넷: 편리함을 제공 → 언제라도 사람들과의 소통할 수 있음 → 기존의 오프라인 환경들을 대체 → 번거로운 과정을 겪지 않아도 됨

구체화 사례

example → cousin's friend moved → signed up for online video chat → useful features to communicate → × travel a long distance in person

예시 → 사촌의 친구가 이사를 갔음 → 온라인 화상 채팅에 가입 함 → 화상 채팅은 소통하기 위한 유용한 기능들을 가지고 있었음 → 친구를 보기 위해 직접 장거리를 이동하지 않아도 되었음

예시 답변

일반적 진술

From my perspective, both made excellent statements, but I would like to add that the Internet would be the most important technological invention by far. The Internet provides people with convenience in terms of communicating with others. It's a proven fact that people can always communicate with others whenever they have Internet access. This has replaced traditional offline settings. Thanks to this, people don't have to go through any tedious processes.

제 시각에서는 두 분 모두 훌륭한 주장을 하셨다고 생각하지만, 저는 인터넷이 현존하는 기술 발명 중에서 가장 중요한 발명일 것이라고 추가하고 싶습니다. 인터넷은 사람들에게 다른 사람들과 소통하는 측면에서 편리함을 제공합니다. 인터넷 접속이 가능한 경우 언제든지 사람들은 다른 사람들과 소통할 수 있다는 것은 입증된 사실입니다. 이것은 전통적인 오프라인 환경을 대체하였습니다. 덕분에 사람들은 귀찮은 과정을 거치지 않아도 됩니다.

구체화 사례

A perfect example of this is my cousin. When his friend moved to another city, he signed up for an online video chat platform that offered a variety of functions. When he visited the website, he found it had useful features that enabled him to communicate with his friend on a daily basis. As a result, he didn't need to travel a long distance in person. This illustrates how the Internet frees people from the inconvenience of offline processes when communicating with others.

이에 대한 완벽한 예시로는 제 사촌입니다. 그의 친구가 다른 도시로 이사를 가자, 그는 다양한 기능을 제공하는 온라인 비디오 채팅 플랫폼에 가입했습니다. 그가 웹사이트를 방문하자, 그는 친구와 매일 소통할 수 있도록 도와주는 유용한 기능이 있다는 것을 발견했습니다. 결과적으로, 그는 직접 멀리 여행할 필요가 없었습니다. 이는 인터넷이 다른 사람들과 소통할 때 오프라인 과정의 불편함에서 사람들을 어떻게 해방해 주는지를 보여 주는 사례입니다.

Lesson 07 시간 활용 관련 주제

본서 | P. 375

01. Making specific plans in advance can significantly contribute to effective time management.

02. Having a specific plan helps individuals utilize their time more efficiently.

03. He ended up saving a substantial amount of time and completed his T.A. work on schedule.

Practice

본서 | P. 376

Your professor is teaching a class. Write a post responding to the professor's question.

In your response, you should:

- express and support your opinion
- make a contribution to the discussion

An effective response will contain at least 100 words.
You will have 10 minutes to write it.

Dr. Joanna: It's interesting to see the contrasting viewpoints regarding the benefits of structured plans versus the advantages of being flexible and open to new experiences. Each approach has its merits, and it ultimately depends on individual preferences and circumstances. Some people make a specific plan for their time in advance, while others make instant plans and just go with the flow. Which lifestyle do you prefer?

Justin: Personally, I prefer making specific plans in advance. Having a well-thought-out schedule allows me to prioritize my tasks, manage my time effectively, and stay organized. By planning ahead, I can set clear goals, allocate sufficient time for each activity, and ensure that I make progress towards my objectives. This approach also helps me maintain a sense of discipline and focus, as I have a road map to guide my actions.

Anna: I personally prefer going with the flow. I find that being spontaneous allows me to embrace new opportunities, adapt to unexpected situations, and remain flexible. Sometimes,

당신의 교수님께서 강의 중입니다. 교수님의 질문에 답하는 글을 쓰세요.

- 당신의 의견을 표현하고 뒷받침하세요
- 토론에 기여하세요

효과적인 답변은 최소한 100단어를 포함할 것입니다.
당신은 10분 동안 글을 작성할 수 있습니다.

조애너 교수: 구조화된 계획과 유연하며 새로운 경험에 열린 태도의 이점에 대한 대조적인 견해를 보는 것은 흥미로운 일입니다. 각 접근법은 각각의 장점이 있으며, 결국 개인의 선호와 상황에 따라 달라집니다. 어떤 사람들은 미리 시간에 대한 구체적인 계획을 세우는 반면, 다른 사람들은 즉흥적인 계획을 세우고 흐름에 맡기는 것을 선호합니다. 여러분은 어떤 생활 방식을 선호하시나요?

저스틴: 개인적으로 저는 사전에 구체적인 계획을 세우는 것을 선호합니다. 신중하게 계획된 일정을 가지면 작업의 우선순위를 정하고 시간을 효과적으로 관리하며 조직적으로 일할 수 있습니다. 사전에 계획을 세우면 명확한 목표를 설정하고 각 활동에 충분한 시간을 할당하며 목표에 대한 진전을 확실히 할 수 있습니다. 또한 이 접근법은 행동을 안내할 로드맵이 있기 때문에 훈련과 집중감을 유지하는 데 도움이 됩니다.

애나: 저는 개인적으로 흐름에 맡기는 것을 선호합니다. 저는 즉흥적으로 행동하는 것이 새로운 기회를 포용하고 예상치 못한 상황에 적응하며 유연할 수 있게 해 준다고 생각합니다. 때로는 엄격한 계획이 창의성

rigid plans can limit creativity and prevent me from exploring different avenues. By going with the flow, I can seize the present moment, follow my instincts, and embrace serendipity. It allows me to be more open-minded, responsive to changes, and comfortable with uncertainty.

을 제한하고 다양한 가능성을 탐험하는 것을 방해할 수 있습니다. 흐름에 따라가면서 현재의 순간을 즐길 수 있으며 직관에 따라 행동할 수 있고 우연을 받아들일 수 있습니다. 이는 저를 더 개방적이고 변화에 민감하며 불확실성에 편안하게 만듭니다.

어휘 structured plan 체계적인 계획 | flexible adj 유연한 | preference n 선호도 | circumstance n 상황 | well-thought-out 신중히 계획된 | ensure v 보장하다 | spontaneous adj 즉흥적인 | seize v 잡다

아웃라인

일반적 진술

making specific plan: effective time management → instant plan: time is wasted → specific plan: utilize time efficiently → handle tasks at a faster pace + focus better + outstanding performance

구체적인 계획을 세우는 것: 효과적인 시간 관리 → 즉석에서 만든 계획: 시간이 낭비 됨 → 구체적 계획: 효과적으로 시간 활용 → 일들을 좀 더 빠른 속도로 다루게 됨 + 집중을 더 잘하게 됨 + 눈에 띄는 성과를 거두게 됨

구체화 사례

example → cousin who used to make instant plans + go with the flow → assist professor as T.A. → x enough time for T.A. work → change lifestyle by making specific plans → save time + complete T.A. work on schedule

예시 → 즉석에서 계획을 세우고 흐름에 맡기는 사촌 → 교수를 조교로서 도움 → 조교 업무를 하기엔 충분치 못한 시간 → 구체적인 계획들을 세우는 것으로 라이프 스타일 변화를 시도함 → 시간 절약 + 일정대로 조교 업무를 완료

예시 답변

일반적 진술

From my perspective, both made excellent statements, but I'm on the same page as Justin. Simply put, making specific plans in advance can significantly contribute to effective time management. It's a proven fact that a considerable amount of time is wasted when people make instant plans and simply go with the flow. Having a specific plan helps individuals utilize their time more efficiently. In detail, it enables workers to handle various tasks at a faster pace, allowing them to focus better and show more outstanding performance.

제 시각에서는 두 분 모두 훌륭한 주장을 하셨다고 생각하지만, 저는 저스틴과 동일한 의견을 가지고 있습니다. 간단히 말해서, 미리 구체적인 계획을 세우는 것은 효과적인 시간 관리에 큰 기여를 할 수 있다고 생각합니다. 즉석에서 계획을 세우고 흐름에 맡기는 경우에는 상당한 시간이 낭비된다는 것이 입증된 사실입니다. 구체적인 계획을 가지는 것은 개인이 시간을 더 효율적으로 활용할 수 있게 도와줍니다. 자세히 말하면, 이는 근로자들이 다양한 업무를 더 빠른 속도로 처리하도록 하여 더 집중하고 뛰어난 성과를 내도록 돕습니다.

구체화 사례

A perfect example of this is my cousin, who used to make instant plans and go with the flow in everything he did. When he worked as a teaching assistant, he had to assist his professor with research. Everything went smoothly except for one thing: he didn't have enough time to complete the T.A. work, which involved collecting a substantial amount of research data, due to his part-time job after school. One day, he decided to change his lifestyle by making specific plans for his time in advance. Thanks to this change, he ended up saving a substantial amount of time and completed his T.A. work on schedule.

이에 대한 완벽한 예시로는 저의 사촌이 있는데, 그는 이전에 모든 것을 즉석에서 계획하고 흐름에 맡기던 사람이었습니다. 그가 교수 조교로 일할 때, 교수님의 연구를 도와야 했습니다. 모든 것은 원활하게 진행되었지만 한 가지 문제가 있었습니다. 방과 후 아르바이트 때문에 많은 연구 데이터를 수집해야 했던 조교 업무를 마무리하는 데 충분한 시간이 없었습니다. 어느 날, 그는 미리 시간에 대한 구체적인 계획을 세우기로 결정했습니다. 이 변화 덕분에 그는 상당한 시간을 절약하고 조교 업무를 예정대로 완료할 수 있었습니다.

Actual Test 1

본서 | P. 378

Question 1

Reading

In the late 14th century, an unknown poet from the Midlands composed four poems titled *Pearl*, *Sir Gawain and the Green Knight*, *Patience*, and *Cleanness*. This collection of poems is referred to as *Cotton Nero A.x* and the author is often referred to as the Pearl Poet. Up to this day, there have been many theories regarding the identity of this poet, and these are three of the most popular ones.

14세기 말, 잉글랜드 중부 지방 출신의 한 무명 시인은 〈진주〉, 〈거웨인 경과 녹색 기사〉, 〈인내〉, 〈순수〉라는 제목의 시 네 편을 썼다. 이 시집은 〈코튼 네로 A.x〉라고 불리며 저자는 흔히 펄 시인이라고 불린다. 오늘날까지 이 시인의 정체에 관한 많은 이론들이 있었고, 다음이 가장 널리 퍼진 세 가지 이론이다.

The first theory is that the author's name was Hugh, and it is based on the *Chronicle of Andrew of Wyntoun*. In the chronicle, an author called Hucheon (little Hugh) is credited with writing three poems, one of which is about the adventures of Gawain. Not only that, but all three poems are written in alliterative verse, as are all four of the poems in *Cotton Nero A.x*. Since they are written in the same style and one poem from each set concerns Gawain, some people contend that all of the *Cotton Nero A.x* poems were written by Hugh.

첫 번째 이론은 저자의 이름이 '휴'라는 것으로, 〈윈턴의 앤드류의 연대기〉에 근거를 둔다. 이 연대기에서는 휴천(작은 휴)이라는 저자가 세 편의 시를 썼다고 하는데, 그중 하나가 거웨인의 모험에 관한 것이다. 그뿐 아니라 세 편의 시는 모두 〈코튼 네로 A.x〉에 있는 네 편의 시와 마찬가지로 두운체로 쓰였다. 그 시들이 같은 문체로 쓰였으며 각 세트에 거웨인을 다루는 시가 한 편씩 있으므로 일부 사람들은 〈코튼 네로 A.x〉에 실려 있는 시를 모두 휴가 썼을 거라고 주장한다.

The second theory is that John Massey was the poet, and it is supported by another poem called *St. Erkenwald* and penmanship. Although the actual authorship of *St. Erkenwald* is unknown, John Massey was a poet who lived in the correct area and time for scholars to attribute it to him. This manuscript was written in very similar handwriting to that of the Pearl Poet, which indicates that one person is likely the author of all five of the poems.

두 번째 이론은 존 매시가 시인이라는 것이며, 이는 〈성 어컨월드〉라는 또 다른 시와 필체가 뒷받침한다. 〈성 어컨월드〉의 실제 원저자는 알려져있지 않지만 존 매시가 해당 지역과 시기에 살았던 시인이었기에 학자들은 그가 저자일 것이라고 추정한다. 이 원고는 펄 시인의 원고와 매우 비슷한 필적으로 쓰였으며, 이는 한 사람이 시 다섯 편을 모두 쓴 저자일 가능성이 높다는 것을 나타낸다.

The third theory is that the poems were actually written by different authors from the same region of England. This comes from the fact that there is little linking the poems to each other. Two are concerned with the Arthur legends, but the only link connecting the other two is that they describe the same area of the countryside. They also seem to be written in the same dialect. Taken together, these facts indicate that they were written in the same region, but they probably were not written by the same person.

세 번째 이론은 그 시들이 잉글랜드의 같은 지역에 살던 각기 다른 저자들의 작품이라는 이론이다. 이는 시들 사이에 연관성이 거의 없다는 사실에서 기인한다. 두 편의 시는 아서 왕의 전설과 관련이 있긴 하지만 다른 두 편의 시를 잇는 연결 고리는 그 시골의 같은 지역을 묘사하고 있다는 것뿐이다. 또한 그 시들은 같은 방언으로 쓰인 것으로 보인다. 종합해보면 이런 사실들은 그 시들이 같은 지역에서 쓰였지만 같은 사람에 의해 쓰인 것은 아닐지도 모른다는 것을 나타낸다.

어휘 poet n 시인 | the Midlands 잉글랜드 중부 지방 | compose v 쓰다, 구성하다 | up to this day 오늘날까지 | identity n 정체, 신원, 정체성 | chronicle n 연대기 | be credited with ~이 있다고 간주되다 | alliterative adj 두운체의 | verse n 운문, 시, (시의) 연, (노래의) 절 | penmanship n 필체, 서법 | authorship n (원)저자 | attribute v ~것이라고 보다 | manuscript n 원고, 필사본 | handwriting n 친필, 필적 | be concerned with ~와 관련이 있다 | dialect n 방언, 사투리

Listening

Due to the fact that the author failed to sign his manuscript,

저자가 자신의 원고에 서명하지 못했다는 사실 때문

the true identity of the Pearl Poet may never be known. The text that you read for your homework detailed three theories that people have suggested regarding his identity, but they are all flawed in serious ways.

에 펄 시인의 정체는 밝혀지지 않을지도 모릅니다. 여러분이 과제를 하기 위해 읽었던 지문에는 그의 신원에 관해 사람들이 제시한 세 가지 이론이 열거되어 있지만 모두 심각한 결함이 있습니다.

The first theory that the author was a man named Hugh seems plausible at first, but upon further examination that idea falls apart. The *Chronicle of Andrew of Wyntoun* speaks of a poet named Hucheon, who was writing around the appropriate time about related topics and in the same style as the poems in *Cotton Nero A.x*. However, this theory overlooks one significant factor, the dialect in which the poems were written. Hucheon's poems were written in a Yorkshire dialect, whereas the Pearl Poet wrote in a Midlands dialect closer to those of Staffordshire or Cheshire. Therefore, it is highly unlikely that Hucheon was the Pearl Poet.

저자가 '휴'라는 사람이었다는 첫 번째 이론은 처음에는 그럴듯해 보이지만, 더 깊이 조사해보면 그 발상은 힘을 잃고 맙니다. 〈윈턴의 앤드류의 연대기〉에서는 휴천이라는 시인에 대해 언급하는데, 그 시인은 적절한 시기에 관련 주제에 대한 저술 활동을 하고 있었으며 〈코튼 네로 A.x〉에 실린 시들과 같은 문체로 썼어요. 그러나 이 이론은 한 가지 중요한 요인, 즉 시에서 쓰인 방언을 간과하고 있습니다. 휴천의 시는 요크셔 방언으로 쓰인 반면, 펄 시인은 스태퍼드셔나 체셔 지방의 것과 가까운 잉글랜드 중부 방언을 사용했어요. 그러므로 휴천이 펄 시인이었을 가능성은 매우 낮습니다.

The second theory that the Pearl Poet was John Massey is also difficult to support. Firstly, there is no concrete proof that Massey wrote *St. Erkenwald*, let alone the Pearl Poet's poems. The theory also points out that the Pearl Poet and John Massey had similar handwriting, but this too is problematic. The poems were all reproduced before the printing press had spread throughout Europe, so they were copied by hand. Therefore, it is possible that they were reproduced by the same scribe, but this in no way clarifies who composed them originally.

펄 시인이 존 매시였다는 두 번째 이론 또한 옹호하기 어렵습니다. 먼저, 존 매시가 펄 시인의 시들은 고사하고 〈성 어컨월드〉의 저자라는 구체적인 증거가 없어요. 이 이론은 또한 펄 시인과 존 매시가 비슷한 필적을 가지고 있었다고 언급하는데, 여기에도 문제가 있습니다. 그 시들은 모두 인쇄기가 유럽 전역에 보급되기 전에 복제되었으므로 손으로 베껴 적었을 것입니다. 그러므로 같은 필경사가 베껴 썼을 가능성은 있습니다만 누가 그 시들을 쓴 원저자인지는 결코 명확하게 말해 주지 않아요.

The third theory that the poems were actually written by four entirely different authors who lived in the same region is also questionable. It allows for the similar landscapes they depict and for them being written in the same dialect. However, their linguistic similarities go beyond dialect. The author actually uses many terms that he invented, and the poems share these terms. It is difficult to believe that four separate poets could have created the same words and used them, so it is clear that there was only one author.

그 시들이 사실 같은 지역에 살았던 네 명의 완전히 다른 저자에 의해 쓰였다는 세 번째 이론 또한 의심의 여지가 있습니다. 이는 그 시들이 비슷한 풍경을 묘사하고 있으며 같은 방언으로 쓰였다는 점을 고려한 것이지요. 그러나 그들의 언어학적 유사성은 방언의 수준을 넘어서고 있습니다. 저자는 실제로 자신이 지어낸 용어들을 다수 사용하고 있으며, 그 시들은 이런 용어들을 함께 사용하고 있습니다. 네 명의 서로 다른 시인들이 같은 단어를 지어내 사용했을 거라고 생각하기 어려우므로 저자는 단 한 명이었음이 분명합니다.

어휘 flawed adj 결함이 있는 | plausible adj 그럴듯한, 이치에 맞는 | fall apart 무너지다 | overlook v 간과하다 | concrete adj 구체적인, 사실에 의거한 | let alone ~은 고사하고 | problematic adj 문제가 있는 | printing press 인쇄기 | scribe n 필경사 | in no way 결코 ~ 않다 | allow for ~을 감안하다 | depict v 묘사하다 | linguistic adj 언어(학)의 | go beyond ~을 넘어서다

강의에서 제시한 요점을 요약하시오. 읽기 지문의 요점에 대해 강의에서 어떻게 반박하는지 설명하시오.

예시 답변

The reading gives three possible theories regarding the identity of the Pearl Poet, who wrote the four poems in a collection titled *Cotton Nero A.x*. However, the lecturer indicates that the reading's theories have flaws and errors in their arguments.

지문은 〈코튼 네로 A.x〉 시집에 있는 네 편의 시를 집필한 펄 시인의 정체에 관해 세 가지 가능한 이론을 제시한다. 그러나 강의자는 지문의 이론에서 주장하는 바에는 결함과 오류가 있다고 말한다.

Firstly, the reading proposes that the Pearl Poet was an author named Hugh. This is because his poems were written in the same style as *Cotton Nero A.x* and some of the poems concern Gawain. However, the lecturer points out that the Pearl Poet and Hugh's dialects are not the same. It is highly likely that they are the two different people who lived in different regions.

첫 번째로, 지문에서는 펄 시인이 휴라는 이름의 저자였다고 제시한다. 이는 그의 시들이 〈코튼 네로 A.x〉와 같은 문체로 쓰였으며 일부 시에서 거웨인을 주제로 하고 있기 때문이다. 그러나 강의자는 펄 시인과 휴가 사용한 방언이 같지 않다는 점을 지적한다. 그들은 다른 지역에 살았던 각기 다른 두 명의 인물일 가능성이 높다.

Secondly, the reading suggests that another poet named John Massey may be the author of *Cotton Nero A.x.* This is supported by the fact that the handwriting of *Cotton Nero A.x* and *St. Erkenwald*, a poem thought to have been written by John Massey, look quite similar. However, the lecturer contradicts this by arguing that the same scribe could have reproduced all the poems.

두 번째로, 지문에서는 존 매시라는 또 다른 시인이 〈코튼 네로 A.x〉의 저자일지도 모른다고 제시한다. 이것은 〈코튼 네로 A.x〉와 존 매시가 쓴 시라고 여겨지는 〈성 어컨월드〉의 필적이 매우 유사해 보인다는 사실에 의해 뒷받침된다. 그러나 강의자는 같은 필경사가 모든 시들을 베껴 썼을 수 있다고 주장하며 이를 반박한다.

Lastly, the reading states that the poems in *Cotton Nero A.x* could have all been written by different authors. This is because there is no clear link among the four poems except for similar landscapes and the same dialect. However, the lecturer undermines this idea by saying that the author used his own invented words in all of his poems. It is hardly likely that four different people created the same words.

마지막으로, 지문은 〈코튼 네로 A.x〉의 시들이 모두 각기 다른 저자에 의해 쓰였을 수 있다고 언급한다. 이는 비슷한 풍경과 동일한 방언을 제외하면 네 편의 시 사이에 분명한 연결 고리가 없기 때문이다. 그러나 강의자는 저자가 모든 시에서 자신이 직접 만들어 낸 단어를 사용했다고 말하면서 이 견해를 일축한다. 네 명의 각기 다른 인물이 같은 단어를 만들어 냈을 것이라고 보기는 어렵다.

어휘 contradict ▣ 반박하다 | except for ~을 제외하고는 | undermine ▣ 훼손시키다

Question 2

Your professor is teaching a class. Write a post responding to the professor's question.

In your response, you should:

- express and support your opinion
- make a contribution to the discussion

An effective response will contain at least 100 words.
You will have 10 minutes to write it.

Dr. Michael: Good day, class. As we navigate through the intricacies of resource allocation in universities, a pressing question emerges: "Should universities give the same amount of money to their students' sports activities as they give to their university libraries?" This topic invites us to consider the equilibrium between physical and intellectual development. In the pursuit of a comprehensive discussion, let's explore the dynamics of funding priorities.

Ian: Thank you, Professor. I find merit in the idea that universities should allocate equal funding to sports activities and libraries. While libraries are crucial for academic pursuits, sports play a pivotal role in students' holistic development. Investing in sports fosters physical well-being, teamwork, and

당신의 교수님께서 강의 중입니다. 교수님의 질문에 답하는 글을 쓰세요.

- 당신의 의견을 표현하고 뒷받침하세요
- 토론에 기여하세요

효과적인 답변은 최소한 100단어를 포함할 것입니다.
당신은 10분 동안 글을 작성할 수 있습니다.

마이클 교수: 안녕하세요, 여러분. 대학에서 자원 할당의 복잡한 사항을 다루다 보면 떠오르는 중요한 질문이 있습니다: "대학은 학생들의 스포츠 활동에 대학 도서관에 주는 것과 같은 금액을 주어야 할까요?" 이 주제는 우리에게 육체적 및 지적 발전 사이의 균형을 고려하도록 합니다. 좀 더 포괄적인 토론을 위해 자원 할당 우선순위의 역학을 다뤄 보겠습니다.

이안: 감사합니다, 교수님. 저는 대학이 도서관과 스포츠 활동에 동일한 자금을 할당해야 한다는 생각에서 장점을 찾았습니다. 도서관은 학문적 추구에 중요하며, 스포츠는 학생들의 종합적인 발전에 중요한 역할을 합니다. 스포츠에 투자하는 것은 신체적 웰빙, 팀워크, 그리고 공동체 의식을 육성합니다. 이러한 측면은 학생의 전반적인 교육 경험에 크게 기여합니다.

a sense of community. These aspects contribute significantly to a student's overall educational experience.

Linda: I appreciate Ian's perspective, but I lean towards a different stance. I believe that universities should prioritize allocating funds based on academic needs rather than equal distribution. Libraries are the heart of academic resources, supporting research, study, and intellectual growth. While sports are valuable for physical well-being, the primary mission of a university is academic excellence. Therefore, a greater allocation to libraries aligns more closely with the core educational mission of universities.

린다: 이안의 관점을 높이 평가하지만, 저는 다른 입장을 가지고 있습니다. 저는 대학이 균등한 분배보다는 학문적 필요에 따라 자금을 할당하는 것이 더 나은 것이라 생각합니다. 도서관은 연구, 공부, 지적 성장을 지원하는 학문적 자원의 중심입니다. 스포츠는 신체적 웰빙에 중요하지만, 대학의 주요 임무는 학문적 우수성입니다. 따라서 도서관에 대한 더 큰 할당이 대학의 핵심 교육 임무와 더 잘 부합한다고 생각합니다.

어휘 intricacy n 복잡한 사항 I emerge v 출현하다, 드러나다 I equilibrium n 균형 I merit n 장점 I pivotal adj 중요한 I allocate v 할당하다 I align v 일치시키다, 맞추다

예시 답변

From my perspective, both made excellent statements, but I'm on the same page as Ian. Simply put, if the university spends its budget on providing various sports activities, students can interact with many people while participating in these activities, creating an optimal condition for broadening their relationships. This is mainly because when they engage in various sports activities at school, they have more opportunities to share diverse experiences and emotions with one another. These shared experiences can potentially create opportunities for various conversations later on. A perfect example of this is a close friend of mine. He used to drift apart from his friends due to his introverted personality, having a serious problem with them. Then, one day, his school decided to allocate more budget to providing students with various sports activities. He decided to participate in these activities not only to maintain his health but also to expand his relationships with friends. At first, it seemed awkward and challenging for him to get close to new people through the activities, but it gradually got better. The people playing sports together slowly opened up to him, and a strong bond was developed between him and his friends.

제 관점에서는 두 사람 모두 훌륭한 주장을 했지만, 저는 이안과 동일한 의견입니다. 간단히 말해서, 대학이 예산을 다양한 스포츠 활동 제공에 사용한다면 학생들은 이러한 활동에 참여하면서 많은 사람들과 상호작용할 수 있어 관계를 확장하기에 최적의 상태를 만들 수 있습니다. 학교에서 다양한 스포츠 활동에 참여할 때 다양한 경험과 감정을 공유할 수 있는 기회가 더 많아집니다. 이러한 공유된 경험은 나중에 다양한 대화의 기회를 만들 수 있습니다. 저의 친한 친구 중 한 명이 이를 완벽하게 보여 줍니다. 그는 내성적인 성격 때문에 친구들과 멀어져 그들과 심각한 문제가 있었습니다. 그런데 어느 날 학교에서는 학생들에게 다양한 스포츠 활동을 제공하기 위해 예산을 더 할당하기로 결정했습니다. 그는 이러한 활동에 참여함으로써 건강을 유지하는 것뿐만 아니라 친구들과의 관계를 확장하기로 결정했습니다. 처음에 그는 새로운 사람들과 가까워지는 것이 서투르고 어려웠지만, 그것은 점차 좋아졌습니다. 함께 스포츠를 하는 사람들이 그에게 마음을 열며 그와 친구들 간에 강한 유대감이 형성되었습니다.

Actual Test 2

본서 I P. 382

Question 1

Reading

Researchers have found that wind turbines kill hundreds of thousands of bats every year. This mostly happens because many migrating bat species fly through areas where wind farms are built, but even non-migrating species are being killed. For this reason, it is important to develop ways to

연구자들은 풍력 발전용 터빈으로 인해 매년 수많은 박쥐가 죽는다는 사실을 발견했다. 이는 대개 이주하는 대다수 박쥐들이 풍력 발전 단지가 세워진 지역들을 통과하여 날아가기 때문에 일어나는 현상인데, 이주하지 않는 박쥐조차 죽임을 당한다. 이러한 이유로

protect bats from wind turbines. Here are three strategies that could help to protect bats.

풍력 발전용 터빈으로부터 박쥐를 보호하는 방법을 강구해 내는 것이 중요하다. 박쥐를 보호하는 데 도움을 줄 수 있는 세 가지 전략들이 있다.

First, the most basic solution is to avoid building wind turbines in areas where bats are common. Since migrating bats follow the same paths every year, it is easy to figure out where they usually fly and not build in those areas. Bat species that do not migrate usually sleep in caves, and these are also easy to locate and avoid. By carefully researching where bats live and fly, we can build wind farms in areas where they will have little effect on bats.

첫째, 가장 기본적인 해결책은 박쥐들이 흔한 지역에 풍력 발전용 터빈을 설치하는 것을 피하는 것이다. 이주하는 박쥐들은 매년 같은 경로를 따라가기 때문에, 그들이 통상 날아가는 곳을 파악해서 그 지역에 설치하지 않는 것은 쉬운 일이다. 이주하지 않는 박쥐들은 보통 동굴에서 잠을 자며, 이 동굴을 찾아내 피하기는 쉽다. 박쥐들이 사는 곳과 날아다니는 곳을 신중히 조사함으로써, 박쥐에게 영향을 거의 주지 않는 지역에 풍력 발전 단지를 조성할 수 있다.

Second, power companies can protect bats by changing their operating schedules. They can shut down their turbines at night, when bats are most active. If the turbines are not moving, the bats can safely fly around them. This would have little effect on the power companies since the demand for electricity is much lower at night. In fact, one wind power company in the U.S. tested out this method, and they reported far fewer bat deaths with only a tiny loss in annual power generation.

둘째, 전력 회사들은 가동 일정을 변경함으로써 박쥐를 보호할 수 있다. 박쥐가 가장 활동적인 밤 시간대에 터빈을 꺼 두면 된다. 터빈이 가동되지 않으면 박쥐들은 그 주변을 안전하게 날아다닐 수 있다. 전기 수요가 밤에는 현저히 낮기 때문에 전력 회사에 별 지장이 없을 것이다. 실제로 미국의 한 풍력 발전소가 이 방법을 시험했는데, 연간 발전량을 극미량만 감소시키면서 박쥐 살상을 상당히 줄였다고 보고했다.

Third, the power companies can use radar to discourage the bats from coming near the turbines. Bats dislike radar waves, which is why they usually avoid areas where radar is used, like airports. So if radar emitters are installed in wind farms and on wind turbines, that will make the bats avoid the area. This method would be ideal, since it keeps the bats safe and allows the wind turbines to operate at any time.

셋째, 전력 회사들은 레이더(전파 탐지기)를 사용하여 박쥐들이 터빈 근처로 오는 것을 막을 수 있다. 박쥐들은 레이더파를 싫어하는데, 이것이 박쥐들이 공항처럼 레이더가 사용되는 지역을 피하는 이유이다. 그래서 레이더 방출기가 풍력 발전 단지와 풍력 발전용 터빈에 설치된다면, 박쥐가 그 지역을 피하게 될 것이다. 이 방법은 박쥐를 안전하게 보호하면서도 풍력 발전용 터빈을 언제든 가동할 수 있다는 점에서 이상적이라고 할 수 있다.

어휘 migrate v 이동하다, 이주하다 | wind farm 풍력 발전 단지 | strategy n 전략, 계획 | locate v ~의 정확한 위치를 찾아내다 | operate v 작동하다, 가동하다 | shut down 정지시키다 | demand n 수요 | annual adj 매년의, 연례의 | power generation 발전(發電) | discourage v 막다, 말리다 | install v 설치하다 | ideal adj 이상적인

Listening

Bats live long lives, but they reproduce slowly. This combination makes them very vulnerable because they cannot respond quickly when a large number of them are killed. This is why it is so important to protect them from wind turbines, which kill hundreds of thousands of them. However, the strategies suggested in the reading would be ineffective.

박쥐는 수명이 길지만, 번식을 느리게 하지요. 이 두 가지 사실 때문에 박쥐들은 매우 취약한데, 많은 수의 박쥐들이 죽으면 빨리 대응을 할 수 없기 때문입니다. 이것이 수많은 박쥐를 살상하는 풍력 발전용 터빈에서 박쥐를 보호하는 것이 아주 중요한 이유입니다. 하지만, 지문에서 제시된 전략들은 효과가 없을 것입니다.

First, the reading explains that it is easy to determine where bats often fly. That is true, but it does not mean that we can simply avoid building wind turbines in those areas. Wind turbines must be built on high ground where the wind is strongest, but these areas are where bats like to fly. Bats do not usually like lowland areas because the air does not move as much, and there are fewer insects to catch. Thus,

첫째로, 지문은 박쥐들이 자주 날아다니는 곳을 알아내기가 쉽다고 설명하고 있습니다. 그것이 사실이긴 하지만, 그렇다고 해서 우리가 그 지역에 풍력 발전용 터빈을 짓는 것을 단순히 피할 수 있다는 건 아닙니다. 풍력 발전용 터빈은 바람이 가장 강한, 고도가 높은 지역에 설치해야만 하는데, 이런 지역은 박쥐들이 즐겨 날아다니는 곳입니다. 박쥐들은 보통 저지대를

separating wind turbines and bats is nearly impossible.

Second, shutting wind turbines down at night would prevent the turbine blades from killing flying bats. But keeping the turbines still at night creates a new problem. During the daytime, bats often sleep in trees or any other tall structure, including wind turbines. Many bats would land on turbines in the early morning to rest. When the turbines started to operate, they would kill the bats that are sleeping in the machinery. Therefore, only operating in the daytime would not protect bats.

Third, it is true that bats dislike radar, and they would definitely avoid wind turbines with radar emitters. However, bats have a very good reason to dislike radar: it hurts them. Even brief exposure to radar waves can damage their reproductive organs, which prevents them from having babies. Radar emitters would keep the turbines from killing bats directly, but the emitters would cause the bat population to decline. So using radar would have the opposite effect from the one it is intended to have.

좋아하지 않는데, 그 이유는 공기가 그만큼 많이 이동하지 않고, 잡아먹을 곤충이 적기 때문입니다. 그래서 풍력 발전용 터빈과 박쥐를 떼어놓기란 거의 불가능해요.

둘째로, 풍력 발전용 터빈을 밤에 중단시키는 것은 날아다니는 박쥐들이 터빈의 날에 맞아 죽는 것을 예방할 수 있을지도 모릅니다. 하지만 밤에 터빈을 중지시키는 것은 인해 새로운 문제를 일으킵니다. 낮에는 박쥐들이 주로 나무나 풍력 발전용 터빈 같은 높은 구조물에서 잠을 잡니다. 많은 박쥐들이 이른 아침에 휴식을 취하기 위해 터빈에 내려앉습니다. 터빈이 작동하기 시작하면 그 장치에서 자고 있던 박쥐들이 죽게 됩니다. 그래서 낮에 가동하는 것만으로는 박쥐를 보호할 수 없습니다.

셋째로, 박쥐들이 레이더를 싫어하는 것은 사실이고, 그래서 레이더 방출기가 달린 풍력 발전용 터빈을 피할 거라는 점은 분명하죠. 하지만 이렇게 박쥐들이 레이더를 싫어하는 데는 그만한 이유가 있습니다. 자신들을 해치기 때문입니다. 레이더파에 잠깐만 노출되어도 생식 기관이 손상될 수 있는데, 이는 임신을 막습니다. 레이더 방출기로 터빈이 박쥐를 직접적으로 죽이는 것을 막을 수 있을지는 모르지만, 방출기가 박쥐의 개체 수 감소를 야기할 수도 있습니다. 그래서 레이더 사용은 의도하는 바와 정반대 효과를 가져올 수도 있습니다.

어휘 reproduce v 번식하다 | vulnerable adj 취약한, 연약한 | ineffective adj 효과 없는 | lowland adj 저지대의 | separate v 분리하다, 떼어놓다 | blade n (칼이나 도구 등의) 날 | exposure n 노출 | reproductive organ 생식 기관 | population n 개체 수 | decline v 감소하다, 줄어들다 | opposite adj 정반대의 | intend to~ 하려고 하다, ~할 작정이다

강의에서 제시한 요점을 요약하시오. 읽기 지문의 요점에 대해 강의에서 어떻게 반박하는지 설명하시오.

예시 답변

The reading and the lecture both talk about the dangers posed to bats by wind turbines. The reading says that it is not difficult to solve this problem by using several strategies. However, the lecturer argues that the strategies suggested in the reading would not be effective.

Firstly, the reading says that it is easy to locate where bats usually fly because they follow the same paths every year when they migrate. We should not build wind turbines in those areas. However, the lecturer says it is almost impossible to separate bats and turbines in that way because the places liked by bats and the ones suitable for building turbines are the same.

Secondly, the reading suggests the strategy of shutting down wind turbines at night when bats are active. Since the demand for electricity is quite low at night, it would not cause much

지문과 강의 모두 풍력 발전용 터빈이 박쥐에게 끼치는 위험에 관해 이야기하고 있다. 지문에서는 몇 가지 전략을 사용하여 이 문제를 해결하는 것이 어렵지 않다고 말한다. 하지만 강의자는 지문에서 제시한 전략들이 효과가 없을 거라고 주장한다.

첫째로, 지문에서는 박쥐들이 매년 이주할 때마다 같은 경로를 따르기 때문에 그들이 통상적으로 날아다니는 곳을 파악하기가 쉽다고 말한다. 그 지역에 터빈을 설치하지 않으면 되는 것이다. 하지만 강의자는 박쥐들이 좋아하는 장소와 풍력 발전용 터빈을 설치하기에 적합한 장소가 일치하기 때문에 이런 식으로 그 둘을 떼어놓기가 거의 불가능하다고 말한다.

둘째로, 지문은 전력 회사들이 박쥐가 주로 활동하는 밤에 터빈을 잠시 꺼 두는 방법을 제시한다. 밤에는 전기 수요가 적기 때문에 전력 회사에 큰 손실을 끼치

harm to power companies. However, according to the lecturer, if they stopped the turbines at night, bats that land on turbines to sleep would be killed by them once the turbines start to work again.

지 않을 것이다. 그러나 강의자에 따르면, 만일 밤에 터빈을 중지시키면 잠을 자기 위해 터빈에 내려앉은 박쥐들이 터빈 가동이 재개됨과 동시에 터빈에 살상될 것이다.

Thirdly, the reading suggests that they can discourage bats from coming near the turbines with devices that send out radar signals, which bats dislike. This is an ideal solution because power companies could operate turbines at any time. However, the lecturer contends that bats dislike radar because it harms them. Radar waves are known to damage their reproductive organs. If the power companies used this strategy, it would lead to a decline in bat populations in the long run.

셋째로, 지문은 박쥐들이 싫어하는 레이더 신호를 방출하는 장치를 이용해서 박쥐들이 터빈 근처로 오는 것을 막을 수 있다고 말한다. 전력 회사들이 풍력 발전용 터빈을 언제든 가동할 수 있다는 점에서 이것은 이상적 해결책이다. 하지만 강의자는 레이더가 자신들에게 해를 입히기 때문에 박쥐들이 레이더를 싫어한다고 주장한다. 레이더파는 박쥐들의 생식 기관을 손상시키는 것으로 알려져 있다. 전력 회사들이 이 전략을 사용한다면 장기적으로 박쥐 개체 수가 감소하게 될 것이다.

어휘 suitable adj 적합한 I cause harm to ~에게 해를 끼치다 I decline n 감소

Question 2

Your professor is teaching a class. Write a post responding to the professor's question.

In your response, you should:

- express and support your opinion
- make a contribution to the discussion

An effective response will contain at least 100 words.
You will have 10 minutes to write it.

당신의 교수님께서 강의 중입니다. 교수님의 질문에 답하는 글을 쓰세요.

- 당신의 의견을 표현하고 뒷받침하세요
- 토론에 기여하세요

효과적인 답변은 최소한 100단어를 포함할 것입니다.
당신은 10분 동안 글을 작성할 수 있습니다.

Dr. Irene: Greetings, class. Today, our focus is on the belief that early exposure to studying abroad is essential for broadening horizons and personal development. The question before us is simple yet profound: Do you agree or disagree with this perspective? Studying overseas at an early age is crucial for evolving as individuals. As we embark on this exploration, let's delve into the dynamics of studying abroad and its potential effects on personal development.

아이린 교수: 안녕하세요, 여러분. 오늘은 해외 유학에 대한 초기 노출이 시야를 확장하고 개인적인 발전에 중요하다는 믿음에 중점을 두겠습니다. 우리 앞에 있는 질문은 간단하면서도 깊은 의미가 담긴 것입니다: 이 관점에 동의하십니까, 동의하지 않으십니까? 어린 나이에 유학을 하는 것은 개인적인 성장에 중요합니다. 이 탐구를 시작할 때, 유학의 역학과 개인적 발전에 미치는 잠재적 영향을 자세히 살펴보겠습니다.

Henry: Thank you, Professor. I wholeheartedly agree with the idea that studying abroad at an early age is crucial for personal development. Experiencing different cultures, meeting diverse people, and navigating unfamiliar environments offer unparalleled opportunities for self-discovery. The challenges and joys of studying abroad shape individuals in ways that traditional education might not.

헨리: 감사합니다, 교수님. 저는 해외에서 조기 교육을 받는 것이 개인적 발전에 중요하다는 생각에 전적으로 동의합니다. 다양한 문화를 경험하고 다양한 사람들을 만나고 익숙하지 않은 환경에서 적응하는 것은 자아 발견에 탁월한 기회를 제공합니다. 해외에서의 공부의 도전과 기쁨은 전통적인 교육이 제공하지 못하는 방식으로 개인을 형성합니다.

Lottie: While I acknowledge the benefits Henry highlights, I find myself leaning towards disagreement. Not everyone has the privilege or inclination to study abroad early in life. Moreover, local education can also foster personal development through exposure to diverse perspectives and cultures. The emphasis should be on creating a globally aware

로티: 헨리가 강조한 이점을 인정하면서도 저는 반대로 기울고 있다고 느낍니다. 모든 사람이 삶 초반에 해외에서 공부할 권리나 경향을 가지고 있지 않습니다. 게다가 현지 교육도 다양한 관점과 문화에 노출함으로써 개인적 성장을 촉진할 수 있습니다. 중점은 지역에서도 모든 학생이 개인적으로 발전할 수 있도록

curriculum locally, ensuring that all students, regardless of their ability to study abroad, can develop as individuals.

전 세계적인 인식을 가진 교육 과정을 만드는 데 있어야 합니다.

어휘 evolve v 진화하다 | delve v 탐구하다 | personal development 개인 발전 | unparalleled adj 비길 데 없는 | disagreement n 불일치 | inclination n 성향 | emphasis n 강조

예시 답변

From my perspective, both made excellent statements, but I'm on the same page as Henry. Simply put, children can gain a lot of advice while studying abroad at an early age. It is obvious that this gives them such valuable and practical advice as they go through unpredictable situations. Through these moments, children can have a chance to evaluate themselves in a more objective way, leading to a better life in the future. A perfect example of this is my own experience. I used to be naive and less sociable due to my introverted personality. This made me segregate myself from people and live in my own world. Then, one day, I got a chance to go to elementary school in the United States. At first, it was uncomfortable and challenging for me to blend in with new friends and learn from a new environment. However, as I was getting used to it, I started to engage in many new experiences I hadn't had before. This not only gave me valuable advice but also made me more grown up mentally.

제 입장에서는 두 사람 모두 훌륭한 주장을 펼쳤지만, 저는 헨리와 의견이 일치합니다. 간단히 말하면, 어린 나이에 해외에서 공부하는 동안 어린이들은 많은 조언을 얻을 수 있습니다. 예측할 수 없는 상황을 겪을 때마다 그들에게 귀중하고 현실적인 조언을 제공한다는 것은 분명합니다. 이러한 순간을 통해 어린이들은 미래에 더 나은 삶으로 이어질 수 있도록 더 객관적으로 자신을 평가할 기회를 갖게 될 것입니다. 이에 대한 완벽한 예는 저의 경험입니다. 저는 예전에 순진하고 내성적인 성격 때문에 사교적이지 못했습니다. 이로 인해 남들과 격리되어 저만의 세계에서 살았습니다. 그러던 어느 날 미국의 초등학교에 다니게 되었습니다. 처음에는 새로운 친구들과 새로운 환경에서 적응하기가 불편하고 어려웠습니다. 그러나 익숙해지면서 저는 이전에 경험하지 못한 많은 새로운 경험에 참여하기 시작했습니다. 이것은 저에게 귀중한 조언뿐만 아니라 정신적으로 더 성숙해지게 만들었습니다.

PAGODA TOEFL

80+ R/L/S/W | 해설서